TAALGIDSEN VAN BERLITZ

Internationaal bekende taalgidsen met een schat aan woorden en zinnen, een grote verscheidenheid aan nuttige wenken en gegevens en een volledige fonetische spelling. Gemakkelijk te lezen en handig in het gebruik.

Duits	Italiaans
Engels	Joegoslavisch
Amerikaans Engels	Portugees
Frans	Russisch
Grieks	Spaans

CASSETTES VAN BERLITZ

De meeste hierboven genoemde titels zijn eveneens verkrijgbaar in combinatie met tweetalige cassettes die u aan een goede uitspraak zullen helpen. Bij de cassettes ingesloten vindt u de complete tekst in twee talen van alle opgenomen woorden en zinnen.

Berlitz Dictionaries

Dansk	Engelsk, Fransk, Italiensk, Spansk, Tysk
Deutsch	Dänisch, Englisch, Finnisch, Französisch, Italienisch, Niederländisch, Norwegisch, Portugiesisch, Schwedisch, Spanisch
English	Danish, Dutch, Finnish, French, German, Italian, Norwegian, Portuguese, Spanish, Swedish
Español	Alemán, Danés, Finlandés, Francés, Holandés, Inglés, Noruego, Sueco
Français	Allemand, Anglais, Danois, Espagnol, Finnois, Italien, Néerlandais, Norvégien, Portugais, Suédois
Italiano	Danese, Finlandese, Francese, Inglese, Norvegese, Olandese, Svedese, Tedesco
Nederlands	Duits, Engels, Frans, Italiaans, Portugees, Spaans
Norsk	Engelsk, Fransk, Italiensk, Spansk, Tysk
Português	Alemão, Francês, Holandês, Inglês, Sueco
Suomi	Englanti, Espanja, Italia, Ranska, Ruotsi, Saksa
Svenska	Engelska, Finska, Franska, Italienska, Portugisiska, Spanska, Tyska

BERLITZ®

engels-nederlands
nederlands-engels
woordenboek

english-dutch
dutch-english
dictionary

By the Staff of Editions Berlitz

Revised edition 1979
Library of Congress Catalog Card Number: 78-78084

3rd printing 1983
Printed in Switzerland

Inhoud

Contents

Voorwoord

Bij het selecteren van de 12 500 woordbegrippen in beide talen voor dit woordenboek stond de redactie in de allereerste plaats de behoeften van de reiziger voor ogen. Dit boekje zal van grote waarde blijken te zijn voor de vele reizigers, toeristen en zakenmensen die het waarderen zich verzekerd te weten van een klein en praktisch woordenboek. Het biedt hen – evenals aan beginners en gevorderden – de benodigde woordenschat, alsook sleutelwoorden en uitdrukkingen voor dagelijks gebruik.

Zoals onze succesvolle taal- en reisgidsen, zijn deze woordenboekjes – tot stand gekomen met behulp van een computer data bank – speciaal ontworpen om in jaszak of handtas gestoken te worden.

Behalve wat u normaliter in woordenboeken vindt, biedt Berlitz nog de volgende extra's:

- een transcriptie van elk grondwoord in het internationale fonetische alfabet (IPA), hetgeen het uitspreken van woorden waarvan de spelling moeilijk lijkt vergemakkelijkt

- een unieke, praktische woordenlijst van culinaire begrippen om het lezen van een menu in een buitenlands restaurant te vereenvoudigen en de mysteries te ontrafelen van bijzondere gerechten

- nuttige informatie over tijdsaanduiding, getallen, de vervoeging van onregelmatige werkwoorden, veel gebruikte afkortingen en een lijst van veel voorkomende uitdrukkingen.

Hoewel geen enkel woordenboek van dit formaat kan pretenderen volledig te zijn, verwachten wij toch dat de gebruiker van dit boek zich goed uitgerust zal voelen om buitenlandse reizen met vertrouwen te ondernemen. Wij zouden het evenwel op prijs stellen opmerkingen, kritiek of suggesties te ontvangen, die mogelijkerwijs kunnen helpen bij het voorbereiden van toekomstige uitgaven.

Preface

In selecting the 12.500 word-concepts in each language for this dictionary, the editors have had the traveller's needs foremost in mind. This book will prove invaluable to all the millions of travellers, tourists and business people who appreciate the reassurance a small and practical dictionary can provide. It offers them—as it does beginners and students—all the basic vocabulary they are going to encounter and to have to use, giving the key words and expressions to allow them to cope in everyday situations.

Like our successful phrase books and travel guides, these dictionaries—created with the help of a computer data bank—are designed to slip into pocket or purse, and thus have a role as handy companions at all times.

Besides just about everything you normally find in dictionaries, there are these Berlitz bonuses:

● imitated pronunciation next to each foreign-word entry, making it easy to read and enunciate words whose spelling may look forbidding

● a unique, practical glossary to simplify reading a foreign restaurant menu and to take the mystery out of complicated dishes and indecipherable names on bills of fare

● useful information on how to tell the time and how to count, on conjugating irregular verbs, commonly seen abbreviations and converting to the metric system, in addition to basic phrases.

While no dictionary of this size can pretend to completeness, we expect the user of this book will feel well armed to affront foreign travel with confidence. We should, however, be very pleased to receive comments, criticism and suggestions that you think may be of help in preparing future editions.

dutch-english
_____

nederlands-engels

Afkortingen

adj	bijvoeglijk naamwoord	*p*	verleden tijd
adv	bijwoord	*pl*	meervoud
Am	Amerikaans	*plAm*	meervoud (Amerikaans)
art	lidwoord	*pp*	voltooid deelwoord
c	gemeenslachtig	*pr*	tegenwoordige tijd
conj	voegwoord	*pref*	voorvoegsel
n	zelfstandig naamwoord	*prep*	voorzetsel
nAm	zelfstandig naamwoord	*pron*	voornaamwoord
	(Amerikaans)	*v*	werkwoord
nt	onzijdig	*vAm*	werkwoord
num	telwoord		(Amerikaans)

Inleiding

Het woordenboek is zodanig opgezet, dat het zoveel mogelijk beantwoordt aan de eisen van de praktijk. Onnodige taalkundige aanduidingen zijn achterwege gelaten. De volgorde van de woorden is strikt alfabetisch, ook als het samengestelde woorden of woorden met een koppelteken betreft. Als enige uitzondering op deze regel zijn enkele idiomatische uitdrukkingen opgenomen als een afzonderlijk artikel, waarbij het meest toonaangevende woord van de uitdrukking bepalend is voor de alfabetische rangschikking. Wanneer bij een grondwoord nog daarvan afgeleide samenstellingen of uitdrukkingen zijn gegeven, staan ook deze weer in alfabetische volgorde.

Achter elk grondwoord vindt u een fonetische transcriptie (zie de Gids voor de uitspraak) en vervolgens, wanneer van toepassing, de woordsoort. Wanneer bij hetzelfde grondwoord meerdere woordsoorten behoren, zijn de vertalingen telkens naar de woordsoort gegroepeerd.

Het meervoud van zelfstandige naamwoorden is altijd opgenomen, wanneer dat onregelmatig is; tevens is het meervoud gegeven van bepaalde woorden waarover de gebruiker in twijfel zou kunnen verkeren.

Wanneer in onregelmatige meervoudsvormen of in afgeleide samenstellingen en uitdrukkingen het teken ~ wordt gebruikt, duidt dit een herhaling aan van het grondwoord als geheel.

In onregelmatige meervoudsvormen van samengestelde woorden wordt alleen het gedeelte, dat verandert, voluit geschreven en het onveranderde deel aangegeven door een liggend streepje (-).

Een sterretje (*) voor een werkwoord geeft aan, dat dit werkwoord onregelmatig is. Voor nadere bijzonderheden kunt u de lijst van onregelmatige werkwoorden raadplegen.

Dit woordenboek is gebaseerd op de Britse spelling. Alle woorden en woordbetekenissen die overwegend Amerikaans zijn, zijn als zodanig aangegeven (zie lijst van gebezigde afkortingen).

Uitspraak

Elk trefwoord in dit deel van het woordenboek wordt gevolgd door een transcriptie in het internationale fonetische alfabet (IPA). In dit alfabet vertegenwoordigt elk teken altijd dezelfde klank. Letters die hieronder niet beschreven zijn worden min of meer op dezelfde wijze uitgesproken als in het Nederlands.

Medeklinkers

b	nooit scherp zoals in he**b**
d	nooit scherp zoals in raa**d**
ð	als de **z** in **z**ee, maar lispend uitgesproken
g	als een zachte **k**, zoals in het Franse **g**arçon
ŋ	als de **ng** in ba**ng**
r	plaats de tong eerst als voor de ʒ (zie beneden), open dan de mond enigszins en beweeg de tong daarbij naar beneden
ʃ	als de **sj** in **sj**ofel
θ	als de **s** in **s**amen, maar lispend uitgesproken
v	als de **w** in **w**aar
w	een korte, zwakke **oe**-klank
ʒ	als de **g** in eta**g**e

N.B. De lettergroep **sj** moet worden uitgesproken als een **s** gevolgd door een **j**-klank, maar *niet* als in **sj**ofel.

Klinkers

α:	als de **aa** in m**aa**t
æ	een klank tussen de **a** in **a**ls en de **e** in b**e**st
ʌ	min of meer als de **a** in **a**ls
e	als in b**e**st
ɛ	als de **e** in b**e**st, maar met de tong wat lager
ə	als de **e** in acht**e**r
ɔ	min of meer als de **o** in p**o**t
u	als de **oe** in g**oe**d, maar korter

1) Een dubbele punt (:) geeft aan dat de voorafgaande klinker lang is.

2) Enkele aan het Frans ontleende Engelse woorden bevatten neusklanken, die aangegeven worden d.m.v. een tilde boven de klinker (b.v. ã). Deze worden door de neus en de mond tegelijkertijd uitgesproken.

Tweeklanken

Een tweeklank bestaat uit twee klinkers, waarvan er één sterk is (beklemtoond) en de andere zwak (niet beklemtoond) en die samen als één klinker worden uitgesproken, zoals ei in het Nederlands. In het Engels is de tweede klinker altijd zwak. Een tweeklank kan soms gevolgd worden door een [ə]. In dergelijke gevallen heeft de tweede klinker van de tweeklank de neiging zeer zwak te worden.

Klemtoon

Het teken (′) geeft aan dat de klemtoon op de volgende lettergreep valt. Als in een woord meer dan één lettergreep wordt beklemtoond, wordt het teken (ˌ) geplaatst vóór de lettergreep, waarop de bijklemtoon valt.

Amerikaanse uitspraak

Onze transcriptie geeft de gebruikelijke Engelse uitspraak aan. De Amerikaanse uitspraak verschilt in enkele opzichten van het Britse Engels en kent daarbij nog belangrijke regionale verschillen. Hier volgen enkele van de meest opvallende afwijkingen:

1) In tegenstelling tot in het Britse Engels wordt de r ook uitgesproken voor een medeklinker en aan het einde van een woord.

2) In vele woorden (b.v. *ask*, *castle*, *laugh* enz.) wordt [ɑ:] uitgesproken als [æ:].

3) De [ɔ]-klank wordt in het Amerikaans uitgesproken als [ɑ], vaak ook als [ɔ:].

4) In woorden als *duty*, *tune*, *new* enz. valt in het Amerikaans de [j]-klank voor de [u:] vaak weg.

5) Bovendien wordt bij een aantal woorden in het Amerikaans de klemtoon anders gelegd.

A

a [ei,ə] *art* (an) een *art*

abbey ['æbi] *n* abdij *c*

abbreviation [ə,bri:vi'eiʃən] *n* afkorting *c*

aberration [,æbə'reiʃən] *n* afwijking *c*

ability [ə'biləti] *n* bekwaamheid *c*; vermogen *nt*

able ['eibl] *adj* in staat; capabel, bekwaam; *be* ~ *to* in staat *zijn om*; *kunnen

abnormal [æb'nɔ:məl] *adj* abnormaal

aboard [ə'bɔ:d] *adv* aan boord

abolish [ə'bɔliʃ] *v* afschaffen

abortion [ə'bɔ:ʃən] *n* abortus *c*

about [ə'baut] *prep* over; betreffende, omtrent; om; *adv* omstreeks, ongeveer; omheen

above [ə'bʌv] *prep* boven; *adv* boven

abroad [ə'brɔ:d] *adv* naar het buitenland, in het buitenland

abscess ['æbses] *n* abces *c*

absence ['æbsəns] *n* afwezigheid *c*

absent ['æbsənt] *adj* afwezig

absolutely ['æbsəlu:tli] *adv* absoluut

abstain from [əb'stein] zich *onthouden van

abstract ['æbstrækt] *adj* abstract

absurd [əb'sə:d] *adj* absurd, ongerijmd

abundance [ə'bʌndəns] *n* overvloed *c*

abundant [ə'bʌndənt] *adj* overvloedig

abuse [ə'bju:s] *n* misbruik *nt*

abyss [ə'bis] *n* afgrond *c*

academy [ə'kædəmi] *n* academie *c*

accelerate [ək'seləreit] *v* versnellen

accelerator [ək'seləreitə] *n* gaspedaal *nt*

accent ['æksənt] *n* accent *nt*; nadruk *c*

accept [ək'sept] *v* aanvaarden, *aannemen; accepteren

access ['ækses] *n* toegang *c*

accessary [ək'sesəri] *n* medeplichtige *c*

accessible [ək'sesəbəl] *adj* toegankelijk

accessories [ək'sesəriz] *pl* toebehoren *pl*, accessoires *pl*

accident ['æksidənt] *n* ongeluk *nt*, ongeval *nt*

accidental [,æksi'dentəl] *adj* toevallig

accommodate [ə'kɔmədeit] *v* *onderbrengen

accommodation [ə,kɔmə'deiʃən] *n* accommodatie *c*, logies *nt*, onderdak *nt*

accompany [ə'kʌmpəni] *v* vergezellen; begeleiden

accomplish [ə'kʌmpliʃ] *v* *volbrengen; bereiken

in accordance with [in ə'kɔ:dəns wið] ingevolge

according to [ə'kɔ:diŋ tu:] volgens; overeenkomstig

account [ə'kaunt] *n* rekening *c*; verslag *nt*; ~ **for** verantwoorden; **on** ~ **of** vanwege

accountable [ə'kauntəbəl] *adj* verklaarbaar

accurate ['ækjurət] *adj* nauwkeurig

accuse [ə'kju:z] *v* beschuldigen; aanklagen

accused [ə'kju:zd] *n* verdachte *c*

accustom [ə'kʌstəm] *v* wennen; **accustomed** gewoon, gewend

ache [eik] *v* pijn *doen; *n* pijn *c*

achieve [ə'tʃi:v] *v* bereiken; presteren

achievement [ə'tʃi:vmənt] *n* prestatie *c*

acid ['æsid] *n* zuur *nt*

acknowledge [ək'nɔlidʒ] *v* erkennen; *toegeven; bevestigen

acne ['ækni] *n* acne *c*

acorn ['eikɔ:n] *n* eikel *c*

acquaintance [ə'kweintəns] *n* bekende *c*, kennis *c*

acquire [ə'kwaiə] *v* *verwerven

acquisition [,ækwi'ziʃən] *n* acquisitie *c*

acquittal [ə'kwitəl] *n* vrijspraak *c*

across [ə'krɔs] *prep* over; aan de andere kant van; *adv* aan de overkant

act [ækt] *n* daad *c*; bedrijf *nt*, akte *c*; nummer *nt*; *v* *optreden, handelen; zich *gedragen; toneelspelen

action ['ækʃən] *n* actie *c*, handeling *c*

active ['æktiv] *adj* actief; bedrijvig

activity [æk'tivəti] *n* activiteit *c*

actor ['æktə] *n* acteur *c*, toneelspeler *c*

actress ['æktris] *n* actrice *c*, toneelspeelster *c*

actual ['æktʃuəl] *adj* eigenlijk, werkelijk

actually ['æktʃuəli] *adv* feitelijk

acute [ə'kju:t] *adj* acuut

adapt [ə'dæpt] *v* aanpassen

add [æd] *v* optellen; toevoegen

adding-machine ['ædiŋmə,ʃi:n] *n* telmachine *c*

addition [ə'diʃən] *n* optelling *c*; toevoeging *c*

additional [ə'diʃənəl] *adj* extra; bijkomend; bijkomstig

address [ə'dres] *n* adres *nt*; *v* adresseren; *aanspreken

addressee [,ædre'si:] *n* geadresseerde *c*

adequate ['ædikwət] *adj* toereikend; adequaat, passend

adjective ['ædʒiktiv] *n* bijvoeglijk naamwoord

adjourn [ə'dʒə:n] *v* uitstellen

adjust [ə'dʒʌst] *v* afstellen; aanpassen

administer [əd'ministə] *v* toedienen

administration [əd,mini'streiʃən] *n* administratie *c*; beheer *nt*

administrative [əd'ministrətiv] *adj* administratief; bestuurlijk; ~ **law** bestuursrecht *nt*

admiral ['ædmərəl] *n* admiraal *c*

admiration [,ædmə'reiʃən] *n* bewondering *c*

admire [əd'maiə] *v* bewonderen

admission [əd'miʃən] *n* toegang *c*; toelating *c*

admit [əd'mit] *v* *toelaten; *toegeven; bekennen

admittance [əd'mitəns] *n* toegang *c*; **no** ~ verboden toegang

adopt [ə'dɔpt] *v* adopteren; *aannemen

adult ['ædʌlt] *n* volwassene *c*; *adj* volwassen

advance [əd'va:ns] *n* vooruitgang *c*; voorschot *nt*; *v* *vooruitgaan; *voorschieten; **in** ~ vooruit, van tevoren

advanced [əd'va:nst] *adj* gevorderd

advantage [əd'va:ntidʒ] *n* voordeel *nt*

advantageous [,ædvən'teidʒəs] *adj* voordelig

adventure [əd'ventʃə] *n* avontuur *nt*

adverb ['ædvə:b] *n* bijwoord *nt*

advertisement [əd'və:tismənt] *n* advertentie c; annonce c

advertising ['ædvətaiziŋ] n reclame c

advice [əd'vais] n advies nt, raad c

advise [əd'vaiz] v adviseren, *aanraden

advocate ['ædvəkət] n voorstander c

aerial ['ɛəriəl] n antenne c

aeroplane ['ɛərəplein] n vliegtuig nt

affair [ə'fɛə] n aangelegenheid c; verhouding c, affaire c

affect [ə'fekt] v beïnvloeden; *betreffen

affected [ə'fektid] adj geaffecteerd

affection [ə'fekʃən] n aandoening c;
genegenheid c

affectionate [ə'fekʃənit] adj lief, aanhankelijk

affiliated [ə'filieitid] adj aangesloten

affirmative [ə'fə:mətiv] adj bevestigend

affliction [ə'flikʃən] n leed nt

afford [ə'fɔ:d] v zich veroorloven

afraid [ə'freid] adj angstig, bang; *be
~ bang *zijn

Africa ['æfrikə] Afrika

African ['æfrikən] adj Afrikaans; n
Afrikaan c

after ['ɑ:ftə] prep na; achter; conj nadat

afternoon [,ɑ:ftə'nu:n] n middag c, namiddag c; **this** ~ vanmiddag

afterwards ['ɑ:ftəwədz] adv later; nadien, naderhand

again [ə'gen] adv weer; opnieuw; ~
and again telkens

against [ə'genst] prep tegen

age [eidʒ] n leeftijd c; ouderdom c;
of ~ meerderjarig; **under** ~ minderjarig

aged ['eidʒid] adj bejaard; oud

agency ['eidʒənsi] n agentschap nt;
bureau nt; vertegenwoordiging c

agenda [ə'dʒendə] n agenda c

agent ['eidʒənt] n vertegenwoordiger

c, agent c

aggressive [ə'gresiv] adj agressief

ago [ə'gou] adv geleden

agrarian [ə'grɛəriən] adj agrarisch,
landbouw-

agree [ə'gri:] v het eens *zijn; toestemmen; *overeenkomen

agreeable [ə'gri:əbəl] adj aangenaam

agreement [ə'gri:mənt] n contract nt;
akkoord nt, overeenkomst c; overeenstemming c

agriculture ['ægrikʌltʃə] n landbouw c

ahead [ə'hed] adv vooruit; ~ **of** voor;
***go** ~ *doorgaan; **straight** ~
rechtuit

aid [eid] n hulp c; v *bijstaan, *helpen

ailment ['eilmənt] n kwaal c; ziekte c

aim [eim] n doel nt; ~ **at** richten op,
mikken op; beogen, nastreven

air [ɛə] n lucht c; v luchten

air-conditioning ['ɛəkən,diʃəniŋ] n
luchtverversing c; **air-conditioned**
adj air conditioned

aircraft ['ɛəkrɑ:ft] n (pl ~) vliegtuig
nt; toestel nt

airfield ['ɛəfi:ld] n vliegveld nt

air-filter ['ɛə,filtə] n luchtfilter nt

airline ['ɛəlain] n luchtvaartmaatschappij c

airmail ['ɛəmeil] n luchtpost c

airplane ['ɛəplein] nAm vliegtuig nt

airport ['ɛəpɔ:t] n luchthaven c

air-sickness ['ɛə,siknəs] n luchtziekte c

airtight ['ɛətait] adj luchtdicht

airy ['ɛəri] adj luchtig

aisle [ail] n zijbeuk c; gangpad nt

alarm [ə'lɑ:m] n alarm nt; v alarmeren

alarm-clock [ə'lɑ:mklɔk] n wekker c

album ['ælbəm] n album nt

alcohol ['ælkəhɔl] n alcohol c

alcoholic [,ælkə'hɔlik] adj alcoholisch

ale [eil] n bier nt

algebra ['ældʒibrə] *n* algebra *c*
Algeria [æl'dʒiəriə] Algerije
Algerian [æl'dʒiəriən] *adj* Algerijns; *n* Algerijn *c*
alien ['eiliən] *n* buitenlander *c*; vreemdeling *c*; *adj* buitenlands
alike [ə'laik] *adj* eender, gelijk
alimony ['æliməni] *n* alimentatie *c*
alive [ə'laiv] *adj* in leven, levend
all [ɔːl] *adj* al; ~ **in** alles inbegrepen; ~ **right!** goed!; **at** ~ helemaal
allergy ['ælədʒi] *n* allergie *c*
alley ['æli] *n* steeg *c*
alliance [ə'laiəns] *n* bondgenootschap *nt*
Allies ['ælaiz] *pl* Geallieerden *pl*
allot [ə'lɔt] *v* *toewijzen
allow [ə'lau] *v* veroorloven, *toestaan; ~ **to** *laten; *be allowed *mogen; *be allowed to *mogen
allowance [ə'lauəns] *n* toelage *c*
all-round [ˌɔːl'raund] *adj* veelzijdig
almanac ['ɔːlmənæk] *n* almanak *c*
almond ['ɑːmənd] *n* amandel *c*
almost ['ɔːlmoust] *adv* bijna; haast
alone [ə'loun] *adv* alleen
along [ə'lɔŋ] *prep* langs
aloud [ə'laud] *adv* hardop
alphabet ['ælfəbet] *n* alfabet *nt*
already [ɔːl'redi] *adv* reeds, al
also ['ɔːlsou] *adv* ook; tevens, eveneens
altar ['ɔːltə] *n* altaar *nt*
alter ['ɔːltə] *v* wijzigen, veranderen
alteration [ˌɔːltə'reiʃən] *n* wijziging *c*, verandering *c*
alternate [ɔːl'təːnət] *adj* afwisselend
alternative [ɔːl'təːnətiv] *n* alternatief *nt*
although [ɔːl'ðou] *conj* ofschoon, hoewel
altitude ['æltitjuːd] *n* hoogte *c*
alto ['æltou] *n* (pl ~s) alt *c*
altogether [ˌɔːltə'geðə] *adv* helemaal; in totaal
always ['ɔːlweiz] *adv* altijd
am [æm] *v* (pr be)
amaze [ə'meiz] *v* verwonderen, verbazen
amazement [ə'meizmənt] *n* verbazing *c*
ambassador [æm'bæsədə] *n* ambassadeur *c*
amber ['æmbə] *n* barnsteen *nt*
ambiguous [æm'bigjuəs] *adj* dubbelzinnig; onduidelijk
ambitious [æm'biʃəs] *adj* ambitieus; eerzuchtig
ambulance ['æmbjuləns] *n* ziekenauto *c*, ambulance *c*
ambush ['æmbuʃ] *n* hinderlaag *c*
America [ə'merikə] Amerika
American [ə'merikən] *adj* Amerikaans; *n* Amerikaan *c*
amethyst ['æmiθist] *n* amethist *c*
amid [ə'mid] *prep* onder; tussen, midden in, te midden van
ammonia [ə'mouniə] *n* ammonia *c*
amnesty ['æmnisti] *n* amnestie *c*
among [ə'mʌŋ] *prep* te midden van; tussen, onder; ~ **other things** onder andere
amount [ə'maunt] *n* hoeveelheid·*c*; som *c*, bedrag *nt*; ~ **to** *bedragen
amuse [ə'mjuːz] *v* amuseren, vermaken
amusement [ə'mjuːzmənt] *n* amusement *nt*, vermaak *nt*
amusing [ə'mjuːzin] *adj* amusant
anaemia [ə'niːmiə] *n* bloedarmoede *c*
anaesthesia [ˌænis'θiːziə] *n* verdoving *c*
anaesthetic [ˌænis'θetik] *n* pijnstillend middel
analyse ['ænəlaiz] *v* ontleden, analyseren
analysis [ə'næləsis] *n* (pl -ses) analyse *c*

analyst ['ænəlist] n analist c; analyticus c

anarchy ['ænəki] n anarchie c

anatomy [ə'nætəmi] n anatomie c

ancestor ['ænsestə] n voorvader c

anchor ['æŋkə] n anker nt

anchovy ['æntʃəvi] n ansjovis c

ancient ['einʃənt] adj oud; ouderwets, verouderd; oeroud

and [ænd, ənd] conj en

angel ['eindʒəl] n engel c

anger ['æŋgə] n toorn c, boosheid c; woede c

angle ['æŋgəl] v hengelen; n hoek c

angry ['æŋgri] adj kwaad

animal ['æniməl] n dier nt

ankle ['æŋkəl] n enkel c

annex¹ ['æneks] n bijgebouw nt; bijlage c

annex² [ə'neks] v annexeren

anniversary [,æni'və:səri] n verjaardag c

announce [ə'nauns] v bekendmaken, aankondigen

announcement [ə'naunsmənt] n aankondiging c, bekendmaking c

annoy [ə'nɔi] v irriteren, ergeren

annoyance [ə'nɔiəns] n ergernis c

annoying [ə'nɔiiŋ] adj vervelend, hinderlijk

annual ['ænjuəl] adj jaarlijks; n jaarboek nt

per annum [pər 'ænəm] jaarlijks

anonymous [ə'nɔniməs] adj anoniem

another [ə'nʌðə] adj nog een; een ander

answer ['ɑ:nsə] v antwoorden; beantwoorden; n antwoord nt

ant [ænt] n mier c

anthology [æn'θɔlədʒi] n bloemlezing c

antibiotic [,æntibai'ɔtik] n antibioticum nt

anticipate [æn'tisipeit] v verwachten,

*voorzien; *voorkomen

antifreeze ['æntifri:z] n antivries c

antipathy [æn'tipəθi] n afkeer c

antique [æn'ti:k] adj antiek; n antiquiteit c; ~ dealer antiquair c

antiquity [æn'tikwəti] n Oudheid c; antiquities pl oudheden pl

antiseptic [,ænti'septik] n antiseptisch middel

antlers ['æntləz] pl gewei nt

anxiety [æŋ'zaiəti] n bezorgdheid c

anxious ['æŋkʃəs] adj verlangend; bezorgd

any ['eni] adj enig

anybody ['enibɔdi] pron wie dan ook

anyhow ['enihau] adv hoe dan ook

anyone ['eniwʌn] pron iedereen

anything ['eniθiŋ] pron wat dan ook

anyway ['eniwei] adv in elk geval

anywhere ['eniweə] adv waar dan ook; overal

apart [ə'pɑ:t] adv apart, afzonderlijk; ~ from afgezien van

apartment [ə'pɑ:tmənt] nAm appartement nt, flat c; etage c; ~ house Am flatgebouw nt

aperitif [ə'perətiv] n aperitief nt/c

apologize [ə'pɔlədʒaiz] v zich verontschuldigen

apology [ə'pɔlədʒi] n excuus nt, verontschuldiging c

apparatus [,æpə'reitəs] n apparaat nt, toestel nt

apparent [ə'pærənt] adj schijnbaar; duidelijk

apparently [ə'pærəntli] adv blijkbaar; klaarblijkelijk

apparition [,æpə'riʃən] n verschijning c

appeal [ə'pi:l] n beroep nt

appear [ə'piə] v *lijken, *schijnen; *blijken; *verschijnen; *optreden

appearance [ə'piərəns] n voorkomen nt; aanblik c; optreden nt

appendicitis [ə,pendi'saitis] *n* blindedarmontsteking *c*

appendix [ə'pendiks] *n* (pl -dices, -dixes) blindedarm *c*

appetite ['æpətait] *n* trek *c*, eetlust *c*

appetizer ['æpətaizə] *n* borrelhapje *nt*

appetizing ['æpətaiziŋ] *adj* smakelijk

applause [ə'plɔ:z] *n* applaus *nt*

apple ['æpəl] *n* appel *c*

appliance [ə'plaiəns] *n* toestel *nt*, apparaat *nt*

application [,æpli'keiʃən] *n* toepassing *c*; aanvraag *c*; sollicitatie *c*

apply [ə'plai] *v* toepassen; gebruiken; solliciteren; *gelden

appoint [ə'pɔint] *v* aanstellen, benoemen

appointment [ə'pɔintmənt] *n* afspraak *c*; benoeming *c*

appreciate [ə'pri:ʃieit] *v* schatten; waarderen, op prijs stellen

appreciation [ə,pri:ʃi'eiʃən] *n* schatting *c*; waardering *c*

approach [ə'proutʃ] *v* naderen; *n* aanpak *c*; toegang *c*

appropriate [ə'proupriət] *adj* juist, geschikt, passend

approval [ə'pru:vəl] *n* goedkeuring *c*; instemming *c*; **on ~** op zicht

approve [ə'pru:v] *v* goedkeuren; **~ of** instemmen met

approximate [ə'prɔksimət] *adj* bij benadering

approximately [ə'prɔksimətli] *adv* circa, ongeveer

apricot ['eiprikɔt] *n* abrikoos *c*

April ['eiprəl] april

apron ['eiprən] *n* schort *c*

Arab ['ærəb] *adj* Arabisch; *n* Arabier *c*

arbitrary ['ɑ:bitrəri] *adj* willekeurig

arcade [ɑ:'keid] *n* zuilengang *c*, galerij *c*

arch [ɑ:tʃ] *n* boog *c*; gewelf *nt*

archaeologist [,ɑ:ki'ɔlədʒist] *n* archeoloog *c*

archaeology [,ɑ:ki'ɔlədʒi] *n* oudheidkunde *c*, archeologie *c*

archbishop [,ɑ:tʃ'biʃəp] *n* aartsbisschop *c*

arched [ɑ:tʃt] *adj* boogvormig

architect ['ɑ:kitekt] *n* architect *c*

architecture ['ɑ:kitektʃə] *n* bouwkunde *c*, architectuur *c*

archives ['ɑ:kaivz] *pl* archief *nt*

are [ɑ:] *v* (pr be)

area ['ɛəriə] *n* streek *c*; gebied *nt*; oppervlakte *c*; **~ code** netnummer *nt*

Argentina [,ɑ:dʒən'ti:nə] Argentinië

Argentinian [,ɑ:dʒən'tiniən] *adj* Argentijns; *n* Argentijn *c*

argue ['ɑ:gju:] *v* argumenteren, debatteren, discussiëren; redetwisten

argument ['ɑ:gjumənt] *n* argument *nt*; discussie *c*; woordenwisseling *c*

arid ['ærid] *adj* dor

*arise [ə'raiz] *v* *oprijzen, *ontstaan

arithmetic [ə'riθmətik] *n* rekenkunde *c*

arm [ɑ:m] *n* arm *c*; wapen *nt*; leuning *c*; *v* bewapenen

armchair ['ɑ:mtʃɛə] *n* fauteuil *c*, leunstoel *c*

armed [ɑ:md] *adj* gewapend; **~ forces** strijdkrachten *pl*

armour ['ɑ:mə] *n* harnas *nt*

army ['ɑ:mi] *n* leger *nt*

aroma [ə'roumə] *n* aroma *nt*

around [ə'raund] *prep* om, rond; *adv* rondom

arrange [ə'reindʒ] *v* rangschikken, ordenen; regelen

arrangement [ə'reindʒmənt] *n* regeling *c*

arrest [ə'rest] *v* arresteren; *n* aanhouding *c*, arrestatie *c*

arrival [ə'raivəl] *n* aankomst *c*; komst *c*

arrive [ə'raiv] *v* *aankomen

arrow ['ærou] *n* pijl *c*

art [ɑ:t] *n* kunst *c*; vaardigheid *c*; ~ **collection** kunstverzameling *c*; ~ **exhibition** kunsttentoonstelling *c*; ~ **gallery** kunstgalerij *c*; ~ **history** kunstgeschiedenis *c*; **arts and crafts** kunstnijverheid *c*; ~ **school** kunstacademie *c*

artery ['ɑ:təri] *n* slagader *c*

artichoke ['ɑ:titʃouk] *n* artisjok *c*

article ['ɑ:tikəl] *n* artikel *nt*; lidwoord *nt*

artifice ['ɑ:tifis] *n* list *c*

artificial [,ɑ:ti'fiʃəl] *adj* kunstmatig

artist ['ɑ:tist] *n* kunstenaar *c*; kunstenares *c*

artistic [ɑ:'tistik] *adj* artistiek, kunstzinnig

as [æz] *conj* als, zoals; even; aangezien, omdat; ~ **from** vanaf; met ingang van; ~ **if** alsof

asbestos [æz'bestɒs] *n* asbest *nt*

ascend [ə'send] *v* omhoog *gaan; *opstijgen; *beklimmen

ascent [ə'sent] *n* stijging *c*; beklimming *c*

ascertain [,æsə'tein] *v* constateren; zich vergewissen van, zich vergewissen van

ash [æʃ] *n* as *c*

ashamed [ə'ʃeimd] *adj* beschaamd; *be ~ zich schamen

ashore [ə'ʃɔ:] *adv* aan land

ashtray ['æʃtrei] *n* asbak *c*

Asia ['eiʃə] Azië

Asian ['eiʃən] *adj* Aziatisch; *n* Aziaat *c*

aside [ə'said] *adv* opzij, terzijde

ask [ɑ:sk] *v* *vragen; *verzoeken; uitnodigen

asleep [ə'sli:p] *adj* in slaap

asparagus [ə'spærəgəs] *n* asperge *c*

aspect ['æspekt] *n* aspect *nt*

asphalt ['æsfælt] *n* asfalt *nt*

aspire [ə'spaiə] *v* streven

aspirin ['æspərin] *n* aspirine *c*

ass [æs] *n* ezel *c*

assassination [ə,sæsi'neiʃən] *n* moord *c*

assault [ə'sɔ:lt] *v* *aanvallen; aanranden

assemble [ə'sembəl] *v* *bijeenbrengen; in elkaar zetten, monteren

assembly [ə'sembli] *n* vergadering *c*, bijeenkomst *c*

assignment [ə'sainmənt] *n* opdracht *c*

assign to [ə'sain] *opdragen aan; *toeschrijven aan

assist [ə'sist] *v* *bijstaan, *helpen; ~ **at** bijwonen

assistance [ə'sistəns] *n* hulp *c*; steun *c*, bijstand *c*

assistant [ə'sistənt] *n* assistent *c*

associate [ə'souʃiət] *n* partner *c*, vennoot *c*; bondgenoot *c*; lid *nt*; *v* associëren; ~ **with** *omgaan met

association [ə,sousi'eiʃən] *n* genootschap *nt*, vereniging *c*

assort [ə'sɔ:t] *v* sorteren

assortment [ə'sɔ:tmənt] *n* assortiment *nt*, sortering *c*

assume [ə'sju:m] *v* *aannemen, veronderstellen

assure [ə'ʃuə] *v* verzekeren

asthma ['æsmə] *n* astma *nt*

astonish [ə'stɒniʃ] *v* verbazen

astonishing [ə'stɒniʃiŋ] *adj* verbazend

astonishment [ə'stɒniʃmənt] *n* verbazing *c*

astronomy [ə'strɒnəmi] *n* sterrenkunde *c*

asylum [ə'sailəm] *n* asiel *nt*; gesticht *nt*, tehuis *nt*

at [æt] *prep* in, bij, op; naar

ate [et] *v* (p eat)

atheist ['eiθiist] *n* atheïst *c*

athlete ['æθli:t] *n* atleet *c*

athletics [æθ'letiks] *pl* atletiek *c*

Atlantic [ət'læntik] Atlantische Oceaan

atmosphere ['ætməsfiə] *n* atmosfeer *c*; sfeer *c*, stemming *c*

atom ['ætəm] *n* atoom *nt*

atomic [ə'tɔmik] *adj* atomisch; atoom-

atomizer ['ætəmaizə] *n* sproeier *c*; spuitbus *c*, verstuiver *c*

attach [ə'tætʃ] *v* hechten, vastmaken; aanhechten; bijvoegen; **attached to** gehecht aan

attack [ə'tæk] *v* *aanvallen; *n* aanval *c*

attain [ə'tein] *v* bereiken

attainable [ə'teinəbəl] *adj* haalbaar; bereikbaar

attempt [ə'tempt] *v* proberen, trachten; beproeven; *n* poging *c*

attend [ə'tend] *v* bijwonen; ~ **on** bedienen; ~ **to** passen op, zich *bezighouden met; letten op, aandacht besteden aan

attendance [ə'tendəns] *n* opkomst *c*

attendant [ə'tendənt] *n* oppasser *c*

attention [ə'tenʃən] *n* aandacht *c*; *pay ~ opletten

attentive [ə'tentiv] *adj* oplettend

attic ['ætik] *n* zolder *c*

attitude ['ætitjuːd] *n* houding *c*

attorney [ə'tɔːni] *n* advocaat *c*

attract [ə'trækt] *v* *aantrekken

attraction [ə'trækʃən] *n* attractie *c*; aantrekking *c*, bekoring *c*

attractive [ə'træktiv] *adj* aantrekkelijk

auburn ['ɔːbən] *adj* kastanjebruin

auction ['ɔːkʃən] *n* veiling *c*

audible ['ɔːdibəl] *adj* hoorbaar

audience ['ɔːdiəns] *n* publiek *nt*

auditor ['ɔːditə] *n* toehoorder *c*

auditorium [,ɔːdi'tɔːriəm] *n* aula *c*

August ['ɔːgəst] augustus

aunt [ɑːnt] *n* tante *c*

Australia [ɔ'streiliə] Australië

Australian [ɔ'streiliən] *adj* Australisch; *n* Australiër *c*

Austria ['ɔstriə] Oostenrijk

Austrian ['ɔstriən] *adj* Oostenrijks; *n* Oostenrijker *c*

authentic [ɔ'θentik] *adj* authentiek; echt

author ['ɔːθə] *n* auteur *c*, schrijver *c*

authoritarian [ɔːˌθɔri'tɛəriən] *adj* autoritair

authority [ɔː'θɔrəti] *n* gezag *nt*; macht *c*; **authorities** *pl* autoriteiten *pl*, overheid *c*

authorization [,ɔːθərai'zeiʃən] *n* machtiging *c*; toestemming *c*

automatic [,ɔːtə'mætik] *adj* automatisch

automation [,ɔːtə'meiʃən] *n* automatisering *c*

automobile ['ɔːtəməbiːl] *n* auto *c*; ~ **club** automobielclub *c*

autonomous [ɔː'tɔnəməs] *adj* autonoom

autopsy ['ɔːtɔpsi] *n* autopsie *c*

autumn ['ɔːtəm] *n* najaar *nt*, herfst *c*

available [ə'veiləbəl] *adj* verkrijgbaar, voorhanden, beschikbaar

avalanche ['ævəlɑːnʃ] *n* lawine *c*

avaricious [,ævə'riʃəs] *adj* gierig

avenue ['ævənjuː] *n* laan *c*

average ['ævəridʒ] *adj* gemiddeld; *n* gemiddelde *nt*; **on the ~** gemiddeld

averse [ə'vəːs] *adj* afkerig

aversion [ə'vəːʃən] *n* tegenzin *c*

avert [ə'vəːt] *v* afwenden

avoid [ə'vɔid] *v* *vermijden; *ontwijken

await [ə'weit] *v* wachten op, afwachten

awake [ə'weik] *adj* wakker

*awake** [ə'weik] *v* wekken

award [ə'wɔːd] *n* prijs *c*; *v* toekennen

aware [ə'wɛə] *adj* bewust

away [ə'wei] *adv* weg; *go ~ *weggaan

awful ['ɔːfəl] *adj* afschuwelijk, ver-

schrikkelijk
awkward ['ɔːkwəd] *adj* pijnlijk; onhandig
awning ['ɔːniŋ] *n* zonnescherm *nt*
axe [æks] *n* bijl *c*
axle ['æksəl] *n* as *c*

B

baby ['beibi] *n* baby *c*; ~ **carriage**
Am kinderwagen *c*
babysitter ['beibi,sitə] *n* babysitter *c*
bachelor ['bætʃələ] *n* vrijgezel *c*
back [bæk] *n* rug *c*; *adv* terug; ** go ~
*teruggaan
backache ['bækeik] *n* rugpijn *c*
backbone ['bækboun] *n* ruggegraat *c*
background ['bækɡraund] *n* achtergrond *c*; vorming *c*
backwards ['bækwədz] *adv* achteruit
bacon ['beikən] *n* spek *nt*
bacterium [bæk'tiːriəm] *n* (pl -ria) bacterie *c*
bad [bæd] *adj* slecht; ernstig, erg;
stout
bag [bæɡ] *n* zak *c*; tas *c*, handtas *c*;
koffer *c*
baggage ['bæɡidʒ] *n* bagage *c*; ~ **deposit office** *Am* bagagedepot *nt*;
hand ~ *Am* handbagage *c*
bail [beil] *n* borgsom *c*
bailiff ['beilif] *n* deurwaarder *c*
bait [beit] *n* aas *nt*
bake [beik] *v* *bakken
baker ['beikə] *n* bakker *c*
bakery ['beikəri] *n* bakkerij *c*
balance ['bæləns] *n* evenwicht *nt*; balans *c*; saldo *nt*
balcony ['bælkəni] *n* balkon *nt*
bald [bɔːld] *adj* kaal
ball [bɔːl] *n* bal *c*; bal *nt*
ballet ['bælei] *n* ballet *nt*

balloon [bə'luːn] *n* ballon *c*
ballpoint-pen ['bɔːlpɔintpen] *n* ballpoint *c*
ballroom ['bɔːlruːm] *n* danszaal *c*
bamboo [bæm'buː] *n* (pl ~s) bamboe
nt
banana [bə'nɑːnə] *n* banaan *c*
band [bænd] *n* orkest *nt*; band *c*
bandage ['bændidʒ] *n* verband *nt*
bandit ['bændit] *n* bandiet *c*
bangle ['bæŋɡəl] *n* armband *c*
banisters ['bænistəz] *pl* trapleuning *c*
bank [bæŋk] *n* oever *c*; bank *c*; *v* deponeren; ~ **account** bankrekening
c
banknote ['bæŋknout] *n* bankbiljet *nt*
bank-rate ['bæŋkreit] *n* disconto *nt*
bankrupt ['bæŋkrʌpt] *adj* failliet,
bankroet
banner ['bænə] *n* vaandel *nt*
banquet ['bæŋkwit] *n* banket *nt*
banqueting-hall ['bæŋkwitiŋhɔːl] *n*
banketzaal *c*
baptism ['bæptizəm] *n* doopsel *nt*,
doop *c*
baptize [bæp'taiz] *v* dopen
bar [bɑː] *n* bar *c*; stang *c*; tralie *c*
barber ['bɑːbə] *n* kapper *c*
bare [bɛə] *adj* naakt, bloot; kaal
barely ['bɛəli] *adv* nauwelijks
bargain ['bɑːgin] *n* koopje *nt*; *v* *afdingen
baritone ['bæritoun] *n* bariton *c*
bark [bɑːk] *n* bast *c*; *v* blaffen
barley ['bɑːli] *n* gerst *c*
barmaid ['bɑːmeid] *n* barjuffrouw *c*
barman ['bɑːmən] *n* (pl -men) barman
c
barn [bɑːn] *n* schuur *c*
barometer [bə'rɔmitə] *n* barometer *c*
baroque [bə'rɔk] *adj* barok
barracks ['bærəks] *pl* kazerne *c*
barrel ['bærəl] *n* ton *c*, vat *nt*
barrier ['bæriə] *n* barrière *c*; slagboom

c

barrister ['bæristə] *n* advocaat *c*

bartender ['bɑ:,tendə] *n* barman *c*

base [beis] *n* basis *c*; grondslag *c*; *v* baseren

baseball ['beisbɔ:l] *n* honkbal *nt*

basement ['beismənt] *n* souterrain *nt*

basic ['beisik] *adj* fundamenteel

basilica [bə'zilikə] *n* basiliek *c*

basin ['beisən] *n* kom *c*, bekken *nt*

basis ['beisis] *n* (pl bases) grondslag *c*, basis *c*

basket ['bɑ:skit] *n* mand *c*

bass¹ [beis] *n* bas *c*

bass² [bæs] *n* (pl ~) baars *c*

bastard ['bɑ:stəd] *n* bastaard *c*; schoft *c*

batch [bætʃ] *n* partij *c*

bath [bɑ:θ] *n* bad *nt*; ~ **salts** badzout *nt*; ~ **towel** badhanddoek *c*

bathe [beið] *v* baden, een bad *nemen

bathing-cap ['beiðiŋkæp] *n* badmuts *c*

bathing-suit ['beiðiŋsu:t] *n* badpak *nt*; zwembroek *c*

bathing-trunks ['beiðiŋtrʌŋks] *n* zwembroek *c*

bathrobe ['bɑ:θroub] *n* badjas *c*

bathroom ['bɑ:θru:m] *n* badkamer *c*; toilet *nt*

batter ['bætə] *n* beslag *nt*

battery ['bætəri] *n* batterij *c*; accu *c*

battle ['bætəl] *n* slag *c*; strijd *c*, gevecht *nt*; *v* *vechten

bay [bei] *n* baai *c*; *v* blaffen

***be** [bi:] *v* *zijn

beach [bi:tʃ] *n* strand *nt*; **nudist** ~ naaktstrand *nt*

bead [bi:d] *n* kraal *c*; **beads** *pl* kralensnoer *nt*; rozenkrans *c*

beak [bi:k] *n* snavel *c*; bek *c*

beam [bi:m] *n* straal *c*; balk *c*

bean [bi:n] *n* boon *c*

bear [bɛə] *n* beer *c*

***bear** [bɛə] *v* *dragen; dulden; *ver-

dragen

beard [biəd] *n* baard *c*

bearer ['bɛərə] *n* drager *c*

beast [bi:st] *n* beest *nt*; ~ **of prey** roofdier *nt*

***beat** [bi:t] *v* *slaan; *verslaan

beautiful ['bju:tifəl] *adj* mooi

beauty ['bju:ti] *n* schoonheid *c*; ~ **parlour** schoonheidssalon *c*; ~ **salon** schoonheidssalon *c*; ~ **treatment** schoonheidsbehandeling *c*

beaver ['bi:və] *n* bever *c*

because [bi'kɔz] *conj* omdat; aangezien; ~ **of** vanwege, wegens

***become** [bi'kʌm] *v* *worden; goed *staan

bed [bed] *n* bed *nt*; ~ **and board** vol pension, kost en inwoning; ~ **and breakfast** logies en ontbijt

bedding ['bediŋ] *n* beddegoed *nt*

bedroom ['bedru:m] *n* slaapkamer *c*

bee [bi:] *n* bij *c*

beech [bi:tʃ] *n* beuk *c*

beef [bi:f] *n* rundvlees *nt*

beehive ['bi:haiv] *n* bijenkorf *c*

been [bi:n] *v* (pp be)

beer [biə] *n* bier *nt*; pils *nt*

beet [bi:t] *n* biet *c*

beetle ['bi:təl] *n* kever *c*

beetroot ['bi:tru:t] *n* beetwortel *c*

before [bi'fɔ:] *prep* voor; *conj* voordat; *adv* van tevoren; eerder, tevoren

beg [beg] *v* bedelen; smeken; *vragen

beggar ['begə] *n* bedelaar *c*

***begin** [bi'gin] *v* *beginnen; *aanvangen

beginner [bi'ginə] *n* beginneling *c*

beginning [bi'giniŋ] *n* begin *nt*; aanvang *c*

on behalf of [ɔn bi'hɑ:f ɔv] namens, in naam van; ten behoeve van

behave [bi'heiv] *v* zich *gedragen

behaviour [bi'heivjə] *n* gedrag *nt*

behind [bi'haind] *prep* achter; *adv* achteraan

beige [beiʒ] *adj* beige

being ['bi:iŋ] *n* wezen *nt*

Belgian ['beldʒən] *adj* Belgisch; *n* Belg *c*

Belgium ['beldʒəm] België

belief [bi'li:f] *n* geloof *nt*

believe [bi'li:v] *v* geloven

bell [bel] *n* klok *c*; bel *c*

bellboy ['belbɔi] *n* piccolo *c*

belly ['beli] *n* buik *c*

belong [bi'lɔŋ] *v* toebehoren

belongings [bi'lɔŋiŋz] *pl* bezittingen *pl*

beloved [bi'lʌvd] *adj* bemind

below [bi'lou] *prep* onder; beneden; *adv* onderaan, beneden

belt [belt] *n* riem *c*; **garter** ~ *Am* jarretelgordel *c*

bench [bentʃ] *n* bank *c*

bend [bend] *n* bocht *c*; kromming *c*

*bend [bend] *v* *buigen; ~ **down** zich bukken

beneath [bi'ni:θ] *prep* onder; *adv* beneden

benefit ['benifit] *n* winst *c*, baat *c*; voordeel *nt*; *v* profiteren

bent [bent] *adj* (pp bend) krom

beret ['berei] *n* baret *c*

berry ['beri] *n* bes *c*

berth [bə:θ] *n* couchette *c*; kooi *c*

beside [bi'said] *prep* naast

besides [bi'saidz] *adv* bovendien; trouwens; *prep* behalve

best [best] *adj* best

bet [bet] *n* weddenschap *c*; inzet *c*

*bet [bet] *v* wedden

betray [bi'trei] *v* *verraden

better ['betə] *adj* beter

between [bi'twi:n] *prep* tussen

beverage ['bevəridʒ] *n* drank *c*

beware [bi'wɛə] *v* zich hoeden, oppassen

bewitch [bi'witʃ] *v* beheksen, betoveren

beyond [bi'jɔnd] *prep* verder dan; voorbij; behalve; *adv* verder

bible ['baibəl] *n* bijbel *c*

bicycle ['baisikəl] *n* fiets *c*; rijwiel *nt*

big [big] *adj* groot; omvangrijk; dik; gewichtig

bile [bail] *n* gal *c*

bilingual [bai'liŋgwəl] *adj* tweetalig

bill [bil] *n* rekening *c*; nota *c*; *v* factureren

billiards ['biljədz] *pl* biljart *nt*

*bind [baind] *v* *binden

binoculars [bi'nɔkjələz] *pl* verrekijker *c*; toneelkijker *c*

biology [bai'ɔlədʒi] *n* biologie *c*

birch [bə:tʃ] *n* berk *c*

bird [bə:d] *n* vogel *c*

Biro ['bairou] *n* ballpoint *c*

birth [bə:θ] *n* geboorte *c*

birthday ['bə:θdei] *n* verjaardag *c*

biscuit ['biskit] *n* koekje *nt*

bishop ['biʃəp] *n* bisschop *c*

bit [bit] *n* stukje *nt*; beetje *nt*

bitch [bitʃ] *n* teef *c*

bite [bait] *n* hap *c*; beet *c*; steek *c*

*bite [bait] *v* *bijten

bitter ['bitə] *adj* bitter

black [blæk] *adj* zwart; ~ **market** zwarte markt

blackberry ['blækbəri] *n* braam *c*

blackbird ['blækbə:d] *n* merel *c*

blackboard ['blækbɔ:d] *n* schoolbord *nt*

black-currant [,blæk'kʌrənt] *n* zwarte bes

blackmail ['blækmeil] *n* chantage *c*; *v* chanteren

blacksmith ['blæksmiθ] *n* smid *c*

bladder ['blædə] *n* blaas *c*

blade [bleid] *n* lemmet *nt*; ~ **of grass** grasspriet *c*

blame [bleim] *n* schuld *c*; verwijt *nt*; *v* de schuld *geven aan, beschuldigen

blank [blæŋk] *adj* blanco

blanket ['blæŋkit] *n* deken *c*

blast [blɑ:st] *n* explosie *c*

blazer ['bleizə] *n* sportjasje *nt*, blazer *c*

bleach [bli:tʃ] *v* bleken

bleak [bli:k] *adj* guur

*****bleed** [bli:d] *v* bloeden; *uitzuigen

bless [bles] *v* zegenen

blessing ['blesiŋ] *n* zegen *c*

blind [blaind] *n* rolgordijn *nt*, jaloezie *c*; *adj* blind; *v* verblinden

blister ['blistə] *n* blaar *c*, blaas *c*

blizzard ['blizəd] *n* sneeuwstorm *c*

block [blɔk] *v* versperren, blokkeren; *n* blok *nt*; ~ **of flats** flatgebouw *nt*

blonde [blɔnd] *n* blondine *c*

blood [blʌd] *n* bloed *nt*; ~ **pressure** bloeddruk *c*

blood-poisoning ['blʌd,pɔizəniŋ] *n* bloedvergiftiging *c*

blood-vessel ['blʌd,vesəl] *n* bloedvat *nt*

blot [blɔt] *n* vlek *c*; smet *c*; **blotting paper** vloeipapier *nt*

blouse [blauz] *n* blouse *c*

blow [blou] *n* klap *c*, slag *c*; windvlaag *c*

*****blow** [blou] *v* *blazen; *waaien

blow-out ['blouaut] *n* bandepech *c*

blue [blu:] *adj* blauw; neerslachtig

blunt [blʌnt] *adj* bot; stomp

blush [blʌʃ] *v* blozen

board [bɔ:d] *n* plank *c*; bord *nt*; pension *nt*; bestuur *nt*; ~ **and lodging** vol pension, kost en inwoning

boarder ['bɔ:də] *n* kostganger *c*

boarding-house ['bɔ:diŋhaus] *n* pension *nt*

boarding-school ['bɔ:diŋsku:l] *n* internaat *nt*

boast [boust] *v* opscheppen

boat [bout] *n* schip *nt*, boot *c*

body ['bɔdi] *n* lichaam *nt*; lijf *nt*

bodyguard ['bɔdigɑ:d] *n* lijfwacht *c*

bog [bɔg] *n* moeras *nt*

boil [bɔil] *v* koken; *n* steenpuist *c*

bold [bould] *adj* stoutmoedig; vrijpostig, brutaal

Bolivia [bə'liviə] Bolivië

Bolivian [bə'liviən] *adj* Boliviaans; *n* Boliviaan *c*

bolt [boult] *n* grendel *c*; bout *c*

bomb [bɔm] *n* bom *c*; *v* bombarderen

bond [bɔnd] *n* obligatie *c*

bone [boun] *n* been *nt*, bot *nt*; graat *c*; *v* uitbenen

bonnet ['bɔnit] *n* motorkap *c*

book [buk] *n* boek *nt*; *v* reserveren, boeken; *inschrijven

booking ['bukiŋ] *n* reservering *c*, bespreking *c*

bookseller ['buk,selə] *n* boekhandelaar *c*

bookstand ['bukstænd] *n* boekenstalletje *nt*

bookstore ['bukstɔ:] *n* boekwinkel *c*, boekhandel *c*

boot [bu:t] *n* laars *c*; bagageruimte *c*

booth [bu:ð] *n* kraam *c*; hokje *nt*

border ['bɔ:də] *n* grens *c*; rand *c*

bore¹ [bɔ:] *v* vervelen; boren; *n* zeurpiet *c*

bore² [bɔ:] *v* (p bear)

boring ['bɔ:riŋ] *adj* vervelend, saai

born [bɔ:n] *adj* geboren

borrow ['bɔrou] *v* lenen; ontlenen

bosom ['buzəm] *n* borst *c*

boss [bɔs] *n* chef *c*, baas *c*

botany ['bɔtəni] *n* plantkunde *c*

both [bouθ] *adj* beide; **both ... and** zowel ... als

bother ['bɔðə] *v* vervelen, hinderen; moeite *doen; *n* last *c*

bottle ['bɔtəl] *n* fles *c*; ~ **opener** flesopener *c*; **hot-water** ~ warmwaterkruik *c*

bottleneck ['bɔtəlnek] *n* flessehals *c*

bottom ['bɔtəm] n bodem c; achterwerk nt, zitvlak nt; adj onderst

bough [bau] n tak c

bought [bɔ:t] v (p, pp buy)

boulder ['bouldə] n rotsblok nt

bound [baund] n grens c; *be ~ to *moeten; ~ for op weg naar

boundary ['baundəri] n grens c; landsgrens c

bouquet [bu'kei] n boeket nt

bourgeois ['buəʒwa:] adj burgerlijk

boutique [bu'ti:k] n boutique c

bow[1] [bau] v *buigen

bow[2] [bou] n boog c; ~ tie vlinderdasje nt, strikje nt

bowels [bauəlz] pl darmen, ingewanden pl

bowl [boul] n schaal c

bowling ['bouliŋ] n bowling c, kegelspel nt; ~ alley kegelbaan c

box[1] [bɔks] v boksen; **boxing match** bokswedstrijd c

box[2] [bɔks] n doos c

box-office ['bɔks,ɔfis] n plaatskaartenbureau nt, kassa c

boy [bɔi] n jongen c; joch nt, knaap c; bediende c; ~ **scout** padvinder c

bra [bra:] n beha c, bustehouder c

bracelet ['breislit] n armband c

braces ['breisiz] pl bretels pl

brain [brein] n hersenen pl; verstand nt

brain-wave ['breinweiv] n inval c

brake [breik] n rem c; ~ **drum** remtrommel c; ~ **lights** remlichten pl

branch [bra:ntʃ] n tak c; filiaal nt

brand [brænd] n merk nt; brandmerk nt

brand-new [,brænd'nju:] adj splinternieuw

brass [bra:s] n messing nt; koper nt, geelkoper nt; ~ **band** n fanfarekorps nt

brassiere ['bræziə] n bustehouder c, beha c

brassware ['bra:swɛə] n koperwerk nt

brave [breiv] adj moedig, dapper; flink

Brazil [brə'zil] Brazilië

Brazilian [brə'ziljən] adj Braziliaans; n Braziliaan c

breach [bri:tʃ] n bres c

bread [bred] n brood nt; **wholemeal** ~ volkorenbrood nt

breadth [bredθ] n breedte c

break [breik] n breuk c; pauze c

*break [breik] v *breken; ~ **down** stuk *gaan; ontleden

breakdown ['breikdaun] n panne c, motorpech c

breakfast ['brekfəst] n ontbijt nt

bream [bri:m] n (pl ~) brasem c

breast [brest] n borst c

breaststroke ['breststrouk] n schoolslag c

breath [breθ] n adem c; lucht c

breathe [bri:ð] v ademen

breathing ['bri:ðiŋ] n ademhaling c

breed [bri:d] n ras nt; soort c/nt

*breed [bri:d] v fokken

breeze [bri:z] n bries c

brew [bru:] v brouwen

brewery ['bru:əri] n brouwerij c

bribe [braib] v *omkopen

bribery ['braibəri] n omkoping c

brick [brik] n steen c, baksteen c

bricklayer ['brik,leiə] n metselaar c

bride [braid] n bruid c

bridegroom ['braidgru:m] n bruidegom c

bridge [bridʒ] n brug c; bridge nt

brief [bri:f] adj kort; beknopt

briefcase ['bri:fkeis] n aktentas c

briefs [bri:fs] pl slip c, onderbroek c

bright [brait] adj helder; blinkend; snugger, pienter

brill [bril] n griet c

brilliant ['briljənt] *adj* schitterend; briljant

brim [brim] *n* rand *c*

*bring [briŋ] *v* *brengen; *meebrengen; ~ back *terugbrengen; ~ up opvoeden, *grootbrengen; ter sprake *brengen

brisk [brisk] *adj* levendig

Britain ['britən] Engeland

British ['britiʃ] *adj* Brits; Engels

Briton ['britən] *n* Brit *c*; Engelsman *c*

broad [brɔːd] *adj* breed; ruim, wijd; globaal

broadcast ['brɔːdkɑːst] *n* uitzending *c*

*broadcast ['brɔːdkɑːst] *v* *uitzenden

brochure ['brouʃuə] *n* brochure *c*

broke¹ [brouk] *v* (p break)

broke² [brouk] *adj* platzak

broken ['broukən] *adj* (pp break) stuk, kapot

broker ['broukə] *n* makelaar *c*

bronchitis [brɔŋ'kaitis] *n* bronchitis *c*

bronze [brɔnz] *n* brons *nt*; *adj* bronzen

brooch [broutʃ] *n* broche *c*

brook [bruk] *n* beek *c*

broom [bruːm] *n* bezem *c*

brothel ['brɔθəl] *n* bordeel *nt*

brother ['brʌðə] *n* broer *c*; broeder *c*

brother-in-law ['brʌðərinlɔː] *n* (pl brothers-) zwager *c*

brought [brɔːt] *v* (p, pp bring)

brown [braun] *adj* bruin

bruise [bruːz] *n* blauwe plek, kneuzing *c*; *v* kneuzen

brunette [bruː'net] *n* brunette *c*

brush [brʌʃ] *n* borstel *c*; kwast *c*; *v* poetsen, borstelen

brutal ['bruːtəl] *adj* beestachtig

bubble ['bʌbəl] *n* bel *c*

bucket ['bʌkit] *n* emmer *c*

buckle ['bʌkəl] *n* gesp *c*

bud [bʌd] *n* knop *c*

budget ['bʌdʒit] *n* begroting *c*, budget

nt

buffet ['bufei] *n* buffet *nt*

bug [bʌg] *n* wandluis *c*; kever *c*; *nAm* insekt *nt*

*build [bild] *v* bouwen

building ['bildiŋ] *n* gebouw *nt*

bulb [bʌlb] *n* bol *c*; bloembol *c*; light ~ gloeilamp *c*

Bulgaria [bʌl'geəriə] Bulgarije

Bulgarian [bʌl'geəriən] *adj* Bulgaars; *n* Bulgaar *c*

bulk [bʌlk] *n* omvang *c*; massa *c*; meerderheid *c*

bulky ['bʌlki] *adj* lijvig, omvangrijk

bull [bul] *n* stier *c*

bullet ['bulit] *n* kogel *c*

bullfight ['bulfait] *n* stierengevecht *nt*

bullring ['bulriŋ] *n* arena *c*

bump [bʌmp] *v* *stoten; botsen; bonzen; *n* stoot *c*, bons *c*

bumper ['bʌmpə] *n* bumper *c*

bumpy ['bʌmpi] *adj* hobbelig

bun [bʌn] *n* broodje *nt*

bunch [bʌntʃ] *n* bos *c*; groep *c*

bundle ['bʌndəl] *n* bundel *c*; *v* *samenbinden, bundelen

bunk [bʌŋk] *n* kooi *c*

buoy [bɔi] *n* boei *c*

burden ['bəːdən] *n* last *c*

bureau ['bjuərou] *n* (pl ~x, ~s) bureau *nt*, schrijftafel *c*; *nAm* commode *c*

bureaucracy [bjuə'rɔkrəsi] *n* bureaucratie *c*

burglar ['bəːglə] *n* inbreker *c*

burgle ['bəːgəl] *v* *inbreken

burial ['beriəl] *n* teraardebestelling *c*, begrafenis *c*

burn [bəːn] *n* brandwond *c*

*burn [bəːn] *v* branden; verbranden; aanbranden

*burst [bəːst] *v* *barsten; *breken

bury ['beri] *v* *begraven; *bedelven

bus [bʌs] *n* bus *c*

bush [buʃ] *n* struik *c*

business ['biznəs] n zaken pl, handel c; bedrijf nt, zaak c; werk nt; aangelegenheid c; ~ **hours** openingstijden pl, kantooruren pl; ~ **trip** zakenreis c; **on** ~ voor zaken

business-like ['biznislaik] adj zakelijk

businessman ['biznəsmən] n (pl -men) zakenman c

bust [bʌst] n buste c

bustle ['bʌsəl] n drukte c

busy ['bizi] adj bezig; druk

but [bʌt] conj maar; doch; prep behalve

butcher ['butʃə] n slager c

butter ['bʌtə] n boter c

butterfly ['bʌtəflai] n vlinder c; ~ **stroke** vlinderslag c

buttock ['bʌtək] n bil c

button ['bʌtən] n knoop c; v knopen

buttonhole ['bʌtənhoul] n knoopsgat nt

*****buy** [bai] v *kopen; aanschaffen

buyer ['baiə] n koper c

by [bai] prep door; met, per; bij

by-pass ['baipɑ:s] n ringweg c; v passeren

C

cab [kæb] n taxi c

cabaret ['kæbərei] n cabaret nt; nachtclub c

cabbage ['kæbidʒ] n kool c

cab-driver ['kæb,draivə] n taxichauffeur c

cabin ['kæbin] n cabine c; hut c; kleedhokje nt; kajuit c

cabinet ['kæbinət] n kabinet nt

cable ['keibəl] n kabel c; telegram nt; v telegraferen

cadre ['kɑ:də] n kader nt

café ['kæfei] n café nt

cafeteria [,kæfə'tiəriə] n cafetaria c

caffeine ['kæfi:n] n coffeïne c

cage [keidʒ] n kooi c

cake [keik] n cake c; gebak nt, taart c, koek c

calamity [kə'læməti] n onheil nt, ramp c

calcium ['kælsiəm] n calcium nt

calculate ['kælkjuleit] v uitrekenen, berekenen

calculation [,kælkju'leiʃən] n berekening c

calendar ['kæləndə] n kalender c

calf [kɑ:f] n (pl calves) kalf nt; kuit c; ~ **skin** kalfsleer nt

call [kɔ:l] v *roepen; noemen; opbellen; n roep c; visite c, bezoek nt; telefoontje nt; *****be called** *heten; ~ **names** *uitschelden; ~ **on** *bezoeken; ~ **up** Am opbellen

callus ['kæləs] n eelt nt

calm [kɑ:m] adj rustig, kalm; ~ **down** kalmeren; bedaren

calorie ['kæləri] n calorie c

Calvinism ['kælvinizəm] n calvinisme nt

came [keim] v (p come)

camel ['kæməl] n kameel c

cameo ['kæmiou] n (pl ~s) camee c

camera ['kæmərə] n fototoestel nt; filmcamera c; ~ **shop** fotowinkel c

camp [kæmp] n kamp nt; v kamperen

campaign [kæm'pein] n campagne c

camp-bed [,kæmp'bed] n veldbed nt, stretcher c

camper ['kæmpə] n kampeerder c

camping ['kæmpiŋ] n camping c; ~ **site** camping c, kampeerterrein nt

camshaft ['kæmʃɑ:ft] n nokkenas c

can [kæn] n blik nt; ~ **opener** blikopener c

*****can** [kæn] v *kunnen

Canada ['kænədə] Canada

Canadian [kə'neidiən] adj Canadees;

n Canadees *c*

canal [kə'næl] *n* kanaal *nt*; gracht *c*, singel *c*

canary [kə'neəri] *n* kanarie *c*

cancel ['kænsəl] *v* annuleren; *afzeggen

cancellation [,kænsə'leiʃən] *n* annulering *c*

cancer ['kænsə] *n* kanker *c*

candelabrum [,kændə'lɑ:brəm] *n* (pl - bra) kandelaber *c*

candidate ['kændidət] *n* kandidaat *c*, gegadigde *c*

candle ['kændəl] *n* kaars *c*

candy ['kændi] *nAm* snoepje *nt*; snoep *nt*, snoepgoed *nt*; ~ **store** *Am* snoepwinkel *c*

cane [kein] *n* riet *nt*; stok *c*

canister ['kænistə] *n* trommel *c*, bus *c*

canoe [kə'nu:] *n* kano *c*

canteen [kæn'ti:n] *n* kantine *c*

canvas ['kænvəs] *n* tentdoek *nt*

cap [kæp] *n* pet *c*, muts *c*

capable ['keipəbəl] *adj* kundig, bekwaam

capacity [kə'pæsəti] *n* capaciteit *c*; vermogen *nt*; bekwaamheid *c*

cape [keip] *n* cape *c*; kaap *c*

capital ['kæpitəl] *n* hoofdstad *c*; kapitaal *nt*; *adj* belangrijk, hoofd-; ~ **letter** hoofdletter *c*

capitalism ['kæpitəlizəm] *n* kapitalisme *nt*

capitulation [kə,pitju'leiʃən] *n* capitulatie *c*

capsule ['kæpsju:l] *n* capsule *c*

captain ['kæptin] *n* kapitein *c*; gezagvoerder *c*

capture ['kæptʃə] *v* gevangen *nemen, *vangen; *innemen; *n* vangst *c*; inneming *c*

car [kɑ:] *n* auto *c*; ~ **hire** autoverhuur *c*; ~ **park** parkeerplaats *c*; ~ **rental** *Am* autoverhuur *c*

carafe [kə'ræf] *n* karaf *c*

caramel ['kærəməl] *n* karamel *c*

carat ['kærət] *n* karaat *nt*

caravan ['kærəvæn] *n* caravan *c*; woonwagen *c*

carburettor [,kɑ:bju'retə] *n* carburateur *c*

card [kɑ:d] *n* kaart *c*; briefkaart *c*

cardboard ['kɑ:dbɔ:d] *n* karton *nt*; *adj* kartonnen

cardigan ['kɑ:digən] *n* vest *nt*

cardinal ['kɑ:dinəl] *n* kardinaal *c*; *adj* kardinaal, hoofd-

care [keə] *n* verzorging *c*; zorg *c*; ~ **about** zich bekommeren om; ~ **for** *houden van; *take ~ **of** zorgen voor, verzorgen

career [kə'riə] *n* loopbaan *c*, carrière *c*

carefree ['keəfri:] *adj* onbezorgd

careful ['keəfəl] *adj* voorzichtig; zorgvuldig, nauwkeurig

careless ['keələs] *adj* achteloos, slordig

caretaker ['keə,teikə] *n* concierge *c*

cargo ['kɑ:gou] *n* (pl ~es) lading *c*, vracht *c*

carnival ['kɑ:nivəl] *n* carnaval *nt*

carp [kɑ:p] *n* (pl ~) karper *c*

carpenter ['kɑ:pintə] *n* timmerman *c*

carpet ['kɑ:pit] *n* vloerkleed *nt*, tapijt *nt*

carriage ['kæridʒ] *n* wagon *c*; koets *c*, rijtuig *nt*

carriageway ['kæridʒwei] *n* rijbaan *c*

carrot ['kærət] *n* peen *c*, wortel *c*

carry ['kæri] *v* *dragen; voeren; ~ **on** voortzetten; *doorgaan; ~ **out** uitvoeren

carry-cot ['kærikɔt] *n* reiswieg *c*

cart [kɑ:t] *n* kar *c*, wagen *c*

cartilage ['kɑ:tilidʒ] *n* kraakbeen *nt*

carton ['kɑ:tən] *n* kartonnen doos; slof *c*

cartoon [kɑ:'tu:n] *n* tekenfilm *c*

cartridge ['kɑ:tridʒ] *n* patroon *c*

carve [ka:v] v *snijden; kerven,
*houtsnijden

carving ['ka:viŋ] n houtsnijwerk nt

case [keis] n geval nt; zaak c; koffer
c; etui nt; **attaché ~** aktentas c;
in ~ indien; in ~ of in geval van

cash [kæʃ] n contanten pl, contant
geld; v verzilveren, incasseren, innen

cashier [kæ'ʃiə] n kassier c; caissière
c

cashmere ['kæʃmiə] n kasjmier nt

casino [kə'si:nou] n (pl ~s) casino nt

cask [ka:sk] n ton c, vat nt

cast [ka:st] n worp c

*cast [ka:st] v gooien, *werpen; **cast
iron** gietijzer nt

castle ['ka:səl] n slot nt, kasteel c

casual ['kæʒuəl] adj ongedwongen;
terloops, toevallig

casualty ['kæʒuəlti] n slachtoffer nt

cat [kæt] n kat c

catacomb ['kætəkoum] n catacombe c

catalogue ['kætələg] n catalogus c

catarrh [kə'ta:] n catarre c

catastrophe [kə'tæstrəfi] n catastrofe c

*catch [kætʃ] v *vangen; *grijpen;
betrappen; *nemen, halen

category ['kætigəri] n categorie c

cathedral [kə'θi:drəl] n dom c, kathedraal c

catholic ['kæθəlik] adj katholiek

cattle ['kætəl] pl vee nt

caught [kɔ:t] v (p, pp catch)

cauliflower ['kɔliflauə] n bloemkool c

cause [kɔ:z] v veroorzaken; aanrichten; n oorzaak c; beweegreden c,
aanleiding c; zaak c; **~ to** *doen

causeway ['kɔ:zwei] n straatweg c

caution ['kɔ:ʃən] n voorzichtigheid c;
v waarschuwen

cautious ['kɔ:ʃəs] adj bedachtzaam

cave [keiv] n grot c; spelonk c

cavern ['kævən] n hol nt

caviar ['kæviɑ:] n kaviaar c

cavity ['kævəti] n holte c

cease [si:s] v *ophouden

ceiling ['si:liŋ] n plafond nt

celebrate ['selibreit] v vieren

celebration [,seli'breiʃən] n viering c

celebrity [si'lebrəti] n roem c

celery ['seləri] n selderij c

celibacy ['selibəsi] n celibaat nt

cell [sel] n cel c

cellar ['selə] n kelder c

cellophane ['seləfein] n cellofaan c

cement [si'ment] n cement nt

cemetery ['semitri] n begraafplaats c,
kerkhof nt

censorship ['sensəʃip] n censuur c

centigrade ['sentigreid] adj celsius

centimetre ['senti,mi:tə] n centimeter c

central ['sentrəl] adj centraal; **~ heating** centrale verwarming; **~ station**
centraal station

centralize ['sentrəlaiz] v centraliseren

centre ['sentə] n centrum nt; middelpunt nt

century ['sentʃəri] n eeuw c

ceramics [si'ræmiks] pl aardewerk nt,
ceramiek c

ceremony ['serəməni] n ceremonie c

certain ['sə:tən] adj zeker; bepaald

certificate [sə'tifikət] n certificaat nt;
attest nt, akte c, diploma nt, getuigschrift nt

chain [tʃein] n keten c, ketting c

chair [tʃɛə] n stoel c; zetel c

chairman ['tʃɛəmən] n (pl -men) voorzitter c

chalet ['ʃælei] n chalet c

chalk [tʃɔ:k] n krijt nt

challenge ['tʃæləndʒ] v uitdagen; n
uitdaging c

chamber ['tʃeimbə] n kamer c

chambermaid ['tʃeimbəmeid] n kamermeisje c

champagne [ʃæm'pein] n champagne

c

champion ['tʃæmpjən] *n* kampioen *c* ; voorvechter *c*

chance [tʃɑ:ns] *n* toeval *nt* ; kans *c*, gelegenheid *c* ; risico *nt* ; gok *c* ; **by ~ toevallig**

change [tʃeindʒ] *v* wijzigen, veranderen ; wisselen ; zich verkleden ; overstappen ; *n* wijziging *c*, verandering *c* ; wisselgeld *nt*, kleingeld *nt*

channel ['tʃænəl] *n* kanaal *nt* ; **English Channel** het Kanaal

chaos ['keiɔs] *n* chaos *c*

chaotic [kei'ɔtik] *adj* chaotisch

chap [tʃæp] *n* vent *c*

chapel ['tʃæpəl] *n* kerk *c*, kapel *c*

chaplain ['tʃæplin] *n* kapelaan *c*

character ['kærəktə] *n* karakter *nt*

characteristic [ˌkærəktə'ristik] *adj* kenmerkend, karakteristiek ; *n* kenmerk *nt* ; karaktertrek *c*

characterize ['kærəktəraiz] *v* kenmerken

charcoal ['tʃɑ:koul] *n* houtskool *c*

charge [tʃɑ:dʒ] *v* berekenen ; belasten ; aanklagen ; *laden ; *n* prijs *c* ; belasting *c*, lading *c*, last *c* ; aanklacht *c* ; ~ **plate** *Am* credit card ; **free of ~** kosteloos ; **in ~ of** belast met ; *take ~ of op zich *nemen

charity ['tʃærəti] *n* liefdadigheid *c*

charm [tʃɑ:m] *n* bekoring *c*, charme *c* ; amulet *c*

charming ['tʃɑ:miŋ] *adj* charmant

chart [tʃɑ:t] *n* tabel *c* ; grafiek *c* ; zeekaart *c* ; **conversion ~** omrekentabel *c*

chase [tʃeis] *v* *najagen ; *verdrijven, *verjagen ; *n* jacht *c*

chasm ['kæzəm] *n* kloof *c*

chassis ['ʃæsi] *n* (pl ~) chassis *nt*

chaste [tʃeist] *adj* kuis

chat [tʃæt] *v* kletsen, babbelen ; *n* babbeltje *nt*, praatje *nt*, geklets *nt*

chatterbox ['tʃætəbɔks] *n* babbelkous *c*

chauffeur ['ʃoufə] *n* chauffeur *c*

cheap [tʃi:p] *adj* goedkoop ; voordelig

cheat [tʃi:t] *v* *bedriegen ; oplichten

check [tʃek] *v* controleren, *nakijken ; *n* ruit *c* ; *nAm* rekening *c* ; cheque *c* ; **check!** schaak! ; ~ **in** zich *inschrijven

check-book ['tʃekbuk] *nAm* chequeboekje *nt*

checkerboard ['tʃekəbɔ:d] *nAm* schaakbord *nt*

checkers ['tʃekəz] *plAm* damspel *nt*

checkroom ['tʃekru:m] *nAm* garderobe *c*

check-up ['tʃekʌp] *n* onderzoek *nt*

cheek [tʃi:k] *n* wang *c*

cheek-bone ['tʃi:kboun] *n* jukbeen *nt*

cheer [tʃiə] *v* juichen ; ~ **up** opvrolijken

cheerful ['tʃiəfəl] *adj* opgewekt, vrolijk

cheese [tʃi:z] *n* kaas *c*

chef [ʃef] *n* chef-kok *c*

chemical ['kemikəl] *adj* scheikundig, chemisch

chemist ['kemist] *n* apotheker *c* ; **chemist's** apotheek *c* ; drogisterij *c*

chemistry ['kemistri] *n* scheikunde *c*, chemie *c*

cheque [tʃek] *n* cheque *c*

cheque-book ['tʃekbuk] *n* chequeboekje *nt*

chequered ['tʃekəd] *adj* geruit, geblokt

cherry ['tʃeri] *n* kers *c*

chess [tʃes] *n* schaakspel *c*

chest [tʃest] *n* borst *c* ; borstkas *c* ; kist *c* ; ~ **of drawers** ladenkast *c*

chestnut ['tʃesnʌt] *n* kastanje *c*

chew [tʃu:] *v* kauwen

chewing-gum ['tʃu:iŋʌm] *n* kauwgom *c/nt*

chicken ['tʃikin] *n* kip *c* ; kuiken *nt*

chickenpox ['tʃikinpɔks] *n* waterpokken *pl*

chief [tʃiːf] *n* chef *c*; *adj* hoofd-, voornaamst

chieftain ['tʃiːftən] *n* opperhoofd *nt*

child [tʃaild] *n* (pl children) kind *nt*

childbirth ['tʃaildbəːθ] *n* bevalling *c*

childhood ['tʃaildhud] *n* jeugd *c*

Chile ['tʃili] Chili

Chilean ['tʃilian] *adj* Chileens; *n* Chileen *c*

chill [tʃil] *n* rilling *c*

chilly ['tʃili] *adj* kil

chimes [tʃaimz] *pl* carillon *nt*

chimney ['tʃimni] *n* schoorsteen *c*

chin [tʃin] *n* kin *c*

China ['tʃainə] China

china ['tʃainə] *n* porselein *nt*

Chinese [tʃaiˈniːz] *adj* Chinees; *n* Chinees *c*

chink [tʃiŋk] *n* kier *c*

chip [tʃip] *n* schilfer *c*; fiche *c*; *v* *afsnijden, *afbreken; **chips** frites *pl*

chiropodist [kiˈrɔpədist] *n* pedicure *c*

chisel ['tʃizəl] *n* beitel *c*

chives [tʃaivz] *pl* bieslook *nt*

chlorine ['klɔːriːn] *n* chloor *nt*

chock-full ['tʃɔkˈful] *adj* afgeladen, stampvol

chocolate ['tʃɔklət] *n* chocola *c*; bonbon *c*; chocolademelk *c*

choice [tʃɔis] *n* keuze *c*; keus *c*

choir [kwaiə] *n* koor *nt*

choke [tʃouk] *v* stikken; wurgen; *n* choke *c*

***choose** [tʃuːz] *v* *kiezen

chop [tʃɔp] *n* kotelet *c*, karbonade *c*; *v* hakken

Christ [kraist] Christus

christen ['krisən] *v* dopen

christening ['krisəniŋ] *n* doop *c*

Christian ['kristʃən] *adj* christelijk; *n* christen *c*; ~ **name** voornaam *c*

Christmas ['krisməs] Kerstmis

chromium ['kroumiəm] *n* chroom *nt*

chronic ['krɔnik] *adj* chronisch

chronological [ˌkrɔnəˈlɔdʒikəl] *adj* chronologisch

chuckle ['tʃʌkəl] *v* grinniken

chunk [tʃʌŋk] *n* stuk *nt*

church [tʃəːtʃ] *n* kerk *c*

churchyard ['tʃəːtʃjɑːd] *n* kerkhof *nt*

cigar [siˈgɑː] *n* sigaar *c*; ~ **shop** sigarenwinkel *c*

cigarette [ˌsigəˈret] *n* sigaret *c*; ~ **tobacco** shag *c*

cigarette-case [ˌsigəˈretkeis] *n* sigarettenkoker *c*

cigarette-holder [ˌsigəˈret,houldə] *n* sigarettepijpje *nt*

cigarette-lighter [ˌsigəˈret,laitə] *n* aansteker *c*

cinema ['sinəmə] *n* bioscoop *c*

cinnamon ['sinəmən] *n* kaneel *c*

circle ['səːkəl] *n* cirkel *c*; kring *c*; balkon *nt*; *v* omringen, *omgeven

circulation [ˌsəːkjuˈleiʃən] *n* circulatie *c*; bloedsomloop *c*; omloop *c*

circumstance ['səːkəmstæns] *n* omstandigheid *c*

circus ['səːkəs] *n* circus *c*

citizen ['sitizən] *n* burger *c*

citizenship ['sitizənʃip] *n* staatsburgerschap *nt*

city ['siti] *n* stad *c*

civic ['sivik] *adj* burger-

civil ['sivəl] *adj* civiel; beleefd; ~ **law** burgerlijk recht; ~ **servant** ambtenaar *c*

civilian [siˈviljən] *adj* burger-; *n* burger *c*

civilization [ˌsivəlaiˈzeiʃən] *n* beschaving *c*

civilized ['sivəlaizd] *adj* beschaafd

claim [kleim] *v* vorderen, opeisen; beweren; *n* eis *c*, aanspraak *c*

clamp [klæmp] *n* klem *c*; klemschroef *c*

clap [klæp] *v* applaudisseren, klappen

clarify ['klærifai] *v* ophelderen, verduidelijken

class [klɑ:s] *n* rang *c*, klasse *c*; klas *c*

classical ['klæsikəl] *adj* klassiek

classify ['klæsifai] *v* indelen

class-mate ['klɑ:smeit] *n* klasgenoot *c*

classroom ['klɑ:sru:m] *n* leslokaal *nt*

clause [klɔ:z] *n* clausule *c*

claw [klɔ:] *n* klauw *c*

clay [klei] *n* klei *c*

clean [kli:n] *adj* zuiver, schoon; *v* schoonmaken, reinigen

cleaning ['kli:niŋ] *n* schoonmaak *c*, reiniging *c*; ~ **fluid** reinigingsmiddel *nt*

clear [kliə] *adj* helder; duidelijk; *v* opruimen

clearing ['kliəriŋ] *n* open plaats

cleft [kleft] *n* kloof *c*

clergyman ['klə:dʒimən] *n* (pl -men) dominee *c*, predikant *c*; geestelijke *c*

clerk [klɑ:k] *n* kantoorbediende *c*, beambte *c*; klerk *c*; secretaris *c*

clever ['klevə] *adj* intelligent; slim, pienter, knap

client ['klaiənt] *n* klant *c*; cliënt *c*

cliff [klif] *n* rots *c*, klip *c*

climate ['klaimit] *n* klimaat *nt*

climb [klaim] *v* *klimmen; *stijgen; *n* stijging *c*

clinic ['klinik] *n* kliniek *c*

cloak [klouk] *n* mantel *c*

cloakroom ['kloukru:m] *n* garderobe *c*

clock [klɔk] *n* klok *c*; **at ... o'clock** om ... uur

cloister ['klɔistə] *n* klooster *nt*

close[1] [klouz] *v* *sluiten; **closed** *adj* toe, dicht, gesloten

close[2] [klous] *adj* nabij

closet ['klɔzit] *n* kast *c*; *nAm* kleerkast *c*

cloth [klɔθ] *n* stof *c*; doek *c*

clothes [klouðz] *pl* kleding *c*, kleren *pl*

clothes-brush ['klouðzbrʌʃ] *n* kleerborstel *c*

clothing ['klouðiŋ] *n* kleding *c*

cloud [klaud] *n* wolk *c*; **clouds** bewolking *c*

cloud-burst ['klaudbə:st] *n* wolkbreuk *c*

cloudy ['klaudi] *adj* betrokken, bewolkt

clover ['klouvə] *n* klaver *c*

clown [klaun] *n* clown *c*

club [klʌb] *n* club *c*; sociëteit *c*, vereniging *c*; knots *c*, knuppel *c*

clumsy ['klʌmzi] *adj* onhandig

clutch [klʌtʃ] *n* koppeling *c*; greep *c*

coach [koutʃ] *n* bus *c*; rijtuig *nt*; koets *c*; trainer *c*

coachwork ['koutʃwə:k] *n* carrosserie *c*

coagulate [kou'ægjuleit] *v* stollen

coal [koul] *n* kolen *pl*

coarse [kɔ:s] *adj* grof

coast [koust] *n* kust *c*

coat [kout] *n* mantel *c*, jas *c*

coat-hanger ['kout,hæŋə] *n* kleerhanger *c*

cobweb ['kɔbweb] *n* spinneweb *nt*

cocaine [kou'kein] *n* cocaïne *c*

cock [kɔk] *n* haan *c*

cocktail ['kɔkteil] *n* cocktail *c*

coconut ['koukənʌt] *n* kokosnoot *c*

cod [kɔd] *n* (pl ~) kabeljauw *c*

code [koud] *n* code *c*

coffee ['kɔfi] *n* koffie *c*

cognac ['kɔnjæk] *n* cognac *c*

coherence [kou'hiərəns] *n* samenhang *c*

coin [kɔin] *n* munt *c*; geldstuk *nt*, muntstuk *nt*

coincide [,kouin'said] *v* *samenvallen

cold [kould] *adj* koud; *n* kou *c*; verkoudheid *c*; **catch a** ~ kou vatten

collapse [kə'læps] *v* *bezwijken, instorten

collar ['kɔlə] n halsband c; boord nt/c, kraag c; ~ **stud** boordeknoopje nt

collarbone ['kɔləboun] n sleutelbeen nt

colleague ['kɔli:g] n collega c

collect [kə'lekt] v verzamelen; ophalen, afhalen; collecteren

collection [kə'lekʃən] n collectie c, verzameling c; lichting c

collective [kə'lektiv] adj collectief

collector [kə'lektə] n verzamelaar c; collectant c

college ['kɔlidʒ] n instelling voor hoger onderwijs; school c

collide [kə'laid] v botsen

collision [kə'liʒən] n aanrijding c, botsing c; aanvaring c

Colombia [kə'lɔmbiə] Colombia

Colombian [kə'lɔmbiən] adj Colombiaans; n Colombiaan c

colonel ['kə:nəl] n kolonel c

colony ['kɔləni] n kolonie c

colour ['kʌlə] n kleur c; v kleuren; ~ **film** kleurenfilm c

colourant ['kʌlərənt] n kleurstof c

colour-blind ['kʌləblaind] adj kleurenblind

coloured ['kʌləd] adj gekleurd

colourful ['kʌləfəl] adj bont, kleurrijk

column ['kɔləm] n pilaar c, zuil c; kolom c; rubriek c; kolonne c

coma ['koumə] n coma nt

comb [koum] v kammen; n kam c

combat ['kɔmbæt] n strijd c, gevecht nt; v *bestrijden, *vechten

combination [,kɔmbi'neiʃən] n combinatie c

combine [kəm'bain] v combineren; *samenbrengen

* come [kʌm] v *komen; ~ **across** *tegenkomen; *vinden

comedian [kə'mi:diən] n toneelspeler c; komiek c

comedy ['kɔmədi] n blijspel nt, komedie c; **musical** ~ musical c

comfort ['kʌmfət] n gemak nt, komfort nt, gerief nt; troost c; v troosten

comfortable ['kʌmfətəbəl] adj geriefelijk, comfortabel

comic ['kɔmik] adj komisch

comics ['kɔmiks] pl stripverhaal nt

coming ['kʌmiŋ] n komst c

comma ['kɔmə] n komma c

command [kə'ma:nd] v *bevelen; n bevel nt

commander [kə'ma:ndə] n bevelhebber c

commemoration [kə,memə'reiʃən] n herdenking c

commence [kə'mens] v *beginnen

comment ['kɔment] n commentaar nt; v aanmerken

commerce ['kɔmə:s] n handel c

commercial [kə'mə:ʃəl] adj handels-, commercieel; n reclamespot c; ~ **law** handelsrecht nt

commission [kə'miʃən] n commissie c

commit [kə'mit] v toevertrouwen; plegen, *begaan

committee [kə'miti] n commissie c, comité nt

common ['kɔmən] adj gemeenschappelijk; gebruikelijk, gewoon; ordinair

commune ['kɔmju:n] n commune c

communicate [kə'mju:nikeit] v meedelen, mededelen

communication [kə,mju:ni'keiʃən] n communicatie c; mededeling c

communiqué [kə'mju:nikei] n communiqué nt

communism ['kɔmjunizəm] n communisme nt

communist ['kɔmjunist] n communist c

community [kə'mju:nəti] n samenleving c, gemeenschap c

commuter [kə'mju:tə] *n* forens *c*

compact ['kompækt] *adj* compact

companion [kəm'pænjən] *n* metgezel *c*

company ['kʌmpəni] *n* gezelschap *nt* ; maatschappij *c* ; firma *c*, onderneming *c*

comparative [kəm'pærətiv] *adj* relatief

compare [kəm'peə] *v* *vergelijken

comparison [kəm'pærisən] *n* vergelijking *c*

compartment [kəm'pɑ:tmənt] *n* coupé *c*

compass ['kʌmpəs] *n* kompas *nt*

compel [kəm'pel] *v* *dwingen

compensate ['kompənseit] *v* compenseren

compensation [,kompən'seiʃən] *n* compensatie *c* ; schadevergoeding *c*

compete [kəm'pi:t] *v* wedijveren

competition [,kompə'tiʃən] *n* wedstrijd *c* ; concurrentie *c*

competitor [kəm'petitər] *n* concurrent *c*

compile [kəm'pail] *v* samenstellen

complain [kəm'plein] *v* klagen

complaint [kəm'pleint] *n* klacht *c* ;
  complaints book klachtenboek *nt*

complete [kəm'pli:t] *adj* compleet, volledig ; *v* voltooien

completely [kəm'pli:tli] *adv* helemaal, volkomen, geheel

complex ['kompleks] *n* complex *nt* ; *adj* ingewikkeld

complexion [kəm'plekʃən] *n* teint *c*

complicated ['komplikeitid] *adj* gecompliceerd, ingewikkeld

compliment ['komplimənt] *n* compliment *nt* ; *v* gelukwensen, feliciteren

compose [kəm'pouz] *v* samenstellen

composer [kəm'pouzə] *n* componist *c*

composition [,kompə'ziʃən] *n* compositie *c* ; samenstelling *c*

comprehensive [,kompri'hensiv] *adj* uitgebreid

comprise [kəm'praiz] *v* omvatten

compromise ['komprəmaiz] *n* compromis *nt*

compulsory [kəm'pʌlsəri] *adj* verplicht

comrade ['komreid] *n* kameraad *c*

conceal [kən'si:l] *v* *verbergen

conceited [kən'si:tid] *adj* verwaand

conceive [kən'si:v] *v* opvatten ; zich voorstellen

concentrate ['konsəntreit] *v* concentreren

concentration [,konsən'treiʃən] *n* concentratie *c*

conception [kən'sepʃən] *n* begrip *nt* ; conceptie *c*

concern [kən'sə:n] *v* *aangaan, *betreffen ; *n* zorg *c* ; aangelegenheid *c* ; bedrijf *nt*, onderneming *c*

concerned [kən'sə:nd] *adj* bezorgd ; betrokken

concerning [kən'sə:niŋ] *prep* omtrent, betreffende

concert ['konsət] *n* concert *nt* ; ~ **hall** concertzaal *c*

concession [kən'seʃən] *n* concessie *c* ; tegemoetkoming *c*

concierge [,kõsi'eəʒ] *n* concierge *c*

concise [kən'sais] *adj* beknopt, summier

conclusion [kən'klu:ʒən] *n* gevolgtrekking *c*, conclusie *c*

concrete ['konkri:t] *adj* concreet ; *n* beton *nt*

concurrence [kən'kʌrəns] *n* samenloop *c*

concussion [kən'kʌʃən] *n* hersenschudding *c*

condition [kən'diʃən] *n* voorwaarde *c* ; toestand *c*, conditie *c* ; omstandigheid *c*

conditional [kən'diʃənəl] *adj* voorwaardelijk

conduct¹ ['kondʌkt] *n* gedrag *nt*

conduct² [kən'dʌkt] *v* leiden ; begeleiden; dirigeren

conductor [kən'dʌktə] n conducteur c; dirigent c

confectioner [kən'fekʃənə] n banketbakker c

conference ['kɔnfərəns] n conferentie c

confess [kən'fes] v bekennen; biechten; *belijden

confession [kən'feʃən] n bekentenis c; biecht c

confidence ['kɔnfidəns] n vertrouwen nt

confident ['kɔnfidənt] adj gerust

confidential [,kɔnfi'denʃəl] adj vertrouwelijk

confirm [kən'fə:m] v bevestigen

confirmation [,kɔnfə'meiʃən] n bevestiging c

confiscate ['kɔnfiskeit] v vorderen, beslag leggen op

conflict ['kɔnflikt] n conflict nt

confuse [kən'fju:z] v verwarren

confusion [kən'fju:ʒən] n verwarring c

congratulate [kən'grætʃuleit] v feliciteren, gelukwensen

congratulation [kən,grætʃu'leiʃən] n felicitatie c, gelukwens c

congregation [,kɔŋgri'geiʃən] n gemeente c; orde c, congregatie c

congress ['kɔŋgres] n congres nt; bijeenkomst c

connect [kə'nekt] v *verbinden; *aansluiten

connection [kə'nekʃən] n relatie c; verband nt; aansluiting c, verbinding c

connoisseur [,kɔnə'sə:] n kenner c

connotation [,kɔnə'teiʃən] n bijbetekenis c

conquer ['kɔŋkə] v veroveren; *overwinnen

conqueror ['kɔŋkərə] n veroveraar c

conquest ['kɔŋkwest] n verovering c

conscience ['kɔnʃəns] n geweten nt

conscious ['kɔnʃəs] adj bewust

consciousness ['kɔnʃəsnəs] n bewustzijn nt

conscript ['kɔnskript] n dienstplichtige c

consent [kən'sent] v toestemmen; instemmen; n instemming c, toestemming c

consequence ['kɔnsikwəns] n consequentie c, gevolg nt

consequently ['kɔnsikwəntli] adv bijgevolg

conservative [kən'sə:vətiv] adj behoudend, conservatief

consider [kən'sidə] v beschouwen; *overwegen; menen, *vinden

considerable [kən'sidərəbəl] adj aanzienlijk; flink, aanmerkelijk

considerate [kən'sidərət] adj attent

consideration [kən,sidə'reiʃən] n overweging c; consideratie c, aandacht c

considering [kən'sidəriŋ] prep gezien

consignment [kən'sainmənt] n zending c

consist of [kən'sist] *bestaan uit

conspire [kən'spaiə] v *samenzweren

constant ['kɔnstənt] adj aanhoudend

constipation [,kɔnsti'peiʃən] n obstipatie c, constipatie c

constituency [kən'stitʃuənsi] n kiesdistrict nt

constitution [,kɔnsti'tju:ʃən] n grondwet c

construct [kən'strʌkt] v bouwen; opbouwen, construeren

construction [kən'strʌkʃən] n constructie c; opbouw c; gebouw nt, bouw c

consul ['kɔnsəl] n consul c

consulate ['kɔnsjulət] n consulaat nt

consult [kən'sʌlt] v raadplegen

consultation [,kɔnsəl'teiʃən] n raadple-

ging c ; consult nt ; ~ **hours** n
spreekuur nt
consumer [kən'sju:mə] n verbruiker c,
consument c
contact ['kɔntækt] n contact nt ; aanraking c ; v zich in verbinding stellen met ; ~ **lenses** contactlenzen pl
contagious [kən'teidʒəs] adj aanstekelijk, besmettelijk
contain [kən'tein] v bevatten ; *inhouden
container [kən'teinə] n reservoir nt ;
container c
contemporary [kən'tempərəri] adj
eigentijds ; toenmalig ; hedendaags ;
n tijdgenoot c
contempt [kən'tempt] n verachting c,
minachting c
content [kən'tent] adj tevreden
contents ['kɔntents] pl inhoud c
contest ['kɔntest] n strijd c ; wedstrijd
c
continent ['kɔntinənt] n continent nt,
werelddeel nt ; vasteland nt
continental [,kɔnti'nentəl] adj continentaal
continual [kən'tinjuəl] adj voortdurend ; **continually** adv steeds
continue [kən'tinju:] v voortzetten,
vervolgen ; *voortgaan, *doorgaan
continuous [kən'tinjuəs] adj voortdurend, doorlopend, onafgebroken
contour ['kɔntuə] n omtrek c
contraceptive [,kɔntrə'septiv] n voorbehoedmiddel nt
contract[1] ['kɔntrækt] n contract nt
contract[2] [kən'trækt] v *oplopen
contractor [kən'træktə] n aannemer c
contradict [,kɔntrə'dikt] v *tegenspreken
contradictory [,kɔntrə'diktəri] adj tegenstrijdig
contrary ['kɔntrəri] n tegendeel nt ;
adj tegengesteld ; **on the** ~ integen-

deel
contrast ['kɔntrɑ:st] n contrast nt ;
verschil nt, tegenstelling c
contribution [,kɔntri'bju:ʃən] n bijdrage c
control [kən'troul] n controle c ; v
controleren
controversial [,kɔntrə'və:ʃəl] adj controversieel, omstreden
convenience [kən'vi:njəns] n gemak nt
convenient [kən'vi:njənt] adj geriefelijk ; geschikt, passend, gemakkelijk
convent ['kɔnvənt] n klooster nt
conversation [,kɔnvə'seiʃən] n conversatie c, gesprek nt
convert [kən'və:t] v bekeren ; omrekenen
convict[1] [kən'vikt] v schuldig *bevinden
convict[2] ['kɔnvikt] n veroordeelde c
conviction [kən'vikʃən] n overtuiging
c ; veroordeling c
convince [kən'vins] v overtuigen
convulsion [kən'vʌlʃən] n kramp c
cook [kuk] n kok c ; v koken ; bereiden, klaarmaken
cookbook ['kukbuk] nAm kookboek
nt
cooker ['kukə] n fornuis nt ; **gas** ~
gasfornuis nt
cookery-book ['kukəribuk] n kookboek nt
cookie ['kuki] nAm biscuit nt
cool [ku:l] adj koel ; **cooling system**
koelsysteem nt
co-operation [kou,ɔpə'reiʃən] n samenwerking c ; medewerking c
co-operative [kou'ɔpərətiv] adj coöperatief ; gewillig, bereidwillig ; n coöperatie c
co-ordinate [kou'ɔ:dineit] v coördineren
co-ordination [kou,ɔ:di'neiʃən] n coördinatie c

copper ['kɔpə] *n* roodkoper *nt*, koper *nt*

copy ['kɔpi] *n* kopie *c*; afschrift *nt*; exemplaar *nt*; *v* kopiëren; namaken; **carbon ~** doorslag *c*

coral ['kɔrəl] *n* koraal *c*

cord [kɔ:d] *n* koord *nt*; snoer *nt*

cordial ['kɔ:diəl] *adj* hartelijk

corduroy ['kɔ:dərɔi] *n* ribfluweel *nt*

core [kɔ:] *n* kern *c*; klokhuis *nt*

cork [kɔ:k] *n* kurk *c*; stop *c*

corkscrew ['kɔ:kskru:] *n* kurketrekker *c*

corn [kɔ:n] *n* korrel *c*; graan *nt*, koren *nt*; eksteroog *nt*, likdoorn *c*; **~ on the cob** maïskolf *c*

corner ['kɔ:nə] *n* hoek *c*

cornfield ['kɔ:nfi:ld] *n* korenveld *nt*

corpse [kɔ:ps] *n* lijk *nt*

corpulent ['kɔ:pjulənt] *adj* corpulent; gezet, dik

correct [kə'rekt] *adj* goed, correct, juist; *v* corrigeren, verbeteren

correction [kə'rekʃən] *n* correctie *c*; verbetering *c*

correctness [kə'rektnəs] *n* juistheid *c*

correspond [,kɔri'spɔnd] *v* corresponderen; *overeenkomen

correspondence [,kɔri'spɔndəns] *n* briefwisseling *c*, correspondentie *c*

correspondent [,kɔri'spɔndənt] *n* correspondent *c*

corridor ['kɔridɔ:] *n* gang *c*

corrupt [kə'rʌpt] *adj* corrupt; *v* *omkopen

corruption [kə'rʌpʃən] *n* omkoping *c*

corset ['kɔ:sit] *n* korset *nt*

cosmetics [kɔz'metiks] *pl* kosmetica *pl*, schoonheidsmiddelen *pl*

cost [kɔst] *n* kosten *pl*; prijs *c*

***cost** [kɔst] *v* kosten

cosy ['kouzi] *adj* knus, gezellig

cot [kɔt] *nAm* stretcher *c*

cottage ['kɔtidʒ] *n* buitenhuis *nt*

cotton ['kɔtən] *n* katoen *nt/c*; katoenen

cotton-wool ['kɔtənwul] *n* watten *pl*

couch [kautʃ] *n* divan *c*

cough [kɔf] *n* hoest *c*; *v* hoesten

could [kud] *v* (p can)

council ['kaunsəl] *n* raad *c*

councillor ['kaunsələ] *n* raadslid *nt*

counsel ['kaunsəl] *n* raad *c*

counsellor ['kaunsələ] *n* raadsman *c*

count [kaunt] *v* tellen; optellen; meetellen; achten; *n* graaf *c*

counter ['kauntə] *n* toonbank *c*; balie *c*

counterfeit ['kauntəfi:t] *v* vervalsen

counterfoil ['kauntəfɔil] *n* controlestrook *c*

counterpane ['kauntəpein] *n* sprei *c*

countess ['kauntis] *n* gravin *c*

country ['kʌntri] *n* land *nt*; platteland *nt*; streek *c*; **~ house** landhuis *nt*

countryman ['kʌntrimən] *n* (pl -men) landgenoot *c*

countryside ['kʌntrisaid] *n* platteland *nt*

county ['kaunti] *n* graafschap *nt*

couple ['kʌpəl] *n* paar *nt*

coupon ['ku:pɔn] *n* coupon *c*, bon *c*

courage ['kʌridʒ] *n* dapperheid *c*, moed *c*

courageous [kə'reidʒəs] *adj* dapper, moedig

course [kɔ:s] *n* koers *c*; gang *c*; loop *c*; cursus *c*; **intensive ~** spoedcursus *c*; **of ~** uiteraard, natuurlijk

court [kɔ:t] *n* rechtbank *c*; hof *nt*

courteous ['kə:tiəs] *adj* hoffelijk

cousin ['kʌzən] *n* nicht *c*, neef *c*

cover ['kʌvə] *v* bedekken; *n* schuilplaats *c*, beschutting *c*; deksel *nt*; omslag *c/nt*

cow [kau] *n* koe *c*

coward ['kauəd] *n* lafaard *c*

cowardly ['kauədli] *adj* laf

cow-hide ['kauhaid] n koeiehuid c
crab [kræb] n krab c
crack [kræk] n gekraak nt; barst c; v
  kraken; *breken, barsten
cracker ['krækə] nAm koekje nt
cradle ['kreidəl] n wieg c; bakermat c
cramp [kræmp] n kramp c
crane [krein] n hijskraan c
crankcase ['kræŋkkeis] n carter nt
crankshaft ['kræŋkʃɑːft] n krukas c
crash [kræʃ] n botsing c; v botsen;
  neerstorten; ~ barrier vangrail c
crate [kreit] n krat c
crater ['kreitə] n krater c
crawl [krɔːl] v *kruipen; n crawl c
craze [kreiz] n rage c
crazy ['kreizi] adj gek; dwaas, krankzinnig
creak [kriːk] v kraken
cream [kriːm] n crème c; room c; adj
  roomkleurig
creamy ['kriːmi] adj romig
crease [kriːs] v kreuken; n vouw c;
  plooi c
create [kriˈeit] v *scheppen; creëren
creature ['kriːtʃə] n schepsel nt; wezen nt
credible ['kredibəl] adj geloofwaardig
credit ['kredit] n krediet nt; v crediteren; ~ card credit card
creditor ['kreditə] n schuldeiser c
credulous ['kredjuləs] adj goedgelovig
creek [kriːk] n inham c, kreek c
*creep [kriːp] v *kruipen
creepy ['kriːpi] adj eng, griezelig
cremate [kriˈmeit] v cremeren
cremation [kriˈmeiʃən] n crematie c
crew [kruː] n bemanning c
cricket ['krikit] n cricket nt; krekel c
crime [kraim] n misdaad c
criminal ['kriminəl] n delinquent c,
  misdadiger c; adj crimineel, misdadig; ~ law strafrecht nt
criminality [ˌkrimiˈnæləti] n criminaliteit c
crimson ['krimzən] adj vuurrood
crippled ['kripəld] adj kreupel
crisis ['kraisis] n (pl crises) crisis c
crisp [krisp] adj croquant, knappend
critic ['kritik] n criticus c
critical ['kritikəl] adj kritisch; kritiek,
  hachelijk, zorgwekkend
criticism ['kritisizəm] n kritiek c
criticize ['kritisaiz] v bekritiseren
crochet ['krouʃei] v haken
crockery ['krɔkəri] n aardewerk nt,
  vaatwerk c
crocodile ['krɔkədail] n krokodil c
crooked ['krukid] adj verdraaid,
  krom; oneerlijk
crop [krɔp] n oogst c
cross [krɔs] v *oversteken; adj kwaad,
  boos; n kruis nt
cross-eyed ['krɔsaid] adj scheel
crossing ['krɔsiŋ] n overtocht c; kruising c; oversteekplaats c; overweg
  c
crossroads ['krɔsroudz] n kruispunt nt
crosswalk ['krɔswɔːk] nAm zebrapad
  nt
crow [krou] n kraai c
crowbar ['kroubaː] n breekijzer nt
crowd [kraud] n massa c, menigte c
crowded ['kraudid] adj druk; overvol
crown [kraun] n kroon c; v kronen;
  bekronen
crucifix ['kruːsifiks] n kruisbeeld nt
crucifixion [ˌkruːsiˈfikʃən] n kruisiging
  c
crucify ['kruːsifai] v kruisigen
cruel [kruəl] adj wreed
cruise [kruːz] n boottocht c, cruise c
crumb [krʌm] n kruimel c
crusade [kruːˈseid] n kruistocht c
crust [krʌst] n korst c
crutch [krʌtʃ] n kruk c
cry [krai] v huilen; schreeuwen; *roepen; n kreet c, schreeuw c; roep c

crystal ['kristəl] *n* kristal *nt*; *adj* kristallen

Cuba ['kju:bə] Cuba

Cuban ['kju:bən] *adj* Cubaans; *n* Cubaan *c*

cube [kju:b] *n* kubus *c*; blokje *nt*

cuckoo ['kuku:] *n* koekoek *c*

cucumber ['kju:kəmbə] *n* komkommer *c*

cuddle ['kʌdəl] *v* knuffelen

cudgel ['kʌdʒəl] *n* knuppel *c*

cuff [kʌf] *n* manchet *c*

cuff-links ['kʌfliŋks] *pl* manchetknopen *pl*

cul-de-sac ['kʌldəsæk] *n* doodlopende weg

cultivate ['kʌltiveit] *v* bebouwen; verbouwen, kweken

culture ['kʌltʃə] *n* cultuur *c*; beschaving *c*

cultured ['kʌltʃəd] *adj* beschaafd

cunning ['kʌniŋ] *adj* sluw

cup [kʌp] *n* kopje *nt*; beker *c*

cupboard ['kʌbəd] *n* kast *c*

curb [kə:b] *n* trottoirband *c*; *v* beteugelen

cure [kjuə] *v* *genezen; *n* kuur *c*; genezing *c*

curio ['kjuəriou] *n* (pl ~s) rariteit *c*

curiosity [,kjuəri'ɔsəti] *n* nieuwsgierigheid *c*

curious ['kjuəriəs] *adj* benieuwd, nieuwsgierig; raar

curl [kə:l] *v* krullen; *n* krul *c*

curler ['kə:lə] *n* krulspeld *c*

curling-tongs ['kə:liŋtɔŋz] *pl* krultang *c*

curly ['kə:li] *adj* krullend

currant ['kʌrənt] *n* krent *c*; bes *c*

currency ['kʌrənsi] *n* valuta *c*; **foreign ~** buitenlands geld

current ['kʌrənt] *n* stroming *c*; stroom *c*; *adj* gangbaar, huidig; **alternating ~** wisselstroom *c*; **direct ~** ge-

lijkstroom *c*

curry ['kʌri] *n* kerrie *c*

curse [kə:s] *v* vloeken; vervloeken; *n* vloek *c*

curtain ['kə:tən] *n* gordijn *nt*; doek *nt*

curve [kə:v] *n* kromming *c*; bocht *c*

curved [kə:vd] *adj* krom, gebogen

cushion ['kuʃən] *n* kussen *c*

custodian [kʌ'stoudiən] *n* suppoost *c*

custody ['kʌstədi] *n* hechtenis *c*; hoede *c*; voogdij *c*

custom ['kʌstəm] *n* gewoonte *c*; gebruik *nt*

customary ['kʌstəməri] *adj* gebruikelijk, gewoon, gewoonlijk

customer ['kʌstəmə] *n* klant *c*; cliënt *c*

Customs ['kʌstəmz] *pl* douane *c*; ~ **duty** accijns *c*; ~ **officer** douanebeambte *c*

cut [kʌt] *n* snee *c*; snijwond *c*

*****cut** [kʌt] *v* *snijden; knippen; verlagen; ~ **off** *afsnijden; afknippen; *afsluiten

cutlery ['kʌtləri] *n* bestek *nt*

cutlet ['kʌtlət] *n* karbonade *c*

cycle ['saikəl] *n* fiets *c*; rijwiel *nt*; kringloop *c*, cyclus *c*

cyclist ['saiklist] *n* fietser *c*; wielrijder *c*

cylinder ['silində] *n* cilinder *c*; ~ **head** cilinderkop *c*

cystitis [si'staitis] *n* blaasontsteking *c*

Czech [tʃek] *adj* Tsjechisch; *n* Tsjech *c*

Czechoslovakia [,tʃekəslə'vɑːkiə] Tsjechoslowakije

D

dad [dæd] *n* vader *c*

daddy ['dædi] *n* papa *c*

daffodil ['dæfədil] n narcis c

daily ['deili] adj dagelijks; n dagblad nt

dairy ['dɛəri] n zuivelwinkel c

dam [dæm] n dam c; dijk c

damage ['dæmidʒ] n schade c; v beschadigen

damp [dæmp] adj vochtig; nat; n vocht nt; v bevochtigen

dance [dɑ:ns] v dansen; n dans c

dandelion ['dændilaiən] n paardebloem c

dandruff ['dændrəf] n roos c

Dane [dein] n Deen c

danger ['deindʒə] n gevaar nt

dangerous ['deindʒərəs] adj gevaarlijk

Danish ['deiniʃ] adj Deens

dare [dɛə] v wagen, durven; uitdagen

daring ['dɛəriŋ] adj gedurfd

dark [dɑ:k] adj duister, donker; n duisternis c

darling ['dɑ:liŋ] n schat c, lieveling c

darn [dɑ:n] v stoppen

dash [dæʃ] v snellen; n gedachtenstreepje nt

dashboard ['dæʃbɔ:d] n dashboard nt

data ['deitə] pl gegeven nt

date¹ [deit] n datum c; afspraak c; v dateren; out of ~ ouderwets

date² [deit] n dadel c

daughter ['dɔ:tə] n dochter c

dawn [dɔ:n] n ochtendschemering c; dageraad c

day [dei] n dag c; by ~ overdag; ~ trip excursie c; per ~ per dag; the ~ before yesterday eergisteren

daybreak ['deibreik] n dageraad c

daylight ['deilait] n daglicht nt

dead [ded] adj dood; gestorven

deaf [def] adj doof

deal [di:l] n transactie c, affaire c

*deal [di:l] v uitdelen; ~ with v te maken *hebben met; zaken *doen met

dealer ['di:lə] n koopman c, handelaar c

dear [diə] adj lief; duur; dierbaar

death [deθ] n dood c; ~ penalty doodstraf c

debate [di'beit] n debat nt

debit ['debit] n debet nt

debt [det] n schuld c

decaffeinated [di:'kæfineitid] adj coffeïnevrij

deceit [di'si:t] n bedrog nt

deceive [di'si:v] v *bedriegen

December [di'sembə] december

decency ['di:sənsi] n fatsoen nt

decent ['di:sənt] adj fatsoenlijk

decide [di'said] v beslissen, *besluiten

decision [di'siʒən] n beslissing c, besluit nt

deck [dek] n dek nt; ~ cabin dekhut c; ~ chair ligstoel c

declaration [,deklə'reiʃən] n verklaring c; aangifte c

declare [di'klɛə] v verklaren; *opgeven; *aangeven

decoration [,dekə'reiʃən] n versiering c

decrease [di:'kri:s] v verminderen; *afnemen; n vermindering c

dedicate ['dedikeit] v toewijden

deduce [di'dju:s] v afleiden

deduct [di'dʌkt] v *aftrekken

deed [di:d] n handeling c, daad c

deep [di:p] adj diep

deep-freeze [,di:p'fri:z] n diepvrieskast c

deer [diə] n (pl ~) hert nt

defeat [di'fi:t] v *verslaan; n nederlaag c

defective [di'fektiv] adj gebrekkig, defect

defence [di'fens] n verdediging c; defensie c

defend [di'fend] v verdedigen

deficiency [di'fiʃənsi] n gebrek nt

deficit ['defisit] n tekort nt

define [di'fain] v *omschrijven, bepalen, definiëren

definite ['definit] adj bepaald; vastomlijnd

definition [,defi'niʃən] n bepaling c, definitie c

deformed [di'fɔ:md] adj misvormd, mismaakt

degree [di'gri:] n graad c; titel c

delay [di'lei] v vertragen; uitstellen; n oponthoud nt, vertraging c; uitstel nt

delegate ['deligət] n gedelegeerde c

delegation [,deli'geiʃən] n delegatie c, afvaardiging c

deliberate¹ [di'libəreit] v beraadslagen, overleggen

deliberate² [di'libərət] adj opzettelijk

deliberation [di,libə'reiʃən] n beraad nt, overleg nt

delicacy ['delikəsi] n lekkernij c

delicate ['delikət] adj fijn; teder; delikaat

delicatessen [,delikə'tesən] n delicatessen pl; delicatessenwinkel c

delicious [di'liʃəs] adj lekker, heerlijk

delight [di'lait] n genot nt, verrukking c; v in verrukking *brengen; **delighted** opgetogen

delightful [di'laitfəl] adj heerlijk, verrukkelijk

deliver [di'livə] v afleveren, bezorgen; verlossen

delivery [di'livəri] n levering c, bezorging c; bevalling c; verlossing c; ~ van bestelauto c

demand [di'ma:nd] v vereisen, eisen; n eis c; navraag c

democracy [di'mɔkrəsi] n democratie c

democratic [,demə'krætik] adj democratisch

demolish [di'mɔliʃ] v slopen

demolition [,demə'liʃən] n afbraak c

demonstrate ['demənstreit] v aantonen; demonstreren, betogen

demonstration [,demən'streiʃən] n demonstratie c; betoging c

den [den] n hol nt

Denmark ['denma:k] Denemarken

denomination [di,nɔmi'neiʃən] n benaming c

dense [dens] adj dicht

dent [dent] n deuk c

dentist ['dentist] n tandarts c

denture ['dentʃə] n kunstgebit nt

deny [di'nai] v ontkennen; *onthouden, weigeren, *ontzeggen

deodorant [di:'oudərənt] n deodorant c

depart [di'pa:t] v *heengaan, *vertrekken; *overlijden

department [di'pa:tmənt] n departement nt, afdeling c; ~ **store** warenhuis nt

departure [di'pa:tʃə] n vertrek nt

dependant [di'pendənt] adj afhankelijk

depend on [di'pend] *afhangen van

deposit [di'pɔzit] n storting c; statiegeld nt; bezinksel nt, afzetting c; v storten

depository [di'pɔzitəri] n bergplaats c

depot ['depou] n opslagplaats c; nAm station nt

depress [di'pres] v deprimeren

depressed [di'prest] adj neerslachtig

depressing [di'presiŋ] adj triest

depression [di'preʃən] n neerslachtigheid c; depressie c; teruggang c

deprive of [di'praiv] *ontnemen

depth [depθ] n diepte c

deputy ['depjuti] n afgevaardigde c; plaatsvervanger c

descend [di'send] v dalen

descendant [di'sendənt] n afstammeling c

descent [di'sent] n afdaling c

describe [di'skraib] v *beschrijven

description [di'skripʃən] n beschrijving

c; signalement nt

desert[1] ['dezət] n woestijn c; adj woest, verlaten

desert[2] [di'zə:t] v deserteren; *verlaten

deserve [di'zə:v] v verdienen

design [di'zain] v *ontwerpen; n ontwerp nt; doel nt

designate ['dezigneit] v *aanwijzen

desirable [di'zaiərəbəl] adj begeerlijk, wenselijk

desire [di'zaiə] n wens c; zin c, begeerte c; v begeren, verlangen, wensen

desk [desk] n bureau nt; lessenaar c; schoolbank c

despair [di'spɛə] n wanhoop c; v wanhopen

despatch [di'spætʃ] v *verzenden

desperate ['despərət] adj wanhopig

despise [di'spaiz] v verachten

despite [di'spait] prep ondanks

dessert [di'zə:t] n dessert nt

destination [,desti'neiʃən] n bestemming c

destine ['destin] v bestemmen

destiny ['destini] n noodlot nt, lot nt

destroy [di'strɔi] v vernielen, vernietigen

destruction [di'strʌkʃən] n vernietiging c; ondergang c

detach [di'tætʃ] v losmaken

detail ['di:teil] n bijzonderheid c, detail nt

detailed ['di:teild] adj uitvoerig, gedetailleerd

detect [di'tekt] v ontdekken

detective [di'tektiv] n detective c; ~ story detectiveroman c

detergent [di'tə:dʒənt] n wasmiddel nt

determine [di'tə:min] v vaststellen, bepalen

determined [di'tə:mind] adj vastbesloten

detour ['di:tuə] n omweg c; omleiding c

devaluation [,di:vælju'eiʃən] n devaluatie c

devalue [,di:'vælju:] v devalueren

develop [di'veləp] v ontwikkelen

development [di'veləpmənt] n ontwikkeling c

deviate ['di:vieit] v *afwijken

devil ['devəl] n duivel c

devise [di'vaiz] v beramen

devote [di'vout] v wijden

dew [dju:] n dauw c

diabetes [,daiə'bi:ti:z] n diabetes c, suikerziekte c

diabetic [,daiə'betik] n suikerzieke c, diabeticus c

diagnose [,daiəg'nouz] v een diagnose stellen; constateren

diagnosis [,daiəg'nousis] n (pl -ses) diagnose c

diagonal [dai'ægənəl] n diagonaal c; adj diagonaal

diagram ['daiəgræm] n schema nt; figuur c, grafiek c

dialect ['daiəlekt] n dialect nt

diamond ['daiəmənd] n diamant c

diaper ['daiəpə] nAm luier c

diaphragm ['daiəfræm] n tussenschot nt

diarrhoea [daiə'riə] n diarree c

diary ['daiəri] n agenda c; dagboek nt

dictaphone ['diktəfoun] n dictafoon c

dictate [dik'teit] v dicteren

dictation [dik'teiʃən] n dictaat nt; dictee nt

dictator [dik'teitə] n dictator c

dictionary ['dikʃənəri] n woordenboek nt

did [did] v (p do)

die [dai] v *sterven; *overlijden

diesel ['di:zəl] n diesel c

diet ['daiət] n dieet nt

differ ['difə] v verschillen

difference ['difərəns] n verschil nt; onderscheid nt

different ['difərənt] adj verschillend; ander

difficult ['difikəlt] adj moeilijk; lastig

difficulty ['difikəlti] n moeilijkheid c; moeite c

***dig** [dig] v *graven; *delven

digest [di'dʒest] v verteren

digestible [di'dʒestəbəl] adj verteerbaar

digestion [di'dʒestʃən] n spijsvertering c

digit ['didʒit] n cijfer nt

dignified ['dignifaid] adj waardig

dike [daik] n dijk c; dam c

dilapidated [di'læpideitid] adj bouwvallig

diligence ['dilidʒəns] n vlijt c, ijver c

diligent ['dilidʒənt] adj vlijtig, ijverig

dilute [dai'lju:t] v aanlengen, verdunnen

dim [dim] adj dof, mat; donker, zwak, vaag

dine [dain] v warm *eten

dinghy ['diŋgi] n bootje nt

dining-car ['dainiŋka:] n restauratiewagen c

dining-room ['dainiŋru:m] n eetkamer c; eetzaal c

dinner ['dinə] n warme maaltijd; avondeten nt, middageten nt

dinner-jacket ['dinə,dʒækit] n smoking c

dinner-service ['dinə,sə:vis] n eetservies nt

diphtheria [dif'θiəriə] n difterie c

diploma [di'ploumə] n diploma nt

diplomat ['dipləmæt] n diplomaat c

direct [di'rekt] adj rechtstreeks, direct; v richten; *wijzen; leiden; regisseren

direction [di'rekʃən] n richting c; instructie c; regie c; bestuur nt; di-

rectional signal Am richtingaanwijzer c; **directions for use** gebruiksaanwijzing c

directive [di'rektiv] n richtlijn c

director [di'rektə] n directeur c; regisseur c

dirt [də:t] n vuil nt

dirty ['də:ti] adj smerig, vies, vuil

disabled [di'seibəld] adj gehandicapt, invalide

disadvantage [,disəd'va:ntidʒ] n nadeel nt

disagree [,disə'gri:] v het oneens *zijn, van mening verschillen

disagreeable [,disə'gri:əbəl] adj onaangenaam

disappear [,disə'piə] v *verdwijnen

disappoint [,disə'point] v teleurstellen; *be disappointing *tegenvallen

disappointment [,disə'pointmənt] n teleurstelling c

disapprove [,disə'pru:v] v afkeuren

disaster [di'za:stə] n ramp c; catastrofe c, onheil nt

disastrous [di'za:strəs] adj rampzalig

disc [disk] n schijf c; grammofoonplaat c; **slipped ~** hernia c

discard [di'ska:d] v afdanken

discharge [dis'tʃa:dʒ] v lossen, *uitladen; **~ of** *ontheffen van

discipline ['disiplin] n discipline c

discolour [di'skʌlə] v verkleuren

disconnect [,diskə'nekt] v ontkoppelen; uitschakelen

discontented [,diskən'tentid] adj ontevreden

discontinue [,diskən'tinju:] v *opheffen, staken

discount ['diskaunt] n korting c, reductie c

discover [di'skʌvə] v ontdekken

discovery [di'skʌvəri] n ontdekking c

discuss [di'skʌs] v *bespreken; discussiëren

discussion [di'skʌʃən] *n* discussie *c*; gesprek *nt*, bespreking *c*, debat *nt*

disease [di'zi:z] *n* ziekte *c*

disembark [,disim'ba:k] *v* van boord *gaan, ontschepen

disgrace [dis'greis] *n* schande *c*

disguise [dis'gaiz] *v* zich vermommen; *n* vermomming *c*

disgusting [dis'gʌstiŋ] *adj* misselijk, walgelijk

dish [diʃ] *n* bord *nt*; schotel *c*, schaal *c*; gerecht *nt*

dishonest [di'sɔnist] *adj* oneerlijk

disinfect [,disin'fekt] *v* ontsmetten

disinfectant [,disin'fektənt] *n* ontsmettingsmiddel *nt*

dislike [di'slaik] *v* een hekel *hebben aan, niet *houden van; *n* afkeer *c*, hekel *c*, antipathie *c*

dislocated ['disləkeitid] *adj* ontwricht

dismiss [dis'mis] *v* *wegzenden; *ontslaan

disorder [di'sɔ:də] *n* wanorde *c*

dispatch [di'spætʃ] *v* versturen, *verzenden

display [di'splei] *v* vertonen; tonen; *n* tentoonstelling *c*, expositie *c*

displease [di'spli:z] *v* ontstemmen, mishagen

disposable [di'spouzəbəl] *adj* wegwerp-

disposal [di'spouzəl] *n* beschikking *c*

dispose of [di'spouz] beschikken over

dispute [di'spju:t] *n* onenigheid *c*; ruzie *c*, geschil *nt*; *v* twisten, betwisten

dissatisfied [di'sætisfaid] *adj* ontevreden

dissolve [di'zɔlv] *v* oplossen; *ontbinden

dissuade from [di'sweid] *afraden

distance ['distəns] *n* afstand *c*; ~ **in kilometres** kilometertal *nt*

distant ['distənt] *adj* ver

distinct [di'stiŋkt] *adj* duidelijk; verschillend

distinction [di'stiŋkʃən] *n* onderscheid *nt*, verschil *nt*

distinguish [di'stiŋwiʃ] *v* onderscheid maken, *onderscheiden

distinguished [di'stiŋwiʃt] *adj* voornaam

distress [di'stres] *n* nood *c*; ~ **signal** noodsein *nt*

distribute [di'stribju:t] *v* uitdelen

distributor [di'stribjutə] *n* agent *c*; stroomverdeler *c*

district ['distrikt] *n* district *nt*; streek *c*; wijk *c*

disturb [di'stə:b] *v* storen, verstoren

disturbance [di'stə:bəns] *n* storing *c*; verwarring *c*

ditch [ditʃ] *n* greppel *c*, sloot *c*

dive [daiv] *v* *duiken

diversion [dai'və:ʃən] *n* wegomlegging *c*; afleiding *c*

divide [di'vaid] *v* delen; verdelen; *scheiden

divine [di'vain] *adj* goddelijk

division [di'viʒən] *n* deling *c*; scheiding *c*; afdeling *c*

divorce [di'vɔ:s] *n* echtscheiding *c*; *v* *scheiden

dizziness ['dizinəs] *n* duizeligheid *c*

dizzy ['dizi] *adj* duizelig

* do [du:] *v* *doen; voldoende *zijn

dock [dɔk] *n* dok *nt*; kade *c*; *v* aanleggen

docker ['dɔkə] *n* havenarbeider *c*

doctor ['dɔktə] *n* arts *c*, dokter *c*; doctor *c*

document ['dɔkjumənt] *n* document *nt*

dog [dɔg] *n* hond *c*

dogged ['dɔgid] *adj* hardnekkig

doll [dɔl] *n* pop *c*

dome [doum] *n* koepel *c*

domestic [də'mestik] *adj* huiselijk; binnenlands; *n* bediende *c*

domicile ['dɔmisail] *n* woonplaats *c*

domination [ˌdɔmi'neiʃən] n overheersing c

dominion [dǝ'minjǝn] n heerschappij c

donate [dou'neit] v *schenken

donation [dou'neiʃǝn] n schenking c, gift c

done [dʌn] v (pp do)

donkey ['dɔŋki] n ezel c

donor ['dounǝ] n donateur c

door [dɔ:] n deur c; **revolving ~** draaideur c; **sliding ~** schuifdeur c

doorbell ['dɔ:bel] n deurbel c

door-keeper ['dɔ:,ki:pǝ] n portier c

doorman ['dɔ:mǝn] n (pl -men) portier c

dormitory ['dɔ:mitri] n slaapzaal c

dose [dous] n dosis c

dot [dɔt] n punt c

double ['dʌbǝl] adj dubbel

doubt [daut] v betwijfelen, twijfelen; n twijfel c; **without ~** zonder twijfel

doubtful ['dautfǝl] adj twijfelachtig; onzeker

dough [dou] n deeg nt

down[1] [daun] adv neer; omlaag, naar beneden, omver; adj neerslachtig; prep langs, van ... af; **~ payment** aanbetaling c

down[2] [daun] n dons nt

downpour ['daunpɔ:] n stortbui c

downstairs [ˌdaun'stɛǝz] adv naar beneden, beneden

downstream [ˌdaun'stri:m] adv stroomafwaarts

down-to-earth [ˌdauntu'ǝ:θ] adj nuchter

downwards ['daunwǝdz] adv neer, naar beneden

dozen ['dʌzǝn] n (pl ~, ~s) dozijn nt

draft [drɑ:ft] n wissel c

drag [dræg] v slepen

dragon ['drægǝn] n draak c

drain [drein] v drooggleggen; afwate-

ren; n afvoer c

drama ['drɑ:mǝ] n drama nt; treurspel nt; toneel nt

dramatic [drǝ'mætik] adj dramatisch

dramatist ['dræmǝtist] n toneelschrijver c

drank [dræŋk] v (p drink)

draper ['dreipǝ] n manufacturier c

drapery ['dreipǝri] n stoffen

draught [drɑ:ft] n tocht c; **draughts** damspel nt

draught-board ['drɑ:ftbɔ:d] n dambord nt

draw [drɔ:] n trekking c

*** draw** [drɔ:] v tekenen; *trekken; *opnemen; **~ up** opstellen

drawbridge ['drɔ:bridʒ] n ophaalbrug c

drawer ['drɔ:ǝ] n la c, lade c; **drawers** onderbroek c

drawing ['drɔ:iŋ] n tekening c

drawing-pin ['drɔ:iŋpin] n punaise c

drawing-room ['drɔ:iŋru:m] n salon c

dread [dred] v vrezen; n vrees c

dreadful ['dredfǝl] adj vreselijk, ontzettend

dream [dri:m] n droom c

*** dream** [dri:m] v dromen

dress [dres] v aankleden; zich kleden; zich aankleden; *verbinden; n japon c, jurk c

dressing-gown ['dresiŋgaun] n kamerjas c

dressing-room ['dresiŋru:m] n kleedkamer c

dressing-table ['dresiŋˌteibǝl] n toilettafel c

dressmaker ['dres,meikǝ] n naaister c

drill [dril] v boren; trainen; n boor c

drink [driŋk] n borrel c, drank c

*** drink** [driŋk] v *drinken

drinking-water ['driŋkiŋˌwɔ:tǝ] n drinkwater nt

drip-dry [ˌdrip'drai] adj zelfstrijkend,

no-iron
drive [draiv] *n* rijweg *c*; autorit *c*
***drive** [draiv] *v* *rijden; besturen
driver ['draivǝ] *n* chauffeur *c*
drizzle ['drizǝl] *n* motregen *c*
drop [drɔp] *v* *laten vallen; *n* druppel *c*
drought [draut] *n* droogte *c*
drown [draun] *v* *verdrinken; *be drowned* *verdrinken
drug [drʌg] *n* verdovend middel; geneesmiddel *nt*
drugstore ['drʌgstɔ:] *nAm* drogisterij *c*, apotheek *c*; warenhuis *nt*
drum [drʌm] *n* trommel *c*
drunk [drʌŋk] *adj* (pp drink) dronken
dry [drai] *adj* droog; *v* drogen; afdrogen
dry-clean [,drai'kli:n] *v* chemisch reinigen
dry-cleaner's [,drai'kli:nǝz] *n* stomerij *c*
dryer ['draiǝ] *n* centrifuge *c*
duchess [dʌtʃis] *n* hertogin *c*
duck [dʌk] *n* eend *c*
due [dju:] *adj* verwacht; verschuldigd; vervallen
dues [dju:z] *pl* schulden *pl*
dug [dʌg] *v* (p, pp dig)
duke [dju:k] *n* hertog *c*
dull [dʌl] *adj* vervelend, saai; flets, mat; bot
dumb [dʌm] *adj* stom; suf, dom
dune [dju:n] *n* duin *nt*
dung [dʌŋ] *n* mest *c*
dunghill ['dʌnhil] *n* mesthoop *c*
duration [dju'reiʃǝn] *n* duur *c*
during ['djuǝriŋ] *prep* gedurende, tijdens
dusk [dʌsk] *n* avondschemering *c*
dust [dʌst] *n* stof *nt*
dustbin ['dʌstbin] *n* vuilnisbak *c*
dusty ['dʌsti] *adj* stoffig
Dutch [dʌtʃ] *adj* Nederlands, Hollands

Dutchman ['dʌtʃmǝn] *n* (pl -men) Nederlander *c*, Hollander *c*
dutiable ['dju:tiǝbǝl] *adj* belastbaar
duty ['dju:ti] *n* plicht *c*; taak *c*; invoerrecht *nt*; **Customs** ~ accijns *c*
duty-free [,dju:ti'fri:] *adj* belastingvrij
dwarf [dwɔ:f] *n* dwerg *c*
dye [dai] *v* verven; *n* verf *c*
dynamo ['dainǝmou] *n* (pl ~s) dynamo *c*
dysentery ['disǝntri] *n* dysenterie *c*

E

each [i:tʃ] *adj* elk, ieder; ~ **other** elkaar
eager ['i:gǝ] *adj* verlangend, ongeduldig
eagle ['i:gǝl] *n* arend *c*
ear [iǝ] *n* oor *nt*
earache ['iǝreik] *n* oorpijn *c*
ear-drum ['iǝdrʌm] *n* trommelvlies *nt*
earl [ǝ:l] *n* graaf *c*
early ['ǝ:li] *adj* vroeg
earn [ǝ:n] *v* verdienen
earnest ['ǝ:nist] *n* ernst *c*
earnings ['ǝ:niŋz] *pl* inkomsten *pl*, verdiensten *pl*
earring ['iǝriŋ] *n* oorbel *c*
earth [ǝ:θ] *n* aarde *c*; grond *c*
earthenware ['ǝ:θǝnwɛǝ] *n* aardewerk *nt*
earthquake ['ǝ:θkweik] *n* aardbeving *c*
ease [i:z] *n* ongedwongenheid *c*, gemak *nt*
east [i:st] *n* oost *c*, oosten *nt*
Easter ['i:stǝ] Pasen
easterly ['i:stǝli] *adj* oostelijk
eastern ['i:stǝn] *adj* oost-, oostelijk
easy ['i:zi] *adj* gemakkelijk; geriefelijk; ~ **chair** leunstoel *c*

easy-going ['i:zi,gouiŋ] adj ontspannen

*eat [i:t] v *eten

eavesdrop ['i:vzdrɔp] v afluisteren

ebony ['ebəni] n ebbehout nt

eccentric [ik'sentrik] adj excentriek

echo ['ekou] n (pl ~es) weerklank c, echo c

eclipse [i'klips] n verduistering c

economic [,i:kə'nɔmik] adj economisch

economical [,i:kə'nɔmikəl] adj spaarzaam, zuinig

economist [i'kɔnəmist] n econoom c

economize [i'kɔnəmaiz] v sparen

economy [i'kɔnəmi] n economie c

ecstasy ['ekstəzi] n extase c

Ecuador ['ekwədɔ:] Ecuador

Ecuadorian [,ekwə'dɔ:riən] n Ecuadoriaan c

eczema ['eksimə] n eczeem nt

edge [edʒ] n kant c, rand c

edible ['edibəl] adj eetbaar

edition [i'diʃən] n editie c, uitgave c; morning ~ ochtendeditie c

editor ['editə] n redakteur c

educate ['edʒukeit] v opleiden, opvoeden

education [,edʒu'keiʃən] n onderwijs nt; opvoeding c

eel [i:l] n aal c, paling c

effect [i'fekt] n gevolg nt, effect nt; v *teweegbrengen; in ~ feitelijk

effective [i'fektiv] adj doeltreffend, effectief

efficient [i'fiʃənt] adj efficiënt, doelmatig

effort ['efət] n inspanning c; poging c

egg [eg] n ei nt

egg-cup ['egkʌp] n eierdopje nt

eggplant ['egpla:nt] n aubergine c

egg-yolk ['egjouk] n eierdooier c

egoistic [,egou'istik] adj zelfzuchtig

Egypt ['i:dʒipt] Egypte

Egyptian [i'dʒipʃən] adj Egyptisch; n Egyptenaar c

eiderdown ['aidədaun] n donzen dekbed

eight [eit] num acht

eighteen [,ei'ti:n] num achttien

eighteenth [,ei'ti:nθ] num achttiende

eighth [eitθ] num achtste

eighty ['eiti] num tachtig

either ['aiðə] pron een van beide; either ... or hetzij ... hetzij, of ... of

elaborate [i'læbəreit] v uitwerken

elastic [i'læstik] adj elastisch; rekbaar; elastiek nt

elasticity [,elæ'stisəti] n rek c

elbow ['elbou] n elleboog c

elder ['eldə] adj ouder

elderly ['eldəli] adj bejaard

eldest ['eldist] adj oudst

elect [i'lekt] v *kiezen, *verkiezen

election [i'lekʃən] n verkiezing c

electric [i'lektrik] adj elektrisch; ~ razor scheerapparaat nt; ~ cord snoer nt

electrician [,ilek'triʃən] n elektricien c

electricity [,ilek'trisəti] n elektriciteit c

electronic [ilek'trɔnik] adj elektronisch

elegance ['eligəns] n elegantie c

elegant ['eligənt] adj elegant

element ['elimənt] n bestanddeel nt, element c

elephant ['elifənt] n olifant c

elevator ['eliveitə] nAm lift c

eleven [i'levən] num elf

eleventh [i'levənθ] num elfde

elf [elf] n (pl elves) elf c

eliminate [i'limineit] v elimineren

elm [elm] n iep c

else [els] adv anders

elsewhere [,el'sweə] adv elders

elucidate [i'lu:sideit] v toelichten

emancipation [i,mænsi'peiʃən] n emancipatie c

embankment [im'bæŋkmənt] n kade c

embargo [em'ba:gou] n (pl ~es) embargo nt

embark [im'ba:k] v inschepen; instappen

embarkation [,emba:'keiʃən] n inscheping c

embarrass [im'bærəs] v in verwarring brengen; in verlegenheid *brengen; hinderen; **embarrassed** verlegen, gegeneerd; **embarrassing** pijnlijk

embassy ['embəsi] n ambassade c

emblem ['embləm] n embleem nt

embrace [im'breis] v omhelzen; n omhelzing c

embroider [im'brɔidə] v borduren

embroidery [im'brɔidəri] n borduurwerk nt

emerald ['emərəld] n smaragd nt

emergency [i'mə:dʒənsi] n spoedgeval nt, noodgeval nt; noodtoestand c; ~ **exit** nooduitgang c

emigrant ['emigrənt] n emigrant c

emigrate ['emigreit] v emigreren

emigration [,emi'greiʃən] n emigratie c

emotion [i'mouʃən] n ontroering c, emotie c

emperor ['empərə] n keizer c

emphasize ['emfəsaiz] v benadrukken

empire ['empaiə] n keizerrijk nt, rijk nt

employ [im'plɔi] v tewerkstellen; gebruiken

employee [,emplɔi'i:] n werknemer c, employé c

employer [im'plɔiə] n werkgever c

employment [im'plɔimənt] n tewerkstelling c, werk nt; ~ **exchange** arbeidsbureau nt

empress ['empris] n keizerin c

empty ['empti] adj leeg; v ledigen

enable [i'neibəl] v in staat stellen

enamel [i'næməl] n email nt

enamelled [i'næməld] adj geëmailleerd

enchanting [in'tʃa:ntiŋ] adj prachtig, betoverend

encircle [in'sə:kəl] v omcirkelen, om-

ringen; *insluiten

enclose [iŋ'klouz] v *bijsluiten, *insluiten

enclosure [iŋ'klouʒə] n bijlage c

encounter [iŋ'kauntə] v ontmoeten; n ontmoeting c

encourage [iŋ'kʌridʒ] v aanmoedigen

encyclopaedia [en,saiklə'pi:diə] n encyclopedie c

end [end] n einde nt; slot nt; v beëindigen; *aflopen

ending ['endiŋ] n einde nt

endless ['endləs] adj oneindig

endorse [in'dɔ:s] v aftekenen, endosseren

endure [in'djuə] v *verdragen

enemy ['enəmi] n vijand c

energetic [,enə'dʒetik] adj energiek

energy ['enədʒi] n energie c; kracht c

engage [iŋ'geidʒ] v in dienst *nemen; *bespreken; zich *verbinden; **engaged** verloofd; bezig, bezet

engagement [iŋ'geidʒmənt] n verloving c; verplichting c; afspraak c; ~ **ring** verlovingsring c

engine ['endʒin] n machine c, motor c; locomotief c

engineer [,endʒi'niə] n ingenieur c

England ['iŋglənd] Engeland

English ['iŋgliʃ] adj Engels

Englishman ['iŋgliʃmən] n (pl -men) Engelsman c

engrave [iŋ'greiv] v graveren

engraver [iŋ'greivə] n graveur c

engraving [iŋ'greiviŋ] n prent c; gravure c

enigma [i'nigmə] n raadsel nt

enjoy [in'dʒɔi] v *genieten van

enjoyable [in'dʒɔiəbəl] adj fijn, prettig, leuk; lekker

enjoyment [in'dʒɔimənt] n genot nt

enlarge [in'la:dʒ] v vergroten; uitbreiden

enlargement [in'la:dʒmənt] n vergroting c

enormous [i'nɔ:məs] *adj* reusachtig, enorm

enough [i'nʌf] *adv* genoeg; *adj* voldoende

enquire [iŋ'kwaiə] *v* informeren; *onderzoeken

enquiry [iŋ'kwaiəri] *n* informatie c; onderzoek *nt*; enquête c

enter ['entə] *v* *betreden, *binnengaan; *inschrijven

enterprise ['entəpraiz] *n* onderneming c

entertain [,entə'tein] *v* vermaken, *onderhouden; *ontvangen

entertainer [,entə'teinə] *n* conferencier c

entertaining [,entə'teiniŋ] *adj* vermakelijk, amusant

entertainment [,entə'teinmənt] *n* vermaak *nt*, amusement *nt*

enthusiasm [in'θju:ziæzəm] *n* enthousiasme *nt*

enthusiastic [in,θju:zi'æstik] *adj* enthousiast

entire [in'taiə] *adj* heel, geheel

entirely [in'taiəli] *adv* helemaal

entrance ['entrəns] *n* ingang c; toegang c; binnenkomst c

entrance-fee ['entrənsfi:] *n* entree c

entry ['entri] *n* ingang c, entree c; toegang c; post c; **no** ~ verboden toegang

envelope ['envəloup] *n* envelop c

envious ['enviəs] *adj* afgunstig, jaloers

environment [in'vaiərənmənt] *n* milieu *nt*; omgeving c

envoy ['envɔi] *n* gezant c

envy ['envi] *n* afgunst c; *v* benijden

epic ['epik] *n* epos *nt*; *adj* episch

epidemic [,epi'demik] *n* epidemie c

epilepsy ['epilepsi] *n* epilepsie c

epilogue ['epilɔg] *n* epiloog c

episode ['episoud] *n* episode c

equal ['i:kwəl] *adj* gelijk; *v* evenaren

equality [i'kwɔləti] *n* gelijkheid c

equalize ['i:kwəlaiz] *v* gelijk maken

equally ['i:kwəli] *adv* even

equator [i'kweitə] *n* evenaar c

equip [i'kwip] *v* uitrusten

equipment [i'kwipmənt] *n* uitrusting c

equivalent [i'kwivələnt] *adj* equivalent, gelijkwaardig

eraser [i'reizə] *n* gom c/nt

erect [i'rekt] *v* opbouwen, oprichten; *adj* overeind, rechtopstaand

err [ə:] *v* zich vergissen; dwalen

errand ['erənd] *n* boodschap c

error ['erə] *n* fout c, vergissing c

escalator ['eskəleitə] *n* roltrap c

escape [i'skeip] *v* ontsnappen; vluchten, ontvluchten, *ontgaan; *n* ontsnapping c

escort[1] ['eskɔ:t] *n* escorte *nt*

escort[2] [i'skɔ:t] *v* escorteren

especially [i'speʃəli] *adv* voornamelijk, vooral

esplanade [,esplə'neid] *n* promenade c

essay ['esei] *n* essay *nt*; verhandeling c, opstel *nt*

essence ['esəns] *n* essentie c; kern c, wezen *nt*

essential [i'senʃəl] *adj* onontbeerlijk; wezenlijk, essentieel

essentially [i'senʃəli] *adv* vooral

establish [i'stæbliʃ] *v* vestigen; vaststellen

estate [i'steit] *n* landgoed *nt*

esteem [i'sti:m] *n* respect *nt*, achting c; *v* achten

estimate[1] ['estimeit] *v* taxeren, schatten

estimate[2] ['estimət] *n* schatting c

estuary ['estʃuəri] *n* riviermonding c

etcetera [et'setərə] enzovoort

etching ['etʃiŋ] *n* ets c

eternal [i'tə:nəl] *adj* eeuwig

eternity [i'tə:nəti] *n* eeuwigheid c

ether ['i:θə] n ether c

Ethiopia [iθi'oupiə] Ethiopië

Ethiopian [iθi'oupiən] adj Ethiopisch;
n Ethiopiër c

Europe ['juərəp] Europa

European [juərə'pi:ən] adj Europees;
n Europeaan c

evacuate [i'vækjueit] v evacueren

evaluate [i'væljueit] v schatten

evaporate [i'væpəreit] v verdampen

even ['i:vən] adj effen, plat, gelijk;
constant; even; adv zelfs

evening ['i:vniŋ] n avond c; ~ **dress**
avondkleding c

event [i'vent] n gebeurtenis c; geval
nt

eventual [i'ventʃuəl] adj eventueel;
uiteindelijk

ever ['evə] adv ooit; altijd

every ['evri] adj ieder, elk

everybody ['evri,bɔdi] pron iedereen

everyday ['evridei] adj alledaags

everyone ['evriwʌn] pron ieder, iedereen

everything ['evriθiŋ] pron alles

everywhere ['evriweə] adv overal

evidence ['evidəns] n bewijs nt

evident ['evidənt] adj duidelijk

evil ['i:vəl] n kwaad nt; adj slecht

evolution [,i:və'lu:ʃən] n evolutie c

exact [ig'zækt] adj nauwkeurig, precies

exactly [ig'zæktli] adv precies

exaggerate [ig'zædʒəreit] v *overdrij-
ven

examination [ig,zæmi'neiʃən] n examen
nt; onderzoek nt; verhoor nt

examine [ig'zæmin] v *onderzoeken

example [ig'zɑ:mpəl] n voorbeeld nt;
for ~ bijvoorbeeld

excavation [,ekskə'veiʃən] n opgraving
c

exceed [ik'si:d] v *overschrijden;
*overtreffen

excel [ik'sel] v *uitblinken

excellent ['eksələnt] adj voortreffelijk,
uitstekend

except [ik'sept] prep uitgezonderd, behalve

exception [ik'sepʃən] n uitzondering c

exceptional [ik'sepʃənəl] adj buitengewoon, uitzonderlijk

excerpt ['eksə:pt] n passage c

excess [ik'ses] n exces nt

excessive [ik'sesiv] adj buitensporig

exchange [iks'tʃeindʒ] v uitwisselen,
wisselen, ruilen; n ruil c; beurs c;
~ **office** wisselkantoor nt; ~ **rate**
koers c

excite [ik'sait] v *opwinden

excitement [ik'saitmənt] n drukte c,
opwinding c

exciting [ik'saitiŋ] adj spannend

exclaim [ik'skleim] v *uitroepen

exclamation [,eksklə'meiʃən] n uitroep
c

exclude [ik'sklu:d] v *uitsluiten

exclusive [ik'sklu:siv] adj exclusief

exclusively [ik'sklu:sivli] adv uitsluitend

excursion [ik'skə:ʃən] n uitstapje nt,
excursie c

excuse[1] [ik'skju:s] n excuus nt

excuse[2] [ik'skju:z] v verontschuldigen,
excuseren

execute ['eksikju:t] v uitvoeren

execution [,eksi'kju:ʃən] n terechtstelling c

executioner [,eksi'kju:ʃənə] n beul c

executive [ig'zekjutiv] adj uitvoerend;
n uitvoerende macht; directeur c

exempt [ig'zempt] v *ontheffen, vrijstellen; adj vrijgesteld

exemption [ig'zempʃən] n vrijstelling c

exercise ['eksəsaiz] n oefening c; thema nt; v oefenen; uitoefenen

exhale [eks'heil] v uitademen

exhaust [ig'zɔ:st] n uitlaatpijp c, uitlaat c; v uitputten; ~ **gases** uit-

exhibit 53 extraordinary

laatgassen *pl*
exhibit [ig'zibit] *v* tentoonstellen; vertonen
exhibition [,eksi'biʃən] *n* expositie *c*, tentoonstelling *c*
exile ['eksail] *n* ballingschap *c*; balling *c*
exist [ig'zist] *v* *bestaan
existence [ig'zistəns] *n* bestaan *nt*
exit ['eksit] *n* uitgang *c*; uitrit *c*
exotic [ig'zɔtik] *adj* exotisch
expand [ik'spænd] *v* uitbreiden; uitspreiden; ontplooien
expect [ik'spekt] *v* verwachten
expectation [,ekspek'teiʃən] *n* verwachting *c*
expedition [,ekspə'diʃən] *n* verzending *c*; expeditie *c*
expel [ik'spel] *v* *uitwijzen
expenditure [ik'spenditʃə] *n* kosten *pl*, uitgave *c*
expense [ik'spens] *n* uitgave *c*; **expenses** *pl* onkosten *pl*
expensive [ik'spensiv] *adj* prijzig, duur; kostbaar
experience [ik'spiəriəns] *n* ervaring *c*; *v* *ervaren, *ondervinden, beleven; **experienced** ervaren
experiment [ik'sperimənt] *n* proef *c*, experiment *nt*; *v* experimenteren
expert ['ekspə:t] *n* deskundige *c*, vakman *c*, expert *c*; *adj* deskundig
expire [ik'spaiə] *v* *vervallen, *aflopen, *verstrijken; uitademen; **expired** vervallen
expiry [ik'spaiəri] *n* vervaldag *c*, afloop *c*
explain [ik'splein] *v* verklaren, uitleggen
explanation [,eksplə'neiʃən] *n* toelichting *c*, uitleg *c*, verklaring *c*
explicit [ik'splisit] *adj* uitdrukkelijk, expliciet
explode [ik'sploud] *v* ontploffen

exploit [ik'splɔit] *v* uitbuiten, exploiteren
explore [ik'splɔ:] *v* verkennen, *onderzoeken
explosion [ik'splouʒən] *n* explosie *c*
explosive [ik'splousiv] *adj* explosief; *n* springstof *c*
export[1] [ik'spɔ:t] *v* uitvoeren, exporteren
export[2] ['ekspɔ:t] *n* export *c*
exportation [,ekspɔ:'teiʃən] *n* uitvoer *c*
exports ['ekspɔ:ts] *pl* export *c*
exposition [,ekspə'ziʃən] *n* tentoonstelling *c*
exposure [ik'spouʒə] *n* blootstelling *c*; belichting *c*; ~ **meter** belichtingsmeter *c*
express [ik'spres] *v* uitdrukken; betuigen, uiten; *adj* expresse-; uitdrukkelijk; ~ **train** sneltrein *c*
expression [ik'spreʃən] *n* uitdrukking *c*; uiting *c*
exquisite [ik'skwizit] *adj* voortreffelijk
extend [ik'stend] *v* verlengen; uitbreiden; verlenen
extension [ik'stenʃən] *n* verlenging *c*; uitbreiding *c*; toestel *nt*; ~ **cord** verlengsnoer *nt*
extensive [ik'stensiv] *adj* omvangrijk; veelomvattend, uitgebreid
extent [ik'stent] *n* omvang *c*
exterior [ek'stiəriə] *adj* uiterlijk; *n* buitenkant *c*
external [ek'stə:nəl] *adj* uiterlijk
extinguish [ik'stiŋwiʃ] *v* blussen, doven
extort [ik'stɔ:t] *v* *afdwingen
extortion [ik'stɔ:ʃən] *n* afpersing *c*
extra ['ekstrə] *adj* extra
extract[1] [ik'strækt] *v* *uittrekken, *trekken
extract[2] ['ekstrækt] *n* fragment *nt*
extradite ['ekstrədait] *v* uitleveren
extraordinary [ik'strɔ:dənri] *adj* bui-

tengewoon

extravagant [ik'strævəgənt] *adj* overdreven, extravagant

extreme [ik'stri:m] *adj* extreem; hoogst, uiterst; *n* uiterste *nt*

exuberant [ig'zju:bərənt] *adj* uitbundig

eye [ai] *n* oog *nt*

eyebrow ['aibrau] *n* wenkbrauw *c*

eyelash ['ailæʃ] *n* wimper *c*

eyelid ['ailid] *n* ooglid *nt*

eye-pencil ['ai,pensəl] *n* wenkbrauwstift *c*

eye-shadow ['ai,ʃædou] *n* ogenschaduw *c*

eye-witness ['ai,witnəs] *n* ooggetuige *c*

F

fable ['feibəl] *n* fabel *c*

fabric ['fæbrik] *n* stof *c*; structuur *c*

façade [fə'sɑ:d] *n* gevel *c*

face [feis] *n* gezicht *nt*; *v* het hoofd *bieden aan; ~ **massage** gezichtsmassage *c*; **facing** tegenover

face-cream ['feiskri:m] *n* gezichtscrème *c*

face-pack ['feispæk] *n* schoonheidsmasker *nt*

face-powder ['feis,paudə] *n* gezichtspoeder *nt/c*

facility [fə'siləti] *n* faciliteit *c*

fact [fækt] *n* feit *nt*; **in** ~ in feite

factor ['fæktə] *n* factor *c*

factory ['fæktəri] *n* fabriek *c*

factual ['fæktʃuəl] *adj* feitelijk

faculty ['fækəlti] *n* vermogen *nt*; gave *c*, talent *nt*, bekwaamheid *c*; faculteit *c*

fad [fæd] *n* gril *c*

fade [feid] *v* verkleuren, *verschieten

faience [fai'ɑ:s] *n* aardewerk *nt*, faience *c*

fail [feil] *v* falen; tekort *schieten; *ontbreken; *nalaten; zakken; **without** ~ beslist

failure ['feiljə] *n* mislukking *c*; fiasco *nt*

faint [feint] *v* *flauwvallen; *adj* zwak, vaag, flauw

fair [feə] *n* kermis *c*; beurs *c*; *adj* billijk, eerlijk; blond; mooi

fairly ['feəli] *adv* vrij, nogal, tamelijk

fairy ['feəri] *n* fee *c*

fairytale ['feəriteil] *n* sprookje *nt*

faith [feiθ] *n* geloof *nt*; vertrouwen *nt*

faithful ['feiθful] *adj* trouw

fake [feik] *n* vervalsing *c*

fall [fɔ:l] *n* val *c*; *nAm* herfst *c*

***fall** [fɔ:l] *v* *vallen

false [fɔ:ls] *adj* vals; verkeerd, onwaar, onecht; ~ **teeth** kunstgebit *nt*

falter ['fɔ:ltə] *v* wankelen; stamelen

fame [feim] *n* faam *c*, roem *c*; reputatie *c*

familiar [fə'miljə] *adj* vertrouwd; familiaar

family ['fæməli] *n* gezin *nt*; familie *c*; ~ **name** achternaam *c*

famous ['feiməs] *adj* beroemd

fan [fæn] *n* ventilator *c*; waaier *c*; fan *c*; ~ **belt** ventilatorriem *c*

fanatical [fə'nætikəl] *adj* fanatiek

fancy ['fænsi] *v* lusten, zin *hebben in; zich verbeelden, zich voorstellen; *n* gril *c*; fantasie *c*

fantastic [fæn'tæstik] *adj* fantastisch

fantasy ['fæntəzi] *n* fantasie *c*

far [fɑ:] *adj* ver; *adv* veel; **by** ~ verreweg; **so** ~ tot nu toe

far-away ['fɑ:rəwei] *adj* ver

farce [fɑ:s] *n* klucht *c*, farce *c*

fare [feə] *n* reiskosten *pl*, tarief *nt*; kost *c*, voedsel *nt*

farm [fɑ:m] *n* boerderij *c*

farmer ['fɑ:mə] *n* boer *c*; **farmer's**

wife boerin *c*
farmhouse ['fɑːmhaus] *n* boerderij *c*
far-off ['fɑːrɔf] *adj* afgelegen
fascinate ['fæsineit] *v* boeien
fascism ['fæʃizəm] *n* fascisme *nt*
fascist ['fæʃist] *adj* fascistisch; *n* fascist *c*
fashion ['fæʃən] *n* mode *c*; manier *c*
fashionable ['fæʃənəbəl] *adj* modieus
fast [fɑːst] *adj* vlug, snel; vast
fast-dyed [‚fɑːst'daid] *adj* wasecht, kleurecht
fasten ['fɑːsən] *v* vastmaken, bevestigen; *hebben
fastener ['fɑːsənə] *n* sluiting *c*
fat [fæt] *adj* vet, dik; *n* vet *nt*
fatal ['feitəl] *adj* fataal, dodelijk, noodlottig
fate [feit] *n* lot *nt*, noodlot *nt*
father ['fɑːðə] *n* vader *c*; pater *c*
father-in-law ['fɑːðərinlɔː] *n* (pl fathers-) schoonvader *c*
fatherland ['fɑːðələnd] *n* vaderland *nt*
fatness ['fætnəs] *n* dikte *c*
fatty ['fæti] *adj* vettig
faucet ['fɔːsit] *nAm* kraan *c*
fault [fɔːlt] *n* schuld *c*; fout *c*, defect *nt*, gebrek *nt*
faultless ['fɔːltləs] *adj* foutloos; feilloos
faulty ['fɔːlti] *adj* gebrekkig, defect
favour ['feivə] *n* gunst *c*; *v* begunstigen, bevoorrechten
favourable ['feivərəbəl] *adj* gunstig
favourite ['feivərit] *n* lieveling *c*, favoriet *c*; *adj* lievelings-
fawn [fɔːn] *adj* lichtbruin; *n* reekalf *nt*
fear [fiə] *n* vrees *c*, angst *c*; *v* vrezen
feasible ['fiːzəbəl] *adj* uitvoerbaar
feast [fiːst] *n* feest *nt*
feat [fiːt] *n* prestatie *c*
feather ['feðə] *n* veer *c*
feature ['fiːtʃə] *n* kenmerk *nt*; gelaats-

trek *c*
February ['februəri] februari
federal ['fedərəl] *adj* federaal
federation [‚fedə'reiʃən] *n* federatie *c*; bond *c*
fee [fiː] *n* honorarium *nt*
feeble ['fiːbəl] *adj* zwak
***feed** [fiːd] *v* voeden; **fed up with** beu
***feel** [fiːl] *v* voelen; betasten; ~ **like** zin *hebben in
feeling ['fiːliŋ] *n* gevoel *nt*
fell [fel] *v* (p fall)
fellow ['felou] *n* kerel *c*
felt[1] [felt] *n* vilt *nt*
felt[2] [felt] *v* (p, pp feel)
female ['fiːmeil] *adj* vrouwelijk
feminine ['feminin] *adj* vrouwelijk
fence [fens] *n* omheining *c*; hek *nt*; *v* schermen
fender ['fendə] *n* bumper *c*
ferment [fə'ment] *v* gisten
ferry-boat ['feribout] *n* veerboot *c*
fertile ['fəːtail] *adj* vruchtbaar
festival ['festivəl] *n* festival *nt*
festive ['festiv] *adj* feestelijk
fetch [fetʃ] *v* halen; afhalen
feudal ['fjuːdəl] *adj* feodaal
fever ['fiːvə] *n* koorts *c*
feverish ['fiːvəriʃ] *adj* koortsig
few [fjuː] *adj* weinig
fiancé [fi'ɑːsei] *n* verloofde *c*
fiancée [fi'ɑːsei] *n* verloofde *c*
fibre ['faibə] *n* vezel *c*
fiction ['fikʃən] *n* fictie *c*, verzinsel *nt*
field [fiːld] *n* akker *c*, veld *nt*; gebied *nt*; ~ **glasses** veldkijker *c*
fierce [fiəs] *adj* wild; woest, fel
fifteen [‚fif'tiːn] *num* vijftien
fifteenth [‚fif'tiːnθ] *num* vijftiende
fifth [fifθ] *num* vijfde
fifty ['fifti] *num* vijftig
fig [fig] *n* vijg *c*
fight [fait] *n* strijd *c*, gevecht *nt*

*fight [fait] *v* *strijden, *vechten

figure ['figə] *n* gestalte *c*, figuur *c*; cijfer *nt*

file [fail] *n* vijl *c*; dossier *nt*; rij *c*

Filipino [,fili'pi:nou] *n* Filippijn *c*

fill [fil] *v* vullen; ~ **in** invullen; **filling station** benzinestation *nt*; ~ **out** *Am* invullen; ~ **up** opvullen

filling ['filiŋ] *n* vulling *c*

film [film] *n* film *c*; *v* filmen

filter ['filtə] *n* filter *nt*

filthy ['filθi] *adj* smerig, vuil

final ['fainəl] *adj* laatst

finance [fai'næns] *v* financieren

finances [fai'nænsiz] *pl* financiën *pl*

financial [fai'nænʃəl] *adj* financieel

finch [fintʃ] *n* vink *c*

*find [faind] *v* *vinden

fine [fain] *n* boete *c*; *adj* fijn; mooi; uitstekend, prachtig; ~ **arts** schone kunsten

finger ['fiŋgə] *n* vinger *c*; **little** ~ pink *c*

fingerprint ['fiŋgəprint] *n* vingerafdruk *c*

finish ['finiʃ] *v* afmaken, beëindigen; eindigen; *n* einde *nt*; eindstreep *c*; **finished** af; op

Finland ['finlənd] Finland

Finn [fin] *n* Fin *c*

Finnish ['finiʃ] *adj* Fins

fire [faiə] *n* vuur *nt*; brand *c*; *v* *schieten; *ontslaan

fire-alarm ['faiərə,la:m] *n* brandalarm *nt*

fire-brigade ['faiəbri,geid] *n* brandweer *c*

fire-escape ['faiəri,skeip] *n* brandtrap *c*

fire-extinguisher ['faiərik,stiŋgwiʃə] *n* brandblusapparaat *nt*

fireplace ['faiəpleis] *n* haard *c*

fireproof ['faiəpru:f] *adj* brandvrij; vuurvast

firm [fə:m] *adj* vast; stevig; *n* firma *c*

first [fə:st] *num* eerst; **at** ~ eerst; aanvankelijk; ~ **name** voornaam *c*

first-aid [,fə:st'eid] *n* eerste hulp; ~ **kit** verbandkist *c*; ~ **post** eerste hulppost

first-class [,fə:st'kla:s] *adj* eersteklas

first-rate [,fə:st'reit] *adj* eersterangs, prima

fir-tree ['fə:tri:] *n* denneboom *c*, den *c*

fish¹ [fiʃ] *n* (pl ~, ~es) vis *c*; ~ **shop** viswinkel *c*

fish² [fiʃ] *v* vissen; hengelen; **fishing gear** vistuig *nt*; **fishing hook** vishaak *c*; **fishing industry** visserij *c*; **fishing licence** visakte *c*; **fishing line** vislijn *c*; **fishing net** visnet *nt*; **fishing rod** hengel *c*; **fishing tackle** vistuig *nt*

fishbone ['fiʃboun] *n* graat *c*, visgraat *c*

fisherman ['fiʃəmən] *n* (pl -men) visser *c*

fist [fist] *n* vuist *c*

fit [fit] *adj* geschikt; *n* aanval *c*; *v* passen; **fitting room** paskamer *c*

five [faiv] *num* vijf

fix [fiks] *v* repareren

fixed [fikst] *adj* vast

fizz [fiz] *n* prik *c*

fjord [fjɔ:d] *n* fjord *c*

flag [flæg] *n* vlag *c*

flame [fleim] *n* vlam *c*

flamingo [flə'miŋgou] *n* (pl ~s, ~es) flamingo *c*

flannel ['flænəl] *n* flanel *nt*

flash [flæʃ] *n* flits *c*

flash-bulb ['flæʃbʌlb] *n* flitslampje *nt*

flash-light ['flæʃlait] *n* zaklantaarn *c*

flask [fla:sk] *n* flacon *c*; **thermos** ~ thermosfles *c*

flat [flæt] *adj* vlak, plat; *n* flat *c*; ~ **tyre** lekke band

flavour ['fleivə] *n* smaak *c*; *v* kruiden

fleet [fli:t] *n* vloot *c*

flesh [fleʃ] *n* vlees *nt*

flew [flu:] *v* (p fly)

flex [fleks] *n* snoer *nt*

flexible ['fleksibəl] *adj* buigbaar; soepel

flight [flait] *n* vlucht *c*; **charter ~** chartervlucht *c*

flint [flint] *n* vuursteen *c*

float [flout] *v* *drijven; *n* vlotter *c*

flock [flɔk] *n* kudde *c*

flood [flʌd] *n* overstroming *c*; vloed *c*

floor [flɔ:] *n* vloer *c*; etage *c*, verdieping *c*; **~ show** floor-show *c*

florist ['flɔrist] *n* bloemist *c*

flour [flauə] *n* bloem *c*, meel *nt*

flow [flou] *v* vloeien, stromen

flower [flauə] *n* bloem *c*

flowerbed ['flauəbed] *n* bloemperk *nt*

flower-shop ['flauəʃɔp] *n* bloemenwinkel *c*

flown [floun] *v* (pp fly)

flu [flu:] *n* griep *c*

fluent ['flu:ənt] *adj* vloeiend

fluid ['flu:id] *adj* vloeibaar; *n* vloeistof *c*

flute [flu:t] *n* fluit *c*

fly [flai] *n* vlieg *c*; gulp *c*

***fly** [flai] *v* *vliegen

foam [foum] *n* schuim *nt*; *v* schuimen

foam-rubber ['foum,rʌbə] *n* schuimrubber *nt*

focus ['foukəs] *n* brandpunt *nt*

fog [fɔg] *n* mist *c*

foggy ['fɔgi] *adj* mistig

foglamp ['fɔglæmp] *n* mistlamp *c*

fold [fould] *v* *vouwen; *opvouwen; *n* vouw *c*

folk [fouk] *n* volk *nt*; **~ song** volkslied *nt*

folk-dance ['foukdɑ:ns] *n* volksdans *c*

folklore ['fouklɔ:] *n* folklore *c*

follow ['fɔlou] *v* volgen; **following** *adj* eerstvolgend, volgend

***be fond of** [bi: fɔnd ɔv] *houden van

food [fu:d] *n* voedsel *nt*; eten *nt*, kost *c*; **~ poisoning** voedselvergiftiging *c*

foodstuffs ['fu:dstʌfs] *pl* levensmiddelen *pl*

fool [fu:l] *n* gek *c*, dwaas *c*; *v* foppen

foolish ['fu:liʃ] *adj* mal, dwaas

foot [fut] *n* (pl feet) voet *c*; **~ powder** voetpoeder *nt/c*; **on ~** te voet

football ['futbɔ:l] *n* voetbal *c*; **~ match** voetbalwedstrijd *c*

foot-brake ['futbreik] *n* voetrem *c*

footpath ['futpɑ:θ] *n* voetpad *nt*

footwear ['futweə] *n* schoeisel *c*

for [fɔ:, fə] *prep* voor; gedurende; naar; vanwege, wegens, uit; *conj* want

***forbid** [fə'bid] *v* *verbieden

force [fɔ:s] *v* noodzaken, *dwingen; forceren; *n* macht *c*, kracht *c*; geweld *nt*; **by ~** noodgedwongen; **driving ~** drijfkracht *c*

ford [fɔ:d] *n* doorwaadbare plaats

forecast ['fɔ:kɑ:st] *n* voorspelling *c*; *v* voorspellen

foreground ['fɔ:graund] *n* voorgrond *c*

forehead ['fɔred] *n* voorhoofd *nt*

foreign ['fɔrin] *adj* buitenlands; vreemd

foreigner ['fɔrinə] *n* buitenlander *c*; vreemdeling *c*

foreman ['fɔ:mən] *n* (pl -men) voorman *c*

foremost ['fɔ:moust] *adj* hoogst

foresail ['fɔ:seil] *n* fok *c*

forest ['fɔrist] *n* woud *nt*, bos *nt*

forester ['fɔristə] *n* boswachter *c*

forge [fɔ:dʒ] *v* vervalsen

***forget** [fə'get] *v* *vergeten

forgetful [fə'getfəl] *adj* vergeetachtig

***forgive** [fə'giv] *v* *vergeven

fork [fɔ:k] *n* vork *c*; tweesprong *c*; *v* zich splitsen

form [fɔ:m] *n* vorm *c*; formulier *nt*;

klas *c*; *v* vormen

formal ['fɔ:məl] *adj* formeel

formality [fɔ:'mæləti] *n* formaliteit *c*

former ['fɔ:mə] *adj* voormalig; vroeger; **formerly** voorheen, vroeger

formula ['fɔ:mjulə] *n* (pl ~e, ~s) formule *c*

fort [fɔ:t] *n* fort *nt*

fortnight ['fɔ:tnait] *n* veertien dagen

fortress ['fɔ:tris] *n* vesting *c*

fortunate ['fɔ:tʃənət] *adj* gelukkig

fortune ['fɔ:tʃu:n] *n* fortuin *nt*; lot *nt*, geluk *nt*

forty ['fɔ:ti] *num* veertig

forward ['fɔ:wəd] *adv* vooruit, voorwaarts; *v* *nazenden

foster-parents ['fɔstə,peərənts] *pl* pleegouders *pl*

fought [fɔ:t] *v* (p, pp fight)

foul [faul] *adj* smerig; gemeen

found¹ [faund] *v* (p, pp find)

found² [faund] *v* oprichten, stichten

foundation [faun'deiʃən] *n* stichting *c*; ~ **cream** basiscrème *c*

fountain ['fauntin] *n* fontein *c*; bron *c*

fountain-pen ['fauntinpen] *n* vulpen *c*

four [fɔ:] *num* vier

fourteen [,fɔ:'ti:n] *num* veertien

fourteenth [,fɔ:'ti:nθ] *num* veertiende

fourth [fɔ:θ] *num* vierde

fowl [faul] *n* (pl ~s, ~) gevogelte *nt*

fox [fɔks] *n* vos *c*

foyer ['fɔiei] *n* foyer *c*

fraction ['frækʃən] *n* fractie *c*

fracture ['fræktʃə] *v* *breken; *n* breuk *c*

fragile ['frædʒail] *adj* breekbaar; broos

fragment ['frægmənt] *n* fragment *nt*; stuk *nt*

frame [freim] *n* lijst *c*; montuur *nt*

France [fra:ns] Frankrijk

franchise ['fræntʃaiz] *n* kiesrecht *nt*

fraternity [frə'tə:nəti] *n* broederschap *c*

fraud [frɔ:d] *n* fraude *c*, bedrog *nt*

fray [frei] *v* rafelen

free [fri:] *adj* vrij; gratis; ~ **of charge** gratis; ~ **ticket** vrijkaart *c*

freedom ['fri:dəm] *n* vrijheid *c*

***freeze** [fri:z] *v* *vriezen; *bevriezen

freezing ['fri:ziŋ] *adj* ijskoud

freezing-point ['fri:ziŋpɔint] *n* vriespunt *nt*

freight [freit] *n* lading *c*, vracht *c*

freight-train ['freittrein] *nAm* goederentrein *c*

French [frentʃ] *adj* Frans

Frenchman ['frentʃmən] *n* (pl -men) Fransman *c*

frequency ['fri:kwənsi] *n* frequentie *c*

frequent ['fri:kwənt] *adj* veelvuldig, frequent; **frequently** dikwijls

fresh [freʃ] *adj* vers; fris; ~ **water** zoet water

friction ['frikʃən] *n* wrijving *c*

Friday ['fraidi] vrijdag *c*

fridge [fridʒ] *n* koelkast *c*, ijskast *c*

friend [frend] *n* vriend *c*; vriendin *c*

friendly ['frendli] *adj* vriendelijk; amicaal, vriendschappelijk

friendship ['frendʃip] *n* vriendschap *c*

fright [frait] *n* angst *c*, schrik *c*

frighten ['fraitən] *v* *doen schrikken

frightened ['fraitənd] *adj* bang; *be ~ *schrikken

frightful ['fraitfəl] *adj* verschrikkelijk, vreselijk

fringe [frindʒ] *n* franje *c*

frock [frɔk] *n* jurk *c*

frog [frɔg] *n* kikker *c*

from [frɔm] *prep* van; uit; vanaf

front [frʌnt] *n* voorkant *c*; **in ~ of** voor

frontier ['frʌntiə] *n* grens *c*

frost [frɔst] *n* vorst *c*

froth [frɔθ] *n* schuim *c*

frozen ['frouzən] *adj* bevroren; ~ **food** diepvries produkten

fruit [fru:t] *n* fruit *nt*; vrucht *c*

fry [frai] *v* *bakken; *braden

frying-pan ['fraiiŋpæn] *n* koekepan *c*

fuel ['fju:əl] *n* brandstof *c*; benzine *c*; ~ **pump** *Am* benzinepomp *c*

full [ful] *adj* vol; ~ **board** vol pension; ~ **stop** punt *c*; ~ **up** vol

fun [fʌn] *n* plezier *nt*, pret *c*; lol *c*

function ['fʌŋkʃən] *n* functie *c*

fund [fʌnd] *n* fonds *nt*

fundamental [,fʌndə'mentəl] *adj* fundamenteel

funeral ['fju:nərəl] *n* begrafenis *c*

funnel ['fʌnəl] *n* trechter *c*

funny ['fʌni] *adj* leuk, grappig; zonderling

fur [fə:] *n* pels *c*; ~ **coat** bontjas *c*; **furs** bont *nt*

furious ['fjuəriəs] *adj* razend, woedend

furnace ['fə:nis] *n* oven *c*

furnish ['fə:niʃ] *v* leveren, verschaffen; inrichten, meubileren; ~ **with** *voorzien van

furniture ['fə:nitʃə] *n* meubilair *nt*

furrier ['fʌriə] *n* bontwerker *c*

further ['fə:ðə] *adj* verder; nader

furthermore ['fə:ðəmɔ:] *adv* bovendien

furthest ['fə:ðist] *adj* verst

fuse [fju:z] *n* zekering *c*; lont *c*

fuss [fʌs] *n* drukte *c*; ophef *c*, herrie *c*

future ['fju:tʃə] *n* toekomst *c*; *adj* toekomstig

G

gable ['geibəl] *n* geveltop *c*

gadget ['gædʒit] *n* technisch snufje

gaiety ['geiəti] *n* vrolijkheid *c*, pret *c*

gain [gein] *v* *winnen; *n* winst *c*

gait [geit] *n* gang *c*, loop *c*

gale [geil] *n* storm *c*

gall [gɔ:l] *n* gal *c*; ~ **bladder** galblaas *c*

gallery ['gæləri] *n* galerij *c*

gallop ['gæləp] *n* galop *c*

gallows ['gælouz] *pl* galg *c*

gallstone ['gɔ:lstoun] *n* galsteen *c*

game [geim] *n* spel *nt*; wild *nt*; ~ **reserve** wildpark *nt*

gang [gæŋ] *n* bende *c*; ploeg *c*

gangway ['gæŋwei] *n* loopplank *c*

gaol [dʒeil] *n* gevangenis *c*

gap [gæp] *n* bres *c*

garage ['gæra:ʒ] *n* garage *c*; *v* stallen

garbage ['ga:bidʒ] *n* vuilnis *nt*, afval *nt*

garden ['ga:dən] *n* tuin *c*; **public** ~ plantsoen *nt*; **zoological gardens** dierentuin *c*

gardener ['ga:dənə] *n* tuinman *c*

gargle ['ga:gəl] *v* gorgelen

garlic ['ga:lik] *n* knoflook *nt/c*

gas [gæs] *n* gas *nt*; *nAm* benzine *c*; ~ **cooker** gasstel *nt*; ~ **pump** *Am* benzinepomp *c*; ~ **station** *Am* benzinestation *nt*; ~ **stove** gaskachel *c*

gasoline ['gæsəli:n] *nAm* benzine *c*

gastric ['gæstrik] *adj* maag-; ~ **ulcer** maagzweer *c*

gasworks ['gæswə:ks] *n* gasfabriek *c*

gate [geit] *n* poort *c*; hek *nt*

gather ['gæðə] *v* verzamelen; *bijeenkomen; oogsten

gauge [geidʒ] *n* meter *c*

gauze [gɔ:z] *n* gaas *nt*

gave [geiv] *v* (p give)

gay [gei] *adj* vrolijk; bont

gaze [geiz] *v* staren

gear [giə] *n* versnelling *c*; uitrusting *c*; **change** ~ schakelen; ~ **lever** versnellingspook *c*

gear-box ['giəbɔks] *n* versnellingsbak *c*

gem [dʒem] *n* juweel *nt*, edelsteen *c*; kleinood *nt*

gender ['dʒendə] *n* geslacht *nt*

general ['dʒenərəl] *adj* algemeen; *n* generaal *c*; ~ **practitioner** huisarts *c*; **in** ~ in het algemeen

generate ['dʒenəreit] *v* verwekken

generation [,dʒenə'reiʃən] *n* generatie *c*

generator ['dʒenəreitər] *n* generator *c*

generosity [,dʒenə'rɔsəti] *n* edelmoedigheid *c*

generous ['dʒenərəs] *adj* gul, royaal

genital ['dʒenitəl] *adj* geslachtelijk

genius ['dʒi:niəs] *n* genie *nt*

gentle ['dʒentəl] *adj* zacht; teer, licht; voorzichtig

gentleman ['dʒentəlmən] *n* (pl -men) heer *c*

genuine ['dʒenjuin] *adj* echt

geography [dʒi'ɔgrəfi] *n* aardrijkskunde *c*

geology [dʒi'ɔlədʒi] *n* geologie *c*

geometry [dʒi'ɔmətri] *n* meetkunde *c*

germ [dʒə:m] *n* bacil *c*; kiem *c*

German ['dʒə:mən] *adj* Duits; *n* Duitser *c*

Germany ['dʒə:məni] Duitsland

gesticulate [dʒi'stikjuleit] *v* gebaren

*get [get] *v* *krijgen; halen; *worden; ~ **back** *teruggaan; ~ **off** uitstappen; ~ **on** instappen; vorderen; ~ **up** *opstaan

ghost [goust] *n* spook *nt*; geest *c*

giant ['dʒaiənt] *n* reus *c*

giddiness ['gidinəs] *n* duizeligheid *c*

giddy ['gidi] *adj* duizelig

gift [gift] *n* geschenk *nt*, cadeau *nt*; gave *c*

gifted ['giftid] *adj* begaafd

gigantic [dʒai'gæntik] *adj* reusachtig

giggle ['gigəl] *v* giechelen

gill [gil] *n* kieuw *c*

gilt [gilt] *adj* verguld

ginger ['dʒindʒə] *n* gember *c*

gipsy ['dʒipsi] *n* zigeuner *c*

girdle ['gə:dəl] *n* step-in *c*

girl [gə:l] *n* meisje *nt*; ~ **guide** padvindster *c*

*give [giv] *v* *geven; *aangeven; ~ **away** verklappen; ~ **in** *toegeven; ~ **up** *opgeven

glacier ['glæsiə] *n* gletsjer *c*

glad [glæd] *adj* verheugd, blij; **gladly** graag, gaarne

gladness ['glædnəs] *n* vreugde *c*

glamorous ['glæmərəs] *adj* betoverend, fascinerend

glamour ['glæmə] *n* charme *c*

glance [glɑ:ns] *n* blik *c*; *v* een blik *werpen

gland [glænd] *n* klier *c*

glare [gleə] *n* scherp licht; schittering *c*

glaring ['gleəriŋ] *adj* verblindend

glass [glɑ:s] *n* glas *nt*; glazen; **glasses** bril *c*; **magnifying** ~ vergrootglas *nt*

glaze [gleiz] *v* emailleren

glen [glen] *n* bergkloof *c*

glide [glaid] *v* *glijden

glider ['glaidə] *n* zweefvliegtuig *nt*

glimpse [glimps] *n* blik *c*; glimp *c*; *v* even *zien

global ['gloubəl] *adj* wereldomvattend

globe [gloub] *n* wereldbol *c*, aardbol *c*

gloom [glu:m] *n* duister *nt*

gloomy ['glu:mi] *adj* somber

glorious ['glɔ:riəs] *adj* prachtig

glory ['glɔ:ri] *n* glorie *c*, roem *c*; eer *c*, lof *c*

gloss [glɔs] *n* glans *c*

glossy ['glɔsi] *adj* glanzend

glove [glʌv] *n* handschoen *c*

glow [glou] *v* gloeien; *n* gloed *c*

glue [glu:] *n* lijm *c*

*go [gou] *v* *gaan; *lopen; *worden; ~ **ahead** *doorgaan; ~ **away** *weggaan; ~ **back** *teruggaan; ~ **home** naar huis *gaan; ~ **in** *binnengaan;

~ on *doorgaan; ~ out *uitgaan;
~ through meemaken, doormaken
goal [goul] n doel nt; doelpunt nt
goalkeeper ['goul,ki:pə] n doelman c
goat [gout] n bok c, geit c
god [gɔd] n god c
goddess ['gɔdis] n godin c
godfather ['gɔd,fɑ:ðə] n peetvader c
goggles ['gɔgəlz] pl duikbril c
gold [gould] n goud nt; ~ leaf bladgoud nt
golden ['gouldən] adj gouden
goldmine ['gouldmain] n goudmijn c
goldsmith ['gouldsmiθ] n goudsmid c
golf [gɔlf] n golf nt
golf-club ['gɔlfklʌb] n golfclub c
golf-course ['gɔlfkɔ:s] n golfbaan c
golf-links ['gɔlfliŋks] n golfbaan c
gondola ['gɔndələ] n gondel c
gone [gɔn] adv (pp go) weg
good [gud] adj goed; lekker; zoet,
braaf
good-bye! [,gud'bai] dag!
good-humoured [,gud'hju:məd] adj opgeruimd
good-looking [,gud'lukiŋ] adj knap
good-natured [,gud'neitʃəd] adj goedhartig
goods [gudz] pl waren pl, goederen
pl; ~ train goederentrein c
good-tempered [,gud'tempəd] adj
goedgestemd
goodwill [,gud'wil] n welwillendheid c
goose [gu:s] n (pl geese) gans c
gooseberry ['guzbəri] n kruisbes c
goose-flesh ['gu:sfleʃ] n kippevel nt
gorge [gɔ:dʒ] n ravijn nt
gorgeous ['gɔ:dʒəs] adj prachtig
gospel ['gɔspəl] n evangelie nt
gossip ['gɔsip] n geroddel nt; v roddelen
got [gɔt] v (p, pp get)
gourmet ['guəmei] n fijnproever c
gout [gaut] n jicht c

govern ['gʌvən] v regeren
governess ['gʌvənis] n gouvernante c
government ['gʌvənmənt] n bewind
nt, regering c
governor ['gʌvənə] n gouverneur c
gown [gaun] n japon c
grace [greis] n gratie c; genade c
graceful ['greisfəl] adj bevallig
grade [greid] n graad c; v rangschikken
gradient ['greidiənt] n helling c
gradual ['grædʒuəl] adj geleidelijk;
gradually adv langzamerhand
graduate ['grædʒueit] v een diploma
behalen
grain [grein] n korrel c, graan nt, koren nt
gram [græm] n gram nt
grammar ['græmə] n grammatica c
grammatical [grə'mætikəl] adj grammaticaal
gramophone ['græməfoun] n grammofoon c
grand [grænd] adj groots
granddad ['grændæd] n opa c
granddaughter ['græn,dɔ:tə] n kleindochter c
grandfather ['græn,fɑ:ðə] n grootvader
c; opa c
grandmother ['græn,mʌðə] n grootmoeder c; oma c
grandparents ['græn,peərənts] pl grootouders pl
grandson ['grænsʌn] n kleinzoon c
granite ['grænit] n graniet nt
grant [grɑ:nt] v gunnen, verlenen; inwilligen; n toelage c, beurs c
grapefruit ['greipfru:t] n pompelmoes
c
grapes [greips] pl druiven pl
graph [græf] n grafiek c
graphic ['græfik] adj grafisch
grasp [grɑ:sp] v *grijpen; n greep c
grass [grɑ:s] n gras nt

grasshopper ['grɑ:s,hɔpə] n sprink-haan c

grate [greit] n rooster nt; v raspen

grateful ['greitfəl] adj erkentelijk, dankbaar

grater ['greitə] n rasp c

gratis ['grætis] adj gratis

gratitude ['grætitju:d] n dankbaarheid c

gratuity [grə'tju:əti] n fooi c

grave [greiv] n graf nt; adj ernstig

gravel ['grævəl] n kiezel c, grind nt

gravestone ['greivstoun] n grafsteen c

graveyard ['greivja:d] n kerkhof nt

gravity ['grævəti] n zwaartekracht c; ernst c

gravy ['greivi] n jus c

graze [greiz] v grazen; n schaafwond c

grease [gri:s] n vet nt; v smeren

greasy ['gri:si] adj vet, vettig

great [greit] adj groot; Great Britain Groot-Brittannië

Greece [gri:s] Griekenland

greed [gri:d] n hebzucht c

greedy ['gri:di] adj hebzuchtig; gulzig

Greek [gri:k] adj Grieks; n Griek c

green [gri:n] adj groen; ~ card groene kaart

greengrocer ['gri:n,grousə] n groente-boer c

greenhouse ['gri:nhaus] n broeikas c, kas c

greens [gri:nz] pl groente c

greet [gri:t] v groeten

greeting ['gri:tiŋ] n groet c

grey [grei] adj grijs; grauw

greyhound ['greihaund] n hazewind c

grief [gri:f] n verdriet nt; bedroefd-heid c, smart c

grieve [gri:v] v treuren

grill [gril] n grill c; v roosteren

grill-room ['grilru:m] n grillroom c

grin [grin] v grijnzen; n grijns c

* grind [graind] v *malen; fijnmalen

grip [grip] v *grijpen; n houvast nt, greep c; nAm handkoffertje nt

grit [grit] n gruis nt

groan [groun] v kreunen

grocer ['grousə] n kruidenier c; gro-cer's kruidenierswinkel c

groceries ['grousəriz] pl kruideniers-waren pl

groin [grɔin] n lies c

groove [gru:v] n groef c

gross¹ [grous] n (pl ~) gros nt

gross² [grous] adj grof; bruto

grotto ['grɔtou] n (pl ~es, ~s) grot c

ground¹ [graund] n bodem c, grond c; ~ floor begane grond; grounds ter-rein nt

ground² [graund] v (p, pp grind)

group [gru:p] n groep c

grouse [graus] n (pl ~) korhoen nt

grove [grouv] n bosje nt

* grow [grou] v groeien; kweken; *worden

growl [graul] v grommen

grown-up ['grounʌp] adj volwassen; n volwassene c

growth [grouθ] n groei c; gezwel nt

grudge [grʌdʒ] v misgunnen

grumble ['grʌmbəl] v mopperen

guarantee [,gærən'ti:] n garantie c; waarborg c; v garanderen

guarantor [,gærən'tɔ:] n borg c

guard [gɑ:d] n bewaker c; v bewaken

guardian ['gɑ:diən] n voogd c

guess [ges] v *raden; *denken, gis-sen; n gissing c

guest [gest] n logé c, gast c

guest-house ['gesthaus] n pension nt

guest-room ['gestru:m] n logeerkamer c

guide [gaid] n gids c; v leiden

guidebook ['gaidbuk] n gids c

guide-dog ['gaiddɔg] n geleidehond c

guilt [gilt] n schuld c

guilty ['gilti] *adj* schuldig
guinea-pig ['ginipig] *n* cavia *c*
guitar [gi'tɑ:] *n* gitaar *c*
gulf [gʌlf] *n* golf *c*
gull [gʌl] *n* meeuw *c*
gum [gʌm] *n* tandvlees *nt*; gom *c*; lijm *c*
gun [gʌn] *n* geweer *nt*, revolver *c*; kanon *nt*
gunpowder ['gʌn,paudə] *n* kruit *nt*
gust [gʌst] *n* windstoot *c*
gusty ['gʌsti] *adj* winderig
gut [gʌt] *n* darm *c*; **guts** lef *nt*
gutter ['gʌtə] *n* goot *c*
guy [gai] *n* vent *c*
gymnasium [dʒim'neiziəm] *n* (pl ~s, -sia) gymnastiekzaal *c*
gymnast ['dʒimnæst] *n* gymnast *c*
gymnastics [dʒim'næstiks] *pl* gymnastiek *c*
gynaecologist [,gainə'kolədʒist] *n* gynaecoloog *c*, vrouwenarts *c*

H

haberdashery ['hæbədæʃəri] *n* garen-en bandwinkel
habit ['hæbit] *n* gewoonte *c*
habitable ['hæbitəbəl] *adj* bewoonbaar
habitual [hə'bitʃuəl] *adj* gewoon
had [hæd] *v* (p, pp have)
haddock ['hædək] *n* (pl ~) schelvis *c*
haemorrhage ['heməridʒ] *n* bloeding *c*
haemorrhoids ['hemərɔidz] *pl* aambeien *pl*
hail [heil] *n* hagel *c*
hair [heə] *n* haar *nt*; ~ **cream** haarcrème *c*; ~ **piece** haarstukje *nt*; ~ **tonic** haartonic *c*
hairbrush ['heəbrʌʃ] *n* haarborstel *c*
hair-do ['heədu:] *n* kapsel *nt*, coiffure *c*

hairdresser ['heə,dresə] *n* kapper *c*
hair-dryer ['heədraiə] *n* haardroger *c*
hair-grip ['heəgrip] *n* haarspeld *c*
hair-net ['heənet] *n* haarnetje *nt*
hair-oil ['heərɔil] *n* haarolie *c*
hairpin ['heəpin] *n* haarspeld *c*
hair-spray ['heəsprei] *n* haarlak *c*
hairy ['heəri] *adj* harig
half¹ [hɑ:f] *adj* half
half² [hɑ:f] *n* (pl halves) helft *c*
half-time [,hɑ:f'taim] *n* rust *c*
halfway [,hɑ:f'wei] *adv* halverwege
halibut ['hælibət] *n* (pl ~) heilbot *c*
hall [hɔ:l] *n* hal *c*; zaal *c*
halt [hɔ:lt] *v* stoppen
halve [hɑ:v] *v* halveren
ham [hæm] *n* ham *c*
hamlet ['hæmlət] *n* gehucht *nt*
hammer ['hæmə] *n* hamer *c*
hammock ['hæmək] *n* hangmat *c*
hamper ['hæmpə] *n* mand *c*
hand [hænd] *n* hand *c*; *v* *aangeven; ~ **cream** handcrème *c*
handbag ['hændbæg] *n* handtas *c*
handbook ['hændbuk] *n* handboek *nt*
hand-brake ['hændbreik] *n* handrem *c*
handcuffs ['hændkʌfs] *pl* handboeien *pl*
handful ['hændful] *n* handvol *c*
handicraft ['hændikrɑ:ft] *n* handenarbeid *c*; handwerk *nt*
handkerchief ['hæŋkətʃif] *n* zakdoek *c*
handle ['hændəl] *n* steel *c*, handvat *nt*; *v* hanteren; behandelen
hand-made [,hænd'meid] *adj* met de hand gemaakt
handshake ['hændʃeik] *n* handdruk *c*
handsome ['hænsəm] *adj* knap
handwork ['hændwə:k] *n* handwerk *nt*
handwriting ['hænd,raitiŋ] *n* handschrift *nt*
handy ['hændi] *adj* handig
***hang** [hæŋ] *v* *ophangen; *hangen
hanger ['hæŋə] *n* kleerhanger *c*

hangover ['hæŋ,ouvə] *n* kater *c*

happen ['hæpən] *v* *voorkomen, ge-beuren

happening ['hæpəniŋ] *n* gebeurtenis *c*

happiness ['hæpinəs] *n* geluk *nt*

happy ['hæpi] *adj* blij, gelukkig

harbour ['ha:bə] *n* haven *c*

hard [ha:d] *adj* hard; moeilijk; **hardly** nauwelijks

hardware ['ha:dwɛə] *n* ijzerwaren *pl*; ~ **store** handel in ijzerwaren

hare [hɛə] *n* haas *c*

harm [ha:m] *n* schade *c*; kwaad *nt*; *v* schaden

harmful ['ha:mfəl] *adj* nadelig, schade-lijk

harmless ['ha:mləs] *adj* onschadelijk

harmony ['ha:məni] *n* harmonie *c*

harp [ha:p] *n* harp *c*

harpsichord ['ha:psikɔ:d] *n* clavecim-bel *c*

harsh [ha:ʃ] *adj* ruw; streng; wreed

harvest ['ha:vist] *n* oogst *c*

has [hæz] *v* (pr have)

haste [heist] *n* spoed *c*, haast *c*

hasten ['heisən] *v* zich haasten

hasty ['heisti] *adj* haastig

hat [hæt] *n* hoed *c*; ~ **rack** kapstok *c*

hatch [hætʃ] *n* luik *nt*

hate [heit] *v* een hekel *hebben aan; haten; *n* haat *c*

hatred ['heitrid] *n* haat *c*

haughty ['hɔ:ti] *adj* hooghartig

haul [hɔ:l] *v* slepen

***have** [hæv] *v* *hebben; *laten; ~ **to** *moeten

haversack ['hævəsæk] *n* broodzak *c*

hawk [hɔ:k] *n* havik *c*; valk *c*

hay [hei] *n* hooi *nt*; ~ **fever** hooi-koorts *c*

hazard ['hæzəd] *n* risico *nt*

haze [heiz] *n* nevel *c*; waas *nt*

hazelnut ['heizəlnʌt] *n* hazelnoot *c*

hazy ['heizi] *adj* heiig; wazig

he [hi:] *pron* hij

head [hed] *n* hoofd *nt*; kop *c*; *v* lei-den; ~ **of state** staatshoofd *nt*; ~ **teacher** schoolhoofd *nt*, hoofdon-derwijzer *c*

headache ['hedeik] *n* hoofdpijn *c*

heading ['hediŋ] *n* titel *c*

headlamp ['hedlæmp] *n* koplamp *c*

headland ['hedlənd] *n* landtong *c*

headlight ['hedlait] *n* koplamp *c*

headline ['hedlain] *n* kop *c*

headmaster [,hed'ma:stə] *n* school-hoofd *nt*; rector *c*, directeur *c*

headquarters [,hed'kwɔ:təz] *pl* hoofd-kwartier *nt*

head-strong ['hedstrɔŋ] *adj* koppig

head-waiter [,hed'weitə] *n* maître d'hôtel

heal [hi:l] *v* *genezen

health [helθ] *n* gezondheid *c*; ~ **centre** consultatiebureau *nt*; ~ **cer-tificate** gezondheidsattest *nt*

healthy ['helθi] *adj* gezond

heap [hi:p] *n* stapel *c*, hoop *c*

***hear** [hiə] *v* horen

hearing ['hiəriŋ] *n* gehoor *nt*

heart [ha:t] *n* hart *nt*; kern *c*; **by** ~ uit het hoofd; ~ **attack** hartaanval *c*

heartburn ['ha:tbə:n] *n* maagzuur *nt*

hearth [ha:θ] *n* haard *c*

heartless ['ha:tləs] *adj* harteloos

hearty ['ha:ti] *adj* hartelijk

heat [hi:t] *n* warmte *c*, hitte *c*; *v* ver-warmen; **heating pad** elektrisch kussen

heater ['hi:tə] *n* kachel *c*; **immersion** ~ dompelaar *c*

heath [hi:θ] *n* heide *c*

heathen ['hi:ðən] *n* heiden *c*; heidens

heather ['heðə] *n* heide *c*

heating ['hi:tiŋ] *n* verwarming *c*

heaven ['hevən] *n* hemel *c*

heavy ['hevi] *adj* zwaar

Hebrew ['hi:bru:] *n* Hebreeuws *nt*
hedge [hedʒ] *n* heg *c*
hedgehog ['hedʒhɔg] *n* egel *c*
heel [hi:l] *n* hiel *c*; hak *c*
height [hait] *n* hoogte *c*; toppunt *nt*, hoogtepunt *nt*
hell [hel] *n* hel *c*
hello! [he'lou] hallo!; dag!
helm [helm] *n* roer *nt*
helmet ['helmit] *n* helm *c*
helmsman ['helmzmən] *n* stuurman *c*
help [help] *v* *helpen; *n* hulp *c*
helper ['helpə] *n* helper *c*
helpful ['helpfəl] *adj* hulpvaardig
helping ['helpiŋ] *n* portie *c*
hem [hem] *n* zoom *c*
hemp [hemp] *n* hennep *c*
hen [hen] *n* hen *c*; kip *c*
henceforth [,hens'fɔ:θ] *adv* voortaan
her [hə:] *pron* haar
herb [hə:b] *n* kruid *c*
herd [hə:d] *n* kudde *c*
here [hiə] *adv* hier; ~ **you are** alstublieft
hereditary [hi'reditəri] *adj* erfelijk
hernia ['hə:niə] *n* breuk *c*
hero ['hiərou] *n* (pl ~es) held *c*
heron ['herən] *n* reiger *c*
herring ['heriŋ] *n* (pl ~, ~s) haring *c*
herself [hə:'self] *pron* zich; zelf
hesitate ['heziteit] *v* aarzelen
heterosexual [,hetərə'sekʃuəl] *adj* heteroseksueel
hiccup ['hikʌp] *n* hik *c*
hide [haid] *n* huid *c*
* **hide** [haid] *v* *verbergen; verstoppen
hideous ['hidiəs] *adj* afschuwelijk
hierarchy ['haiəra:ki] *n* hiërarchie *c*
high [hai] *adj* hoog
highway ['haiwei] *n* hoofdweg *c*; *nAm* autoweg *c*
hijack ['haidʒæk] *v* kapen
hijacker ['haidʒækə] *n* kaper *c*
hike [haik] *v* *trekken

hill [hil] *n* heuvel *c*
hillock ['hilək] *n* lage heuvel *nt*
hillside ['hilsaid] *n* helling *c*
hilltop ['hiltɔp] *n* heuveltop *c*
hilly ['hili] *adj* heuvelachtig
him [him] *pron* hem
himself [him'self] *pron* zich; zelf
hinder ['hində] *v* hinderen
hinge [hindʒ] *n* scharnier *nt*
hip [hip] *n* heup *c*
hire [haiə] *v* huren; **for** ~ te huur
hire-purchase [,haiə'pə:tʃəs] *n* huurkoop *c*
his [hiz] *adj* zijn
historian [hi'stɔ:riən] *n* geschiedkundige *c*
historic [hi'stɔrik] *adj* historisch
historical [hi'stɔrikəl] *adj* geschiedkundig
history ['histəri] *n* geschiedenis *c*
hit [hit] *n* hit *c*
* **hit** [hit] *v* *slaan; raken, *treffen
hitchhike ['hitʃhaik] *v* liften
hitchhiker ['hitʃˌhaikə] *n* lifter *c*
hoarse [hɔ:s] *adj* schor, hees
hobby ['hɔbi] *n* liefhebberij *c*, hobby *c*
hobby-horse ['hɔbihɔ:s] *n* stokpaardje *nt*
hockey ['hɔki] *n* hockey *nt*
hoist [hɔist] *v* *hijsen
hold [hould] *n* ruim *nt*
* **hold** [hould] *v* *vasthouden, *houden; bewaren; ~ **on** zich *vasthouden; ~ **up** ondersteunen
hold-up ['houldʌp] *n* overval *c*
hole [houl] *n* kuil *c*, gat *nt*
holiday ['hɔlədi] *n* vakantie *c*; feestdag *c*; ~ **camp** vakantiekamp *nt*; ~ **resort** vakantieoord *nt*; **on** ~ met vakantie
Holland ['hɔlənd] Holland
hollow ['hɔlou] *adj* hol
holy ['houli] *adj* heilig
homage ['hɔmidʒ] *n* hulde *c*

home [houm] *n* thuis *nt*; tehuis *nt*, huis *nt*; *adv* thuis, naar huis; **at ~** thuis

home-made [,houm'meid] *adj* eigengemaakt

homesickness ['houm,siknəs] *n* heimwee *nt*

homosexual [,houmə'sekʃuəl] *adj* homoseksueel

honest ['ɔnist] *adj* eerlijk; oprecht

honesty ['ɔnisti] *n* eerlijkheid *c*

honey ['hʌni] *n* honing *c*

honeymoon ['hʌnimu:n] *n* huwelijksreis *c*, wittebroodsweken *pl*

honk [hʌŋk] *vAm* claxonneren

honour ['ɔnə] *n* eer *c*; *v* eren, huldigen

honourable ['ɔnərəbəl] *adj* eervol, eerzaam; rechtschapen

hood [hud] *n* kap *c*; *nAm* motorkap *c*

hoof [hu:f] *n* hoef *c*

hook [huk] *n* haak *c*

hoot [hu:t] *v* claxonneren

hooter ['hu:tə] *n* claxon *c*

hoover ['hu:və] *v* stofzuigen

hop[1] [hɔp] *v* huppelen; *n* sprong *c*

hop[2] [hɔp] *n* hop *c*

hope [houp] *n* hoop *c*; *v* hopen

hopeful ['houpfəl] *adj* hoopvol

hopeless ['houpləs] *adj* hopeloos

horizon [hə'raizən] *n* kim *c*, horizon *c*

horizontal [,hɔri'zɔntəl] *adj* horizontaal

horn [hɔ:n] *n* hoorn *c*; claxon *c*

horrible ['hɔribəl] *adj* vreselijk; verschrikkelijk, gruwelijk, afschuwelijk

horror ['hɔrə] *n* afgrijzen *nt*, afschuw *c*

hors-d'œuvre [ɔ:'də:vr] *n* hors d'œuvre *c*, voorgerecht *nt*

horse [hɔ:s] *n* paard *nt*

horseman ['hɔ:smən] *n* (pl -men) ruiter *c*

horsepower ['hɔ:s,pauə] *n* paardekracht *c*

horserace ['hɔ:sreis] *n* harddraverij *c*

horseradish ['hɔ:s,rædiʃ] *n* mierikswortel *c*

horseshoe ['hɔ:sʃu:] *n* hoefijzer *nt*

horticulture ['hɔ:tikʌltʃə] *n* tuinbouw *c*

hosiery ['houʒəri] *n* tricotgoederen *pl*

hospitable ['hɔspitəbəl] *adj* gastvrij

hospital ['hɔspitəl] *n* hospitaal *nt*, ziekenhuis *nt*

hospitality [,hɔspi'tæləti] *n* gastvrijheid *c*

host [houst] *n* gastheer *c*

hostage ['hɔstidʒ] *n* gijzelaar *c*

hostel ['hɔstəl] *n* herberg *c*

hostess ['houstis] *n* gastvrouw *c*

hostile ['hɔstail] *adj* vijandig

hot [hɔt] *adj* warm, heet

hotel [hou'tel] *n* hotel *nt*

hot-tempered [,hɔt'tempəd] *adj* driftig

hour [auə] *n* uur *nt*

hourly ['auəli] *adj* uur-

house [haus] *n* huis *nt*; woning *c*; pand *nt*; **~ agent** makelaar *c*; **~ block** *Am* huizenblok *nt*; **public ~** kroeg *c*

houseboat ['hausbout] *n* woonboot *c*

household ['haushould] *n* huishouden *nt*

housekeeper ['haus,ki:pə] *n* huishoudster *c*

housekeeping ['haus,ki:piŋ] *n* huishouden *nt*

housemaid ['hausmeid] *n* meid *c*

housewife ['hauswaif] *n* huisvrouw *c*

housework ['hauswə:k] *n* huishouden *nt*

how [hau] *adv* hoe; wat; **~ many** hoeveel; **~ much** hoeveel

however [hau'evə] *conj* evenwel, echter

hug [hʌg] *v* omhelzen; *n* omhelzing *c*

huge [hju:dʒ] *adj* geweldig, enorm, reusachtig

hum [hʌm] v neuriën

human ['hju:mən] adj menselijk; ~ **being** menselijk wezen

humanity [hju'mænəti] n mensheid c

humble ['hʌmbəl] adj nederig

humid ['hju:mid] adj vochtig

humidity [hju'midəti] n vochtigheid c

humorous ['hju:mərəs] adj grappig, geestig, humoristisch

humour ['hju:mə] n humor c

hundred ['hʌndrəd] n honderd

Hungarian [hʌŋ'gɛəriən] adj Hongaars; n Hongaar c

Hungary ['hʌŋgəri] Hongarije

hunger ['hʌŋgə] n honger c

hungry ['hʌŋgri] adj hongerig

hunt [hʌnt] v jagen; n jacht c; ~ **for** *zoeken

hunter ['hʌntə] n jager c

hurricane ['hʌrikən] n orkaan c; ~ **lamp** stormlamp c

hurry ['hʌri] v *opschieten, zich haasten; n haast c; **in a** ~ haastig

***hurt** [hə:t] v pijn *doen, bezeren; kwetsen

hurtful ['hə:tfəl] adj schadelijk

husband ['hʌzbənd] n echtgenoot c, man c

hut [hʌt] n hut c

hydrogen ['haidrədʒən] n waterstof c

hygiene ['haidʒi:n] n hygiëne c

hygienic [hai'dʒi:nik] adj hygiënisch

hymn [him] n gezang nt

hyphen ['haifən] n koppelteken nt

hypocrisy [hi'pɔkrəsi] n huichelarij c

hypocrite ['hipəkrit] n huichelaar c

hypocritical [,hipə'kritikəl] adj huichelachtig, hypocriet, schijnheilig

hysterical [hi'sterikəl] adj hysterisch

I

I [ai] pron ik

ice [ais] n ijs nt

ice-bag ['aisbæg] n koeltas c

ice-cream ['aiskri:m] n ijs nt, ijsje nt

Iceland ['aislənd] IJsland

Icelander ['aisləndə] n IJslander c

Icelandic [ais'lændik] adj IJslands

icon ['aikɔn] n ikoon c

idea [ai'diə] n idee nt/c; inval c, gedachte c; denkbeeld nt, begrip nt

ideal [ai'diəl] adj ideaal; n ideaal nt

identical [ai'dentikəl] adj identiek

identification [ai,dentifi'keiʃən] n identificatie c

identify [ai'dentifai] v identificeren

identity [ai'dentəti] n identiteit c; ~ **card** identiteitskaart c

idiom ['idiəm] n idioom nt

idiomatic [,idiə'mætik] adj idiomatisch

idiot ['idiət] n idioot c

idiotic [,idi'ɔtik] adj idioot

idle ['aidəl] adj werkeloos; lui; ijdel

idol ['aidəl] n afgod c; idool nt

if [if] conj als; indien

ignition [ig'niʃən] n ontsteking c; ~ **coil** ontsteking c

ignorant ['ignərənt] adj onwetend

ignore [ig'nɔ:] v negeren

ill [il] adj ziek; slecht; kwaad

illegal [i'li:gəl] adj illegaal, onwettig

ill gible [i'ledʒəbəl] adj onleesbaar

illiterate [i'litərət] n analfabeet c

illness ['ilnəs] n ziekte c

illuminate [i'lu:mineit] v verlichten

illumination [i,lu:mi'neiʃən] n verlichting c

illusion [i'lu:ʒən] n illusie c; droombeeld nt

illustrate ['iləstreit] v illustreren

illustration [,ilə'streiʃən] n illustratie c

image ['imidʒ] n beeld nt

imaginary [i'mædʒinəri] *adj* denkbeeldig

imagination [i,mædʒi'neiʃən] *n* verbeelding *c*

imagine [i'mædʒin] *v* zich voorstellen;
zich verbeelden; zich *indenken

imitate ['imiteit] *v* nabootsen, imiteren

imitation [,imi'teiʃən] *n* namaak *c*, imitatie *c*

immediate [i'mi:djət] *adj* onmiddellijk

immediately [i'mi:djətli] *adv* meteen,
dadelijk, onmiddellijk

immense [i'mens] *adj* oneindig, reusachtig, onmetelijk

immigrant ['imigrənt] *n* immigrant *c*

immigrate ['imigreit] *v* immigreren

immigration [,imi'greiʃən] *n* immigratie *c*

immodest [i'mɔdist] *adj* onbescheiden

immunity [i'mju:nəti] *n* immuniteit *c*

immunize ['imjunaiz] *v* immuun maken

impartial [im'pɑ:ʃəl] *adj* onpartijdig

impassable [im'pɑ:səbəl] *adj* onbegaanbaar

impatient [im'peiʃənt] *adj* ongeduldig

impede [im'pi:d] *v* belemmeren

impediment [im'pedimənt] *n* beletsel
nt

imperfect [im'pə:fikt] *adj* onvolmaakt

imperial [im'piəriəl] *adj* keizerlijk;
rijks-

impersonal [im'pə:sənəl] *adj* onpersoonlijk

impertinence [im'pə:tinəns] *n* onbeschaamdheid *c*

impertinent [im'pə:tinənt] *adj* brutaal,
onbeschoft, onbeschaamd

implement[1] ['implimənt] *n* werktuig
nt, gereedschap *nt*

implement[2] ['impliment] *v* uitvoeren

imply [im'plai] *v* impliceren; *inhouden

impolite [,impə'lait] *adj* onbeleefd

import[1] [im'pɔ:t] *v* invoeren, importeren

import[2] ['impɔ:t] *n* import *c*, invoer *c*;
~ duty invoerrecht *nt*

importance [im'pɔ:təns] *n* belang *nt*

important [im'pɔ:tənt] *adj* gewichtig,
belangrijk

importer [im'pɔ:tə] *n* importeur *c*

imposing [im'pouziŋ] *adj* indrukwekkend

impossible [im'pɔsəbəl] *adj* onmogelijk

impotence ['impətəns] *n* impotentie *c*

impotent ['impətənt] *adj* impotent

impound [im'paund] *v* beslag leggen
op

impress [im'pres] *v* imponeren, indruk
maken op

impression [im'preʃən] *n* indruk *c*

impressive [im'presiv] *adj* indrukwekkend

imprison [im'prizən] *v* gevangen zetten

imprisonment [im'prizənmənt] *n* gevangenschap *c*

improbable [im'prɔbəbəl] *adj* onwaarschijnlijk

improper [im'prɔpə] *adj* ongepast

improve [im'pru:v] *v* verbeteren

improvement [im'pru:vmənt] *n* verbetering *c*

improvise ['imprəvaiz] *v* improviseren

impudent ['impjudənt] *adj* onbeschaamd

impulse ['impʌls] *n* impuls *c*; prikkel
c

impulsive [im'pʌlsiv] *adj* impulsief

in [in] *prep* in; over, op; *adv* binnen

inaccessible [i,næk'sesəbəl] *adj* ontoegankelijk

inaccurate [i'nækjurət] *adj* onnauwkeurig

inadequate [i'nædikwət] *adj* onvoldoende

incapable [iŋ'keipəbəl] *adj* onbekwaam

incense ['insens] *n* wierook *c*

incident ['insidənt] n incident nt

incidental [,insi'dentəl] adj toevallig

incite [in'sait] v aansporen

inclination [,iŋkli'neiʃən] n neiging c

incline [iŋ'klain] n helling c

inclined [iŋ'klaind] adj genegen, geneigd; *be ~ to v neigen

include [iŋ'klu:d] v bevatten, *insluiten; included inbegrepen

inclusive [iŋ'klu:siv] adj inclusief

income ['iŋkəm] n inkomen nt

income-tax ['iŋkəmtæks] n inkomstenbelasting c

incompetent [iŋ'kɔmpətənt] adj onbekwaam

incomplete [,iŋkəm'pli:t] adj onvolledig, incompleet

inconceivable [,iŋkən'si:vəbəl] adj ondenkbaar

inconspicuous [,iŋkən'spikjuəs] adj onopvallend

inconvenience [,iŋkən'vi:njəns] n ongemak nt, ongerief nt

inconvenient [,iŋkən'vi:njənt] adj ongelegen; lastig

incorrect [,iŋkə'rekt] adj onnauwkeurig, onjuist

increase[1] [iŋ'kri:s] v vermeerderen; *oplopen, *toenemen

increase[2] ['iŋkri:s] n toename c; verhoging c

incredible [iŋ'kredəbəl] adj ongelofelijk

incurable [iŋ'kjuərəbəl] adj ongeneeslijk

indecent [in'di:sənt] adj onfatsoenlijk

indeed [in'di:d] adv inderdaad

indefinite [in'definit] adj onbepaald

indemnity [in'demnəti] n schadeloosstelling c, schadevergoeding c

independence [,indi'pendəns] n onafhankelijkheid c

independent [,indi'pendənt] adj onafhankelijk; zelfstandig

index ['indeks] n register nt, index c; ~ finger wijsvinger c

India ['indiə] India

Indian ['indiən] adj Indisch; Indiaans; n Indiër c; Indiaan c

indicate ['indikeit] v *aangeven, aanduiden

indication [,indi'keiʃən] n teken nt, aanwijzing c

indicator ['indikeitə] n richtingaanwijzer c

indifferent [in'difərənt] adj onverschillig

indigestion [,indi'dʒestʃən] n indigestie c

indignation [,indig'neiʃən] n verontwaardiging c

indirect [,indi'rekt] adj indirect

individual [,indi'vidʒuəl] adj afzonderlijk, individueel; n enkeling c, individu nt

Indonesia [,ində'ni:ziə] Indonesië

Indonesian [,ində'ni:ziən] adj Indonesisch; n Indonesiër c

indoor ['indɔ:] adj binnen

indoors [,in'dɔ:z] adv binnen

indulge [in'dʌldʒ] v *toegeven

industrial [in'dʌstriəl] adj industrieel; ~ area industriegebied nt

industrious [in'dʌstriəs] adj vlijtig

industry ['indəstri] n industrie c

inedible [i'nedibəl] adj oneetbaar

inefficient [,ini'fiʃənt] adj ondoeltreffend

inevitable [i'nevitəbəl] adj onvermijdelijk

inexpensive [,inik'spensiv] adj goedkoop

inexperienced [,inik'spiəriənst] adj onervaren

infant ['infənt] n zuigeling c

infantry ['infəntri] n infanterie c

infect [in'fekt] v besmetten, *aansteken

infection [in'fekʃən] n infectie c

infectious [in'fekʃəs] adj besmettelijk

infer [in'fə:] v afleiden

inferior [in'fiəriə] adj inferieur, minderwaardig; lager

infinite ['infinət] adj oneindig

infinitive [in'finitiv] n onbepaalde wijs

infirmary [in'fə:məri] n ziekenzaal c

inflammable [in'flæməbəl] adj ontvlambaar

inflammation [,inflə'meiʃən] n ontsteking c

inflatable [in'fleitəbəl] adj opblaasbaar

inflate [in'fleit] v *opblazen

inflation [in'fleiʃən] n inflatie c

influence ['influəns] n invloed c; v beïnvloeden

influential [,influ'enʃəl] adj invloedrijk

influenza [,influ'enzə] n griep c

inform [in'fɔ:m] v informeren; inlichten, mededelen

informal [in'fɔ:məl] adj informeel

information [,infə'meiʃən] n informatie c; inlichting c, mededeling c; ~ bureau inlichtingenkantoor nt

infra-red [,infrə'red] adj infrarood

infrequent [in'fri:kwənt] adj zeldzaam

ingredient [in'gri:diənt] n ingrediënt nt, bestanddeel nt

inhabit [in'hæbit] v bewonen

inhabitable [in'hæbitəbəl] adj bewoonbaar

inhabitant [in'hæbitənt] n inwoner c; bewoner c

inhale [in'heil] v inademen

inherit [in'herit] v erven

inheritance [in'heritəns] n erfenis c

initial [i'niʃəl] adj begin-, eerst; n voorletter c; v paraferen

initiative [i'niʃətiv] n initiatief nt

inject [in'dʒekt] v *inspuiten

injection [in'dʒekʃən] n injectie c

injure ['indʒə] v verwonden, kwetsen; krenken

injured ['indʒəd] adj gewond

injury ['indʒəri] n verwonding c; letsel nt, blessure c

injustice [in'dʒʌstis] n onrecht nt

ink [ink] n inkt c

inlet ['inlet] n inham c

inn [in] n herberg c

inner ['inə] adj inwendig; ~ tube binnenband c

inn-keeper ['in,ki:pə] n herbergier c

innocence ['inəsəns] n onschuld c

innocent ['inəsənt] adj onschuldig

inoculate [i'nɔkjuleit] v inenten

inoculation [i,nɔkju'leiʃən] n inenting c

inquire [iŋ'kwaiə] v *navragen, informatie *inwinnen

inquiry [iŋ'kwaiəri] n vraag c, navraag c; onderzoek nt; ~ office informatiebureau nt

inquisitive [iŋ'kwizətiv] adj nieuwsgierig

insane [in'sein] adj krankzinnig

inscription [in'skripʃən] n inscriptie c

insect ['insekt] n insekt nt; ~ repellent insektenwerend middel

insecticide [in'sektisaid] n insekticide c

insensitive [in'sensətiv] adj ongevoelig

insert [in'sə:t] v invoegen

inside [,in'said] n binnenkant c; adj binnenst; adv binnen; van binnen; prep in, binnen; ~ out binnenste buiten; insides ingewanden pl

insight ['insait] n inzicht nt

insignificant [,insig'nifikənt] adj onbelangrijk; onbeduidend, nietsbetekenend; nietig

insist [in'sist] v *aandringen; *aanhouden, *volhouden

insolence ['insələns] n onbeschaamdheid c

insolent ['insələnt] adj brutaal, onbeschaamd

insomnia [in'sɔmniə] n slapeloosheid c

inspect [in'spekt] v inspecteren

inspection [in'spekʃən] n inspectie c; controle c

inspector [in'spektə] n inspecteur c

inspire [in'spaiə] v bezielen

install [in'stɔ:l] v installeren

installation [,instə'leiʃən] n installatie c

instalment [in'stɔ:lmənt] n afbetaling c

instance ['instəns] n voorbeeld nt; geval nt; for ~ bijvoorbeeld

instant ['instənt] n ogenblik nt

instantly ['instəntli] adv ogenblikkelijk, onmiddellijk, meteen

instead of [in'sted ɔv] in plaats van

instinct ['instiŋkt] n instinct nt

institute ['institju:t] n instituut nt; instelling c; v instellen

institution [,insti'tju:ʃən] n inrichting c, instelling c

instruct [in'strʌkt] v onderrichten

instruction [in'strʌkʃən] n onderwijs nt

instructive [in'strʌktiv] adj leerzaam

instructor [in'strʌktə] n leraar c

instrument [,insə'fiʃənt] n instrument nt; musical ~ muziekinstrument nt

insufficient ['insə'fiʃənt] adj onvoldoende

insulate ['insjuleit] v isoleren

insulation [,insju'leiʃən] n isolatie c

insulator ['insjuleitə] n isolator c

insult[1] [in'sʌlt] v beledigen

insult[2] ['insʌlt] n belediging c

insurance [in'ʃuərəns] n assurantie c, verzekering c; ~ policy verzekeringspolis c

insure [in'ʃuə] v verzekeren

intact [in'tækt] adj intact

intellect ['intəlekt] n intellect nt

intellectual [,intə'lektʃuəl] adj intellectueel

intelligence [in'telidʒəns] n intelligen-

tie c

intelligent [in'telidʒənt] adj intelligent

intend [in'tend] v van plan *zijn, bedoelen

intense [in'tens] adj intens; hevig

intention [in'tenʃən] n bedoeling c

intentional [in'tenʃənəl] adj opzettelijk

intercourse ['intəkɔ:s] n omgang c

interest ['intrəst] n interesse c, belangstelling c; belang nt; rente c; v interesseren; interested geïnteresseerd, belangstellend

interesting ['intrəstiŋ] adj interessant

interfere [,intə'fiə] v tussenbeide *komen; ~ with zich bemoeien met

interference [,intə'fiərəns] n inmenging c

interim ['intərim] n tussentijd c

interior [in'tiəriə] n binnenkant c

interlude ['intəlu:d] n intermezzo nt

intermediary [,intə'mi:djəri] n tussenpersoon c

intermission [,intə'miʃən] n pauze c

internal [in'tə:nəl] adj intern, inwendig

international [,intə'næʃənəl] adj internationaal

interpret [in'tə:prit] v tolken; vertolken

interpreter [in'tə:pritə] n tolk c

interrogate [in'terəgeit] v *ondervragen

interrogation [in,terə'geiʃən] n verhoor nt

interrogative [,intə'rɔgətiv] adj vragend

interrupt [,intə'rʌpt] v *onderbreken

interruption [,intə'rʌpʃən] n onderbreking c

intersection [,intə'sekʃən] n kruispunt nt

interval ['intəvəl] n pauze c; tussenpoos c

intervene [,intə'vi:n] v *ingrijpen

interview ['intəvju:] *n* interview *nt*, vraaggesprek *nt*

intestine [in'testin] *n* darm *c*; **intestines** ingewanden *pl*

intimate ['intimət] *adj* intiem

into ['intu] *prep* in

intolerable [in'tɔlərəbəl] *adj* onuitstaanbaar

intoxicated [in'tɔksikeitid] *adj* dronken

intrigue [in'tri:g] *n* komplot *nt*

introduce [,intrə'dju:s] *v* introduceren, voorstellen; inleiden; invoeren

introduction [,intrə'dʌkʃən] *n* inleiding *c*

invade [in'veid] *v* *binnenvallen

invalid[1] ['invəli:d] *n* invalide *c*; *adj* invalide

invalid[2] [in'vælid] *adj* ongeldig

invasion [in'veiʒən] *n* inval *c*, invasie *c*

invent [in'vent] *v* *uitvinden; *verzinnen

invention [in'venʃən] *n* uitvinding *c*

inventive [in'ventiv] *adj* vindingrijk

inventor [in'ventə] *n* uitvinder *c*

inventory [in'ventri] *n* inventaris *c*

invert [in'və:t] *v* omdraaien

invest [in'vest] *v* investeren; beleggen

investigate [in'vestigeit] *v* *onderzoeken

investigation [in,vesti'geiʃən] *n* onderzoek *nt*

investment [in'vestmənt] *n* investering *c*; belegging *c*, geldbelegging *c*

investor [in'vestə] *n* investeerder *c*

invisible [in'vizəbəl] *adj* onzichtbaar

invitation [,invi'teiʃən] *n* uitnodiging *c*

invite [in'vait] *v* inviteren, uitnodigen

invoice ['invɔis] *n* factuur *c*

involve [in'vɔlv] *v* impliceren; **involved** betrokken

inwards ['inwədz] *adv* naar binnen

iodine ['aiədi:n] *n* jodium *nt*

Iran [i'rɑ:n] Iran

Iranian [i'reiniən] *adj* Iraans; *n* Iraniër

c

Iraq [i'rɑ:k] Irak

Iraqi [i'rɑ:ki] *adj* Iraaks; *n* Irakees *c*

irascible [i'ræsibəl] *adj* driftig

Ireland ['aiələnd] Ierland

Irish ['aiəriʃ] *adj* Iers

Irishman ['aiəriʃmən] *n* (pl -men) Ier *c*

iron ['aiən] *n* ijzer *nt*; strijkijzer *nt*; ijzeren; *v* *strijken

ironical [ai'rɔnikəl] *adj* ironisch

ironworks ['aiənwə:ks] *n* hoogovens *pl*

irony ['aiərəni] *n* ironie *c*

irregular [i'regjulə] *adj* onregelmatig

irreparable [i'repərəbəl] *adj* onherstelbaar

irrevocable [i'revəkəbəl] *adj* onherroepelijk

irritable ['iritəbəl] *adj* prikkelbaar

irritate ['iriteit] *v* prikkelen, irriteren

is [iz] *v* (pr be)

island ['ailənd] *n* eiland *nt*

isolate ['aisəleit] *v* isoleren

isolation [,aisə'leiʃən] *n* isolement *nt*; isolatie *c*

Israel ['izreil] Israël

Israeli [iz'reili] *adj* Israëlisch; *n* Israëliër *c*

issue ['iʃu:] *v* *uitgeven; *n* uitgifte *c*, oplage *c*, uitgave *c*; kwestie *c*, punt *nt*; uitkomst *c*, resultaat *nt*, gevolg *nt*, slot *nt*, einde *nt*; uitgang *c*

isthmus ['isməs] *n* landengte *c*

it [it] *pron* het

Italian [i'tæljən] *adj* Italiaans; *n* Italiaan *c*

italics [i'tæliks] *pl* cursiefschrift *nt*

Italy ['itəli] Italië

itch [itʃ] *n* jeuk *c*; kriebel *c*; *v* jeuken

item ['aitəm] *n* artikel *nt*; punt *nt*

itinerant [ai'tinərənt] *adj* rondreizend

itinerary [ai'tinərəri] *n* reisplan *nt*, reisroute *c*

ivory ['aivəri] *n* ivoor *nt*

ivy ['aivi] *n* klimop *c*

J

jack [dʒæk] *n* krik *c*

jacket ['dʒækit] *n* jasje *nt*, colbert *c*, vest *nt*; omslag *c/nt*

jade [dʒeid] *n* jade *nt/c*

jail [dʒeil] *n* gevangenis *c*

jailer ['dʒeilə] *n* cipier *c*

jam [dʒæm] *n* jam *c*; verkeersopstopping *c*

janitor ['dʒænitə] *n* concierge *c*

January ['dʒænjuəri] januari

Japan [dʒə'pæn] Japan

Japanese [,dʒæpə'ni:z] *adj* Japans; *n* Japanner *c*

jar [dʒɑ:] *n* pot *c*

jaundice ['dʒɔ:ndis] *n* geelzucht *c*

jaw [dʒɔ:] *n* kaak *c*

jealous ['dʒeləs] *adj* jaloers

jealousy ['dʒeləsi] *n* jaloezie *c*

jeans [dʒi:nz] *pl* spijkerbroek *c*

jelly ['dʒeli] *n* gelei *c*

jelly-fish ['dʒelifiʃ] *n* kwal *c*

jersey ['dʒə:zi] *n* jersey *c*; trui *c*

jet [dʒet] *n* straal *c*; straalvliegtuig *nt*

jetty ['dʒeti] *n* pier *c*

Jew [dʒu:] *n* jood *c*

jewel ['dʒu:əl] *n* juweel *nt*

jeweller ['dʒu:ələ] *n* juwelier *c*

jewellery ['dʒu:əlri] *n* juwelen; bijouterie *c*

Jewish ['dʒu:iʃ] *adj* joods

job [dʒɔb] *n* karwei *nt*; betrekking *c*, baan *c*

jockey ['dʒɔki] *n* jockey *c*

join [dʒɔin] *v* *verbinden; zich voegen bij, zich *aansluiten bij; samenvoegen, verenigen

joint [dʒɔint] *n* gewricht *nt*; las *c*; *adj* verenigd, gezamenlijk

jointly ['dʒɔintli] *adv* gezamenlijk

joke [dʒouk] *n* mop *c*, grap *c*

jolly ['dʒɔli] *adj* leuk

Jordan ['dʒɔ:dən] Jordanië

Jordanian [dʒɔ:'deiniən] *adj* Jordaans; *n* Jordaniër *c*

journal ['dʒə:nəl] *n* tijdschrift *nt*

journalism ['dʒə:nəlizəm] *n* journalistiek *c*

journalist ['dʒə:nəlist] *n* journalist *c*

journey ['dʒə:ni] *n* reis *c*

joy [dʒɔi] *n* genot *nt*, vreugde *c*

joyful ['dʒɔifəl] *adj* blij, vrolijk

jubilee ['dʒu:bili:] *n* jubileum *nt*

judge [dʒʌdʒ] *n* rechter *c*; *v* oordelen; beoordelen

judgment ['dʒʌdʒmənt] *n* oordeel *nt*; beoordeling *c*

jug [dʒʌg] *n* kan *c*

Jugoslav [ju:gə'slɑ:v] *adj* Joegoslavisch; *n* Joegoslaaf *c*

Jugoslavia [ju:gə'slɑ:viə] Joegoslavië

juice [dʒu:s] *n* sap *nt*

juicy ['dʒu:si] *adj* sappig

July [dʒu'lai] juli

jump [dʒʌmp] *v* *springen; *n* sprong *c*

jumper ['dʒʌmpə] *n* jumper *c*

junction ['dʒʌŋkʃən] *n* kruising *c*; knooppunt *nt*

June [dʒu:n] juni

jungle ['dʒʌŋgəl] *n* oerwoud *nt*, jungle *c*

junior ['dʒu:njə] *adj* jonger

junk [dʒʌŋk] *n* rommel *c*

jury ['dʒuəri] *n* jury *c*

just [dʒʌst] *adj* terecht, rechtvaardig; juist; *adv* pas; precies

justice ['dʒʌstis] *n* recht *nt*; gerechtigheid *c*, rechtvaardigheid *c*

juvenile ['dʒu:vənail] *adj* jeugdig

K

kangaroo [ˌkæŋgəˈruː] *n* kangoeroe *c*

keel [kiːl] *n* kiel *c*

keen [kiːn] *adj* enthousiast; scherp

*keep [kiːp] *v* *houden; bewaren; *blijven; ~ **away from** niet *betreden; ~ **off** *afblijven; ~ **on** *doorgaan met; ~ **quiet** *zwijgen; ~ **up** *volhouden; ~ **up with** *bijhouden

keg [keg] *n* vaatje *nt*

kennel [ˈkenəl] *n* hondehok *nt*; kennel *c*

Kenya [ˈkenjə] Kenya

kerosene [ˈkerəsiːn] *n* petroleum *c*

kettle [ˈketəl] *n* ketel *c*

key [kiː] *n* sleutel *c*

keyhole [ˈkiːhoul] *n* sleutelgat *nt*

khaki [ˈkɑːki] *n* kaki *nt*

kick [kik] *v* trappen, schoppen; *n* trap *c*, schop *c*

kick-off [ˌkiˈkɔf] *n* aftrap *c*

kid [kid] *n* kind *nt*; geiteleer *nt*; *v* *beetnemen

kidney [ˈkidni] *n* nier *c*

kill [kil] *v* *ombrengen, doden

kilogram [ˈkiləgræm] *n* kilo *nt*

kilometre [ˈkiləˌmiːtə] *n* kilometer *c*

kind [kaind] *adj* aardig, vriendelijk; goed; *n* soort *c/nt*

kindergarten [ˈkindəˌgɑːtən] *n* kleuterschool *c*

king [kiŋ] *n* koning *c*

kingdom [ˈkiŋdəm] *n* koninkrijk *nt*; rijk *nt*

kiosk [ˈkiːɔsk] *n* kiosk *c*

kiss [kis] *n* zoen *c*, kus *c*; *v* kussen

kit [kit] *n* uitrusting *c*

kitchen [ˈkitʃin] *n* keuken *c*; ~ **garden** moestuin *c*

kleenex [ˈkliːneks] *n* papieren zakdoek *c*

knapsack [ˈnæpsæk] *n* knapzak *c*

knave [neiv] *n* boer *c*

knee [niː] *n* knie *c*

kneecap [ˈniːkæp] *n* knieschijf *c*

*kneel [niːl] *v* knielen

knew [njuː] *v* (p know)

knickers [ˈnikəz] *pl* onderbroek *c*

knife [naif] *n* (pl knives) mes *nt*

knight [nait] *n* ridder *c*

*knit [nit] *v* breien

knob [nɔb] *n* knop *c*

knock [nɔk] *v* kloppen; *n* klop *c*; ~ **against** *stoten tegen; ~ **down** *neerslaan

knot [nɔt] *n* knoop *c*; *v* knopen

*know [nou] *v* *weten, kennen

knowledge [ˈnɔlidʒ] *n* kennis *c*

knuckle [ˈnʌkəl] *n* knokkel *c*

L

label [ˈleibəl] *n* etiket *nt*; *v* etiketteren

laboratory [ləˈbɔrətəri] *n* laboratorium *nt*

labour [ˈleibə] *n* werk *nt*, arbeid *c*; weeën *pl*; *v* zwoegen; **labor permit** *Am* werkvergunning *c*

labourer [ˈleibərə] *n* arbeider *c*

labour-saving [ˈleibəˌseiviŋ] *adj* arbeidbesparend

labyrinth [ˈlæbərinθ] *n* doolhof *nt*

lace [leis] *n* kant *nt*; veter *c*

lack [læk] *n* gemis *nt*, gebrek *nt*; *v* missen

lacquer [ˈlækə] *n* lak *c*

lad [læd] *n* jongen *c*, joch *nt*

ladder [ˈlædə] *n* ladder *c*

lady [ˈleidi] *n* dame *c*; **ladies' room** damestoilet *nt*

lagoon [ləˈguːn] *n* lagune *c*

lake [leik] *n* meer *nt*

lamb [læm] *n* lam *nt*; lamsvlees *nt*

lame [leim] *adj* lam, mank, kreupel

lamentable [ˈlæməntəbəl] *adj* erbarmelijk

lamp [læmp] n lamp c

lamp-post ['læmppoust] n lantaarnpaal c

lampshade ['læmpʃeid] n lampekap c

land [lænd] n land nt; v landen; aan land *gaan

landlady ['lænd,leidi] n hospita c

landlord ['lændlɔ:d] n huisbaas c; hospes c

landmark ['lændmɑ:k] n baken nt; mijlpaal c

landscape ['lændskeip] n landschap nt

lane [lein] n steeg c, pad nt; rijstrook c

language ['læŋgwidʒ] n taal c; ~ laboratory talenpracticum nt

lantern ['læntən] n lantaarn c

lapel [lə'pel] n revers c

larder ['lɑ:də] n provisiekast c

large [lɑ:dʒ] adj groot; ruim

lark [lɑ:k] n leeuwerik c

laryngitis [,lærin'dʒaitis] n keelontsteking c

last [lɑ:st] adj laatst; vorig; v duren; at ~ eindelijk; tenslotte, uiteindelijk

lasting ['lɑ:stiŋ] adj blijvend, duurzaam

latchkey ['lætʃki:] n huissleutel c

late [leit] adj laat; te laat

lately ['leitli] adv de laatste tijd, onlangs, laatst

lather ['lɑ:ðə] n schuim nt

Latin America ['lætin ə'merikə] Latijns-Amerika

Latin-American [,lætinə'merikən] adj Latijns-Amerikaans

latitude ['lætitju:d] n breedtegraad c

laugh [lɑ:f] v *lachen; n lach c

laughter ['lɑ:ftə] n gelach nt

launch [lɔ:ntʃ] v inzetten; lanceren; n motorschip nt

launching ['lɔ:ntʃiŋ] n tewaterlating c

launderette [,lɔ:ndə'ret] n wasserette c

laundry ['lɔ:ndri] n wasserij c; was c

lavatory ['lævətəri] n toilet nt

lavish ['læviʃ] adj kwistig

law [lɔ:] n wet c; recht nt; ~ court gerecht nt

lawful ['lɔ:fəl] adj wettig

lawn [lɔ:n] n grasveld nt, gazon nt

lawsuit ['lɔ:su:t] n proces nt, geding nt

lawyer ['lɔ:jə] n advocaat c; jurist c

laxative ['læksətiv] n laxeermiddel nt

*lay [lei] v plaatsen, zetten, leggen; ~ bricks metselen

layer [leiə] n laag c

layman ['leimən] n leek c

lazy ['leizi] adj lui

lead[1] [li:d] n voorsprong c; leiding c; riem c

lead[2] [led] n lood nt

*lead [li:d] v leiden

leader ['li:də] n aanvoerder c, leider c

leadership ['li:dəʃip] n leiderschap nt

leading ['li:diŋ] adj vooraanstaand, voornaamst

leaf [li:f] n (pl leaves) blad nt

league [li:g] n bond c

leak [li:k] v lekken; n lek nt

leaky ['li:ki] adj lek

lean [li:n] adj mager

*lean [li:n] v leunen

leap [li:p] n sprong c

*leap [li:p] v *springen

leap-year ['li:pjiə] n schrikkeljaar nt

*learn [lə:n] v leren

learner ['lə:nə] n beginneling c, beginner c

lease [li:s] n huurcontract nt; pacht c; v verpachten, verhuren; huren

leash [li:ʃ] n lijn c

least [li:st] adj geringst, minst; kleinst; at ~ minstens; tenminste

leather ['leðə] n leer nt; lederen, leren

leave [li:v] n verlof nt

*leave [li:v] v *vertrekken, *verlaten; *laten; ~ behind *achterlaten; ~ out *weglaten

Lebanese [,lebə'ni:z] adj Libanees; n Libanees c

Lebanon ['lebənən] Libanon

lecture ['lektʃə] n college nt, lezing c

left¹ [left] adj links

left² [left] v (p, pp leave)

left-hand ['lefthænd] adj links

left-handed [,left'hændid] adj linkshandig

leg [leg] n poot c, been nt

legacy ['legəsi] n erfenis c

legal ['li:gəl] adj wettig, wettelijk; juridisch

legalization [,li:gəlai'zeiʃən] n legalisatie c

legation [li'geiʃən] n legatie c

legible ['ledʒibəl] adj leesbaar

legitimate [li'dʒitimət] adj wettig

leisure ['leʒə] n vrije tijd; gemak nt

lemon ['lemən] n citroen c

lemonade [,lemə'neid] n limonade c

*lend [lend] v lenen, uitlenen

length [leŋθ] n lengte c

lengthen ['leŋθən] v verlengen

lengthways ['leŋθweiz] adv in de lengte

lens [lenz] n lens c; telephoto ~ telelens c; zoom ~ zoomlens c

leprosy ['leprəsi] n lepra c

less [les] adv minder

lessen ['lesən] v verminderen

lesson ['lesən] n les c

*let [let] v *laten; verhuren; ~ down teleurstellen

letter ['letə] n brief c; letter c; ~ of credit kredietbrief c; ~ of recommendation aanbevelingsbrief c

letter-box ['letəbɔks] n brievenbus c

lettuce ['letis] n sla c

level ['levəl] adj egaal; plat, vlak, effen, gelijk; n peil nt, niveau nt; wa-terpas c; v egaliseren, nivelleren; ~ crossing overweg c

lever ['li:və] n hefboom c, hendel c

Levis ['li:vaiz] pl jeans pl

liability [,laiə'biləti] n aansprakelijkheid c

liable ['laiəbəl] adj aansprakelijk; ~ to onderhevig aan

liberal ['libərəl] adj liberaal; mild, royaal, vrijgevig

liberation [,libə'reiʃən] n bevrijding c

Liberia [lai'biəriə] Liberia

Liberian [lai'biəriən] adj Liberiaans; n Liberiaan c

liberty ['libəti] n vrijheid c

library ['laibrəri] n bibliotheek c

licence ['laisəns] n licentie c; vergunning c; driving ~ rijbewijs nt; ~ number Am kenteken nt; ~ plate Am nummerbord nt

license ['laisəns] v een vergunning verlenen

lick [lik] v likken

lid [lid] n deksel nt

lie [lai] v *liegen; n leugen c

*lie [lai] v *liggen; ~ down *gaan liggen

life [laif] n (pl lives) leven nt; ~ insurance levensverzekering c

lifebelt ['laifbelt] n reddingsgordel c

lifetime ['laiftaim] n leven nt

lift [lift] v optillen; n lift c

light [lait] n licht nt; adj licht; ~ bulb peer c

*light [lait] v *aansteken

lighter ['laitə] n aansteker c

lighthouse ['laithaus] n vuurtoren c

lighting ['laitiŋ] n verlichting c

lightning ['laitniŋ] n bliksem c

like [laik] v *houden van; *mogen, lusten; adj gelijk; conj zoals; prep als

likely ['laikli] adj waarschijnlijk

like-minded [,laik'maindid] adj gelijkgezind

likewise ['laikwaiz] *adv* evenzo, even-eens

lily ['lili] *n* lelie *c*

limb [lim] *n* ledemaat *c*

lime [laim] *n* kalk *c*; linde *c*; limoen *c*

limetree ['laimtri:] *n* linde *c*

limit ['limit] *n* limiet *c*; *v* beperken

limp [limp] *v* hinken; *adj* slap

line [lain] *n* regel *c*; streep *c*; snoer *nt*; lijn *c*; rij *c*; **stand in** ~ *Am* in de rij *staan

linen ['linin] *n* linnen *nt*; linnengoed *nt*

liner ['lainə] *n* lijnboot *c*

lingerie ['lõʒəri:] *n* lingerie *c*

lining ['lainiŋ] *n* voering *c*

link [liŋk] *v* *verbinden; *n* verbinding *c*; schakel *c*

lion ['laiən] *n* leeuw *c*

lip [lip] *n* lip *c*

lipsalve ['lipsɑ:v] *n* lippenboter *c*

lipstick ['lipstik] *n* lippenstift *c*

liqueur [li'kjuə] *n* likeur *c*

liquid ['likwid] *adj* vloeibaar; *n* vloei-stof *c*

liquor ['likə] *n* sterke drank

liquorice ['likəris] *n* drop *c*

list [list] *n* lijst *c*; *v* noteren

listen ['lisən] *v* aanhoren, luisteren

listener ['lisnə] *n* luisteraar *c*

literary ['litrəri] *adj* letterkundig, lite-rair

literature ['litrətʃə] *n* literatuur *c*

litre ['li:tə] *n* liter *c*

litter ['litə] *n* afval *nt*; rommel *c*; nest *nt*

little ['litəl] *adj* klein; weinig

live[1] [liv] *v* leven; wonen

live[2] [laiv] *adj* levend

livelihood ['laivlihud] *n* kost *c*

lively ['laivli] *adj* levendig

liver ['livə] *n* lever *c*

living-room ['liviŋru:m] *n* huiskamer *c*,

woonkamer *c*

load [loud] *n* lading *c*; last *c*; *v* *la-den

loaf [louf] *n* (pl loaves) brood *nt*

loan [loun] *n* lening *c*

lobby ['lɔbi] *n* hal *c*; foyer *c*

lobster ['lɔbstə] *n* kreeft *c*

local ['loukəl] *adj* lokaal, plaatselijk; ~ **call** lokaal gesprek; ~ **train** stop-trein *c*

locality [lou'kæləti] *n* plaats *c*

locate [lou'keit] *v* plaatsen

location [lou'keiʃən] *n* ligging *c*

lock [lɔk] *v* op slot *doen; *n* slot *nt*; sluis *c*; ~ **up** *opsluiten

locomotive [,loukə'moutiv] *n* locomo-tief *c*

lodge [lɔdʒ] *v* herbergen; *n* jachthuis *nt*

lodger ['lɔdʒə] *n* kamerbewoner *c*

lodgings ['lɔdʒiŋz] *pl* logies *nt*

log [lɔg] *n* houtblok *nt*

logic ['lɔdʒik] *n* logica *c*

logical ['lɔdʒikəl] *adj* logisch

lonely ['lounli] *adj* eenzaam

long [lɔŋ] *adj* lang; langdurig; ~ **for** verlangen naar; **no longer** niet meer

longing ['lɔŋiŋ] *n* verlangen *nt*

longitude ['lɔndʒitju:d] *n* lengtegraad *c*

look [luk] *v* *kijken; *lijken, er uit *zien; *n* kijkje *nt*, blik *c*; uiterlijk *nt*, voorkomen *nt*; ~ **after** verzor-gen, zorgen voor, passen op; ~ **at** *aankijken, *kijken naar; ~ **for** *zoeken; ~ **out** *uitkijken, oppas-sen; ~ **up** *opzoeken

looking-glass ['lukiŋglɑ:s] *n* spiegel *c*

loop [lu:p] *n* lus *c*

loose [lu:s] *adj* los

loosen ['lu:sən] *v* losmaken

lord [lɔ:d] *n* lord *c*

lorry ['lɔri] *n* vrachtwagen *c*

***lose** [lu:z] *v* kwijtraken, *verliezen

loss [lɔs] *n* verlies *nt*

lost [lɔst] *adj* verdwaald; weg; ~ **and found** gevonden voorwerpen; ~ **property office** bureau voor gevonden voorwerpen

lot [lɔt] *n* lot *nt*; hoop *c*, boel *c*

lotion ['louʃən] *n* lotion *c*; **aftershave** ~ after shave

lottery ['lɔtəri] *n* loterij *c*

loud [laud] *adj* hard, luid

loud-speaker [,laud'spi:kə] *n* luidspreker *c*

lounge [laundʒ] *n* salon *c*

louse [laus] *n* (pl lice) luis *c*

love [lʌv] *v* *houden van, *liefhebben; *n* liefde *c*; **in** ~ verliefd

lovely ['lʌvli] *adj* heerlijk, prachtig, mooi

lover ['lʌvə] *n* minnaar *c*

love-story ['lʌv,stɔ:ri] *n* liefdesgeschiedenis *c*

low [lou] *adj* laag; diep; neerslachtig; ~ **tide** eb *c*

lower ['louə] *v* *neerlaten; verlagen; *strijken; *adj* onderst, lager

lowlands ['louləndz] *pl* laagland *nt*

loyal ['lɔiəl] *adj* loyaal

lubricate ['lu:brikeit] *v* oliën, smeren

lubrication [,lu:bri'keiʃən] *n* smering *c*; ~ **oil** smeerolie *c*; ~ **system** smeersysteem *nt*

luck [lʌk] *n* geluk *nt*; toeval *nt*; **bad** ~ pech *c*

lucky charm amulet *c*

ludicrous ['lu:dikrəs] *adj* belachelijk, bespottelijk

luggage ['lʌgidʒ] *n* bagage *c*; **hand** ~ handbagage *c*; **left** ~ **office** bagagedepot *nt*; ~ **rack** bagagerek *nt*, bagagenet *nt*; ~ **van** bagagewagen *c*

lukewarm ['lu:kwɔ:m] *adj* lauw

lumbago [lʌm'beigou] *n* spit *nt*

luminous ['lu:minəs] *adj* lichtgevend

lump [lʌmp] *n* brok *nt*, klont *c*, stuk

nt; bult *c*; ~ **of sugar** suikerklontje *nt*; ~ **sum** ronde som

lumpy ['lʌmpi] *adj* klonterig

lunacy ['lu:nəsi] *n* krankzinnigheid *c*

lunatic ['lu:nətik] *adj* krankzinnig; *n* krankzinnige *c*

lunch [lʌntʃ] *n* lunch *c*, middageten *nt*

luncheon ['lʌntʃən] *n* middageten *nt*

lung [lʌŋ] *n* long *c*

lust [lʌst] *n* wellust *c*

luxurious [lʌg'ʒuəriəs] *adj* luxueus

luxury ['lʌkʃəri] *n* luxe *c*

M

machine [mə'ʃi:n] *n* apparaat *nt*, machine *c*

machinery [mə'ʃi:nəri] *n* machinerie *c*; mechanisme *nt*

mackerel ['mækrəl] *n* (pl ~) makreel *c*

mackintosh ['mækintɔʃ] *n* regenjas *c*

mad [mæd] *adj* krankzinnig, waanzinnig, gek; kwaad

madam ['mædəm] *n* mevrouw

madness ['mædnəs] *n* waanzin *c*

magazine [,mægə'zi:n] *n* blad *nt*

magic ['mædʒik] *n* toverkunst *c*, magie *c*; *adj* tover-

magician [mə'dʒiʃən] *n* goochelaar *c*

magistrate ['mædʒistreit] *n* magistraat *c*

magnetic [mæg'netik] *adj* magnetisch

magneto [mæg'ni:tou] *n* (pl ~s) magneet *c*

magnificent [mæg'nifisənt] *adj* prachtig; groots, luisterrijk

magpie ['mægpai] *n* ekster *c*

maid [meid] *n* meid *c*

maiden name ['meidən neim] meisjesnaam *c*

mail [meil] *n* post *c*; *v* posten; ~ **order** *Am* postwissel *c*

mailbox ['meilbɔks] *nAm* brievenbus *c*

main [mein] *adj* hoofd-, voornaamst; grootst; ~ **deck** bovendek *nt*; ~ **line** hoofdlijn *c*; ~ **road** hoofdweg *c*; ~ **street** hoofdstraat *c*

mainland ['meinlənd] *n* vasteland *nt*

mainly ['meinli] *adv* hoofdzakelijk

mains [meinz] *pl* hoofdleiding *c*

maintain [mein'tein] *v* handhaven

maintenance ['meintənəns] *n* onderhoud *nt*

maize [meiz] *n* maïs *c*

major ['meidʒə] *adj* groter; grootst; *n* majoor *c*

majority [mə'dʒɔrəti] *n* meerderheid *c*

***make** [meik] *v* maken; verdienen; halen; ~ **do with** zich *behelpen met; ~ **good** vergoeden; ~ **up** opstellen

make-up ['meikʌp] *n* make-up *c*

malaria [mə'lɛəriə] *n* malaria *c*

Malay [mə'lei] *n* Maleis *nt*

Malaysia [mə'leiziə] Maleisië

Malaysian [mə'leiziən] *adj* Maleisisch

male [meil] *adj* mannelijk

malicious [mə'liʃəs] *adj* boosaardig

malignant [mə'lignənt] *adj* kwaadaardig

mallet ['mælit] *n* houten hamer

malnutrition [,mælnju'triʃən] *n* ondervoeding *c*

mammal ['mæməl] *n* zoogdier *nt*

mammoth ['mæməθ] *n* mammoet *c*

man [mæn] *n* (pl men) man *c*; mens *c*; **men's room** herentoilet *nt*

manage ['mænidʒ] *v* beheren; slagen

manageable ['mænidʒəbəl] *adj* hanteerbaar

management ['mænidʒmənt] *n* directie *c*; beheer *nt*

manager ['mænidʒə] *n* chef *c*, directeur *c*

mandarin ['mændərin] *n* mandarijn *c*

mandate ['mændeit] *n* mandaat *nt*

manger ['meindʒə] *n* kribbe *c*

manicure ['mænikjuə] *n* manicure *c*; *v* manicuren

mankind [mæn'kaind] *n* mensheid *c*

mannequin ['mænəkin] *n* mannequin *c*

manner ['mænə] *n* wijze *c*, manier *c*; **manners** *pl* manieren

man-of-war [,mænəv'wɔ:] *n* oorlogsschip *nt*

manor-house ['mænəhaus] *n* herenhuis *nt*

mansion ['mænʃən] *n* herenhuis *nt*

manual ['mænjuəl] *adj* hand-

manufacture [,mænju'fæktʃə] *v* vervaardigen, fabriceren

manufacturer [,mænju'fæktʃərə] *n* fabrikant *c*

manure [mə'njuə] *n* mest *c*

manuscript ['mænjuskript] *n* manuscript *nt*

many ['meni] *adj* veel

map [mæp] *n* kaart *c*; landkaart *c*; plattegrond *c*

maple ['meipəl] *n* esdoorn *c*

marble ['mɑ:bəl] *n* marmer *nt*; knikker *c*

March [mɑ:tʃ] maart

march [mɑ:tʃ] *v* marcheren; *n* mars *c*

mare [mɛə] *n* merrie *c*

margarine [,mɑ:dʒə'ri:n] *n* margarine *c*

margin ['mɑ:dʒin] *n* kantlijn *c*, marge *c*

maritime ['mæritaim] *adj* maritiem

mark [mɑ:k] *v* aankruisen; merken; kenmerken; *n* merkteken *nt*; cijfer *nt*; schietschijf *c*

market ['mɑ:kit] *n* markt *c*

market-place ['mɑ:kitpleis] *n* marktplein *nt*

marmalade ['mɑ:məleid] *n* marmelade *c*

marriage ['mæridʒ] *n* huwelijk *nt*

marrow ['mærou] n merg nt
marry ['mæri] v huwen, trouwen;
married couple echtpaar nt
marsh [mɑ:ʃ] n moeras nt
marshy ['mɑ:ʃi] adj moerassig
martyr ['mɑ:tə] n martelaar c
marvel ['mɑ:vəl] n wonder nt; v zich
verbazen
marvellous ['mɑ:vələs] adj prachtig
mascara [mæ'skɑ:rə] n mascara c
masculine ['mæskjulin] adj mannelijk
mash [mæʃ] v fijnstampen
mask [mɑ:sk] n masker nt
Mass [mæs] n mis c
mass [mæs] n massa c; ~ production
massaproduktie c
massage ['mæsɑ:ʒ] n massage c; v
masseren
masseur [mæ'sə:] n masseur c
massive ['mæsiv] adj massief
mast [mɑ:st] n mast c
master ['mɑ:stə] n meester c; baas c;
leraar c, onderwijzer c; v beheersen
masterpiece ['mɑ:stəpi:s] n meesterwerk nt
mat [mæt] n mat c; adj mat, dof
match [mætʃ] n lucifer c; wedstrijd c;
v passen bij
match-box ['mætʃbɔks] n lucifersdoosje nt
material [mə'tiəriəl] n materiaal nt;
stof c; adj stoffelijk, materieel
mathematical [,mæθə'mætikəl] adj
wiskundig
mathematics [,mæθə'mætiks] n wiskunde c
matrimonial [,mætri'mouniəl] adj echtelijk
matrimony ['mætriməni] n echt c
matter ['mætə] n stof c, materie c;
aangelegenheid c, kwestie c, zaak c;
v van belang *zijn; as a ~ of fact
feitelijk, eigenlijk
matter-of-fact [,mætərəv'fækt] adj

nuchter
mattress ['mætrəs] n matras c
mature [mə'tjuə] adj rijp
maturity [mə'tjuərəti] n rijpheid c
mausoleum [,mɔ:sə'li:əm] n mausoleum nt
mauve [mouv] adj lichtpaars
May [mei] mei
*may [mei] v *kunnen; *mogen
maybe ['meibi:] adv misschien
mayor [mɛə] n burgemeester c
maze [meiz] n doolhof nt
me [mi:] pron me
meadow ['medou] n wei c
meal [mi:l] n maaltijd c, maal nt
mean [mi:n] adj gemeen; n gemiddelde nt
*mean [mi:n] v betekenen; bedoelen;
menen
meaning ['mi:niŋ] n betekenis c
meaningless ['mi:niŋləs] adj nietszeggend
means [mi:nz] n middel nt; by no ~
zeker niet, geenszins
in the meantime [in ðə 'mi:ntaim] inmiddels, ondertussen
meanwhile ['mi:nwail] adv intussen,
ondertussen
measles ['mi:zəlz] n mazelen pl
measure ['meʒə] v *meten; n maat c;
maatregel c
meat [mi:t] n vlees nt
mechanic [mi'kænik] n monteur c
mechanical [mi'kænikəl] adj mechanisch
mechanism ['mekənizəm] n mechanisme nt
medal ['medəl] n medaille c
mediaeval [,medi'i:vəl] adj middeleeuws
mediate ['mi:dieit] v bemiddelen
mediator ['mi:dieitə] n bemiddelaar c
medical ['medikəl] adj geneeskundig,
medisch

medicine ['medsin] *n* geneesmiddel *nt*; geneeskunde *c*

meditate ['mediteit] *v* mediteren

Mediterranean [,meditə'reiniən] Middellandse Zee

medium ['mi:diəm] *adj* middelmatig, gemiddeld, midden-

*****meet** [mi:t] *v* ontmoeten; *tegenkomen

meeting ['mi:tiŋ] *n* vergadering *c*, bijeenkomst *c*; ontmoeting *c*

meeting-place ['mi:tiŋpleis] *n* trefpunt *nt*

melancholy ['melənkəli] *n* weemoed *c*

mellow ['melou] *adj* zacht

melodrama ['melə,drɑ:mə] *n* melodrama *nt*

melody ['melədi] *n* melodie *c*

melon ['melən] *n* meloen *c*

melt [melt] *v* *smelten

member ['membə] *n* lid *nt*; **Member of Parliament** kamerlid *nt*

membership ['membəʃip] *n* lidmaatschap *nt*

memo ['memou] *n* (pl ~s) memorandum *nt*

memorable ['memərəbəl] *adj* gedenkwaardig

memorial [mə'mɔ:riəl] *n* gedenkteken *nt*

memorize ['meməraiz] *v* uit het hoofd leren

memory ['meməri] *n* geheugen *nt*; herinnering *c*; nagedachtenis *c*

mend [mend] *v* herstellen, repareren

menstruation [,menstru'eiʃən] *n* menstruatie *c*

mental ['mentəl] *adj* geestelijk

mention ['menʃən] *v* noemen, vermelden; *n* melding *c*, vermelding *c*

menu ['menju:] *n* spijskaart *c*, menukaart *c*

merchandise ['mə:tʃəndaiz] *n* handelswaar *c*, koopwaar *c*

merchant ['mə:tʃənt] *n* handelaar *c*, koopman *c*

merciful ['mə:sifəl] *adj* barmhartig

mercury ['mə:kjuri] *n* kwik *nt*

mercy ['mə:si] *n* genade *c*, clementie *c*

mere [miə] *adj* louter

merely ['miəli] *adv* slechts

merger ['mə:dʒə] *n* fusie *c*

merit ['merit] *v* verdienen; *n* verdienste *c*

mermaid ['mə:meid] *n* zeemeermin *c*

merry ['meri] *adj* vrolijk

merry-go-round ['merigou,raund] *n* draaimolen *c*

mesh [meʃ] *n* maas *c*

mess [mes] *n* rommel *c*, warboel *c*; ~ up *bederven

message ['mesidʒ] *n* boodschap *c*, bericht *nt*

messenger ['mesindʒə] *n* bode *c*

metal ['metəl] *n* metaal *nt*; metalen

meter ['mi:tə] *n* meter *c*

method ['meθəd] *n* aanpak *c*, methode *c*; orde *c*

methodical [mə'θɔdikəl] *adj* methodisch

methylated spirits ['meθəleitid 'spirits] brandspiritus *c*

metre ['mi:tə] *n* meter *c*

metric ['metrik] *adj* metrisch

Mexican ['meksikən] *adj* Mexicaans; Mexicaan *c*

Mexico ['meksikou] Mexico

mezzanine ['mezəni:n] *n* entresol *c*

microphone ['maikrəfoun] *n* microfoon *c*

midday ['middei] *n* middag *c*

middle ['midəl] *n* midden *nt*; *adj* middelst; **Middle Ages** middeleeuwen *pl*; **middle-class** *adj* burgerlijk

midnight ['midnait] *n* middernacht *c*

midst [midst] *n* midden *nt*

midsummer ['mid,sʌmə] *n* midzomer *c*

midwife ['midwaif] *n* (pl -wives) vroed-

vrouw c
might [mait] n macht c
*might [mait] v *kunnen
mighty ['maiti] adj machtig
migraine ['migrein] n migraine c
mild [maild] adj zacht
mildew ['mildju] n schimmel c
mile [mail] n mijl c
mileage ['mailidʒ] n afstand in mijlen
milepost ['mailpoust] n wegwijzer c
milestone ['mailstoun] n mijlpaal c
milieu ['mi:ljə:] n milieu nt
military ['militəri] adj militair; ~
force krijgsmacht c
milk [milk] n melk c
milkman ['milkmən] n (pl -men) melkboer c
milk-shake ['milkʃeik] n milk shake
mill [mil] n molen c; fabriek c
miller ['milə] n molenaar c
milliner ['milinə] n modiste c
million ['miljən] n miljoen nt
millionaire [,miljə'neə] n miljonair c
mince [mins] v fijnhakken
mind [maind] n geest c; v bezwaar
*hebben tegen; letten op, *geven
om
mine [main] n mijn c
miner ['mainə] n mijnwerker c
mineral ['minərəl] n delfstof c, mineraal nt; ~ **water** mineraalwater nt
miniature ['minjətʃə] n miniatuur c
minimum ['miniməm] n minimum nt
mining ['maining] n mijnbouw c
minister ['ministə] n minister c; predikant c; **Prime Minister** premier c
ministry ['ministri] n ministerie nt
mink [miŋk] n nerts c
minor ['mainə] adj klein, gering, kleiner; ondergeschikt; n minderjarige
c
minority [mai'nɔrəti] n minderheid c
mint [mint] n munt c
minus ['mainəs] prep min

minute[1] ['minit] n minuut c; **minutes**
notulen pl
minute[2] [mai'nju:t] adj minuscuul
miracle ['mirəkəl] n wonder nt
miraculous [mi'rækjuləs] adj wonderbaarlijk
mirror ['mirə] n spiegel c
misbehave [,misbi'heiv] v zich *misdragen
miscarriage [mis'kæridʒ] n miskraam
c
miscellaneous [,misə'leiniəs] adj gemengd
mischief ['mistʃif] n kattekwaad nt;
onheil nt, schade c, kwaad nt
mischievous ['mistʃivəs] adj ondeugend
miserable ['mizərəbəl] adj beroerd, ellendig
misery ['mizəri] n narigheid c, ellende
c; nood c
misfortune [mis'fɔ:tʃən] n tegenslag c,
ongeluk nt
*mislay [mis'lei] v kwijtraken
misplaced [mis'pleist] adj misplaatst
mispronounce [,misprə'nauns] v verkeerd *uitspreken
miss[1] [mis] mejuffrouw, juffrouw c
miss[2] [mis] v missen
missing ['misiŋ] adj ontbrekend; ~
person vermiste c
mist [mist] n nevel c, mist c
mistake [mi'steik] n abuis nt, vergissing c, fout c
*mistake [mi'steik] v verwarren
mistaken [mi'steikən] adj fout; ***be** ~
zich vergissen
mister ['mistə] n meneer, mijnheer
mistress ['mistrəs] n vrouw des hui-
zes; meesteres c; maîtresse c
mistrust [mis'trʌst] v wantrouwen
misty ['misti] adj mistig
*misunderstand [,misʌndə'stænd] v
*misverstaan

misunderstanding [,misʌndə'stændiŋ] n misverstand nt

misuse [mis'ju:s] n misbruik nt

mittens ['mitənz] pl wanten pl

mix [miks] v mengen; ~ with *omgaan met

mixed [mikst] adj gemêleerd, gemengd

mixer ['miksə] n mixer c

mixture ['mikstʃə] n mengsel nt

moan [moun] v kreunen

moat [mout] n gracht c

mobile ['moubail] adj beweeglijk, mobiel

mock [mɔk] v bespotten

mockery ['mɔkəri] n spot c

model ['mɔdəl] n model nt; mannequin c; v modelleren, boetseren

moderate ['mɔdərət] adj gematigd, matig; middelmatig

modern ['mɔdən] adj modern

modest ['mɔdist] adj discreet, bescheiden

modesty ['mɔdisti] n bescheidenheid c

modify ['mɔdifai] v wijzigen

mohair ['mouhɛə] n mohair nt

moist [mɔist] adj nat, vochtig

moisten ['mɔisən] v bevochtigen

moisture ['mɔistʃə] n vochtigheid c; moisturizing cream vochtinbrengende crème

molar ['moulə] n kies c

moment ['moumənt] n moment nt, ogenblik nt

momentary ['mouməntəri] adj kortstondig

monarch ['mɔnək] n vorst c

monarchy ['mɔnəki] n monarchie c

monastery ['mɔnəstri] n klooster nt

Monday ['mʌndi] maandag c

monetary ['mʌnitəri] adj monetair; ~ unit munteenheid c

money ['mʌni] n geld nt; ~ exchange wisselkantoor nt; ~ order overschrijving c

monk [mʌŋk] n monnik c

monkey ['mʌŋki] n aap c

monologue ['mɔnɔlɔg] n monoloog c

monopoly [mə'nɔpəli] n monopolie nt

monotonous [mə'nɔtənəs] adj eentonig

month [mʌnθ] n maand c

monthly ['mʌnθli] adj maandelijks; ~ magazine maandblad nt

monument ['mɔnjumənt] n gedenkteken nt, monument nt

mood [mu:d] n humeur nt, stemming c

moon [mu:n] n maan c

moonlight ['mu:nlait] n maanlicht nt

moor [muə] n heide c, veen nt

moose [mu:s] n (pl ~, ~s) eland c

moped ['mouped] n bromfiets c

moral ['mɔrəl] n moraal c; adj zedelijk, moreel; morals zeden pl

morality [mə'ræləti] n moraliteit c

more [mɔ:] adj meer; once ~ nogmaals

moreover [mɔ:'rouvə] adv voorts, bovendien

morning ['mɔ:niŋ] n ochtend c, morgen c; ~ paper ochtendblad nt; this ~ vanmorgen

Moroccan [mə'rɔkən] adj Marokkaans; n Marokkaan c

Morocco [mə'rɔkou] Marokko

morphia ['mɔ:fiə] n morfine c

morphine ['mɔ:fi:n] n morfine c

morsel ['mɔ:səl] n brok nt

mortal ['mɔ:təl] adj dodelijk, sterfelijk

mortgage ['mɔ:gidʒ] n hypotheek c

mosaic [mə'zeiik] n mozaïek nt

mosque [mɔsk] n moskee c

mosquito [mə'ski:tou] n (pl ~es) mug c; muskiet c

mosquito-net [mə'ski:tounet] n muskietennet nt

moss [mɔs] n mos nt

most [moust] adj meest; at ~ hoogstens, hooguit; ~ of all vooral

mostly ['moustli] *adv* meestal

motel [mou'tel] *n* motel *nt*

moth [mɔθ] *n* mot *c*

mother ['mʌðə] *n* moeder *c*; ~ **tongue** moedertaal *c*

mother-in-law ['mʌðərinlɔ:] *n* (pl mothers-) schoonmoeder *c*

mother-of-pearl [,mʌðərəv'pə:l] *n* paarlemoer *nt*

motion ['mouʃən] *n* beweging *c*; motie *c*

motive ['moutiv] *n* motief *nt*

motor ['moutə] *n* motor *c*; *v* *autorijden; ~ **body** *Am* carrosserie *c*; **starter** ~ startmotor *c*

motorbike ['moutəbaik] *nAm* brommer *c*

motor-boat ['moutəbout] *n* motorboot *c*

motor-car ['moutəka:] *n* auto *c*

motor-cycle ['moutə,saikəl] *n* motorfiets *c*

motoring ['moutəriŋ] *n* automobilisme *nt*

motorist ['moutərist] *n* automobilist *c*

motorway ['moutəwei] *n* snelweg *c*

motto ['mɔtou] *n* (pl ~es, ~s) devies *nt*

mouldy ['mouldi] *adj* beschimmeld

mound [maund] *n* heuvel *c*

mount [maunt] *v* *bestijgen; *n* berg *c*

mountain ['mauntin] *n* berg *c*; ~ **pass** bergpas *c*; ~ **range** bergketen *c*

mountaineering [,maunti'niəriŋ] *n* bergsport *c*

mountainous ['mauntinəs] *adj* bergachtig

mourning ['mɔ:niŋ] *n* rouw *c*

mouse [maus] *n* (pl mice) muis *c*

moustache [mə'sta:ʃ] *n* snor *c*

mouth [mauθ] *n* mond *c*; muil *c*, bek *c*; monding *c*

mouthwash ['mauθwɔʃ] *n* mondspoeling *c*

movable ['mu:vəbəl] *adj* roerend

move [mu:v] *v* *bewegen; verplaatsen; verhuizen; ontroeren; *n* zet *c*, stap *c*; verhuizing *c*

movement ['mu:vmənt] *n* beweging *c*

movie ['mu:vi] *n* film *c*; **movies** *Am* bioscoop *c*; ~ **theater** *Am* bioscoop *c*

much [mʌtʃ] *adj* veel; **as** ~ evenveel; evenzeer

muck [mʌk] *n* drek *c*

mud [mʌd] *n* modder *c*

muddle ['mʌdəl] *n* wirwar *c*, warboel *c*; *v* verknoeien

muddy ['mʌdi] *adj* modderig

mud-guard ['mʌdga:d] *n* spatbord *nt*

muffler ['mʌflə] *nAm* knalpot *c*

mug [mʌg] *n* beker *c*, kroes *c*

mulberry ['mʌlbəri] *n* moerbei *c*

mule [mju:l] *n* muildier *nt*, muilezel *c*

mullet ['mʌlit] *n* mul *c*

multiplication [,mʌltipli'keiʃən] *n* vermenigvuldiging *c*

multiply ['mʌltiplai] *v* vermenigvuldigen

mumps [mʌmps] *n* bof *c*

municipal [mju:'nisipəl] *adj* gemeentelijk

municipality [mju:,nisi'pæləti] *n* gemeentebestuur *nt*

murder ['mə:də] *n* moord *c*; *v* vermoorden

murderer ['mə:dərə] *n* moordenaar *c*

muscle ['mʌsəl] *n* spier *c*

muscular ['mʌskjulə] *adj* gespierd

museum [mju:'zi:əm] *n* museum *nt*

mushroom ['mʌʃru:m] *n* champignon *c*; paddestoel *c*

music ['mju:zik] *n* muziek *c*; ~ **academy** conservatorium *nt*

musical ['mju:zikəl] *adj* muzikaal; *n* musical *c*

music-hall ['mju:zikhɔ:l] *n* variététheater *nt*

musician [mju:'ziʃən] *n* musicus *c*
muslin ['mʌzlin] *n* mousseline *c*
mussel ['mʌsəl] *n* mossel *c*
* **must** [mʌst] *v* *moeten
mustard ['mʌstəd] *n* mosterd *c*
mute [mju:t] *adj* stom
mutiny ['mju:tini] *n* muiterij *c*
mutton ['mʌtən] *n* schapevlees *nt*
mutual ['mju:tʃuəl] *adj* onderling, wederzijds
my [mai] *adj* mijn
myself [mai'self] *pron* me; zelf
mysterious [mi'stiəriəs] *adj* mysterieus, geheimzinnig
mystery ['mistəri] *n* raadsel *nt*, mysterie *nt*
myth [miθ] *n* mythe *c*

N

nail [neil] *n* nagel *c*; spijker *c*
nailbrush ['neilbrʌʃ] *n* nagelborstel *c*
nail-file ['neilfail] *n* nagelvijl *c*
nail-polish ['neil,pɔliʃ] *n* nagellak *c*
nail-scissors ['neil,sizəz] *pl* nagelschaar *c*
naïve [na:'i:v] *adj* naïef
naked ['neikid] *adj* bloot, naakt; kaal
name [neim] *n* naam *c*; *v* noemen; **in the ~ of** namens
namely ['neimli] *adv* namelijk
nap [næp] *n* dutje *nt*
napkin ['næpkin] *n* servet *nt*
nappy ['næpi] *n* luier *c*
narcosis [na:'kousis] *n* (pl -ses) narcose *c*
narcotic [na:'kɔtik] *n* narcoticum *nt*
narrow ['nærou] *adj* eng, smal, nauw
narrow-minded [,nærou'maindid] *adj* bekrompen
nasty ['na:sti] *adj* naar, akelig
nation ['neiʃən] *n* natie *c*; volk *nt*

national ['næʃənəl] *adj* nationaal; volks-; staats-; ~ **anthem** volkslied *nt*; ~ **dress** nationale klederdracht; ~ **park** natuurreservaat *nt*
nationality [,næʃə'næləti] *n* nationaliteit *c*
nationalize ['næʃənəlaiz] *v* nationaliseren
native ['neitiv] *n* inboorling *c*; *adj* inheems; ~ **country** vaderland *nt*, geboorteland *nt*; ~ **language** moedertaal *c*
natural ['nætʃərəl] *adj* natuurlijk; aangeboren
naturally ['nætʃərəli] *adv* natuurlijk, uiteraard
nature ['neitʃə] *n* natuur *c*; aard *c*
naughty ['nɔ:ti] *adj* ondeugend, stout
nausea ['nɔ:siə] *n* misselijkheid *c*
naval ['neivəl] *adj* marine-
navel ['neivəl] *n* navel *c*
navigable ['nævigəbəl] *adj* bevaarbaar
navigate ['nævigeit] *v* *varen; sturen
navigation [,nævi'geiʃən] *n* navigatie *c*; scheepvaart *c*
navy ['neivi] *n* marine *c*
near [niə] *prep* bij; *adj* nabij, dichtbij
nearby ['niəbai] *adj* nabijzijnd
nearly ['niəli] *adv* haast, bijna
neat [ni:t] *adj* keurig, net; puur
necessary ['nesəsəri] *adj* nodig, noodzakelijk
necessity [nə'sesəti] *n* noodzaak *c*
neck [nek] *n* hals *c*; **nape of the ~** nek *c*
necklace ['nekləs] *n* halsketting *c*
necktie ['nektai] *n* das *c*
need [ni:d] *v* hoeven, behoeven, nodig *hebben; *n* nood *c*, behoefte *c*; noodzaak *c*; ~ **to** *moeten
needle ['ni:dəl] *n* naald *c*
needlework ['ni:dəlwə:k] *n* handwerk *nt*
negative ['negətiv] *adj* ontkennend,

negatief; *n* negatief *nt*

neglect [ni'glekt] *v* verwaarlozen; *n* verwaarlozing *c*

neglectful [ni'glektfəl] *adj* nalatig

negligee ['negliʒei] *n* négligé *nt*

negotiate [ni'gouʃieit] *v* onderhandelen

negotiation [ni,gouʃi'eiʃən] *n* onderhandeling *c*

Negro ['ni:grou] *n* (pl ~es) neger *c*

neighbour ['neibə] *n* buur *c*, buurman *c*

neighbourhood ['neibəhud] *n* buurt *c*

neighbouring ['neibəriŋ] *adj* aangrenzend, naburig

neither ['naiðə] *pron* geen van beide; **neither ... nor** noch ... noch

neon ['ni:ɔn] *n* neon *nt*

nephew ['nefju:] *n* neef *c*

nerve [nə:v] *n* zenuw *c*; durf *c*

nervous ['nə:vəs] *adj* nerveus, zenuwachtig

nest [nest] *n* nest *nt*

net [net] *n* net *nt*; *adj* netto

the Netherlands ['neðələndz] Nederland

network ['netwə:k] *n* netwerk *nt*

neuralgia [njuə'rældʒə] *n* zenuwpijn *c*

neurosis [njuə'rousis] *n* neurose *c*

neuter ['nju:tə] *adj* onzijdig

neutral ['nju:trəl] *adj* neutraal

never ['nevə] *adv* nimmer, nooit

nevertheless [,nevəðə'les] *adv* niettemin

new [nju:] *adj* nieuw; **New Year** nieuwjaar

news [nju:z] *n* nieuwsberichten *pl*, nieuws *nt*; journaal *nt*

newsagent ['nju:,zeidʒənt] *n* krantenverkoper *c*

newspaper ['nju:z,peipə] *n* krant *c*

newsreel ['nju:zri:l] *n* filmjournaal *nt*

newsstand ['nju:zstænd] *n* krantenkiosk *c*

New Zealand [nju: 'zi:lənd] Nieuw-Zeeland

next [nekst] *adj* volgend; ~ **to** naast

nice [nais] *adj* aardig, mooi, prettig; lekker; sympathiek

nickel ['nikəl] *n* nikkel *nt*

nickname ['nikneim] *n* bijnaam *c*

nicotine ['nikəti:n] *n* nicotine *c*

niece [ni:s] *n* nicht *c*

Nigeria [nai'dʒiəriə] Nigeria

Nigerian [nai'dʒiəriən] *adj* Nigeriaans; *n* Nigeriaan *c*

night [nait] *n* nacht *c*; avond *c*; **by ~** 's nachts; ~ **flight** nachtvlucht *c*; ~ **rate** nachttarief *nt*; ~ **train** nachttrein *c*

nightclub ['naitklʌb] *n* nachtclub *c*

night-cream ['naitkri:m] *n* nachtcrème *c*

nightdress ['naitdres] *n* nachtjapon *c*

nightingale ['naitiŋgeil] *n* nachtegaal *c*

nightly ['naitli] *adj* nachtelijk

nil [nil] *niets*

nine [nain] *num* negen

nineteen [,nain'ti:n] *num* negentien

nineteenth [,nain'ti:nθ] *num* negentiende

ninety ['nainti] *num* negentig

ninth [nainθ] *num* negende

nitrogen ['naitrədʒən] *n* stikstof *c*

no [nou] neen, nee; *adj* geen; ~ **one** niemand

nobility [nou'biləti] *n* adel *c*

noble ['noubəl] *adj* adellijk; edel

nobody ['noubɔdi] *pron* niemand

nod [nɔd] *n* knik *c*; *v* knikken

noise [nɔiz] *n* geluid *nt*; herrie *c*, rumoer *nt*, lawaai *nt*

noisy ['nɔizi] *adj* lawaaierig; gehorig

nominal ['nɔminəl] *adj* nominaal

nominate ['nɔmineit] *v* benoemen

nomination [,nɔmi'neiʃən] *n* nominatie *c*; benoeming *c*

none [nʌn] *pron* geen

nonsense ['nɔnsəns] *n* onzin *c*
noon [nu:n] *n* middag *c*
normal ['nɔ:məl] *adj* gewoon, normaal
north [nɔ:θ] *n* noorden *nt*; noord *c*; *adj* noordelijk; **North Pole** noordpool *c*
north-east [,nɔ:θ'i:st] *n* noordoosten *nt*
northerly ['nɔ:ðəli] *adj* noordelijk
northern ['nɔ:ðən] *adj* noordelijk
north-west [,nɔ:θ'west] *n* noordwesten *nt*
Norway ['nɔ:wei] Noorwegen
Norwegian [nɔ:'wi:dʒən] *adj* Noors; *n* Noor *c*
nose [nouz] *n* neus *c*
nosebleed ['nouzbli:d] *n* neusbloeding *c*
nostril ['nɔstril] *n* neusgat *nt*
not [nɔt] *adv* niet
notary ['noutəri] *n* notaris *c*
note [nout] *n* aantekening *c*, notitie *c*; noot *c*; toon *c*; *v* noteren; opmerken, constateren
notebook ['noutbuk] *n* notitieboek *nt*
noted ['noutid] *adj* befaamd
notepaper ['nout,peipə] *n* schrijfpapier *nt*, briefpapier *nt*
nothing ['nʌθiŋ] *n* niks, niets
notice ['noutis] *v* bemerken, merken, opmerken; *zien; *n* aankondiging *c*, bericht *nt*; notitie *c*, aandacht *c*
noticeable ['noutisəbəl] *adj* merkbaar; opmerkelijk
notify ['noutifai] *v* mededelen; waarschuwen
notion ['nouʃən] *n* begrip *nt*, notie *c*
notorious [nou'tɔ:riəs] *adj* berucht
nougat ['nu:ga:] *n* noga *c*
nought [nɔ:t] *n* nul *c*
noun [naun] *n* zelfstandig naamwoord *nt*
nourishing ['nʌriʃiŋ] *adj* voedzaam
novel ['nɔvəl] *n* roman *c*
novelist ['nɔvəlist] *n* romanschrijver *c*

November [nou'vembə] november
now [nau] *adv* nu; thans; ~ **and then** nu en dan
nowadays ['nauədeiz] *adv* tegenwoordig
nowhere ['nouweə] *adv* nergens
nozzle ['nɔzəl] *n* tuit *c*
nuance [nju:'ã:s] *n* nuance *c*
nuclear ['nju:kliə] *adj* kern-, nucleair; ~ **energy** kernenergie *c*
nucleus ['nju:kliəs] *n* kern *c*
nude [nju:d] *adj* naakt; *n* naakt *nt*
nuisance ['nju:səns] *n* last *c*
numb [nʌm] *adj* gevoelloos; verstijfd
number ['nʌmbə] *n* nummer *nt*; cijfer *nt*, getal *nt*; aantal *nt*
numeral ['nju:mərəl] *n* telwoord *nt*
numerous ['nju:mərəs] *adj* talrijk
nun [nʌn] *n* non *c*
nunnery ['nʌnəri] *n* nonnenklooster *nt*
nurse [nə:s] *n* zuster *c*, verpleegster *c*; kinderjuffrouw *c*; *v* verplegen; zogen
nursery ['nə:səri] *n* kinderkamer *c*; crèche *c*; boomkwekerij *c*
nut [nʌt] *n* noot *c*; moer *c*
nutcrackers ['nʌt,krækəz] *pl* notekraker *c*
nutmeg ['nʌtmeg] *n* nootmuskaat *c*
nutritious [nju:'triʃəs] *adj* voedzaam
nutshell ['nʌtʃel] *n* notedop *c*
nylon ['nailən] *n* nylon *c*

O

oak [ouk] *n* eik *c*
oar [ɔ:] *n* roeiriem *c*
oasis [ou'eisis] *n* (pl oases) oase *c*
oath [ouθ] *n* eed *c*
oats [outs] *pl* haver *c*
obedience [ə'bi:diəns] *n* gehoorzaamheid *c*

obedient [ə'bi:diənt] *adj* gehoorzaam

obey [ə'bei] *v* gehoorzamen

object¹ ['ɔbdʒikt] *n* object *nt*; voorwerp *nt*; doel *nt*

object² [əb'dʒekt] *v* *tegenwerpen; ~ to bezwaar *hebben tegen

objection [əb'dʒekʃən] *n* bezwaar *nt*, tegenwerping *c*

objective [əb'dʒektiv] *adj* objectief; *n* doel *nt*

obligatory [ə'bligətəri] *adj* verplicht

oblige [ə'blaidʒ] *v* verplichten; *be obliged to verplicht *zijn om; *moeten

obliging [ə'blaidʒiŋ] *adj* voorkomend

oblong ['ɔblɔŋ] *adj* langwerpig; *n* rechthoek *c*

obscene [əb'si:n] *adj* obsceen

obscure [əb'skjuə] *adj* obscuur, duister

observation [,ɔbzə'veiʃən] *n* observatie *c*, waarneming *c*

observatory [əb'zə:vətri] *n* observatorium *nt*

observe [əb'zə:v] *v* observeren, *waarnemen

obsession [əb'seʃən] *n* obsessie *c*

obstacle ['ɔbstəkəl] *n* hindernis *c*

obstinate ['ɔbstinət] *adj* koppig; hardnekkig

obtain [əb'tein] *v* behalen, *verkrijgen

obtainable [əb'teinəbəl] *adj* verkrijgbaar

obvious ['ɔbviəs] *adj* duidelijk

occasion [ə'keiʒən] *n* gelegenheid *c*; aanleiding *c*

occasionally [ə'keiʒənəli] *adv* af en toe, nu en dan

occupant ['ɔkjupənt] *n* bewoner *c*

occupation [,ɔkju'peiʃən] *n* werk *nt*; bezetting *c*

occupy ['ɔkjupai] *v* *innemen, bezetten; occupied *adj* bezet

occur [ə'kə:] *v* gebeuren, *voorkomen, zich *voordoen

occurrence [ə'kʌrəns] *n* gebeurtenis *c*

ocean ['ouʃən] *n* oceaan *c*

October [ɔk'toubə] oktober

octopus ['ɔktəpəs] *n* octopus *c*

oculist ['ɔkjulist] *n* oogarts *c*

odd [ɔd] *adj* raar, vreemd; oneven

odour ['oudə] *n* geur *c*

of [ɔv, əv] *prep* van

off [ɔf] *adv* af; weg; *prep* van

offence [ə'fens] *n* overtreding *c*; belediging *c*, aanstoot *c*

offend [ə'fend] *v* krenken, beledigen; *overtreden

offensive [ə'fensiv] *adj* offensief; beledigend, aanstootgevend; *n* offensief *nt*

offer ['ɔfə] *v* *aanbieden; *bieden; *n* aanbieding *c*, aanbod *nt*

office ['ɔfis] *n* bureau *nt*, kantoor *nt*; ambt *nt*; ~ hours kantooruren *pl*

officer ['ɔfisə] *n* officier *c*

official [ə'fiʃəl] *adj* officieel

off-licence ['ɔf,laisəns] *n* slijterij *c*

often ['ɔfən] *adv* vaak, dikwijls

oil [ɔil] *n* olie *c*; fuel ~ stookolie *c*; ~ filter oliefilter *nt*; ~ pressure oliedruk *c*

oil-painting [,ɔil'peintiŋ] *n* olieverfschilderij *nt*

oil-refinery ['ɔilri,fainəri] *n* olieraffinaderij *c*

oil-well ['ɔilwel] *n* oliebron *c*

oily ['ɔili] *adj* olieachtig

ointment ['ɔintmənt] *n* zalf *c*

okay! ['ou'kei] in orde!

old [ould] *adj* oud; ~ age ouderdom *c*

old-fashioned [,ould'fæʃənd] *adj* ouderwets

olive ['ɔliv] *n* olijf *c*; ~ oil olijfolie *c*

omelette ['ɔmlət] *n* omelet *nt*

ominous ['ɔminəs] *adj* onheilspellend

omit [ə'mit] *v* *weglaten

omnipotent [ɔm'nipətənt] *adj* almachtig

on [ɔn] *prep* op; aan

once [wʌns] *adv* eenmaal, eens; **at ~** meteen, dadelijk; **~ more** nog eens

oncoming ['ɔn,kʌmiŋ] *adj* tegemoetkomend, naderend

one [wʌn] *num* een; *pron* men

oneself [wʌn'self] *pron* zelf

onion ['ʌnjən] *n* ui *c*

only ['ounli] *adj* enig; *adv* slechts, alleen, maar; *conj* maar

onwards ['ɔnwədz] *adv* voorwaarts

onyx ['ɔniks] *n* onyx *nt*

opal ['oupəl] *n* opaal *c*

open ['oupən] *v* openen; *adj* open; openhartig

opening ['oupəniŋ] *n* opening *c*

opera ['ɔpərə] *n* opera *c*; **~ house** opera *c*

operate ['ɔpəreit] *v* opereren, werken

operation [,ɔpə'reiʃən] *n* werking *c*; operatie *c*

operator ['ɔpəreitə] *n* telefoniste *c*

operetta [,ɔpə'retə] *n* operette *c*

opinion [ə'pinjən] *n* opinie *c*, mening *c*

opponent [ə'pounənt] *n* tegenstander *c*

opportunity [,ɔpə'tju:nəti] *n* gelegenheid *c*, kans *c*

oppose [ə'pouz] *v* zich verzetten

opposite ['ɔpəzit] *prep* tegenover; *adj* tegengesteld

opposition [,ɔpə'ziʃən] *n* oppositie *c*

oppress [ə'pres] *v* beklemmen, verdrukken

optician [ɔp'tiʃən] *n* opticien *c*

optimism ['ɔptimizəm] *n* optimisme *nt*

optimist ['ɔptimist] *n* optimist *c*

optimistic [,ɔpti'mistik] *adj* optimistisch

optional ['ɔpʃənəl] *adj* facultatief

or [ɔ:] *conj* of

oral ['ɔ:rəl] *adj* mondeling

orange ['ɔrindʒ] *n* sinaasappel *c*; *adj* oranje

orchard ['ɔ:tʃəd] *n* boomgaard *c*

orchestra ['ɔ:kistrə] *n* orkest *nt*; **~ seat** *Am* stalles *pl*

order ['ɔ:də] *v* *bevelen; bestellen; *n* volgorde *c*, orde *c*; opdracht *c*, bevel *nt*; bestelling *c*; **in ~** in orde; **in ~ to** om te; **made to ~** op maat gemaakt; **out of ~** buiten werking; **postal ~** postwissel *c*

order-form ['ɔ:dəfɔ:m] *n* bestelformulier *nt*

ordinary ['ɔ:dənri] *adj* alledaags, gewoon

ore [ɔ:] *n* erts *nt*

organ ['ɔ:gən] *n* orgaan *nt*; orgel *nt*

organic [ɔ:'gænik] *adj* organisch

organization [,ɔ:gənai'zeiʃən] *n* organisatie *c*

organize ['ɔ:gənaiz] *v* organiseren

Orient ['ɔ:riənt] *n* Oosten *nt*

oriental [,ɔ:ri'entəl] *adj* oosters

orientate ['ɔ:riənteit] *v* zich oriënteren

origin ['ɔridʒin] *n* origine *c*, oorsprong *c*; afstamming *c*, herkomst *c*

original [ə'ridʒinəl] *adj* oorspronkelijk, origineel

originally [ə'ridʒinəli] *adv* aanvankelijk

orlon ['ɔ:lɔn] *n* orlon *nt*

ornament ['ɔ:nəmənt] *n* versiersel *nt*

ornamental [,ɔ:nə'mentəl] *adj* ornamenteel

orphan ['ɔ:fən] *n* wees *c*

orthodox ['ɔ:θədɔks] *adj* orthodox

ostrich ['ɔstritʃ] *n* struisvogel *c*

other ['ʌðə] *adj* ander

otherwise ['ʌðəwaiz] *conj* anders

*ought to [ɔ:t] *moeten

our [auə] *adj* ons

ourselves [auə'selvz] *pron* ons; zelf

out [aut] *adv* buiten, uit; **~ of** buiten, uit

outbreak ['autbreik] *n* uitbarsting *c*

outcome ['autkʌm] *n* resultaat *nt*

*outdo [,aut'du:] *v* *overtreffen

outdoors [,aut'dɔ:z] adv buiten

outer ['autə] adj buitenst

outfit ['autfit] n uitrusting c

outline ['autlain] n omtrek c; v schetsen

outlook ['autluk] n verwachting c; zienswijze c

output ['autput] n produktie c

outrage ['autreidʒ] n gewelddaad c

outside [,aut'said] adv buiten; prep buiten; n uiterlijk nt, buitenkant c

outsize ['autsaiz] n extra grote maat

outskirts ['autskə:ts] pl buitenwijk c

outstanding [,aut'stændiŋ] adj eminent, vooraanstaand

outward ['autwəd] adj uiterlijk

outwards ['autwədz] adv naar buiten

oval ['ouvəl] adj ovaal

oven ['ʌvən] n oven c

over ['ouvə] prep boven, over; meer dan; adv over; omver; adj voorbij; ~ there ginds

overall ['ouvərɔ:l] adj totaal

overalls ['ouvərɔ:lz] pl overall c

overcast [,ouvə'ka:st] adj betrokken

overcoat ['ouvəkout] n overjas c

*overcome [,ouvə'kʌm] v *overwinnen

overdue [,ouvə'dju:] adj te laat; achterstallig

overgrown [,ouvə'groun] adj begroeid

overhaul [,ouvə'hɔ:l] v reviseren

overlook [,ouvə'luk] v over het hoofd *zien

overnight [,ouvə'nait] adv 's nachts

overseas [,ouvə'si:z] adj overzees

oversight ['ouvəsait] n vergissing c

*oversleep [,ouvə'sli:p] v zich *verslapen

overstrung [,ouvə'strʌŋ] adj overspannen

*overtake [,ouvə'teik] v inhalen; no overtaking inhalen verboden

over-tired [,ouvə'taiəd] adj oververmoeid

overture ['ouvətʃə] n ouverture c

overweight ['ouvəweit] n bagageoverschot nt

overwhelm [,ouvə'welm] v onthutsen, overweldigen

overwork [,ouvə'wə:k] v zich overwerken

owe [ou] v verschuldigd *zijn, schuldig *zijn; te danken *hebben aan; owing to vanwege, ten gevolge van

owl [aul] n uil c

own [oun] v *bezitten; adj eigen

owner ['ounə] n bezitter c, eigenaar c

ox [ɔks] n (pl oxen) os c

oxygen ['ɔksidʒən] n zuurstof c

oyster ['ɔistə] n oester c

P

pace [peis] n gang c; schrede c, stap c; tempo nt

Pacific Ocean [pə'sifik 'ouʃən] Stille Oceaan

pacifism ['pæsifizəm] n pacifisme nt

pacifist ['pæsifist] n pacifist c; pacifistisch

pack [pæk] v inpakken; ~ up inpakken

package ['pækidʒ] n pak nt

packet ['pækit] n pakje nt

packing ['pækiŋ] n verpakking c

pad [pæd] n kussentje nt; blocnote c

paddle ['pædəl] n peddel c

padlock ['pædlɔk] n hangslot nt

pagan ['peigən] adj heidens; n heiden c

page [peidʒ] n pagina c, bladzijde c

page-boy ['peidʒbɔi] n piccolo c

pail [peil] n emmer c

pain [pein] n pijn c; pains moeite c

painful ['peinfəl] adj pijnlijk

painless ['peinləs] adj pijnloos

paint [peint] n verf c; v schilderen; verven

paint-box ['peintbɔks] n verfdoos c

paint-brush ['peintbrʌʃ] n penseel nt

painter ['peintə] n schilder c

painting ['peintiŋ] n schilderij nt

pair [peə] n paar nt

Pakistan [,pɑːki'stɑːn] Pakistan

Pakistani [,pɑːki'stɑːni] adj Pakistaans; n Pakistaan c

palace ['pæləs] n paleis nt

pale [peil] adj bleek; licht

palm [pɑːm] n palm c; handpalm c

palpable ['pælpəbəl] adj tastbaar

palpitation [,pælpi'teiʃən] n hartklopping c

pan [pæn] n pan c

pane [pein] n ruit c

panel ['pænəl] n paneel nt

panelling ['pænəliŋ] n lambrizering c

panic ['pænik] n paniek c

pant [pænt] v hijgen

panties ['pæntiz] pl onderbroek c, slip c

pants [pænts] pl onderbroek c; plAm broek c

pant-suit ['pæntsuːt] n broekpak nt

panty-hose ['pæntihouz] n panty c

paper ['peipə] n papier nt; krant c; papieren; carbon ~ carbonpapier nt; ~ bag papieren zak; ~ napkin papieren servet; typing ~ schrijfmachinepapier nt; wrapping ~ pakpapier nt

paperback ['peipəbæk] n pocketboek nt

paper-knife ['peipənaif] n briefopener c

parade [pə'reid] n parade c, optocht c

paraffin ['pærəfin] n petroleum c

paragraph ['pærəgrɑːf] n alinea c, paragraaf c

parakeet ['pærəkiːt] n parkiet c

paralise ['pærəlaiz] v verlammen

parallel ['pærəlel] adj evenwijdig, parallel; n parallel c

parcel ['pɑːsəl] n pakket nt, pakje nt

pardon ['pɑːdən] n vergiffenis c; gratie c

parents ['peərənts] pl ouders pl

parents-in-law ['peərəntsinlɔː] pl schoonouders pl

parish ['pæriʃ] n parochie c

park [pɑːk] n park nt; v parkeren; no parking verboden te parkeren; parking fee parkeertarief nt; parking light stadslicht nt; parking lot Am parkeerplaats c; parking meter parkeermeter c; parking zone parkeerzone c

parliament ['pɑːləmənt] n parlement nt

parliamentary [,pɑːlə'mentəri] adj parlementair

parrot ['pærət] n papegaai c

parsley ['pɑːsli] n peterselie c

parson ['pɑːsən] n dominee c

parsonage ['pɑːsənidʒ] n pastorie c

part [pɑːt] n gedeelte nt, deel nt; stuk nt; v *scheiden; spare ~ onderdeel nt

partial ['pɑːʃəl] adj gedeeltelijk; partijdig

participant [pɑː'tisipənt] n deelnemer c

participate [pɑː'tisipeit] v *deelnemen

particular [pə'tikjulə] adj bijzonder, speciaal; kieskeurig; in ~ in het bijzonder

parting ['pɑːtiŋ] n afscheid nt; scheiding c

partition [pɑː'tiʃən] n tussenschot nt

partly ['pɑːtli] adv deels, gedeeltelijk

partner ['pɑːtnə] n partner c; compagnon c

partridge ['pɑːtridʒ] n patrijs c

party ['pɑːti] n partij c; fuif c, feestje nt; groep c

pass [pɑːs] *v* *voorbijgaan, passeren; *aangeven; slagen; *vAm* inhalen; **no passing** *Am* inhalen verboden; ~ **by** passeren; ~ **through** *gaan door

passage ['pæsidʒ] *n* doorgang *c*; overtocht *c*; passage *c*; doorreis *c*

passenger ['pæsəndʒə] *n* passagier *c*; ~ **car** *Am* wagon *c*; ~ **train** personentrein *c*

passer-by [,pɑːsə'bai] *n* voorbijganger *c*

passion ['pæʃən] *n* hartstocht *c*, passie *c*; drift *c*

passionate ['pæʃənət] *adj* hartstochtelijk

passive ['pæsiv] *adj* passief

passport ['pɑːspɔːt] *n* paspoort *nt*; ~ **control** paspoortcontrole *c*; ~ **photograph** pasfoto *c*

password ['pɑːswɔːd] *n* wachtwoord *nt*

past [pɑːst] *n* verleden *nt*; *adj* vorig, afgelopen, voorbij; *prep* langs, voorbij

paste [peist] *n* pasta *c*; *v* plakken

pastry ['peistri] *n* gebak *nt*; ~ **shop** banketbakkerij *c*

pasture ['pɑːstʃə] *n* weiland *nt*

patch [pætʃ] *v* verstellen

patent ['peitənt] *n* patent *nt*, octrooi *nt*

path [pɑːθ] *n* pad *nt*

patience ['peiʃəns] *n* geduld *nt*

patient ['peiʃənt] *adj* geduldig; *n* patiënt *c*

patriot ['peitriət] *n* patriot *c*

patrol [pə'troul] *n* patrouille *c*; *v* patrouilleren; surveilleren

pattern ['pætən] *n* motief *nt*, patroon *nt*

pause [pɔːz] *n* pauze *c*; *v* pauzeren

pave [peiv] *v* plaveien, bestraten

pavement ['peivmənt] *n* trottoir *nt*; plaveisel *nt*

pavilion [pə'viljən] *n* paviljoen *nt*

paw [pɔː] *n* poot *c*

pawn [pɔːn] *v* verpanden; *n* pion *c*

pawnbroker ['pɔːn,broukə] *n* pandjesbaas *c*

pay [pei] *n* salaris *nt*, loon *nt*

*pay [pei] *v* betalen; lonen; ~ **attention to** letten op; **paying** rendabel; ~ **off** aflossen; ~ **on account** afbetalen

pay-desk ['peidesk] *n* kassa *c*

payee [pei'iː] *n* begunstigde *c*

payment ['peimənt] *n* betaling *c*

pea [piː] *n* erwt *c*

peace [piːs] *n* vrede *c*

peaceful ['piːsfəl] *adj* vreedzaam

peach [piːtʃ] *n* perzik *c*

peacock ['piːkɔk] *n* pauw *c*

peak [piːk] *n* top *c*; spits *c*; ~ **hour** spitsuur *nt*; ~ **season** hoogseizoen *nt*

peanut ['piːnʌt] *n* pinda *c*

pear [peə] *n* peer *c*

pearl [pəːl] *n* parel *c*

peasant ['pezənt] *n* boer *c*

pebble ['pebəl] *n* kiezel *c*

peculiar [pi'kjuːljə] *adj* eigenaardig; speciaal, bijzonder

peculiarity [pi,kjuːli'ærəti] *n* eigenaardigheid *c*

pedal ['pedəl] *n* pedaal *nt/c*

pedestrian [pi'destriən] *n* voetganger *c*; **no pedestrians** verboden voor voetgangers; ~ **crossing** zebrapad *nt*

pedicure ['pedikjuə] *n* pedicure *c*

peel [piːl] *v* schillen *c*; *n* schil *c*

peep [piːp] *v* gluren

peg [peg] *n* klerenhaak *c*

pelican ['pelikən] *n* pelikaan *c*

pelvis ['pelvis] *n* bekken *nt*

pen [pen] *n* pen *c*

penalty ['penəlti] *n* boete *c*; straf *c*; ~

kick strafschop c

pencil ['pensəl] n potlood nt

pencil-sharpener ['pensəl‚ʃɑ:pnə] n punteslijper c

penetrate ['penitreit] v *doordringen

penguin ['peŋgwin] n pinguin c

penicillin [‚peni'silin] n penicilline c

peninsula [pə'ninsjulə] n schiereiland nt

penknife ['pennaif] n (pl -knives) zakmes nt

pension¹ ['pɑ̃:siɔ̃:] n pension nt

pension² ['penʃən] n pensioen nt

people ['pi:pəl] pl mensen; n volk nt

pepper ['pepə] n peper c

peppermint ['pepəmint] n pepermunt c

perceive [pə'si:v] v bemerken

percent [pə'sent] n procent nt

percentage [pə'sentidʒ] n percentage nt

perceptible [pə'septibəl] adj merkbaar

perception [pə'sepʃən] n gewaarwording c

perch [pə:tʃ] (pl ~) baars c

percolator ['pə:kəleitə] n percolator c

perfect ['pə:fikt] adj volkomen, volmaakt

perfection [pə'fekʃən] n perfectie c, volmaaktheid c

perform [pə'fɔ:m] v uitvoeren, verrichten

performance [pə'fɔ:məns] n voorstelling c

perfume ['pə:fju:m] n parfum nt

perhaps [pə'hæps] adv misschien; wellicht

peril ['peril] n gevaar nt

perilous ['periləs] adj gevaarlijk

period ['piəriəd] n tijdperk nt, periode c; punt nt

periodical [‚piəri'ɔdikəl] n tijdschrift nt; adj periodiek

perish ['periʃ] v *omkomen

perishable ['periʃəbəl] adj aan bederf onderhevig

perjury ['pə:dʒəri] n meineed c

permanent ['pə:mənənt] adj blijvend, permanent, duurzaam; bestendig, vast; ~ press plooihoudend; ~ wave permanent c

permission [pə'miʃən] n toestemming c, permissie c; verlof nt, vergunning c

permit¹ [pə'mit] v *toestaan, veroorloven

permit² ['pə:mit] n vergunning c

peroxide [pə'rɔksaid] n waterstofperoxyde nt

perpendicular [‚pə:pən'dikjulə] adj loodrecht

Persia ['pə:ʃə] Perzië

Persian ['pə:ʃən] adj Perzisch; n Pers c

person ['pə:sən] n persoon c; per ~ per persoon

personal ['pə:sənəl] adj persoonlijk

personality [‚pə:sə'næləti] n persoonlijkheid c

personnel [‚pə:sə'nel] n personeel nt

perspective [pə'spektiv] n perspectief nt

perspiration [‚pə:spə'reiʃən] n transpiratie c, zweet nt

perspire [pə'spaiə] v transpireren, zweten

persuade [pə'sweid] v overreden, overhalen; overtuigen

persuasion [pə'sweiʒən] n overtuiging c

pessimism ['pesimizəm] n pessimisme nt

pessimist ['pesimist] n pessimist c

pessimistic [‚pesi'mistik] adj pessimistisch

pet [pet] n huisdier nt; lieveling c

petal ['petəl] n bloemblad nt

petition [pi'tiʃən] n petitie c

petrol ['petrǝl] n benzine c; ~ **pump** benzinepomp c; ~ **station** benzine-station nt; ~ **tank** benzinetank c

petroleum [pi'trouliǝm] n petroleum c

petty ['peti] adj klein, nietig, onbedui-dend; ~ **cash** kleingeld nt

pewit ['pi:wit] n kievit c

pewter ['pju:tǝ] n tin nt

phantom ['fæntǝm] n spook nt

pharmacology [,fɑ:mǝ'kɔlǝdʒi] n far-macologie c

pharmacy ['fɑ:mǝsi] n apotheek c; drogisterij c

phase [feiz] n fase c

pheasant ['fezǝnt] n fazant c

Philippine ['filipain] adj Filippijns

Philippines ['filipi:nz] pl Filippijnen pl

philosopher [fi'lɔsǝfǝ] n wijsgeer c, fi-losoof c

philosophy [fi'lɔsǝfi] n wijsbegeerte c, filosofie c

phone [foun] n telefoon c; v opbellen, telefoneren

phonetic [fǝ'netik] adj fonetisch

photo ['foutou] n (pl ~s) foto c

photograph ['foutǝgrɑ:f] n foto c; v fotograferen

photographer [fǝ'tɔgrǝfǝ] n fotograaf c

photography [fǝ'tɔgrǝfi] n fotografie c

photostat ['foutǝstæt] n fotocopie c

phrase [freiz] n uitdrukking c

phrase-book ['freizbuk] n taalgids c

physical ['fizikǝl] adj fysiek

physician [fi'ziʃǝn] n dokter c

physicist ['fizisist] n natuurkundige c

physics ['fiziks] n fysica c, natuurkun-de c

physiology [,fizi'ɔlǝdʒi] n fysiologie c

pianist ['pi:ǝnist] n pianist c

piano [pi'ænou] n piano c; **grand** ~ vleugel c

pick [pik] v plukken; *kiezen; n keus c; ~ **up** oprapen; ophalen; **pick-up**

van bestelauto c

pick-axe ['pikæks] n houweel nt

pickles ['pikǝlz] pl zoetzuur nt, pickles pl

picnic ['piknik] n picknick c; v pick-nicken

picture ['piktʃǝ] n schilderij nt; plaat c, prent c; beeld nt, afbeelding c; ~ **postcard** ansichtkaart c, prent-briefkaart c; **pictures** bioscoop c

picturesque [,piktʃǝ'resk] adj pittoresk, schilderachtig

piece [pi:s] n stuk nt

pier [piǝ] n pier c

pierce [piǝs] v doorboren

pig [pig] n varken nt; zwijn nt

pigeon ['pidʒǝn] n duif c

pig-headed ['pig'hedid] adj eigenwijs

piglet ['piglǝt] n big c

pigskin ['pigskin] n varkensleer nt

pike [paik] (pl ~) snoek c

pile [pail] n stapel c; v opstapelen; **piles** pl aambeien pl

pilgrim ['pilgrim] n pelgrim c

pilgrimage ['pilgrimidʒ] n bedevaart c

pill [pil] n pil c

pillar ['pilǝ] n zuil c, pilaar c

pillar-box ['pilǝbɔks] n brievenbus c

pillow ['pilou] n kussen nt, hoofdkus-sen nt

pillow-case ['piloukeis] n kussensloop c/nt

pilot ['pailǝt] n piloot c; loods c

pimple ['pimpǝl] n puistje nt

pin [pin] n speld c; v vastspelden; **bobby** ~ Am haarspeld c

pincers ['pinsǝz] pl nijptang c

pinch [pintʃ] v *knijpen

pineapple ['pai,næpǝl] n ananas c

ping-pong ['piŋpɔŋ] n tafeltennis nt

pink [piŋk] adj roze

pioneer [,paiǝ'niǝ] n pionier c

pious ['paiǝs] adj vroom

pip [pip] n pit c

pipe [paip] *n* pijp *c*; leiding *c*; ~ **cleaner** pijpestoker *c*; ~ **tobacco** pijptabak *c*

pirate ['paiərət] *n* piraat *c*

pistol ['pistəl] *n* pistool *nt*

piston ['pistən] *n* zuiger *c*; ~ **ring** zuigerring *c*

piston-rod ['pistənrod] *n* zuigerstang *c*

pit [pit] *n* kuil *c*; groeve *c*

pitcher ['pitʃə] *n* kruik *c*

pity ['piti] *n* medelijden *nt*; *v* medelijden *hebben met, beklagen; **what a pity!** jammer!

placard ['plækɑ:d] *n* aanplakbiljet *nt*

place [pleis] *n* plaats *c*; *v* zetten, plaatsen; ~ **of birth** geboorteplaats *c*; *take ~ *plaatshebben

plague [pleig] *n* plaag *c*

plaice [pleis] (pl ~) schol *c*

plain [plein] *adj* duidelijk; gewoon, eenvoudig; *n* vlakte *c*

plan [plæn] *n* plan *nt*; plattegrond *c*; *v* plannen

plane [plein] *adj* vlak; *n* vliegtuig *nt*; ~ **crash** vliegramp *c*

planet ['plænit] *n* planeet *c*

planetarium [,plæni'teəriəm] *n* planetarium *nt*

plank [plæŋk] *n* plank *c*

plant [plɑ:nt] *n* plant *c*; bedrijf *nt*; *v* planten

plantation [plæn'teiʃən] *n* plantage *c*

plaster ['plɑ:stə] *n* pleister *nt*, gips *nt*; pleister *c*

plastic ['plæstik] *adj* plastic; *n* plastic *nt*

plate [pleit] *n* bord *nt*; plaat *c*

plateau ['plætou] *n* (pl ~x, ~s) hoogvlakte *c*

platform ['plætfɔ:m] *n* perron *nt*; ~ **ticket** perronkaartje *nt*

platinum ['plætinəm] *n* platina *nt*

play [plei] *v* spelen; bespelen; *n* spel *nt*; toneelstuk *nt*; **one-act** ~ eenakter *c*; ~ **truant** spijbelen

player [pleiə] *n* speler *c*

playground ['pleigraund] *n* speelplaats *c*

playing-card ['pleiiŋkɑ:d] *n* speelkaart *c*

playwright ['pleirait] *n* toneelschrijver *c*

plea [pli:] *n* pleidooi *nt*

plead [pli:d] *v* pleiten

pleasant ['plezənt] *adj* prettig, aardig, aangenaam

please [pli:z] alstublieft; *v* *bevallen; **pleased** ingenomen; **pleasing** aangenaam

pleasure ['pleʒə] *n* genoegen *nt*, pret *c*, plezier *nt*

plentiful ['plentifəl] *adj* overvloedig

plenty ['plenti] *n* overvloed *c*; heleboel *c*

pliers [plaiəz] *pl* tang *c*

plimsolls ['plimsəlz] *pl* gymschoenen *pl*

plot [plot] *n* samenzwering *c*, komplot *nt*; handeling *c*; perceel *nt*

plough [plau] *n* ploeg *c*; *v* ploegen

plucky ['plʌki] *adj* flink

plug [plʌg] *n* stekker *c*; ~ **in** inschakelen

plum [plʌm] *n* pruim *c*

plumber ['plʌmə] *n* loodgieter *c*

plump [plʌmp] *adj* mollig

plural ['pluərəl] *n* meervoud *nt*

plus [plʌs] *prep* plus

pneumatic [nju:'mætik] *adj* pneumatisch

pneumonia [nju:'mouniə] *n* longontsteking *c*

poach [poutʃ] *v* stropen

pocket ['pokit] *n* zak *c*

pocket-book ['pokitbuk] *n* portefeuille *c*

pocket-comb ['pokitkoum] *n* zakkam *c*

pocket-knife ['pokitnaif] *n* (pl -knives)

zakmes *nt*

pocket-watch ['pɔkitwɔtʃ] *n* zakhorloge *nt*

poem ['pouim] *n* gedicht *nt*

poet ['pouit] *n* dichter *c*

poetry ['pouitri] *n* dichtkunst *c*

point [pɔint] *n* punt *nt*; punt *c*; *v* *wijzen; ~ of view standpunt *nt*; ~ out *aanwijzen

pointed ['pɔintid] *adj* spits

poison ['pɔizən] *n* vergif *nt*; *v* vergiftigen

poisonous ['pɔizənəs] *adj* giftig

Poland ['poulənd] Polen

Pole [poul] *n* Pool *c*

pole [poul] *n* paal *c*

police [pə'liːs] *pl* politie *c*

policeman [pə'liːsmən] *n* (pl -men) agent *c*, politieagent *c*

police-station [pə'liːs,steiʃən] *n* politiebureau *nt*

policy ['pɔlisi] *n* beleid *nt*, politiek *c*; polis *c*

polio ['pouliou] *n* polio *c*, kinderverlamming *c*

Polish ['pouliʃ] *adj* Pools

polish ['pɔliʃ] *v* poetsen

polite [pə'lait] *adj* beleefd

political [pə'litikəl] *adj* politiek

politician [,pɔli'tiʃən] *n* politicus *c*

politics ['pɔlitiks] *n* politiek *c*

pollution [pə'luːʃən] *n* vervuiling *c*, verontreiniging *c*

pond [pɔnd] *n* vijver *c*

pony ['pouni] *n* pony *c*

poor [puə] *adj* arm; armoedig; slecht

pope [poup] *n* paus *c*

poplin ['pɔplin] *n* popeline *nt/c*

pop music [pɔp 'mjuːzik] popmuziek *c*

poppy ['pɔpi] *n* klaproos *c*; papaver *c*

popular ['pɔpjulə] *adj* populair; volks-

population [,pɔpju'leiʃən] *n* bevolking *c*

populous ['pɔpjuləs] *adj* dichtbevolkt

porcelain ['pɔːsəlin] *n* porselein *nt*

porcupine ['pɔːkjupain] *n* stekelvarken *nt*

pork [pɔːk] *n* varkensvlees *nt*

port [pɔːt] *n* haven *c*; bakboord *nt*

portable ['pɔːtəbəl] *adj* draagbaar

porter ['pɔːtə] *n* kruier *c*; portier *c*

porthole ['pɔːthoul] *n* patrijspoort *c*

portion ['pɔːʃən] *n* portie *c*

portrait ['pɔːtrit] *n* portret *nt*

Portugal ['pɔːtjugəl] Portugal

Portuguese [,pɔːtju'giːz] *adj* Portugees; *n* Portugees *c*

position [pə'ziʃən] *n* positie *c*; houding *c*; betrekking *c*

positive ['pɔzətiv] *adj* positief; *n* positief *nt*

possess [pə'zes] *v* *bezitten; **possessed** *adj* bezeten

possession [pə'zeʃən] *n* bezit *nt*; **possessions** eigendom *nt*

possibility [,pɔsə'biləti] *n* mogelijkheid *c*

possible ['pɔsəbəl] *adj* mogelijk; eventueel

post [poust] *n* paal *c*; betrekking *c*; post *c*; *v* posten; **post-office** postkantoor *nt*

postage ['poustidʒ] *n* frankering *c*; ~ **paid** franko; ~ **stamp** postzegel *c*

postcard ['poustkaːd] *n* briefkaart *c*; ansichtkaart *c*

poster ['poustə] *n* affiche *nt*, poster *c*

poste restante [poust re'stãːt] poste restante

postman ['poustmən] *n* (pl -men) postbode *c*

post-paid [,poust'peid] *adj* franko

postpone [pə'spoun] *v* uitstellen

pot [pɔt] *n* pot *c*

potato [pə'teitou] *n* (pl ~es) aardappel *c*

pottery ['pɔtəri] *n* aardewerk *nt*

pouch [pautʃ] *n* buidel *c*

poulterer ['poultərə] n poelier c

poultry ['poultri] n gevogelte nt

pound [paund] n pond nt

pour [pɔ:] v *inschenken, *schenken, *gieten

poverty ['pɔvəti] n armoede c

powder ['paudə] n poeder nt/c; ~ compact poederdoos c; talc ~ talkpoeder nt/c

powder-puff ['paudəpʌf] n poederdons c

powder-room ['paudəru:m] n damestoilet nt

power [pauə] n kracht c; energie c; macht c; mogendheid c

powerful ['pauəfəl] adj machtig; sterk

powerless ['pauələs] adj machteloos

power-station ['pauə,steiʃən] n elektriciteitscentrale c

practical ['præktikəl] adj praktisch

practically ['præktikli] adv vrijwel

practice ['præktis] n praktijk c

practise ['præktis] v beoefenen; oefenen

praise [preiz] v *prijzen; n lof c

pram [præm] n kinderwagen c

prawn [prɔ:n] n garnaal c, steurgarnaal c

pray [prei] v *bidden

prayer [prɛə] n gebed nt

preach [pri:tʃ] v preken

precarious [pri'kɛəriəs] adj hachelijk

precaution [pri'kɔ:ʃən] n voorzorg c; voorzorgsmaatregel c

precede [pri'si:d] v *voorafgaan

preceding [pri'si:diŋ] adj voorgaand

precious ['preʃəs] adj kostbaar; dierbaar

precipice ['presipis] n afgrond c

precipitation [pri,sipi'teiʃən] n neerslag c

precise [pri'sais] adj precies, exact, nauwkeurig; secuur

predecessor ['pri:disesə] n voorganger

c

predict [pri'dikt] v voorspellen

prefer [pri'fə:] v de voorkeur *geven aan, liever *hebben

preferable ['prefərəbəl] adj te verkiezen, verkieselijker, de voorkeur verdienend

preference ['prefərəns] n voorkeur c

prefix ['pri:fiks] n voorvoegsel nt

pregnant ['pregnənt] adj in verwachting, zwanger

prejudice ['predʒədis] n vooroordeel nt

preliminary [pri'liminəri] adj inleidend; voorlopig

premature ['premətʃuə] adj voorbarig

premier ['premiə] n premier c

premises ['premisiz] pl pand nt

premium ['pri:miəm] n premie c

prepaid [,pri:'peid] adj vooruitbetaald

preparation [,prepə'reiʃən] n voorbereiding c

prepare [pri'pɛə] v voorbereiden; klaarmaken

prepared [pri'pɛəd] adj bereid

preposition [,prepə'ziʃən] n voorzetsel nt

prescribe [pri'skraib] v *voorschrijven

prescription [pri'skripʃən] n recept nt

presence ['prezəns] n aanwezigheid c; tegenwoordigheid c

present[1] ['prezənt] n geschenk nt, cadeau nt; heden nt; adj tegenwoordig; aanwezig

present[2] [pri'zent] v voorstellen; *aanbieden

presently ['prezəntli] adv meteen, dadelijk

preservation [,prezə'veiʃən] n bewaring c

preserve [pri'zə:v] v bewaren; inmaken

president ['prezidənt] n president c; voorzitter c

press [pres] n pers c; v indrukken,

drukken; persen; ~ **conference**
persconferentie *c*

pressing ['presiŋ] *adj* urgent, dringend

pressure ['preʃə] *n* druk *c*; spanning
c; **atmospheric** ~ luchtdruk *c*

pressure-cooker ['preʃə,kukə] *n* snelkookpan *c*

prestige [pre'sti:ʒ] *n* prestige *nt*

presumable [pri'zju:məbəl] *adj* vermoedelijk

presumptuous [pri'zʌmpʃəs] *adj* overmoedig; arrogant

pretence [pri'tens] *n* voorwendsel *nt*

pretend [pri'tend] *v* *doen alsof, voorwenden

pretext ['pri:tekst] *n* voorwendsel *nt*

pretty ['priti] *adj* mooi, knap; *adv*
vrij, tamelijk, nogal

prevent [pri'vent] *v* beletten, verhinderen; *voorkomen

preventive [pri'ventiv] *adj* preventief

previous ['pri:viəs] *adj* verleden, vroeger, voorgaand

pre-war [,pri:'wɔ:] *adj* vooroorlogs

price [prais] *v* prijzen; ~ **list** prijslijst
c

priceless ['praisləs] *adj* onschatbaar

price-list ['prais,list] *n* prijs *c*

prick [prik] *v* prikken

pride [praid] *n* trots *c*

priest [pri:st] *n* priester *c*

primary ['praiməri] *adj* primair; eerst,
hoofd-; elementair

prince [prins] *n* prins *c*

princess [prin'ses] *n* prinses *c*

principal ['prinsəpəl] *adj* voornaamst;
n rector *c*, directeur *c*

principle ['prinsəpəl] *n* beginsel *nt*,
principe *nt*

print [print] *v* drukken; *n* afdruk *c*;
prent *c*; **printed matter** drukwerk
nt

prior [praiə] *adj* vroeger

priority [prai'ɔrəti] *n* prioriteit *c*, voor-

rang *c*

prison ['prizən] *n* gevangenis *c*

prisoner ['prizənə] *n* gedetineerde *c*,
gevangene *c*; ~ **of war** krijgsgevangene *c*

privacy ['praivəsi] *n* privacy *c*, privéleven *nt*

private ['praivit] *adj* particulier, privé;
persoonlijk

privilege ['priviliʤ] *n* voorrecht *nt*

prize [praiz] *n* prijs *c*; beloning *c*

probable ['prɔbəbəl] *adj* vermoedelijk,
waarschijnlijk

probably ['prɔbəbli] *adv* waarschijnlijk

problem ['prɔbləm] *n* probleem *nt*;
vraagstuk *nt*

procedure [prə'si:dʒə] *n* procedure *c*

proceed [prə'si:d] *v* *voortgaan; te
werk *gaan

process ['prouses] *n* proces *nt*, procédé *nt*

procession [prə'seʃən] *n* processie *c*,
stoet *c*

proclaim [prə'kleim] *v* afkondigen

produce[1] [prə'dju:s] *v* produceren

produce[2] ['prɔdju:s] *n* opbrengst *c*,
produkt *nt*

producer [prə'dju:sə] *n* producent *c*

product ['prɔdʌkt] *n* produkt *nt*

production [prə'dʌkʃən] *n* produktie *c*

profession [prə'feʃən] *n* vak *nt*, beroep
nt

professional [prə'feʃənəl] *adj* beroeps-

professor [prə'fesə] *n* hoogleraar *c*,
professor *c*

profit ['prɔfit] *n* voordeel *nt*, winst *c*;
baat *c*; *v* profiteren

profitable ['prɔfitəbəl] *adj* winstgevend

profound [prə'faund] *adj* diepzinnig

programme ['prougræm] *n* programma
nt

progress[1] ['prougres] *n* vooruitgang *c*

progress[2] [prə'gres] *v* vorderen

progressive [prə'gresiv] *adj* vooruitstrevend, progressief; toenemend

prohibit [prəˈhibit] v *verbieden

prohibition [ˌprouiˈbiʃən] n verbod nt

prohibitive [prəˈhibitiv] adj onoverkomelijk

project [ˈprɔdʒekt] n plan nt, project nt

promenade [ˌprɔməˈnɑːd] n promenade c

promise [ˈprɔmis] n belofte c; v beloven

promote [prəˈmout] v bevorderen

promotion [prəˈmouʃən] n promotie c

prompt [prɔmpt] adj onmiddellijk, prompt

pronoun [ˈprounaun] n voornaamwoord nt

pronounce [prəˈnauns] v *uitspreken

pronunciation [ˌprənʌnsiˈeiʃən] n uitspraak c

proof [pruːf] n bewijs nt

propaganda [ˌprɔpəˈgændə] n propaganda c

propel [prəˈpel] v *aandrijven

propeller [prəˈpelə] n schroef c, propeller c

proper [ˈprɔpə] adj juist; behoorlijk, passend, geschikt, gepast

property [ˈprɔpəti] n bezit nt, eigendom nt; eigenschap c

prophet [ˈprɔfit] n profeet c

proportion [prəˈpɔːʃən] n proportie c

proportional [prəˈpɔːʃənəl] adj evenredig

proposal [prəˈpouzəl] n voorstel nt

propose [prəˈpouz] v voorstellen

proposition [ˌprɔpəˈziʃən] n voorstel nt

proprietor [prəˈpraiətə] n eigenaar c

prospect [ˈprɔspekt] n vooruitzicht nt

prospectus [prəˈspektəs] n prospectus c

prosperity [prɔˈsperəti] n voorspoed c, welvaart c

prosperous [ˈprɔspərəs] adj welvarend

prostitute [ˈprɔstitjuːt] n prostituée c

protect [prəˈtekt] v beschermen

protection [prəˈtekʃən] n bescherming c

protein [ˈproutiːn] n eiwit nt

protest¹ [ˈproutest] n protest nt

protest² [prəˈtest] v protesteren

Protestant [ˈprɔtistənt] adj protestants

proud [praud] adj trots; hoogmoedig

prove [pruːv] v aantonen, *bewijzen; *blijken

proverb [ˈprɔvəːb] n spreekwoord nt

provide [prəˈvaid] v leveren, verschaffen; **provided that** mits

province [ˈprɔvins] n provincie c; gewest nt

provincial [prəˈvinʃəl] adj provinciaal

provisional [prəˈviʒənəl] adj voorlopig

provisions [prəˈviʒənz] pl voorraad c

prune [pruːn] n pruim c

psychiatrist [saiˈkaiətrist] n psychiater c

psychic [ˈsaikik] adj psychisch

psychoanalyst [ˌsaikouˈænəlist] n analyticus c

psychological [ˌsaikəˈlɔdʒikəl] adj psychologisch

psychologist [saiˈkɔlədʒist] n psycholoog c

psychology [saiˈkɔlədʒi] n psychologie c

pub [pʌb] n café nt; kroeg c

public [ˈpʌblik] adj publiek, openbaar; algemeen; n publiek nt; ~ **garden** plantsoen nt; ~ **house** café nt

publication [ˌpʌbliˈkeiʃən] n publikatie c

publicity [pʌˈblisəti] n reclame c

publish [ˈpʌbliʃ] v publiceren, *uitgeven

publisher [ˈpʌbliʃə] n uitgever c

puddle [ˈpʌdəl] n plas c

pull [pul] v *trekken; ~ **out** *vertrekken; ~ **up** stoppen

pulley ['puli] *n* (pl ~s) katrol *c*

Pullman ['pulmən] *n* slaaprijtuig *nt*

pullover ['pu,louvə] *n* pullover *c*

pulpit ['pulpit] *n* kansel *c*, preekstoel *c*

pulse [pʌls] *n* polsslag *c*, pols *c*

pump [pʌmp] *n* pomp *c*; *v* pompen

punch [pʌntʃ] *v* stompen; *n* vuistslag *c*

punctual ['pʌŋktʃuəl] *adj* stipt, punctueel

puncture ['pʌŋktʃə] *n* lekke band, bandepech *c*

punctured ['pʌŋktʃəd] *adj* lek

punish ['pʌniʃ] *v* straffen

punishment ['pʌniʃmənt] *n* straf *c*

pupil ['pju:pəl] *n* leerling *c*

puppet-show ['pʌpitʃou] *n* poppenkast *c*

purchase ['pə:tʃəs] *v* *kopen; *n* aankoop *c*, koop *c*; ~ **price** koopprijs *c*; ~ **tax** omzetbelasting *c*

purchaser ['pə:tʃəsə] *n* koper *c*

pure [pjuə] *adj* rein, zuiver

purple ['pə:pəl] *adj* paars

purpose ['pə:pəs] *n* bedoeling *c*, doel *nt*; **on** ~ opzettelijk

purse [pə:s] *n* beurs *c*, portemonnee *c*

pursue [pə'sju:] *v* vervolgen; nastreven

pus [pʌs] *n* etter *c*

push [puʃ] *n* zet *c*, duw *c*; *v* duwen; *schuiven; *dringen

push-button ['puʃ,bʌtən] *n* drukknop *c*

put [put] *v* plaatsen, leggen, zetten; stoppen; stellen; ~ **away** *opbergen; ~ **off** opschorten; ~ **on** *aantrekken; ~ **out** *uitdoen

puzzle ['pʌzəl] *n* puzzel *c*; raadsel *nt*; *v* in verwarring *brengen; **jigsaw** ~ legpuzzel *c*

puzzling ['pʌzliŋ] *adj* onbegrijpelijk

pyjamas [pə'dʒɑ:məz] *pl* pyjama *c*

Q

quack [kwæk] *n* kwakzalver *c*, charlatan *c*

quail [kweil] *n* (pl ~, ~s) kwartel *c*

quaint [kweint] *adj* raar; ouderwets

qualification [,kwɔlifi'keiʃən] *n* bevoegdheid *c*; voorbehoud *nt*, restrictie *c*

qualified ['kwɔlifaid] *adj* gediplomeerd; bevoegd

qualify ['kwɔlifai] *v* geschikt *zijn

quality ['kwɔləti] *n* kwaliteit *c*; eigenschap *c*

quantity ['kwɔntəti] *n* hoeveelheid *c*; aantal *nt*

quarantine ['kwɔrənti:n] *n* quarantaine *c*

quarrel ['kwɔrəl] *v* twisten, ruzie maken; *n* twist *c*, ruzie *c*

quarry ['kwɔri] *n* steengroeve *c*

quarter ['kwɔ:tə] *n* kwart *c*; kwartaal *nt*; wijk *c*; ~ **of an hour** kwartier *nt*

quarterly ['kwɔ:təli] *adj* driemaandelijks

quay [ki:] *n* kade *c*

queen [kwi:n] *n* koningin *c*

queer [kwiə] *adj* zonderling, raar; vreemd

query ['kwiəri] *n* vraag *c*; *v* *navragen; betwijfelen

question ['kwestʃən] *n* vraag *c*; kwestie *c*, vraagstuk *nt*; *v* *ondervragen; in twijfel *trekken; ~ **mark** vraagteken *nt*

queue [kju:] *n* rij *c*; *v* in de rij *staan

quick [kwik] *adj* vlug

quick-tempered [,kwik'tempəd] *adj* driftig

quiet ['kwaiət] *adj* stil, kalm, bedaard, rustig; *n* stilte *c*, rust *c*

quilt [kwilt] *n* sprei *c*

quinine [kwi'ni:n] *n* kinine *c*

quit [kwit] *v* *ophouden met, *uit-scheiden

quite [kwait] *adv* helemaal; tamelijk, vrij, nogal; zeer, heel

quiz [kwiz] *n* (pl ~zes) quiz *c*

quota ['kwoutə] *n* quota *c*

quotation [kwou'teiʃən] *n* citaat *nt*; ~ **marks** aanhalingstekens *pl*

quote [kwout] *v* citeren, aanhalen

R

rabbit ['ræbit] *n* konijn *nt*

rabies ['reibiz] *n* hondsdolheid *c*

race [reis] *n* wedloop *c*, race *c*; ras *nt*

race-course ['reiskɔ:s] *n* renbaan *c*

race-horse ['reishɔ:s] *n* renpaard *nt*

race-track ['reistræk] *n* renbaan *c*

racial ['reiʃəl] *adj* rassen-

racket ['rækit] *n* kabaal *nt*

racquet ['rækit] *n* racket *nt*

radiator ['reidieitə] *n* radiator *c*

radical ['rædikəl] *adj* radicaal

radio ['reidiou] *n* radio *c*

radish ['rædiʃ] *n* radijs *c*

radius ['reidiəs] *n* (pl radii) straal *c*

raft [rɑ:ft] *n* vlot *nt*

rag [ræg] *n* vod *nt*

rage [reidʒ] *n* razernij *c*, woede *c*; *v* razen, woeden

raid [reid] *n* inval *c*

rail [reil] *n* leuning *c*, reling *c*

railing ['reiliŋ] *n* hek *nt*

railroad ['reilroud] *nAm* spoorbaan *c*, spoorweg *c*

railway ['reilwei] *n* spoorweg *c*, spoorbaan *c*

rain [rein] *n* regen *c*; *v* regenen

rainbow ['reinbou] *n* regenboog *c*

raincoat ['reinkout] *n* regenjas *c*

rainproof ['reinpru:f] *adj* waterdicht

rainy ['reini] *adj* regenachtig

raise [reiz] *v* optillen; verhogen; *grootbrengen, verbouwen, fokken; *heffen; *nAm* loonsverhoging *c*, opslag *c*

raisin ['reizən] *n* rozijn *c*

rake [reik] *n* hark *c*

rally ['ræli] *n* bijeenkomst *c*

ramp [ræmp] *n* glooiing *c*

ramshackle ['ræm,ʃækəl] *adj* gammel

rancid ['rænsid] *adj* ranzig

rang [ræŋ] *v* (p ring)

range [reindʒ] *n* bereik *nt*

range-finder ['reindʒ,faində] *n* af-standsmeter *c*

rank [ræŋk] *n* rang *c*; rij *c*

ransom ['rænsəm] *n* losgeld *nt*

rape [reip] *v* verkrachten

rapid ['ræpid] *adj* vlug, snel

rapids ['ræpidz] *pl* stroomversnelling *c*

rare [reə] *adj* zeldzaam

rarely ['reəli] *adv* zelden

rascal ['rɑ:skəl] *n* schelm *c*, deugniet *c*

rash [ræʃ] *n* uitslag *c*, huiduitslag *c*; *adj* overhaast, onbezonnen

raspberry ['rɑ:zbəri] *n* framboos *c*

rat [ræt] *n* rat *c*

rate [reit] *n* prijs *c*, tarief *nt*; snelheid *c*; **at any** ~ hoe dan ook, in elk geval; ~ **of exchange** wisselkoers *c*

rather ['rɑ:ðə] *adv* vrij, tamelijk, nogal; liever, eerder

ration ['ræʃən] *n* rantsoen *nt*

rattan [ræ'tæn] *n* rotan *nt*

raven ['reivən] *n* raaf *c*

raw [rɔ:] *adj* rauw; ~ **material** grondstof *c*

ray [rei] *n* straal *c*

rayon ['reiɔn] *n* kunstzijde *c*

razor ['reizə] *n* scheerapparaat *nt*

razor-blade ['reizəbleid] *n* scheermesje *nt*

reach [ri:tʃ] *v* bereiken; *n* bereik *nt*

reaction [ri'ækʃən] n reactie c

* read [ri:d] v *lezen

reading-lamp ['ri:diŋlæmp] n leeslamp c

reading-room ['ri:diŋru:m] n leeszaal c

ready ['redi] adj gereed, klaar

ready-made [,redi'meid] adj confectie-real [riəl] adj echt

real [riəl] adj echt

reality [ri'æləti] n werkelijkheid c

realizable ['riəlaizəbəl] adj haalbaar

realize ['riəlaiz] v beseffen; tot stand *brengen, verwezenlijken

really ['riəli] adv echt, werkelijk; eigenlijk

rear [riə] n achterkant c; v *groot-brengen

rear-light [riə'lait] n achterlicht nt

reason ['ri:zən] n oorzaak c, reden c; verstand nt, rede c; v redeneren

reasonable ['ri:zənəbəl] adj redelijk; billijk

reassure [,ri:ə'ʃuə] v geruststellen

rebate ['ri:beit] n korting c, reductie c

rebellion [ri'beljən] n opstand c, op-roer nt

recall [ri'kɔ:l] v zich herinneren; *te-rugroepen; *herroepen

receipt [ri'si:t] n kwitantie c, reçu nt; ontvangst c

receive [ri'si:v] v *krijgen, *ontvangen

receiver [ri'si:və] n telefoonhoorn c

recent ['ri:sənt] adj recent

recently ['ri:səntli] adv kort geleden, onlangs

reception [ri'sepʃən] n ontvangst c; onthaal nt; ~ **office** receptie c

receptionist [ri'sepʃənist] n receptioni-ste c

recession [ri'seʃən] n teruggang c

recipe ['resipi] n recept nt

recital [ri'saitəl] n recital nt

reckon ['rekən] v rekenen; beschou-wen; *denken

recognition [,rekəg'niʃən] n erkenning

c

recognize ['rekəgnaiz] v herkennen; erkennen

recollect [,rekə'lekt] v zich herinneren

recommence [,ri:kə'mens] v hervatten

recommend [,rekə'mend] v *aanprij-zen, *aanbevelen; *aanraden

recommendation [,rekəmen'deiʃən] n aanbeveling c

reconciliation [,rekənsili'eiʃən] n ver-zoening c

record[1] ['rekɔ:d] n grammofoonplaat c; record nt; register nt; **long-playing** ~ langspeelplaat c

record[2] [ri'kɔ:d] v registreren

recorder [ri'kɔ:də] n bandrecorder c

recording [ri'kɔ:diŋ] n opname c

record-player ['rekɔ:d,pleiə] n platen-speler c, pick-up c

recover [ri'kʌvə] v *terugvinden; zich herstellen, *genezen

recovery [ri'kʌvəri] n genezing c, her-stel nt

recreation [,rekri'eiʃən] n recreatie c, ontspanning c; ~ **centre** recreatie-centrum nt; ~ **ground** speelterrein nt

recruit [ri'kru:t] n rekruut c

rectangle ['rektæŋgəl] n rechthoek c

rectangular [rek'tæŋgjulə] adj recht-hoekig

rector ['rektə] n predikant c, dominee c

rectory ['rektəri] n pastorie c

rectum ['rektəm] n endeldarm c

red [red] adj rood

redeem [ri'di:m] v verlossen

reduce [ri'dju:s] v reduceren, vermin-deren, verlagen

reduction [ri'dʌkʃən] n korting c, re-ductie c

redundant [ri'dʌndənt] adj overbodig

reed [ri:d] n riet nt

reef [ri:f] n rif nt

reference ['refrəns] *n* referentie *c*, verwijzing *c*; betrekking *c*; **with ~ to** met betrekking tot

refer to [ri'fə:] *verwijzen naar

refill ['ri:fil] *n* vulling *c*

refinery [ri'fainəri] *n* raffinaderij *c*

reflect [ri'flekt] *v* weerkaatsen

reflection [ri'flekʃən] *n* weerkaatsing *c*; spiegelbeeld *nt*

reflector [ri'flektə] *n* reflector *c*

reformation [,refə'meiʃən] *n* reformatie *c*

refresh [ri'freʃ] *v* verfrissen

refreshment [ri'freʃmənt] *n* verfrissing *c*

refrigerator [ri'fridʒəreitə] *n* koelkast *c*, ijskast *c*

refund¹ [ri'fʌnd] *v* terugbetalen

refund² ['ri:fʌnd] *n* terugbetaling *c*

refusal [ri'fju:zəl] *n* weigering *c*

refuse¹ [ri'fju:z] *v* weigeren

refuse² ['refju:s] *n* afval *nt*

regard [ri'ga:d] *v* beschouwen; *bekijken; *n* respect *nt*; **as regards** betreffende, aangaande, wat betreft

regarding [ri'ga:diŋ] *prep* met betrekking tot, betreffende; ten aanzien van

regatta [ri'gætə] *n* regatta *c*

régime [rei'ʒi:m] *n* regime *nt*

region ['ri:dʒən] *n* streek *c*; gebied *nt*

regional ['ri:dʒənəl] *adj* plaatselijk

register ['redʒistə] *v* zich *inschrijven; aantekenen; **registered letter** aangetekende brief

registration [,redʒi'streiʃən] *n* registratie *c*; ~ **form** inschrijvingsformulier *nt*; ~ **number** kenteken *nt*; ~ **plate** nummerbord *nt*

regret [ri'gret] *v* betreuren; *n* spijt *c*

regular ['regjulə] *adj* geregeld, regelmatig; gewoon, normaal

regulate ['regjuleit] *v* regelen

regulation [,regju'leiʃən] *n* reglement

nt, voorschrift *nt*; regeling *c*

rehabilitation [,ri:hə,bili'teiʃən] *n* revalidatie *c*

rehearsal [ri'hə:səl] *n* repetitie *c*

rehearse [ri'hə:s] *v* repeteren

reign [rein] *n* regering *c*; *v* regeren

reimburse [,ri:im'bə:s] *v* terugbetalen, vergoeden

reindeer ['reindiə] *n* (pl ~) rendier *nt*

reject [ri'dʒekt] *v* *afwijzen, *verwerpen; afkeuren

relate [ri'leit] *v* vertellen

related [ri'leitid] *adj* verwant

relation [ri'leiʃən] *n* relatie *c*, verband *nt*; verwante *c*

relative ['relətiv] *n* familielid *nt*; *adj* betrekkelijk, relatief

relax [ri'læks] *v* zich ontspannen

relaxation [,rilæk'seiʃən] *n* ontspanning *c*

reliable [ri'laiəbəl] *adj* betrouwbaar

relic ['relik] *n* relikwie *c*

relief [ri'li:f] *n* verademing *c*, verlichting *c*; steun *c*; reliëf *nt*

relieve [ri'li:v] *v* verlichten; aflossen

religion [ri'lidʒən] *n* godsdienst *c*

religious [ri'lidʒəs] *adj* godsdienstig

rely on [ri'lai] vertrouwen op

remain [ri'mein] *v* *blijven; *overblijven

remainder [ri'meində] *n* restant *nt*, rest *c*

remaining [ri'meiniŋ] *adj* overig, overblijvend

remark [ri'ma:k] *n* opmerking *c*; *v* opmerken

remarkable [ri'ma:kəbəl] *adj* opmerkelijk

remedy ['remədi] *n* geneesmiddel *nt*; middel *nt*

remember [ri'membə] *v* zich herinneren; *onthouden

remembrance [ri'membrəns] *n* aandenken *nt*, herinnering *c*

remind [ri'maind] v herinneren

remit [ri'mit] v overmaken

remittance [ri'mitəns] n storting c

remnant ['remnənt] n overblijfsel nt, restant nt, rest c

remote [ri'mout] adj afgelegen, ver

removal [ri'mu:vəl] n verwijdering c

remove [ri'mu:v] v verwijderen

remunerate [ri'mju:nəreit] v vergoeden

remuneration [ri,mju:nə'reiʃən] n vergoeding c

renew [ri'nju:] v vernieuwen; verlengen

rent [rent] v huren; n huur c

repair [ri'peə] v herstellen, repareren; n herstel nt

reparation [,repə'reiʃən] n reparatie c

*repay [ri'pei] v terugbetalen

repayment [ri'peimənt] n terugbetaling c

repeat [ri'pi:t] v herhalen

repellent [ri'pelənt] adj weerzinwekkend, afstotelijk

repentance [ri'pentəns] n berouw nt

repertory ['repətəri] n repertoire nt

repetition [,repə'tiʃən] n herhaling c

replace [ri'pleis] v *vervangen

reply [ri'plai] v antwoorden; n antwoord nt; in ~ als antwoord

report [ri'pɔ:t] v rapporteren; melden; zich aanmelden; n verslag nt, rapport nt

reporter [ri'pɔ:tə] n verslaggever c

represent [,repri'zent] v vertegenwoordigen; voorstellen

representation [,reprizen'teiʃən] n vertegenwoordiging c

representative [,repri'zentətiv] adj representatief

reprimand ['reprimɑ:nd] v berispen

reproach [ri'proutʃ] n verwijt nt; v *verwijten

reproduce [,ri:prə'dju:s] v reproduceren

reproduction [,ri:prə'dʌkʃən] n reproduktie c

reptile ['reptail] n reptiel nt

republic [ri'pʌblik] n republiek c

republican [ri'pʌblikən] adj republikeins

repulsive [ri'pʌlsiv] adj weerzinwekkend

reputation [,repju'teiʃən] n reputatie c; naam c

request [ri'kwest] n verzoek nt; v *verzoeken

require [ri'kwaiə] v vereisen

requirement [ri'kwaiəmənt] n vereiste c

requisite ['rekwizit] adj vereist

rescue ['reskju:] v redden; n redding c

research [ri'sə:tʃ] n onderzoek nt

resemblance [ri'zembləns] n gelijkenis c

resemble [ri'zembəl] v *lijken op

resent [ri'zent] v kwalijk *nemen

reservation [,rezə'veiʃən] n reservering c

reserve [ri'zə:v] v reserveren; *bespreken; n reserve c

reserved [ri'zə:vd] adj gereserveerd

reservoir ['rezəvwɑ:] n reservoir nt

reside [ri'zaid] v wonen

residence ['rezidəns] n woonplaats c; ~ permit verblijfsvergunning c

resident ['rezidənt] n inwoner c; adj woonachtig; intern

resign [ri'zain] v ontslag *nemen

resignation [,rezig'neiʃən] n ontslagneming c

resin ['rezin] n hars nt/c

resist [ri'zist] v zich verzetten

resistance [ri'zistəns] n verzet nt

resolute ['rezəlu:t] adj resoluut, vastberaden

respect [ri'spekt] n respect nt; ontzag nt, achting c, eerbied c; v respecteren

respectable [ri'spektəbəl] *adj* eerzaam, respectabel

respectful [ri'spektfəl] *adj* eerbiedig

respective [ri'spektiv] *adj* respectievelijk

respiration [,respə'reiʃən] *n* ademhaling *c*

respite ['respait] *n* uitstel *nt*

responsibility [ri,sponsə'biləti] *n* verantwoordelijkheid *c*; aansprakelijkheid *c*

responsible [ri'sponsəbəl] *adj* verantwoordelijk; aansprakelijk

rest [rest] *n* rust *c*; rest *c*; *v* uitrusten, rusten

restaurant ['restərɔ̃:] *n* restaurant *nt*

restful ['restfəl] *adj* rustig

rest-home ['resthoum] *n* rusthuis *nt*

restless ['restləs] *adj* onrustig; ongedurig

restrain [ri'strein] *v* *inhouden, *weerhouden

restriction [ri'strikʃən] *n* beperking *c*

result [ri'zʌlt] *n* resultaat *nt*; gevolg *nt*; uitslag *c*; *v* resulteren

resume [ri'zju:m] *v* hervatten

résumé ['rezjumei] *n* samenvatting *c*

retail ['ri:teil] *v* in het klein *verkopen; ~ **trade** kleinhandel *c*, detailhandel *c*

retailer ['ri:teilə] *n* detaillist *c*, kleinhandelaar *c*; wederverkoper *c*

retina ['retinə] *n* netvlies *nt*

retired [ri'taiəd] *adj* gepensioneerd

return [ri'tə:n] *v* *terugkomen, terugkeren; *n* terugkeer *c*; ~ **flight** retourvlucht *c*; ~ **journey** terugreis *c*

reunite [,ri:ju:'nait] *v* herenigen

reveal [ri'vi:l] *v* openbaren, onthullen

revelation [,revə'leiʃən] *n* onthulling *c*

revenge [ri'vendʒ] *n* wraak *c*

revenue ['revənju:] *n* inkomen *nt*

reverse [ri'və:s] *n* tegendeel *nt*; keerzijde *c*; omkeer *c*, tegenslag *c*; *adj* omgekeerd; *v* *achteruitrijden

review [ri'vju:] *n* bespreking *c*; tijdschrift *nt*

revise [ri'vaiz] *v* *herzien

revision [ri'viʒən] *n* herziening *c*

revival [ri'vaivəl] *n* herstel *nt*

revolt [ri'voult] *v* in opstand *komen; *n* opstand *c*, oproer *nt*

revolting [ri'voultiŋ] *adj* walgelijk, stuitend, weerzinwekkend

revolution [,revə'lu:ʃən] *n* revolutie *c*; omwenteling *c*

revolutionary [,revə'lu:ʃənəri] *adj* revolutionair

revolver [ri'volvə] *n* revolver *c*

revue [ri'vju:] *n* revue *c*

reward [ri'wɔ:d] *n* beloning *c*; *v* belonen

rheumatism ['ru:mətizəm] *n* reumatiek *c*

rhinoceros [rai'nosərəs] *n* (pl ~, ~es) neushoorn *c*

rhubarb ['ru:ba:b] *n* rabarber *c*

rhyme [raim] *n* rijm *nt*

rhythm ['riðəm] *n* ritme *nt*

rib [rib] *n* rib *c*

ribbon ['ribən] *n* lint *nt*

rice [rais] *n* rijst *c*

rich [ritʃ] *adj* rijk

riches ['ritʃiz] *pl* rijkdom *c*

riddle ['ridəl] *n* raadsel *nt*

ride [raid] *n* rit *c*

* **ride** [raid] *v* *rijden; *paardrijden

rider ['raidə] *n* ruiter *c*

ridge [ridʒ] *n* bergrug *c*

ridicule ['ridikju:l] *v* bespotten

ridiculous [ri'dikjuləs] *adj* bespottelijk, belachelijk

riding ['raidiŋ] *n* paardesport *c*

riding-school ['raidiŋsku:l] *n* manege *c*

rifle ['raifəl] *v* geweer *nt*

right [rait] *n* recht *nt*; *adj* goed, juist; recht; rechts; billijk, rechtvaardig; **all right!** in orde!; * **be** ~ gelijk *hebben; ~ **of way** voorrang *c*

righteous ['raitʃəs] *adj* rechtvaardig

right-hand ['raithænd] *adj* rechter, rechts

rightly ['raitli] *adv* terecht

rim [rim] *n* velg *c*; rand *c*

ring [riŋ] *n* ring *c*; kring *c*; piste *c*

* **ring** [riŋ] *v* bellen; ~ **up** opbellen

rinse [rins] *v* spoelen; *n* spoeling *c*

riot ['raiət] *n* rel *c*

rip [rip] *v* scheuren

ripe [raip] *adj* rijp

rise [raiz] *n* opslag *c*, verhoging *c*; stijging *c*; opkomst *c*

* **rise** [raiz] *v* *opstaan; *opgaan; *stijgen

rising ['raiziŋ] *n* opstand *c*

risk [risk] *n* risico *nt*; gevaar *nt*; *v* wagen

risky ['riski] *adj* gewaagd, riskant

rival ['raivəl] *n* rivaal *c*; concurrent *c*; *v* rivaliseren

rivalry ['raivəlri] *n* rivaliteit *c*; concurrentie *c*

river ['rivə] *n* rivier *c*; ~ **bank** oever *c*

riverside ['rivəsaid] *n* rivieroever *c*

roach [routʃ] *n* (pl ~) blankvoren *c*

road [roud] *n* straat *c*, weg *c*; ~ **fork** *n* tweesprong *c*; ~ **map** wegenkaart *c*; ~ **system** wegennet *nt*; ~ **up** werk in uitvoering

roadhouse ['roudhaus] *n* wegrestaurant *nt*

roadside ['roudsaid] *n* wegkant *c*; ~ **restaurant** wegrestaurant *nt*

roadway ['roudwei] *nAm* rijbaan *c*

roam [roum] *v* *zwerven

roar [rɔː] *v* loeien, brullen; *n* gebrul *nt*, geraas *nt*

roast [roust] *v* *braden, roosteren

rob [rɔb] *v* beroven

robber ['rɔbə] *n* dief *c*

robbery ['rɔbəri] *n* roof *c*, diefstal *c*, beroving *c*

robe [roub] *n* jurk *c*; gewaad *nt*

robin ['rɔbin] *n* roodborstje *nt*

robust [rou'bʌst] *adj* fors

rock [rɔk] *n* rots *c*; *v* schommelen

rocket ['rɔkit] *n* raket *c*

rock-'n-roll [,rɔkən'roul] *n* rock en roll *c*

rocky ['rɔki] *adj* rotsachtig

rod [rɔd] *n* stang *c*, roede *c*

roe [rou] *n* kuit *c*, viskuit *c*

roll [roul] *v* rollen; *n* rol *c*; broodje *nt*

Roman Catholic ['roumən 'kæθəlik] rooms-katholiek

romance [rə'mæns] *n* romance *c*

romantic [rə'mæntik] *adj* romantisch

roof [ruːf] *n* dak *nt*; **thatched** ~ strodak *nt*

room [ruːm] *n* vertrek *nt*, kamer *c*; ruimte *c*, plaats *c*; ~ **and board** kost en inwoning; ~ **service** bediening op de kamer; ~ **temperature** kamertemperatuur *c*

roomy ['ruːmi] *adj* ruim

root [ruːt] *n* wortel *c*

rope [roup] *n* touw *nt*

rosary ['rouzəri] *n* rozenkrans *c*

rose [rouz] *n* roos *c*; *adj* roze

rotten ['rɔtən] *adj* rot

rouge [ruːʒ] *n* rouge *c/nt*

rough [rʌf] *adj* ruw

roulette [ruː'let] *n* roulette *c*

round [raund] *adj* rond; *prep* rondom, om; *n* ronde *c*; ~ **trip** *Am* retour

roundabout ['raundəbaut] *n* rotonde *c*

rounded ['raundid] *adj* afgerond

route [ruːt] *n* route *c*

routine [ruː'tiːn] *n* routine *c*

row[1] [rou] *n* rij *c*; *v* roeien

row[2] [rau] *n* ruzie *c*

rowdy ['raudi] *adj* baldadig

rowing-boat ['rouiŋbout] *n* roeiboot *c*

royal ['rɔiəl] *adj* koninklijk

rub [rʌb] *v* *wrijven

rubber ['rʌbə] *n* rubber *nt*; vlakgom

c/nt; ~ **band** elastiek nt

rubbish ['rʌbiʃ] n afval nt; geklets nt, onzin c; **talk** ~ kletsen

rubbish-bin ['rʌbiʃbin] n vuilnisbak c

ruby ['ru:bi] n robijn c

rucksack ['rʌksæk] n rugzak c

rudder ['rʌdə] n roer nt

rude [ru:d] adj grof

rug [rʌg] n kleedje nt

ruin ['ru:in] v ruïneren; n ondergang c; **ruins** ruïne c

ruination [,ru:i'neiʃən] n ondergang c

rule [ru:l] n regel c; bewind nt, bestuur nt, heerschappij c; v heersen, regeren; **as a** ~ gewoonlijk, in de regel

ruler ['ru:lə] n vorst c, heerser c; liniaal c

Rumania [ru:'meiniə] Roemenië

Rumanian [ru:'meiniən] adj Roemeens; n Roemeen c

rumour ['ru:mə] n gerucht nt

***run** [rʌn] v rennen; ~ **into** *tegenkomen

runaway ['rʌnəwei] n ontsnapte gevangene

rung [rʌn] v (pp ring)

runway ['rʌnwei] n startbaan c

rural ['ruərəl] adj plattelands-

ruse [ru:z] n list c

rush [rʌʃ] v zich haasten; n bies c

rush-hour ['rʌʃauə] n spitsuur nt

Russia ['rʌʃə] Rusland

Russian ['rʌʃən] adj Russisch; n Rus c

rust [rʌst] n roest nt

rustic ['rʌstik] adj rustiek

rusty ['rʌsti] adj roestig

S

saccharin ['sækərin] n sacharine c

sack [sæk] n zak c

sacred ['seikrid] adj heilig

sacrifice ['sækrifais] n offer nt; v opofferen

sacrilege ['sækrilidʒ] n heiligschennis c

sad [sæd] adj bedroefd; verdrietig, droevig, treurig

saddle ['sædəl] n zadel nt

sadness ['sædnəs] n bedroefdheid c

safe [seif] adj veilig; n brandkast c, kluis c

safety ['seifti] n veiligheid c

safety-belt ['seiftibelt] n veiligheidsgordel c

safety-pin ['seiftipin] n veiligheidsspeld c

safety-razor ['seifti,reizə] n scheerapparaat nt

sail [seil] v *bevaren, *varen; n zeil nt

sailing-boat ['seiliŋbout] n zeilboot c

sailor ['seilə] n matroos c

saint [seint] n heilige c

salad ['sæləd] n sla c

salad-oil ['sælədɔil] n slaolie c

salary ['sæləri] n loon nt, salaris nt

sale [seil] n verkoop c; **clearance** ~ opruiming c; **for** ~ te koop; **sales** uitverkoop c; **sales tax** omzetbelasting c

saleable ['seiləbəl] adj verkoopbaar

salesgirl ['seilzgə:l] n verkoopster c

salesman ['seilzmən] n (pl -men) verkoper c

salmon ['sæmən] n (pl ~) zalm c

salon ['sælɔ̃:] n salon c

saloon [sə'lu:n] n bar c

salt [sɔ:lt] n zout nt

salt-cellar ['sɔ:lt,selə] n zoutvaatje nt

salty ['sɔ:lti] adj zout

salute [sə'lu:t] v groeten

salve [sɑ:v] n zalf c

same [seim] adj zelfde

sample ['sɑ:mpəl] n monster nt

sanatorium [,sænə'tɔ:riəm] n (pl ~s, -ria) sanatorium nt

sand [sænd] n zand nt

sandal ['sændəl] n sandaal c

sandpaper ['sænd,peipə] n schuurpapier nt

sandwich ['sænwidʒ] n boterham c

sandy ['sændi] adj zanderig

sanitary ['sænitəri] adj sanitair; ~ towel maandverband nt

sapphire ['sæfaiə] n saffier nt

sardine [sɑ:'di:n] n sardine c

satchel ['sætʃəl] n schooltas c

satellite ['sætəlait] n satelliet c

satin ['sætin] n satijn nt

satisfaction [,sætis'fækʃən] n bevrediging c, voldoening c

satisfy ['sætisfai] v bevredigen; satisfied voldaan, tevreden

Saturday ['sætədi] zaterdag c

sauce [sɔ:s] n saus c

saucepan ['sɔ:spən] n steelpan c

saucer ['sɔ:sə] n schoteltje c

Saudi Arabia [,saudiə'reibiə] Saoedi-Arabië

Saudi Arabian [,saudiə'reibiən] adj Saoedi-Arabisch

sauna ['sɔ:nə] n sauna c

sausage ['sɔsidʒ] n worst c

savage ['sævidʒ] adj wild

save [seiv] v redden; sparen

savings ['seivinz] pl spaargeld nt; ~ bank spaarbank c

saviour ['seivjə] n redder c

savoury ['seivəri] adj smakelijk; pikant

saw[1] [sɔ:] v (p see)

saw[2] [sɔ:] n zaag c

sawdust ['sɔ:dʌst] n zaagsel nt

saw-mill ['sɔ:mil] n houtzagerij c

*say [sei] v *zeggen

scaffolding ['skæfəldiŋ] n steigers pl

scale [skeil] n schaal c; toonladder c; schub c; scales pl weegschaal c

scandal ['skændəl] n schandaal nt

Scandinavia [,skændi'neiviə] Scandinavië

Scandinavian [,skændi'neiviən] adj Scandinavisch; n Scandinaviër c

scapegoat ['skeipgout] n zondebok c

scar [skɑ:] n litteken nt

scarce [skɛəs] adj schaars

scarcely ['skɛəsli] adv nauwelijks

scarcity ['skɛəsəti] n schaarste c

scare [skɛə] v *doen schrikken; n schrik c

scarf [skɑ:f] n (pl ~s, scarves) das c, sjaal c

scarlet ['skɑ:lət] adj vuurrood

scary ['skɛəri] adj griezelig

scatter ['skætə] v verspreiden

scene [si:n] n scène c

scenery ['si:nəri] n landschap nt

scenic ['si:nik] adj schilderachtig

scent [sent] n geur c

schedule ['ʃedju:l] n dienstregeling c, rooster nt

scheme [ski:m] n schema nt; plan nt

scholar ['skɔlə] n geleerde c; leerling c

scholarship ['skɔləʃip] n studiebeurs c

school [sku:l] n school c

schoolboy ['sku:lbɔi] n schooljongen c

schoolgirl ['sku:lgə:l] n schoolmeisje nt

schoolmaster ['sku:l,mɑ:stə] n onderwijzer c, meester c

schoolteacher ['sku:l,ti:tʃə] n onderwijzer c

science ['saiəns] n wetenschap c

scientific [,saiən'tifik] adj wetenschappelijk

scientist ['saiəntist] n geleerde c

scissors ['sizəz] pl schaar c

scold [skould] v berispen; *schelden

scooter ['sku:tə] *n* scooter *c*; autoped *c*

score [skɔ:] *n* stand *c*; *v* scoren

scorn [skɔ:n] *n* hoon *c*, verachting *c*; *v* verachten

Scot [skɔt] *n* Schot *c*

Scotch [skɔtʃ] *adj* Schots; **scotch tape** plakband *nt*

Scotland ['skɔtlənd] Schotland

Scottish ['skɔtiʃ] *adj* Schots

scout [skaut] *n* padvinder *c*

scrap [skræp] *n* snipper *c*

scrap-book ['skræpbuk] *n* plakboek *nt*

scrape [skreip] *v* schrappen

scrap-iron ['skræpaiən] *n* schroot *nt*

scratch [skrætʃ] *v* krassen, krabben; *n* kras *c*, schram *c*

scream [skri:m] *v* gillen, schreeuwen; *n* gil *c*, schreeuw *c*

screen [skri:n] *n* scherm *nt*; beeld-scherm *nt*

screw [skru:] *n* schroef *c*; *v* schroeven

screw-driver ['skru:,draivə] *n* schroeve-draaier *c*

scrub [skrʌb] *v* schrobben; *n* struik *c*

sculptor ['skʌlptə] *n* beeldhouwer *c*

sculpture ['skʌlptʃə] *n* beeldhouwwerk *nt*

sea [si:] *n* zee *c*

sea-bird ['si:bə:d] *n* zeevogel *c*

sea-coast ['si:koust] *n* zeekust *c*

seagull ['si:gʌl] *n* meeuw *c*, zeemeeuw *c*

seal [si:l] *n* zegel *nt*; rob *c*, zeehond *c*

seam [si:m] *n* naad *c*

seaman ['si:mən] *n* (pl -men) zeeman *c*

seamless ['si:mləs] *adj* naadloos

seaport ['si:pɔ:t] *n* zeehaven *c*

search [sə:tʃ] *v* *zoeken; fouilleren, *doorzoeken

searchlight ['sə:tʃlait] *n* schijnwerper *c*

seascape ['si:skeip] *n* zeegezicht *nt*

sea-shell ['si:ʃel] *n* zeeschelp *c*

seashore ['si:ʃɔ:] *n* kust *c*

seasick ['si:sik] *adj* zeeziek

seasickness ['si:,siknəs] *n* zeeziekte *c*

seaside ['si:said] *n* kust *c*; ~ **resort** badplaats *c*

season ['si:zən] *n* jaargetijde *nt*, sei-zoen *nt*; **high** ~ hoogseizoen *nt*; **low** ~ naseizoen *nt*; **off** ~ buiten het seizoen

season-ticket ['si:zən,tikit] *n* abonne-mentskaart *c*

seat [si:t] *n* stoel *c*; plaats *c*, zitplaats *c*; zetel *c*

seat-belt ['si:tbelt] *n* veiligheidsgordel *c*

sea-urchin ['si:,ə:tʃin] *n* zeeëgel *c*

sea-water ['si:,wɔ:tə] *n* zeewater *nt*

second ['sekənd] *num* tweede; *n* se-conde *c*; tel *c*

secondary ['sekəndəri] *adj* secundair, ondergeschikt; ~ **school** middelba-re school

second-hand [,sekənd'hænd] *adj* twee-dehands

secret ['si:krət] *n* geheim *nt*; *adj* ge-heim

secretary ['sekrətri] *n* secretaresse *c*; secretaris *c*

section ['sekʃən] *n* sectie *c*; afdeling *c*, vak *nt*

secure [si'kjuə] *adj* veilig; *v* bemachti-gen

security [si'kjuərəti] *n* veiligheid *c*; pand *nt*

sedate [si'deit] *adj* kalm

sedative ['sedətiv] *n* kalmerend middel

seduce [si'dju:s] *v* verleiden

* see [si:] *v* *zien; *begrijpen, *in-zien; ~ **to** zorgen voor

seed [si:d] *n* zaad *nt*

* seek [si:k] *v* *zoeken

seem [si:m] *v* *lijken, *schijnen

seen [si:n] *v* (pp see)

seesaw ['si:sɔ:] *n* wip *c*

seize [si:z] *v* *grijpen

seldom ['seldəm] *adv* zelden

select [si'lekt] *v* selecteren, *uitkiezen; *adj* select, uitgelezen

selection [si'lekʃən] *n* keuze *c*, selectie *c*

self-centred [,self'sentəd] *adj* egocentrisch

self-employed [,selfim'plɔid] *adj* zelfstandig

self-evident [,sel'fevidənt] *adj* vanzelfsprekend

self-government [,self'gʌvəmənt] *n* zelfbestuur *nt*

selfish ['selfiʃ] *adj* egoïstisch

selfishness ['selfiʃnəs] *n* egoïsme *nt*

self-service [,self'sə:vis] *n* zelfbediening *c*; ~ **restaurant** zelfbedieningsrestaurant *nt*

* **sell** [sel] *v* *verkopen

semblance ['sembləns] *n* schijn *c*

semi- ['semi] half

semicircle ['semi,sə:kəl] *n* halve cirkel

semi-colon [,semi'koulən] *n* puntkomma *c*

senate ['senət] *n* senaat *c*

senator ['senətə] *n* senator *c*

* **send** [send] *v* sturen, *zenden; ~ **back** terugsturen, *terugzenden; ~ **for** *laten halen; ~ **off** versturen

senile ['si:nail] *adj* seniel

sensation [sen'seiʃən] *n* sensatie *c*; gewaarwording *c*, gevoel *nt*

sensational [sen'seiʃənəl] *adj* sensationeel, opzienbarend

sense [sens] *n* zintuig *nt*; gezond verstand, rede *c*; zin *c*, betekenis *c*; *v* voelen; ~ **of honour** eergevoel *nt*

senseless ['sensləs] *adj* zinloos

sensible ['sensəbəl] *adj* verstandig

sensitive ['sensitiv] *adj* gevoelig

sentence ['sentəns] *n* zin *c*; vonnis *nt*; *v* veroordelen

sentimental [,senti'mentəl] *adj* sentimenteel

separate¹ ['separeit] *v* *scheiden

separate² ['sepərət] *adj* afzonderlijk, gescheiden

separately ['sepərətli] *adv* apart

September [sep'tembə] september

septic ['septik] *adj* septisch; * **become** ~ *ontsteken

sequel ['si:kwəl] *n* vervolg *nt*

sequence ['si:kwəns] *n* volgorde *c*; reeks *c*

serene [sə'ri:n] *adj* kalm; helder

serial ['siəriəl] *n* feuilleton *nt*

series ['siəri:z] *n* (pl ~) reeks *c*, serie *c*

serious ['siəriəs] *adj* serieus, ernstig

seriousness ['siəriəsnəs] *n* ernst *c*

sermon ['sə:mən] *n* preek *c*

serum ['siərəm] *n* serum *nt*

servant ['sə:vənt] *n* bediende *c*

serve [sə:v] *v* bedienen

service ['sə:vis] *n* dienst *c*; bediening *c*; ~ **charge** bedieningsgeld *nt*; ~ **station** benzinestation *nt*

serviette [,sə:vi'et] *n* servet *nt*

session ['seʃən] *n* zitting *c*

set [set] *n* stel *nt*, groep *c*

* **set** [set] *v* zetten; ~ **menu** vast menu; ~ **out** *vertrekken

setting ['setiŋ] *n* omgeving *c*; ~ **lotion** haarversteviger *c*

settle ['setəl] *v* afhandelen, regelen; ~ **down** zich vestigen

settlement ['setəlmənt] *n* regeling *c*, schikking *c*, overeenkomst *c*

seven ['sevən] *num* zeven

seventeen [,sevən'ti:n] *num* zeventien

seventeenth [,sevən'ti:nθ] *num* zeventiende

seventh ['sevənθ] *num* zevende

seventy ['sevənti] *num* zeventig

several ['sevərəl] *adj* ettelijk, verscheidene

severe [si'viə] *adj* hevig, streng, ernstig

sew [sou] v naaien; ~ **up** hechten

sewer ['su:ə] n riool nt

sewing-machine ['souiŋmə,ʃi:n] n naaimachine c

sex [seks] n geslacht nt; sex c

sexton ['sekstən] n koster c

sexual ['sekʃuəl] adj seksueel

sexuality [,sekʃu'æləti] n seksualiteit c

shade [ʃeid] n schaduw c; tint c

shadow ['ʃædou] n schaduw c

shady ['ʃeidi] adj schaduwrijk

* **shake** [ʃeik] v schudden

shaky ['ʃeiki] adj gammel

* **shall** [ʃæl] v *zullen; *moeten

shallow ['ʃælou] adj ondiep

shame [ʃeim] n schaamte c; schande c; **shame!** foei!

shampoo [ʃæm'pu:] n shampoo c

shamrock ['ʃæmrɔk] n klaver c

shape [ʃeip] n vorm c; v vormen

share [ʃeə] v delen; n deel nt; aandeel nt

shark [ʃɑ:k] n haai c

sharp [ʃɑ:p] adj scherp

sharpen ['ʃɑ:pən] v *slijpen

shave [ʃeiv] v zich *scheren

shaver ['ʃeivə] n scheerapparaat nt

shaving-brush ['ʃeiviŋbrʌʃ] n scheerkwast c

shaving-cream ['ʃeiviŋkri:m] n scheercrème c

shaving-soap ['ʃeiviŋsoup] n scheerzeep c

shawl [ʃɔ:l] n omslagdoek c, sjaal c

she [ʃi:] pron ze

shed [ʃed] n schuur c

* **shed** [ʃed] v storten; verspreiden

sheep [ʃi:p] n (pl ~) schaap nt

sheer [ʃiə] adj absoluut, puur; dun, doorzichtig

sheet [ʃi:t] n laken nt; blad nt; plaat c

shelf [ʃelf] n (pl shelves) plank c

shell [ʃel] n schelp c; dop c

shellfish ['ʃelfiʃ] n schaaldier nt

shelter ['ʃeltə] n beschutting c, schuilplaats c; v beschutten

shepherd ['ʃepəd] n herder c

shift [ʃift] n ploeg c

* **shine** [ʃain] v *schijnen; glanzen, *blinken

ship [ʃip] n schip nt; v verschepen; **shipping line** scheepvaartlijn c

shipowner ['ʃi,pounə] n reder c

shipyard ['ʃipjɑ:d] n scheepswerf c

shirt [ʃə:t] n hemd nt, overhemd nt

shiver ['ʃivə] v bibberen, rillen; n rilling c

shivery ['ʃivəri] adj rillerig

shock [ʃɔk] n schok c; v schokken; ~ **absorber** schokbreker c

shocking ['ʃɔkiŋ] adj schokkend

shoe [ʃu:] n schoen c; **gym shoes** gymschoenen pl; ~ **polish** schoensmeer c

shoe-lace ['ʃu:leis] n schoenveter c

shoemaker ['ʃu:,meikə] n schoenmaker c

shoe-shop ['ʃu:ʃɔp] n schoenwinkel c

shook [ʃuk] v (p shake)

* **shoot** [ʃu:t] v *schieten

shop [ʃɔp] n winkel c; v winkelen; ~ **assistant** verkoper c; **shopping bag** boodschappentas c; **shopping centre** winkelcentrum nt

shopkeeper ['ʃɔp,ki:pə] n winkelier c

shop-window [,ʃɔp'windou] n etalage c

shore [ʃɔ:] n oever c, kust c

short [ʃɔ:t] adj kort; klein; ~ **circuit** kortsluiting c

shortage ['ʃɔ:tidʒ] n tekort nt, gebrek nt

shortcoming ['ʃɔ:t,kʌmiŋ] n tekortkoming c

shorten ['ʃɔ:tən] v verkorten

shorthand ['ʃɔ:thænd] n stenografie c

shortly ['ʃɔ:tli] adv weldra, binnenkort, spoedig

shorts [ʃɔːts] *pl* korte broek; *plAm* onderbroek *c*

short-sighted [ˌʃɔːt'saitid] *adj* bijziend

shot [ʃɔt] *n* schot *nt*; injectie *c*; opname *c*

*__should__ [ʃud] *v* *moeten

shoulder ['ʃouldə] *n* schouder *c*

shout [ʃaut] *v* schreeuwen, *roepen; *n* schreeuw *c*

shovel ['ʃʌvəl] *n* schop *c*

show [ʃou] *n* voorstelling *c*; tentoonstelling *c*

*__show__ [ʃou] *v* tonen; *laten zien, tentoonstellen; aantonen

show-case ['ʃoukeis] *n* vitrine *c*

shower [ʃauə] *n* douche *c*; bui *c*, regenbui *c*

showroom ['ʃouruːm] *n* toonzaal *c*

shriek [ʃriːk] *v* gillen; *n* gil *c*

shrimp [ʃrimp] *n* garnaal *c*

shrine [ʃrain] *n* heiligdom *nt*, schrijn *c*

*__shrink__ [ʃriŋk] *v* *krimpen

shrinkproof ['ʃriŋkpruːf] *adj* krimpvrij

shrub [ʃrʌb] *n* struik *c*

shudder ['ʃʌdə] *n* rilling *c*

shuffle ['ʃʌfəl] *v* schudden

*__shut__ [ʃʌt] *v* *sluiten; **shut** dicht, gesloten; ~ **in** *insluiten

shutter ['ʃʌtə] *n* luik *nt*, blind *c*

shy [ʃai] *adj* schuw, verlegen

shyness ['ʃainəs] *n* verlegenheid *c*

Siam [sai'æm] Siam

Siamese [ˌsaiə'miːz] *adj* Siamees; *n* Siamees *c*

sick [sik] *adj* ziek; misselijk

sickness ['siknəs] *n* ziekte *c*; misselijkheid *c*

side [said] *n* kant *c*, zijde *c*; partij *c*; **one-sided** *adj* eenzijdig

sideburns ['saidbəːnz] *pl* bakkebaarden *pl*

sidelight ['saidlait] *n* zijlicht *nt*

side-street ['saidstriːt] *n* zijstraat *c*

sidewalk ['saidwɔːk] *nAm* stoep *c*,

trottoir *nt*

sideways ['saidweiz] *adv* opzij

siege [siːdʒ] *n* belegering *c*

sieve [siv] *n* zeef *c*; *v* zeven

sift [sift] *v* zeven

sight [sait] *n* zicht *nt*; gezicht *nt*, aanblik *c*; bezienswaardigheid *c*

sign [sain] *n* teken *nt*; gebaar *nt*, wenk *c*; *v* ondertekenen, tekenen

signal ['signəl] *n* signaal *nt*; sein *nt*, teken *nt*; *v* seinen

signature ['signətʃə] *n* handtekening

significant [sig'nifikənt] *adj* veelbetekenend

signpost ['sainpoust] *n* wegwijzer *c*

silence ['sailəns] *n* stilte *c*; *v* tot zwijgen *brengen

silencer ['sailənsə] *n* knalpot *c*

silent ['sailənt] *adj* zwijgend, stil; *__be__ ~ *zwijgen

silk [silk] *n* zijde *c*

silken ['silkən] *adj* zijden

silly ['sili] *adj* mal, dwaas

silver ['silvə] *n* zilver *nt*; zilveren

silversmith ['silvəsmiθ] *n* zilversmid *c*

silverware ['silvəwɛə] *n* zilverwerk *nt*

similar ['similə] *adj* dergelijk, overeenkomstig

similarity [ˌsimi'lærəti] *n* gelijkenis *c*

simple ['simpəl] *adj* simpel, eenvoudig; gewoon

simply ['simpli] *adv* eenvoudig, gewoonweg

simulate ['simjuleit] *v* huichelen

simultaneous [ˌsiməl'teiniəs] *adj* gelijktijdig; **simultaneously** *adv* tegelijkertijd

sin [sin] *n* zonde *c*

since [sins] *prep* sedert; *adv* sindsdien; *conj* sinds; aangezien

sincere [sin'siə] *adj* oprecht

sinew ['sinjuː] *n* pees *c*

*__sing__ [siŋ] *v* *zingen

singer ['siŋə] *n* zanger *c*; zangeres *c*

single ['siŋgəl] adj enkel; ongetrouwd

singular ['siŋgjulə] n enkelvoud nt; adj eigenaardig

sinister ['sinistə] adj onheilspellend

sink [siŋk] n gootsteen c

*sink [siŋk] v *zinken

sip [sip] n slokje nt

siphon ['saifən] n sifon c

sir [sə:] meneer

siren ['saiərən] n sirene c

sister ['sistə] n zuster c, zus c

sister-in-law ['sistərinlɔ:] n (pl sisters-) schoonzuster c

*sit [sit] v *zitten; ~ down *gaan zit-
ten

site [sait] n plaats c; ligging c

sitting-room ['sitiŋru:m] n zitkamer c

situated ['sitʃueitid] adj gelegen

situation [,sitʃu'eiʃən] n situatie c; ligging c

six [siks] num zes

sixteen [,siks'ti:n] num zestien

sixteenth [,siks'ti:nθ] num zestiende

sixth [siksθ] num zesde

sixty ['siksti] num zestig

size [saiz] n grootte c, maat c; afmeting c, omvang c; formaat nt

skate [skeit] v schaatsen; n schaats c

skating-rink ['skeitiŋriŋk] n kunstijsbaan c, ijsbaan c

skeleton ['skelitən] n skelet nt, geraamte nt

sketch [sketʃ] n tekening c, schets c; v tekenen, schetsen

sketch-book ['sketʃbuk] n schetsboek nt

ski¹ [ski:] v skiën

ski² [ski:] n (pl ~, ~s) ski c; ~ boots skischoenen pl; ~ pants skibroek c; ~ poles Am skistokken pl; ~ sticks skistokken pl

skid [skid] v slippen

skier ['ski:ə] n skiër c

skilful ['skilfəl] adj bekwaam, behen-

dig, vaardig

ski-lift ['ski:lift] n skilift c

skill [skil] n vaardigheid c

skilled [skild] adj vaardig, vakkundig

skin [skin] n vel nt, huid c; schil c; ~ cream huidcrème c

skip [skip] v huppelen; *overslaan

skirt [skə:t] n rok c

skull [skʌl] n schedel c

sky [skai] n hemel c; lucht c

skyscraper ['skai,skreipə] n wolkenkrabber c

slack [slæk] adj traag

slacks [slæks] pl broek c

slam [slæm] v *dichtslaan

slander ['slɑ:ndə] n laster c

slant [slɑ:nt] v hellen

slanting ['slɑ:ntiŋ] adj schuin, hellend, scheef

slap [slæp] v *slaan; n klap c

slate [sleit] n lei nt

slave [sleiv] n slaaf c

sledge [sledʒ] n slee c, slede c

sleep [sli:p] n slaap c

*sleep [sli:p] v *slapen

sleeping-bag ['sli:piŋbæg] n slaapzak c

sleeping-car ['sli:piŋkɑ:] n slaapwagen c

sleeping-pill ['sli:piŋpil] n slaappil c

sleepless ['sli:pləs] adj slapeloos

sleepy ['sli:pi] adj slaperig

sleeve [sli:v] n mouw c; hoes c

sleigh [slei] n slee c, ar c

slender ['slendə] adj slank

slice [slais] n snee c

slide [slaid] n glijbaan c; dia c

*slide [slaid] v *glijden

slight [slait] adj licht; gering

slim [slim] adj slank; v vermageren

slip [slip] v slippen, *uitglijden; ontglippen; n misstap c; onderrok c

slipper ['slipə] n slof c, pantoffel c

slippery ['slipəri] adj glibberig, glad

slogan ['slougən] n leus c, slagzin c

slope [sloup] *n* helling *c*; *v* glooien
sloping ['sloupiŋ] *adj* afhellend
sloppy ['slɔpi] *adj* slordig
slot [slɔt] *n* gleuf *c*
slot-machine ['slɔt,məʃi:n] *n* automaat *c*
slovenly ['slʌvənli] *adj* slordig
slow [slou] *adj* traag, langzaam; ~ **down** vertragen; afremmen
sluice [slu:s] *n* sluis *c*
slum [slʌm] *n* achterbuurt *c*
slump [slʌmp] *n* prijsdaling *c*
slush [slʌʃ] *n* sneeuwslik *nt*
sly [slai] *adj* listig
smack [smæk] *v* *slaan; *n* klap *c*
small [smɔ:l] *adj* klein; gering
smallpox ['smɔ:lpɔks] *n* pokken *pl*
smart [smɑ:t] *adj* chic; knap, pienter
smell [smel] *n* geur *c*
***smell** [smel] *v* *ruiken; *stinken
smelly ['smeli] *adj* stinkend
smile [smail] *v* glimlachen; *n* glimlach *c*
smith [smiθ] *n* smid *c*
smoke [smouk] *v* roken; *n* rook *c*; **no smoking** verboden te roken
smoker ['smoukə] *n* roker *c*; rookcoupé *c*
smoking-compartment ['smoukiŋkəm,pɑ:tmənt] *n* coupé voor rokers
smoking-room ['smoukiŋru:m] *n* rookkamer *c*
smooth [smu:ð] *adj* effen, vlak, glad; zacht
smuggle ['smʌgəl] *v* smokkelen
snack [snæk] *n* snack *c*
snack-bar ['snækbɑ:] *n* snackbar *c*
snail [sneil] *n* slak *c*
snake [sneik] *n* slang *c*
snapshot ['snæpʃɔt] *n* kiekje *nt*, momentopname *c*
sneakers ['sni:kəz] *plAm* gymschoenen *pl*
sneeze [sni:z] *v* niezen

sniper ['snaipə] *n* sluipschutter *c*
snooty ['snu:ti] *adj* verwaand
snore [snɔ:] *v* snurken
snorkel ['snɔ:kəl] *n* snorkel *c*
snout [snaut] *n* snuit *c*
snow [snou] *n* sneeuw *c*; *v* sneeuwen
snowstorm ['snoustɔ:m] *n* sneeuwstorm *c*
snowy ['snoui] *adj* besneeuwd
so [sou] *conj* dus; *adv* zo; dermate; **and** ~ **on** enzovoort; ~ **far** tot zover; ~ **that** zodat, opdat
soak [souk] *v* weken, doorweken
soap [soup] *n* zeep *c*; ~ **powder** zeeppoeder *nt*
sober ['soubə] *adj* nuchter; bezonnen
so-called [,sou'kɔ:ld] *adj* zogenaamd
soccer ['sɔkə] *n* voetbal *nt*; ~ **team** elftal *nt*
social ['souʃəl] *adj* maatschappelijk, sociaal
socialism ['souʃəlizəm] *n* socialisme *nt*
socialist ['souʃəlist] *adj* socialistisch; *n* socialist *c*
society [sə'saiəti] *n* maatschappij *c*; genootschap *nt*, vereniging *c*; gezelschap *nt*
sock [sɔk] *n* sok *c*
socket ['sɔkit] *n* fitting *c*
soda-water ['soudə,wɔ:tə] *n* spuitwater *nt*, sodawater *nt*
sofa ['soufə] *n* sofa *c*
soft [sɔft] *adj* zacht; ~ **drink** frisdrank *c*
soften ['sɔfən] *v* verzachten
soil [sɔil] *n* grond *c*; bodem, aarde *c*
soiled [sɔild] *adj* bevuild
sold [sould] *v* (p, pp sell); ~ **out** uitverkocht
solder ['sɔldə] *v* solderen
soldering-iron ['sɔldəriŋaiən] *n* soldeerbout *c*
soldier ['souldʒə] *n* militair *c*, soldaat *c*

sole¹ [soul] *adj* enig

sole² [soul] *n* zool c; tong c

solely ['soulli] *adv* uitsluitend

solemn ['sɔləm] *adj* plechtig

solicitor [sə'lisitə] *n* raadsman c, advocaat c

solid ['sɔlid] *adj* stevig, solide; massief; *n* vaste stof

soluble ['sɔljubəl] *adj* oplosbaar

solution [sə'lu:ʃən] *n* oplossing c

solve [sɔlv] *v* oplossen

sombre ['sɔmbə] *adj* somber

some [sʌm] *adj* enige, enkele; *pron* sommige; iets; ~ **day** eens; ~ **more** nog wat; ~ **time** eens

somebody ['sʌmbədi] *pron* iemand

somehow ['sʌmhau] *adv* op de een of andere manier

someone ['sʌmwʌn] *pron* iemand

something ['sʌmθiŋ] *pron* iets

sometimes ['sʌmtaimz] *adv* soms

somewhat ['sʌmwɔt] *adv* enigszins

somewhere ['sʌmwɛə] *adv* ergens

son [sʌn] *n* zoon c

song [sɔŋ] *n* lied *nt*

son-in-law ['sʌninlɔ:] *n* (pl sons-) schoonzoon c

soon [su:n] *adv* vlug, gauw, weldra, spoedig; **as** ~ **as** zodra

sooner ['su:nə] *adv* liever

sore [sɔ:] *adj* pijnlijk, zeer; *n* zere plek; zweer c; ~ **throat** keelpijn c

sorrow ['sɔrou] *n* droefheid c, leed *nt*, verdriet *nt*

sorry ['sɔri] *adj* bedroefd; **sorry!** neem me niet kwalijk!, sorry!, pardon!

sort [sɔ:t] *v* sorteren, rangschikken; *n* slag *nt*, soort c/*nt*; **all sorts of** allerlei

soul [soul] *n* ziel c; geest c

sound [saund] *n* klank c, geluid *nt*; *v* *klinken; *adj* degelijk

soundproof ['saundpru:f] *adj* geluiddicht

soup [su:p] *n* soep c

soup-plate ['su:ppleit] *n* soepbord *nt*

soup-spoon ['su:pspu:n] *n* soeplepel c

sour [sauə] *adj* zuur

source [sɔ:s] *n* bron c

south [sauθ] *n* zuid c, zuiden *nt*; **South Pole** zuidpool c

South Africa [sauθ 'æfrikə] Zuid-Afrika

south-east [,sauθ'i:st] *n* zuidoosten *nt*

southerly ['sʌðəli] *adj* zuidelijk

southern ['sʌðən] *adj* zuidelijk

south-west [,sauθ'west] *n* zuidwesten *nt*

souvenir ['su:vəniə] *n* souvenir *nt*

sovereign ['sɔvrin] *n* vorst c

Soviet ['souviət] *adj* Sovjet-

Soviet Union ['souviət 'ju:njən] Sovjet-Unie

*** sow** [sou] *v* zaaien

spa [spa:] *n* geneeskrachtige bron

space [speis] *n* ruimte c; afstand c, tussenruimte c; *v* spatiëren

spacious ['speiʃəs] *adj* ruim

spade [speid] *n* schop c, spade c

Spain [spein] Spanje

Spaniard ['spænjəd] *n* Spanjaard c

Spanish ['spæniʃ] *adj* Spaans

spanking ['spæŋkiŋ] *n* pak slaag

spanner ['spænə] *n* schroefsleutel c

spare [spɛə] *adj* reserve-, extra; *v* missen; ~ **part** onderdeel *nt*; ~ **room** logeerkamer c; ~ **time** vrije tijd; ~ **tyre** reserveband c; ~ **wheel** reservewiel *nt*

spark [spa:k] *n* vonk c

sparking-plug ['spa:kiŋplʌg] *n* bougie c

sparkling ['spa:kliŋ] *adj* fonkelend; mousserend

sparrow ['spærou] *n* mus c

*** speak** [spi:k] *v* *spreken

spear [spiə] *n* speer c

special ['speʃəl] *adj* bijzonder, spe-

ciaal; ~ **delivery** expresse-
specialist ['speʃəlist] n specialist c
speciality [,speʃi'æləti] n specialiteit c
specialize ['speʃəlaiz] v zich specialiseren
specially ['speʃəli] adv in het bijzonder
species ['spiːʃiːz] n (pl ~) soort c/nt
specific [spə'sifik] adj specifiek
specimen ['spesimən] n exemplaar nt,
specimen nt
speck [spek] n spat c
spectacle ['spektəkəl] n schouwspel
nt; **spectacles** bril c
spectator [spek'teitə] n kijker c, toeschouwer c
speculate ['spekjuleit] v speculeren
speech [spiːtʃ] n spraak c; rede c, toespraak c; taal c
speechless ['spiːtʃləs] adj sprakeloos
speed [spiːd] n snelheid c; vaart c,
spoed c; **cruising** ~ kruissnelheid
c; ~ **limit** maximum snelheid, snelheidsbeperking c
*****speed** [spiːd] v hard *rijden; te hard
*rijden
speeding ['spiːdiŋ] n snelheidsovertreding c
speedometer [spiː'dɔmitə] n snelheidsmeter c
spell [spel] n betovering c
*****spell** [spel] v spellen
spelling ['speliŋ] n spelling c
*****spend** [spend] v *uitgeven, besteden;
*doorbrengen
sphere [sfiə] n bol c; sfeer c
spice [spais] n specerij c; **spices** kruiden
spiced [spaist] adj gekruid
spicy ['spaisi] adj pikant
spider ['spaidə] n spin c; **spider's
web** spinneweb nt
*****spill** [spil] v morsen
*****spin** [spin] v *spinnen; draaien
spinach ['spinidʒ] n spinazie c

spine [spain] n ruggegraat c
spinster ['spinstə] n oude vrijster
spire [spaiə] n spits c
spirit ['spirit] n geest c; bui c; **spirits**
sterke drank; stemming c; ~ **stove**
spiritusbrander c
spiritual ['spiritʃuəl] adj geestelijk
spit [spit] n spuug nt, speeksel nt;
spit nt
*****spit** [spit] v spuwen
in spite of [in spait ɔv] ongeacht, ondanks
spiteful ['spaitfəl] adj hatelijk
splash [splæʃ] v spatten
splendid ['splendid] adj schitterend,
prachtig
splendour ['splendə] n pracht c
splint [splint] n spalk c
splinter ['splintə] n splinter c
*****split** [split] v *splijten
*****spoil** [spɔil] v *bederven; verwennen
spoke[1] [spouk] v (p speak)
spoke[2] [spouk] n spaak c
sponge [spʌndʒ] n spons c
spook [spuːk] n spook nt
spool [spuːl] n spoel c
spoon [spuːn] n lepel c
sport [spɔːt] n sport c
sports-car ['spɔːtskaː] n sportwagen c
sports-jacket ['spɔːts,dʒækit] n sportjasje nt
sportsman ['spɔːtsmən] n (pl -men)
sportman c
sportswear ['spɔːtsweə] n sportkleding
c
spot [spɔt] n spat c, vlek c; plek c,
plaats c
spotless ['spɔtləs] adj vlekkeloos
spotlight ['spɔtlait] n schijnwerper c
spotted ['spɔtid] adj gespikkeld
spout [spaut] n straal c
sprain [sprein] v verstuiken, verzwikken; n verstuiking c
*****spread** [spred] v spreiden

spring [spriŋ] *n* voorjaar *nt*, lente *c*; veer *c*; bron *c*

springtime ['spriŋtaim] *n* voorjaar *nt*

sprouts [sprauts] *pl* spruitjes *pl*

spy [spai] *n* spion *c*

squadron ['skwɔdrən] *n* eskader *nt*

square [skweə] *adj* vierkant; *n* kwadraat *nt*, vierkant *nt*; plein *nt*

squash [skwɔʃ] *n* vruchtensap *nt*

squirrel ['skwirəl] *n* eekhoorn *c*

squirt [skwə:t] *n* straal *c*

stable ['steibəl] *adj* stabiel; *n* stal *c*

stack [stæk] *n* stapel *c*

stadium ['steidiəm] *n* stadion *nt*

staff [sta:f] *n* staf *c*

stage [steidʒ] *n* toneel *nt*; fase *c*, stadium *nt*; etappe *c*

stain [stein] *v* vlekken; *n* spat *c*, vlek *c*; **stained glass** gebrandschilderd glas; ~ **remover** vlekkenwater *nt*

stainless ['steinləs] *adj* vlekkeloos; ~ **steel** roestvrij staal

staircase ['steəkeis] *n* trap *c*

stairs [steəz] *pl* trap *c*

stale [steil] *adj* oudbakken

stall [stɔ:l] *n* kraam *c*; stalles *pl*

stamina ['stæminə] *n* uithoudingsvermogen *nt*

stamp [stæmp] *n* postzegel *c*; stempel *c*; *v* frankeren; stampen; ~ **machine** postzegelautomaat *c*

stand [stænd] *n* kraam *c*; tribune *c*

*****stand** [stænd] *v* *staan

standard ['stændəd] *n* norm *c*, maatstaf *c*; standaard-; ~ **of living** levensstandaard *c*

stanza ['stænzə] *n* couplet *nt*

staple ['steipəl] *n* nietje *nt*

star [sta:] *n* ster *c*

starboard ['sta:bəd] *n* stuurboord *nt*

starch [sta:tʃ] *n* stijfsel *nt*; *v* *stijven

stare [steə] *v* staren

starling ['sta:liŋ] *n* spreeuw *c*

start [sta:t] *v* *beginnen; *n* begin *nt*;

starter motor startmotor *c*

starting-point ['sta:tiŋpɔint] *n* uitgangspunt *nt*

state [steit] *n* staat *c*; toestand *c*; *v* verklaren

the States Verenigde Staten

statement ['steitmənt] *n* verklaring *c*

statesman ['steitsmən] *n* (pl -men) staatsman *c*

station ['steiʃən] *n* station *nt*; plaats *c*

stationary ['steiʃənəri] *adj* stilstaand

stationer's ['steiʃənəz] *n* kantoorboekhandel *c*

stationery ['steiʃənəri] *n* schrijfbehoeften *pl*

station-master ['steiʃən,ma:stə] *n* stationschef *c*

statistics [stə'tistiks] *pl* statistiek *c*

statue ['stætʃu:] *n* standbeeld *nt*

stay [stei] *v* *blijven; logeren, *verblijven; *n* verblijf *nt*

steadfast ['stedfa:st] *adj* standvastig

steady ['stedi] *adj* vast

steak [steik] *n* biefstuk *c*

*****steal** [sti:l] *v* *stelen

steam [sti:m] *n* stoom *c*

steamer ['sti:mə] *n* stoomboot *c*

steel [sti:l] *n* staal *nt*

steep [sti:p] *adj* steil

steeple ['sti:pəl] *n* kerktoren *c*

steering-column ['stiəriŋ,kɔləm] *n* stuurkolom *c*

steering-wheel ['stiəriŋwi:l] *n* stuurwiel *nt*

steersman ['stiəzmən] *n* (pl -men) stuurman *c*

stem [stem] *n* steel *c*

stenographer [ste'nɔgrəfə] *n* stenograaf *c*

step [step] *n* pas *c*, stap *c*; trede *c*; *v* stappen

stepchild ['steptʃaild] *n* (pl -children) stiefkind *nt*

stepfather ['step,fa:ðə] *n* stiefvader *c*

stepmother ['step,mʌðə] *n* stiefmoeder *c*

sterile ['sterail] *adj* steriel

sterilize ['sterilaiz] *v* steriliseren

steward ['stju:əd] *n* steward *c*

stewardess ['stju:ədes] *n* stewardess *c*

stick [stik] *n* stok *c*

* **stick** [stik] *v* kleven, plakken

sticky ['stiki] *adj* kleverig

stiff [stif] *adj* stijf

still [stil] *adv* nog; toch; *adj* stil

stillness ['stilnəs] *n* stilte *c*

stimulant ['stimjulənt] *n* stimulerend middel

stimulate ['stimjuleit] *v* stimuleren

sting [stiŋ] *n* prik *c*, steek *c*

* **sting** [stiŋ] *v* *steken

stingy ['stindʒi] *adj* gierig

* **stink** [stiŋk] *v* *stinken

stipulate ['stipjuleit] *v* bepalen

stipulation [,stipju'leiʃən] *n* bepaling *c*

stir [stə:] *v* *bewegen; roeren

stirrup ['stirəp] *n* stijgbeugel *c*

stitch [stitʃ] *n* steek *c*; hechting *c*

stock [stɔk] *n* voorraad *c*; *v* in voorraad *hebben; ~ exchange effectenbeurs *c*, beurs *c*; ~ market effectenbeurs *c*; stocks and shares effecten

stocking ['stɔkiŋ] *n* kous *c*

stole[1] [stoul] *v* (p steal)

stole[2] [stoul] *n* stola *c*

stomach ['stʌmək] *n* maag *c*

stomach-ache ['stʌməkeik] *n* buikpijn *c*, maagpijn *c*

stone [stoun] *n* steen *c*; edelsteen *c*; pit *c*; stenen; **pumice ~** puimsteen *nt*

stood [stud] *v* (p, pp stand)

stop [stɔp] *v* stoppen; *ophouden met, staken; *n* halte *c*; **stop!** halt!

stopper ['stɔpə] *n* stop *c*

storage ['stɔ:ridʒ] *n* opslag *c*

store [stɔ:] *n* voorraad *c*; winkel *c*; *v* *opslaan

store-house ['stɔ:haus] *n* magazijn *nt*

storey ['stɔ:ri] *n* etage *c*, verdieping *c*

stork [stɔ:k] *n* ooievaar *c*

storm [stɔ:m] *n* storm *c*

stormy ['stɔ:mi] *adj* stormachtig

story ['stɔ:ri] *n* verhaal *nt*

stout [staut] *adj* dik, gezet, corpulent

stove [stouv] *n* kachel *c*; fornuis *nt*

straight [streit] *adj* recht; eerlijk; *adv* recht; ~ **ahead** rechtdoor; ~ **away** direct, meteen; ~ **on** rechtdoor

strain [strein] *n* inspanning *c*; spanning *c*; *v* forceren; zeven

strainer ['streinə] *n* vergiet *nt*

strange [streindʒ] *adj* vreemd; raar

stranger ['streindʒə] *n* vreemdeling *c*; vreemde *c*

strangle ['stræŋgəl] *v* wurgen

strap [stræp] *n* riem *c*

straw [strɔ:] *n* stro *nt*

strawberry ['strɔ:bəri] *n* aardbei *c*

stream [stri:m] *n* beek *c*; stroom *c*; *v* stromen

street [stri:t] *n* straat *c*

streetcar ['stri:tka:] *nAm* tram *c*

street-organ ['stri:,tɔ:gən] *n* draaiorgel *nt*

strength [streŋθ] *n* sterkte *c*, kracht *c*

stress [stres] *n* spanning *c*; nadruk *c*; *v* benadrukken

stretch [stretʃ] *v* rekken; *n* stuk *nt*

strict [strikt] *adj* strikt; streng

strife [straif] *n* strijd *c*

strike [straik] *n* staking *c*

* **strike** [straik] *v* *slaan; *toeslaan; *treffen; staken; *strijken

striking ['straikiŋ] *adj* frappant, opmerkelijk, opvallend

string [striŋ] *n* touw *nt*; snaar *c*

strip [strip] *n* strook *c*

stripe [straip] *n* streep *c*

striped [straipt] *adj* gestreept

stroke [strouk] *n* beroerte *c*

stroll [stroul] v wandelen; n wandeling c

strong [strɔŋ] adj sterk; krachtig

stronghold ['strɔŋhould] n burcht c

structure ['strʌktʃə] n structuur c

struggle ['strʌgəl] n strijd c, worsteling c; v worstelen, *strijden

stub [stʌb] n controlestrook c

stubborn ['stʌbən] adj hardnekkig

student ['stju:dənt] n student c; studente c

study ['stʌdi] v studeren; n studie c; studeerkamer c

stuff [stʌf] n stof c; spul nt

stuffed [stʌft] adj gevuld

stuffing ['stʌfiŋ] n vulling c

stuffy ['stʌfi] adj benauwd

stumble ['stʌmbəl] v struikelen

stung [stʌŋ] v (p, pp sting)

stupid ['stju:pid] adj dom

style [stail] n stijl c

subject[1] ['sʌbdʒikt] n onderwerp nt; onderdaan c; ~ to onderhevig aan

subject[2] [səb'dʒekt] v *onderwerpen

submit [səb'mit] v zich *onderwerpen

subordinate [sə'bɔ:dinət] adj ondergeschikt; bijkomstig

subscriber [səb'skraibə] n abonnee c

subscription [səb'skripʃən] n abonnement nt

subsequent ['sʌbsikwənt] adj volgend

subsidy ['sʌbsidi] n subsidie c

substance ['sʌbstəns] n substantie c

substantial [səb'stænʃəl] adj stoffelijk; werkelijk; aanzienlijk

substitute ['sʌbstitju:t] v *vervangen; n vervanging c; plaatsvervanger c

subtitle ['sʌb,taitəl] n ondertitel c

subtle ['sʌtəl] adj subtiel

subtract [səb'trækt] v *aftrekken

suburb ['sʌbə:b] n buitenwijk c, voorstad c

suburban [sə'bə:bən] adj van de voorstad

subway ['sʌbwei] nAm ondergrondse c

succeed [sək'si:d] v slagen; opvolgen

success [sək'ses] n succes nt

successful [sək'sesfəl] adj succesvol

succumb [sə'kʌm] v *bezwijken

such [sʌtʃ] adj dergelijk, zulk; adv zo; ~ as zoals

suck [sʌk] v *zuigen

sudden ['sʌdən] adj plotseling

suddenly ['sʌdənli] adv opeens

suede [sweid] n suède nt/c

suffer ['sʌfə] v *lijden; *ondergaan

suffering ['sʌfəriŋ] n lijden nt

suffice [sə'fais] v voldoende *zijn

sufficient [sə'fiʃənt] adj voldoende, genoeg

suffrage ['sʌfridʒ] n stemrecht nt, kiesrecht nt

sugar ['ʃugə] n suiker c

suggest [sə'dʒest] v voorstellen

suggestion [sə'dʒestʃən] n voorstel nt

suicide ['su:isaid] n zelfmoord c

suit [su:t] v schikken; aanpassen; goed *staan; n kostuum nt

suitable ['su:təbəl] adj gepast, geschikt

suitcase ['su:tkeis] n koffer c

suite [swi:t] n suite c

sum [sʌm] n som c

summary ['sʌməri] n resumé nt, samenvatting c

summer ['sʌmə] n zomer c; ~ time zomertijd c

summit ['sʌmit] n top c

summons ['sʌmənz] n (pl ~es) dagvaarding c

sun [sʌn] n zon c

sunbathe ['sʌnbeið] v zonnebaden

sunburn ['sʌnbə:n] n zonnebrand c

Sunday ['sʌndi] zondag c

sun-glasses ['sʌn,glɑ:siz] pl zonnebril c

sunlight ['sʌnlait] n zonlicht nt

sunny ['sʌni] adj zonnig

sunrise ['sʌnraiz] n zonsopgang c

sunset ['sʌnset] n zonsondergang c

sunshade ['sʌnʃeid] n parasol c

sunshine ['sʌnʃain] n zonneschijn c

sunstroke ['sʌnstrouk] n zonnesteek c

suntan oil ['sʌntænɔil] zonnebrandolie c

superb [su'pə:b] adj groots, prachtig

superficial [,su:pə'fiʃəl] adj oppervlakkig

superfluous [su'pə:fluəs] adj overbodig

superior [su'piəriə] adj beter, groter, hoger, superieur

superlative [su'pə:lətiv] adj overtreffend; n superlatief c

supermarket ['su:pə,ma:kit] n supermarkt c

superstition [,su:pə'stiʃən] n bijgeloof nt

supervise ['su:pəvaiz] v toezicht *houden op

supervision [,su:pə'viʒən] n controle c, toezicht nt

supervisor ['su:pəvaizə] n opzichter c

supper ['sʌpə] n avondeten nt

supple ['sʌpəl] adj soepel, lenig, buigzaam

supplement ['sʌplimənt] n supplement nt

supply [sə'plai] n aanvoer c, levering c; voorraad c; aanbod nt; v leveren, bezorgen

support [sə'pɔ:t] v ondersteunen, steunen; n steun c; ~ hose steunkousen pl

supporter [sə'pɔ:tə] n supporter c

suppose [sə'pouz] v *aannemen, veronderstellen; supposing that aangenomen dat

suppository [sə'pɔzitəri] n zetpil c

suppress [sə'pres] v onderdrukken

surcharge ['sə:tʃɑ:dʒ] n toeslag c

sure [ʃuə] adj zeker

surely ['ʃuəli] adv zeker

surface ['sə:fis] n oppervlakte c

surf-board ['sə:fbɔ:d] n surfplank c

surgeon ['sə:dʒən] n chirurg c; veterinary ~ veearts c

surgery ['sə:dʒəri] n operatie c; spreekkamer c

surname ['sə:neim] n achternaam c

surplus ['sə:pləs] n overschot nt

surprise [sə'praiz] n verrassing c; verbazing c; v verrassen; verbazen

surrender [sə'rendə] v zich *overgeven; n overgave c

surround [sə'raund] v omringen, *omgeven

surrounding [sə'raundiŋ] adj omliggend

surroundings [sə'raundiŋz] pl omgeving c

survey ['sə:vei] n overzicht nt

survival [sə'vaivəl] n overleving c

survive [sə'vaiv] v overleven

suspect[1] [sə'spekt] v *verdenken; vermoeden

suspect[2] ['sʌspekt] n verdachte c

suspend [sə'spend] v schorsen

suspenders [sə'spendəz] plAm bretels pl; suspender belt jarretelgordel c

suspension [sə'spenʃən] n vering c, ophanging c; ~ bridge hangbrug c

suspicion [sə'spiʃən] n verdenking c; wantrouwen nt, argwaan c

suspicious [sə'spiʃəs] adj verdacht; argwanend, achterdochtig

sustain [sə'stein] v *verdragen

Swahili [swɑ'hi:li] n Swahili nt

swallow ['swɔlou] v inslikken, slikken; n zwaluw c

swam [swæm] v (p swim)

swamp [swɔmp] n moeras nt

swan [swɔn] n zwaan c

swap [swɔp] v ruilen

*swear [sweə] v *zweren; vloeken

sweat [swet] n zweet nt; v zweten

sweater ['swetə] n sweater c

Swede [swi:d] *n* Zweed *c*
Sweden ['swi:dən] Zweden
Swedish ['swi:diʃ] *adj* Zweeds
*****sweep** [swi:p] *v* vegen
sweet [swi:t] *adj* zoet; lief; *n* snoepje *nt*; toetje *nt*; **sweets** snoep *nt*, snoepgoed *nt*
sweeten ['swi:tən] *v* zoet maken
sweetheart ['swi:tha:t] *n* liefje *nt*, lieveling *c*
sweetshop ['swi:tʃɔp] *n* snoepwinkel *c*
swell [swel] *adj* prachtig
*****swell** [swel] *v* *zwellen
swelling ['sweliŋ] *n* zwelling *c*
swift [swift] *adj* snel
*****swim** [swim] *v* *zwemmen
swimmer ['swimə] *n* zwemmer *c*
swimming ['swimiŋ] *n* zwemsport *c*; ~ **pool** zwembad *nt*
swimming-trunks ['swimiŋtrʌŋks] *n* zwembroek *c*
swim-suit ['swimsu:t] *n* zwempak *nt*
swindle ['swindəl] *v* oplichten; *n* zwendelarij *c*
swindler ['swindlə] *n* oplichter *c*
swing [swiŋ] *n* schommel *c*
*****swing** [swiŋ] *v* zwaaien; schommelen
Swiss [swis] *adj* Zwitsers; *n* Zwitser *c*
switch [switʃ] *n* schakelaar *c*; *v* omwisselen; ~ **off** uitschakelen; ~ **on** inschakelen
switchboard ['switʃbɔ:d] *n* schakelbord *nt*
Switzerland ['switsələnd] Zwitserland
sword [sɔ:d] *n* zwaard *nt*
swum [swʌm] *v* (pp swim)
syllable ['siləbəl] *n* lettergreep *c*
symbol ['simbəl] *n* symbool *nt*
sympathetic [,simpə'θetik] *adj* hartelijk, begrijpend
sympathy ['simpəθi] *n* sympathie *c*; medegevoel *nt*
symphony ['simfəni] *n* symfonie *c*
symptom ['simtəm] *n* symptoom *nt*

synagogue ['sinəgɔg] *n* synagoge *c*
synonym ['sinənim] *n* synoniem *nt*
synthetic [sin'θetik] *adj* synthetisch
syphon ['saifən] *n* sifon *c*
Syria ['siriə] Syrië
Syrian ['siriən] *adj* Syrisch; *n* Syriër *c*
syringe [si'rindʒ] *n* spuit *c*
syrup ['sirəp] *n* stroop *c*, siroop *c*
system ['sistəm] *n* systeem *nt*; stelsel *nt*; **decimal** ~ tientallig stelsel
systematic [,sistə'mætik] *adj* systematisch

T

table ['teibəl] *n* tafel *c*; tabel *c*; ~ **of contents** inhoudsopgave *c*; ~ **tennis** tafeltennis *nt*
table-cloth ['teibəlklɔθ] *n* tafellaken *nt*
tablespoon ['teibəlspu:n] *n* eetlepel *c*
tablet ['tæblit] *n* tablet *nt*
taboo [tə'bu:] *n* taboe *nt*
tactics ['tæktiks] *pl* tactiek *c*
tag [tæg] *n* etiket *nt*
tail [teil] *n* staart *c*
tail-light ['teillait] *n* achterlicht *nt*
tailor ['teilə] *n* kleermaker *c*
tailor-made ['teiləmeid] *adj* op maat gemaakt
*****take** [teik] *v* *nemen; pakken; *brengen; *begrijpen, snappen; ~ **away** *meenemen; *afnemen, *wegnemen; ~ **off** starten; ~ **out** *wegnemen; ~ **over** *overnemen; ~ **place** *plaatshebben; ~ **up** *innemen
take-off ['teikɔf] *n* start *c*
tale [teil] *n* verhaal *nt*, vertelling *c*
talent ['tælənt] *n* aanleg *c*, talent *nt*
talented ['tæləntid] *adj* begaafd
talk [tɔ:k] *v* *spreken, praten; *n* gesprek *nt*

talkative ['tɔ:kətiv] adj spraakzaam

tall [tɔ:l] adj hoog; lang, groot

tame [teim] adj mak, tam; v temmen

tampon ['tæmpən] n tampon c

tangerine [,tændʒə'ri:n] n mandarijn c

tangible ['tændʒibəl] adj tastbaar

tank [tæŋk] n tank c

tanker ['tæŋkə] n tankschip nt

tanned [tænd] adj gebruind

tap [tæp] n kraan c; klop c; v kloppen

tape [teip] n band c; lint nt; adhesive ~ plakband nt; hechtpleister c

tape-measure ['teip,meʒə] n centimeter c

tape-recorder ['teipri,kɔ:də] n bandrecorder c

tapestry ['tæpistri] n wandkleed nt, gobelin c

tar [ta:] n teer c/nt

target ['ta:git] n doel nt, mikpunt nt

tariff ['tærif] n tarief nt

tarpaulin [ta:'pɔ:lin] n dekzeil nt

task [ta:sk] n taak c

taste [teist] n smaak c; v smaken; proeven

tasteless ['teistləs] adj smakeloos

tasty ['teisti] adj lekker, smakelijk

taught [tɔ:t] v (p, pp teach)

tavern ['tævən] n herberg c

tax [tæks] n belasting c; v belasten

taxation [tæk'seiʃən] n belasting c

tax-free ['tæksfri:] adj belastingvrij

taxi ['tæksi] n taxi c; ~ rank taxistandplaats c; ~ stand Am taxistandplaats c

taxi-driver ['tæksi,draivə] n taxichauffeur c

taxi-meter ['tæksi,mi:tə] n taximeter c

tea [ti:] n thee c

*teach [ti:tʃ] v leren, *onderwijzen

teacher ['ti:tʃə] n docent c, leraar c; lerares c; onderwijzer c, meester c, schoolmeester c

teachings ['ti:tʃiŋz] pl leer c

tea-cloth ['ti:klɔθ] n theedoek c

teacup ['ti:kʌp] n theekopje nt

team [ti:m] n equipe c, ploeg c

teapot ['ti:pɔt] n theepot c

tear¹ [tiə] n traan c

tear² [teə] n scheur c; *tear v scheuren

tear-jerker ['tiə,dʒə:kə] n smartlap c

tease [ti:z] v plagen

tea-set ['ti:set] n theeservies nt

tea-shop ['ti:ʃɔp] n tearoom c

teaspoon ['ti:spu:n] n theelepel c

teaspoonful ['ti:spu:n,ful] n theelepel c

technical ['teknikəl] adj technisch

technician [tek'niʃən] n technicus c

technique [tek'ni:k] n techniek c

technology [tek'nɔlədʒi] n technologie c

teenager ['ti:,neidʒə] n tiener c

teetotaller [ti:'toutələ] n geheelonthouder c

telegram ['teligræm] n telegram nt

telegraph ['teligra:f] v telegraferen

telepathy [ti'lepəθi] n telepathie c

telephone ['telifoun] n telefoon c; ~ book Am telefoongids c, telefoonboek nt; ~ booth telefooncel c; ~ call telefoongesprek nt; ~ directory telefoonboek nt, telefoongids c; ~ exchange telefooncentrale c; ~ operator telefoniste c

telephonist [ti'lefənist] n telefoniste c

television ['teliviʒən] n televisie c; ~ set televisietoestel nt

telex ['teleks] n telex c

*tell [tel] v *zeggen; vertellen

temper ['tempə] n boosheid c

temperature ['temprətʃə] n temperatuur c

tempest ['tempist] n storm c

temple ['tempəl] n tempel c; slaap c

temporary ['tempərəri] adj voorlopig, tijdelijk

tempt [tempt] v *aantrekken

temptation [temp'teifən] n verleiding c

ten [ten] num tien

tenant ['tenənt] n huurder c

tend [tend] v de neiging *hebben; verzorgen; ~ to neigen tot

tendency ['tendənsi] n neiging c, tendens c

tender ['tendə] adj teder, teer; mals

tendon ['tendən] n pees c

tennis ['tenis] n tennis nt; ~ shoes tennisschoenen pl

tennis-court ['teniskɔ:t] n tennisbaan c

tense [tens] adj gespannen

tension ['tenʃən] n spanning c

tent [tent] n tent c

tenth [tenθ] num tiende

tepid ['tepid] adj lauw

term [tə:m] n term c; periode c, termijn c; voorwaarde c

terminal ['tə:minəl] n eindpunt nt

terrace ['terəs] n terras nt

terrain [te'rein] n terrein nt

terrible ['teribəl] adj verschrikkelijk, ontzettend, vreselijk

terrific [tə'rifik] adj geweldig

terrify ['terifai] v schrik *aanjagen; terrifying angstwekkend

territory ['teritəri] n gebied nt

terror ['terə] n angst c

terrorism ['terərizəm] n terrorisme nt, terreur c

terrorist ['terərist] n terrorist c

terylene ['terili:n] n terylene nt

test [test] n proef c, test c; v proberen, testen

testify ['testifai] v getuigen

text [tekst] n tekst c

textbook ['teksbuk] n leerboek nt

textile ['tekstail] n textiel c/nt

texture ['tekstʃə] n structuur c

Thai [tai] adj Thailands; n Thailander c

Thailand ['tailænd] Thailand

than [ðæn] conj dan

thank [θæŋk] v bedanken, danken; ~ you dank u

thankful ['θæŋkfəl] adj dankbaar

that [ðæt] adj die, dat; conj dat

thaw [θɔ:] v dooien, ontdooien; n dooi c

the [ðə,ði] art de art; the ... the hoe ... hoe

theatre ['θiətə] n schouwburg c, theater nt

theft [θeft] n diefstal c

their [ðeə] adj hun

them [ðem] pron hen

theme [θi:m] n thema nt, onderwerp nt

themselves [ðəm'selvz] pron zich; zelf

then [ðen] adv toen; vervolgens, dan

theology [θi'ɔlədʒi] n theologie c

theoretical [θiə'retikəl] adj theoretisch

theory ['θiəri] n theorie c

therapy ['θerəpi] n therapie c

there [ðeə] adv daar; daarheen

therefore ['ðeəfɔ:] conj daarom

thermometer [θə'mɔmitə] n thermometer c

thermostat ['θə:məstæt] n thermostaat c

these [ði:z] adj deze

thesis ['θi:sis] n (pl theses) stelling c

they [ðei] pron ze

thick [θik] adj dik; dicht

thicken ['θikən] v verdikken

thickness ['θiknəs] n dikte c

thief [θi:f] n (pl thieves) dief c

thigh [θai] n dij c

thimble ['θimbəl] n vingerhoed c

thin [θin] adj dun; mager

thing [θiŋ] n ding nt

* think [θiŋk] v *denken; *nadenken; ~ of *denken aan; *bedenken; ~ over *overdenken

thinker ['θiŋkə] n denker c

third [θəːd] *num* derde
thirst [θəːst] *n* dorst *c*
thirsty ['θəːsti] *adj* dorstig
thirteen [,θəː'tiːn] *num* dertien
thirteenth [,θəː'tiːnθ] *num* dertiende
thirtieth ['θəːtiəθ] *num* dertigste
thirty ['θəːti] *num* dertig
this [ðis] *adj* dit, deze
thistle ['θisəl] *n* distel *c*
thorn [θɔːn] *n* doorn *c*
thorough ['θʌrə] *adj* grondig, degelijk
thoroughbred ['θʌrəbred] *adj* volbloed
thoroughfare ['θʌrəfɛə] *n* hoofdweg *c*, hoofdstraat *c*
those [ðouz] *adj* die
though [ðou] *conj* hoewel, ofschoon, alhoewel; *adv* overigens
thought[1] [θɔːt] *v* (p, pp think)
thought[2] [θɔːt] *n* gedachte *c*
thoughtful ['θɔːtfəl] *adj* nadenkend; zorgzaam
thousand ['θauzənd] *num* duizend
thread [θred] *n* draad *c*; garen *nt*; *v* *rijgen
threadbare ['θredbɛə] *adj* versleten
threat [θret] *n* dreigement *nt*, bedreiging *c*
threaten ['θretən] *v* dreigen, bedreigen; **threatening** dreigend
three [θriː] *num* drie
three-quarter [,θriː'kwɔːtə] *adj* driekwart
threshold ['θreʃould] *n* drempel *c*
threw [θruː] *v* (p throw)
thrifty ['θrifti] *adj* zuinig
throat [θrout] *n* keel *c*; hals *c*
throne [θroun] *n* troon *c*
through [θruː] *prep* door
throughout [θruː'aut] *adv* overal
throw [θrou] *n* gooi *c*
***throw** [θrou] *v* *werpen, gooien
thrush [θrʌʃ] *n* lijster *c*
thumb [θʌm] *n* duim *c*
thumbtack ['θʌmtæk] *nAm* punaise *c*

thump [θʌmp] *v* stampen
thunder ['θʌndə] *n* donder *c*; *v* donderen
thunderstorm ['θʌndəstɔːm] *n* onweer *nt*
thundery ['θʌndəri] *adj* onweerachtig
Thursday ['θəːzdi] donderdag *c*
thus [ðʌs] *adv* zo
thyme [taim] *n* tijm *c*
tick [tik] *n* streepje *nt*; ~ **off** aanstrepen
ticket ['tikit] *n* kaartje *nt*; bon *c*; ~ **collector** conducteur *c*; ~ **machine** kaartenautomaat *c*
tickle ['tikəl] *v* kietelen
tide [taid] *n* getij *nt*; **high** ~ hoog water; **low** ~ laag water
tidings ['taidiŋz] *pl* nieuws *nt*
tidy ['taidi] *adj* net; ~ **up** opruimen
tie [tai] *v* knopen, *binden; *n* das *c*
tiger ['taigə] *n* tijger *c*
tight [tait] *adj* strak; nauw, krap; *adv* vast
tighten ['taitən] *v* aanhalen, *aantrekken; strakker maken; strakker *worden
tights [taits] *pl* maillot *c*
tile [tail] *n* tegel *c*; dakpan *c*
till [til] *prep* tot aan, tot; *conj* tot, totdat
timber ['timbə] *n* timmerhout *nt*
time [taim] *n* tijd *c*; maal *c*, keer *c*; **all the** ~ aldoor; **in** ~ op tijd; ~ **of arrival** aankomsttijd *c*; ~ **of departure** vertrektijd *c*
time-saving ['taim,seiviŋ] *adj* tijdbesparend
timetable ['taim,teibəl] *n* dienstregeling *c*
timid ['timid] *adj* bedeesd
timidity [ti'midəti] *n* verlegenheid *c*
tin [tin] *n* tin *nt*; bus *c*, blik *nt*; **tinned food** conserven *pl*
tinfoil ['tinfɔil] *n* zilverpapier *nt*

tin-opener ['ti,noupənə] *n* blikopener *c*

tiny ['taini] *adj* minuscuul

tip [tip] *n* punt *c* ; fooi *c*

tire[1] [taiə] *n* band *c*

tire[2] [taiə] *v* vermoeien

tired [taiəd] *adj* vermoeid, moe ; ~ **of** beu

tiring ['taiəriŋ] *adj* vermoeiend

tissue ['tiʃu:] *n* weefsel *nt* ; papieren zakdoek

title ['taitəl] *n* titel *c*

to [tu:] *prep* tot ; aan, voor, bij, naar ; om te

toad [toud] *n* pad *c*

toadstool ['toudstu:l] *n* paddestoel *c*

toast [toust] *n* toast *c*

tobacco [tə'bækou] *n* (pl ~s) tabak *c* ; ~ **pouch** tabakszak *c*

tobacconist [tə'bækənist] *n* sigarenwinkelier *c* ; **tobacconist's** tabakswinkel *c*

today [tə'dei] *adv* vandaag

toddler ['tɔdlə] *n* peuter *c*

toe [tou] *n* teen *c*

toffee ['tɔfi] *n* toffee *c*

together [tə'geðə] *adv* bijeen, samen

toilet ['tɔilət] *n* toilet *nt* ; ~ **case** toilettas *c*

toilet-paper ['tɔilət,peipə] *n* closetpapier *nt*, toiletpapier *nt*

toiletry ['tɔilətri] *n* toiletbenodigdheden *pl*

token ['toukən] *n* teken *nt* ; bewijs *nt* ; munt *c*

told [tould] *v* (p, pp tell)

tolerable ['tɔlərəbəl] *adj* draaglijk

toll [toul] *n* tol *c*

tomato [tə'mɑ:tou] *n* (pl ~es) tomaat *c*

tomb [tu:m] *n* graf *nt*

tombstone ['tu:mstoun] *n* grafsteen *c*

tomorrow [tə'mɔrou] *adv* morgen

ton [tʌn] *n* ton *c*

tone [toun] *n* toon *c* ; klank *c*

tongs [tɔŋz] *pl* tang *c*

tongue [tʌŋ] *n* tong *c*

tonic ['tɔnik] *n* tonicum *nt*

tonight [tə'nait] *adv* vannacht, vanavond

tonsilitis [,tɔnsə'laitis] *n* amandelontsteking *c*

tonsils ['tɔnsəlz] *pl* amandelen

too [tu:] *adv* te ; ook

took [tuk] *v* (p take)

tool [tu:l] *n* werktuig *nt*, gereedschap *nt* ; ~ **kit** gereedschapskist *c*

toot [tu:t] *vAm* claxonneren

tooth [tu:θ] *n* (pl teeth) tand *c*

toothache ['tu:θeik] *n* tandpijn *c*

toothbrush ['tu:θbrʌʃ] *n* tandenborstel *c*

toothpaste ['tu:θpeist] *n* tandpasta *c/nt*

toothpick ['tu:θpik] *n* tandestoker *c*

toothpowder ['tu:θ,paudə] *n* tandpoeder *nt/c*

top [tɔp] *n* top *c* ; bovenkant *c* ; deksel *nt* ; bovenst ; **on** ~ **of** bovenop ; ~ **side** bovenkant *c*

topcoat ['tɔpkout] *n* overjas *c*

topic ['tɔpik] *n* onderwerp *nt*

topical ['tɔpikəl] *adj* actueel

torch [tɔ:tʃ] *n* fakkel *c* ; zaklantaarn *c*

torment[1] [tɔ:'ment] *v* kwellen

torment[2] ['tɔ:ment] *n* kwelling *c*

torture ['tɔ:tʃə] *n* marteling *c* ; *v* martelen

toss [tɔs] *v* gooien

tot [tɔt] *n* kleuter *c*

total ['toutəl] *adj* totaal ; geheel, volslagen ; *n* totaal *nt*

totalitarian [,toutæli'tɛəriən] *adj* totalitair

totalizator ['toutəlaizeitə] *n* totalisator *c*

touch [tʌtʃ] *v* aanraken ; *betreffen ; *n* contact *nt*, aanraking *c* ; tastzin *c*

touching ['tʌtʃiŋ] *adj* aandoenlijk

tough [tʌf] *adj* taai

tour [tuə] *n* rondreis *c*

tourism ['tuərizəm] *n* toerisme *nt*

tourist ['tuərist] *n* toerist *c*; ~ **class** toeristenklasse *c*; ~ **office** verkeersbureau *nt*

tournament ['tuənəmənt] *n* toernooi *nt*

tow [tou] *v* slepen

towards [tə'wɔ:dz] *prep* naar; jegens

towel [tauəl] *n* handdoek *c*

towelling ['tauəliŋ] *n* badstof *c*

tower [tauə] *n* toren *c*

town [taun] *n* stad *c*; ~ **centre** stadscentrum *nt*; ~ **hall** stadhuis *nt*

townspeople ['taunz,pi:pəl] *pl* stadsmensen *pl*

toxic ['tɔksik] *adj* vergiftig

toy [tɔi] *n* speelgoed *nt*

toyshop ['tɔiʃɔp] *n* speelgoedwinkel *c*

trace [treis] *n* spoor *nt*; *v* opsporen

track [træk] *n* spoor *nt*; renbaan *c*

tractor ['træktə] *n* tractor *c*

trade [treid] *n* koophandel *c*, handel *c*; ambacht *nt*, vak *nt*; *v* handel *drijven

trademark ['treidma:k] *n* handelsmerk *nt*

trader ['treidə] *n* handelaar *c*

tradesman ['treidzmən] *n* (pl -men) handelaar *c*

trade-union [,treid'ju:njən] *n* vakbond *c*

tradition [trə'diʃən] *n* traditie *c*

traditional [trə'diʃənəl] *adj* traditioneel

traffic ['træfik] *n* verkeer *nt*; ~ **jam** verkeersopstopping *c*; ~ **light** stoplicht *nt*

trafficator ['træfikeitə] *n* richtingaanwijzer *c*

tragedy ['trædʒədi] *n* tragedie *c*

tragic ['trædʒik] *adj* tragisch

trail [treil] *n* spoor *nt*, pad *nt*

trailer ['treilə] *n* aanhangwagen *c*;

nAm kampeerwagen *c*

train [trein] *n* trein *c*; *v* dresseren, trainen; **stopping** ~ stoptrein *c*; **through** ~ doorgaande trein

training ['treiniŋ] *n* training *c*

trait [treit] *n* trek *c*

traitor ['treitə] *n* verrader *c*

tram [træm] *n* tram *c*

tramp [træmp] *n* landloper *c*, vagebond *c*; *v* *rondtrekken

tranquil ['træŋkwil] *adj* rustig

tranquillizer ['træŋkwilaizə] *n* kalmerend middel

transaction [træn'zækʃən] *n* transactie *c*

transatlantic [,trænzət'læntik] *adj* transatlantisch

transfer [træns'fə:] *v* *overbrengen

transform [træns'fɔ:m] *v* veranderen

transformer [træns'fɔ:mə] *n* transformator *c*

transition [træn'siʃən] *n* overgang *c*

translate [træns'leit] *v* vertalen

translation [træns'leiʃən] *n* vertaling *c*

translator [træns'leitə] *n* vertaler *c*

transmission [trænz'miʃən] *n* uitzending *c*

transmit [trænz'mit] *v* *uitzenden

transmitter [trænz'mitə] *n* zender *c*

transparent [træn'spɛərənt] *adj* doorzichtig

transport[1] ['trænspɔ:t] *n* vervoer *nt*

transport[2] [træn'spɔ:t] *v* transporteren

transportation [,trænspɔ:'teiʃən] *n* transport *nt*

trap [træp] *n* val *c*

trash [træʃ] *n* rommel *c*; ~ **can** *Am* vuilnisbak *c*

travel ['trævəl] *v* reizen; ~ **agency** reisbureau *nt*; ~ **agent** reisagent *c*; ~ **insurance** reisverzekering *c*; **travelling expenses** reiskosten *pl*

traveller ['trævələ] *n* reiziger *c*; **traveller's cheque** reischeque *c*

tray [trei] n dienblad nt

treason ['tri:zən] n verraad nt

treasure ['treʒə] n schat c

treasurer ['treʒərə] n penningmeester c

treasury ['treʒəri] n schatkist c

treat [tri:t] v behandelen

treatment ['tri:tmənt] n behandeling c

treaty ['tri:ti] n verdrag nt

tree [tri:] n boom c

tremble ['trembəl] v rillen, beven; trillen

tremendous [tri'mendəs] adj enorm

trespasser ['trespəsə] n indringer c

trial [traiəl] n rechtszaak c; proef c

triangle ['traiæŋgəl] n driehoek c

triangular [trai'æŋgjulə] adj driehoekig

tribe [traib] n stam c

tributary ['tribjutəri] n zijrivier c

tribute ['tribju:t] n hulde c

trick [trik] n streek c; foefje nt, kunstje nt

trigger ['trigə] n trekker c

trim [trim] v bijknippen

trip [trip] n uitstapje nt, reis c

triumph ['traiəmf] n triomf c; v zegevieren

triumphant [trai'ʌmfənt] adj triomfantelijk

trolley-bus ['trolibʌs] n trolleybus c

troops [tru:ps] pl troepen pl

tropical ['tropikəl] adj tropisch

tropics ['tropiks] pl tropen pl

trouble ['trʌbəl] n zorg c, moeite c, last c; v storen

troublesome ['trʌbəlsəm] adj lastig

trousers ['trauzəz] pl broek c

trout [traut] n (pl ~) forel c

truck [trʌk] nAm vrachtwagen c

true [tru:] adj waar; werkelijk, echt; getrouw, trouw

trumpet ['trʌmpit] n trompet c

trunk [trʌŋk] n koffer c; stam c; nAm kofferruimte c; trunks pl

gymnastiekbroek c

trunk-call ['trʌŋkkɔ:l] n interlokaal gesprek

trust [trʌst] v vertrouwen; n vertrouwen nt

trustworthy ['trʌst,wə:ði] adj betrouwbaar

truth [tru:θ] n waarheid c

truthful ['tru:θfəl] adj waarheidsgetrouw

try [trai] v proberen; trachten, pogen; n poging c; ~ on passen

tube [tju:b] n pijp c, buis c; tube c

tuberculosis [tju:,bə:kju'lousis] n tuberculose c

Tuesday ['tju:zdi] dinsdag c

tug [tʌg] v slepen; n sleepboot c; ruk c

tuition [tju:'iʃən] n onderwijs nt

tulip ['tju:lip] n tulp c

tumbler ['tʌmblə] n beker c

tumour ['tju:mə] n gezwel nt, tumor c

tuna ['tju:nə] n (pl ~, ~s) tonijn c

tune [tju:n] n wijs c, melodie c; ~ in afstemmen

tuneful ['tju:nfəl] adj melodieus

tunic ['tju:nik] n tuniek c

Tunisia [tju:'niziə] Tunesië

Tunisian [tju:'niziən] adj Tunesisch; n Tunesiër c

tunnel ['tʌnəl] n tunnel c

turbine ['tə:bain] n turbine c

turbojet [,tə:bou'dʒet] n straalvliegtuig nt

Turk [tə:k] n Turk c

Turkey ['tə:ki] Turkije

turkey ['tə:ki] n kalkoen c

Turkish ['tə:kiʃ] adj Turks; ~ bath Turks bad

turn [tə:n] v draaien, keren; omkeren, omdraaien; n wending c, draai c; bocht c; beurt c; ~ back terugkeren; ~ down *verwerpen; ~ into veranderen in; ~ off dichtdraaien;

~ **on** aanzetten; opendraaien; ~
over omkeren; ~ **round** omkeren;
zich omdraaien

turning ['tə:niŋ] *n* bocht *c*

turning-point ['tə:niŋpɔint] *n* keerpunt
nt

turnover ['tə:,nouvə] *n* omzet *c*; ~ **tax**
omzetbelasting *c*

turnpike ['tə:npaik] *nAm* tolweg *c*

turpentine ['tə:pəntain] *n* terpentijn *c*

turtle ['tə:təl] *n* schildpad *c*

tutor ['tju:tə] *n* huisonderwijzer *c*;
voogd *c*

tuxedo [tʌk'si:dou] *nAm* (pl ~s, ~es)
smoking *c*

tweed [twi:d] *n* tweed *nt*

tweezers ['twi:zəz] *pl* pincet *c*

twelfth [twelfθ] *num* twaalfde

twelve [twelv] *num* twaalf

twentieth ['twentiəθ] *num* twintigste

twenty ['twenti] *num* twintig

twice [twais] *adv* tweemaal

twig [twig] *n* twijg *c*

twilight ['twailait] *n* schemering *c*

twine [twain] *n* touw *nt*

twins [twinz] *pl* tweeling *c*; **twin beds**
lits-jumeaux *nt*

twist [twist] *v* *winden; draaien; *n*
draai *c*

two [tu:] *num* twee

two-piece [,tu:'pi:s] *adj* tweedelig

type [taip] *v* tikken, typen; *n* type *nt*

typewriter ['taipraitə] *n* schrijfmachine *c*

typewritten ['taipritən] getypt

typhoid ['taifɔid] *n* tyfus *c*

typical ['tipikəl] *adj* kenmerkend, typisch

typist ['taipist] *n* typiste *c*

tyrant ['taiərənt] *n* tiran *c*

tyre [taiə] *n* band *c*; ~ **pressure** bandenspanning *c*

U

ugly ['ʌgli] *adj* lelijk

ulcer ['ʌlsə] *n* zweer *c*

ultimate ['ʌltimət] *adj* laatst

ultraviolet [,ʌltrə'vaiələt] *adj* ultraviolet

umbrella [ʌm'brelə] *n* paraplu *c*

umpire ['ʌmpaiə] *n* scheidsrechter *c*

unable [ʌ'neibəl] *adj* onbekwaam

unacceptable [,ʌnək'septəbəl] *adj* onaanvaardbaar

unaccountable [,ʌnə'kauntəbəl] *adj* onverklaarbaar

unaccustomed [,ʌnə'kʌstəmd] *adj* niet
gewend

unanimous [ju:'næniməs] *adj* unaniem

unanswered [,ʌ'nɑ:nsəd] *adj* onbeantwoord

unauthorized [,ʌ'nɔ:θəraizd] *adj* onbevoegd

unavoidable [,ʌnə'vɔidəbəl] *adj* onvermijdelijk

unaware [,ʌnə'wɛə] *adj* onbewust

unbearable [ʌn'bɛərəbəl] *adj* ondraaglijk

unbreakable [,ʌn'breikəbəl] *adj* onbreekbaar

unbroken [,ʌn'broukən] *adj* heel

unbutton [,ʌn'bʌtən] *v* losknopen

uncertain [ʌn'sə:tən] *adj* onzeker

uncle ['ʌŋkəl] *n* oom *c*

unclean [,ʌn'kli:n] *adj* onrein

uncomfortable [ʌn'kʌmfətəbəl] *adj* ongemakkelijk

uncommon [ʌn'kɔmən] *adj* ongewoon,
zeldzaam

unconditional [,ʌnkən'diʃənəl] *adj* onvoorwaardelijk

unconscious [ʌn'kɔnʃəs] *adj* bewusteloos

uncork [,ʌn'kɔ:k] *v* ontkurken

uncover [ʌn'kʌvə] *v* blootleggen

uncultivated [ˌʌn'kʌltiveitid] adj onbebouwd

under ['ʌndə] prep beneden, onder

undercurrent ['ʌndəˌkʌrənt] n onderstroom c

underestimate [ˌʌndə'restimeit] v onderschatten

underground ['ʌndəgraund] adj ondergronds; n metro c

underline [ˌʌndə'lain] v onderstrepen

underneath [ˌʌndə'ni:θ] adv beneden

underpants ['ʌndəpænts] plAm onderbroek c

undershirt ['ʌndəʃə:t] n hemd nt

undersigned ['ʌndəsaind] n ondergetekende c

*understand [ˌʌndə'stænd] v *begrijpen

understanding [ˌʌndə'stændiŋ] n begrip nt

*undertake [ˌʌndə'teik] v *ondernemen

undertaking [ˌʌndə'teikiŋ] n onderneming c

underwater ['ʌndəˌwɔ:tə] adj onderwater-

underwear ['ʌndəwɛə] n ondergoed nt

undesirable [ˌʌndi'zaiərəbəl] adj ongewenst

*undo [ˌʌn'du:] v losmaken

undoubtedly [ʌn'dautidli] adv ongetwijfeld

undress [ˌʌn'dres] v zich uitkleden

undulating ['ʌndjuleitiŋ] adj golvend

unearned [ˌʌ'nə:nd] adj onverdiend

uneasy [ʌ'ni:zi] adj onbehaaglijk

uneducated [ˌʌ'nedjukeitid] adj ongeschoold

unemployed [ˌʌnim'plɔid] adj werkeloos

unemployment [ˌʌnim'plɔimənt] n werkeloosheid c

unequal [ˌʌ'ni:kwəl] adj ongelijk

uneven [ˌʌ'ni:vən] adj ongelijk, oneffen

unexpected [ˌʌnik'spektid] adj onvoorzien, onverwacht

unfair [ˌʌn'fɛə] adj oneerlijk, onbillijk

unfaithful [ˌʌn'feiθfəl] adj ontrouw

unfamiliar [ˌʌnfə'miljə] adj onbekend

unfasten [ˌʌn'fa:sən] v losmaken

unfavourable [ˌʌn'feivərəbəl] adj ongunstig

unfit [ˌʌn'fit] adj ongeschikt

unfold [ʌn'fould] v ontvouwen

unfortunate [ʌn'fɔ:tʃənət] adj ongelukkig

unfortunately [ʌn'fɔ:tʃənətli] adv helaas, ongelukkigerwijs

unfriendly [ˌʌn'frendli] adj onvriendelijk

unfurnished [ˌʌn'fə:niʃt] adj ongemeubileerd

ungrateful [ʌn'greitfəl] adj ondankbaar

unhappy [ʌn'hæpi] adj ongelukkig

unhealthy [ʌn'helθi] adj ongezond

unhurt [ʌn'hə:t] adj heelhuids

uniform ['ju:nifɔ:m] n uniform nt/c; adj uniform

unimportant [ˌʌnim'pɔ:tənt] adj onbelangrijk

uninhabitable [ˌʌnin'hæbitəbəl] adj onbewoonbaar

uninhabited [ˌʌnin'hæbitid] adj onbewoond

unintentional [ˌʌnin'tenʃənəl] adj onopzettelijk

union ['ju:njən] n vereniging c; verbond nt, unie c

unique [ju:'ni:k] adj uniek

unit ['ju:nit] n eenheid c

unite [ju:'nait] v verenigen

United States [ju:'naitid steits] Verenigde Staten

unity ['ju:nəti] n eenheid c

universal [ˌju:ni'və:səl] adj algemeen, universeel

universe ['juːnivəːs] *n* heelal *nt*

university [ˌjuːni'vəːsəti] *n* universiteit *c*

unjust [ˌʌn'dʒʌst] *adj* onrechtvaardig

unkind [ʌn'kaind] *adj* onaardig, onvriendelijk

unknown [ˌʌn'noun] *adj* onbekend

unlawful [ˌʌn'lɔːfəl] *adj* onwettig

unlearn [ˌʌn'ləːn] *v* afleren

unless [ən'les] *conj* tenzij

unlike [ˌʌn'laik] *adj* verschillend

unlikely [ʌn'laikli] *adj* onwaarschijnlijk

unlimited [ʌn'limitid] *adj* grenzeloos, onbeperkt

unload [ˌʌn'loud] *v* lossen, *uitladen

unlock [ˌʌn'lɔk] *v* openen

unlucky [ʌn'lʌki] *adj* ongelukkig

unnecessary [ʌn'nesəsəri] *adj* onnodig

unoccupied [ʌ'nɔkjupaid] *adj* onbezet

unofficial [ˌʌnə'fiʃəl] *adj* officieus

unpack [ˌʌn'pæk] *v* uitpakken

unpleasant [ʌn'plezənt] *adj* onaangenaam, onplezierig; naar, vervelend

unpopular [ˌʌn'pɔpjulə] *adj* impopulair, onbemind

unprotected [ˌʌnprə'tektid] *adj* onbeschermd

unqualified [ʌn'kwɔlifaid] *adj* onbevoegd

unreal [ˌʌn'riəl] *adj* onwerkelijk

unreasonable [ʌn'riːzənəbəl] *adj* onredelijk

unreliable [ˌʌnri'laiəbəl] *adj* onbetrouwbaar

unrest [ˌʌn'rest] *n* onrust *c*; rusteloosheid *c*

unsafe [ˌʌn'seif] *adj* onveilig

unsatisfactory [ˌʌnsætis'fæktəri] *adj* onbevredigend

unscrew [ˌʌn'skruː] *v* losschroeven

unselfish [ˌʌn'selfiʃ] *adj* onzelfzuchtig

unskilled [ˌʌn'skild] *adj* ongeschoold

unsound [ˌʌn'saund] *adj* ongezond

unstable [ˌʌn'steibəl] *adj* labiel

unsteady [ˌʌn'stedi] *adj* wankel, onvast; onevenwichtig

unsuccessful [ˌʌnsək'sesfəl] *adj* mislukt

unsuitable [ˌʌn'suːtəbəl] *adj* ongepast

unsurpassed [ˌʌnsə'pɑːst] *adj* onovertroffen

untidy [ʌn'taidi] *adj* slordig

untie [ˌʌn'tai] *v* losknopen

until [ən'til] *prep* tot

untrue [ˌʌn'truː] *adj* onwaar

untrustworthy [ˌʌn'trʌst,wəː ði] *adj* onbetrouwbaar

unusual [ʌn'juːʒuəl] *adj* ongebruikelijk, ongewoon

unwell [ˌʌn'wel] *adj* onwel

unwilling [ˌʌn'wiliŋ] *adj* onwillig

unwise [ˌʌn'waiz] *adj* onverstandig

unwrap [ˌʌn'ræp] *v* uitpakken

up [ʌp] *adv* naar boven, omhoog, op

upholster [ʌp'houlstə] *v* bekleden

upkeep ['ʌpkiːp] *n* onderhoud *nt*

uplands ['ʌpləndz] *pl* hoogvlakte *c*

upon [ə'pɔn] *prep* op

upper ['ʌpə] *adj* hoger, bovenst

upright ['ʌprait] *adj* rechtopstaand; *adv* overeind

upset [ʌp'set] *v* verstoren; *adj* overstuur

upside-down [ˌʌpsaid'daun] *adv* ondersteboven

upstairs [ˌʌp'steəz] *adv* boven; naar boven

upstream [ˌʌp'striːm] *adv* stroomopwaarts

upwards ['ʌpwədz] *adv* naar boven

urban ['əːbən] *adj* stedelijk

urge [əːdʒ] *v* aansporen; *n* drang *c*

urgency ['əːdʒənsi] *n* urgentie *c*

urgent ['əːdʒənt] *adj* dringend

urine ['juərin] *n* urine *c*

Uruguay ['juərəgwai] Uruguay

Uruguayan [ˌjuərə'gwaiən] *adj* Uru-

guayaans; *n* Uruguayaan *c*
us [ʌs] *pron* ons
usable ['ju:zəbəl] *adj* bruikbaar
usage ['ju:zidʒ] *n* gebruik *nt*
use¹ [ju:z] *v* gebruiken; *be used to
gewoon *zijn; ~ up verbruiken
use² [ju:s] *n* gebruik *nt*; nut *nt*; *be
of ~ baten
useful ['ju:sfəl] *adj* bruikbaar, nuttig
useless ['ju:sləs] *adj* nutteloos
user ['ju:zə] *n* gebruiker *c*
usher ['ʌʃə] *n* suppoost *c*
usherette [ˌʌʃə'ret] *n* ouvreuse *c*
usual ['ju:ʒuəl] *adj* gebruikelijk
usually ['ju:ʒuəli] *adv* gewoonlijk
utensil [ju:'tensəl] *n* gereedschap *nt*,
werktuig *nt*; gebruiksvoorwerp *nt*
utility [ju:'tiləti] *n* nut *nt*
utilize ['ju:tilaiz] *v* benutten
utmost ['ʌtmoust] *adj* uiterst
utter ['ʌtə] *adj* volslagen, totaal; *v* uiten

V

vacancy ['veikənsi] *n* vacature *c*
vacant ['veikənt] *adj* vacant
vacate [və'keit] *v* ontruimen
vacation [və'keiʃən] *n* vakantie *c*
vaccinate ['væksineit] *v* inenten
vaccination [ˌvæksi'neiʃən] *n* inenting
c
vacuum ['vækjuəm] *n* vacuüm *nt*;
vAm stofzuigen; ~ cleaner stofzuiger *c*; ~ flask thermosfles *c*
vagrancy ['veigrənsi] *n* landloperij *c*
vague [veig] *adj* vaag
vain [vein] *adj* ijdel; vergeefs; in ~
vergeefs, tevergeefs
valet ['vælit] *n* bediende *c*
valid ['vælid] *adj* geldig
valley ['væli] *n* dal *nt*, vallei *c*

valuable ['væljubəl] *adj* waardevol,
kostbaar; valuables *pl* kostbaarheden *pl*
value ['vælju:] *n* waarde *c*; *v* schatten
valve [vælv] *n* ventiel *nt*
van [væn] *n* bestelauto *c*
vanilla [və'nilə] *n* vanille *c*
vanish ['væniʃ] *v* *verdwijnen
vapour ['veipə] *n* damp *c*
variable ['veəriəbəl] *adj* veranderlijk
variation [ˌveəri'eiʃən] *n* afwisseling *c*;
verandering *c*
varied ['veərid] *adj* gevarieerd
variety [və'raiəti] *n* verscheidenheid *c*;
~ show variétévoorstelling *c*; ~
theatre variététheater *nt*
various ['veəriəs] *adj* allerlei, verscheidene
varnish ['vɑ:niʃ] *n* lak *c*, vernis *nt/c*;
v lakken
vary ['veəri] *v* variëren, afwisselen;
veranderen; verschillen
vase [vɑ:z] *n* vaas *c*
vaseline ['væsəli:n] *n* vaseline *c*
vast [vɑ:st] *adj* onmetelijk, uitgestrekt
vault [vɔ:lt] *n* gewelf *nt*; kluis *c*
veal [vi:l] *n* kalfsvlees *nt*
vegetable ['vedʒətəbəl] *n* groente *c*; ~
merchant groenteboer *c*
vegetarian [ˌvedʒi'teəriən] *n* vegetariër
c
vegetation [ˌvedʒi'teiʃən] *n* plantengroei *c*
vehicle ['vi:əkəl] *n* voertuig *nt*
veil [veil] *n* sluier *c*
vein [vein] *n* ader *c*; varicose ~ spatader *c*
velvet ['velvit] *n* fluweel *nt*
velveteen [ˌvelvi'ti:n] *n* katoenfluweel
nt
venerable ['venərəbəl] *adj* eerbiedwaardig
venereal disease [vi'niəriəl di'zi:z] geslachtsziekte *c*

Venezuela [ˌveniˈzweilə] Venezuela

Venezuelan [ˌveniˈzweilən] adj Venezolaans; n Venezolaan c

ventilate [ˈventileit] v ventileren; luchten

ventilation [ˌventiˈleiʃən] n ventilatie c; luchtverversing c

ventilator [ˈventileitə] n ventilator c

venture [ˈventʃə] v wagen

veranda [vəˈrændə] n veranda c

verb [vəːb] n werkwoord nt

verbal [ˈvəːbəl] adj mondeling

verdict [ˈvəːdikt] n vonnis nt, uitspraak c

verge [vəːdʒ] n rand c

verify [ˈverifai] v verifiëren

verse [vəːs] n vers nt

version [ˈvəːʃən] n versie c; vertaling c

versus [ˈvəːsəs] prep contra

vertical [ˈvəːtikəl] adj verticaal

vertigo [ˈvəːtigou] n duizeling c

very [ˈveri] adv erg, zeer; adj precies, waar, werkelijk; uiterst

vessel [ˈvesəl] n vaartuig nt, schip nt; vat nt

vest [vest] n hemd nt; nAm vest nt

veterinary surgeon [ˈvetrinəri ˈsəːdʒən] dierenarts c

via [vaiə] prep via

viaduct [ˈvaiədʌkt] n viaduct c/nt

vibrate [vaiˈbreit] v trillen

vibration [vaiˈbreiʃən] n vibratie c

vicar [ˈvikə] n predikant c

vicarage [ˈvikəridʒ] n pastorie c

vice-president [ˌvaisˈprezidənt] n vice-president c

vicinity [viˈsinəti] n nabijheid c, buurt c

vicious [ˈviʃəs] adj boosaardig

victim [ˈviktim] n slachtoffer nt; dupe c

victory [ˈviktəri] n overwinning c

view [vjuː] n uitzicht nt; opvatting c,

mening c; v *bekijken

view-finder [ˈvjuːˌfaində] n zoeker c

vigilant [ˈvidʒilənt] adj waakzaam

villa [ˈvilə] n villa c

village [ˈvilidʒ] n dorp nt

villain [ˈvilən] n boef c

vine [vain] n wijnstok c

vinegar [ˈvinigə] n azijn c

vineyard [ˈvinjəd] n wijngaard c

vintage [ˈvintidʒ] n wijnoogst c

violation [vaiəˈleiʃən] n schending c

violence [ˈvaiələns] n geweld nt

violent [ˈvaiələnt] adj gewelddadig; hevig, heftig

violet [ˈvaiələt] n viooltje nt; adj violet

violin [vaiəˈlin] n viool c

virgin [ˈvəːdʒin] n maagd c

virtue [ˈvəːtʃuː] n deugd c

visa [ˈviːzə] n visum c

visibility [ˌvizəˈbiləti] n zicht nt

visible [ˈvizəbəl] adj zichtbaar

vision [ˈviʒən] n visie c

visit [ˈvizit] v *bezoeken; n visite c, bezoek nt; **visiting hours** bezoekuren pl

visiting-card [ˈvizitiŋkaːd] n visitekaartje nt

visitor [ˈvizitə] n bezoeker c

vital [ˈvaitəl] adj essentieel

vitamin [ˈvitəmin] n vitamine c

vivid [ˈvivid] adj levendig

vocabulary [vəˈkæbjuləri] n vocabulaire nt, woordenschat c; woordenlijst c

vocal [ˈvoukəl] adj vocaal

vocalist [ˈvoukəlist] n zanger c

voice [vɔis] n stem c

void [vɔid] adj nietig

volcano [vɔlˈkeinou] n (pl ~es, ~s) vulkaan c

volt [voult] n volt c

voltage [ˈvoultidʒ] n voltage c/nt

volume [ˈvɔljum] n volume nt; deel nt

voluntary ['vɔləntəri] *adj* vrijwillig

volunteer [,vɔlən'tiə] *n* vrijwilliger *c*

vomit ['vɔmit] *v* braken, *overgeven

vote [vout] *v* stemmen; *n* stem *c*; stemming *c*

voucher ['vautʃə] *n* bon *c*, bewijs *nt*

vow [vau] *n* gelofte *c*, eed *c*; *v* *zweren

vowel [vauəl] *n* klinker *c*

voyage ['vɔiidʒ] *n* reis *c*

vulgar ['vʌlgə] *adj* vulgair; volks-, ordinair

vulnerable ['vʌlnərəbəl] *adj* kwetsbaar

vulture ['vʌltʃə] *n* gier *c*

W

wade [weid] *v* waden

wafer ['weifə] *n* wafel *c*

waffle ['wɔfəl] *n* wafel *c*

wages ['weidʒiz] *pl* loon *nt*

waggon ['wægən] *n* wagon *c*

waist [weist] *n* taille *c*, middel *nt*

waistcoat ['weiskout] *n* vest *nt*

wait [weit] *v* wachten; ~ on bedienen

waiter ['weitə] *n* ober *c*, kelner *c*

waiting *n* het wachten

waiting-list ['weitiŋlist] *n* wachtlijst *c*

waiting-room ['weitiŋru:m] *n* wachtkamer *c*

waitress ['weitris] *n* serveerster *c*

*wake [weik] *v* wekken; ~ up ontwaken, wakker *worden

walk [wɔ:k] *v* *lopen; wandelen; *n* wandeling *c*; loop *c*; walking te voet

walker ['wɔ:kə] *n* wandelaar *c*

walking-stick ['wɔ:kiŋstik] *n* wandelstok *c*

wall [wɔ:l] *n* muur *c*; wand *c*

wallet ['wɔlit] *n* portefeuille *c*

wallpaper ['wɔ:l,peipə] *n* behang *nt*

walnut ['wɔ:lnʌt] *n* walnoot *c*

waltz [wɔ:ls] *n* wals *c*

wander ['wɔndə] *v* *rondzwerven, *zwerven

want [wɔnt] *v* *willen; wensen; *n* behoefte *c*; gebrek *nt*, gemis *nt*

war [wɔ:] *n* oorlog *c*

warden ['wɔ:dən] *n* bewaker *c*, opzichter *c*

wardrobe ['wɔ:droub] *n* klerenkast *c*, garderobe *c*

warehouse ['weəhaus] *n* magazijn *nt*, pakhuis *nt*

wares [weəz] *pl* waren *pl*

warm [wɔ:m] *adj* heet, warm; *v* verwarmen

warmth [wɔ:mθ] *n* warmte *c*

warn [wɔ:n] *v* waarschuwen

warning ['wɔ:niŋ] *n* waarschuwing *c*

wary ['weəri] *adj* behoedzaam

was [wɔz] *v* (p be)

wash [wɔʃ] *v* *wassen; ~ and wear zelfstrijkend; ~ up afwassen

washable ['wɔʃəbəl] *adj* wasbaar

wash-basin ['wɔʃ,beisən] *n* wasbekken *nt*

washing ['wɔʃiŋ] *n* was *c*; wasgoed *nt*

washing-machine ['wɔʃiŋmə,ʃi:n] *n* wasmachine *c*

washing-powder ['wɔʃiŋ,paudə] *n* waspoeder *nt*

washroom ['wɔʃru:m] *nAm* toilet *nt*

wash-stand ['wɔʃstænd] *n* wastafel *c*

wasp [wɔsp] *n* wesp *c*

waste [weist] *v* verspillen; *n* verspilling *c*; *adj* braak

wasteful ['weistfəl] *adj* verkwistend

wastepaper-basket [weist'peipə,bɑ:-skit] *n* prullenmand *c*

watch [wɔtʃ] *v* *kijken naar, *gadeslaan; letten op; *n* horloge *nt*; ~ for *uitkijken naar; ~ out *uitkijken

watch-maker ['wɔtʃ,meikə] *n* horlogemaker c

watch-strap ['wɔtʃstræp] n horloge-bandje nt

water ['wɔːtə] n water nt; **iced** ~ ijs-water nt; **running** ~ stromend wa-ter; ~ **pump** waterpomp c; ~ **ski** waterski c

water-colour ['wɔːtə,kʌlə] n waterverf c; aquarel c

watercress ['wɔːtəkres] n waterkers c

waterfall ['wɔːtəfɔːl] n waterval c

watermelon ['wɔːtə,melən] n waterme-loen c

waterproof ['wɔːtəpruːf] adj water-dicht

water-softener [,wɔːtə,sɔfnə] n wasver-zachter c

waterway ['wɔːtəwei] n vaarwater nt

watt [wɔt] n watt c

wave [weiv] n golf c; v zwaaien

wave-length ['weivleŋθ] n golflengte c

wavy ['weivi] adj golvend

wax [wæks] n was c

waxworks ['wækswɔːks] pl wassenbeel-denmuseum nt

way [wei] n manier c, wijze c; weg c; kant c, richting c; afstand c; **any** ~ hoe dan ook; **by the** ~ tussen twee haakjes; **one-way traffic** eenrich-tingsverkeer nt; **out of the** ~ afge-legen; **the other** ~ **round** anders-om; ~ **back** terugweg c; ~ **in** in-gang c; ~ **out** uitgang c

wayside ['weisaid] n wegkant c

we [wiː] pron we

weak [wiːk] adj zwak; slap

weakness ['wiːknəs] n zwakheid c

wealth [welθ] n rijkdom c

wealthy ['welθi] adj rijk

weapon ['wepən] n wapen nt

* **wear** [weə] v *aanhebben, *dragen; ~ **out** *verslijten

weary ['wiəri] adj moe, vermoeid

weather ['weðə] n weer nt; ~ **fore-**

cast weerbericht nt

* **weave** [wiːv] v *weven

weaver ['wiːvə] n wever c

wedding ['wediŋ] n huwelijk nt, brui-loft c

wedding-ring ['wediŋriŋ] n trouwring c

wedge [wedʒ] n wig c

Wednesday ['wenzdi] woensdag c

weed [wiːd] n onkruid nt

week [wiːk] n week c

weekday ['wiːkdei] n weekdag c

weekly ['wiːkli] adj wekelijks

* **weep** [wiːp] v huilen

weigh [wei] v *wegen

weighing-machine ['weiiŋmə,ʃiːn] n weegschaal c

weight [weit] n gewicht nt

welcome ['welkəm] adj welkom; n welkom nt; v verwelkomen

weld [weld] v lassen

welfare ['welfeə] n welzijn c

well[1] [wel] adv goed; adj gezond; **as** ~ ook, eveneens; **as** ~ **as** evenals; **well!** welnu!

well[2] [wel] n bron c, put c

well-founded [,wel'faundid] adj ge-grond

well-known ['welnoun] adj bekend

well-to-do [,weltə'duː] adj bemiddeld

went [went] v (p go)

were [wɔː] v (p be)

west [west] n west c, westen nt

westerly ['westəli] adj westelijk

western ['westən] adj westers

wet [wet] adj nat; vochtig

whale [weil] n walvis c

wharf [wɔːf] n (pl ~s, wharves) kade c

what [wɔt] pron wat; ~ **for** waarom

whatever [wɔ'tevə] pron wat dan ook

wheat [wiːt] n tarwe c

wheel [wiːl] n wiel nt

wheelbarrow ['wiːl,bærou] n kruiwa-gen c

wheelchair ['wi:ltʃɛə] n rolstoel c

when [wen] adv wanneer; conj als, toen, wanneer

whenever [we'nevə] conj wanneer ook

where [wɛə] adv waar; conj waar

wherever [wɛə'revə] conj waar ook

whether ['weðə] conj of; whether ... or of ... of

which [witʃ] pron welk; dat

whichever [wi'tʃevə] adj welk ook

while [wail] conj terwijl; n poosje nt

whilst [wailst] conj terwijl

whim [wim] n gril c, bevlieging c

whip [wip] n zweep c; v kloppen

whiskers ['wiskəz] pl bakkebaarden pl

whisper ['wispə] v fluisteren; n gefluister nt

whistle ['wisəl] v *fluiten; n fluitje nt

white [wait] adj wit; blank

whitebait ['waitbeit] n witvis c

whiting ['waitiŋ] n (pl ~) wijting c

Whitsun ['witsən] Pinksteren

who [hu:] pron wie; die

whoever [hu:'evə] pron wie ook

whole [houl] adj geheel, heel; n geheel nt

wholesale ['houlseil] n groothandel c; ~ dealer grossier c

wholesome ['houlsəm] adj gezond

wholly ['houlli] adv helemaal

whom [hu:m] pron wie

whore [hɔ:] n hoer c

whose [hu:z] pron wiens; van wie

why [wai] adv waarom

wicked ['wikid] adj slecht

wide [waid] adj wijd, breed

widen ['waidən] v verwijden

widow ['widou] n weduwe c

widower ['widouə] n weduwnaar c

width [widθ] n breedte c

wife [waif] n (pl wives) echtgenote c, vrouw c

wig [wig] n pruik c

wild [waild] adj wild; woest

will [wil] n wil c; testament nt

*will [wil] v *willen; *zullen

willing ['wiliŋ] adj bereid

willingly ['wiliŋli] adv graag

will-power ['wilpauə] n wilskracht c

*win [win] v *winnen

wind [wind] n wind c

*wind [waind] v kronkelen; *opwinden, *winden

winding ['waindiŋ] adj kronkelig

windmill ['windmil] n molen c, windmolen c

window ['windou] n raam c

window-sill ['windousil] n vensterbank c

windscreen ['windskri:n] n voorruit c; ~ wiper ruitenwisser c

windshield ['windʃi:ld] nAm voorruit c; ~ wiper Am ruitenwisser c

windy ['windi] adj winderig

wine [wain] n wijn c

wine-cellar ['wain,selə] n wijnkelder c

wine-list ['wainlist] n wijnkaart c

wine-merchant ['wain,mə:tʃənt] n wijnkoper c

wine-waiter ['wain,weitə] n wijnkelner c

wing [wiŋ] n vleugel c

winkle ['wiŋkəl] n alikruik c

winner ['winə] n winnaar c

winning ['winiŋ] adj winnend; winnings pl winst c

winter ['wintə] n winter c; ~ sports wintersport c

wipe [waip] v vegen, afvegen

wire [waiə] n draad c; ijzerdraad nt

wireless ['waiələs] n radio c

wisdom ['wizdəm] n wijsheid c

wise [waiz] adj wijs

wish [wiʃ] v verlangen, wensen; n verlangen nt, wens c

witch [witʃ] n heks c

with [wið] prep met; bij; van

*withdraw [wið'drɔ:] v *terugtrekken

within [wi'ðin] *prep* binnen ; *adv* van binnen

without [wi'ðaut] *prep* zonder

witness ['witnəs] *n* getuige *c*

wits [wits] *pl* verstand *nt*

witty ['witi] *adj* geestig

wolf [wulf] *n* (pl wolves) wolf *c*

woman ['wumən] *n* (pl women) vrouw *c*

womb [wu:m] *n* baarmoeder *c*

won [wʌn] *v* (p, pp win)

wonder ['wʌndə] *n* wonder *nt* ; verwondering *c* ; *v* zich *afvragen

wonderful ['wʌndəfəl] *adj* prachtig, verrukkelijk ; heerlijk

wood [wud] *n* hout *nt* ; bos *nt*

wood-carving ['wud,ka:viŋ] *n* houtsnijwerk *nt*

wooded ['wudid] *adj* bebost

wooden ['wudən] *adj* houten ; ~ **shoe** klomp *c*

woodland ['wudlənd] *n* bebost gebied

wool [wul] *n* wol *c* ; **darning** ~ stopgaren *nt*

woollen ['wulən] *adj* wollen

word [wə:d] *n* woord *nt*

wore [wɔ:] *v* (p wear)

work [wə:k] *n* werk *nt* ; arbeid *c* ; *v* werken ; functioneren ; **working day** werkdag *c* ; ~ **of art** kunstwerk *nt* ; ~ **permit** werkvergunning *c*

worker ['wə:kə] *n* arbeider *c*

working ['wə:kiŋ] *n* werking *c*

workman ['wə:kmən] *n* (pl -men) arbeider *c*

works [wə:ks] *pl* fabriek *c*

workshop ['wə:kʃɔp] *n* werkplaats *c*

world [wə:ld] *n* wereld *c* ; ~ **war** wereldoorlog *c*

world-famous [,wə:ld'feiməs] *adj* wereldberoemd

world-wide ['wə:ldwaid] *adj* wereldomvattend

worm [wə:m] *n* worm *c*

worn [wɔ:n] *adj* (pp wear) versleten

worn-out [,wɔ:n'aut] *adj* versleten

worried ['wʌrid] *adj* ongerust

worry ['wʌri] *v* zich ongerust maken ; *n* zorg *c*, bezorgdheid *c*

worse [wə:s] *adj* slechter ; *adv* erger

worship ['wə:ʃip] *v* *aanbidden ; *n* eredienst *c*

worst [wə:st] *adj* slechtst ; *adv* ergst

worsted ['wustid] *n* kamgaren *nt*

worth [wə:θ] *n* waarde *c* ; *be ~ waard *zijn ; *be worth-while de moeite waard *zijn

worthless ['wə:θləs] *adj* waardeloos

worthy of ['wə:ði əv] waard

would [wud] *v* (p will) gewoon *zijn

wound¹ [wu:nd] *n* wond *c* ; *v* kwetsen, verwonden

wound² [waund] *v* (p, pp wind)

wrap [ræp] *v* inpakken

wreck [rek] *n* wrak *nt* ; *v* vernielen

wrench [rentʃ] *n* sleutel *c* ; ruk *c* ; *v* verdraaien

wrinkle ['riŋkəl] *n* rimpel *c*

wrist [rist] *n* pols *c*

wrist-watch ['ristwɔtʃ] *n* polshorloge *nt*

*write [rait] *v* *schrijven ; **in writing** schriftelijk ; ~ **down** *opschrijven

writer ['raitə] *n* schrijver *c*

writing-pad ['raitiŋpæd] *n* blocnote *c*, schrijfblok *nt*

writing-paper ['raitiŋ,peipə] *n* schrijfpapier *nt*

written ['ritən] *adj* (pp write) schriftelijk

wrong [rɔŋ] *adj* verkeerd, fout ; *n* onrecht *nt* ; *v* onrecht *aandoen ; *be ~ ongelijk *hebben

wrote [rout] *v* (p write)

X

Xmas ['krisməs] Kerstmis
X-ray ['eksrei] *n* röntgenfoto *c*; *v* doorlichten

Y

yacht [jɔt] *n* jacht *nt*
yacht-club ['jɔtklʌb] *n* zeilclub *c*
yachting ['jɔtiŋ] *n* zeilsport *c*
yard [jɑːd] *n* erf *nt*
yarn [jɑːn] *n* garen *nt*
yawn [jɔːn] *v* gapen, geeuwen
year [jiə] *n* jaar *nt*
yearly ['jiəli] *adj* jaarlijks
yeast [jiːst] *n* gist *c*
yell [jel] *v* gillen; *n* gil *c*
yellow ['jelou] *adj* geel
yes [jes] ja
yesterday ['jestədi] *adv* gisteren
yet [jet] *adv* nog; *conj* toch, echter, maar
yield [jiːld] *v* *opbrengen; *toegeven
yoke [jouk] *n* juk *nt*

yolk [jouk] *n* dooier *c*
you [juː] *pron* je; jou; u; jullie
young [jʌŋ] *adj* jong
your [jɔː] *adj* uw; jouw; jullie
yourself [jɔː'self] *pron* je; zelf
yourselves [jɔː'selvz] *pron* je; zelf
youth [juːθ] *n* jeugd *c*; ~ **hostel** jeugdherberg *c*
Yugoslav [ˌjuːgə'slɑːv] *n* Joegoslaaf *c*
Yugoslavia [ˌjuːgə'slɑːviə] Joegoslavië

Z

zeal [ziːl] *n* ijver *c*
zealous ['zeləs] *adj* ijverig
zebra ['ziːbrə] *n* zebra *c*
zenith ['zeniθ] *n* zenit *nt*; toppunt *nt*
zero ['ziərou] *n* (pl ~s) nul *c*
zest [zest] *n* animo *c*
zinc [ziŋk] *n* zink *nt*
zip [zip] *n* ritssluiting *c*; ~ **code** *Am* postcode *c*
zipper ['zipə] *n* ritssluiting *c*
zodiac ['zoudiæk] *n* dierenriem *c*
zone [zoun] *n* zone *c*; gebied *nt*
zoo [zuː] *n* (pl ~s) dierentuin *c*
zoology [zou'ɔlədʒi] *n* zoölogie *c*

Culinaire woordenlijst

Spijzen

almond amandel
anchovy ansjovis
angel food cake witte, ronde cake, gemaakt van suiker, eiwit en bloem
angels on horseback geroosterde, met spek omwikkelde oesters
appetizer borrelhapje
apple appel
  ~ **charlotte** lagen van appels en sneetjes boord met vanille en slagroom
  ~ **dumpling** appelbol
  ~ **sauce** appelmoes
apricot abrikoos
Arbroath smoky gerookte schelvis
artichoke artisjok
asparagus asperge
  ~ **tip** aspergepunt
aspic koude schotel in gelei
assorted gevarieerd, gemengd
bacon spek
  ~ **and eggs** spiegeleieren met spek
bagel klein kransvormig broodje
baked in de oven gebakken, gebraden
  ~ **Alaska** omelette sibérienne
  ~ **beans** witte bonen in tomatensaus

  ~ **potato** hele, ongeschilde aardappel, in de oven gebakken
Bakewell tart amandeltaart met jam
baloney worstsoort
banana banaan
  ~ **split** in de lengte gehalveerde banaan met ijs, noten en overgoten met vruchtensiroop of vloeibare chocolade
barbecue 1) gehakt rundvlees in tomatensaus in een broodje geserveerd 2) maaltijd van geroosterd vlees in de open lucht
  ~ **sauce** zeer scherpe tomatensaus
barbecued geroosterd op houtskool
basil basilicum
bass baars
bean boon
beef rundvlees
  ~ **olive** blinde vink
beefburger gehakte, geroosterde biefstuk geserveerd in een broodje
beet, beetroot rode biet
bilberry blauwe bosbes
bill rekening
  ~ **of fare** menu

biscuit 1) koekje (GB) 2) broodje (US)

black pudding bloedworst

blackberry braam

blackcurrant zwarte bes

bloater verse bokking

blood sausage bloedworst

blueberry blauwe bosbes

boiled gekookt

Bologna (sausage) worstsoort

bone bot

boned ontbeend

Boston baked beans witte bonen met stukjes spek en stroop

Boston cream pie taart met vlavulling en chocoladeglazuur

brains hersenen

braised gestoofd

bramble pudding bramenpudding, vaak met schijfjes appel erin

braunschweiger gerookte leverworst

bread brood

breaded gepaneerd

breakfast ontbijt

bream brasem

breast borst (stuk)

brisket borststuk

broad bean tuinboon

broth bouillon

brown Betty afwisselende lagen appel, perzik of kers en paneermeel, met suiker en kruiderijen, in de oven gebakken

brunch ontbijt en lunch gecombineerd

brussels sprout spruitje

bubble and squeak soort pannekoek van gebakken aardappelen en kool, soms met vlees

bun 1) krentebroodje (GB) 2) klein, luchtig broodje (US)

butter boter

buttered beboterd

cabbage kool

Caesar salad sla met geroosterde, naar knoflook smakende brooddobbelsteentjes, anjovis en geraspte kaas

cake gebak, koek, cake, taart

cakes koekjes, taartjes

calf kalfsvlees

Canadian bacon gerookt spek in dikke plakken gesneden

canapé belegd sneetje brood

cantaloupe wratmeloen, kanteloep

caper kappertje

capercaillie, capercailzie auerhoen

carp karper

carrot wortel

cashew vrucht van de cajouboom

casserole gestoofd

catfish meerval (vis)

catsup ketchup

cauliflower bloemkool

celery selderie

cereal graansoorten voor bij het ontbijt, zoals maïsvlokken, havermout, met melk en suiker
hot ~ havermoutpap

chateaubriand dubbele biefstuk van de haas

check rekening

Cheddar (cheese) stevige kaas met een milde, zurige smaak

cheese kaas
~ board kaasassortiment
~ cake kaaskoekje

cheeseburger gehakte, geroosterde biefstuk met schijfje kaas, opgediend in een broodje

chef's salad salade van ham, kip, eieren, tomaten, sla en kaas

cherry kers

chestnut tamme kastanje

chicken kip

chicory 1) Brussels lof (GB) 2) andijvie (US)

chili con carne gehakt rundvlees gestoofd met bruine bonen, Spaanse pepers en komijn

chili pepper rode Spaanse pepers

chips 1) patates frites (GB) 2) aardappel chips (US)

chitt(er)lings varkensspens

chive bieslook

chocolate chocolade
~ **pudding** 1) chocoladepudding bereid met verkruimelde koekjes, suiker, eieren en bloem (GB) 2) chocolademousse (US)

choice keus

chop kotelet
~ **suey** gerecht, bereid uit fijngesneden varkensvlees en kip, groenten en rijst (tjap tjoy)

chopped fijngehakt

chowder dikke soep van vis, schaal- en schelpdieren of kip, met groenten

Christmas pudding speciaal Kerstgebak, soms geflambeerd

chutney sterke Indische kruiderij

cinnamon kaneel

clam steenmossel

club sandwich dubbele sandwich met kip, spek, sla, tomaat en mayonaise

cobbler vruchtenmoes met deeg, soms met ijs

cock-a-leekie soup preisoep met kip

coconut kokosnoot

cod kabeljauw

Colchester oyster beste soort Engelse oester

cold cuts/meat koud vlees

coleslaw koolsla

compote vruchten op sap

condiment kruiderij

consommé heldere soep

cooked gekookt

cookie koekje

corn 1) koren (GB) 2) maïs (US)
~ **on the cob** maïskolf

cornflakes maïsvlokken

cottage cheese witte, verse kaas

cottage pie gehakt vlees met uien, bedekt met aardappelpuree in de oven gebakken

course gerecht

cover charge couvert

crab krab

cracker droog beschuit van bladerdeeg

cranberry veenbes
~ **sauce** veenbessengelei

crawfish, crayfish 1) rivierkreeft 2) langoest (GB) 3) steurgarnaal (US)

cream 1) room 2) vlaai (dessert) 3) gebonden soep
~ **cheese** roomkaas
~ **puff** roomsoes

creamed potatoes aardappelen in witte roomsaus

creole op Creoolse wijze bereid; over het algemeen zeer pikant, met tomaten, paprika's en uien, geserveerd met rijst

cress waterkers

crisps chips

croquette kroket

crumpet rond, licht broodje, geroosterd en beboterd

cucumber komkommer

Cumberland ham zeer fijne, gerookte Engelse ham

Cumberland sauce rode bessengelei, op smaak gemaakt met wijn, sinaasappelsap en kruiderijen

cupcake klein rond gebakje

cured gezouten, gerookt, gepekeld (vis en vlees)

currant krent
curried met kerrie
curry kerrie
custard custardvla
cutlet vleeslapje, kotelet
dab schar
Danish pastry soort luchtig koffie-
brood
date dadel
Derby cheese gele kaas met pi-
kante smaak
devilled sterk gekruid
devil's food cake machtige choco-
ladetaart
devils on horseback gekookte
pruimen, gevuld met amandelen en ansjovis, omwikkeld met
spek, geroosterd en geserveerd
op toost
Devonshire cream dikke, klonte-
rige room
diced in dobbelsteentjes gesneden
diet food volgens voedselleer bereid
dill dille
dinner diner, avondeten
dish schotel, gerecht
donut, doughnut soort oliebol
double cream volle room
Dover sole tong uit Dover, in Engeland zeer gewaardeerd
dressing 1) slasaus 2) vulsel voor
kalkoen (US)
Dublin Bay prawn steurgarnaal
duck eend
duckling jonge eend
dumpling knoedel
Dutch apple pie appeltaart bedekt
met een mengsel van boter en
bruine suiker
éclair langwerpig, met chocolade
of caramel geglaceerd room-
taartje
eel paling

egg ei
  boiled ~ gekookt
  fried ~ spiegelei
  hard-boiled ~ hardgekookt
  poached ~ gepocheerd
  scrambled ~ roerei
  soft-boiled ~ zachtgekookt
eggplant aubergine, eierplant
endive 1) andijvie (GB) 2) Brussels lof (US)
entrecôte tussenrib
entrée 1) voorgerecht (GB) 2)
hoofdgerecht (US)
escalope schnitzel
fennel venkel
fig vijg
filet mignon kalfs- of varkens-
haasje
fillet filet van vlees of vis
finnan haddock gerookte schelvis
fish vis
  ~ **and chips** gebakken vis met
  frites
  ~ **cake** viskoekje
flan vla, ronde taart met vruchten
flapjack (appel)flap
flounder bot
forcemeat farce, gehakt
fowl gevogelte
frankfurter knakworst
French bean slaboon
French bread stokbrood
French dressing 1) slasaus in olie,
azijn en tuinkruiden (GB) 2)
romige slasaus met ketchup
(US)
french fries patates frites
French toast wentelteefje
fresh vers
fricassée ragoût, vleeshachee
fried gebakken in een koekepan of
in de olie
fritter beignet, poffertje
frogs' legs kikkerbilletjes

frosting suikerglazuur

fruit vrucht

fry bakken

game wild

gammon gerookte ham

garfish geep (snoekachtige zeevis)

garlic knoflook

garnish garnituur

gherkin augurkje

giblets afval van gevogelte

ginger gember

goose gans

  ~ **berry** kruisbes

grape druif

  ~ **fruit** pompelmoes

grated geraspt

gravy vleesjus

grayling vlagzalm

green bean slaboon

green pepper groene paprika

green salad sla

greens groenten

grilled geroosterd

grilse jonge zalm

grouse korhoen

gumbo 1) groente van Afrikaanse afkomst 2) Creools gerecht van vlees, kip of vis, met *okra*zaden, uien, tomaten en kruiden

haddock gerookte schelvis

haggis hart, longen en lever van een schaap fijn gehakt en in de maag gekookt met reuzel, havermeel en uien

hake stokvis

halibut heilbot

ham and eggs spiegeleieren met ham

hamburger gehakt, geroosterd rundvlees opgediend in een broodje

hare haas

haricot bean prinsessenboon, witte boon

hash 1) gehakt of fijngesneden vlees 2) hachee met aardappelen en groenten

hazelnut hazelnoot

heart hart

herb tuinkruid

herring haring

home-made eigengemaakt, van het huis

hominy grits brij van maïsgrutten

honey honing

  ~ **dew melon** zoete meloen met geelgroen vruchtvlees

hors-d'œuvre voorgerecht (Engeland)

horse-radish mierikswortel

hot 1) heet, warm 2) sterk gekruid

  ~ **cross bun** fijn broodje gevuld met rozijnen en kruisvormig bedekt met glazuur, wordt in de vastentijd gegeten (brioche)

  ~ **dog** hot dog, warme worst in een broodje

huckleberry blauwe bosbes

hush puppy beignet van maïsmeel en uien

ice-cream ijs

iced gekoeld

icing suikerglazuur

Idaho baked potato soort bintje, ongeschild in de oven gepoft

Irish stew hutspot van schapevlees, aardappelen en uien

Italian dressing slasaus van olie, azijn en tuinkruiden

jellied in gelei

Jell-O gelatinedessert

jelly jam; gelei

Jerusalem artichoke aardpeer

John Dory zonnevis (zeevis)

jugged hare hazepeper

juice sap

juniper berry jeneverbes

junket gestremde melk (wrongel),

gesuikerd
kale boerenkool
kedgeree stukjes vis met rijst, eiren, boter, wordt vaak als warm gerecht aan het ontbijt geserveerd
kidney nier
kipper bokking
lamb lamsvlees
Lancashire hot pot schotel in de oven van ragoût van lamsvlees en nieren met uien, kruiderijen en aardappelen
larded gelardeerd
lean mager
leek prei
leg bout
lemon citroen
~ **sole** scharretong
lentil linze
lettuce kropsla, veldsla
lima bean tuinboon
lime limoen, kleine groene citroen
liver lever
loaf brood
lobster kreeft
loin lendestuk
Long Island duck eend van Long Island, in de VS zeer goed bekend staande soort
low-calorie laag caloriegehalte
lox gerookte zalm
macaroon bitterkoekje
mackerel makreel
maize maïs
mandarin mandarijntje
maple syrup ahornstroop
marinated gemarineerd
marjoram marjolein
marmalade marmelade van sinaasappelen of andere citrusvruchten
marrow beenmerg
~ **bone** mergpijp

marshmallow Amerikaans snoepgoed; *marshmallows* worden vaak aan warme chocola en allerlei soorten desserts toegevoegd
marzipan marsepein
mashed potatoes aardappelpuree
meal maaltijd
meat vlees
~ **ball** gehaktbal
~ **loaf** gehaktbrood
~ **pâté** vleespastei
medium (done) net gaar
melon meloen
melted gesmolten
Melton Mowbray pie pastei bestaande uit gehakt vlees en kruiden
meringue schuimgebak, schuimpje
milk melk
mince fijnhakken
~ **pie** pasteitje met krenten, rozijnen, fijngehakte geconfijte vruchten en appelen (met of zonder vlees)
minced fijngehakt
~ **meat** fijngehakt vlees
mint munt (kruid)
minute steak kort gebakken biefstuk
mixed gemengd
~ **grill** aan een stokje geregen, geroosterde stukjes vlees
molasses melasse, stroop
morel morille, zeer gewaardeerde paddestoelsoort
mousse 1) dessert van geklopte eieren en slagroom 2) luchtig pasteitje
mulberry moerbei
mullet harder (vis gelijkend op een karper)
mulligatawny soup zeer sterk ge

kruide soep van Indische afkomst met wortels, uien, *chutney* en kip met kerrie
mushroom paddestoel
muskmelon meloen
mussel mossel
mustard mosterd
mutton schapevlees
noodle noedel
nut noot
oatmeal (porridge) havermoutpap
oil olie
okra zaad van de *gumbo*, wordt
gebruikt om soepen en ragoût-
sausen aan te dikken
olive olijf
onion ui
orange sinaasappel
ox tongue ossetong
oxtail ossestaart
oyster oester
pancake pannekoek
Parmesan (cheese) Parmezaanse
kaas
parsley peterselie
parsnip pastinaak, witte peen
partridge patrijs
pastry banket, gebakje, taartje
pasty pastei
pea doperwt
peach perzik
peanut olienoot, pinda
  ~ **butter** pindakaas
pear peer
pearl barley parelgerst
pepper peper
  ~ **mint** pepermunt
perch baars
persimmon dadelpruim
pheasant fazant
pickerel jonge snoek
pickle 1) groente of geconfijte
vrucht in pekelzuur 2) in het
bijzonder augurkje (US)

pickled in pekel bewaard
pie pastei, vaak met een deksel
van bladerdeeg, gevuld met
vlees, groenten of vruchten
pig varken
pigeon duif
pike snoek
pineapple ananas
plaice schol
plain natuur, zonder iets erin
plate bord, schaal
plum pruim
  ~ **pudding** speciaal Kerstgebak, soms geflambeerd
poached gepocheerd
popcorn gepofte maïskorrels
popover klein, luchtig broodje
pork varkensvlees
porridge havermoutpap
porterhouse steak biefstuk van de
haas
pot roast met groenten gesmoord
rundvlees
potato aardappel
  ~ **chips** 1) patates frites (GB)
2) aardappel chips (US)
  ~ **in its jacket** aardappel in de
schil gekookt en opgediend
potted shrimps garnalen in gesmolten boter, koud opgediend
in een vorm
poultry gevogelte, pluimvee
prawn grote garnaal
prune gedroogde pruim
ptarmigan sneeuwhoen
pudding soepel of stevig beslag
van meel en eieren, gegarneerd
met vlees, vis, groenten of
vruchten, in de oven gebakken
of gaargestoomd; nagerecht
pumpernickel zwart roggebrood
pumpkin pompoen
quail kwartel
quince kweepeer

rabbit konijn
radish radijs
rainbow trout regenboogforel
raisin rozijn
rare ongaar
raspberry framboos
raw rauw
red mullet soort harder (zeevis)
red (sweet) pepper rode paprika
redcurrant rode bes
relish kruiderij gemaakt van fijn-
    gesneden groente in azijn
rhubarb rabarber
rib (of beef) ribstuk (van het rund)
ribe-eye steak entrecôte
rice rijst
rissole vlees- of viskroket
river trout rivierforel
roast braadstuk
roasted gebraden
Rock Cornish hen piepkuiken
roe viskuit
roll broodje
rollmop herring rolmops, gemari-
    neerde haringfilet
round steak runderschijf
Rubens sandwich cornedbeef op
    een toostje, met zuurkool, kaas
    en slasaus; warm opgediend
rump steak biefstuk
rusk beschuit
rye bread roggebrood
saddle lendestuk
saffron saffraan
sage salie
salad sla
    ~ **bar** verschillende soorten
    slaatjes, tomaten, prinsessen-
    bonen
    ~ **cream** slasaus, licht gezoet
    ~ **dressing** slasaus
salmon zalm
    ~ **trout** zalmforel
salt zout

salted gezouten
sardine sardien
sauce saus
sauerkraut zuurkool
sausage worst
sauté(ed) snel in boter, olie of vet
    gebakken
scallop 1) kamschelp 2) kalfslapje
scampi steurgarnaal
scone zacht broodje, warm geser-
    veerd, met boter en jam
Scotch broth runder- of schape-
    bouillon met groenten
Scotch woodcock toost met roerei
    en ansjovis
sea bass zeebaars
sea kale zeekool
seafood zeebanket
(in) season (in het) seizoen
seasoning kruiderij
service bediening
    ~ **charge** bedieningstarief
    ~ **included** inclusief bediening
    ~ **not included** exclusief bedie-
    ning
set menu menu van de dag
shad elft (zeevis)
shallot sjalot
shellfish schelp- en schaaldieren
sherbet sorbet
shoulder schouderstuk
shredded wheat gesponnen tarwe,
    wordt bij het ontbijt gegeten
shrimp garnaal
silverside (of beef) onderste deel
    van runderschenkel
sirloin steak lendestuk (van het
    rund)
skewer vleespen
slice sneet(je), plak
sliced in plakken gesneden
sloppy Joe gehakt vlees in scherpe
    tomatensaus, geserveerd in een
    broodje

smelt spiering
smoked gerookt
snack hapje, snack
sole tong (vis)
soup soep
sour zuur
soused herring gepekelde haring
spare rib krabbetje
spice kruiderij
spinach spinazie
spiny lobster langoest
(on a) spit (aan het) spit
sponge cake Moscovisch gebak
sprat sprot
squash mergpompoen
starter voorgerecht
steak and kidney pie pastei in bladerdeeg van niertjes en rundvlees
steamed gekookt
stew stoofschotel
Stilton (cheese) een van de beste Engelse kazen, wit of blauw geaderd
strawberry aardbei
string bean slaboon
stuffed gevuld
stuffing vulling
suck(l)ing pig speenvarken
sugar suiker
sugarless zonder suiker
sundae roomijs met vruchten, noten, slagroom en siroop
supper avondmaaltijd
swede knolraap
sweet 1) zoet 2) dessert
 ~ **corn** zoete maïs
 ~ **potato** bataat, knol van een oorspronkelijk tropisch gewas, rijk aan zetmeel en suiker
sweetbread zwezerik
Swiss cheese Emmentaler kaas
Swiss roll opgerold gebak met jam ertussen (koninginnebrood)

Swiss steak met groenten en kruiderijen gestoofde runderlappen
T-bone steak lendestuk van het rund met een T-vormig bot erin
table d'hôte open tafel in een hotel
tangerine mandarijntje
tarragon dragon
tart (vruchten)taart
tenderloin filet van vlees
Thousand Island dressing slasaus, bestaande uit mayonaise met piment, noten, olijven, selderie, uien, peterselie en eieren
thyme tijm
toad-in-the-hole rundvlees (of worstjes) in beslag gedoopt en in de oven gebakken
toast geroosterd brood
toasted getoost
 ~ **cheese** toost met gesmolten kaas
tomato tomaat
tongue tong (vlees)
tournedos ossehaas in dikke plakken
treacle melasse, stroop
trifle cake met amandelen en gelei, in sherry (of brandewijn) gedrenkt, opgediend met vla of slagroom
tripe pens
trout forel
truffle truffel (paddestoel)
tuna, tunny tonijn
turbot tarbot
turkey kalkoen
turnip raap, knol
turnover flap
turtle schildpad
underdone ongaar
vanilla vanille
veal kalfsvlees
 ~ **bird** blinde vink
 ~ **escalope** kalfsoester

vegetable groente
~ **marrow** mergpompoen, courgette
venison wildbraad
vichyssoise preisoep, koud geserveerd
vinegar azijn
Virginia baked ham ham in de
oven geroosterd, in inkepingen
in het vel worden stukjes ananas, kersen en kruidnagels
gestoken waarna de ham
met het vruchtesap geglaceerd
wordt
wafer wafeltje
waffle warme wafel met boter,
stroop of honing
walnut walnoot
water ice sorbet
watercress waterkers

watermelon watermeloen
well-done gaar
Welsh rabbit/rarebit gesmolten
kaas op geroosterd brood
whelk kinkhoorn (wulk)
whipped cream slagroom
whitebait witvis
wine list wijnkaart
woodcock (hout)snip
Worcestershire sauce zoetzure
saus bestaande uit soja en vele
andere ingrediënten
York ham zeer goed bekend staande ham, opgediend in dunne
plakken
Yorkshire pudding knappend gebakken deeg, geserveerd met
rosbief
zucchini mergpompoen, courgette
zwieback beschuit

Dranken

ale donker, zoetachtig bier, onder
hoge temperatuur gegist
bitter ~ bitter bier, nogal zwaar
brown ~ gebotteld, zoetachtig
donker bier
light ~ gebotteld licht bier
mild ~ donker bier van het
vat met een zeer uitgesproken
smaak
pale ~ gebotteld licht bier
applejack Amerikaanse appel-
brandewijn
Athol Brose haver vermengd met
kokend water, honing en whisky

Bacardi cocktail cocktail van rum
en gin met grenadinesiroop en
limoensap
barley water frisdrank gemaakt
van parelgerst met citroen-
smaak
barley wine donker bier met hoog
alcoholgehalte
beer bier
bottled ~ gebotteld bier
draft, draught ~ getapt bier,
bier van het vat
bitters kruidenaperitieven, de
spijsvertering bevorderende
alcoholische dranken

black velvet champagne met toevoeging van *stout* (vaak ter begeleiding van oesters)

bloody Mary cocktail van wodka, tomatesap en kruiderijen

bourbon Amerikaanse whisky, hoofdzakelijk van mais gestookt

brandy 1) verzamelnaam voor brandewijnsoorten gemaakt van druiven en andere vruchten 2) cognac

~ **Alexander** cocktail van brandewijn, crème de cacao en room

British wines wijnen in Engeland gegist; gemaakt van geïmporteerde druiven (of van geïmporteerd druivesap)

cherry brandy kersenlikeur

chocolate chocolademelk

cider cider

~ **cup** mengsel van cider, kruiderijen, suiker en ijs

claret rode Bordeauxwijn

cobbler *long drink* gemaakt van vruchten, waaraan men wijn of alcohol toevoegt

coffee koffie

~ **with cream** met room

black ~ zonder melk

caffeine-free ~ cafeïnevrij

white ~ half koffie, half melk; koffie verkeerd

cordial hartversterking

cream room

cup verfrissende drank gemaakt van gekoelde wijn, sodawater en een likeur of andere sterkedrank met een schijfje citroen of sinaasappel

daiquiri cocktail van rum, suiker, limoensap

double dubbele portie

Drambuie likeur gemaakt van whisky en honing

dry martini 1) droge vermouth (GB) 2) cocktail van droge vermouth en gin (US)

egg-nog alcoholische drank op basis van rum of andere sterkedrank, vermengd met geklopt eigeel en suiker

gin and it gin met Italiaanse vermouth

gin-fizz gin met citroensap, sodawater en suiker

ginger ale frisdrank met gembersmaak

ginger beer gemberbier

grasshopper cocktail van crème de menthe, crème de cacao en room

Guinness (stout) donker zoetsmakend bier met een hoog mout- en hopgehalte

half pint ongeveer 3 dl

highball alcoholische drank, zoals whisky, vermengd met water, sodawater of *ginger ale*

iced gekoeld, ijskoud

Irish coffee koffie met suiker en slagroom, waaraan men een scheut Ierse whisky toevoegt

Irish Mist Ierse likeur van whisky en honing

Irish whiskey Ierse whisky minder scherp dan Schotse whisky, bevat naast gerst ook rogge, haver en tarwe

juice sap

lager licht bier, koud geserveerd

lemon squash kwast

lemonade limonade

lime juice limoensap

liqueur likeur

liquor sterkedrank

long drink sterkedrank met tonic, sodawater of gewoon water en

ijsblokjes
madeira madera
Manhattan cocktail van Amerikaanse whisky en vermouth met
angostura
milk melk
mineral water mineraalwater
mulled wine bisschopswijn; warme, gekruide wijn
neat onvermengd. puur, zonder
water of ijs
old-fashioned cocktail van whisky,
angostura, sinaasappel schijfje,
suiker en maraskijnkersen
on the rocks met ijsblokjes
Ovaltine ovomaltine
Pimm's cup(s) sterkedrank met
vruchtesap, eventueel aange-
lengd met sodawater
~ **No. 1** met gin
~ **No. 2** met whisky
~ **No. 3** met rum
~ **No. 4** met brandewijn
pink champagne roze champagne
pink lady cocktail van eiwit, calva-
dos, citroensap, grenadine en
gin
pint ongeveer 6 dl
porter donker, bitter bier
quart 1,14 l (US 0,95 l)
root beer gezoete frisdrank met
aromat uit plantenwortels en
kruiden
rye (whiskey) whisky uit rogge
gestookt; zwaarder en scherper
van smaak dan *bourbon*
scotch (whisky) Schotse whisky,
een uit gerst en maïs (grain
whisky) gestookte sterkedrank,

vaak vermengd met malt whisky, uitsluitend uit gemoute gerst
gestookt
screwdriver wodka met sinaasappelsap
shandy *bitter ale* vermengd met
limonade of met *ginger beer*
short drink sterkedrank, onverdund gedronken
shot scheut sterkedrank
sloe gin-fizz sleepruimlikeur
(vrucht van de sleedoorn) met
citroensap en sodawater
soda water sodawater, spuitwater
soft drink frisdrank
spirits spiritualiën, gedistilleerde
dranken
stinger cognac en crème de
menthe
stout donker bier met veel hop
gebrouwen
straight sterkedrank onverdund
gedronken, puur
tea thee
toddy grog
Tom Collins *long drink* van gin,
citroensap, spuitwater en suiker
tonic (water) tonic, spuitwater met
kininesmaak
vodka wodka
whisky sour whisky, citroensap,
suiker en sodawater
wine wijn
dessert ~ zoete
dry ~ droge
red ~ rode
sparkling ~ mousserende
sweet ~ zoete (dessertwijn)
white ~ witte

Engelse onregelmatige werkwoorden

De onderstaande lijst geeft de Engelse onregelmatige werkwoorden aan. De samengestelde werkwoorden of werkwoorden met een voorvoegsel worden als de grondwerkwoorden vervoegd, bijvoorbeeld: *withdraw* wordt vervoegd als *draw* en *rebuild* als *build*.

Onbepaalde wijs	Onvoltooid verleden tijd	Verleden deelwoord	
arise	arose	arisen	*opstaan*
awake	awoke	awoken	*ontwaken*
be	was	been	*zijn*
bear	bore	borne	*dragen*
beat	beat	beaten	*slaan*
become	became	become	*worden*
begin	began	begun	*aanvangen*
bend	bent	bent	*buigen*
bet	bet	bet	*wedden*
bid	bade/bid	bidden/bid	*verzoeken*
bind	bound	bound	*binden*
bite	bit	bitten	*bijten*
bleed	bled	bled	*bloeden*
blow	blew	blown	*blazen*
break	broke	broken	*breken*
breed	bred	bred	*fokken*
bring	brought	brought	*brengen*
build	built	built	*bouwen*
burn	burnt/burned	burnt/burned	*branden*
burst	burst	burst	*barsten*
buy	bought	bought	*kopen*
can*	could	—	*kunnen*
cast	cast	cast	*werpen*
catch	caught	caught	*vangen*
choose	chose	chosen	*kiezen*
cling	clung	clung	*vastklemmen*
clothe	clothed/clad	clothed/clad	*kleden*
come	came	come	*komen*
cost	cost	cost	*kosten*
creep	crept	crept	*kruipen*
cut	cut	cut	*snijden*
deal	dealt	dealt	*uitdelen*
dig	dug	dug	*graven*
do (he does)	did	done	*doen*
draw	drew	drawn	*trekken*
dream	dreamt/dreamed	dreamt/dreamed	*dromen*
drink	drank	drunk	*drinken*
drive	drove	driven	*rijden*
dwell	dwelt	dwelt	*vertoeven*

* tegenwoordige tijd

eat	ate	eaten	*eten*
fall	fell	fallen	*vallen*
feed	fed	fed	*voeden*
feel	felt	felt	*voelen*
fight	fought	fought	*vechten*
find	found	found	*vinden*
flee	fled	fled	*vluchten*
fling	flung	flung	*werpen*
fly	flew	flown	*vliegen*
forsake	forsook	forsaken	*verzaken*
freeze	froze	frozen	*vriezen*
get	got	got	*krijgen*
give	gave	given	*geven*
go	went	gone	*gaan*
grind	ground	ground	*malen*
grow	grew	grown	*groeien*
hang	hung	hung	*(op)hangen*
have	had	had	*hebben*
hear	heard	heard	*horen*
hew	hewed	hewed/hewn	*hakken*
hide	hid	hidden	*verstoppen*
hit	hit	hit	*slaan*
hold	held	held	*houden*
hurt	hurt	hurt	*pijn doen*
keep	kept	kept	*houden*
kneel	knelt	knelt	*knielen*
knit	knitted/knit	knitted/knit	*breien*
know	knew	known	*weten*
lay	laid	laid	*leggen*
lead	led	led	*leiden*
lean	leant/leaned	leant/leaned	*leunen*
leap	leapt/leaped	leapt/leaped	*springen*
learn	learnt/learned	learnt/learned	*leren*
leave	left	left	*verlaten*
lend	lent	lent	*lenen(aan)*
let	let	let	*laten*
lie	lay	lain	*liggen*
light	lit/lighted	lit/lighted	*aansteken*
lose	lost	lost	*verliezen*
make	made	made	*maken*
may*	might	—	*mogen, kunnen*
mean	meant	meant	*bedoelen*
meet	met	met	*ontmoeten*
mow	mowed	mowed/mown	*maaien*
must*	—	—	*moeten*
ought (to)*	—	—	*moeten*
pay	paid	paid	*betalen*
put	put	put	*zetten*
read	read	read	*lezen*

* tegenwoordige tijd

rid	rid	rid	*zich ontdoen (van)*
ride	rode	ridden	*rijden*
ring	rang	rung	*bellen*
rise	rose	risen	*opstaan*
run	ran	run	*rennen*
saw	sawed	sawn	*zagen*
say	said	said	*zeggen*
see	saw	seen	*zien*
seek	sought	sought	*zoeken*
sell	sold	sold	*verkopen*
send	sent	sent	*verzenden*
set	set	set	*zetten*
sew	sewed	sewed/sewn	*naaien*
shake	shook	shaken	*schudden*
shall*	should	—	*zullen*
shed	shed	shed	*vergieten*
shine	shone	shone	*schijnen*
shoot	shot	shot	*schieten*
show	showed	shown	*tonen*
shrink	shrank	shrunk	*krimpen*
shut	shut	shut	*sluiten*
sing	sang	sung	*zingen*
sink	sank	sunk	*zinken*
sit	sat	sat	*zitten*
sleep	slept	slept	*slapen*
slide	slid	slid	*glijden*
sling	slung	slung	*slingeren*
slink	slunk	slunk	*sluipen*
slit	slit	slit	*opensnijden*
smell	smelled/smelt	smelled/smelt	*ruiken*
sow	sowed	sown/sowed	*zaaien*
speak	spoke	spoken	*spreken*
speed	sped/speeded	sped/speeded	*zich haasten*
spell	spelt/spelled	spelt/spelled	*spellen*
spend	spent	spent	*uitgeven*
spill	spilt/spilled	spilt/spilled	*morsen*
spin	spun	spun	*spinnen*
spit	spat	spat	*spuwen*
split	split	split	*splijten*
spoil	spoilt/spoiled	spoilt/spoiled	*bederven*
spread	spread	spread	*spreiden*
spring	sprang	sprung	*ontspringen*
stand	stood	stood	*staan*
steal	stole	stolen	*stelen*
stick	stuck	stuck	*kleven*
sting	stung	stung	*steken*
stink	stank/stunk	stunk	*stinken*
strew	strewed	strewed/strewn	*strooien*
stride	strode	stridden	*schrijden*

* tegenwoordige tijd

strike	struck	struck/stricken	*slaan*
string	strung	strung	*rijgen*
strive	strove	striven	*streven*
swear	swore	sworn	*zweren*
sweep	swept	swept	*vegen*
swell	swelled	swollen	*zwellen*
swim	swam	swum	*zwemmen*
swing	swung	swung	*slingeren*
take	took	taken	*nemen*
teach	taught	taught	*onderwijzen*
tear	tore	torn	*scheuren*
tell	told	told	*vertellen*
think	thought	thought	*denken*
throw	threw	thrown	*werpen*
thrust	thrust	thrust	*duwen*
tread	trod	trodden	*treden*
wake	woke/waked	woken/waked	*wekken*
wear	wore	worn	*dragen*
weave	wove	woven	*weven*
weep	wept	wept	*huilen*
will*	would	—	*zullen*
win	won	won	*winnen*
wind	wound	wound	*opwinden*
wring	wrung	wrung	*wringen*
write	wrote	written	*schrijven*

---

* tegenwoordige tijd

Engelse afkortingen

AA	*Automobile Association*	Britse Automobielclub
AAA	*American Automobile Association*	Amerikaanse Automobielclub
ABC	*American Broadcasting Company*	Amerikaanse radio- en televisiemaatschappij
A.D.	*anno Domini*	na Christus
Am.	*America; American*	Amerika; Amerikaans
a.m.	*ante meridiem (before noon)*	de tijd tussen 0 en 12 uur
Amtrak	*American railroad corporation*	Amerikaanse spoorwegmaatschappij
AT & T	*American Telephone and Telegraph Company*	Amerikaanse telefoon- en telegraafmaatschappij
Ave.	*avenue*	avenue
BBC	*British Broadcasting Corporation*	Britse radio- en televisie- maatschappij
B.C.	*before Christ*	voor Christus
bldg.	*building*	gebouw
Blvd.	*boulevard*	boulevard
B.R.	*British Rail*	Britse Spoorwegen
Brit.	*Britain; British*	Groot-Brittannië, Brits
Bros.	*brothers*	gebroeders
¢	*cent*	1/100 van een dollar
Can.	*Canada; Canadian*	Canada; Canadees
CBS	*Columbia Broadcasting System*	Amerikaanse radio- en televisiemaatschappij
CID	*Criminal Investigation Department*	afdeling criminele recherche van Scotland Yard
CNR	*Canadian National Railway*	Canadese Nationale Spoorwegen
c/o	*(in) care of*	per adres
Co.	*company*	maatschappij
Corp.	*corporation*	vennootschap
CPR	*Canadian Pacific Railways*	Canadese spoorweg- maatschappij
D.C.	*District of Columbia*	district in de V.S. waarin de hoofdstad Washington ligt
DDS	*Doctor of Dental Science*	doctor in de tandheelkunde
dept.	*department*	departement, afdeling
EEC	*European Economic Community*	EEG, Europese Economische Gemeenschap
e.g.	*for instance*	bijvoorbeeld

Eng.	*England; English*	Engeland; Engels
excl.	*excluding; exclusive*	exclusief
ft.	*foot/feet*	voet
GB	*Great Britain*	Groot-Brittannië
H.E.	*His/Her Excellency;*	Zijne/Hare Excellentie;
	His Eminence	Zijne Eminentie
H.H.	*His Holiness*	Zijne Heiligheid
H.M.	*His/Her Majesty*	Zijne/Hare Majesteit
H.M.S.	*Her Majesty's ship*	Harer Majesteits schip
		(Brits oorlogsschip)
hp	*horsepower*	paardekracht
Hwy	*highway*	autoweg
i.e.	*that is to say*	d.w.z., dat wil zeggen
in.	*inch*	duim (2,54 cm)
Inc.	*incorporated*	naamloze vennootschap
incl.	*including, inclusive*	inclusief
£	*pound sterling*	pond sterling
L.A.	*Los Angeles*	Los Angeles
Ltd.	*limited*	naamloze vennootschap
M.D.	*Doctor of Medicine*	arts
M.P.	*Member of Parliament*	lid van het Lagerhuis
		(Engeland)
mph	*miles per hour*	Engelse mijl per uur
Mr.	*Mister*	meneer
Mrs.	*Missis*	mevrouw
Ms.	*Missis/Miss*	mevrouw/mejuffrouw
nat.	*national*	nationaal
NBC	*National Broadcasting*	Amerikaanse radio- en
	Company	televisiemaatschappij
No.	*number*	nummer
N.Y.C.	*New York City*	New York City
O.B.E.	*Officer (of the Order)*	Officier in de Orde
	of the British Empire	van het Britse Imperium
p.	*page; penny/pence*	bladzijde; 1/100 van een pond
p.a.	*per annum*	per jaar
Ph.D.	*Doctor of Philosophy*	doctor in de wijsbegeerte
p.m.	*post meridiem*	de tijd tussen 12 en 24 uur
	(after noon)	
PO	*Post Office*	postkantoor
POO	*post office order*	postorder
pop.	*population*	bevolking
P.T.O.	*please turn over*	zie ommezijde, a.u.b.
RAC	*Royal Automobile Club*	Koninklijke Britse
		Automobielclub

RCMP	*Royal Canadian Mounted Police*	Koninklijke Canadese Bereden Politie
Rd.	*road*	weg
ref.	*reference*	verwijzing
Rev.	*reverend*	dominee
RFD	*rural free delivery*	landelijke postbus
RR	*railroad*	spoorweg
RSVP	*please reply*	verzoeke gaarne antwoord
$	*dollar*	dollar
Soc.	*society*	maatschappij, genootschap
St.	*saint ; street*	sint; straat
STD	*Subscriber Trunk Dialling*	automatisch telefoonverkeer
UN	*United Nations*	V.N., Verenigde Naties
UPS	*United Parcel Service*	Amerikaanse pakketdienst
US	*United States*	Verenigde Staten
USS	*United States Ship*	Amerikaans oorlogsschip
VAT	*value added tax*	B.T.W.
VIP	*very important person*	zeer belangrijke persoon
Xmas	*Christmas*	Kerstmis
yd.	*yard*	yard (91,44 cm)
YMCA	*Young Men's Christian Association*	Christelijke Jongeren Vereniging
YWCA	*Young Women's Christian Association*	Christelijke Meisjes Vereniging
ZIP	*ZIP code*	postnummer

Telwoorden

Hoofdtelwoorden

0	zero
1	one
2	two
3	three
4	four
5	five
6	six
7	seven
8	eight
9	nine
10	ten
11	eleven
12	twelve
13	thirteen
14	fourteen
15	fifteen
16	sixteen
17	seventeen
18	eighteen
19	nineteen
20	twenty
21	twenty-one
22	twenty-two
23	twenty-three
24	twenty-four
25	twenty-five
30	thirty
40	forty
50	fifty
60	sixty
70	seventy
80	eighty
90	ninety
100	a/one hundred
230	two hundred and thirty
1,000	a/one thousand
10,000	ten thousand
100,000	a/one hundred thousand
1,000,000	a/one million

Rangtelwoorden

1st	first
2nd	second
3rd	third
4th	fourth
5th	fifth
6th	sixth
7th	seventh
8th	eighth
9th	ninth
10th	tenth
11th	eleventh
12th	twelfth
13th	thirteenth
14th	fourteenth
15th	fifteenth
16th	sixteenth
17th	seventeenth
18th	eighteenth
19th	nineteenth
20th	twentieth
21st	twenty-first
22nd	twenty-second
23rd	twenty-third
24th	twenty-fourth
25th	twenty-fifth
26th	twenty-sixth
27th	twenty-seventh
28th	twenty-eighth
29th	twenty-ninth
30th	thirtieth
40th	fortieth
50th	fiftieth
60th	sixtieth
70th	seventieth
80th	eightieth
90th	ninetieth
100th	hundredth
230th	two hundred and thirtieth
1,000th	thousandth

Tijd

De Engelsen en Amerikanen gebruiken het twaalf-uren systeem. De uitdrukking *a.m. (ante meridiem)* duidt op de uren tussen middernacht en 12 uur 's middags; *p.m. (post meridiem)* op de uren tussen 12 uur 's middags en middernacht. Engeland gaat momenteel geleidelijk over op het continentale systeem.

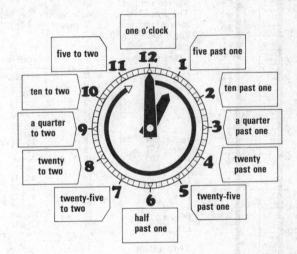

I'll come at seven a.m.	Ik kom om 7 uur 's morgens.
I'll come at two p.m.	Ik kom om 2 uur 's middags.
I'll come at eight p.m.	Ik kom om 8 uur 's avonds.

Dagen van de week

Sunday	zondag	*Thursday*	donderdag
Monday	maandag	*Friday*	vrijdag
Tuesday	dinsdag	*Saturday*	zaterdag
Wednesday	woensdag		

Conversion tables/Omrekentabellen

Meters en voeten
Het middelste cijfer geeft zowel meters als voeten aan, bijvoorbeeld 1 meter = 3,281 voet en 1 voet = 0,30 m.

Metres and feet
The figure in the middle stands for both metres and feet, e.g. 1 metre = 3.281 ft. and 1 foot = 0.30 m.

Meters/Metres		Voeten/Feet
0.30	1	3.281
0.61	2	6.563
0.91	3	9.843
1.22	4	13.124
1.52	5	16.403
1.83	6	19.686
2.13	7	22.967
2.44	8	26.248
2.74	9	29.529
3.05	10	32.810
3.66	12	39.372
4.27	14	45.934
6.10	20	65.620
7.62	25	82.023
15.24	50	164.046
22.86	75	246.069
30.48	100	328.092

Temperatuur
Voor het omrekenen van Celsius in Fahrenheit, moet u het aantal graden Celsius met 1,8 vermenigvuldigen en er dan 32 bij optellen.
Voor het omrekenen van Fahrenheit in Celsius, moet u 32 van het aantal graden Fahrenheit aftrekken en dan delen door 1,8.

Temperature
To convert Centigrade to Fahrenheit, multiply by 1.8 and add 32.
To convert Fahrenheit to Centigrade, subtract 32 from Fahrenheit and divide by 1.8.

Enkele nuttige zinnen	**Some Basic Phrases**
Alstublieft.	Please.
Hartelijk dank.	Thank you very much.
Niets te danken.	Don't mention it.
Goedemorgen.	Good morning.
Goedemiddag.	Good afternoon.
Goedenavond.	Good evening.
Goedenacht.	Good night.
Tot ziens.	Good-bye.
Tot straks.	See you later.
Waar is/Waar zijn…?	Where is/Where are…?
Hoe noemt u dit?	What do you call this?
Wat betekent dat?	What does that mean?
Spreekt u Engels?	Do you speak English?
Spreekt u Duits?	Do you speak German?
Spreekt u Frans?	Do you speak French?
Spreekt u Spaans?	Do you speak Spanish?
Spreekt u Italiaans?	Do you speak Italian?
Kunt u wat langzamer spreken, alstublieft?	Could you speak more slowly, please?
Ik begrijp het niet.	I don't understand.
Mag ik…hebben?	Can I have…?
Kunt u mij…tonen?	Can you show me…?
Kunt u mij zeggen…?	Can you tell me…?
Kunt u me helpen?	Can you help me, please?
Ik wil graag…	I'd like…
Wij willen graag…	We'd like…
Geeft u me…, alstublieft.	Please give me…
Brengt u me…, alstublieft.	Please bring me…
Ik heb honger.	I'm hungry.
Ik heb dorst.	I'm thirsty.
Ik ben verdwaald.	I'm lost.
Vlug!	Hurry up!
Er is/Er zijn…	There is/There are…
Er is geen/Er zijn geen…	There isn't/There aren't…

Aankomst	Arrival
Uw paspoort, alstublieft.	Your passport, please.
Hebt u iets aan te geven?	Have you anything to declare?
Nee, helemaal niets.	No, nothing at all.
Kunt u me met mijn bagage helpen, alstublieft?	Can you help me with my luggage, please?
Waar is de bus naar het centrum?	Where's the bus to the centre of town, please?
Hierlangs, alstublieft.	This way, please.
Waar kan ik een taxi krijgen?	Where can I get a taxi?
Wat kost het naar…?	What's the fare to…?
Breng me naar dit adres, alstublieft.	Take me to this address, please.
Ik heb haast.	I'm in a hurry.

Hotel	Hotel
Mijn naam is…	My name is…
Hebt u gereserveerd?	Have you a reservation?
Ik wil graag een kamer met bad.	I'd like a room with a bath.
Hoeveel kost het per nacht?	What's the price per night?
Mag ik de kamer zien?	May I see the room?
Wat is mijn kamernummer?	What's my room number, please?
Er is geen warm water.	There's no hot water.
Mag ik de directeur spreken, alstublieft?	May I see the manager, please?
Heeft er iemand voor mij opgebeld?	Did anyone telephone me?
Is er post voor mij?	Is there any mail for me?
Mag ik de rekening, alstublieft?	May I have my bill (check), please?

Uit eten	Eating out
Hebt u een menu à prix fixe?	Do you have a fixed-price menu?
Mag ik de spijskaart zien?	May I see the menu?
Kunt u ons een asbak brengen, alstublieft?	May we have an ashtray, please?

Waar is het toilet?	Where's the toilet, please?
Ik wil graag een voorgerecht.	I'd like an hors d'œuvre (starter).
Hebt u soep?	Have you any soup?
Ik wil graag vis.	I'd like some fish.
Wat voor vis hebt u?	What kind of fish do you have?
Ik wil graag een biefstuk.	I'd like a steak.
Wat voor groenten hebt u?	What vegetables have you got?
Niets meer, dank u.	Nothing more, thanks.
Wat wilt u drinken?	What would you like to drink?
Een pils, alstublieft.	I'll have a beer, please.
Ik wil graag een fles wijn.	I'd like a bottle of wine.
Mag ik de rekening, alstublieft?	May I have the bill (check), please?
Is de bediening inbegrepen?	Is service included?
Dank u, het was een uitstekende maaltijd.	Thank you, that was a very good meal.

Reizen

Travelling

Waar is het station?	Where's the railway station, please?
Waar is het loket?	Where's the ticket office, please?
Ik wil graag een kaartje naar...	I'd like a ticket to...
Eerste of tweede klas?	First or second class?
Eerste klas, alstublieft.	First class, please.
Enkele reis of retour?	Single or return (one way or roundtrip)?
Moet ik overstappen?	Do I have to change trains?
Van welk perron vertrekt de trein naar...?	What platform does the train for... leave from?
Waar is het dichtstbijzijnde metrostation?	Where's the nearest underground (subway) station?
Waar is het busstation?	Where's the bus station, please?
Hoe laat vertrekt de eerste bus naar...?	When's the first bus to...?
Wilt u me bij de volgende halte laten uitstappen?	Please let me off at the next stop.

Ontspanning	**Relaxing**
Wat wordt er in de bioscoop gegeven?	What's on at the cinema (movies)?
Hoe laat begint de film?	What time does the film begin?
Zijn er nog plaatsen vrij voor vanavond?	Are there any tickets for tonight?
Waar kunnen we gaan dansen?	Where can we go dancing?
Ontmoetingen	**Meeting people**
Dag mevrouw/juffrouw/ mijnheer.	How do you do.
Hoe maakt u het?	How are you?
Uitstekend, dank u. En u?	Very well, thank you. And you?
Mag ik u... voorstellen?	May I introduce...?
Mijn naam is...	My name is...
Prettig kennis met u te maken.	I'm very pleased to meet you.
Hoelang bent u al hier?	How long have you been here?
Het was mij een genoegen.	It was nice meeting you.
Hindert het u als ik rook?	Do you mind if I smoke?
Hebt u een vuurtje, alstublieft?	Do you have a light, please?
Mag ik u iets te drinken aanbieden?	May I get you a drink?
Mag ik u vanavond ten eten uitnodigen?	May I invite you for dinner tonight?
Waar spreken we af?	Where shall we meet?
Winkels en diensten	**Shops, stores and services**
Waar is de dichtstbijzijnde bank?	Where's the nearest bank, please?
Waar kan ik reischeques inwisselen?	Where can I cash some travellers' cheques?
Kunt u me wat kleingeld geven, alstublieft?	Can you give me some small change, please?
Waar is de dichtstbijzijnde apotheek?	Where's the nearest chemist's (pharmacy)?
Hoe kom ik daar?	How do I get there?
Is het te lopen?	Is it within walking distance?

Kunt u mij helpen, alstublieft?	Can you help me, please?
Hoeveel kost dit? En dat?	How much is this? And that?
Het is niet precies wat ik zoek.	It's not quite what I want.
Het bevalt me.	I like it.
Kunt u mij iets tegen zonnebrand aanbevelen?	Can you recommend something for sunburn?
Knippen, alstublieft.	I'd like a haircut, please.
Ik wil een manicure, alstublieft.	I'd like a manicure, please.

De weg vragen — **Street directions**

Kunt u mij op de kaart aanwijzen waar ik ben?	Can you show me on the map where I am?
U bent op de verkeerde weg.	You are on the wrong road.
Rij/Ga rechtuit.	Go/Walk straight ahead.
Het is aan de linkerkant/aan de rechterkant.	It's on the left/on the right.

Spoedgevallen — **Emergencies**

Roep vlug een dokter.	Call a doctor quickly.
Roep een ambulance.	Call an ambulance.
Roep de politie, alstublieft.	Please call the police.

Introduction

The dictionary has been designed to take account of your practical needs. Unnecessary linguistic information has been avoided. The entries are listed in alphabetical order regardless of whether the entry word is printed in a single word, is hyphened or is in two or more separate words. The only exception to this rule, reflexive verbs, are listed as main entries alphabetically according to the verb, e.g. *zich afvragen* is found under **a**.

When an entry is followed by sub-entries such as expressions and locutions, these, too, have been listed in alphabetical order.

Each main-entry word is followed by a phonetic transcription (see Guide to pronunciation). Following the transcription is the part of speech of the entry word whenever applicable. When an entry word may be used as more then one part of speech, the translations are grouped together after the respective part of speech.

Considering the complexity of the rules for constructing the plural of Dutch nouns, we have supplied the plural form whenever in current use.

Each time an entry word is repeated in plurals or in sub-entries, a tilde (~) is used to represent the full entry word.

In plurals of long words, only the part that changes is written out fully, whereas the unchanged part is represented by a hyphen.

Entry:	beker (pl ~s)	Plural:	bekers
	kind (pl ~eren)		kinderen
	leslokaal (pl -kalen)		leslokalen

An asterisk (*) in front of a verb indicates that the verb is irregular. For details, refer to the lists of irregular verbs.

Abbreviations

adj	adjective	*p*	past tense
adv	adverb	*pl*	plural
Am	American	*plAm*	plural (American)
art	article	*pp*	past participle
c	common gender	*pr*	present tense
conj	conjunction	*pref*	prefix
n	noun	*prep*	preposition
nAm	noun (American)	*pron*	pronoun
nt	neuter	*v*	verb
num	numeral	*vAm*	verb (American)

Guide to Pronunciation

Each main entry in this part of the dictionary is followed by a phonetic transcription which shows you how to pronounce the words. This transcription should be read as if it were English. It is based on Standard British pronunciation, though we have tried to take account of General American pronunciation also. Below, only those letters and symbols are explained which we consider likely to be ambiguous or not immediately understood.

The syllables are separated by hyphens, and stressed syllables are printed in *italics*.

Of course, the sounds of any two languages are never exactly the same, but if you follow carefully our indications, you should be able to pronounce the foreign words in such a way that you'll be understood. To make your task easier, our transcriptions occasionally simplify slightly the sound system of the language while still reflecting the essential sound differences.

Consonants

g	a g-sound where the tongue doesn't quite close the air passage between itself and the roof of the mouth, so that the escaping air produces audible friction; often fairly hard, so that it resembles **kh**
kh	like **g**, but based on a **k**-sound; therefore hard and voiceless, like **ch** in Scottish lo**ch**
ñ	as in Spanish se**ñ**or, or like **ni** in o**ni**on
s	always hard, as in **s**o
zh	a soft, voiced **sh**, like **s** in plea**s**ure

1) In everyday speech, the **n** in the ending of verbs and plurals of nouns is usually dropped.

2) We use the transcription **v** for two different sounds (written **v** and **w** in Dutch) because the difference between them is often inaudible to foreigners.

Vowels and Diphthongs

aa	long **a**, as in c**a**r, without any **r**-sound
ah	a short version of **aa**; between **a** in c**a**t and **u** in c**u**t
ai	like **air**, without any **r**-sound

eh	like **e** in g**e**t
er	as in oth**er**, without any **r**-sound
ew	a "rounded **ee**-sound"; say the vowel sound **ee** (as in s**ee**), and while saying it, round your lips as for **oo** (as in s**oo**n), without moving your tongue; when your lips are in the **oo** position, but your tongue is in the **ee** position, you should be pronouncing the correct sound
ı	like **i** in b**i**t
igh	as in s**igh**
o	always as in h**o**t (British pronunciation)
ou	as in l**ou**d
ur	as in f**ur**, but with rounded lips and no **r**-sound

1) A bar over a vowel symbol (e.g. $\overline{oo}$) shows that this sound is long.

2) Raised letters (e.g. **aa**^ee, **t**^y, ^y**eh**) should be pronounced only fleetingly.

3) Dutch vowels (i.e. not diphthongs) are pure. Therefore, you should try to read a transcription like $\overline{oa}$ without moving tongue or lips while pronouncing the sound.

4) Some Dutch words borrowed from French contain nasal vowels, which we transcribe with a vowel symbol plus **ng** (e.g. **ahng**). This **ng** should *not* be pronounced, and serves solely to indicate nasal quality of the preceding vowel. A nasal vowel is pronounced simultaneously through the mouth and the nose.

A

aal (aal) *c* (pl alen) eel

aambeien (*aam*-bay-ern) *pl* haemorrhoids *pl*, piles *pl*

aan (aan) *prep* to; on

aanbetaling (*aam*-ber-taa-lɪng) *c* (pl ~en) down payment

* **aanbevelen** (*aam*-ber-vāy-lern) *v* recommend

aanbeveling (*aam*-ber-vāy-lɪng) *c* (pl ~en) recommendation

aanbevelingsbrief (*aam*-ber-vāy-lɪngs-breef) *c* (pl -brieven) letter of recommendation

* **aanbidden** (*aam*-bɪ-dern) *v* worship

* **aanbieden** (*aam*-bee-dern) *v* offer; present

aanbieding (*aam*-bee-dɪng) *c* (pl ~en) offer

aanblik (*aam*-blɪk) *c* sight; appearance

aanbod (*aam*-bot) *nt* offer; supply

aanbranden (*aam*-brahn-dern) *v* *burn

aandacht (*aan*-dahkht) *c* attention; notice, consideration; ~ **besteden aan** attend to

aandeel (*aan*-dāyl) *nt* (pl -delen) share

aandenken (*aan*-dehng-kern) *nt* (pl ~s) remembrance

aandoening (*aan*-dōō-nɪng) *c* (pl ~en) affection

aandoenlijk (aan-*dōōn*-lerk) *adj* touching

* **aandrijven** (*aan*-dray-vern) *v* propel

* **aandringen** (*aan*-drɪ-ngern) *v* insist

aanduiden (*aan*-dur^(ew)-dern) *v* indicate

* **aangaan** (*aang*-gaan) *v* concern

aangaande (aang-*gaan*-der) *prep* as regards

aangeboren (aang-ger-*bōa*-rern) *adj* natural

aangelegenheid (aang-ger-*lāy*-gern-hayt) *c* (pl -heden) matter, concern; affair, business

aangenaam (aang-ger-naam) *adj* agreeable, pleasing, pleasant

aangesloten (aang-ger-*slōā*-tern) *adj* affiliated

* **aangeven** (*aang*-gāy-vern) *v* indicate; declare; *give, hand, pass

aangezien (aang-ger-*zeen*) *conj* as, since; because

aangifte (*aang*-gɪf-ter) *c* (pl ~n) declaration

aangrenzend (aang-*grehn*-zernt) *adj* neighbouring

aanhalen (*aan*-haa-lern) *v* tighten; quote

aanhalingstekens (*aan*-haa-lɪngs-tāy-kerns) *pl* quotation marks

aanhangwagen (*aan*-hahng-vaa-gern) *c* (pl ~s) trailer

aanhankelijk (aan-*hahng*-ker-lerk) *adj*

affectionate

*aanhebben (aan-heh-bern) v *wear

aanhechten (aan-hehkh-tern) v attach

aanhoren (aan-hōa-rern) v listen

*aanhouden (aan-hou-dern) v insist;
aanhoudend constant

aanhouding (aan-hou-dɪng) c (pl ~en)
arrest

*aankijken (aang-kay-kern) v look at

aanklacht (aang-klahkht) c (pl ~en)
charge

aanklagen (aang-klaa-gern) v accuse,
charge

aankleden (aang-klāy-dern) v dress;
*get dressed

*aankomen (aang-kōa-mern) v arrive

aankomst (aang-komst) c arrival

aankomsttijd (aang-koms-tayt) c (pl
~en) time of arrival

aankondigen (aang-kon-der-gern) v
announce

aankondiging (aang-kon-der-gɪng) c
(pl ~en) notice, announcement

aankoop (aang-kōap) c (pl -kopen)
purchase

aankruisen (aang-krur^{ew}-sern) v mark

aanleg (aan-lehkh) c talent

aanleggen (aan-leh-gern) v dock

aanleiding (aan-lay-dɪng) c (pl ~en)
cause, occasion

aanlengen (aan-leh-ngern) v dilute

zich aanmelden (aan-mehl-dern) report

aanmerkelijk (aa-mehr-ker-lerk) adj
considerable

aanmerken (aa-mehr-kern) v comment

aanmoedigen (aa-mōō-der-gern) v encourage

*aannemen (aa-nāy-mern) v accept;
assume, suppose; adopt; aangenomen dat supposing that

aannemer (aa-nāy-merr) c (pl ~s)
contractor

aanpak (aam-pahk) c method, ap-

proach

aanpassen (aam-pah-sern) v adapt;
suit; adjust

aanplakbiljet (aam-plahk-bɪl-^yeht) nt
(pl ~ten) placard

*aanprijzen (aam-pray-zern) v recom-
mend

*aanraden (aan-raa-dern) v advise,
recommend

aanraken (aan-raa-kern) v touch

aanraking (aan-raa-kɪng) c (pl ~en)
touch; contact

aanranden (aan-rahn-dern) v assault

aanrichten (aan-rɪkh-tern) v cause

aanrijding (aan-ray-dɪng) c (pl ~en)
collision

aanschaffen (aan-skhah-fern) v *buy

*aansluiten (aan-slur^{ew}-tern) v con-
nect

aansluiting (aan-slur^{ew}-tɪng) c (pl
~en) connection

aansporen (aan-spōa-rern) v incite;
urge

aanspraak (aan-spraak) c (pl -spra-
ken) claim

aansprakelijk (aan-spraa-ker-lerk) adj
liable; responsible

aansprakelijkheid (aan-spraa-ker-lerk-
hayt) c liability; responsibility

*aanspreken (aan-sprāy-kern) v ad-
dress

aanstekelijk (aan-stāy-ker-lerk) adj
contagious

*aansteken (aan-stāy-kern) v *light;
infect

aansteker (aan-stāy-kerr) c (pl ~s)
lighter, cigarette-lighter

aanstellen (aan-steh-lern) v appoint

aanstoot (aan-stōat) c offence

aanstootgevend (aan-stōat-khāy-vernt)
adj offensive

aanstrepen (aan-strāy-pern) v tick off

aantal (aan-tahl) nt (pl ~len) number; quantity

aantekenen (*aan*-tāy-ker-nern) v record; register

aantekening (*aan*-tāy-ker-nıng) c (pl ~en) note

aantonen (*aan*-tōā-nern) v prove; demonstrate; *show

aantrekkelijk (aan-*treh*-ker-lerk) adj attractive

***aantrekken** (*aan*-treh-kern) v attract; tempt; *put on; tighten

aantrekking (*aan*-treh-kıng) c attraction

aanvaarden (aan-*vaar*-dern) v accept

aanval (*aan*-vahl) c (pl ~len) attack; fit

***aanvallen** (*aan*-vah-lern) v attack; assault

aanvang (*aan*-vahng) c beginning

***aanvangen** (*aan*-vah-ngern) v *begin

aanvankelijk (aan-*vahng*-ker-lerk) adv originally, at first

aanvaring (*aan*-vaa-rıng) c (pl ~en) collision

aanvoer (*aan*-vōōr) c supply

aanvoerder (*aan*-vōōr-derr) c (pl ~s) leader

aanvraag (*aan*-vraakh) c (pl -vragen) application

aanwezig (aan-*vāy*-zerkh) adj present

aanwezigheid (aan-*vāy*-zerkh-hayt) c presence

***aanwijzen** (*aan*-vay-zern) v point out; designate

aanwijzing (*aan*-vay-zıng) c (pl ~en) indication

aanzetten (*aan*-zeh-tern) v turn on

aanzien (*aan*-zeen) nt aspect; esteem; **ten ~ van** regarding

aanzienlijk (aan-*zeen*-lerk) adj considerable, substantial

aap (aap) c (pl apen) monkey

aard (aart) c nature

aardappel (*aar*-dah-perl) c (pl ~s, ~en) potato

aardbei (*aart*-bay) c (pl ~en) strawberry

aardbeving (*aart*-bāy-vıng) c (pl ~en) earthquake

aardbol (*aart*-bol) c globe

aarde (*aar*-der) c earth; soil

aardewerk (*aar*-der-vehrk) nt crockery, pottery, faience, earthenware, ceramics pl

aardig (*aar*-derkh) adj pleasant; nice, kind

aardrijkskunde (*aar*-drayks-kern-der) c geography

aartsbisschop (*aarts*-bı-skhop) c (pl ~pen) archbishop

aarzelen (*aar*-zer-lern) v hesitate

aas (aass) nt bait

abces (ahp-*sehss*) nt (pl ~sen) abscess

abdij (ahb-*day*) c (pl ~en) abbey

abnormaal (ahp-nor-*maal*) adj abnormal

abonnee (ah-bo-*nāy*) c (pl ~s) subscriber

abonnement (ah-bo-ner-*mehnt*) nt (pl ~en) subscription

abonnementskaart (ah-bo-ner-*mehnts*-kaart) c (pl ~en) season-ticket

abortus (ah-*bor*-terss) c (pl ~sen) abortion

abrikoos (ah-bree-*kōāss*) c (pl -kozen) apricot

absoluut (ahp-sōā-*lewt*) adj sheer; adv absolutely

abstract (ahp-*strahkt*) adj abstract

absurd (ahp-*serrt*) adj absurd

abuis (aa-*bur^ew^ss*) nt (pl abuizen) mistake

academie (aa-kaa-*dāy*-mee) c (pl ~s) academy

accent (ahk-*sehnt*) nt (pl ~en) accent

accepteren (ahk-sehp-*tāy*-rern) v accept

accessoires (ahk-seh-*svaa*-rerss) pl accessories pl

accijns (ahk-*sayns*) *c* (pl -cijnzen) Customs duty

accommodatie (ah-ko-mōa-*daa*-tsee) *c* accommodation

accu (*ah*-kew) *c* (pl ~'s) battery

acht (ahkht) *num* eight

achteloos (*ahkh*-ter-lōass) *adj* careless

achten (*ahkh*-tern) *v* esteem; count

achter (*ahkh*-terr) *prep* behind; after

achteraan (ahkh-ter-*raan*) *adv* behind

achterbuurt (*ahkh*-terr-bēwrt) *c* (pl ~en) slum

achterdochtig (ahkh-terr-*dokh*-terkh) *adj* suspicious

achtergrond (*ahkh*-terr-gront) *c* (pl ~en) background

achterkant (*ahkh*-terr-kahnt) *c* (pl ~en) rear

* **achterlaten** (*ahkh*-terr-laa-tern) *v* *leave behind

achterlicht (*ahkh*-terr-likht) *nt* (pl ~en) tail-light, rear-light

achternaam (*ahkh*-terr-naam) *c* (pl -namen) family name, surname

achterstallig (ahkh-terr-*stah*-lerkh) *adj* overdue

achteruit (ahkh-ter-*rur*ᵉʷt) *adv* backwards

* **achteruitrijden** (ahkh-ter-*rur*ᵉʷt-ray-dern) *v* reverse

achterwerk (*ahkh*-terr-vehrk) *nt* (pl ~en) bottom

achting (*ahkh*-tıng) *c* respect, esteem

achtste (*ahkht*-ster) *num* eighth

achttien (*ahkh*-teen) *num* eighteen

achttiende (*ahkh*-teen-der) *num* eighteenth

acne (*ahk*-nāy) *c* acne

acquisitie (ah-kvee-*zee*-tsee) *c* (pl ~s) acquisition

acteur (ahk-*tūrr*) *c* (pl ~s) actor

actie (*ahk*-see) *c* (pl ~s) action

actief (ahk-*teef*) *adj* active

activiteit (ahk-tee-vee-*tayt*) *c* (pl ~en) activity

actrice (ahk-*tree*-ser) *c* (pl ~s) actress

actueel (ahk-tēw-*vāyl*) *adj* topical

acuut (ah-*kewt*) *adj* acute

adel (*aa*-derl) *c* nobility

adellijk (*aa*-der-lerk) *adj* noble

adem (*aa*-derm) *c* breath

ademen (*aa*-der-mern) *v* breathe

ademhaling (*aa*-derm-haa-lıng) *c* breathing, respiration

adequaat (ah-dāy-*kvaat*) *adj* adequate

ader (*aa*-derr) *c* (pl ~s, ~en) vein

administratie (aht-mee-nee-*straa*-tsee) *c* (pl ~s) administration

administratief (aht-mee-nee-straa-*teef*) *adj* administrative

admiraal (aht-mee-*raal*) *c* (pl ~s) admiral

adopteren (ah-dop-*tāy*-rern) *v* adopt

adres (aa-*drehss*) *nt* (pl ~sen) address

adresseren (aa-dreh-*sāy*-rern) *v* address

advertentie (aht-ferr-*tehn*-see) *c* (pl ~s) advertisement

advies (aht-*feess*) *nt* (pl adviezen) advice

adviseren (aht-fee-*zāy*-rern) *v* advise

advocaat (aht-fōa-*kaat*) *c* (pl -caten) lawyer; barrister; solicitor; attorney

af (ahf) *adv* off; finished; ~ **en toe** occasionally

afbeelding (*ahf*-bāyl-dıng) *c* (pl ~en) picture

afbetalen (*ahf*-ber-taa-lern) *v* *pay on account

afbetaling (*ahf*-ber-taa-lıng) *c* (pl ~en) instalment

* **afblijven** (*ahf*-blay-vern) *v* *keep off

afbraak (*ahf*-braak) *c* demolition

* **afbreken** (*ahf*-brāy-kern) *v* chip

afdaling (*ahf*-daa-lıng) *c* (pl ~en) descent

afdanken (*ahf*-dahng-kern) *v* discard

afdeling (ahf-dāy-lıng) c (pl ~en) division, department; section

*afdingen (ahf-dı-ngern) v bargain

afdrogen (ahf-drōā-gern) v dry

afdruk (ahf-drerk) c (pl ~ken) print

*afdwingen (ahf-dvı-ngern) v extort

affaire (ah-fai-rer) c (pl ~s) deal; affair

affiche (ah-fee-sher) nt (pl ~s) poster

afgeladen (ahf-kher-laa-dern) adj chock-full

afgelegen (ahf-kher-lāy-gern) adj remote, far-off, out of the way

afgelopen (ahf-kher-lōā-pern) adj past

afgerond (ahf-kher-ront) adj rounded

afgevaardigde (ahf-kher-vaar-derg-der) c (pl ~n) deputy

afgezien van (ahf-kher-zeen vahn) apart from

afgod (ahf-khot) c (pl ~en) idol

afgrijzen (ahf-khray-zern) nt horror

afgrond (ahf-khront) c (pl ~en) precipice, abyss

afgunst (ahf-khernst) c envy

afgunstig (ahf-khern-sterkh) adj envious

afhalen (ahf-haa-lern) v collect, fetch

afhandelen (ahf-hahn-der-lern) v settle

*afhangen van (ahf-hah-ngern) depend on

afhankelijk (ahf-hahng-ker-lerk) adj dependant

afhellend (ahf-heh-lernt) adj sloping

afkeer (ahf-kāyr) c dislike; antipathy

afkerig (ahf-kāy-rerkh) adj averse

afkeuren (ahf-kūr-rern) v disapprove; reject

afknippen (ahf-knı-pern) v *cut off

afkondigen (ahf-kon-der-gern) v proclaim

afkorting (ahf-kor-tıng) c (pl ~en) abbreviation

afleiden (ahf-lay-dern) v deduce, infer

afleiding (ahf-lay-dıng) c diversion

afleren (ahf-lāy-rern) v unlearn

afleveren (ahf-lāy-ver-rern) v deliver

afloop (ahf-lōāp) c expiry

*aflopen (ahf-lōā-pern) v end; expire

aflossen (ahf-lo-sern) v relieve; *pay off

afluisteren (ahf-lur^ew-ster-rern) v eavesdrop

afmaken (ahf-maa-kern) v finish

afmeting (ahf-māy-tıng) c (pl ~en) size

*afnemen (ahf-nāy-mern) v decrease; *take away

afpersing (ahf-pehr-sıng) c (pl ~en) extortion

*afraden (ahf-raa-dern) v dissuade from

afremmen (ahf-reh-mern) v slow down

Afrika (aa-free-kaa) Africa

Afrikaan (aa-free-kaan) c (pl -kanen) African

Afrikaans (aa-free-kaans) adj African

afschaffen (ahf-skhah-fern) v abolish

afscheid (ahf-skhayt) nt parting

afschrift (ahf-skhrıft) nt (pl ~en) copy

afschuw (ahf-skhew^oo) c horror

afschuwelijk (ahf-skhew-ver-lerk) adj horrible, awful; hideous

*afsluiten (ahf-slur^ew-tern) v *cut off

*afsnijden (ahf-snay-dern) v *cut off; chip

afspraak (ahf-spraak) c (pl -spraken) date, appointment; engagement

afstammeling (ahf-stah-mer-lıng) c (pl ~en) descendant

afstamming (ahf-stah-mıng) c origin

afstand (ahf-stahnt) c (pl ~en) distance; space, way

afstandsmeter (ahf-stahnts-māy-terr) c (pl ~s) range-finder

afstellen (ahf-steh-lern) v adjust

afstemmen (ahf-steh-mern) v tune in

afstotelijk (ahf-stōā-ter-lerk) adj repellent

aftekenen (*ahf*-tāy-ker-nern) v endorse
aftrap (*ahf*-trahp) c kick-off
***aftrekken** (*ahf*-treh-kern) v deduct; subtract
afvaardiging (*ah*-faar-der-gɪng) c (pl ~en) delegation
afval (*ah*-fahl) nt garbage, litter, rubbish, refuse
afvegen (*ah*-fāy-gern) v wipe
afvoer (*ah*-fōōr) c drain
zich ***afvragen** (*ah*-fraa-gern) wonder
afwachten (*ahf*-vahkh-tern) v await
afwassen (*ahf*-vah-sern) v wash up
afwateren (*ahf*-vaa-ter-rern) v drain
afwenden (*ahf*-vehn-dern) v avert
afwezig (ahf-*vāy*-zerkh) adj absent
afwezigheid (ahf-*vāy*-zerkh-hayt) c absence
***afwijken** (*ahf*-vay-kern) v deviate
afwijking (*ahf*-vay-kɪng) c (pl ~en) aberration
***afwijzen** (*ahf*-vay-zern) v reject
afwisselen (*ahf*-vɪ-ser-lern) v vary; **afwisselend** alternate
afwisseling (*ahf*-vɪ-ser-lɪng) c variation
***afzeggen** (*ahf*-seh-gern) v cancel
afzetting (*ahf*-seh-tɪng) c (pl ~en) deposit
afzonderlijk (ahf-*son*-derr-lerk) adj individual; separate; adv apart
agenda (aa-*gehn*-daa) c (pl ~'s) diary; agenda
agent (aa-*gehnt*) c (pl ~en) policeman; distributor, agent
agentschap (aa-*gehnt*-skhahp) nt (pl ~pen) agency
agrarisch (aa-*graa*-reess) adj agrarian
agressief (ah-greh-*seef*) adj aggressive
akelig (*aa*-ker-lerkh) adj nasty
akker (*ah*-kerr) c (pl ~s) field
akkoord (ah-*kōārt*) nt (pl ~en) agreement
akte (*ahk*-ter) c (pl ~n, ~s) act, cer-

tificate
aktentas (*ahk*-tern-tahss) c (pl ~sen) briefcase, attaché case
al (ahl) adj all; adv already
alarm (aa-*lahrm*) nt alarm
alarmeren (aa-lahr-*māy*-rern) v alarm
album (*ahl*-berm) nt (pl ~s) album
alcohol (*ahl*-kōā-hol) c alcohol
alcoholisch (ahl-kōā-*hōā*-leess) adj alcoholic
aldoor (*ahl*-dōār) adv all the time
alfabet (*ahl*-faa-beht) nt alphabet
algebra (*ahl*-ger-braa) c algebra
algemeen (ahl-ger-*māyn*) adj general; universal, public; **in het ~** in general
Algerije (ahl-ger-*ray*-er) Algeria
Algerijn (ahl-ger-*rayn*) c (pl ~en) Algerian
Algerijns (ahl-ger-*rayns*) adj Algerian
alhoewel (ahl-hōō-*vehl*) conj though
alikruik (*aa*-lee-krur^{ewk}) c (pl ~en) winkle
alimentatie (ah-lee-mehn-*taa*-tsee) c alimony
alinea (aa-*lee*-nāy-aa) c (pl ~'s) paragraph
alledaags (ah-ler-*daakhs*) adj ordinary; everyday
alleen (ah-*lāyn*) adv only; alone
allemaal (ah-ler-*maal*) num ALL
allergie (ah-lehr-*gee*) c (pl ~ën) allergy
allerlei (*ah*-lerr-lay) adj various; all sorts of
alles (*ah*-lerss) pron everything
almachtig (ahl-*mahkh*-terkh) adj omnipotent
almanak (*ahl*-maa-nahk) c (pl ~ken) almanac
als (ahls) conj if; when; as, like
alsof (ahl-*zof*) conj as if; ***doen ~** pretend
alstublieft (ahl-stēw-*bleeft*) here you

are; please
alt (ahlt) *c* (pl ~en) alto
altaar (*ahl*-taar) *nt* (pl altaren) altar
alternatief (ahl-terr-naa-*teef*) *nt* (pl -tieven) alternative
altijd (*ahl*-tayt) *adv* always, ever
amandel (aa-*mahn*-derl) *c* (pl ~en, ~s) almond; **amandelen** tonsils *pl*
amandelontsteking (aa-*mahn*-derl-ont-stāy-kɪng) *c* (pl ~en) tonsilitis
ambacht (*ahm*-bahkht) *nt* (pl ~en) trade
ambassade (ahm-bah-*saa*-der) *c* (pl ~s) embassy
ambassadeur (ahm-bah-saa-*dūrr*) *c* (pl ~s) ambassador
ambitieus (ahm-bee-*ts*ʸ*ūrss*) *adj* ambitious
ambt (ahmt) *nt* (pl ~en) office
ambtenaar (*ahm*-ter-naar) *c* (pl -naren) civil servant
ambulance (ahm-bēw-*lahn*-ser) *c* (pl ~s) ambulance
Amerika (aa-*māy*-ree-kaa) America
Amerikaan (aa-māy-ree-*kaan*) *c* (pl -kanen) American
Amerikaans (aa-māy-ree-*kaans*) *adj* American
amethist (ah-mer-*tist*) *c* (pl ~en) amethyst
amicaal (aa-mee-*kaal*) *adj* friendly
ammonia (ah-*mōā*-nee-ʸaa) *c* ammonia
amnestie (ahm-nehss-*tee*) *c* amnesty
amulet (aa-mēw-*leht*) *c* (pl ~ten) lucky charm, charm
amusant (aa-mēw-*zahnt*) *adj* amusing; entertaining
amusement (aa-mēw-zer-*mehnt*) *nt* amusement; entertainment
amuseren (aa-mēw-*zāy*-rern) *v* amuse
analfabeet (ahn-ahl-faa-*bāyt*) *c* (pl -beten) illiterate
analist (ah-naa-*list*) *c* (pl ~en) analyst

analyse (ah-naa-*lee*-zer) *c* (pl ~n, ~s) analysis
analyseren (ah-naa-lee-*zāy*-rern) *v* analyse
analyticus (ah-naa-*lee*-tee-kerss) *c* (pl -ci) analyst, psychoanalyst
ananas (ah-nah-nahss) *c* (pl ~sen) pineapple
anarchie (ah-nahr-*khee*) *c* anarchy
anatomie (ah-naa-tōā-*mee*) *c* anatomy
ander (*ahn*-derr) *adj* other; different; **een ~** another; **onder andere** among other things
anders (*ahn*-derrs) *adv* else; otherwise
andersom (ahn-derr-*som*) *adv* the other way round
angst (ahngst) *c* (pl ~en) fright, fear; terror
angstig (*ahng*-sterkh) *adj* afraid
angstwekkend (ahngst-*veh*-kernt) *adj* terrifying
animo (aa-nee-*mōā*) *c* zest
anker (*ahng*-kerr) *nt* (pl ~s) anchor
annexeren (ah-nehk-*sāy*-rern) *v* annex
annonce (ah-*nawng*-ser) *c* (pl ~s) advertisement
annuleren (ah-nēw-*lāy*-rern) *v* cancel
annulering (ah-nēw-*lāy*-rɪng) *c* (pl ~en) cancellation
anoniem (ah-nōā-*neem*) *adj* anonymous
ansichtkaart (*ahn*-zɪkht-kaart) *c* (pl ~en) postcard, picture postcard
ansjovis (ahn-*shōā*-vɪss) *c* (pl ~sen) anchovy
antenne (ahn-*teh*-ner) *c* (pl ~s) aerial
antibioticum (ahn-tee-bee-ʸ*ōā*-tee-kerm) *nt* (pl -ca) antibiotic
antiek (ahn-*teek*) *adj* antique
antipathie (ahn-tee-paa-*tee*) *c* dislike
antiquair (ahn-tee-*kair*) *c* (pl ~s) antique dealer
antiquiteit (ahn-tee-kvee-*tayt*) *c* (pl ~en) antique

antivries (ahn-tee-*vreess*) c antifreeze

antwoord (ahnt-*vōart*) nt (pl ~en) reply, answer; **als** ~ in reply

antwoorden (ahnt-*vōar*-dern) v reply, answer

apart (aa-*pahrt*) adv apart, separately

aperitief (aa-*pāy*-ree-*teef*) nt/c (pl -tieven) aperitif

apotheek (aa-pōa-*tāyk*) c (pl -theken) pharmacy, chemist's; drugstore *nAm*

apotheker (aa-pōa-*tāy*-kerr) c (pl ~s) chemist

apparaat (ah-paa-*raat*) nt (pl -raten) appliance; machine; apparatus

appartement (ah-pahr-ter-*mehnt*) nt (pl ~en) apartment *nAm*

appel (*ah*-perl) c (pl ~s) apple

applaudisseren (ah-plou-dee-*sāy*-rern) v clap

applaus (ah-*plouss*) nt applause

april (ah-*prıl*) April

aquarel (aa-kvaa-*rehl*) c (pl ~len) water-colour

ar (ahr) c (pl ~ren) sleigh

Arabier (aa-raa-*beer*) c (pl ~en) Arab

Arabisch (aa-*raa*-beess) adj Arab

arbeid (*ahr*-bayt) c labour, work

arbeidbesparend (*ahr*-bayt-ber-spaa-rernt) adj labour-saving

arbeider (*ahr*-bay-derr) c (pl ~s) labourer, workman, worker

arbeidsbureau (*ahr*-bayts-bēw-rōa) nt (pl ~s) employment exchange

archeologie (ahr-khāy-ōa-lōa-*gee*) c archaeology

archeoloog (ahr-khāy-ōa-*lōakh*) c (pl -logen) archaeologist

archief (ahr-*kheef*) nt (pl -chieven) archives pl

architect (ahr-shee-*tehkt*) c (pl ~en) architect

architectuur (ahr-shee-tehk-*tēwr*) c architecture

arena (aa-*rāy*-naa) c (pl ~'s) bullring

arend (*aa*-rernt) c (pl ~en) eagle

Argentijn (ahr-gern-*tayn*) c (pl ~en) Argentinian

Argentijns (ahr-gern-*tayns*) adj Argentinian

Argentinië (ahr-gern-*tee*-nee-Yer) Argentina

argument (ahr-gēw-*mehnt*) nt (pl ~en) argument

argumenteren (ahr-gēw-mehn-*tāy*-rern) v argue

argwaan (*ahrkh*-vaan) c suspicion

argwanend (*ahrkh*-vaa-nernt) adj suspicious

arm[1] (ahrm) adj poor

arm[2] (ahrm) c (pl ~en) arm

armband (*ahrm*-bahnt) c (pl ~en) bracelet; bangle

armoede (*ahr*-mōō-der) c poverty

armoedig (*ahr*-mōō-derkh) adj poor

aroma (aa-*rōa*-maa) nt aroma

arrestatie (ah-rehss-*taa*-tsee) c (pl ~s) arrest

arresteren (ah-rehss-*tāy*-rern) v arrest

arrogant (ah-rōa-*gahnt*) adj presumptuous

artikel (ahr-*tee*-kerl) nt (pl ~en, ~s) article; item

artisjok (ahr-tee-*shok*) c (pl ~ken) artichoke

artistiek (ahr-tıss-*teek*) adj artistic

arts (ahrts) c (pl ~en) doctor

as[1] (ahss) c (pl ~sen) axle

as[2] (ahss) c ash

asbak (*ahss*-bahk) c (pl ~ken) ashtray

asbest (*ahss*-behst) nt asbestos

asfalt (*ahss*-fahlt) nt asphalt

asiel (aa-*zeel*) nt asylum

aspect (ahss-*pehkt*) nt (pl ~en) aspect

asperge (ahss-*pehr*-zher) c (pl ~s) asparagus

aspirine (ahss-pee-*ree*-ner) c aspirin

assistent (ah-see-*stehnt*) c (pl ~en)

assistant

associëren (ah-sōa-*shāy*-rern) v associate

assortiment (ah-sor-tee-*mehnt*) nt (pl ~en) assortment

assurantie (ah-sēw-*rahn*-see) c (pl -ties, -tiën) insurance

astma (*ahss*-maa) nt asthma

atheïst (aa-tāy-*ist*) c (pl ~en) atheist

Atlantische Oceaan (aht-*lahn*-tee-ser ōa-say-*aan*) Atlantic

atleet (aht-*lāyt*) c (pl -leten) athlete

atletiek (aht-lāy-*teek*) c athletics pl

atmosfeer (aht-moss-*fāyr*) c atmosphere

atomisch (aa-*tōa*-meess) adj atomic

atoom (aa-*tōam*) nt (pl atomen) atom; **atoom-** atomic

attent (ah-*tehnt*) adj considerate

attest (ah-*tehst*) nt (pl ~en) certificate

attractie (ah-*trahk*-see) c (pl ~s) attraction

aubergine (ōa-behr-*zhee*-ner) c (pl ~s) eggplant

augustus (ou-*gerss*-terss) August

aula (*ou*-laa) c (pl ~'s) auditorium

Australië (ou-*straa*-lee-Yer) Australia

Australiër (ou-*straa*-lee-Yerr) c (pl ~s) Australian

Australisch (ou-*straa*-leess) adj Australian

auteur (ōa-*tūrr*) c (pl ~s) author

authentiek (ōa-tehn-*teek*) adj authentic

auto (*ōa*-tōa) c (pl ~'s) car; motorcar, automobile

automaat (ōa-tōa-*maat*) c (pl -maten) slot-machine

automatisch (ōa-tōa-*maa*-teess) adj automatic

automatisering (ōa-tōa-maa-tee-*zāy*-ring) c automation

automobielclub (ōa-tōa-mōa-*beel*-klerp) c (pl ~s) automobile club

automobilisme (ōa-tōa-mōa-bee-*liss*-mer) nt motoring

automobilist (ōa-tōa-mōa-bee-*list*) c (pl ~en) motorist

autonoom (ōa-tōa-*nōam*) adj autonomous

autoped (*ōa*-tōa-peht) c (pl ~s) scooter

autopsie (ōa-top-*see*) c autopsy

*****autorijden** (*ōa*-tōa-ray-dern) v motor

autorit (*ōa*-tōa-rit) c (pl ~ten) drive

autoritair (ōa-tōa-ree-*tair*) adj authoritarian

autoriteiten (ōa-tōa-ree-*tay*-tern) pl authorities pl

autoverhuur (*ōa*-tōa-verr-hēwr) c car hire; car rental Am

autoweg (*ōa*-tōa-vehkh) c (pl ~en) highway nAm

avond c (pl ~en) night, evening

avondeten (*aa*-vernt-āy-tern) nt dinner; supper

avondkleding (*aa*-vernt-klāy-ding) c evening dress

avondschemering (*aa*-vernt-skhāy-mer-ring) c dusk

avontuur (aa-von-*tēwr*) nt (pl -turen) adventure

Aziaat (aa-zee-*Yaat*) c (pl Aziaten) Asian

Aziatisch (aa-zee-*Yaa*-teess) adj Asian

Azië (*aa*-zee-Yer) Asia

azijn (aa-*zayn*) c vinegar

B

baai (baa^ee) c (pl ~en) bay

baan (baan) c (pl banen) job

baard (baart) c (pl ~en) beard

baarmoeder (*baar*-mōo-derr) c womb

baars (baars) c (pl baarzen) bass,

perch

baas (baass) c (pl bazen) boss; master

baat (baat) c benefit; profit

babbelen (bah-ber-lern) v chat

babbelkous (bah-berl-kouss) c (pl ~en) chatterbox

babbeltje (bah-berl-t^yer) nt (pl ~s) chat

baby (bāy-bee) c (pl ~'s) baby

bacil (bah-sil) c (pl ~len) germ

bacterie (bahk-tāy-ree) c (pl -riën) bacterium

bad (baht) nt (pl ~en) bath; **een ~ *nemen** bathe

baden (baa-dern) v bathe

badhanddoek (baht-hahn-dōōk) c (pl ~en) bath towel

badjas (baht-^yahss) c (pl ~sen) bathrobe

badkamer (baht-kaa-merr) c (pl ~s) bathroom

badmuts (baht-merts) c (pl ~en) bathing-cap

badpak (baht-pahk) nt (pl ~ken) bathing-suit

badplaats (baht-plaats) c (pl ~en) seaside resort

badstof (baht-stof) c towelling

badzout (baht-sout) nt bath salts

bagage (bah-gaa-zher) c baggage; luggage

bagagedepot (bah-gaa-zher-dāy-pōa) nt (pl ~s) left luggage office; baggage deposit office Am

bagagenet (bah-gaa-zher-neht) nt (pl ~ten) luggage rack

bagageoverschot (bah-gaa-zher-ōa-verr-skhot) nt overweight

bagagerek (bah-gaa-zher-rehk) nt (pl ~ken) luggage rack

bagageruimte (bah-gaa-zher-rur^{ew}m-ter) c (pl ~n, ~s) boot

bagagewagen (bah-gaa-zher-vaa-gern) c (pl ~s) luggage van

bakboord (bahk-bōart) nt port

baken (baa-kern) nt (pl ~s) landmark

bakermat (baa-kerr-maht) c cradle

bakkebaarden (bah-ker-baar-dern) pl whiskers pl, sideburns pl

*bakken (bah-kern) v bake; fry

bakker (bah-kerr) c (pl ~s) baker

bakkerij (bah-ker-ray) c (pl ~en) bakery

baksteen (bahk-stāyn) c (pl -stenen) brick

bal¹ (bahl) c (pl ~len) ball

bal² (bahl) nt (pl ~s) ball

balans (bah-lahns) c (pl ~en) balance

baldadig (bahl-daa-derkh) adj rowdy

balie (baa-lee) c (pl ~s) counter

balk (bahlk) c (pl ~en) beam

balkon (bahl-kon) nt (pl ~s) balcony; circle

ballet (bah-leht) nt (pl ~ten) ballet

balling (bah-ling) c (pl ~en) exile

ballingschap (bah-ling-skhahp) c exile

ballon (bah-lon) c (pl ~s) balloon

ballpoint (bol-po^ynt) c (pl ~s) ballpoint-pen; Biro

bamboe (bahm-bōō) nt bamboo

banaan (baa-naan) c (pl bananen) banana

band (bahnt) c (pl ~en) tape; band; tyre, tire; **lekke ~** flat tyre, puncture

bandenspanning (bahn-der-spah-ning) c tyre pressure

bandepech (bahn-der-pehkh) c blowout, puncture

bandiet (bahn-deet) c (pl ~en) bandit

bandrecorder (bahnt-rer-kor-derr) c (pl ~s) tape-recorder, recorder

bang (bahng) adj frightened, afraid

bank (bahngk) c (pl ~en) bank; bench

bankbiljet (bahngk-bil-^yeht) nt (pl ~ten) banknote

banket (bahng-keht) nt (pl ~ten) banquet

banketbakker (bahng-*keht*-bah-kerr) *c*
(pl ~s) confectioner

banketbakkerij (bahng-keht-bah-ker-
ray) *c* (pl ~en) pastry shop

banketzaal (bahng-*keht*-saal) *c* (pl -za-
len) banqueting-hall

bankrekening (*bahngk*-rāy-ker-nıng) *c*
(pl ~en) bank account

bankroet (bahngk-*rōōt*) *adj* bankrupt

bar (bahr) *c* (pl ~s) bar; saloon

baret (baa-*reht*) *c* (pl ~ten) beret

bariton (*baa*-ree-ton) *c* (pl ~s) baritone

barjuffrouw (*bahr*-ʸer-frou) *c* (pl ~en)
barmaid

barman (*bahr*-mahn) *c* (pl ~nen) bartender, barman

barmhartig (bahr-*mahr*-terkh) *adj* merciful

barnsteen (*bahrn*-stāyn) *nt* amber

barok (baa-*rok*) *adj* baroque

barometer (*bah*-rōa-māy-terr) *c* (pl ~s)
barometer

barrière (bah-ree-ʸai-rer) *c* (pl ~s) barrier

barst (bahrst) *c* (pl ~en) crack

* **barsten** (*bahrs*-tern) *v* crack, *burst,
*split; *get cracked

bas (bahss) *c* (pl ~sen) bass

baseren (baa-*zāy*-rern) *v* base

basiliek (baa-zee-*leek*) *c* (pl ~en) basilica

basis (*baa*-zerss) *c* (pl bases) basis;
base

basiscrème (*baa*-zerss-kraim) *c* (pl ~s)
foundation cream

bast (bahst) *c* (pl ~en) bark

bastaard (*bahss*-taart) *c* (pl ~en, ~s)
bastard

baten (*baa*-tern) *v* *be of use

batterij (bah-ter-*ray*) *c* (pl ~en) battery

beambte (ber-*ahm*-ter) *c* (pl ~n) clerk

beantwoorden (ber-*ahnt*-vōar-dern) *v*
answer

bebost (ber-*bost*) *adj* wooded

bebouwen (ber-*bou*-ern) *v* cultivate

bed (beht) *nt* (pl ~den) bed

bedaard (ber-*daart*) *adj* quiet

bedachtzaam (ber-*dahkht*-saam) *adj*
cautious

bedanken (ber-*dahng*-kern) *v* thank

bedaren (ber-*daa*-rern) *v* calm down

beddegoed (*beh*-der-gōōt) *nt* bedding

bedeesd (ber-*dāyst*) *adj* timid

bedekken (ber-*deh*-kern) *v* cover

bedelaar (*bāy*-der-laar) *c* (pl ~s) beggar

bedelen (*bāy*-der-lern) *v* beg

* **bedelven** (ber-*dehl*-vern) *v* bury

* **bedenken** (ber-*dehng*-kern) *v* *think
of

* **bederven** (ber-*dehr*-vern) *v* *spoil;
mess up

bedevaart (*bāy*-der-vaart) *c* (pl ~en)
pilgrimage

bediende (ber-*deen*-der) *c* (pl ~n, ~s)
domestic, servant; valet; boy

bedienen (ber-*dee*-nern) *v* serve; wait
on; attend on

bediening (ber-*dee*-nıng) *c* service

bedieningsgeld (ber-*dee*-nıngs-khehlt)
nt service charge

bedoelen (ber-*dōō*-lern) *v* *mean; intend

bedoeling (ber-*dōō*-ling) *c* (pl ~en)
purpose, intention

bedrag (ber-*drahkh*) *nt* (pl ~en)
amount

* **bedragen** (ber-*draa*-gern) *v* amount
to

bedreigen (ber-*dray*-gern) *v* threaten

bedreiging (ber-*dray*-gıng) *c* (pl ~en)
threat

* **bedriegen** (ber-*dree*-gern) *v* deceive;
cheat

bedrijf (ber-*drayf*) *nt* (pl bedrijven)

business, concern; plant; act

bedrijvig (ber-*dray*-verkh) *adj* active

bedroefd (ber-*drōōft*) *adj* sad, sorry

bedroefdheid (ber-*drōōft*-hayt) *c* sadness; grief

bedrog (ber-*drokh*) *nt* deceit; fraud

beëindigen (ber-*ayn*-der-gern) *v* end, finish

beek (bāyk) *c* (pl beken) brook, stream

beeld (bāylt) *nt* (pl ~en) picture, image

beeldhouwer (*bāylt*-hou-err) *c* (pl ~s) sculptor

beeldhouwwerk (*bāylt*-hou-vehrk) *nt* (pl ~en) sculpture

beeldscherm (*bāylt*-skhehrm) *nt* (pl ~en) screen

been[1] (bāyn) *nt* (pl benen) leg

been[2] (bāyn) *nt* (pl beenderen, benen) bone

beer (bāyr) *c* (pl beren) bear

beest (bāyst) *nt* (pl ~en) beast

beestachtig (*bāyst*-ahkh-terkh) *adj* brutal

beet (bāyt) *c* (pl beten) bite

beetje (*bāy*-tᵉer) *nt* bit

*****beetnemen** (*bāyt*-nāy-mern) *v* kid

beetwortel (*bāyt*-vor-terl) *c* (pl ~s, ~en) beetroot

befaamd (ber-*faamt*) *adj* noted

begaafd (ber-*gaaft*) *adj* gifted, talented

*****begaan** (ber-*gaan*) *v* commit

begeerlijk (ber-*gāyr*-lerk) *adj* desirable

begeerte (ber-*gāyr*-ter) *c* (pl ~n) desire

begeleiden (ber-ger-*lay*-dern) *v* accompany; conduct

begeren (ber-*gāy*-rern) *v* desire

begin (ber-*gin*) *nt* start, beginning; **begin-** initial

beginneling (ber-*gi*-ner-ling) *c* (pl ~en) learner, beginner

*****beginnen** (ber-*gi*-nern) *v* start, commence, *begin

beginner (ber-*gi*-nerr) *c* (pl ~s) learner

beginsel (ber-*gin*-serl) *nt* (pl ~en, ~s) principle

begraafplaats (ber-*graaf*-plaats) *c* (pl ~en) cemetery

begrafenis (ber-*graa*-fer-niss) *c* (pl ~sen) burial; funeral

*****begraven** (ber-*graa*-vern) *v* bury

*****begrijpen** (ber-*gray*-pern) *v* *understand; *see, *take; **begrijpend** sympathetic

begrip (ber-*grip*) *nt* (pl ~pen) notion; idea, conception; understanding

begroeid (ber-*grōōᵉᵉt*) *adj* overgrown

begroting (ber-*grōa*-ting) *c* (pl ~en) budget

begunstigde (ber-*gern*-sterkh-der) *c* (pl ~n) payee

begunstigen (ber-*gern*-ster-gern) *v* favour

beha (bāy-*haa*) *c* (pl ~'s) brassiere, bra

behalen (ber-*haa*-lern) *v* obtain

behalve (ber--*hahl*-ver) *prep* but, except; beyond, besides

behandelen (ber-*hahn*-der-lern) *v* treat, handle

behandeling (ber-*hahn*-der-ling) *c* (pl ~en) treatment

behang (ber-*hahng*) *nt* wallpaper

beheer (ber-*hāyr*) *nt* management; administration

beheersen (ber-*hāyr*-sern) *v* master

beheksen (ber-*hehk*-sern) *v* bewitch

zich *****behelpen met** (ber-*hehl*-pern) *make do with

behendig (ber-*hehn*-derkh) *adj* skilful

beheren (ber-*hāy*-rern) *v* manage

behoedzaam (ber-*hōōt*-saam) *adj* wary

behoefte (ber-*hōōf*-ter) *c* (pl ~n) need, want

behoeven (ber-*hōō*-vern) *v* need; **ten behoeve van** on behalf of

behoorlijk (ber-*hōār*-lerk) *adj* proper

behoren (ber-*hōā*-rern) *v* belong to; **ought

behoudend (ber-*hou*-dernt) *adj* conservative

beide (*bay*-der) *adj* both; either; **een van ~** either; **geen van ~** neither

beige (*bai*-zher) *adj* beige

beïnvloeden (ber-*in*-vlōō-dern) *v* influence; affect

beitel (*bay*-terl) *c* (pl ~s) chisel

bejaard (ber-*Yaart*) *adj* aged; elderly

bek (behk) *c* (pl ~ken) mouth; beak

bekend (ber-*kehnt*) *adj* well-known

bekende (ber-*kehn*-der) *c* (pl ~n) acquaintance

bekendmaken (ber-*kehnt*-maa-kern) *v* announce

bekendmaking (ber-*kehnt*-maa-king) *c* (pl ~en) announcement

bekennen (ber-*keh*-nern) *v* admit, confess

bekentenis (ber-*kehn*-ter-niss) *c* (pl ~sen) confession

beker (*bāy*-kerr) *c* (pl ~s) mug; tumbler; cup

bekeren (ber-*kāy*-rern) *v* convert

****bekijken** (ber-*kay*-kern) *v* regard, view

bekken (*beh*-kern) *nt* (pl ~s) basin; pelvis

beklagen (ber-*klaa*-gern) *v* pity

bekleden (ber-*klāy*-dern) *v* upholster

beklemmen (ber-*kleh*-mern) *v* oppress

****beklimmen** (ber-*kli*-mern) *v* ascend

beklimming (ber-*kli*-ming) *c* (pl ~en) ascent

beknopt (ber-*knopt*) *adj* concise; brief

zich bekommeren om (ber-*ko*-mer-rern) care about

bekoring (ber-*kōā*-ring) *c* (pl ~en) attraction, charm

bekritiseren (ber-kree-tee-*zāy*-rern) *v* criticize

bekrompen (ber-*krom*-pern) *adj* narrow-minded

bekronen (ber-*krōā*-nern) *v* crown

bekwaam (ber-*kvaam*) *adj* able, capable; skilful

bekwaamheid (ber-*kvaam*-hayt) *c* (pl -heden) ability, faculty, capacity

bel (behl) *c* (pl ~len) bell; bubble

belachelijk (ber-*lah*-kher-lerk) *adj* ridiculous, ludicrous

belang (ber-*lahng*) *nt* (pl ~en) interest; importance; **van ~** **zijn* matter

belangrijk (ber-*lahng*-rayk) *adj* important; capital

belangstellend (ber-lahng-*steh*-lernt) *adj* interested

belangstelling (ber-*lahng*-steh-ling) *c* interest

belastbaar (ber-*lahst*-baar) *adj* dutiable

belasten (ber-*lahss*-tern) *v* charge; tax; **belast met** in charge of

belasting (ber-*lahss*-ting) *c* (pl ~en) charge; tax; taxation

belastingvrij (ber-lahss-ting-*vray*) *adj* duty-free; tax-free

beledigen (ber-*lāy*-der-gern) *v* insult; offend; **beledigend** offensive

belediging (ber-*lāy*-der-ging) *c* (pl ~en) insult; offence

beleefd (ber-*lāyft*) *adj* polite; civil

belegering (ber-*lāy*-ger-ring) *c* (pl ~en) siege

beleggen (ber-*leh*-gern) *v* invest

belegging (ber-*leh*-ging) *c* (pl ~en) investment

beleid (ber-*layt*) *nt* policy

belemmeren (ber-*leh*-mer-rern) *v* impede

beletsel (ber-*leht*-serl) *nt* (pl ~s, ~en) impediment

beletten (ber-*leh*-tern) *v* prevent

beleven (ber-*lay*-vern) *v* experience

Belg (behlkh) *c* (pl ~en) Belgian

België (*behl*-gee-Yer) Belgium

Belgisch (*behl*-geess) *adj* Belgian

belichting (ber-*lıkh*-tıng) *c* exposure

belichtingsmeter (ber-*lıkh*-tıngs-may-terr) *c* (pl ~s) exposure meter

*belijden** (ber-*lay*-dern) *v* confess

bellen (*beh*-lern) *v* *ring

belofte (ber-*lof*-ter) *c* (pl ~n) promise

belonen (ber-*loa*-nern) *v* reward

beloning (ber-*loa*-nıng) *c* (pl ~en) reward; prize

beloven (ber-*loa*-vern) *v* promise

bemachtigen (ber-*mahkh*-ter-gern) *v* secure

bemanning (ber-*mah*-nıng) *c* (pl ~en) crew

bemerken (ber-*mehr*-kern) *v* notice; perceive

bemiddelaar (ber-*mı*-der-laar) *c* (pl ~s) mediator

bemiddeld (ber-*mı*-derlt) *adj* well-to-do

bemiddelen (ber-*mı*-der-lern) *v* mediate

bemind (ber-*mınt*) *adj* beloved

zich bemoeien met (ber-*moo*ᵉᵉ-ern) interfere with

benadrukken (ber-*naa*-drer-kern) *v* emphasize, stress

benaming (ber-*naa*-mıng) *c* (pl ~en) denomination

benauwd (ber-*nout*) *adj* stuffy

bende (*behn*-der) *c* (pl ~n, ~s) gang

beneden (ber-*nay*-dern) *prep* under, below; *adv* underneath, beneath; below; downstairs; **naar** ~ downwards, down; downstairs

benieuwd (ber-*nee*ᵒᵒt) *adj* curious

benijden (ber-*nay*-dern) *v* envy

benoemen (ber-*noo*-mern) *v* nominate, appoint

benoeming (ber-*noo*-mıng) *c* (pl ~en) nomination, appointment

benutten (ber-*ner*-tern) *v* utilize

benzine (behn-*zee*-ner) *c* petrol; fuel; gasoline *nAm*, gas *nAm*

benzinepomp (behn-*zee*-ner-pomp) *c* (pl ~en) petrol pump; fuel pump *Am*; gas pump *Am*

benzinestation (behn-*zee*-ner-staa-shon) *nt* (pl ~s) service station, petrol station, filling station; gas station *Am*

benzinetank (behn-*zee*-ner-tehngk) *c* (pl ~s) petrol tank

beoefenen (ber-*oo*-fer-nern) *v* practise

beogen (ber-*oa*-gern) *v* aim at

beoordelen (ber-*oar*-day-lern) *v* judge

beoordeling (ber-*oar*-day-lıng) *c* (pl ~en) judgment

bepaald (ber-*paalt*) *adj* definite; certain

bepalen (ber-*paa*-lern) *v* define, determine; stipulate

bepaling (ber-*paa*-lıng) *c* (pl ~en) stipulation; definition

beperken (ber-*pehr*-kern) *v* limit

beperking (ber-*pehr*-kıng) *c* (pl ~en) restriction

beproeven (ber-*proo*-vern) *v* attempt

beraad (ber-*raat*) *nt* deliberation

beraadslagen (ber-*raat*-slaa-gern) *v* deliberate

beramen (ber-*raa*-mern) *v* devise

bereid (ber-*rayt*) *adj* prepared, willing

bereiden (ber-*ray*-dern) *v* cook

bereidwillig (ber-*rayt*-vı-lerkh) *adj* cooperative

bereik (ber-*rayk*) *nt* reach; range

bereikbaar (ber-*rayk*-baar) *adj* attainable

bereiken (ber-*ray*-kern) *v* reach; achieve, accomplish, attain

berekenen (ber-*ray*-ker-nern) *v* calculate; charge

berekening (ber-*rāy*-ker-nıng) *c* (pl ~en) calculation

berg (behrkh) *c* (pl ~en) mountain; mount

bergachtig (*behrkh*-ahkh-terkh) *adj* mountainous

bergketen (*behrkh*-kāy-tern) *c* (pl ~s) mountain range

bergkloof (*behrkh*-klōaf) *c* (pl -kloven) glen

bergpas (*behrkh*-pahss) *c* (pl ~sen) mountain pass

bergplaats (*behrkh*-plaats) *c* (pl ~en) depository

bergrug (*behrkh*-rerg) *c* (pl ~gen) ridge

bergsport (*behrkh*-sport) *c* mountain-eering

bericht (ber-*rıkht*) *nt* (pl ~en) mess-age; notice

berispen (ber-*rıss*-pern) *v* reprimand, scold

berk (behrk) *c* (pl ~en) birch

beroemd (ber-*rōōmt*) *adj* famous

beroep (ber-*rōōp*) *nt* (pl ~en) pro-fession; appeal; **beroeps**- pro-fessional

beroerd (ber-*rōōrt*) *adj* miserable

beroerte (ber-*rōōr*-ter) *c* (pl ~n, ~s) stroke

berouw (ber-*rou*) *nt* repentance

beroven (ber-*rōā*-vern) *v* rob

beroving (ber-*rōā*-vıng) *c* (pl ~en) robbery

berucht (ber-*rerkht*) *adj* notorious

bes (behss) *c* (pl ~sen) berry; cur-rant; **zwarte** ~ black-currant

beschaafd (ber-*skhaaft*) *adj* civilized; cultured

beschaamd (ber-*skhaamt*) *adj* ashamed

beschadigen (ber-*skhaa*-der-gern) *v* damage

beschaving (ber-*skhaa*-vıng) *c* (pl ~en) civilization; culture

bescheiden (ber-*skhay*-dern) *adj* mod-est

bescheidenheid (ber-*skhay*-dern-hayt) *c* modesty

beschermen (ber-*skhehr*-mern) *v* pro-tect

bescherming (ber-*skhehr*-mıng) *c* pro-tection

beschikbaar (ber-*skhık*-baar) *adj* avail-able

beschikken over (ber-*skhı*-kern) dis-pose of

beschikking (ber-*skhı*-king) *c* disposal

beschimmeld (ber-*skhı*-merlt) *adj* mouldy

beschouwen (ber-*skhou*-ern) *v* con-sider; regard; reckon

* **beschrijven** (ber-*skhray*-vern) *v* de-scribe

beschrijving (ber-*skhray*-vıng) *c* (pl ~en) description

beschuldigen (ber-*skherl*-der-gern) *v* accuse; blame

beschutten (ber-*skher*-tern) *v* shelter

beschutting (ber-*skher*-ting) *c* cover, shelter

beseffen (ber-*seh*-fern) *v* realize

beslag (ber-*slahkh*) *nt* batter; **beslag leggen op** impound, confiscate

beslissen (ber-*slı*-sern) *v* decide

beslissing (ber-*slı*-sing) *c* (pl ~en) decision

beslist (ber-*slıst*) *adv* without fail

besluit (ber-*slur^{ew}*-t) *nt* (pl ~en) deci-sion

* **besluiten** (ber-*slur^{ew}*-tern) *v* decide

besmettelijk (ber-*smeh*-ter-lerk) *adj* contagious, infectious

besmetten (ber-*smeh*-tern) *v* infect

besneeuwd (ber-*snāy^{oo}*t) *adj* snowy

bespelen (ber-*spāy*-lern) *v* play

bespottelijk (ber-*spo*-ter-lerk) *adj* rid-iculous, ludicrous

bespotten (ber-*spo*-tern) v ridicule;
mock

*bespreken (ber-*spray*-kern) v engage,
reserve; discuss

bespreking (ber-*spray*-king) c (pl ~en)
booking; review; discussion

best (behst) adj best

bestaan (ber-*staan*) nt existence

*bestaan (ber-*staan*) v exist; ~ uit
consist of

bestanddeel (ber-*stahn*-dayl) nt (pl
-delen) ingredient; element

besteden (ber-*stay*-dern) v *spend

bestek (ber-*stehk*) nt (pl ~ken) cutlery

bestelauto (ber-stehl-ōa-tōa) c (pl ~'s)
van; delivery van, pick-up van

bestelformulier (ber-stehl-for-mew-
leer) nt (pl ~en) order-form

bestellen (ber-*steh*-lern) v order

bestelling (ber-*steh*-ling) c (pl ~en)
order

bestemmen (ber-*steh*-mern) v destine

bestemming (ber-*steh*-ming) c (pl
~en) destination

bestendig (ber-*stehn*-derkh) adj permanent

*bestijgen (ber-*stay*-gern) v mount

bestraten (ber-*straa*-tern) v pave

*bestrijden (ber-*stray*-dern) v combat

besturen (ber-*stew*-rern) v *drive

bestuur (ber-*stewr*) nt (pl besturen)
direction; board; rule

bestuurlijk (ber-*stewr*-lerk) adj administrative

bestuursrecht (ber-*stewrs*-rehkht) nt
administrative law

betalen (ber-*taa*-lern) v *pay

betaling (ber-*taa*-ling) c (pl ~en) payment

betasten (ber-*tahss*-tern) v *feel

betekenen (ber-*tay*-ker-nern) v *mean

betekenis (ber-*tay*-ker-niss) c (pl
~sen) meaning; sense

beter (*bay*-terr) adj better; superior

beteugelen (ber-*tur*-ger-lern) v curb

betogen (ber-*tōa*-gern) v demonstrate

betoging (ber-*tōa*-ging) c (pl ~en)
demonstration

beton (ber-*ton*) nt concrete

betoveren (ber-*tōa*-ver-rern) v bewitch; **betoverend** enchanting,
glamorous

betovering (ber-*tōa*-ver-ring) c (pl
~en) spell

betrappen (ber-*trah*-pern) v *catch

*betreden (ber-*tray*-dern) v enter

*betreffen (ber-*treh*-fern) v concern;
affect, touch; **wat betreft** as regards

betreffende (ber-*treh*-fern-der) prep as
regards, regarding, about, concerning

betrekkelijk (ber-*treh*-ker-lerk) adj
relative

*betrekken (ber-*treh*-kern) v impli-
cate, *get involved; obtain

betrekking (ber-*treh*-king) c (pl ~en)
post, position, job; reference; **met
~ tot** regarding, with reference to

betreuren (ber-*trur*-rern) v regret

betrokken (ber-*tro*-kern) adj cloudy,
overcast; concerned, involved

betrouwbaar (ber-*trou*-baar) adj trustworthy, reliable

betuigen (ber-*tur*ew-gern) v express

betwijfelen (ber-*tvay*-fer-lern) v doubt,
query

betwisten (ber-*tviss*-tern) v dispute

beu (būr) adj tired of, fed up with

beuk (būrk) c (pl ~en) beech

beul (būrl) c (pl ~en) executioner

beurs (būrrs) c (pl beurzen) purse;
stock exchange; fair; grant

beurt (būrrt) c (pl ~en) turn

bevaarbaar (ber-*vaar*-baar) adj navigable

*bevallen (ber-*vah*-lern) v please

bevallig (ber-*vah*-lerkh) *adj* graceful

bevalling (ber-*vah*-ling) *c* (pl ~en) delivery, childbirth

*****bevaren** (ber-*vaa*-rern) *v* sail

bevatten (ber-*vah*-tern) *v* contain; include

bevel (ber-*vehl*) *nt* (pl ~en) command, order

*****bevelen** (ber-*vāy*-lern) *v* command, order

bevelhebber (ber-*vehl*-heh-berr) *c* (pl ~s) commander

beven (*bāy*-vern) *v* tremble

bever (*bāy*-verr) *c* (pl ~s) beaver

bevestigen (ber-*vehss*-ter-gern) *v* acknowledge, confirm; fasten; **bevestigend** affirmative

bevestiging (ber-*vehss*-ter-ging) *c* (pl ~en) confirmation

zich *****bevinden (ber-*vin*-dern) *****be

bevlieging (ber-*vlee*-ging) *c* (pl ~en) whim

bevochtigen (ber-*vokh*-ter-gern) *v* damp, moisten

bevoegd (ber-*vōōkht*) *adj* qualified

bevoegdheid (ber-*vōōkht*-hayt) *c* (pl -heden) qualification

bevolking (ber-*vol*-king) *c* population

bevoorrechten (ber-*vōā*-raykh-tern) *v* favour

bevorderen (ber-*vor*-der-rern) *v* promote

bevredigen (ber-*vrāy*-der-gern) *v* satisfy

bevrediging (ber-*vrāy*-der-ging) *c* (pl ~en) satisfaction

*****bevriezen** (ber-*vree*-zern) *v* *****freeze

bevrijding (ber-*vray*-ding) *c* liberation

bevuild (ber-*vur*^ew^*/t*) *adj* soiled

bewaken (ber-*vaa*-kern) *v* guard

bewaker (ber-*vaa*-kerr) *c* (pl ~s) guard; warden

bewapenen (ber-*vaa*-per-nern) *v* arm

bewaren (ber-*vaa*-rern) *v* *****hold; preserve; *****keep

bewaring (ber-*vaa*-ring) *c* preservation

beweeglijk (ber-*vāykh*-lerk) *adj* mobile

beweegreden (ber-*vāykh*-rāy-dern) *c* (pl ~en) cause

*****bewegen** (ber-*vāy*-gern) *v* move; stir

beweging (ber-*vāy*-ging) *c* (pl ~en) movement; motion

beweren (ber-*vāy*-rern) *v* claim

bewijs (ber-*vayss*) *nt* (pl bewijzen) proof, evidence; token; voucher

*****bewijzen** (ber-*vay*-zern) *v* prove

bewind (ber-*vint*) *nt* rule, government

bewolking (ber-*vol*-king) *c* clouds

bewolkt (ber-*volkt*) *adj* cloudy

bewonderen (ber-*von*-der-rern) *v* admire

bewondering (ber-*von*-der-ring) *c* admiration

bewonen (ber-*vōā*-nern) *v* inhabit

bewoner (ber-*vōā*-nerr) *c* (pl ~s) inhabitant; occupant

bewoonbaar (ber-*vōān*-baar) *adj* habitable, inhabitable

bewust (ber-*verst*) *adj* conscious, aware

bewusteloos (ber-*verss*-ter-lōass) *adj* unconscious

bewustzijn (ber-*verst*-sayn) *nt* consciousness

bezem (*bāy*-zerm) *c* (pl ~s) broom

bezeren (ber-*zāy*-rern) *v* *****hurt

bezet (ber-*zeht*) *adj* engaged, occupied

bezetten (ber-*zeh*-tern) *v* occupy

bezetting (ber-*zeh*-ting) *c* (pl ~en) occupation

bezielen (ber-*zee*-lern) *v* inspire

bezienswaardigheid (ber-zeen-*svaar*-derkh-hayt) *c* (pl -heden) sight

bezig (*bāy*-zerkh) *adj* engaged, busy

zich *****bezighouden met (*bāy*-zerkh-hou-dern) attend to

bezinksel (ber-*zingk*-serl) *nt* (pl ~s) deposit

bezit (ber-*zit*) *nt* property; possession

*bezitten (ber-*zi*-tern) *v* possess, own

bezitter (ber-*zi*-terr) *c* (pl ~s) owner

bezittingen (ber-*zi*-ting-ern) *pl* belongings *pl*

bezoek (ber-*zōōk*) *nt* (pl ~en) call, visit

*bezoeken (ber-*zōō*-kern) *v* visit; call on

bezoeker (ber-*zōō*-kerr) *c* (pl ~s) visitor

bezoekuren (ber-*zōōk*-ēw-rern) *pl* visiting hours

bezonnen (ber-*zo*-nern) *adj* sober

bezorgd (ber-*zorkht*) *adj* anxious, concerned

bezorgdheid (ber-*zorkht*-hayt) *c* worry, anxiety

bezorgen (ber-*zor*-gern) *v* deliver; supply

bezorging (ber-*zor*-ging) *c* delivery

bezwaar (ber-*zvaar*) *nt* (pl bezwaren) objection; ~ *hebben tegen object to; mind

*bezwijken (ber-*zvay*-kern) *v* collapse; succumb

bibberen (*bi*-ber-rern) *v* shiver

bibliotheek (bee-blee-ᵛōā-*tāyk*) *c* (pl -theken) library

*bidden (*bi*-dern) *v* pray

biecht (beekht) *c* (pl ~en) confession

biechten (*beekh*-tern) *v* confess

*bieden (*bee*-dern) *v* offer

biefstuk (*beef*-sterk) *c* (pl ~ken) steak

bier (beer) *nt* (pl ~en) beer; ale

bies (beess) *c* (pl biezen) rush

bieslook (*beess*-lōāk) *nt* chives *pl*

biet (beet) *c* (pl ~en) beet

big (bikh) *c* (pl ~gen) piglet

bij¹ (bay) *prep* near, at, with, by; to

bij² (bay) *c* (pl ~en) bee

bijbel (*bay*-berl) *c* (pl ~s) bible

bijbetekenis (*bay*-ber-tāy-ker-niss) *c* (pl ~sen) connotation

bijdrage (*bay*-draa-ger) *c* (pl ~n) contribution

bijeen (bay-*āyn*) *adv* together

*bijeenbrengen (bay-*āyn*-breh-ngern) *v* assemble

*bijeenkomen (bay-*āyng*-kōā-mern) *v* gather

bijeenkomst (bay-*āyng*-komst) *c* (pl ~en) meeting; rally; assembly, congress

bijenkorf (*bay*-er-korf) *c* (pl -korven) beehive

bijgebouw (*bay*-ger-bou) *nt* (pl ~en) annex

bijgeloof (*bay*-ger-lōāf) *nt* superstition

bijgevolg (bay-ger-*volkh*) *adv* consequently

*bijhouden (*bay*-hou-dern) *v* *keep up with

bijknippen (*bay*-kni-pern) *v* trim

bijkomend (*bay*-kōā-mernt) *adj* additional

bijkomstig (bay-*kom*-sterkh) *adj* additional; subordinate

bijl (bayl) *c* (pl ~en) axe

bijlage (*bay*-laa-ger) *c* (pl ~n) annex; enclosure

bijna (*bay*-naa) *adv* nearly, almost

bijnaam (*bay*-naam) *c* (pl -namen) nickname

bijouterie (bee-zhōō-ter-*ree*) *c* jewellery

*bijsluiten (*bay*-slur^ew-tern) *v* enclose

*bijstaan (*bay*-staan) *v* assist, aid

bijstand (*bay*-stahnt) *c* assistance

*bijten (*bay*-tern) *v* *bite

bijvoegen (*bay*-vōō-gern) *v* attach

bijvoeglijk naamwoord (bay-*vōōkh*-lerk naam-vōārt) adjective

bijvoorbeeld (ber-*vōār*-bāylt) *adv* for instance, for example

bijwonen (*bay*-vōā-nern) *v* assist at, attend

bijwoord (*bay*-vōārt) *nt* (pl ~en) adverb

bijziend (bay-*zeent*) *adj* short-sighted

bijzonder (bee-*zon*-derr) *adj* special, particular; peculiar; **in het ~** in particular, specially

bijzonderheid (bee-*zon*-derr-hayt) *c* (pl -heden) detail

bil (bil) *c* (pl ~len) buttock

biljart (bil-*Yahrt*) *nt* billiards *pl*

billijk (*bi*-lerk) *adj* right, fair, reasonable

*****binden** (*bin*-dern) *v* *bind; tie

binnen (*bi*-nern) *prep* within, inside; *adv* inside, indoors; in; indoor; **naar ~** inwards; **van ~** within, inside

binnenband (*bi*-ner-bahnt) *c* (pl ~en) inner tube

*****binnengaan** (*bi*-ner-gaan) *v* enter, *go in

binnenkant (*bi*-ner-kahnt) *c* interior, inside

*****binnenkomen** (*bi*-nern-kōa-mern) *v* enter

binnenkomst (*bi*-ner-komst) *c* entrance

binnenkort (bi-ner-*kort*) *adv* shortly

binnenlands (*bi*-ner-lahnts) *adj* domestic

binnenst (*bi*-nerst) *adj* inside; **binnenste buiten** *adv* inside out

*****binnenvallen** (*bi*-ner-vah-lern) *v* invade

biologie (bee-Yōa-lōa-*gee*) *c* biology

bioscoop (bee-Yoss-*kōap*) *c* (pl -scopen) cinema; pictures; movie theater *Am*, movies *Am*

biscuit (biss-*kvee*) *nt* (pl ~s) cookie *nAm*

bisschop (*biss*-khop) *c* (pl ~pen) bishop

bitter (*bi*-terr) *adj* bitter

blaar (blaar) *c* (pl blaren) blister

blaas (blaass) *c* (pl blazen) bladder; blister

blaasontsteking (*blaass*-ont-stāy-king) *c* (pl ~en) cystitis

blad[1] (blaht) *nt* (pl ~eren, blaren) leaf

blad[2] (blaht) *nt* (pl ~en) sheet; magazine

bladgoud (*blaht*-khout) *nt* gold leaf

bladzijde (*blaht*-say-der) *c* (pl ~n) page

blaffen (*blah*-fern) *v* bark; bay

blanco (*blahng*-kōa) *adj* blank

blank (blahngk) *adj* white

blankvoren (*blahngk*-fōa-rern) *c* (pl ~s) roach

blauw (blou) *adj* blue

*****blazen** (*blaa*-zern) *v* *blow

blazer (*blāy*-zerr) *c* (pl ~s) blazer

bleek (blāyk) *adj* pale

bleken (*blāy*-kern) *v* bleach

blessure (bleh-*sēw*-rer) *c* (pl ~s) injury

blij (blay) *adj* glad; happy, joyful

blijkbaar (*blayk*-baar) *adv* apparently

*****blijken** (*blay*-kern) *v* prove; appear

blijspel (*blay*-spehl) *nt* (pl ~en) comedy

*****blijven** (*blay*-vern) *v* stay, remain; *keep; **blijvend** lasting; permanent

blik (blik) *nt* (pl ~ken) tin, can; *c* look; glimpse, glance; **een ~** *werpen** glance

blikopener (*blik*-ōa-per-nerr) *c* (pl ~s) tin-opener, can opener

bliksem (*blik*-serm) *c* lightning

blind[1] (blint) *nt* (pl ~en) shutter

blind[2] (blint) *adj* blind

blindedarm (blin-der-*dahrm*) *c* (pl ~en) appendix

blindedarmontsteking (blin-der-*dahrm*-ont-stāy-king) *c* (pl ~en) appendicitis

*****blinken** (*bling*-kern) *v* *shine; **blinkend** bright

blocnote (*blok*-nōat) *c* (pl ~s) writing-pad

bloed (blo͞ot) *nt* blood

bloedarmoede (blo͞ot-ahr-mo͞o-der) *c* anaemia

bloeddruk (blo͞o-drerk) *c* blood pressure

bloeden (blo͞o-dern) *v* *bleed

bloeding (blo͞o-dıng) *c* (pl ~en) haemorrhage

bloedsomloop (blo͞ot-som-lo͞ap) *c* circulation

bloedvat (blo͞ot-faht) *nt* (pl ~en) blood-vessel

bloedvergiftiging (blo͞ot-ferr-gıf-ter-gıng) *c* blood-poisoning

bloem¹ (blo͞om) *c* flour

bloem² (blo͞om) *c* (pl ~en) flower

bloemblad (blo͞om-blaht) *nt* (pl ~en) petal

bloembol (blo͞om-bol) *c* (pl ~len) bulb

bloemenwinkel (blo͞o-mer-vıng-kerl) *c* (pl ~s) flower-shop

bloemist (blo͞o-mıst) *c* (pl ~en) florist

bloemkool (blo͞om-ko͞al) *c* (pl -kolen) cauliflower

bloemlezing (blo͞om-lāy-zıng) *c* (pl ~en) anthology

bloemperk (blo͞om-pehrk) *nt* (pl ~en) flowerbed

blok (blok) *nt* (pl ~ken) block; **blokje** *nt* cube

blokkeren (blo-kāy-rern) *v* block

blond (blont) *adj* fair

blondine (blon-dee-ner) *c* (pl ~s) blonde

bloot (blo͞at) *adj* bare; naked

blootleggen (blo͞at-leh-gern) *v* uncover

blootstelling (blo͞at-steh-lıng) *c* (pl ~en) exposure

blouse (blo͞o-zer) *c* (pl ~s) blouse

blozen (blo͞a-zern) *v* blush

blussen (bler-sern) *v* extinguish

bocht (bokht) *c* (pl ~en) turning, bend; curve, turn

bode (bo͞a-der) *c* (pl ~n, ~s) messenger

bodem (bo͞a-derm) *c* (pl ~s) bottom; ground; soil

boef (bo͞of) *c* (pl boeven) villain

boei (bo͞oee) *c* (pl ~en) buoy

boeien (bo͞oee-ern) *v* fascinate

boek (bo͞ok) *nt* (pl ~en) book

boeken (bo͞o-kern) *v* book

boekenstalletje (bo͞o-ker-stah-ler-tYer) *nt* (pl ~s) bookstand

boeket (bo͞o-keht) *nt* (pl ~ten) bouquet

boekhandel (bo͞ok-hahn-derl) *c* (pl ~s) bookstore

boekhandelaar (bo͞ok-hahn-der-laar) *c* (pl -laren) bookseller

boekwinkel (bo͞ok-vıng-kerl) *c* (pl ~s) bookstore

boel (bo͞ol) *c* lot

boer (bo͞or) *c* (pl ~en) farmer; peasant; knave

boerderij (bo͞or-der-ray) *c* (pl ~en) farm; farmhouse

boerin (bo͞o-rın) *c* (pl ~nen) farmer's wife

boete (bo͞o-ter) *c* (pl ~n, ~s) penalty, fine

boetseren (bo͞ot-sāy-rern) *v* model

bof (bof) *c* mumps

bok (bok) *c* (pl ~ken) goat

boksen (bok-sern) *v* box

bokswedstrijd (boks-veht-strayt) *c* (pl ~en) boxing match

bol (bol) *c* (pl ~len) bulb; sphere

Boliviaan (bo͞a-lee-vee-Yaan) *c* (pl -vianen) Bolivian

Boliviaans (bo͞a-lee-vee-Yaans) *adj* Bolivian

Bolivië (bo͞a-lee-vee-Yer) Bolivia

bom (bom) *c* (pl ~men) bomb

bombarderen (bom-bahr-dāy-rern) *v* bomb

bon (bon) *c* (pl ~nen) coupon; ticket; voucher

bonbon (bom-*bon*) *c* (pl ~s) chocolate

bond (bont) *c* (pl ~en) league, federation

bondgenoot (*bont*-kher-nōat) *c* (pl -noten) associate

bondgenootschap (*bont*-kher-nōat-skhahp) *nt* (pl ~pen) alliance

bons (bons) *c* (pl bonzen) bump

bont (bont) *adj* gay, colourful; *nt* furs

bontjas (*bon*-t^Yahss) *c* (pl ~sen) fur coat

bontwerker (*bon*-tvehr-kerr) *c* (pl ~s) furrier

bonzen (*bon*-zern) *v* bump

boodschap (*bōat*-skhahp) *c* (pl ~pen) errand; message

boodschappentas (*bōat*-skhah-per-tahss) *c* (pl ~sen) shopping bag

boog (bōakh) *c* (pl bogen) arch; bow

boogvormig (*bōakh*-for-merkh) *adj* arched

boom (bōam) *c* (pl bomen) tree

boomgaard (*bōam*-gaart) *c* (pl ~en) orchard

boomkwekerij (bōam-kvāy-ker-*ray*) *c* (pl ~en) nursery

boon (bōan) *c* (pl bonen) bean

boor (bōar) *c* (pl boren) drill

boord (bōart) *nt/c* (pl ~en) collar; **aan boord** aboard; **van boord *gaan** disembark

boordeknoopje (*bōar*-der-knōa-p^Yer) *nt* (pl ~s) collar stud

boos (bōass) *adj* cross

boosaardig (bōa-*zaar*-derkh) *adj* malicious, vicious

boosheid (*bōass*-hayt) *c* anger, temper

boot (bōat) *c* (pl boten) boat

bootje (*bōa*-t^Yer) *nt* (pl ~s) dinghy

boottocht (*bōa*-tokht) *c* (pl ~en) cruise

bord (bort) *nt* (pl ~en) dish, plate; board

bordeel (bor-*dāyl*) *nt* (pl -delen) brothel

borduren (bor-*deW*-rern) *v* embroider

borduurwerk (bor-*deWr*-vehrk) *nt* (pl ~en) embroidery

boren (*bōa*-rern) *v* drill, bore

borg (borkh) *c* (pl ~en) guarantor

borgsom (*borkh*-som) *c* (pl ~men) bail

borrel (*boa*-rerl) *c* (pl ~s) drink

borrelhapje (*bo*-rerl-hahp-^Yer) *nt* (pl ~s) appetizer

borst (borst) *c* (pl ~en) chest; breast, bosom

borstel (*bor*-sterl) *c* (pl ~s) brush

borstelen (*bor*-ster-lern) *v* brush

borstkas (*borst*-kahss) *c* (pl ~sen) chest

bos (boss) *nt* (pl ~sen) forest, wood; *c* bunch

bosje (*bo*-sher) *nt* (pl ~s) grove

boswachter (*boss*-vahkh-terr) *c* (pl ~s) forester

bot¹ (bot) *adj* dull, blunt

bot² (bot) *nt* (pl ~ten) bone

boter (*bōa*-terr) *c* butter

boterham (*bōa*-terr-hahm) *c* (pl ~men) sandwich

botsen (*bot*-sern) *v* bump; collide, crash

botsing (*bot*-sing) *c* (pl ~en) collision, crash

bougie (bōo-*zhee*) *c* (pl ~s) sparking-plug

bout (bout) *c* (pl ~en) bolt

boutique (bōo-*teek*) *c* (pl ~s) boutique

bouw (bou) *c* construction

bouwen (*bou*-ern) *v* *build; construct

bouwkunde (*bou*-kern-der) *c* architecture

bouwvallig (bou-*vah*-lerkh) *adj* dilapidated

boven (*bōa*-vern) *prep* above, over;

adv above; upstairs; **naar** ~ upwards, up; upstairs

bovendek (*boā*-vern-dehk) *nt* main deck

bovendien (boa-vern-*deen*) *adv* furthermore, moreover, besides

bovenkant (*boā*-verng-kahnt) *c* (pl ~en) top side, top

bovenop (boā-vern-*op*) *prep* on top of

bovenst (*boā*-verst) *adj* upper, top

braaf (braaf) *adj* good

braak (braak) *adj* waste

braam (braam) *c* (pl bramen) blackberry

*braden (*braa*-dern) *v* fry; roast

braken (*braa*-kern) *v* vomit

brand (brahnt) *c* (pl ~en) fire

brandalarm (*brahnt*-aa-lahrm) *nt* fire-alarm

brandblusapparaat (brahnt-blerss-ah-paa-raat) *nt* (pl -raten) fire-extinguisher

branden (*brahn*-dern) *v* *burn

brandkast (*brahnt*-kahst) *c* (pl ~en) safe

brandmerk (*brahnt*-mehrk) *nt* (pl ~en) brand

brandpunt (*brahnt*-pernt) *nt* (pl ~en) focus

brandspiritus (*brahnt*-spee-ree-terss) *c* methylated spirits

brandstof (*brahnt*-stof) *c* (pl ~fen) fuel

brandtrap (*brahn*-trahp) *c* (pl ~pen) fire-escape

brandvrij (*brahnt*-fray) *adj* fireproof

brandweer (*brahn*-tvayr) *c* fire-brigade

brandwond (*brahn*-tvont) *c* (pl ~en) burn

brasem (*braa*-serm) *c* (pl ~s) bream

Braziliaan (braa-zee-lee-*Yaan*) *c* (pl -lianen) Brazilian

Braziliaans (braa-zee-lee-*Yaans*) *adj* Brazilian

Brazilië (braa-zee-lee-*Yer*) Brazil

breed (brayt) *adj* broad, wide

breedte (*bray*-ter) *c* (pl ~n, ~s) breadth, width

breedtegraad (*bray*-ter-graat) *c* (pl -graden) latitude

breekbaar (*brayk*-baar) *adj* fragile

breekijzer (*bray*-kay-zerr) *nt* (pl ~s) crowbar

breien (bray-ern) *v* *knit

*breken (*bray*-kern) *v* *break; *burst; crack; fracture

*brengen (*breh*-ngern) *v* *bring; *take

bres (brehss) *c* (pl ~sen) gap, breach

bretels (brer-*tehls*) *pl* braces *pl*; suspenders *plAm*

breuk (brurk) *c* (pl ~en) break; fracture; hernia

brief (breef) *c* (pl brieven) letter; **aangetekende** ~ registered letter

briefkaart (*breef*-kaart) *c* (pl ~en) card, postcard

briefopener (*breef*-oā-per-nerr) *c* (pl ~s) paper-knife

briefpapier (*breef*-paa-peer) *nt* notepaper

briefwisseling (*breef*-vi-ser-ling) *c* correspondence

bries (breess) *c* breeze

brievenbus (*bree*-ver-berss) *c* (pl ~sen) letter-box, pillar-box; mailbox *nAm*

bril (bril) *c* (pl ~len) spectacles, glasses

briljant (bril-*Yahnt*) *adj* brilliant

Brit (brit) *c* (pl ~ten) Briton

Brits (brits) *adj* British

broche (bro-sher) *c* (pl ~s) brooch

brochure (bro-*shew*-rer) *c* (pl ~s) brochure

broeder (*broō*-derr) *c* (pl ~s) brother

broederschap (*broō*-derr-skhahp) *c*

fraternity

broeikas (*broͦee*-kahss) *c* (pl ~sen) greenhouse

broek (brōͦk) *c* (pl ~en) trousers *pl*, slacks *pl*; pants *plAm*; **korte ~** shorts *pl*

broekpak (*brōͦk*-pahk) *nt* (pl ~ken) pant-suit

broer (brōͦor) *c* (pl ~s) brother

brok (brok) *nt* (pl ~ken) morsel; lump

bromfiets (*brom*-feets) *c* (pl ~en) moped

brommer (*bro*-merr) *c* (pl ~s) motorbike *nAm*

bron (bron) *c* (pl ~nen) well; fountain, source, spring; **geneeskrachtige ~** spa

bronchitis (brong-*khee*-terss) *c* bronchitis

brons (brons) *nt* bronze

bronzen (*bron*-zern) *adj* bronze

brood (brōͦat) *nt* (pl broden) bread; loaf

broodje (*brōͦa*-tᵛer) *nt* (pl ~s) roll, bun

broos (brōͦass) *adj* fragile

brouwen (*brou*-ern) *v* brew

brouwerij (brou-er-*ray*) *c* (pl ~en) brewery

brug (brerkh) *c* (pl ~gen) bridge

bruid (brur^ewt) *c* (pl ~en) bride

bruidegom (*brur^ew*-der-gom) *c* (pl ~s) bridegroom

bruikbaar (*brur^ew*k-baar) *adj* usable; useful

bruiloft (*brur^ew*-loft) *c* (pl ~en) wedding

bruin (brur^ewn) *adj* brown

brullen (*brer*-lern) *v* roar

brunette (brew-*neh*-ter) *c* (pl ~s) brunette

brutaal (brew-*taal*) *adj* bold, impertinent, insolent

bruto (*brōͦ*-tōͦa) *adj* gross

budget (ber-*jeht*) *nt* (pl ~ten, ~s) budget

buffet (bew-*feht*) *nt* (pl ~ten) buffet

bui (bur^ew) *c* (pl ~en) shower; spirit

buidel (*bur^ew*-derl) *c* (pl ~s) pouch

buigbaar (*bur^ew*kh-baar) *adj* flexible

***buigen** (*bur^ew*-gern) *v* *bend; bow

buigzaam (*bur^ew*kh-saam) *adj* supple

buik (bur^ewk) *c* (pl ~en) belly

buikpijn (*bur^ew*k-payn) *c* stomachache

buis (bur^ewss) *c* (pl buizen) tube

buiten (*bur^ew*-tern) *prep* outside, out of; *adv* out; outside, outdoors; **naar ~** outwards

buitengewoon (*bur^ew*-ter-ger-vōͦan) *adj* extraordinary, exceptional

buitenhuis (*bur^ew*-ter-hur^ewss) *nt* (pl -huizen) cottage

buitenkant (*bur^ew*-ter-kahnt) *c* (pl ~en) outside, exterior

in het buitenland (ın ert *bur^ew*-tern-lahnt) abroad

buitenlander (*bur^ew*-ter-lahn-derr) *c* (pl ~s) alien, foreigner

buitenlands (*bur^ew*-ter-lahnts) *adj* alien, foreign

buitensporig (bur^ew-ter-*spōͦa*-rerkh) *adj* excessive

buitenwijk (*bur^ew*-ter-vayk) *c* (pl ~en) suburb; outskirts *pl*

zich bukken (*ber*-kern) *bend down

Bulgaar (berl-*gaar*) *c* (pl -garen) Bulgarian

Bulgaars (berl-*gaars*) *adj* Bulgarian

Bulgarije (berl-gaa-*ray*-er) Bulgaria

bult (berlt) *c* (pl ~en) lump

bumper (*berm*-perr) *c* (pl ~s) bumper, fender

bundel (*bern*-derl) *c* (pl ~s) bundle

bundelen (*bern*-der-lern) *v* bundle

burcht (berrkht) *c* (pl ~en) stronghold

bureau (bew-*rōͦa*) *nt* (pl ~s) agency, office; bureau, desk; **~ voor ge-**

vonden voorwerpen lost property office

bureaucratie (bew-rōa-kraa-*tsee*) *c* bureaucracy

burgemeester (berr-ger-*mǎyss*-terr) *c* (pl ~s) mayor

burger (*berr*-gerr) *c* (pl ~s) citizen; civilian; **burger**- civilian, civic

burgerlijk (*berr*-gerr-lerk) *adj* bourgeois, middle-class; ~ **recht** civil law

bus (berss) *c* (pl ~sen) coach, bus; tin, canister

buste (*bew*-ster) *c* (pl ~s, ~n) bust

bustehouder (*bew*-ster-hou-derr) *c* (pl ~s) brassiere, bra

buur (bewr) *c* (pl buren) neighbour

buurman (*bewr*-mahn) *c* neighbour

buurt (bewrt) *c* (pl ~en) neighbourhood, vicinity

C

cabaret (kaa-baa-*reht*) *nt* (pl ~s) cabaret

cabine (kaa-*bee*-ner) *c* (pl ~s) cabin

cadeau (kaa-*dōā*) *nt* (pl ~s) gift, present

café (kah-*fǎy*) *nt* (pl ~s) café; public house, pub

cafetaria (kah-fer-*taa*-ree-ᵞaa) *c* (pl ~'s) cafeteria

caissière (kah-*shai*-rer) *c* (pl ~s) cashier

cake (kǎyk) *c* (pl ~s) cake

calcium (*kahl*-see-ᵞerm) *nt* calcium

calorie (kah-lōa-*ree*) *c* (pl ~ën) calorie

calvinisme (kahl-vee-*niss*-mer) *nt* Calvinism

camee (kaa-*mǎy*) *c* (pl ~ën) cameo

campagne (kahm-*pah*-ñer) *c* (pl ~s) campaign

camping (*kehm*-pɪng) *c* (pl ~s) camping site, camping

Canada (*kaa*-naa-daa) Canada

Canadees (kaa-naa-*dǎyss*) *adj* Canadian

capabel (kaa-*paa*-berl) *adj* able

capaciteit (kaa-paa-see-*tayt*) *c* (pl ~en) capacity

cape (kǎyp) *c* (pl ~s) cape

capitulatie (kah-pee-tēw-*laa*-tsee) *c* (pl ~s) capitulation

capsule (kahp-*sēw*-ler) *c* (pl ~s) capsule

caravan (*keh*-rer-vern) *c* (pl ~s) caravan

carbonpapier (kahr-*bon*-paa-peer) *nt* carbon paper

carburateur (kahr-bēw-raa-*tūrr*) *c* (pl ~s) carburettor

carillon (kaa-rɪl-ᵞon) *nt* (pl ~s) chimes *pl*

carnaval (*kahr*-naa-vahl) *nt* carnival

carrière (kah-ree-ᵞai-rer) *c* (pl ~s) career

carrosserie (kah-ro-ser-*ree*) *c* (pl ~ën) coachwork; motor body *Am*

carter (*kahr*-terr) *nt* crankcase

casino (kaa-*zee*-nōā) *nt* (pl ~'s) casino

catacombe (kah-tah-*kom*-ber) *c* (pl ~n) catacomb

catalogus (kah-*taa*-lōā-gerss) *c* (pl -gussen, -gi) catalogue

catarre (kaa-*tahr*) *c* catarrh

catastrofe (kaa-taa-*straw*-fer) *c* (pl ~s) catastrophe, disaster

categorie (kaa-ter-gōā-*ree*) *c* (pl ~ën) category

cavia (*kaa*-vee-ᵞaa) *c* (pl ~'s) guinea-pig

cel (sehl) *c* (pl ~len) cell

celibaat (sǎy-lee-*baat*) *nt* celibacy

cellofaan (seh-loa-*faan*) *nt* cellophane

celsius (*sehl*-see-ᵞerss) centigrade

cement (ser-*mehnt*) *nt* cement

censuur (sehn-*zewr*) *c* censorship

centimeter (*sehn-tee-māy-terr*) *c* (pl ~s) centimetre; tape-measure

centraal (sehn-*traal*) *adj* central; ~ **station** central station; **centrale verwarming** central heating

centraliseren (sehn-traa-lee-*zāy*-rern) *v* centralize

centrifuge (sehn-tree-*few*-zher) *c* (pl ~s) dryer

centrum (*sehn*-trerm) *nt* (pl centra) centre

ceramiek (sāy-raa-*meek*) *c* ceramics *pl*

ceremonie (sāy-rer-*mōa*-nee) *c* (pl -niën, -nies) ceremony

certificaat (sehr-tee-fee-*kaat*) *nt* (pl -caten) certificate

chalet (shaa-*leht*) *nt* (pl ~s) chalet

champagne (shahm-*pah*-ñer) *c* (pl ~s) champagne

champignon (shahm-pee-*ñon*) *c* (pl ~s) mushroom

chantage (shahn-*taa*-zher) *c* blackmail

chanteren (shahn-*tāy*-rern) *v* blackmail

chaos (*khaa*-oss) *c* chaos

chaotisch (khaa-*ōa*-teess) *adj* chaotic

charlatan (*shahr*-laa-tahn) *c* (pl ~s) quack

charmant (shahr-*mahnt*) *adj* charming

charme (*shahr*-mer) *c* (pl ~s) charm; glamour

chartervlucht (*chahr*-terr-vlerkht) *c* (pl ~en) charter flight

chassis (shah-*see*) *nt* (pl ~) chassis

chauffeur (shōa-*fūrr*) *c* (pl ~s) driver, chauffeur

chef (shehf) *c* (pl ~s) boss, manager, chief

chef-kok (shehf-*kok*) *c* (pl ~s) chef

chemie (khāy-*mee*) *c* chemistry

chemisch (*khāy*-meess) *adj* chemical

cheque (shehk) *c* (pl ~s) cheque; check *nAm*

chequeboekje (shehk-bōo-k^yer) *nt* (pl ~s) cheque-book; check-book *nAm*

chic (sheek) *adj* smart

Chileen (shee-*lāyn*) *c* (pl -lenen) Chilean

Chileens (shee-*lāyns*) *adj* Chilean

Chili (*shee*-lee) Chile

China (*shee*-naa) China

Chinees (shee-*nāyss*) *adj* Chinese

chirurg (shee-*rerrkh*) *c* (pl ~en) surgeon

chloor (khlōar) *nt* chlorine

chocola (shōa-kōa-*laa*) *c* chocolate

chocolademelk (shōa-kōa-*laa*-der-mehlk) *c* chocolate

christelijk (*kriss*-ter-lerk) *adj* Christian

christen (*kriss*-tern) *c* (pl ~en) Christian

Christus (*kriss*-terss) Christ

chronisch (*khrōa*-neess) *adj* chronic

chronologisch (khrōa-nōa-*lōa*-geess) *adj* chronological

chroom (khrōam) *nt* chromium

cijfer (*say*-ferr) *nt* (pl ~s) number, figure; digit; mark

cilinder (see-*lin*-derr) *c* (pl ~s) cylinder

cilinderkop (see-*lin*-derr-kop) *c* (pl ~pen) cylinder head

cipier (see-*peer*) *c* (pl ~s) jailer

circa (*sir*-kaa) *adv* approximately

circulatie (sir-kew-*laa*-tsee) *c* circulation

circus (*sir*-kerss) *nt* (pl ~sen) circus

cirkel (*sir*-kerl) *c* (pl ~s) circle

citaat (see-*taat*) *nt* (pl citaten) quotation

citeren (see-*tāy*-rern) *v* quote

citroen (see-*trōon*) *c* (pl ~en) lemon

civiel (see-*veel*) *adj* civil

clausule (klou-*sew*-ler) *c* (pl ~s) clause

clavecimbel (klaa-ver-*sim*-berl) *c* (pl ~s) harpsichord

claxon (*klahk*-son) *c* (pl ~s) horn, hooter

claxonneren (klahk-so-*nay*-rern) *v* hoot ; toot *vAm*, honk *vAm*

clementie (klay-*mehn*-tsee) *c* mercy

cliënt (klee-*ᵞehnt*) *c* (pl ~en) customer, client

closetpapier (kloa-*zeht*-pah-peer) *nt* toilet-paper

cocaïne (koa-kaa-*ee*-ner) *c* cocaine

code (*koa*-der) *c* (pl ~s) code

coffeïne (ko-fay-*ee*-ner) *c* caffeine

coffeïnevrij (ko-fay-*ee*-ner-vray) *adj* decaffeinated

cognac (ko-*ñahk*) *c* cognac

coiffure (kvah-*few*-rer) *c* (pl ~s) hair-do

colbert (kol-*bair*) *c* (pl ~s) jacket

collectant (ko-lehk-*tahnt*) *c* (pl ~en) collector

collecteren (ko-lehk-*tay*-rern) *v* collect

collectie (ko-*lehk*-see) *c* (pl ~s) collection

collectief (ko-lehk-*teef*) *adj* collective

collega (ko-*lay*-gaa) *c* (pl ~'s) colleague

college (ko-*lay*-zher) *nt* (pl ~s) lecture

Colombia (koa-*lom*-bee-ᵞaa) Colombia

Colombiaan (koa-lom-bee-ᵞaan) *c* (pl -bianen) Colombian

Colombiaans (koa-lom-bee-ᵞaans) *adj* Colombian

coma (*koa*-maa) *nt* coma

combinatie (kom-bee-*naa*-tsee) *c* (pl ~s) combination

combineren (kom-bee-*nay*-rern) *v* combine

comfortabel (kom-for-*taa*-berl) *adj* comfortable

comité (ko-mee-*tay*) *nt* (pl ~s) committee

commentaar (ko-mehn-*taar*) *nt* (pl -taren) comment

commercieel (ko-mehr-*shayl*) *adj* commercial

commissie (ko-*mi*-see) *c* (pl ~s) committee ; commission

commode (ko-*moa*-der) *c* (pl ~s) bureau *nAm*

commune (ko-*mew*-ner) *c* (pl ~s) commune

communicatie (ko-mew-nee-*kaa*-tsee) *c* communication

communiqué (ko-mew-nee-*kay*) *nt* (pl ~s) communiqué

communisme (ko-mew-*niss*-mer) *nt* communism

communist (ko-mew-*nist*) *c* (pl ~en) communist

compact (kom-*pahkt*) *adj* compact

compagnon (kom-pah-*ñon*) *c* (pl ~s) partner

compensatie (kom-pehn-*zaa*-tsee) *c* (pl ~s) compensation

compenseren (kom-pehn-*zay*-rern) *v* compensate

compleet (kom-*playt*) *adj* complete

complex (kom-*plehks*) *nt* (pl ~en) complex

compliment (kom-plee-*mehnt*) *nt* (pl ~en) compliment

componist (kom-poa-*nist*) *c* (pl ~en) composer

compositie (kom-poa-*zee*-tsee) *c* (pl ~s) composition

compromis (kom-proa-*mee*) *nt* (pl ~sen) compromise

concentratie (kon-sehn-*traa*-tsee) *c* (pl ~s) concentration

concentreren (kon-sehn-*tray*-rern) *v* concentrate

conceptie (kon-*sehp*-see) *c* conception

concert (kon-*sehrt*) *nt* (pl ~en) concert

concertzaal (kon-*sehrt*-saal) *c* (pl -zalen) concert hall

concessie (kon-*seh*-see) *c* (pl ~s) concession

concierge (kon-*shehr*-zheh) c (pl ~s) janitor; caretaker, concierge

conclusie (kong-*klew*-zee) c (pl ~s) conclusion

concreet (kong-*krayt*) adj concrete

concurrent (kong-kew-*rehnt*) c (pl ~en) competitor; rival

concurrentie (kong-kew-*rehn*-tsee) c competition; rivalry

conditie (kon-*dee*-tsee) c (pl ~s) condition

conducteur (kon-derk-*turr*) c (pl ~s) conductor; ticket collector

conferencier (kon-fer-rahng-*shay*) c (pl ~s) entertainer

conferentie (kon-fer-*rehn*-see) c (pl ~s) conference

conflict (kon-*flikt*) nt (pl ~en) conflict

congregatie (kong-gray-*gaa*-tsee) c (pl ~s) congregation

congres (kong-*grehss*) nt (pl ~sen) congress

consequentie (kon-ser-*kvehn*-see) c (pl ~s) consequence

conservatief (kon-zerr-vaa-*teef*) adj conservative

conservatorium (kon-zerr-vaa-*tōa*-ree-Yerm) nt (pl -ria) music academy

conserven (kon-*sehr*-vern) pl tinned food

consideratie (kon-see-der-*raa*-tsee) c consideration

constant (kon-*stahnt*) adj even

constateren (koan-staa-*tay*-rern) v note, ascertain; diagnose

constipatie (kon-stee-*paa*-tsee) c constipation

constructie (kon-*strerk*-see) c (pl ~s) construction

construeren (kon-strew°°-*ay*-rern) v construct

consul (*kon*-zerl) c (pl ~s) consul

consulaat (kon-zew-*laat*) nt (pl -laten) consulate

consult (kon-*zerlt*) nt (pl ~en) consultation

consultatiebureau (kon-zerl-*taa*-tsee-bew-rōa) nt (pl ~s) health centre

consument (kon-zew-*mehnt*) c (pl ~en) consumer

contact (kon-*tahkt*) nt (pl ~en) contact; touch

contactlenzen (kon-*tahkt*-lehn-zern) pl contact lenses

contanten (kon-*tahn*-tern) pl cash

continent (kon-tee-*nehnt*) nt (pl ~en) continent

continentaal (kon-tee-nehn-*taal*) adj continental

contra (*kon*-traa) prep versus

contract (kon-*trahkt*) nt (pl ~en) agreement, contract

contrast (kon-*trahst*) nt (pl ~en) contrast

controle (kon-*traw*-ler) c (pl ~s) control; supervision, inspection

controleren (kon-trōa-*lay*-rern) v control, check

controlestrook (kon-*traw*-ler-strōak) c (-stroken) counterfoil, stub

controversieel (kon-trōa-vehr-*zhayl*) adj controversial

conversatie (kon-verr-*zaa*-tsee) c (pl ~s) conversation

coöperatie (kōa-ōa-per-*raa*-tsee) c (pl ~s) co-operative

coöperatief (kōa-ōa-per-raa-*teef*) adj co-operative

coördinatie (kōa-or-dee-*naa*-tsee) c co-ordination

coördineren (kōa-or-dee-*nay*-rern) v co-ordinate

corpulent (kor-pew-*lehnt*) adj corpulent, stout

correct (ko-*rehkt*) adj correct

correctie (ko-*rehk*-see) c (pl ~s) correction

correspondent (ko-rehss-pon-*dehnt*) c

(pl ~en) correspondent

correspondentie (ko-rehss-pon-*dehn*-see) *c* correspondence

corresponderen (ko-rehss-pon-*dāy*-rern) *v* correspond

corrigeren (ko-ree-*zhāy*-rern) *v* correct

corrupt (ko-*rerpt*) *adj* corrupt

couchette (kōō-*sheh*-ter) *c* (pl ~s) berth

coupé (kōō-*pāy*) *c* (pl ~s) compartment; ~ **voor rokers** smoking-compartment

couplet (kōō-*pleht*) *nt* (pl ~ten) stanza

coupon (kōō-*pon*) *c* (pl ~s) coupon

crèche (krehsh) *c* (pl ~s) nursery

crediteren (krāy-dee-*tāy*-rern) *v* credit

creëren (krāy-*āy*-rern) *v* create

crematie (krāy-*maa*-tsee) *c* (pl ~s) cremation

crème (kraim) *c* (pl ~s) cream; **vochtinbrengende** ~ moisturizing cream

cremeren (krāy-*māy*-rern) *v* cremate

criminaliteit (kree-mee-naa-lee-*tayt*) *c* criminality

crimineel (kree-mee-*nāyl*) *adj* criminal

crisis (*kree*-serss) *c* (pl -ses) crisis

criticus (*kree*-tee-kerss) *c* (pl -ci) critic

croquant (krōa-*kahnt*) *adj* crisp

Cuba (*kēw*-baa) Cuba

Cubaan (kēw-*baan*) *c* (pl -banen) Cuban

Cubaans (kēw-*baans*) *adj* Cuban

cultuur (kerl-*tēwr*) *c* (pl -turen) culture

cursiefschrift (kerr-*zeef*-skhrift) *nt* italics *pl*

cursus (*kerr*-zerss) *c* (pl ~sen) course

cyclus (*see*-klerss) *c* (pl ~sen) cycle

D

daad (daat) *c* (pl daden) deed, act

daar (daar) *adv* there

daarheen (*daar*-hāyn) *adv* there

daarom (*daa*-rom) *conj* therefore

dadel (*daa*-derl) *c* (pl ~s) date

dadelijk (*daa*-der-lerk) *adv* at once, immediately; presently

dag (dahkh) *c* (pl ~en) day; **dag!** hello!; good-bye!; **per** ~ per day

dagblad (*dahkh*-blaht) *nt* (pl ~en) daily

dagboek (*dahkh*-bōōk) *nt* (pl ~en) diary

dagelijks (*daa*-ger-lerks) *adj* daily

dageraad (*daa*-ger-raat) *c* daybreak, dawn

daglicht (*dahkh*-likht) *nt* daylight

dagvaarding (*dahkh*-vaar-ding) *c* (pl ~en) summons

dak (dahk) *nt* (pl ~en) roof

dakpan (*dahk*-pahn) *c* (pl ~nen) tile

dal (dahl) *nt* (pl ~en) valley

dalen (*daa*-lern) *v* descend

dam (dahm) *c* (pl ~men) dam; dike

dambord (*dahm*-bort) *nt* (pl ~en) draught-board

dame (*daa*-mer) *c* (pl ~s) lady

damestoilet (*daa*-merss-tvah-leht) *nt* (pl ~ten) powder-room, ladies' room

damp (dahmp) *c* (pl ~en) vapour

damspel (*dahm*-spehl) *nt* draughts; checkers *plAm*

dan (dahn) *adv* then; *conj* than; **nu en** ~ occasionally

dankbaar (*dahngk*-baar) *adj* grateful, thankful

dankbaarheid (*dahngk*-baar-hayt) *c* gratitude

danken (*dahng*-kern) *v* thank; **dank u**

thank you; **te ~ *hebben aan** owe

dans (dahns) c (pl ~en) dance

dansen (dahn-sern) v dance

danszaal (dahn-saal) c (pl -zalen) ballroom

dapper (dah-perr) adj brave, courageous

dapperheid (dah-perr-hayt) c courage

darm (dahrm) c (pl ~en) gut, intestine; **darmen** bowels pl

das (dahss) c (pl ~sen) necktie, tie; scarf

dat (daht) pron which; conj that

datum (daa-term) c (pl data) date

dauw (dou) c dew

de (der) art the art

debat (der-baht) nt (pl ~ten) discussion, debate

debatteren (day-bah-tay-rern) v argue

debet (day-beht) nt debit

december (day-sehm-berr) December

deeg (daykh) nt dough

deel (dayl) nt (pl delen) part; share; volume

*deelnemen (dayl-nay-mern) v participate

deelnemer (dayl-nay-merr) c (pl ~s) participant

deels (dayls) adv partly

Deen (dayn) c (pl Denen) Dane

Deens (dayns) adj Danish

defect¹ (der-fehkt) adj defective, faulty

defect² (der-fehkt) nt (pl ~en) fault

defensie (day-fehn-zee) c defence

definiëren (day-fi-ni-ay-rern) v define

definitie (day-fee-nee-tsee) c (pl ~s) definition

degelijk (day-ger-lerk) adj thorough; sound

dek (dehk) nt deck

deken (day-kern) c (pl ~s) blanket

dekhut (dehk-hert) c (pl ~ten) deck cabin

deksel (dehk-serl) nt (pl ~s) lid; cover, top

dekzeil (dehk-sayl) nt (pl ~en) tarpaulin

delegatie (day-ler-gaa-tsee) c (pl ~s) delegation

delen (day-lern) v divide; share

delfstof (dehlf-stof) c (pl ~fen) mineral

delicatessen (day-lee-kaa-teh-sern) pl delicatessen

delicatessenwinkel (day-lee-kaa-teh-ser-ving-kerl) c (pl ~s) delicatessen

delikaat (day-lee-kaat) adj delicate

deling (day-ling) c (pl ~en) division

delinquent (day-ling-kvehnt) c (pl ~en) criminal

*delven (dehl-vern) v *dig

democratie (day-moa-kraa-tsee) c (pl ~ën) democracy

democratisch (day-moa-kraa-teess) adj democratic

demonstratie (day-mon-straa-tsee) c (pl ~s) demonstration

demonstreren (day-mon-stray-rern) v demonstrate

den (dehn) c (pl ~nen) fir-tree

Denemarken (day-ner-mahr-kern) Denmark

denkbeeld (dehngk-bayld) nt (pl ~en) idea

denkbeeldig (dehngk-bayl-derkh) adj imaginary

*denken (dehng-kern) v *think; guess, reckon; **~ aan** *think of

denker (dehng-kerr) c (pl ~s) thinker

denneboom (deh-ner-boam) c (pl -bomen) fir-tree

deodorant (day-Yoa-doa-rahnt) c deodorant

departement (day-pahr-ter-mehnt) nt (pl ~en) department

deponeren (day-poa-nay-rern) v bank

depressie (day-preh-see) c (pl ~s) depression

deprimeren (*dāy*-pree-*māy*-rern) *v* depress

derde (*dehr*-der) *num* third

dergelijk (*dehr*-ger-lerk) *adj* such; similar

dermate (*dehr*-maa-ter) *adv* so

dertien (*dehr*-teen) *num* thirteen

dertiende (*dehr*-teen-der) *num* thirteenth

dertig (*dehr*-terkh) *num* thirty

dertigste (*dehr*-terkh-ster) *num* thirtieth

deserteren (*dāy*-zehr-*tāy*-rern) *v* desert

deskundig (dehss-*kern*-derkh) *adj* expert

deskundige (dehss-*kern*-der-ger) *c* (pl ~n) expert

dessert (deh-*sair*) *nt* (pl ~s) dessert

detail (dāy-*tigh*) *nt* (pl ~s) detail

detailhandel (dāy-*tigh*-hahn-derl) *c* retail trade

detaillist (dāy-tah-*Yıst*) *c* (pl ~en) retailer

detectiveroman (dāy-*tehk*-tıf-rōā-mahn) *c* (pl ~s) detective story

deugd (dūrkht) *c* (pl ~en) virtue

deugniet (*dūrkh*-neet) *c* (pl ~en) rascal

deuk (dūrk) *c* (pl ~en) dent

deur (dūrr) *c* (pl ~en) door

deurbel (*dūrr*-behl) *c* (pl ~len) doorbell

deurwaarder (*dūrr*-vaar-derr) *c* (pl ~s) bailiff

devaluatie (dāy-vaa-lēw-*vaa*-tsee) *c* (pl ~s) devaluation

devalueren (dāy-vaa-lēw-*vāy*-rern) *v* devalue

devies (der-*veess*) *nt* (pl deviezen) motto

deze (*dāy*-zer) *pron* this; these

dia (*dee*-Yaa) *c* (pl ~'s) slide

diabetes (dee-Yaa-*bāy*-terss) *c* diabetes

diabeticus (dee-Yaa-*bāy*-tee-kerss) *c* (pl -ci) diabetic

diagnose (dee-Yahkh-*nōā*-zer) *c* (pl ~n, ~s) diagnosis; **een ~ stellen** diagnose

diagonaal[1] (dee-Yaa-gōā-*naal*) *adj* diagonal

diagonaal[2] (dee-Yaa-gōā-*naal*) *c* (pl -nalen) diagonal

dialect (dee-Yaa-*lehkt*) *nt* (pl ~en) dialect

diamant (dee-Yaa-*mahnt*) *c* (pl ~en) diamond

diarree (dee-Yah-*rāy*) *c* diarrhoea

dicht (dıkht) *adj* dense; thick; closed, shut

dichtbevolkt (dıkht-ber-*volkt*) *adj* populous

dichtbij (dıkht-*bay*) *adj* near

dichtdraaien (*dıkh*-draa-ee-ern) *v* turn off

dichter (*dıkh*-terr) *c* (pl ~s) poet

dichtkunst (*dıkht*-kernst) *c* poetry

*dichtslaan (*dıkht*-slaan) *v* slam

dictaat (dık-*taat*) *nt* (pl -taten) dictation

dictafoon (dık-taa-*fōān*) *c* (pl ~s) dictaphone

dictator (dık-*taa*-tor) *c* (pl ~s) dictator

dictee (dık-*tāy*) *nt* (pl ~s) dictation

dicteren (dık-*tāy*-rern) *v* dictate

die (dee) *pron* that; those; who

dieet (dee-*Yāyt*) *nt* diet

dief (deef) *c* (pl dieven) robber, thief

diefstal (*deef*-stahl) *c* (pl ~len) robbery, theft

dienblad (*deen*-blaht) *nt* (pl ~en) tray

dienen (*dee*-nern) *v* serve

dienst (deenst) *c* (pl ~en) service; **in ~ *nemen** engage

dienstplichtige (deenst-*plıkh*-ter-ger) *c* (pl ~n) conscript

dienstregeling (deenst-rāy-ger-lıng) *c* (pl ~en) schedule, timetable

diep (deep) *adj* deep; low

diepte (*deep*-ter) *c* (pl ~n, ~s) depth

diepvrieskast (*deep*-freess-kahst) *c* (pl ~en) deep-freeze

diepzinnig (deep-*si*-nerkh) *adj* profound

dier (deer) *nt* (pl ~en) animal

dierbaar (*deer*-baar) *adj* dear; precious

dierenarts (*dee*-rern-ahrts) *c* (pl ~en) veterinary surgeon

dierenriem (*dee*-rer-reem) *c* zodiac

dierentuin (*dee*-rer-tur^(ew)n) *c* (pl ~en) zoological gardens; zoo

diesel (*dee*-serl) *c* diesel

difterie (dif-ter-*ree*) *c* diphtheria

dij (day) *c* (pl ~en) thigh

dijk (dayk) *c* (pl ~en) dike; dam

dik (dik) *adj* corpulent; thick; fat, stout, big

dikte (*dik*-ter) *c* (pl ~n, ~s) thickness; fatness

dikwijls (*dik*-verls) *adv* frequently, often

ding (ding) *nt* (pl ~en) thing

dinsdag (*dins*-dahkh) *c* Tuesday

diploma (dee-*plōa*-maa) *nt* (pl ~'s) certificate, diploma; **een ~ behalen** graduate

diplomaat (dee-plōa-*maat*) *c* (pl -maten) diplomat

direct (dee-*rehkt*) *adj* direct; *adv* straight away

directeur (dee-rerk-*tūrr*) *c* (pl ~en, ~s) executive, manager, director; headmaster, principal

directie (dee-*rehk*-see) *c* (pl ~s) management

dirigent (dee-ree-*gehnt*) *c* (pl ~en) conductor

dirigeren (dee-ree-*gāy*-rern) *v* conduct

discipline (di-see-*plee*-ner) *c* discipline

disconto (diss-kon-*tōa*) *nt* (pl ~'s) bank-rate

discreet (diss-*krāyt*) *adj* modest

discussie (diss-*ker*-see) *c* (pl ~s) discussion, argument

discussiëren (diss-ker-*shāy*-rern) *v* discuss; argue

distel (*diss*-terl) *c* (pl ~s) thistle

district (diss-*trikt*) *nt* (pl ~en) district

dit (dit) *pron* this

divan (*dee*-vahn) *c* (pl ~s) couch

docent (dōa-*sehnt*) *c* (pl ~en) teacher

doch (dokh) *conj* but

dochter (*dokh*-terr) *c* (pl ~s) daughter

doctor (*dok*-tor) *c* (pl ~en, ~s) doctor

document (dōa-kew-*mehnt*) *nt* (pl ~en) document

dodelijk (*dōa*-der-lerk) *adj* mortal, fatal

doden (*dōa*-dern) *v* kill

doek (dōok) *c* (pl ~en) cloth; *nt* curtain

doel (dōol) *nt* (pl ~en) objective, aim, purpose; object, goal, design, target

doelman (*dōol*-mahn) *c* (pl ~nen) goalkeeper

doelmatig (*dōol*-*maa*-terkh) *adj* efficient

doelpunt (*dōol*-pernt) *nt* (pl ~en) goal

doeltreffend (*dōol*-*treh*-fernt) *adj* effective

***doen** (dōon) *v* *do; cause to

dof (dof) *adj* mat, dim

dok (dok) *nt* (pl ~ken) dock

dokter (*dok*-terr) *c* (pl ~s) doctor, physician

dom¹ (dom) *adj* dumb, stupid

dom² (dom) *c* cathedral

dominee (*dōa*-mee-nāy) *c* (pl ~s) clergyman, parson, rector

dompelaar (*dom*-per-laar) *c* (pl ~s) immersion heater

donateur (dōa-naa-*tūrr*) *c* (pl ~s) donor

donder (*don*-derr) *c* thunder

donderdag (*don*-derr-dahkh) *c* Thurs-

day
donderen (*don*-der-rern) v thunder
donker (*dong*-kerr) adj dark, dim
dons (dons) nt down; **donzen dek-bed** eiderdown
dood (dōat) adj dead; c death
doodstraf (*dōat*-strahf) c death penalty
doof (dōaf) adj deaf
dooi (dōa^ee) c thaw
dooien (*dōa^ee*-ern) v thaw
dooier (*dōa^ee*-err) c (pl ~s) yolk
doolhof (*dōal*-hof) nt (pl -hoven) maze; labyrinth
doop (dōap) c baptism, christening
doopsel (*dōap*-serl) nt baptism
door (dōar) prep through; by
doorboren (dōar-*bōa*-rern) v pierce
*****doorbrengen** (*dōar*-breh-ngern) v *spend
doordat (dōar-*daht*) conj because
*****doordringen** (*dōar*-drı-ngern) v penetrate
*****doorgaan** (*dōar*-gaan) v continue, *go on; carry on; *go ahead; ~ **met** *keep on
doorgang (*dōar*-gahng) c (pl ~en) passage
doorlichten (*dōar*-lıkh-tern) v X-ray
doorlopend (dōar-*lōa*-pernt) adj continuous
doormaken (*dōar*-maa-kern) v *go through
doorn (dōarn) c (pl ~en, ~s) thorn
doorreis (*dōa*-rayss) c passage
doorslag (*dōar*-slahkh) c (pl ~en) carbon copy
doorweken (dōar-*vāy*-kern) v soak
doorzichtig (dōar-*zıkh*-terkh) adj transparent, sheer
*****doorzoeken** (dōar-*zōō*-kern) v search
doos (dōass) c (pl dozen) box
dop (dop) c (pl ~pen) shell
dopen (*dōa*-pern) v baptize, christen

dor (dor) adj arid
dorp (dorp) nt (pl ~en) village
dorst (dorst) c thirst
dorstig (*dors*-terkh) adj thirsty
dosis (*dōa*-zerss) c (pl doses) dose
dossier (do-*shāy*) nt (pl ~s) file
douane (dōō-*vaa*-ner) c Customs pl
douanebeambte (dōō-*vaa*-ner-ber-ahm-ter) c (pl ~n) Customs officer
douche (dōōsh) c (pl ~s) shower
doven (*dōa*-vern) v extinguish
dozijn (dōa-*zayn*) nt (pl ~en) dozen
draad (draat) c (pl draden) thread; wire
draagbaar (*draakh*-baar) adj portable
draaglijk (*draakh*-lerk) adj tolerable
draai (draa^ee) c (pl ~en) turn; twist
draaideur (*draa^ee*-dūrr) c (pl ~en) revolving door
draaien (*draa^ee*-ern) v turn; twist; *spin
draaimolen (*draa^ee*-mōa-lern) c (pl ~s) merry-go-round
draaiorgel (*draa^ee*-or-gerl) nt (pl ~s) street-organ
draak (draak) c (pl draken) dragon
*****dragen** (*draa*-gern) v carry, *bear; *wear
drager (*draa*-gerr) c (pl ~s) bearer
drama (*draa*-maa) nt (pl ~'s) drama
dramatisch (draa-*maa*-teess) adj dramatic
drang (drahng) c urge
drank (drahngk) c (pl ~en) drink, beverage; **sterke** ~ spirits, liquor
dreigement (dray-ger-*mernt*) nt (pl ~en) threat
dreigen (*dray*-gern) v threaten
drek (drehk) c muck
drempel (*drehm*-perl) c (pl ~s) threshold
dresseren (dreh-*sāy*-rern) v train
drie (dree) num three
driehoek (*dree*-hōōk) c (pl ~en) tri-

angle

driehoekig (dree-_hoo_-kerkh) _adj_ triangular

driekwart (_dree_-kvahrt) _adj_ three-quarter

driemaandelijks (_dree_-maan-der-lerks) _adj_ quarterly

drift (drıft) _c_ passion

driftig (_drıf_-terkh) _adj_ quick-tempered; hot-tempered, irascible

drijfkracht (_drayf_-krahkht) _c_ driving force

* **drijven** (_dray_-vern) _v_ float

* **dringen** (_drı_-ngern) _v_ push; **dringend** pressing, urgent

drinkbaar (_drıngk_-baar) _adj_ for drinking

* **drinken** (_drıng_-kern) _v_ *drink

drinkwater (_drıngk_-vaa-terr) _nt_ drinking-water

droefheid (_droof_-hayt) _c_ sorrow

droevig (_droo_-verkh) _adj_ sad

drogen (_droa_-gern) _v_ dry

drogisterij (droa-gıss-ter-_ray_) _c_ (pl ~en) pharmacy, chemist's; drugstore _nAm_

dromen (_droa_-mern) _v_ *dream

dronken (_drong_-kern) _adj_ drunk; intoxicated

droog (droakh) _adj_ dry

droogleggen (_droakh_-leh-gern) _v_ drain

droogte (_droakh_-ter) _c_ drought

droom (droam) _c_ (pl dromen) dream

droombeeld (_droam_-baylt) _nt_ (pl ~en) illusion

drop (drop) _c_ liquorice

druiven (_drurew_-vern) _pl_ grapes _pl_

druk (drerk) _adj_ busy; crowded; _c_ pressure

drukken (_drer_-kern) _v_ press; print

drukknop (_drer_-knop) _c_ (pl ~pen) push-button

drukte (_drerk_-ter) _c_ bustle; fuss, excitement

drukwerk (_drerk_-vehrk) _nt_ printed matter

druppel (_drer_-perl) _c_ (pl ~s) drop

dubbel (_der_-berl) _adj_ double

dubbelzinnig (der-berl-_zı_-nerkh) _adj_ ambiguous

duidelijk (_durew_-der-lerk) _adj_ distinct, plain, clear; apparent, evident; obvious

duif (durewf) _c_ (pl duiven) pigeon

duikbril (_durew_k-brıl) _c_ (pl ~len) goggles _pl_

* **duiken** (_durew_-kern) _v_ dive

duim (durewm) _c_ (pl ~en) thumb

duin (durewn) _nt_ (pl ~en) dune

duister (_durew_-sterr) _adj_ obscure, dark; _nt_ gloom

duisternis (_durew_-sterr-nıss) _c_ dark

Duits (durewts) _adj_ German

Duitser (_durew_t-serr) _c_ (pl ~s) German

Duitsland (_durew_ts-lahnt) Germany

duivel (_durew_-verl) _c_ (pl ~s) devil

duizelig (_durew_-zer-lerkh) _adj_ giddy, dizzy

duizeligheid (_durew_-zer-lerkh-hayt) _c_ giddiness, dizziness

duizeling (_durew_-zer-lıng) _c_ (pl ~en) vertigo

duizend (_durew_-zernt) _num_ thousand

dulden (_derl_-dern) _v_ *bear

dun (dern) _adj_ thin; sheer

dupe (_dew_-per) _c_ (pl ~s) victim

duren (_dew_-rern) _v_ last

durf (derrf) _c_ nerve

durven (_derr_-vern) _v_ dare

dus (derss) _conj_ so

dutje (_der_-tʸer) _nt_ (pl ~s) nap

duur (dewr) _adj_ dear, expensive; _c_ duration

duurzaam (_dewr_-zaam) _adj_ lasting, permanent

duw (dewᵒᵒ) _c_ (pl ~en) push

duwen (_dewᵒᵒ_-ern) _v_ push

dwaas¹ (dvaass) *adj* foolish, crazy, silly

dwaas² (dvaass) *c* (pl dwazen) fool

dwalen (*dvaa*-lern) *v* err

dwerg (dvehrkh) *c* (pl ~en) dwarf

*dwingen (*dvi*-ngern) *v* force; compel

dynamo (dee-*naa*-mōa) *c* (pl ~'s) dynamo

dysenterie (dee-sehn-ter-*ree*) *c* dysentery

E

eb (ehp) *c* low tide

ebbehout (*eh*-ber-hout) *nt* ebony

echo (*eh*-khōa) *c* (pl ~'s) echo

echt (ehkht) *adj* genuine, true, authentic, real; *adv* really; *c* matrimony

echtelijk (*ehkh*-ter-lerk) *adj* matrimonial

echter (*ehkh*-terr) *conj* however, yet

echtgenoot (*ehkht*-kher-nōat) *c* (pl -noten) husband

echtgenote (*ehkht*-kher-nōa-ter) *c* (pl ~n) wife

echtpaar (*ehkht*-paar) *nt* (pl -paren) married couple

echtscheiding (*ehkht*-skhay-ding) *c* (pl ~en) divorce

economie (āy-kōa-nōa-*mee*) *c* economy

economisch (āy-kōa-*nōa*-meess) *adj* economic

econoom (āy-kōa-*nōam*) *c* (pl -nomen) economist

Ecuador (āy-kvaa-*dor*) Ecuador

Ecuadoriaan (āy-kvaa-dōa-ree-*Yaan*) *c* (pl -rianen) Ecuadorian

eczeem (ehk-*sāym*) *nt* eczema

edel (*āy*-derl) *adj* noble

edelmoedigheid (āy-derl-*mōo*-derkh-hayt) *c* generosity

edelsteen (*āy*-derl-stāyn) *c* (pl -stenen) gem, stone

editie (āy-*dee*-tsee) *c* (pl ~s) edition

eed (āyt) *c* (pl eden) oath, vow

eekhoorn (*āyk*-hōarn) *c* (pl ~s) squirrel

eelt (āylt) *nt* callus

een¹ (ern) *art* a *art*

een² (āyn) *num* one

eenakter (*āyn*-ahk-terr) *c* (pl ~s) one-act play

eend (āynt) *c* (pl ~en) duck

eender (*āyn*-derr) *adj* alike

eenheid (*āyn*-hayt) *c* (pl -heden) unit; unity

eenmaal (*āyn*-maal) *adv* once

eenrichtingsverkeer (āyn-*rikh*-tings-ferr-kāyr) *nt* one-way traffic

eens (āyns) *adv* once; some time, some day; **het ~ *zijn** agree

eentonig (āyn-*tōa*-nerkh) *adj* monotonous

eenvoudig (āyn-*vou*-derkh) *adj* plain, simple; *adv* simply

eenzaam (*āyn*-zaam) *adj* lonely

eenzijdig (āyn-*zay*-derkh) *adj* one-sided

eer (āyr) *c* honour; glory

eerbied (*āyr*-beet) *c* respect

eerbiedig (āyr-*bee*-derkh) *adj* respectful

eerbiedwaardig (āyr-beet-*vaar*-derkh) *adj* venerable

eerder (*āyr*-derr) *adv* before; rather

eergevoel (*āyr*-ger-vōōl) *nt* sense of honour

eergisteren (*āyr*-giss-ter-rern) *adv* the day before yesterday

eerlijk (*āyr*-lerk) *adj* honest; fair, straight

eerlijkheid (*āyr*-lerk-hayt) *c* honesty

eerst (āyrst) *adj* first; primary, initial; *adv* at first

eersteklas (*āyr*-ster-klahss) *adj* first-class

eersterangs (*āyr*-ster-rahngs) *adj* first-rate

eerstvolgend (*āyrst*-*fol*-gernt) *adj* following

eervol (*āyr*-vol) *adj* honourable

eerzaam (*āyr*-zaam) *adj* respectable; honourable

eerzuchtig (*āyr*-*zerkh*-terkh) *adj* ambitious

eetbaar (*āyt*-baar) *adj* edible

eetkamer (*āyt*-kaa-merr) *c* (pl ~s) dining-room

eetlepel (*āyt*-lāy-perl) *c* (pl ~s) table-spoon

eetlust (*āyt*-lerst) *c* appetite

eetservies (*āyt*-sehr-veess) *nt* (pl -viezen) dinner-service

eetzaal (*āyt*-saal) *c* (pl -zalen) dining-room

eeuw (āy⁰⁰) *c* (pl ~en) century

eeuwig (*āy*⁰⁰-erkh) *adj* eternal

eeuwigheid (*āy*⁰⁰-erkh-hayt) *c* eternity

effect (eh-*fehkt*) *nt* (pl ~en) effect; **effecten** stocks and shares

effectenbeurs (eh-*fehk*-term-būrrs) *c* (pl -beurzen) stock market, stock exchange

effectief (eh-fehk-*teef*) *adj* effective

effen (*eh*-fern) *adj* level; smooth, even

efficiënt (eh-fee-*shehnt*) *adj* efficient

egaal (āy-*gaal*) *adj* level

egaliseren (āy-gaa-lee-*zāy*-rern) *v* level

egel (*āy*-gerl) *c* (pl ~s) hedgehog

egocentrisch (āy-gōa-*sehn*-treess) *adj* self-centred

egoïsme (āy-gōa-*viss*-mer) *nt* selfishness

egoïstisch (āy-gōa-*viss*-teess) *adj* selfish

Egypte (āy-*gip*-ter) Egypt

Egyptenaar (āy-*gip*-ter-naar) *c* (pl -naren) Egyptian

Egyptisch (āy-*gip*-teess) *adj* Egyptian

ei (ay) *nt* (pl ~eren) egg

eierdooier (ay-err-dōa⁰⁰-err) *c* (pl ~s) egg-yolk

eierdopje (ay-err-dop-ʸer) *nt* (pl ~s) egg-cup

eigen (ay-gern) *adj* own

eigenaar (ay-ger-naar) *c* (pl ~s, -naren) owner, proprietor

eigenaardig (ay-ger-*naar*-derkh) *adj* singular, peculiar

eigenaardigheid (ay-ger-*naar*-derkh-hayt) *c* (pl -heden) peculiarity

eigendom (ay-gern-dom) *nt* (pl ~men) property; possessions

eigengemaakt (ay-gern-ger-maakt) *adj* home-made

eigenlijk (ay-gern-lerk) *adj* actual; *adv* as a matter of fact, really

eigenschap (ay-gern-skhahp) *c* (pl ~pen) property, quality

eigentijds (ay-gern-*tayts*) *adj* contemporary

eigenwijs (ay-gern-*vayss*) *adj* pig-headed

eik (ayk) *c* (pl ~en) oak

eikel (ay-kerl) *c* (pl ~s) acorn

eiland (ay-lahnt) *nt* (pl ~en) island

einde (ayn-der) *nt* end, finish; ending, issue

eindelijk (ayn-der-lerk) *adv* at last

eindigen (ayn-der-gern) *v* finish

eindpunt (aynt-pernt) *nt* (pl ~en) terminal

eindstreep (aynt-strāyp) *c* (pl -strepen) finish

eis (ayss) *c* (pl ~en) demand, claim

eisen (ay-sern) *v* demand

eiwit (ay-vit) *nt* (pl ~ten) protein

ekster (*ehk*-sterr) *c* (pl ~s) magpie

eksteroog (*ehk*-sterr-ōakh) *nt* (pl -ogen) corn

eland (*āy*-lahnt) *c* (pl ~en) moose

elastiek (āy-lahss-*teek*) *nt* (pl ~en) rubber band, elastic

elastisch (āy-*lahss*-teess) *adj* elastic

elders (*ehl*-derrs) *adv* elsewhere

elegant (āy-ler-*gahnt*) *adj* elegant

elegantie (āy-ler-*gahnt*-see) *c* elegance

elektricien (āy-lehk-tree-*shang*) *c* (pl ~s) electrician

elektriciteit (āy-lehk-tree-see-*tayt*) *c* electricity

elektriciteitscentrale (āy-lehk-tree-see-*tayt*-sehn-traa-ler) *c* power-station

elektrisch (āy-*lehk*-treess) *adj* electric

elektronisch (āy-lehk-*trōā*-neess) *adj* electronic

element (āy-ler-*mehnt*) *nt* (pl ~en) element

elementair (āy-ler-mehn-*tair*) *adj* primary

elf¹ (ehlf) *num* eleven

elf² (ehlf) *c* (pl ~en) elf

elfde (*ehlf*-der) *num* eleventh

elftal (*ehlf*-tahl) *nt* (pl ~len) soccer team

elimineren (āy-lee-mee-*nāy*-rern) *v* eliminate

elk (ehlk) *adj* each, every

elkaar (ehl-*kaar*) *pron* each other

elleboog (*eh*-ler-*bōāk*h) *c* (pl -bogen) elbow

ellende (eh-*lehn*-der) *c* misery

ellendig (eh-*lehn*-derkh) *adj* miserable

email (āy-*migh*) *nt* enamel

emailleren (āy-migh-*āy*-rern) *v* glaze

emancipatie (āy-mahn-see-*paa*-tsee) *c* emancipation

embargo (ehm-*bahr*-gōa) *nt* embargo

embleem (ehm-*blāym*) *nt* (pl -blemen) emblem

emigrant (āy-mee-*grahnt*) *c* (pl ~en) emigrant

emigratie (āy-mee-*graa*-tsee) *c* emigration

emigreren (āy-mee-*grāy*-rern) *v* emigrate

eminent (āy-mee-*nehnt*) *adj* outstanding

emmer (*eh*-merr) *c* (pl ~s) bucket, pail

emotie (āy-*mōā*-tsee) *c* (pl ~s) emotion

employé (ahm-plvah-*ʸāy*) *c* (pl ~s) employee

en (ehn) *conj* and

encyclopedie (ehn-see-klōa-pāy-*dee*) *c* (pl ~ën) encyclopaedia

endeldarm (*ehn*-derl-dahrm) *c* (pl ~en) rectum

endosseren (ahn-do-*sāy*-rern) *v* endorse

energie (āy-nehr-*zhee*) *c* energy; power

energiek (āy-nehr-*zheek*) *adj* energetic

eng (ehng) *adj* narrow; creepy

engel (*eh*-ngerl) *c* (pl ~en) angel

Engeland (*eh*-nger-lahnt) England; Britain

Engels (*eh*-ngerls) *adj* English; British

Engelsman (*eh*-ngerls-mahn) *c* (pl Engelsen) Englishman; Briton

enig (*āy*-nerkh) *adj* sole, only; *pron* any; **enige** *pron* some

enigszins (*āy*-nerkh-sɪns) *adv* somewhat

enkel¹ (*ehng*-kerl) *adj* single; **enkele** *pron* some

enkel² (*ehng*-kerl) *c* (pl ~s) ankle

enkeling (*ehng*-ker-lɪng) *c* (pl ~en) individual

enkelvoud (*ehng*-kerl-vout) *nt* singular

enorm (āy-*norm*) *adj* tremendous, enormous, huge

enquête (ahng-*kai*-ter) *c* (pl ~s) enquiry

enthousiasme (ahn-tōō-*zhahss*-mer) *nt* enthusiasm

enthousiast (ahn-tōō-*zhahst*) *adj* enthusiastic; keen

entree (ahn-*trāy*) *c* entry; entrance-fee

entresol (ahng-trer-*sol*) *c* (pl ~s) mezzanine

envelop (ahng-ver-*lop*) *c* (pl ~pen) envelope

enzovoort (ehn-zōa-*vōart*) and so on, etcetera

epidemie (āy-pee-der-*mee*) *c* (pl ~ën) epidemic

epilepsie (āy-pee-lehp-*see*) *c* epilepsy

epiloog (āy-pee-*lōakh*) *c* (pl -logen) epilogue

episch (*āy*-peess) *adj* epic

episode (āy-pee-*zōa*-der) *c* (pl ~n, ~s) episode

epos (*āy*-poss) *nt* (pl epen, ~sen) epic

equipe (āy-*keep*) *c* (pl ~s) team

equivalent (āy-kvee-vaa-*lehnt*) *adj* equivalent

er (ehr) *adv* there; *pron* of them

erbarmelijk (ehr-*bahr*-mer-lerk) *adj* lamentable

eredienst (*āy*-rer-deenst) *c* (pl ~en) worship

eren (*āy*-rern) *v* honour

erf (ehrf) *nt* (pl erven) yard

erfelijk (*ehr*-fer-lerk) *adj* hereditary

erfenis (*ehr*-fer-niss) *c* (pl ~sen) inheritance; legacy

erg (ehrkh) *adj* bad; *adv* very; **erger** worse; **ergst** worst

ergens (*ehr*-gerns) *adv* somewhere

ergeren (*ehr*-ger-rern) *v* annoy

ergernis (*ehr*-gerr-niss) *c* annoyance

erkennen (ehr-*keh*-nern) *v* recognize; acknowledge

erkenning (ehr-*keh*-ning) *c* (pl ~en) recognition

erkentelijk (ehr-*kehn*-ter-lerk) *adj* grateful

ernst (ehrnst) *c* seriousness; gravity

ernstig (*ehrn*-sterkh) *adj* serious; grave, bad, severe

erts (ehrts) *nt* (pl ~en) ore

* **ervaren** (ehr-*vaa*-rern) *v* experience

ervaring (ehr-*vaa*-ring) *c* (pl ~en) experience

erven (*ehr*-vern) *v* inherit

erwt (ehrt) *c* (pl ~en) pea

escorte (ehss-*kor*-ter) *nt* (pl ~s) escort

escorteren (ehss-kor-*tāy*-rern) *v* escort

esdoorn (ehss-dōarn) *c* (pl ~s) maple

eskader (ehss-*kaa*-derr) *nt* (pl ~s) squadron

essay (eh-*sāy*) *nt* (pl ~s) essay

essentie (eh-*sehn*-see) *c* essence

essentieel (eh-sehn-*shāyl*) *adj* vital, essential

etage (āy-*taa*-zher) *c* (pl ~s) floor, storey; apartment *nAm*

etalage (āy-taa-*laa*-zher) *c* (pl ~s) shop-window

etappe (āy-*tah*-per) *c* (pl ~n, ~s) stage

eten (*āy*-tern) *nt* food

* **eten** (*āy*-tern) *v* *eat

ether (*āy*-terr) *c* ether

Ethiopië (āy-tee-*Yōa*-pee-Yer) Ethiopia

Ethiopiër (āy-tee-*Yōa*-pee-Yerr) *c* (pl ~s) Ethiopian

Ethiopisch (āy-tee-*Yōa*-peess) *adj* Ethiopian

etiket (āy-tee-*keht*) *nt* (pl ~ten) label, tag

etiketteren (āy-tee-keh-*tāy*-rern) *v* label

etmaal (*eht*-maal) *nt* (pl -malen) twenty-four hours

ets (ehts) *c* (pl ~en) etching

ettelijk (*eh*-ter-lerk) *adj* several

etter (*eh*-terr) *c* pus

etui (āy-*tvee*) *nt* (pl ~s) case

Europa (ūr-*rōa*-paa) Europe

Europeaan (ūr-rōa-pāy-*aan*) *c* (pl -anen) European

Europees (ūr-rōa-*pāyss*) *adj* European

evacueren (āy-vaa-kēw-*vāy*-rern) *v* evacuate

evangelie (āy-vahng-*gāy*-lee) *nt* (pl -liën, ~s) gospel

even (*āȳ*-vern) *adj* even; *adv* equally, as

evenaar (*āȳ*-ver-naar) *c* equator

evenals (*āȳ*-ver-nahls) *conj* as well as

evenaren (*āȳ*-ver-*naa*-rern) *v* equal

eveneens (*āȳ*-ver-*nāȳns*) *adv* as well, likewise, also

evenredig (*āȳ*-ver-*rāȳ*-derkh) *adj* proportional

eventueel (*āȳ*-vern-tew-*vāȳl*) *adj* possible, eventual

evenveel (*āȳ*-ver-*vāȳl*) *adv* as much

evenwel (*āȳ*-ver-*vehl*) *adv* however

evenwicht (*āȳ*-ver-*vɪkht*) *nt* balance

evenwijdig (*āȳ*-ver-*vay*-derkh) *adj* parallel

evenzeer (*āȳ*-ver-zāȳr) *adv* as much

evenzo (*āȳ*-ver-*zōā*) *adv* likewise

evolutie (*āȳ*-vōā-*lēw*-tsee) *c* (pl ~s) evolution

exact (ehk-*sahkt*) *adj* precise

examen (ehk-*saa*-mern) *nt* (pl ~s) examination

excentriek (ehk-sehn-*treek*) *adj* eccentric

exces (ehk-*sehss*) *nt* (pl ~sen) excess

exclusief (ehks-klēw-*zeef*) *adj* exclusive

excursie (ehks-*kerr*-zee) *c* (pl ~s) day trip, excursion

excuseren (ehks-kēw-*zāȳ*-rern) *v* excuse

excuus (ehks-*kēwss*) *nt* (pl excuses) apology, excuse

exemplaar (ehk-serm-*plaar*) *nt* (pl -plaren) specimen; copy

exotisch (ehk-*sōā*-teess) *adj* exotic

expeditie (ehks-per-*dee*-tsee) *c* (pl ~s) expedition

experiment (ehks-pāȳ-ree-*mehnt*) *nt* (pl ~en) experiment

experimenteren (ehks-pāȳ-ree-mehn-*tāȳ*-rern) *v* experiment

expert (ehks-*pair*) *c* (pl ~s) expert

expliciet (ehks-plee-*seet*) *adj* explicit

exploiteren (ehks-plvah-*tāȳ*-rern) *v* exploit

explosie (ehks-*plōā*-zee) *c* (pl ~s) blast, explosion

explosief (ehks-plōā-*zeef*) *adj* explosive

export (*ehk*-sport) *c* exports *pl*, export

exporteren (ehk-spor-*tāȳ*-rern) *v* export

expositie (ehk-spōā-*zee*-tsee) *c* (pl ~s) exhibition; display

expresse- (ehk-*spreh*-ser) express; special delivery

extase (ehk-*staa*-zer) *c* ecstasy

extra (*ehk*-straa) *adj* additional, extra; spare

extravagant (ehk-straa-vaa-*gahnt*) *adj* extravagant

extreem (ehk-*strāȳm*) *adj* extreme

ezel (*āȳ*-zerl) *c* (pl ~s) ass; donkey

F

faam (faam) *c* fame

fabel (*faa*-berl) *c* (pl ~s, ~en) fable

fabriceren (faa-bree-*sāȳ*-rern) *v* manufacture

fabriek (faa-*breek*) *c* (pl ~en) factory; mill, works *pl*

fabrikant (faa-bree-*kahnt*) *c* (pl ~en) manufacturer

faciliteit (faa-see-lee-*tayt*) *c* (pl ~en) facility

factor (*fahk*-tor) *c* (pl ~en) factor

factureren (fahk-tēw-*rāȳ*-rern) *v* bill

factuur (fahk-*tēwr*) *c* (pl -turen) invoice

facultatief (faa-kerl-taa-*teef*) *adj* optional

faculteit (faa-kerl-*tayt*) *c* (pl ~en) faculty

faience (faa-ʸahng-ser) c faience

failliet (fah-ʸeet) adj bankrupt

fakkel (fah-kerl) c (pl ~s) torch

falen (faa-lern) v fail

familiaar (fah-mee-lee-ʸaar) adj familiar

familie (faa-mee-lee) c (pl ~s) family

familielid (faa-mee-lee-lıt) nt (pl -leden) relative

fanatiek (faa-naa-teek) adj fanatical

fanfarekorps (fahm-faa-rer-korps) nt (pl ~en) brass band

fantasie (fahn-taa-zee) c (pl ~ën) fantasy, fancy

fantastisch (fahn-tahss-teess) adj fantastic

farce (fahrs) c (pl ~n) farce

farmacologie (fahr-maa-kōā-lōā-gee) c pharmacology

fascinerend (fah-see-nāy-rernt) adj glamorous

fascisme (fah-sıss-mer) nt fascism

fascist (fah-sıst) c (pl ~en) fascist

fascistisch (fah-sıss-teess) adj fascist

fase (faa-zer) c (pl ~s, ~n) stage, phase

fataal (faa-taal) adj fatal

fatsoen (faht-sōōn) nt decency

fatsoenlijk (faht-sōōn-lerk) adj decent

fauteuil (fōā-tur^ew) c (pl ~s) armchair

favoriet (faa-vōā-reet) c (pl ~en) favourite

fazant (faa-zahnt) c (pl ~en) pheasant

februari (fāy-brēw-vaa-ree) February

federaal (fāy-der-raal) adj federal

federatie (fāy-der-raa-tsee) c (pl ~s) federation

fee (fāy) c (pl ~ën) fairy

feest (fāyst) nt (pl ~en) feast

feestdag (fāyss-dahkh) c (pl ~en) holiday

feestelijk (fāy-ster-lerk) adj festive

feestje (fāy-sher) nt (pl ~s) party

feilloos (fay-lōāss) adj faultless

feit (fayt) nt (pl ~en) fact; **in feite** in fact

feitelijk (fay-ter-lerk) adj factual; adv as a matter of fact, actually, in effect

fel (fehl) adj fierce

felicitatie (fāy-lee-see-taa-tsee) c (pl ~s) congratulation

feliciteren (fāy-lee-see-tāy-rern) v congratulate; compliment

feodaal (fāy-ʸōā-daal) adj feudal

festival (fehss-tee-vahl) nt (pl ~s) festival

feuilleton (fur^ew-er-ton) nt (pl ~s) serial

fiasco (fee-ʸahss-kōā) nt (pl ~'s) failure

fiche (fee-sher) c (pl ~s) chip

fictie (fık-see) c (pl ~s) fiction

fiets (feets) c (pl ~en) cycle, bicycle

fietser (fee-tserr) c (pl ~s) cyclist

figuur (fee-gēwr) c (pl -guren) figure; diagram

fijn (fayn) adj enjoyable; fine; delicate

fijnhakken (fayn-hah-kern) v mince

***fijnmalen** (fayn-maa-lern) v *grind

fijnproever (faym-prōō-verr) c (pl ~s) gourmet

fijnstampen (fayn-stahm-pern) v mash

filiaal (fee-lee-ʸaal) nt (-ialen) branch

Filippijn (fee-lı-payn) c (pl ~en) Filipino

Filippijnen (fee-lı-pay-nern) pl Philippines pl

Filippijns (fee-lı-payns) adj Philippine

film (film) c (pl ~s) film; movie

filmcamera (film-kaa-mer-raa) c (pl ~'s) camera

filmen (fıl-mern) v film

filmjournaal (film-zhōōr-naal) nt newsreel

filosofie (fee-lōā-zōā-fee) c (pl ~ën) philosophy

filosoof (fee-lōa-*zōāf*) *c* (pl -sofen) philosopher

filter (*fil*-terr) *nt* (pl ~s) filter

Fin (fin) *c* (pl ~nen) Finn

financieel (fee-nahn-*shāyl*) *adj* financial

financiën (fee-nahn-see-Yern) *pl* finances *pl*

financieren (fee-nahn-*see*-rern) *v* finance

Finland (*fin*-lahnt) Finland

Fins (fins) *adj* Finnish

firma (*fir*-maa) *c* (pl ~'s) company, firm

fitting (*fi*-ting) *c* (pl ~en) socket

fjord (fYort) *c* (pl ~en) fjord

flacon (flaa-*kon*) *c* (pl ~s) flask

flamingo (flaa-*ming*-gōa) *c* (pl ~'s) flamingo

flanel (flaa-*nehl*) *nt* flannel

flat (fleht) *c* (pl ~s) flat; apartment *nAm*

flatgebouw (*fleht*-kher-bou) *nt* (pl ~en) block of flats; apartment house *Am*

flauw (flou) *adj* faint

*****flauwvallen** (*flou*-vah-lern) *v* faint

fles (flehss) *c* (pl ~sen) bottle

flesopener (*fleh*-zōa-per-nerr) *c* (pl ~s) bottle opener

flessehals (*fleh*-ser-hahls) *c* bottleneck

flets (flehts) *adj* dull

flink (flingk) *adj* considerable; brave, plucky

flits (flits) *c* (pl ~en) flash

flitslampje (*flits*-lahm-pYer) *nt* (pl ~s) flash-bulb

fluisteren (*flur*ewss-ter-rern) *v* whisper

fluit (flurewt) *c* (pl ~en) flute

*****fluiten** (*flur*ew-tern) *v* whistle

fluitje (*flur*ew-tYer) *nt* (pl ~s) whistle

fluweel (flēw-*vāyl*) *nt* velvet

foefje (*fōō*-fYer) *nt* (pl ~s) trick

foei! (fōōee) shame!

fok (fok) *c* (pl ~ken) foresail

fokken (*fo*-kern) *v* *breed; raise

folklore (fol-*klōa*-rer) *c* folklore

fonds (fons) *nt* (pl ~en) fund

fonetisch (fōa-*nāy*-teess) *adj* phonetic

fonkelend (*fong*-ker-lernt) *adj* sparkling

fontein (fon-*tayn*) *c* (pl ~en) fountain

fooi (fōaee) *c* (pl ~en) tip; gratuity

foppen (*fo*-pern) *v* fool

forceren (for-*sāy*-rern) *v* strain; force

forel (fōa-*rehl*) *c* (pl ~len) trout

forens (fōa-*rehns*) *c* (pl ~en, forenzen) commuter

formaat (for-*maat*) *nt* (pl -maten) size

formaliteit (for-maa-lee-*tayt*) *c* (pl ~en) formality

formeel (for-*māyl*) *adj* formal

formule (for-*mēw*-ler) *c* (pl ~s) formula

formulier (for-mēw-*leer*) *nt* (pl ~en) form

fornuis (for-*nur*ewss) *nt* (pl -nuizen) cooker, stove

fors (fors) *adj* robust

fort (fort) *nt* (pl ~en) fort

fortuin (for-*tur*ewn) *nt* (pl ~en) fortune

foto (*fōa*-tōa) *c* (pl ~'s) photograph, photo

fotocopie (fōa-tōa-kōa-*pee*) *c* (pl ~ën) photostat

fotograaf (fōa-tōa-*graaf*) *c* (pl -grafen) photographer

fotograferen (fōa-tōa-graa-*fāy*-rern) *v* photograph

fotografie (fōa-tōa-graa-*fee*) *c* photography

fototoestel (*fōa*-tōa-tōō-stehl) *nt* (pl ~len) camera

fotowinkel (*fōa*-tōa-ving-kerl) *c* (pl ~s) camera shop

fouilleren (fōō-*Yāy*-rern) *v* search

fout¹ (fout) *adj* mistaken, wrong

fout² (fout) *c* (pl ~en) error, mistake, fault

foutloos (*fout*-lōass) *adj* faultless

foyer (fvah-*Yay*) *c* (pl ~s) foyer; lobby

fractie (*frahk*-see) *c* (pl ~s) fraction

fragment (frahkh-*mehnt*) *nt* (pl ~en) fragment; extract

framboos (frahm-*bōass*) *c* (pl -bozen) raspberry

franje (*frah*-ñer) *c* (pl ~s) fringe

frankeren (frahng-*kay*-rern) *v* stamp

frankering (frahng-*kay*-rɪng) *c* (pl ~en) postage

franko (*frahng*-kōa) *adj* postage paid, post-paid

Frankrijk (*frahng*-krayk) France

Frans (frahns) *adj* French

Fransman (*frahns*-mahn) *c* (pl Fransen) Frenchman

frappant (frah-*pahnt*) *adj* striking

fraude (*frou*-der) *c* (pl ~s) fraud

frequent (frer-*kvehnt*) *adj* frequent

frequentie (frer-*kvehn*-tsee) *c* (pl ~s) frequency

fris (frɪss) *adj* fresh

frisdrank (*frɪss*-drahngk) *c* soft drink

frites (freet) *pl* chips

fruit (frur^ewt) *nt* fruit

fuif (fur^ewf) *c* (pl fuiven) party

functie (*ferngk*-see) *c* (pl ~s) function

functioneren (ferngk-shōa-*nay*-rern) *v* work

fundamenteel (fern-daa-mehn-*tayl*) *adj* fundamental, basic

fusie (*few*-zee) *c* (pl ~s) merger

fysica (*fee*-zee-kaa) *c* physics

fysiek (fee-*zeek*) *adj* physical

fysiologie (fee-zee-Yōa-lōa-*gee*) *c* physiology

G

* **gaan** (gaan) *v* *go; *~ **door** pass through

gaarne (*gaar*-ner) *adv* gladly

gaas (gaass) *nt* gauze

* **gadeslaan** (*gaa*-der-slaan) *v* watch

gal (gahl) *c* gall, bile

galblaas (*gahl*-blaass) *c* (pl -blazen) gall bladder

galerij (gah-ler-*ray*) *c* (pl ~en) arcade; gallery

galg (gahlkh) *c* (pl ~en) gallows *pl*

galop (gaa-*lop*) *c* gallop

galsteen (*gahl*-stayn) *c* (pl -stenen) gallstone

gammel (*gah*-merl) *adj* ramshackle, shaky

gang (gahng) *c* (pl ~en) corridor; gait, pace; course

gangbaar (*gahng*-baar) *adj* current

gangpad (*gahng*-paht) *nt* (pl ~en) aisle

gans (gahns) *c* (pl ganzen) goose

gapen (*gaa*-pern) *v* yawn

garage (gaa-*raa*-zher) *c* (pl ~s) garage

garanderen (gaa-rahn-*day*-rern) *v* guarantee

garantie (gaa-*rahn*-tsee) *c* (pl ~s) guarantee

garderobe (gahr-der-*raw*-ber) *c* (pl ~s) wardrobe, cloakroom; checkroom *nAm*

garen (*gaa*-rern) *nt* (pl ~s) thread, yarn; **garen- en bandwinkel** haberdashery

garnaal (gahr-*naal*) *c* (pl -nalen) prawn, shrimp

gas (gahss) *nt* (pl ~sen) gas

gasfabriek (*gahss*-faa-breek) *c* (pl ~en) gasworks

gasfornuis (*gahss*-for-nur^ewss) *nt* (pl

-nuizen) gas cooker

gaskachel (*gahss*-kah-kherl) *c* (pl ~s) gas stove

gaspedaal (*gahss*-per-daal) *nt* (pl -dalen) accelerator

gasstel (*gah*-stehl) *nt* (pl ~len) gas cooker

gast (gahst) *c* (pl ~en) guest

gastheer (*gahst*-hāyr) *c* (pl -heren) host

gastvrij (gahst-*fray*) *adj* hospitable

gastvrijheid (gahst-*fray*-hayt) *c* hospitality

gastvrouw (*gahst*-frou) *c* (pl ~en) hostess

gat (gaht) *nt* (pl ~en) hole

gauw (gou) *adv* soon

gave (*gaa*-ver) *c* (pl ~n) gift, faculty

gazon (gaa-*zon*) *nt* (pl ~s) lawn

geadresseerde (ger-ah-dreh-*sāy*-der) *c* (pl ~n) addressee

geaffecteerd (ger-ah-fehk-*tāyrt*) *adj* affected

Geallieerden (ger-ah-lee-*ʸāy*-dern) *pl* Allies *pl*

gearmd (ger-*ahrmt*) *adv* arm-in-arm

gebaar (ger-*baar*) *nt* (pl gebaren) sign

gebak (ger-*bahk*) *nt* cake, pastry

gebaren (ger-*baa*-rern) *v* gesticulate

gebed (ger-*beht*) *nt* (pl ~en) prayer

gebergte *nt* mountain range

gebeuren (ger-*bū̄r*-rern) *v* occur; happen

gebeurtenis (ger-*bū̄rr*-ter-nɪss) *c* (pl ~sen) event; happening, occurrence

gebied (ger-*beet*) *nt* (pl ~en) region; zone, area, field, territory

geblokt (ger-*blokt*) *adj* chequered

gebogen (ger-*bōā*-gern) *adj* curved

geboorte (ger-*bōār*-ter) *c* (pl ~n) birth

geboorteland (ger-*bōār*-ter-lahnt) *nt* native country

geboorteplaats (ger-*bōār*-ter-plaats) *c* place of birth

geboren (ger-*bōā*-rern) *adj* born

gebouw (ger-*bou*) *nt* (pl ~en) construction, building

gebrek (ger-*brehk*) *nt* (pl ~en) deficiency, fault; want, lack, shortage

gebrekkig (ger-*breh*-kerkh) *adj* defective, faulty

gebruik (ger-*brurᵉʷk*) *nt* (pl ~en) use, usage; custom

gebruikelijk (ger-*brurᵉʷ*-ker-lerk) *adj* customary; common, usual

gebruiken (ger-*brurᵉʷ*-kern) *v* use; employ; apply

gebruiker (ger-*brurᵉʷ*-kerr) *c* (pl ~s) user

gebruiksaanwijzing (ger-*brurᵉʷk*-saan-vay-zɪng) *c* (pl ~en) directions for use

gebruiksvoorwerp (ger-*brurᵉʷ*ks-fōār-vehrp) *nt* (pl ~en) utensil

gebruind (ger-*brurᵉʷnt*) *adj* tanned

gebrul (ger-*brerl*) *nt* roar

gecompliceerd (ger-kom-plee-*sāyrt*) *adj* complicated

gedachte (ger-*dahkh*-ter) *c* (pl ~n) thought; idea

gedachtenstreepje (ger-*dahkh*-ter-strāyp-ʸer) *nt* (pl ~s) dash

gedeelte (ger-*dāyl*-ter) *nt* (pl ~n, ~s) part

gedeeltelijk (ger-*dāyl*-ter-lerk) *adj* partial; *adv* partly

gedelegeerde (ger-dāy-ler-*gāy*-der) *c* (pl ~n) delegate

gedenkteken (ger-*dehngk*-tāy-kern) *nt* (pl ~s) memorial; monument

gedenkwaardig (ger-dehngk-*vaar*-derkh) *adj* memorable

gedetailleerd (ger-dāy-tah-*ʸāyrt*) *adj* detailed

gedetineerde (ger-dāy-tee-*nāyr*-der) *c* (pl ~n) prisoner

gedicht (ger-*dɪkht*) *nt* (pl ~en) poem

geding (ger-*dɪng*) *nt* (pl ~en) lawsuit

gediplomeerd (ger-dee-plōa-*māyrt*) *adj* qualified

gedrag (ger-*drahkh*) *nt* conduct, behaviour

zich *gedragen (ger-*draa*-gern) act, behave

geduld (ger-*derlt*) *nt* patience

geduldig (ger-*derl*-derkh) *adj* patient

gedurende (ger-*dēw*-rern-der) *prep* during; for

gedurfd (ger-*derrft*) *adj* daring

geel (gāyl) *adj* yellow

geelkoper (*gāyl*-kōa-perr) *nt* brass

geelzucht (*gāyl*-zerkht) *c* jaundice

geëmailleerd (ger-āy-mah-*yāyrt*) *adj* enamelled

geen (gāyn) *adj* no

geenszins (*gāyn*-sɪns) *adv* by no means

geest (gāyst) *c* (pl ~en) spirit, mind; soul; ghost

geestelijk (*gāy*-ster-lerk) *adj* spiritual, mental

geestelijke (*gāy*-ster-ler-ker) *c* (pl ~n) clergyman

geestig (*gāy*-sterkh) *adj* witty, humorous

geeuwen (*gāy*ᵒᵒ-ern) *v* yawn

gefluister (ger-*flur*ᵉʷ-sterr) *nt* whisper

gegadigde (ger-*gaa*-derkh-der) *c* (pl ~n) candidate

gegeneerd (ger-zher-*nāyrt*) *adj* embarrassed

gegeven (ger-*gāy*-vern) *nt* (pl ~s) data *pl*

gegrond (ger-*gront*) *adj* well-founded

gehandicapt (ger-*hehn*-dee-kehpt) *adj* disabled

geheel (ger-*hāyl*) *adj* entire, whole, total; *adv* completely; *nt* whole

geheelonthouder (ger-*hāyl*-ont-hou-derr) *c* (pl ~s) teetotaller

geheim¹ (ger-*haym*) *adj* secret

geheim² (ger-*haym*) *nt* (pl ~en) secret

geheimzinnig (ger-haym-zɪ-nerkh) *adj* mysterious

geheugen (ger-*hūr*-gern) *nt* memory

gehoor (ger-*hōar*) *nt* hearing

gehoorzaam (ger-*hōar*-zaam) *adj* obedient

gehoorzaamheid (ger-*hōar*-zaam-hayt) *c* obedience

gehoorzamen (ger-*hōar*-zaa-mern) *v* obey

gehorig (ger-*hōa*-rerkh) *adj* noisy

gehucht (ger-*herkht*) *nt* (pl ~en) hamlet

geïnteresseerd (ger-ɪn-trer-*sāyrt*) *adj* interested

geïsoleerd (ger-ee-zōa-*lāyrt*) *adj* isolated

geit (gayt) *c* (pl ~en) goat

geiteleer (gay-ter-*lāyr*) *nt* kid

gek¹ (gehk) *adj* crazy, mad

gek² (gehk) *c* (pl ~ken) fool

geklets (ger-*klehts*) *nt* chat; rubbish

gekleurd (ger-*klūrrt*) *adj* coloured

gekraak (ger-*kraak*) *nt* crack

gekruid (ger-*krur*ᵉʷt) *adj* spiced

gelaatstrek (ger-*laats*-trehk) *c* (pl ~ken) feature

gelach (ger-*lahkh*) *nt* laughter

geld (gehlt) *nt* money; **buitenlands** ~ foreign currency; **contant** ~ cash

geldbelegging (*gehlt*-ber-leh-gɪng) *c* (pl ~en) investment

*gelden (*gehl*-dern) *v* apply

geldig (*gehl*-derkh) *adj* valid

geldstuk (*gehlt*-sterk) *nt* (pl ~ken) coin

geleden (ger-*lāy*-dern) ago; **kort** ~ recently

geleerde (ger-*lāyr*-der) *c* (pl ~n) scholar, scientist

gelegen (ger-*lay*-gern) *adj* situated

gelegenheid (ger-*lāy*-gern-hayt) *c* (pl -heden) occasion, chance, opportunity

gelei (zher-*lay*) *c* (pl ~en) jelly

geleidehond (ger-*lay*-der-hont) *c* (pl ~en) guide-dog

geleidelijk (ger-*lay*-der-lerk) *adj* gradual

gelijk (ger-*layk*) *adj* equal, like, alike; level, even; ~ *hebben* * be right; ~ *maken* equalize

gelijkenis (ger-*lay*-ker-nıss) *c* (pl ~sen) resemblance, similarity

gelijkgezind (ger-layk-kher-*zınt*) *adj* like-minded

gelijkheid (ger-*layk*-hayt) *c* equality

gelijkstroom (ger-*layk*-strōam) *c* direct current

gelijktijdig (ger-layk-*tay*-derkh) *adj* simultaneous

gelijkwaardig (ger-layk-*vaar*-derkh) *adj* equivalent

gelofte (ger-*lof*-ter) *c* (pl ~n) vow

geloof (ger-*lōaf*) *nt* belief; faith

geloofwaardig (ger-lōaf-*vaar*-derkh) *adj* credible

geloven (ger-*lōa*-vern) *v* believe

geluid (ger-*lur^{ew}t*) *nt* (pl ~en) sound; noise

geluiddicht (ger-lur^{ew}-*dıkht*) *adj* soundproof

geluk (ger-*lerk*) *nt* happiness; luck, fortune

gelukkig (ger-*ler*-kerkh) *adj* happy; fortunate

gelukwens (ger-*lerk*-vehns) *c* (pl ~en) congratulation

gelukwensen (ger-*lerk*-vehn-sern) *v* congratulate, compliment

gemak (ger-*mahk*) *nt* leisure; ease; comfort

gemakkelijk (ger-*mah*-ker-lerk) *adj* easy; convenient

gematigd (ger-*maa*-terkht) *adj* moderate

gember (*gehm*-berr) *c* ginger

gemeen (ger-*māyn*) *adj* foul, mean

gemeenschap (ger-*māyn*-skhahp) *c* (pl ~pen) community

gemeenschappelijk (ger-māyn-*skhah*-per-lerk) *adj* common

gemeente (ger-*māyn*-ter) *c* (pl ~n, ~s) congregation

gemeentebestuur (ger-*māyn*-ter-ber-stēwr) *nt* municipality

gemeentelijk (ger-*māyn*-ter-lerk) *adj* municipal

gemêleerd (ger-meh-*lāyrt*) *adj* mixed

gemengd (ger-*mehngt*) *adj* mixed; miscellaneous

gemiddeld (ger-mı-derlt) *adj* average, medium; *adv* on the average

gemiddelde (ger-mı-derl-der) *nt* (pl ~n) average, mean

gemis (ger-*mıss*) *nt* want, lack

genade (ger-*naa*-der) *c* mercy; grace

geneeskunde (ger-*nāyss*-kern-der) *c* medicine

geneeskundig (ger-nāyss-*kern*-derkh) *adj* medical

geneesmiddel (ger-*nāyss*-mı-derl) *nt* (pl ~en) medicine; remedy, drug

genegen (ger-*nāy*-gern) *adj* inclined

genegenheid (ger-*nāy*-gern-hayt) *c* affection

geneigd (ger-*naykht*) *adj* inclined

generaal (gāy-ner-*raal*) *c* (pl ~s) general

generatie (gāy-ner-*raa*-tsee) *c* (pl ~s) generation

generator (gāy-ner-*raa*-tor) *c* (pl ~en, ~s) generator

* **genezen** (ger-*nāy*-zern) *v* heal; cure; • recover

genezing (ger-*nāy*-zıng) *c* (pl ~en) cure; recovery

genie (zher-*nee*) *nt* (pl ~ën) genius

* **genieten van** (ger-*nee*-tern) enjoy

genoeg (ger-*nōōkh*) *adv* enough; sufficient

genoegen (ger-*nōō*-gern) *nt* (pl ~s)

pleasure

genootschap (ger-*nōat*-skhahp) *nt* (pl ~pen) society; association

genot (ger-*not*) *nt* joy; delight; enjoyment

geologie (gāy-ʸōa-lōa-*gee*) *c* geology

gepast (ger-*pahst*) *adj* suitable, proper

gepensioneerd (ger-pehn-shōa-*nāȳrt*) *adj* retired

geraamte (ger-*raam*-ter) *nt* (pl ~n, ~s) skeleton

geraas (ger-*raass*) *nt* roar

gerecht (ger-*rehkht*) *nt* (pl ~en) dish; law court

gerechtigheid (ger-*rehkh*-terkh-hayt) *c* justice

gereed (ger-*rāȳt*) *adj* ready

gereedschap (ger-*rāȳt*-skhahp) *nt* (pl ~pen) tool; utensil, implement

gereedschapskist (ger-*rāȳt*-skhahps-kıst) *c* (pl ~en) tool kit

geregeld (ger-*rāȳ*-gerlt) *adj* regular

gereserveerd (ger-rāȳ-zehr-*vāȳrt*) *adj* reserved

gerief (ger-*reef*) *nt* comfort

geriefelijk (ger-*ree*-fer-lerk) *adj* comfortable, easy; convenient

gering (ger-*rıng*) *adj* minor; slight, small; **geringst** least

geroddel (ger-*ro*-derl) *nt* gossip

gerst (gehrst) *c* barley

gerucht (ger-*rerkht*) *nt* (pl ~en) rumour

geruit (ger-*rur*ᵉʷt) *adj* chequered

gerust (ger-*rerst*) *adj* confident

geruststellen (ger-*rerst*-steh-lern) *v* reassure

gescheiden (ger-*skhay*-dern) *adj* separate

geschenk (ger-*skhehngk*) *nt* (pl ~en) gift, present

geschiedenis (ger-*skhee*-der-nıss) *c* history

geschiedkundig (ger-skheet-*kern*-

derkh) *adj* historical

geschiedkundige (ger-skheet-*kern*-der-ger) *c* (pl ~n) historian

geschikt (ger-*skhıkt*) *adj* convenient, suitable, proper, appropriate, fit; ~ *zijn qualify

geschil (ger-*skhıl*) *nt* (pl ~len) dispute

geslacht (ger-*slahkht*) *nt* (pl ~en) sex; gender

geslachtsziekte (ger-*slahkht*-seek-ter) *c* (pl ~n, ~s) venereal disease

gesloten (ger-*slōa*-tern) *adj* closed, shut

gesp (gehsp) *c* (pl ~en) buckle

gespannen (ger-*spah*-nern) *adj* tense

gespierd (ger-*speert*) *adj* muscular

gespikkeld (ger-*spı*-kerlt) *adj* spotted

gesprek (ger-*sprehk*) *nt* (pl ~ken) discussion, conversation, talk; **interlokaal** ~ trunk-call; **lokaal** ~ local call

gestalte (ger-*stahl*-ter) *c* (pl ~n, ~s) figure

gesticht (ger-*stıkht*) *nt* (pl ~en) asylum

gestorven (ger-*stor*-vern) *adj* dead

gestreept (ger-*strāȳpt*) *adj* striped

getal (ger-*tahl*) *nt* (pl ~len) number

getij (ger-*tay*) *nt* (pl ~en) tide

getrouw (ger-*trou*) *adj* true

getuige (ger-*tur*ᵉʷ-ger) *c* (pl ~n) witness

getuigen (ger-*tur*ᵉʷ-gern) *v* testify

getuigschrift (ger-*tur*ᵉʷkh-skhrıft) *nt* (pl ~en) certificate

getypt (ger-*teept*) *adj* typewritten

geur (gūrr) *c* (pl ~en) smell, odour; scent

gevaar (ger-*vaar*) *nt* (pl -varen) danger; risk, peril

gevaarlijk (ger-*vaar*-lerk) *adj* dangerous; perilous

geval (ger-*vahl*) *nt* (pl ~len) case; instance; event; **in elk** ~ at any rate, anyway; **in ~ van** in case of

gevangene (ger-*vah*-nger-ner) *c* (pl ~n) prisoner

gevangenis (ger-*vah*-nger-niss) *c* (pl ~sen) prison; gaol, jail

gevangenschap (ger-*vah*-ngern-skhahp) *c* imprisonment

gevarieerd (ger-vaa-ree-ᵞa̅yrt) *adj* varied

gevecht (ger-*vehkht*) *nt* (pl ~en) combat, battle, fight

gevel (*ga̅y*-verl) *c* (pl ~s) façade

geveltop (*ga̅y*-verl-top) *c* (pl ~pen) gable

* **geven** (*ga̅y*-vern) *v* *give; ~ **om** mind

gevoel (ger-*vo̅o̅l*) *nt* feeling; sensation

gevoelig (ger-*vo̅o̅*-lerkh) *adj* sensitive

gevoelloos (ger-*vo̅o̅*-lo̅ass) *adj* numb

gevogelte (ger-*vo̅a̅*-gerl-ter) *nt* fowl; poultry

gevolg (ger-*volkh*) *nt* (pl ~en) result, consequence; issue, effect; **ten gevolge van** owing to

gevolgtrekking (ger-*volkh*-treh-king) *c* (pl ~en) conclusion

gevorderd (ger-*vor*-derrt) *adj* advanced

gevuld (ger-*verlt*) *adj* stuffed

gewaad (ger-*vaat*) *nt* (pl gewaden) robe

gewaagd (ger-*vaakht*) *adj* risky

gewaarwording (ger-*vaar*-vor-ding) *c* (pl ~en) perception; sensation

gewapend (ger-*vaa*-pernt) *adj* armed

geweer (ger-*va̅yr*) *nt* (pl geweren) rifle, gun

gewei (ger-*vay*) *nt* (pl ~en) antlers *pl*

geweld (ger-*vehlt*) *nt* violence; force

gewelddaad (ger-*vehl*-daat) *c* (pl -daden) outrage

gewelddadig (ger-vehl-*daa*-derkh) *adj* violent

geweldig (ger-*vehl*-derkh) *adj* terrific; huge

gewelf (ger-*vehlf*) *nt* (pl gewelven) arch, vault

gewend (ger-*vehnt*) *adj* accustomed

gewest (ger-*vehst*) *nt* (pl ~en) province

geweten (ger-*va̅y*-tern) *nt* conscience

gewicht (ger-*vikht*) *nt* (pl ~en) weight

gewichtig (ger-*vikh*-terkh) *adj* important; big

gewillig (ger-*vi*-lerkh) *adj* co-operative

gewond (ger-*vont*) *adj* injured

gewoon (ger-*vo̅a̅n*) *adj* normal, ordinary; common, regular, plain, simple; customary, habitual; accustomed; ~ *zijn* *be used to; would

gewoonlijk (ger-*vo̅a̅n*-lerk) *adj* customary; *adv* as a rule, usually

gewoonte (ger-*vo̅a̅n*-ter) *c* (pl ~n, ~s) habit; custom

gewoonweg (ger-*vo̅a̅n*-vehkh) *adv* simply

gewricht (ger-*vrikht*) *nt* (pl ~en) joint

gezag (ger-*zahkh*) *nt* authority

gezagvoerder (ger-*zahkh*-fo̅o̅r-derr) *c* (pl ~s) captain

gezamenlijk (ger-*zaa*-mer-lerk) *adj* joint

gezang (ger-*zahng*) *nt* (pl ~en) hymn

gezant (ger-*zahnt*) *c* (pl ~en) envoy

gezellig (ger-*zeh*-lerkh) *adj* cosy

gezelschap (ger-*zehl*-skhahp) *nt* (pl ~pen) company; society

gezet (ger-*zeht*) *adj* corpulent; stout

gezicht (ger-*zikht*) *nt* (pl ~en) face; sight

gezichtscrème (ger-*zikhts*-kraim) *c* (pl ~s) face-cream

gezichtsmassage (ger-*zikhts*-mah-saa-zher) *c* (pl ~s) face massage

gezichtspoeder (ger-*zikhts*-po̅o̅-derr) *nt/c* (pl ~s) face-powder

gezien (ger-*zeen*) *prep* considering

gezin (ger-*zin*) *nt* (pl ~nen) family

gezond (ger-*zont*) *adj* healthy; well; wholesome

gezondheid (ger-*zont*-hayt) *c* health

gezondheidsattest (ger-*zont*-hayts-ah-tehst) *nt* (pl ~en) health certificate

gezwel (ger-*zvehl*) *nt* (pl ~len) tumour, growth

gids (gɪts) *c* (pl ~en) guide; guide-book

giechelen (*gee*-kher-lern) *v* giggle

gier (geer) *c* (pl ~en) vulture

gierig (*gee*-rerkh) *adj* avaricious; stingy

** **gieten** (*gee*-tern) *v* pour

gietijzer (*gee*-tay-zerr) *nt* cast iron

gift (gɪft) *c* (pl ~en) donation

giftig (*gɪf*-terkh) *adj* poisonous

gijzelaar (*gay*-zer-laar) *c* (pl ~s) hostage

gil (gɪl) *c* (pl ~len) scream, yell, shriek

gillen (*gɪ*-lern) *v* scream, yell, shriek

ginds (gɪns) *adv* over there

gips (gɪps) *nt* plaster

gissen (*gɪ*-sern) *v* guess

gissing (*gɪ*-sɪng) *c* (pl ~en) guess

gist (gɪst) *c* yeast

gisten (*gɪss*-tern) *v* ferment

gisteren (*gɪss*-ter-rern) *adv* yesterday

gitaar (gee-*taar*) *c* (pl -taren) guitar

glad (glaht) *adj* slippery; smooth

glans (glahns) *c* gloss

glanzen (*glahn*-zern) *v* *shine; **glanzend** glossy

glas (glahss) *nt* (pl glazen) glass; **gebrandschilderd** ~ stained glass

glazen (*glaa*-zern) *adj* glass

gletsjer (*gleht*-sherr) *c* (pl ~s) glacier

gleuf (glůrf) *c* (pl gleuven) slot

glibberig (*glɪ*-ber-rerkh) *adj* slippery

glijbaan (*glay*-baan) *c* (pl -banen) slide

** **glijden** (*glay*-dern) *v* glide, *slide

glimlach (*glɪm*-lahkh) *c* smile

glimlachen (*glɪm*-lah-khern) *v* smile

glimp (glɪmp) *c* glimpse

globaal (glōa-*baal*) *adj* broad

gloed (glōot) *c* glow

gloeien (*glōō*ee-ern) *v* glow

gloeilamp (*glōō*ee-lahmp) *c* (pl ~en) light bulb

glooien (*glōā*ee-ern) *v* slope

glooiing (*glōā*ee-ɪng) *c* (pl ~en) ramp

glorie (*glōā*-ree) *c* glory

gluren (*glůw*-rern) *v* peep

gobelin (gōa-ber-*lang*) *c* (pl ~s) tapestry

god (got) *c* (pl ~en) god

goddelijk (*go*-der-lerk) *adj* divine

godin (gōa-*dɪn*) *c* (pl ~nen) goddess

godsdienst (*gots*-deenst) *c* (pl ~en) religion

godsdienstig (gots-*deen*-sterkh) *adj* religious

goed (gōot) *adj* good; right, correct; kind; *adv* well; **goed!** all right!

goederen (*gōō*-der-rern) *pl* goods *pl*

goederentrein (*gōō*-der-rern-trayn) *c* (pl ~en) goods train; freight-train *nAm*

goedgelovig (gōot-kher-*lōā*-verkh) *adj* credulous

goedgestemd (gōot-kher-*stehmt*) *adj* good-tempered

goedhartig (gōot-*hahr*-terkh) *adj* good-natured

goedkeuren (*gōōt*-kūr-rern) *v* approve

goedkeuring (*gōōt*-kur-rɪng) *c* (pl ~en) approval

goedkoop (gōot-*kōap*) *adj* cheap; inexpensive

gok (gok) *c* chance

golf[1] (golf) *c* (pl golven) wave; gulf

golf[2] (golf) *nt* golf

golfbaan (*golf*-baan) *c* (pl -banen) golf-links, golf-course

golfclub (*golf*-klerp) *c* (pl ~s) golf-club

golflengte (*golf*-lehng-ter) *c* (pl ~n, ~s) wave-length

golvend (*gol*-vernt) *adj* wavy, undulating

gom (gom) *c/nt* (pl ~men) eraser

gondel (*gon*-derl) *c* (pl ~s) gondola

goochelaar (*gōa̅*-kher-laar) *c* (pl ~s) magician

gooi (gōa̅ee) *c* (pl ~en) throw

gooien (*gōa̅*ee-ern) *v* *throw; *cast; toss

goot (gōa̅t) *c* (pl goten) gutter

gootsteen (*gōa̅t*-stāyn) *c* (pl -stenen) sink

gordijn (gor-*dayn*) *nt* (pl ~en) curtain

gorgelen (*gor*-ger-lern) *v* gargle

goud (gout) *nt* gold

gouden (*gou*-dern) *adj* golden

goudmijn (*gout*-mayn) *c* (pl ~en) goldmine

goudsmid (*gout*-smɪt) *c* (pl -smeden) goldsmith

gouvernante (gōō-verr-*nahn*-ter) *c* (pl ~s) governess

gouverneur (gōō-verr-*nūrr*) *c* (pl ~s) governor

graad (graat) *c* (pl graden) degree; grade

graaf (graaf) *c* (pl graven) count; earl

graafschap (*graaf*-skhahp) *nt* (pl ~pen) county

graag (graakh) *adv* gladly, willingly

graan (graan) *nt* (pl granen) corn, grain

graat (graat) *c* (pl graten) bone, fishbone

gracht (grahkht) *c* (pl ~en) canal; moat

graf (grahf) *nt* (pl graven) grave; tomb

grafiek (graa-*feek*) *c* (pl ~en) graph, diagram; chart

grafisch (*graa*-feess) *adj* graphic

grafsteen (*grahf*-stāyn) *c* (pl -stenen) tombstone, gravestone

gram (grahm) *nt* (pl ~men) gram

grammatica (grah-*maa*-tee-kaa) *c* grammar

grammaticaal (grah-maa-tee-*kaal*) *adj* grammatical

grammofoon (grah-mōa̅-*fōa̅n*) *c* (pl ~s) gramophone

grammofoonplaat (grah-mōa̅-*fōa̅n*-plaat) *c* (pl -platen) disc, record

graniet (graa-*neet*) *nt* granite

grap (grahp) *c* (pl ~pen) joke

grappig (*grah*-perkh) *adj* funny, humorous

gras (grahss) *nt* grass

grasspriet (*grahss*-spreet) *c* (pl ~en) blade of grass

grasveld (*grahss*-fehlt) *nt* (pl ~en) lawn

gratie (*graa*-tsee) *c* grace; pardon

gratis (*graa*-terss) *adv* free of charge, free, gratis

grauw (grou) *adj* grey

***graven** (*graa*-vern) *v* *dig

graveren (graa-*vāy*-rern) *v* engrave

graveur (graa-*vūrr*) *c* (pl ~s) engraver

gravin (graa-*vɪn*) *c* (pl ~nen) countess

gravure (graa-*vew̅*-rer) *c* (pl ~s, ~n) engraving

grazen (*graa*-zern) *v* graze

greep (grāyp) *c* (pl grepen) grip; grasp, clutch

grendel (*grehn*-derl) *c* (pl ~s) bolt

grens (grehns) *c* (pl grenzen) frontier, border; boundary, bound

grenzeloos (*grehn*-zer-lōass) *adj* unlimited

greppel (*greh*-perl) *c* (pl ~s) ditch

Griek (greek) *c* (pl ~en) Greek

Griekenland (*gree*-kern-lahnt) Greece

Grieks (greeks) *adj* Greek

griep (greep) *c* flu, influenza

griet (greet) *c* (pl ~en) brill

griezelig (*gree*-zer-lerkh) *adj* scary,

creepy

grijns (grayns) *c* grin

grijnzen (grayn-zern) *v* grin

***grijpen** (gray-pern) *v* *catch, grip, grasp, seize

grijs (grayss) *adj* grey

gril (gril) *c* (pl ~len) whim, fancy, fad

grind (grint) *nt* gravel

grinniken (gri-ner-kern) *v* chuckle

groef (groof) *c* (pl groeven) groove

groei (groo^ee) *c* growth

groeien (groo^ee-ern) *v* *grow

groen (groon) *adj* green

groente *c* (pl ~n, ~s) greens *pl*, vegetable

groenteboer (groon-ter-boor) *c* (pl ~en) greengrocer; vegetable merchant

groep (groop) *c* (pl ~en) group; bunch, set, party

groet (groot) *c* (pl ~en) greeting

groeten (groo-tern) *v* greet; salute

groeve (groo-ver) *c* (pl ~n) pit

grof (grof) *adj* gross, coarse; rude

grommen (gro-mern) *v* growl

grond (gront) *c* ground; earth, soil; **begane ~** ground floor

grondig (gron-derkh) *adj* thorough

grondslag (gront-slahkh) *c* (pl ~en) basis, base

grondstof (gront-stof) *c* (pl ~fen) raw material

grondwet (gront-veht) *c* (pl ~ten) constitution

groot (groot) *adj* big; great, large, tall; major; **grootst** major, main; **groter** major; superior

***grootbrengen** (groot-breh-ngern) *v* *bring up, raise; rear

Groot-Brittannië (groot-bri-tah-nee-Yer) Great Britain

groothandel (groot-hahn-derl) *c* wholesale

grootmoeder (groot-moo-derr) *c* (pl

~s) grandmother

grootouders (groot-ou-derrs) *pl* grandparents *pl*

groots (groots) *adj* grand, superb, magnificent

grootte (groo-ter) *c* (pl ~n, ~s) size

grootvader (groot-faa-derr) *c* (pl ~s) grandfather

gros (gross) *nt* (pl ~sen) gross

grossier (gro-seer) *c* (pl ~s) wholesale dealer

grot (grot) *c* (pl ~ten) cave; grotto

gruis (grur^ewss) *nt* grit

gruwelijk (grew-ver-lerk) *adj* horrible

gul (gerl) *adj* generous

gulp (gerlp) *c* (pl ~en) fly

gulzig (gerl-zerkh) *adj* greedy

gunnen (ger-nern) *v* grant

gunst (gernst) *c* (pl ~en) favour

gunstig (gern-sterkh) *adj* favourable

guur (gewr) *adj* bleak

gymnast (gim-nahst) *c* (pl ~en) gymnast

gymnastiek (gim-nahss-teek) *c* gymnastics *pl*

gymnastiekbroek (gim-nahss-teek-brook) *c* (pl ~en) trunks *pl*

gymnastiekzaal (gim-nahss-teek-saal) *c* (pl -zalen) gymnasium

gymschoenen (gim-skhoo-nern) *pl* gym shoes, plimsolls *pl*; sneakers *plAm*

gynaecoloog (gee-nāy-kōa-lōakh) *c* (pl -logen) gynaecologist

H

haai (haa^ee) *c* (pl ~en) shark

haak (haak) *c* (pl haken) hook; **tussen twee haakjes** by the way

haalbaar (haal-baar) *adj* attainable, realizable

haan (haan) *c* (pl hanen) cock

haar¹ (haar) *nt* (pl haren) hair

haar² (haar) *pron* her

haarborstel (*haar*-bor-sterl) *c* (pl ~s) hairbrush

haarcrème (*haar*-kraim) *c* (pl ~s) hair cream

haard (haart) *c* (pl ~en) hearth, fireplace

haardroger (*haar*-drōā-gerr) *c* (pl ~s) hair-dryer

haarlak (*haar*-lahk) *c* (pl ~ken) hairspray

haarnetje (*haar*-neh-tᵛer) *nt* (pl ~s) hair-net

haarolie (*haar*-ōā-lee) *c* hair-oil

haarspeld (*haar*-spehlt) *c* (pl ~en) hairpin, hair-grip; bobby pin *Am*

haarstukje (*haar*-ster-kᵛer) *nt* (pl ~s) hair piece

haarversteviger (*haar*-verr-stāȳ-ver-gerr) *c* setting lotion

haas (haass) *c* (pl hazen) hare

haast¹ (haast) *adv* nearly, almost

haast² (haast) *c* haste, hurry

zich haasten (*haass*-tern) hasten, rush, hurry

haastig (*haass*-terkh) *adj* hasty; *adv* in a hurry

haat (haat) *c* hatred, hate

hachelijk (*hah*-kher-lerk) *adj* precarious, critical

hagel (*haa*-gerl) *c* hail

hak (hahk) *c* (pl ~ken) heel

haken (*haa*-kern) *v* crochet

hakken (*hah*-kern) *v* chop

hal (hahl) *c* (pl ~len) lobby, hall

halen (*haa*-lern) *v* *get, fetch; *make; *catch; *laten ~ *send for

half (hahlf) *adj* half; semi-; *adv* half

hallo! (hah-*lōā*) hello!

hals (hahls) *c* (pl halzen) throat; neck

halsband (*hahls*-bahnt) *c* (pl ~en) collar

halsketting (*hahls*-keh-tɪng) *c* (pl ~en) necklace

halt! (hahlt) stop!

halte (*hahl*-ter) *c* (pl ~n, ~s) stop

halveren (hahl-*vāȳ*-rern) *v* halve

halverwege (*hahl*-verr-vāȳ-ger) *adv* halfway

ham (hahm) *c* (pl ~men) ham

hamer (*haa*-merr) *c* (pl ~s) hammer; **houten ~** mallet

hand (hahnt) *c* (pl ~en) hand; **hand-** manual; **met de ~ gemaakt** hand-made

handbagage (*hahnt*-bah-gaa-zher) *c* hand luggage; hand baggage *Am*

handboeien (*hahnt*-bōōᵉᵉ-ern) *pl* handcuffs *pl*

handboek (*hahnt*-bōōk) *nt* (pl ~en) handbook

handcrème (*hahnt*-kraim) *c* (pl ~s) hand cream

handdoek (*hahn*-dōōk) *c* (pl ~en) towel

handdruk (*hahn*-drerk) *c* handshake

handel (*hahn*-derl) *c* commerce, trade; business; ~ ***drijven** trade; **handels-** commercial

handelaar (*hahn*-der-laar) *c* (pl ~s, -laren) tradesman, merchant; dealer, trader

handelen (*hahn*-der-lern) *v* act

handeling (*hahn*-der-lɪng) *c* (pl ~en) action; deed, plot

handelsmerk (*hahn*-derls-mehrk) *nt* (pl ~en) trademark

handelsrecht (*hahn*-derls-rehkht) *nt* commercial law

handelswaar (*hahn*-derls-vaar) *c* merchandise

handenarbeid (*hahn*-der-nahr-bayt) *c* handicraft

handhaven (*hahnt*-haa-vern) *v* maintain

handig (*hahn*-derkh) *adj* handy

creepy

grijns (grayns) *c* grin

grijnzen (grayn-zern) *v* grin

*****grijpen** (gray-pern) *v* *catch, grip, grasp, seize

grijs (grayss) *adj* grey

gril (grɪl) *c* (pl ~len) whim, fancy, fad

grind (grɪnt) *nt* gravel

grinniken (grɪ-ner-kern) *v* chuckle

groef (grōof) *c* (pl groeven) groove

groei (grōo^ee) *c* growth

groeien (grōo^ee-ern) *v* *grow

groen (grōon) *adj* green

groente *c* (pl ~n, ~s) greens *pl*, vegetable

groenteboer (grōon-ter-bōor) *c* (pl ~en) greengrocer; vegetable merchant

groep (grōop) *c* (pl ~en) group; bunch, set, party

groet (grōot) *c* (pl ~en) greeting

groeten (grōo-tern) *v* greet; salute

groeve (grōo-ver) *c* (pl ~n) pit

grof (grof) *adj* gross, coarse; rude

grommen (gro-mern) *v* growl

grond (gront) *c* ground; earth, soil; **begane** ~ ground floor

grondig (gron-derkh) *adj* thorough

grondslag (gront-slahkh) *c* (pl ~en) basis, base

grondstof (gront-stof) *c* (pl ~fen) raw material

grondwet (gront-veht) *c* (pl ~ten) constitution

groot (grōat) *adj* big; great, large, tall; major; **grootst** major, main; **groter** major; superior

*****grootbrengen** (grōat-breh-ngern) *v* *bring up, raise; rear

Groot-Brittannië (grōat-brɪ-tah-nee-^yer) Great Britain

groothandel (grōat-hahn-derl) *c* wholesale

grootmoeder (grōat-mōo-derr) *c* (pl

~s) grandmother

grootouders (grōat-ou-derrs) *pl* grandparents *pl*

groots (grōats) *adj* grand, superb, magnificent

grootte (grōa-ter) *c* (pl ~n, ~s) size

grootvader (grōat-faa-derr) *c* (pl ~s) grandfather

gros (gross) *nt* (pl ~sen) gross

grossier (gro-seer) *c* (pl ~s) wholesale dealer

grot (grot) *c* (pl ~ten) cave; grotto

gruis (grur^ewss) *nt* grit

gruwelijk (grew-ver-lerk) *adj* horrible

gul (gerl) *adj* generous

gulp (gerlp) *c* (pl ~en) fly

gulzig (gerl-zerkh) *adj* greedy

gunnen (ger-nern) *v* grant

gunst (gernst) *c* (pl ~en) favour

gunstig (gern-sterkh) *adj* favourable

guur (gewr) *adj* bleak

gymnast (gɪm-nahst) *c* (pl ~en) gymnast

gymnastiek (gɪm-nahss-teek) *c* gymnastics *pl*

gymnastiekbroek (gɪm-nahss-teek-brōok) *c* (pl ~en) trunks *pl*

gymnastiekzaal (gɪm-nahss-teek-saal) *c* (pl -zalen) gymnasium

gymschoenen (gɪm-skhōo-nern) *pl* gym shoes, plimsolls *pl*; sneakers *plAm*

gynaecoloog (gee-nāy-kōa-lōakh) *c* (pl -logen) gynaecologist

H

haai (haa^ee) *c* (pl ~en) shark

haak (haak) *c* (pl haken) hook; **tussen twee haakjes** by the way

haalbaar (haal-baar) *adj* attainable, realizable

haan (haan) *c* (pl hanen) cock

haar[1] (haar) *nt* (pl haren) hair

haar[2] (haar) *pron* her

haarborstel (*haar*-bor-sterl) *c* (pl ~s) hairbrush

haarcrème (*haar*-kraim) *c* (pl ~s) hair cream

haard (haart) *c* (pl ~en) hearth, fireplace

haardroger (*haar*-drōā-gerr) *c* (pl ~s) hair-dryer

haarlak (*haar*-lahk) *c* (pl ~ken) hairspray

haarnetje (*haar*-neh-t^yer) *nt* (pl ~s) hair-net

haarolie (*haar*-ōā-lee) *c* hair-oil

haarspeld (*haar*-spehlt) *c* (pl ~en) hairpin, hair-grip; bobby pin *Am*

haarstukje (*haar*-ster-k^yer) *nt* (pl ~s) hair piece

haarversteviger (*haar*-verr-stāy-ver-gerr) *c* setting lotion

haas (haass) *c* (pl hazen) hare

haast[1] (haast) *adv* nearly, almost

haast[2] (haast) *c* haste, hurry

zich haasten (*haass*-tern) hasten, rush, hurry

haastig (*haass*-terkh) *adj* hasty; *adv* in a hurry

haat (haat) *c* hatred, hate

hachelijk (*hah*-kher-lerk) *adj* precarious, critical

hagel (*haa*-gerl) *c* hail

hak (hahk) *c* (pl ~ken) heel

haken (*haa*-kern) *v* crochet

hakken (*hah*-kern) *v* chop

hal (hahl) *c* (pl ~len) lobby, hall

halen (*haa*-lern) *v* *get, fetch; *make; *catch; *laten ~ *send for

half (hahlf) *adj* half; semi-; *adv* half

hallo! (hah-*lōā*) hello!

hals (hahls) *c* (pl halzen) throat; neck

halsband (*hahls*-bahnt) *c* (pl ~en) collar

halsketting (*hahls*-keh-tɪng) *c* (pl ~en) necklace

halt! (hahlt) stop!

halte (*hahl*-ter) *c* (pl ~n, ~s) stop

halveren (hahl-*vāy*-rern) *v* halve

halverwege (*hahl*-verr-vāy-ger) *adv* halfway

ham (hahm) *c* (pl ~men) ham

hamer (*haa*-merr) *c* (pl ~s) hammer; **houten ~** mallet

hand (hahnt) *c* (pl ~en) hand; **hand**-manual; **met de ~ gemaakt** handmade

handbagage (*hahnt*-bah-gaa-zher) *c* hand luggage; hand baggage *Am*

handboeien (*hahnt*-bōō^{ee}-ern) *pl* handcuffs *pl*

handboek (*hahnt*-bōōk) *nt* (pl ~en) handbook

handcrème (*hahnt*-kraim) *c* (pl ~s) hand cream

handdoek (*hahn*-dōōk) *c* (pl ~en) towel

handdruk (*hahn*-drerk) *c* handshake

handel (*hahn*-derl) *c* commerce, trade; business; ~ *drijven trade; **handels**- commercial

handelaar (*hahn*-der-laar) *c* (pl ~s, -laren) tradesman, merchant; dealer, trader

handelen (*hahn*-der-lern) *v* act

handeling (*hahn*-der-lɪng) *c* (pl ~en) action; deed, plot

handelsmerk (*hahn*-derls-mehrk) *nt* (pl ~en) trademark

handelsrecht (*hahn*-derls-rehkht) *nt* commercial law

handelswaar (*hahn*-derls-vaar) *c* merchandise

handenarbeid (*hahn*-der-nahr-bayt) *c* handicraft

handhaven (*hahnt*-haa-vern) *v* maintain

handig (*hahn*-derkh) *adj* handy

handkoffertje (*hahnt*-ko-ferr-t^yer) *nt* (pl ~s) grip *nAm*

handpalm (*hahnt*-pahlm) *c* (pl ~en) palm

handrem (*hahnt*-rehm) *c* (pl ~men) hand-brake

handschoen (*hahnt*-skhoōn) *c* (pl ~en) glove

handschrift (*hahnt*-skhrift) *nt* (pl ~en) handwriting

handtas (*hahn*-tahss) *c* (pl ~sen) handbag, bag

handtekening (*hahn*-tāy-ker-ning) *v* (pl ~en) signature

handvat (*hahnt*-faht) *nt* (pl ~ten) handle

handvol (*hahnt*-fol) *c* (pl ~en) handful

handwerk (*hahnt*-vehrk) *nt* handwork, handicraft; needlework

hangbrug (*hahng*-brerkh) *c* (pl ~gen) suspension bridge

*****hangen** (*hah*-ngern) *v* *hang

hangmat (*hahng*-maht) *c* (pl ~ten) hammock

hangslot (*hahng*-slot) *nt* (pl ~en) padlock

hanteerbaar (hahn-*tāyr*-baar) *adj* manageable

hanteren (hahn-*tāy*-rern) *v* handle

hap (hahp) *c* (pl ~pen) bite

hard (hahrt) *adj* hard; loud

harddraverij (hahr-draa-ver-*ray*) *c* (pl ~en) horserace

hardnekkig (hahrt-*neh*-kerkh) *adj* obstinate, dogged, stubborn

hardop (hahrt-*op*) *adv* aloud

harig (*haa*-rerkh) *adj* hairy

haring (*haa*-ring) *c* (pl ~en) herring

hark (hahrk) *c* (pl ~en) rake

harmonie (hahr-moā-*nee*) *c* harmony

harnas (*hahr*-nahss) *nt* (pl ~sen) armour

harp (hahrp) *c* (pl ~en) harp

hars (hahrs) *nt/c* resin

hart (hahrt) *nt* (pl ~en) heart

hartaanval (*hahr*-taan-vahl) *c* (pl ~len) heart attack

hartelijk (*hahr*-ter-lerk) *adj* hearty, cordial; sympathetic

harteloos (*hahr*-ter-loāss) *adj* heartless

hartklopping (*hahrt*-klo-ping) *c* (pl ~en) palpitation

hartstocht (*hahrts*-tokht) *c* passion

hartstochtelijk (hahrts-*tokh*-ter-lerk) *adj* passionate

hatelijk (*haa*-ter-lerk) *adj* spiteful

haten (*haa*-tern) *v* hate

haven (*haa*-vern) *c* (pl ~s) port, harbour

havenarbeider (*haa*-vern-ahr-bay-derr) *c* (pl ~s) docker

haver (*haa*-verr) *c* oats *pl*

havik (*haa*-vik) *c* (pl ~en) hawk

hazelnoot (*haa*-zerl-noāt) *c* (pl -noten) hazelnut

hazewind (haa-zer-*vint*) *c* (pl ~en) greyhound

*****hebben** (*heh*-bern) *v* *have

Hebreeuws (hāy-*brāy*^{oo}ss) *nt* Hebrew

hebzucht (*hehp*-serkht) *c* greed

hebzuchtig (hehp-*serkh*-terkh) *adj* greedy

hechten (*hehkh*-tern) *v* attach; sew up

hechtenis (*hehkh*-ter-niss) *c* custody

hechting (*hehkh*-ting) *c* (pl ~en) stitch

hechtpleister (*hehkht*-play-sterr) *c* (pl ~s) adhesive tape

heden (*hāy*-dern) *nt* present

hedendaags (*hāy*-dern-daakhs) *adj* contemporary

heel (hāyl) *adj* entire, whole; unbroken; *adv* quite

heelal (*hāy*-*lahl*) *nt* universe

heelhuids (*hāyl*-hur^{ew}ts) *adj* unhurt

*****heengaan** (*hāyng*-gaan) *v* depart

heer (hāyr) *c* (pl heren) gentleman

heerlijk (*hāyr*-lerk) *adj* lovely, wonderful; delightful, delicious

heerschappij (hāȳr-skhah-*pay*) c (pl ~en) rule; dominion

heersen (hāȳr-sern) v rule

heerser (hāȳr-serr) c (pl ~s) ruler

hees (hāyss) adj hoarse

heet (hāyt) adj hot; warm

hefboom (hehf-bōam) c (pl -bomen) lever

*heffen (heh-fern) v raise

heftig (hehf-terkh) adj violent

heg (hehkh) c (pl ~gen) hedge

heide (hay-der) c (pl ~n) heath; moor; heather

heiden (hay-dern) c (pl ~en) heathen, pagan

heidens (hay-derns) adj heathen, pagan

heiig (hay-erkh) adj hazy

heilbot (hayl-bot) c (pl ~ten) halibut

heilig (hay-lerkh) adj holy, sacred

heiligdom (hay-lerkh-dom) nt (pl ~men) shrine

heilige (hay-ler-ger) c (pl ~n) saint

heiligschennis (hay-lerkh-skheh-nerss) c sacrilege

heimwee (haym-vāȳ) nt homesickness

hek (hehk) nt (pl ~ken) fence; gate; railing

hekel (hāȳ-kerl) c dislike; **een ~ *hebben aan** hate, dislike

heks (hehks) c (pl ~en) witch

hel (hehl) c hell

helaas (hāy-laass) adv unfortunately

held (hehlt) c (pl ~en) hero

helder (hehl-derr) adj clear; serene; bright

heleboel (hāȳ-ler-bōol) c plenty

helemaal (hāȳ-ler-maal) adv entirely, altogether, completely, wholly; quite; at all

helft (hehlft) c (pl ~en) half

hellen (heh-lern) v slant; **hellend** slanting

helling (heh-lɪng) c (pl ~en) slope; hillside; gradient, incline

helm (hehlm) c (pl ~en) helmet

*helpen (hehl-pern) v help; assist, aid

helper (hehl-perr) c (pl ~s) helper

hem (hehm) pron him

hemd (hehmt) nt (pl ~en) shirt; vest; undershirt

hemel (hāȳ-merl) c (pl ~s, ~en) sky; heaven

hen[1] (hehn) pron them

hen[2] (hehn) c (pl ~nen) hen

hendel (hehn-derl) c (pl ~s) lever

hengel (heh-ngerl) c (pl ~s) fishing rod

hengelen (heh-nger-lern) v angle, fish

hennep (heh-nerp) c hemp

herberg (hehr-behrkh) c (pl ~en) hostel, tavern, inn

herbergen (hehr-behr-gern) v lodge

herbergier (hehr-behr-*geer*) c (pl ~s) inn-keeper

herdenking (hehr-*dehng*-kɪng) c (pl ~en) commemoration

herder (hehr-derr) c (pl ~s) shepherd

herenhuis (hāȳ-rern-hur^ewss) nt (pl -huizen) mansion, manor-house

herenigen (heh-rāȳ-ner-gern) v reunite

herentoilet (hāȳ-rern-tvah-leht) nt (pl ~ten) men's room

herfst (hehrfst) c autumn; fall nAm

herhalen (hehr-haa-lern) v repeat

herhaling (hehr-haa-lɪng) c (pl ~en) repetition

herinneren (heh-rɪ-ner-rern) v remind; **zich ~** remember, recollect, recall

herinnering (heh-rɪ-ner-rɪng) c (pl ~en) memory; remembrance

herkennen (hehr-keh-nern) v recognize

herkomst (hehr-komst) c origin

hernia (hehr-nee-Yaa) c slipped disc

herrie (heh-ree) c noise; fuss

*herroepen (heh-rōō-pern) v recall

hersenen (*hehr*-ser-nern) *pl* brain

hersenschudding (*hehr*-sern-skher-ding) *c* (pl ~en) concussion

herstel (hehr-*stehl*) *nt* repair; recovery; revival

herstellen (hehr-*steh*-lern) *v* repair, mend; **zich ~** recover

hert (hehrt) *nt* (pl ~en) deer

hertog (*hehr*-tokh) *c* (pl ~en) duke

hertogin (hehr-tōa-*gin*) *c* (pl ~nen) duchess

hervatten (hehr-*vah*-tern) *v* resume, recommence

*****herzien** (hehr-*zeen*) *v* revise

herziening (hehr-*zee*-ning) *c* (pl ~en) revision

het (heht, ert) *art* the; *pron* it

*****heten** (*hāy*-tern) *v* *be called

heteroseksueel (hāy-ter-rōa-sehk-sew-*vāyl*) *adj* heterosexual

hetzij ... hetzij (heht-*say*) either ... or

heup (hūrp) *c* (pl ~en) hip

heuvel (*hūr*-verl) *c* (pl ~s) hill; mound

heuvelachtig (*hūr*-ver-lahkh-terkh) *adj* hilly

heuveltop (*hūr*-verl-top) *c* (pl ~pen) hilltop

hevig (*hāy*-verkh) *adj* severe, violent; intense

hiel (heel) *c* (pl ~en) heel

hier (heer) *adv* here

hiërarchie (hee-Yer-rahr-*khee*) *c* (pl ~ën) hierarchy

hij (hay) *pron* he

hijgen (*hay*-gern) *v* pant

*****hijsen** (*hay*-sern) *v* hoist

hijskraan (*hayss*-kraan) *c* (pl -kranen) crane

hik (hik) *c* hiccup

hinderen (*hin*-der-rern) *v* hinder; bother, embarrass

hinderlaag (*hin*-derr-laakh) *c* (pl -lagen) ambush

hinderlijk (*hin*-derr-lerk) *adj* annoying

hindernis (*hin*-derr-niss) *c* (pl ~sen) obstacle

hinken (*hing*-kern) *v* limp

historisch (hee-*stōa*-reess) *adj* historic

hitte (*hi*-ter) *c* heat

hobbelig (*ho*-ber-lerkh) *adj* bumpy

hobby (*ho*-bee) *c* (pl ~'s) hobby

hoe (hōō) *adv* how; **~ ... hoe** the ... the; **~ dan ook** anyhow, any way; at any rate

hoed (hōōt) *c* (pl ~en) hat

hoede (*hōō*-der) *c* custody

zich hoeden (*hōō*-dern) *v* beware

hoef (hōōf) *c* (pl hoeven) hoof

hoefijzer (*hōōf*-ay-zerr) *nt* (pl ~s) horseshoe

hoek (hōōk) *c* (pl ~en) corner; angle

hoer (hōōr) *c* (pl ~en) whore

hoes (hōōss) *c* (pl hoezen) sleeve

hoest (hōōst) *c* cough

hoesten (*hōōss*-tern) *v* cough

hoeveel (hōō-*vāyl*) *pron* how much; how many

hoeveelheid (hōō-*vāyl*-hayt) *c* (pl -heden) quantity; amount

hoeven (*hōō*-vern) *v* need

hoewel (hōō-*vehl*) *conj* although, though

hof (hof) *nt* (pl hoven) court

hoffelijk (*ho*-fer-lerk) *adj* courteous

hokje (*ho*-kYer) *nt* (pl ~s) booth

hol¹ (hol) *nt* (pl ~en) den; cavern

hol² (hol) *adj* hollow

Holland (*ho*-lahnt) Holland

Hollander (*ho*-lahn-derr) *c* (pl ~s) Dutchman

Hollands (*ho*-lahnts) *adj* Dutch

holte (*hol*-ter) *c* (pl ~s, ~n) cavity

homoseksueel (hōa-mōa-sehk-sew-*vāyl*) *adj* homosexual

hond (hont) *c* (pl ~en) dog

hondehok (*hon*-der-hok) *nt* (pl ~ken) kennel

honderd (*hon*-derrt) *num* hundred

hondsdolheid (honts-*dol*-hayt) *c* rabies

Hongaar (hong-*gaar*) *c* (pl -garen) Hungarian

Hongaars (hong-*gaars*) *adj* Hungarian

Hongarije (hong-gaa-*ray*-er) *c* Hungary

honger (*ho*-ngerr) *c* hunger

hongerig (*ho*-nger-rerkh) *adj* hungry

honing (*hōa*-nıng) *c* honey

honkbal (*hongk*-bahl) *nt* baseball

honorarium (hōa-nōa-*raa*-ree-Yerm) *nt* (pl -ria) fee

hoofd (hōaft) *nt* (pl ~en) head; **het ~ * bieden aan** face; **hoofd-** primary, main, chief; cardinal, capital; **over het ~ * zien** overlook; **uit het ~** by heart; **uit het ~ leren** memorize

hoofdkussen (*hōaft*-ker-sern) *nt* (pl ~s) pillow

hoofdkwartier (*hōaft*-kvahr-teer) *nt* (pl ~en) headquarters *pl*

hoofdleiding (*hōaft*-lay-dıng) *c* (pl ~en) mains *pl*

hoofdletter (*hōaft*-leh-terr) *c* (pl ~s) capital letter

hoofdlijn (*hōaft*-layn) *c* (pl ~en) main line

hoofdonderwijzer (*hōaft*-on-derr-vay-zerr) *c* (pl ~s) head teacher

hoofdpijn (*hōaft*-payn) *c* headache

hoofdstad (*hōaft*-staht) *c* (pl -steden) capital

hoofdstraat (*hōaft*-straat) *c* (pl -straten) main street, thoroughfare

hoofdweg (*hōaft*-vehkh) *c* (pl ~en) main road, thoroughfare; highway

hoofdzakelijk (hōaft-*saa*-ker-lerk) *adv* mainly

hoog (hōakh) *adj* high; tall; **hoger** upper; superior; **hoogst** foremost, extreme

hooghartig (hōakh-*hahr*-terkh) *adj* haughty

hoogleraar (hōakh-*lāy*-raar) *c* (pl -leraren, ~s) professor

hoogmoedig (hōakh-*mōō*-derkh) *adj* proud

hoogovens (*hōakh*-ōa-verns) *pl* iron-works

hoogseizoen (*hōakh*-say-zōōn) *nt* high season, peak season

hoogstens (*hōakh*-sterns) *adv* at most

hoogte (*hōakh*-ter) *c* (pl ~n, ~s) height; altitude

hoogtepunt (*hōakh*-ter-pernt) *nt* (pl ~en) height

hooguit (hōakh-ur^{ew}t) *adv* at most

hoogvlakte (*hōakh*-flahk-ter) *c* (pl ~n, ~s) uplands *pl*; plateau

hooi (hōa^{ee}) *nt* hay

hooikoorts (*hōa^{ee}*-kōarts) *c* hay fever

hoon (hōan) *c* scorn

hoop¹ (hōap) *c* (pl hopen) heap, lot

hoop² (hōap) *c* hope

hoopvol (*hōap*-fol) *adj* hopeful

hoorbaar (*hōar*-baar) *adj* audible

hoorn (*hōa*-rern) *c* (pl ~en, ~s) horn

hop (hop) *c* hop

hopeloos (*hōa*-per-lōass) *adj* hopeless

hopen (*hōa*-pern) *v* hope

horen (*hōa*-rern) *v* *hear

horizon (*hōa*-ree-zon) *c* horizon

horizontaal (hōa-ree-zon-*taal*) *adj* horizontal

horloge (hor-*lōa*-zher) *nt* (pl ~s) watch

horlogebandje (hor-*lōa*-zher-bahn-t^yer) *nt* (pl ~s) watch-strap

horlogemaker (hor-*lōa*-zher-maa-kerr) *c* (pl ~s) watch-maker

hors d'œuvre (awr-*dūr*-vrer) *c* (pl ~s) hors-d'œuvre

hospes (*hoss*-perss) *c* (pl ~sen) land-lord

hospita (*hoss*-pee-taa) *c* (pl ~'s) land-lady

hospitaal (*hoss*-pee-taal) *nt* (pl -talen) hospital

hotel (hōa-*tehl*) *nt* (pl ~s) hotel
***houden** (*hou*-dern) *v* *hold; *keep; ~ **van** love; like, care for, *be fond of; **niet ~ van** dislike
houding (*hou*-dɪng) *c* (pl ~en) position; attitude
hout (hout) *nt* wood
houtblok (*hout*-blok) *nt* (pl ~ken) log
houten (*hou*-tern) *adj* wooden
houtskool (*houts*-kōal) *c* charcoal
***houtsnijden** (*hout*-snay-dern) *v* carve
houtsnijwerk (*hout*-snay-vehrk) *nt* wood-carving
houtzagerij (hout-saa-ger-*ray*) *c* (pl ~en) saw-mill
houvast (hou-*vahst*) *nt* grip
houweel (hou-*vāyl*) *nt* (pl -welen) pick-axe
huichelaar (hur*ew*-kher-laar) *c* (pl ~s) hypocrite
huichelachtig (hur*ew*-kherl-ahkh-terkh) *adj* hypocritical
huichelarij (hur*ew*-kher-laa-*ray*) *c* hypocrisy
huichelen (hur*ew*-kher-lern) *v* simulate
huid (hur*ew*t) *c* (pl ~en) skin; hide
huidcrème (hur*ew*t-kraim) *c* (pl ~s) skin cream
huidig (hur*ew*-derkh) *adj* current
huiduitslag (hur*ew*t-ur*ew*t-slahkh) *c* rash
huilen (hur*ew*-lern) *v* cry, *weep
huis (hur*ew*ss) *nt* (pl huizen) house; home; **naar ~** home
huisarts (hur*ew*ss-ahrts) *c* (pl ~en) general practitioner
huisbaas (hur*ew*ss-baass) *c* (pl -bazen) landlord
huisdier (hur*ew*ss-deer) *nt* (pl ~en) pet
huiselijk (hur*ew*-ser-lerk) *adj* domestic
huishouden (hur*ew*ss-hou-dern) *nt* (pl ~s) household; housework, housekeeping
huishoudster (hur*ew*ss-hout-sterr) *c* (pl

~s) housekeeper
huiskamer (hur*ew*ss-kaa-merr) *c* (pl ~s) living-room
huisonderwijzer (hur*ew*ss-on-derr-vay-zerr) *c* (pl ~s) tutor
huissleutel (hur*ew*-slur-terl) *c* (pl ~s) latchkey
huisvrouw (hur*ew*ss-frou) *c* (pl ~en) housewife
huizenblok (hur*ew*-zern-blok) *nt* (pl ~ken) house block *Am*
hulde (*herl*-der) *c* tribute, homage
huldigen (*herl*-der-gern) *v* honour
hulp (herlp) *c* help; assistance, aid; **eerste ~** first-aid; **eerste hulppost** first-aid post
hulpvaardig (herlp-*faar*-derkh) *adj* helpful
humeur (hew-*mūrr*) *nt* (pl ~en) mood
humor (*hew*-mor) *c* humour
humoristisch (hew-mōa-*riss*-teess) *adj* humorous
hun (hern) *pron* their
huppelen (*her*-per-lern) *v* hop, skip
huren (*hew*-rern) *v* hire, rent; lease
hut (hert) *c* (pl ~ten) hut; cabin
huur (hewr) *c* (pl huren) rent; **te ~** for hire
huurcontract (*hewr*-kon-trahkt) *nt* (pl ~en) lease
huurder (*hewr*-derr) *c* (pl ~s) tenant
huurkoop (*hewr*-kōap) *c* hire-purchase
huwelijk (*hew*-ver-lerk) *nt* (pl ~en) wedding, marriage
huwelijksreis (*hew*-ver-lerks-rayss) *c* (pl -reizen) honeymoon
huwen (*hew*⁰⁰-ern) *v* marry
hygiëne (hee-gee-*ʸāy*-ner) *c* hygiene
hygiënisch (hee-gee-*ʸāy*-neess) *adj* hygienic
hypocriet (hee-pōa-*kreet*) *adj* hypocritical
hypotheek (hee-pōa-*tāyk*) *c* (pl -theken) mortgage

hysterisch (hee-*stāy*-reess) *adj* hysterical

I

ideaal[1] (ee-*dāy*-ⱼ*aal*) *adj* ideal
ideaal[2] (ee-*dāy*-ⱼ*aal*) *nt* (pl idealen) ideal
idee (ee-*dāy*) *nt/c* (pl ~ën, ~s) idea
identiek (ee-dehn-*teek*) *adj* identical
identificatie (ee-dehn-tee-fi-*kaa*-tsee) *c* identification
identificeren (ee-dehn-tee-fee-*sāy*-rern) *v* identify
identiteit (ee-dehn-ti-*tayt*) *c* identity
identiteitskaart (ee-dehn-tee-*tayts*-kaart) *c* (pl ~en) identity card
idiomatisch (ee-dee-ⱼ*ōa*-*maa*-teess) *adj* idiomatic
idioom (ee-dee-ⱼ*ōam*) *nt* (pl idiomen) idiom
idioot[1] (ee-dee-ⱼ*ōat*) *adj* idiotic
idioot[2] (ee-dee-ⱼ*ōat*) *c* (pl idioten) idiot
idool (ee-*dōal*) *nt* (pl idolen) idol
ieder (*ee*-derr) *pron* each, every; everyone
iedereen (ee-der-*rāyn*) *pron* everyone, everybody; anyone
iemand (*ee*-mahnt) *pron* someone, somebody
iep (eep) *c* (pl ~en) elm
Ier (eer) *c* (pl ~en) Irishman
Ierland (*eer*-lahnt) Ireland
Iers (eers) *adj* Irish
iets (eets) *pron* something; some
ijdel (*ay*-derl) *adj* vain; idle
ijs (ayss) *nt* ice; ice-cream
ijsbaan (*ayss*-baan) *c* (pl -banen) skating-rink
ijsje (*ay*-sher) *nt* (pl ~s) ice-cream
ijskast (*ayss*-kahst) *c* (pl ~en) fridge,

refrigerator
ijskoud (*ayss*-kout) *adj* freezing
IJsland (*ayss*-lahnt) Iceland
IJslander (*ayss*-lahn-derr) *c* (pl ~s) Icelander
IJslands (*ayss*-lahnts) *adj* Icelandic
ijswater (*ayss*-vaa-terr) *nt* iced water
ijver (*ay*-verr) *c* zeal; diligence
ijverig (*ay*-ver-rerkh) *adj* zealous; diligent
ijzer (*ay*-zerr) *nt* iron
ijzerdraad (*ay*-zerr-draat) *nt* wire
ijzeren (*ay*-zer-rern) *adj* iron
ijzerwaren (*ay*-zerr-vaa-rern) *pl* hardware
ik (ık) *pron* I
ikoon (ee-*kōan*) *c* (pl ikonen) icon
illegaal (ee-ler-*gaal*) *adj* illegal
illusie (ı-*lēw*-zee) *c* (pl ~s) illusion
illustratie (ı-lēw-*straa*-tsee) *c* (pl ~s) illustration
illustreren (ı-lēw-*strāy*-rern) *v* illustrate
imitatie (ee-mee-*taa*-tsee) *c* (pl ~s) imitation
imiteren (ee-mee-*tāy*-rern) *v* imitate
immigrant (ı-mee-*grahnt*) *c* (pl ~en) immigrant
immigratie (ı-mee-*graa*-tsee) *c* immigration
immigreren (ı-mee-*grāy*-rern) *v* immigrate
immuniteit (ı-mēw-nee-*tayt*) *c* immunity
impliceren (ım-plee-*sāy*-rern) *v* imply, involve
imponeren (ım-pōa-*nāy*-rern) *v* impress
impopulair (ım-pōa-pēw-*lair*) *adj* unpopular
import (*ım*-port) *c* import
importeren (ım-por-*tāy*-rern) *v* import
importeur (ım-por-*tūrr*) *c* (pl ~s) importer

impotent (ɪm-pōa-*tehnt*) *adj* impotent

impotentie (ɪm-pōa-*tehn*-see) *c* impotence

improviseren (ɪm-prōa-vee-*sā̄y*-rern) *v* improvise

impuls (ɪm-*perls*) *c* (pl ~en) impulse

impulsief (ɪm-perl-*zeef*) *adj* impulsive

in (ɪn) *prep* in; into, inside; at

inademen (*ɪn*-aa-der-mern) *v* inhale

inbegrepen (ɪn-ber-grā̄y-pern) *adj* included; **alles ~** all in

inboorling (ɪm-bōar-lɪng) *c* (pl ~en) native

*** inbreken** (ɪm-brā̄y-kern) *v* burgle

inbreker (ɪm-brā̄y-kerr) *c* (pl ~s) burglar

incasseren (ɪng-kah-*sā̄y*-rern) *v* cash

incident (ɪn-see-*dehnt*) *nt* (pl ~en) incident

inclusief (ɪng-klēw-*zeef*) *adv* inclusive

incompleet (ɪng-kom-*plā̄yt*) *adj* incomplete

indelen (*ɪn*-dā̄y-lern) *v* classify

zich * indenken (*ɪn*-dehng-kern) *v* imagine

inderdaad (ɪn-derr-*daat*) *adv* indeed

index (*ɪn*-dehks) *c* (pl ~en) index

India (*ɪn*-dee-Yah) India

Indiaan (ɪn-dee-*Yaan*) *c* (pl Indianen) Indian

Indiaans (ɪn-dee-*Yaans*) *adj* Indian

indien (ɪn-*deen*) *conj* in case, if

Indiër (*ɪn*-dee-Yerr) *c* (pl ~s) Indian

indigestie (ɪn-dee-*gehss*-tee) *c* indigestion

indirect (*ɪn*-dee-rehkt) *adj* indirect

Indisch (*ɪn*-deess) *adj* Indian

individu (ɪn-dee-vee-*dēw̄*) *nt* (pl ~en, ~'s) individual

individueel (ɪn-dee-vee-dēw̄-*vā̄yl*) *adj* individual

Indonesië (ɪn-dōa-*nā̄y*-zee-Yer) Indonesia

Indonesiër (ɪn-dōa-*nā̄y*-zee-Yerr) *c* (pl

~s) Indonesian

Indonesisch (ɪn-dōa-*nā̄y*-zeess) *adj* Indonesian

indringer (*ɪn*-drɪ-ngerr) *c* (pl ~s) trespasser

indruk (*ɪn*-drerk) *c* (pl ~ken) impression; **~ maken op** impress

indrukken (*ɪn*-drer-kern) *v* press

indrukwekkend (ɪn-drerk-*veh*-kernt) *adj* impressive, imposing

industrie (ɪn-derss-*tree*) *c* (pl ~ën) industry

industrieel (ɪn-derss-tree-*Yā̄yl*) *adj* industrial

industriegebied (ɪn-derss-*tree*-ger-beet) *nt* (pl ~en) industrial area

ineens (ɪ-*nā̄yns*) *adv* suddenly; at once

inenten (*ɪn*-ehn-tern) *v* vaccinate, inoculate

inenting (*ɪn*-ehn-tɪng) *c* (pl ~en) vaccination, inoculation

infanterie (*ɪn*-fahn-ter-ree) *c* infantry

infectie (ɪn-*fehk*-see) *c* (pl ~s) infection

inferieur (ɪn-fā̄y-ree-*Yūrr*) *adj* inferior

inflatie (ɪn-*flaa*-tsee) *c* inflation

informatie (ɪn-for-*maa*-tsee) *c* (pl ~s) information; enquiry; **~ * inwinnen** *v* inquire

informatiebureau (ɪn-for-*maa*-tsee-bēw̄-rōa) *nt* (pl ~s) inquiry office

informeel (ɪn-for-*mā̄yl*) *adj* informal

informeren (ɪn-for-*mā̄y*-rern) *v* enquire; inform

infrarood (ɪn-fraa-*rōat*) *adj* infra-red

*** ingaan** (*ɪng*-gaan) *v* enter; * take effect

ingang (*ɪng*-gahng) *c* (pl ~en) entrance, way in; entry; **met ~ van** as from

ingenieur (ɪn-zhern-*Yūrr*) *c* (pl ~s) engineer

ingenomen (*ɪng*-ger-nōa-mern) *adj*

pleased

ingevolge (ıng-ger-*vol*-ger) *prep* in accordance with

ingewanden (*ıng*-ger-vahn-dern) *pl* bowels *pl*, intestines, insides

ingewikkeld (ıng-ger-vı-kerlt) *adj* complicated; complex

ingrediënt (ıng-grāy-dee-*Yehnt*) *nt* (pl ~en) ingredient

*****ingrijpen** (*ıng*-gray-pern) *v* intervene

inhalen (*ın*-haa-lern) *v* *overtake; pass *vAm*; ~ **verboden** no overtaking; no passing *Am*

inham (*ın*-hahm) *c* (pl ~men) creek, inlet

inheems (ın-*hāyms*) *adj* native

inhoud (*ın*-hout) *c* contents *pl*

*****inhouden** (*ın*-hou-dern) *v* contain; imply; restrain

inhoudsopgave (*ın*-houts-op-khaa-ver) *c* (pl ~n) table of contents

initiatief (ee-nee-shaa-*teef*) *nt* (pl -tieven) initiative

injectie (ın-*Yehk*-see) *c* (pl ~s) shot, injection

inkomen (*ıng*-kōa-mern) *nt* (pl ~s) revenue, income

inkomsten (*ın*-kom-stern) *pl* earnings *pl*

inkomstenbelasting (*ıng*-kom-ster-ber-lahss-tıng) *c* income-tax

inkt (ıngkt) *c* ink

inleiden (*ın*-lay-dern) *v* introduce; **inleidend** preliminary

inleiding (*ın*-lay-dıng) *c* (pl ~en) introduction

inlichten (*ın*-lıkh-tern) *v* inform

inlichting (*ın*-lıkh-tıng) *c* (pl ~en) information

inlichtingenkantoor (*ın*-lıkh-tı-nger-kahn-tōar) *nt* (pl -toren) information bureau

inmaken (*ın*-maa-kern) *v* preserve

inmenging (*ın*-mehng-ıng) *c* (pl ~en) interference

inmiddels (ın-*mı*-derls) *adv* in the meantime

*****innemen** (*ı*-nāy-mern) *v* *take up; occupy; capture

inneming (*ı*-nāy-mıng) *c* capture

innen (*ı*-nern) *v* cash

inpakken (*ım*-pah-kern) *v* wrap; pack up, pack

inrichten (*ın*-rıkh-tern) *v* furnish

inrichting (*ın*-rıkh-tıng) *c* (pl ~en) institution

inschakelen (*ın*-skhaa-ker-lern) *v* switch on; plug in

*****inschenken** (*ın*-skhehng-kern) *v* pour

inschepen (*ın*-skhāy-pern) *v* embark

inscheping (*ın*-skhāy-pıng) *c* embarkation

*****inschrijven** (*ın*-skhray-vern) *v* enter, book; **zich** ~ register, check in

inschrijvingsformulier (*ın*-skhray-vıngs-for-mēw-leer) *nt* (pl ~en) registration form

inscriptie (ın-*skrıp*-see) *c* (pl ~s) inscription

insekt (ın-*sehkt*) *nt* (pl ~en) insect; bug *nAm*

insekticide (ın-sehk-tee-*see*-der) *c* (pl ~n) insecticide

inslikken (*ın*-slı-kern) *v* swallow

*****insluiten** (*ın*-slur^ew-tern) *v* *shut in; encircle; include; enclose

inspanning (*ın*-spah-nıng) *c* (pl ~en) strain, effort

inspecteren (ın-spehk-*tāy*-rern) *v* inspect

inspecteur (ın-spehk-*tŭrr*) *c* (pl ~s) inspector

inspectie (ın-*spehk*-see) *c* (pl ~s) inspection

*****inspuiten** (*ın*-spur^ew-tern) *v* inject

installatie (ın-stah-*laa*-tsee) *c* (pl ~s) installation

installeren (ın-stah-*lāy*-rern) *v* install

instappen (ɪn-stah-pern) v *get on; embark

instellen (ɪn-steh-lern) v institute

instelling (ɪn-steh-lɪng) c (pl ~en) institution, institute

instemmen (ɪn-steh-mern) v consent; ~ met approve of

instemming (ɪn-steh-mɪng) c approval, consent

instinct (ɪn-stɪngkt) nt (pl ~en) instinct

instituut (ɪn-stee-tēwt) nt (pl -tuten) institute

instorten (ɪn-stor-tern) v collapse

instructie (ɪn-strerk-see) c (pl ~s) direction

instrument (ɪn-strēw-mehnt) nt (pl ~en) instrument

intact (ɪn-tahkt) adj intact

integendeel (ɪn-tāy-gern-dāyl) on the contrary

intellect (ɪn-ter-lehkt) nt intellect

intellectueel (ɪn-ter-lehk-tēw-vāyl) adj intellectual

intelligent (ɪn-ter-lee-gehnt) adj clever, intelligent

intelligentie (ɪn-ter-lee-gehn-see) c intelligence

intens (ɪn-tehns) adj intense

interessant (ɪn-ter-rer-sahnt) adj interesting

interesse (ɪn-ter-reh-ser) c interest

interesseren (ɪn-ter-reh-sāy-rern) v interest

intermezzo (ɪn-terr-mehd-zōa) nt (pl ~'s) interlude

intern (ɪn-tehrn) adj internal; resident

internaat (ɪn-terr-naat) nt (pl -naten) boarding-school

internationaal (ɪn-terr-naht-shōa-naal) adj international

intiem (ɪn-teem) adj intimate

introduceren (ɪn-trōa-dēw-sāy-rern) v introduce

intussen (ɪn-ter-sern) adv meanwhile

inval (ɪn-vahl) c (pl ~len) brain-wave, idea; raid, invasion

invalide[1] (ɪn-vaa-lee-der) adj disabled, invalid

invalide[2] (ɪn-vaa-lee-der) c (pl ~n) invalid

invasie (ɪn-vaa-zee) c (pl ~s) invasion

inventaris (ɪn-vehn-taa-rerss) c (pl ~sen) inventory

investeerder (ɪn-vehss-tāyr-derr) c (pl ~s) investor

investeren (ɪn-vehss-tāy-rern) v invest

investering (ɪn-vehss-tāy-rɪng) c (pl ~en) investment

inviteren (ɪn-vee-tāy-rern) v invite

invloed (ɪn-vlōot) c (pl ~en) influence

invloedrijk (ɪn-vlōot-rayk) adj influential

invoegen (ɪn-vōo-gern) v insert

invoer (ɪn-vōor) c import

invoeren (ɪn-vōo-rern) v introduce; import

invoerrecht (ɪn-vōo-rehkht) nt (pl ~en) duty, import duty

invullen (ɪn-ver-lern) v fill in; fill out Am

inwendig (ɪn-vehn-derkh) adj inner; internal

inwilligen (ɪn-vɪ-ler-gern) v grant

inwoner (ɪn-vōa-nerr) c (pl ~s) inhabitant; resident

inzet (ɪn-zeht) c (pl ~ten) bet

inzetten (ɪn-zeh-tern) v launch

inzicht (ɪn-zɪkht) nt (pl ~en) insight

***inzien** (ɪn-zeen) v *see

Iraaks (ee-raaks) adj Iraqi

Iraans (ee-raans) adj Iranian

Irak (ee-raak) Iraq

Irakees (ee-raa-kāyss) c (pl -kezen) Iraqi

Iran (ee-raan) Iran

Iraniër (ee-raa-nee-Yerr) c (pl ~s) Iranian

ironie (ee-róa-*nee*) *c* irony

ironisch (ee-róa-neess) *adj* ironical

irriteren (ɪ-ree-*tāy*-rern) *v* annoy, irritate

isolatie (ee-zóa-*laa*-tsee) *c* insulation; isolation

isolator (ee-zóa-*laa*-tor) *c* (pl ~en, ~s) insulator

isolement (ee-zóa-ler-*mehnt*) *nt* isolation

isoleren (ee-zóa-*lāy*-rern) *v* insulate; isolate

Israël (ɪss-raa-ehl) Israel

Israëliër (ɪss-raa-*āy*-lee-ᵞerr) *c* (pl ~s) Israeli

Israëlisch (ɪss-raa-*āy*-leess) *adj* Israeli

Italiaan (ee-taa-lee-ᵞaan) *c* (pl -lianen) Italian

Italiaans (ee-taa-lee-ᵞaans) *adj* Italian

Italië (ee-*taa*-lee-ᵞer) Italy

ivoor (ee-*vóar*) *nt* ivory

J

ja (ᵞaa) yes

jaar (ᵞaar) *nt* (pl jaren) year

jaarboek (ᵞaar-bóok) *nt* (pl ~en) annual

jaargetijde (ᵞaar-ger-tay-der) *nt* (pl ~n) season

jaarlijks (ᵞaar-lerks) *adj* annual, yearly; *adv* per annum

jacht[1] (ᵞahkht) *c* hunt; chase

jacht[2] (ᵞahkht) *nt* (pl ~en) yacht

jachthuis (ᵞahkht-hurᵉʷss) *nt* (pl -huizen) lodge

jade (ᵞaa-der) *nt/c* jade

jagen (ᵞaa-gern) *v* hunt

jager (ᵞaa-gerr) *c* (pl ~s) hunter

jaloers (ᵞaa-*lóors*) *adj* envious, jealous

jaloezie (ᵞaa-lóo-*zee*) *c* (pl ~ën) jealousy; blind

jam (zhehm) *c* jam

jammer! (ᵞah-merr) what a pity!

januari (ᵞah-neʷ-*vaa*-ree) January

Japan (ᵞaa-*pahn*) Japan

Japanner (ᵞaa-*pah*-nerr) *c* (pl ~s) Japanese

Japans (ᵞaa-*pahns*) *adj* Japanese

japon (ᵞaa-*pon*) *c* (pl ~nen) dress; gown

jarretelgordel (zhah-rer-*tehl*-gor-derl) *c* (pl ~s) suspender belt; garter belt *Am*

jas (ᵞahss) *c* (pl ~sen) coat

jasje (ᵞah-sher) *nt* (pl ~s) jacket

je (ᵞer) *pron* you; yourself; yourselves

jegens (ᵞāy-gerns) *prep* towards

jeugd (ᵞūrkht) *c* youth

jeugdherberg (ᵞūrkht-hehr-behrkh) *c* (pl ~en) youth hostel

jeugdig (ᵞūrkh-derkh) *adj* juvenile

jeuk (ᵞūrk) *c* itch

jeuken (ᵞūr-kern) *v* itch

jicht (ᵞɪkht) *c* gout

joch (ᵞokh) *nt* boy, lad

jodium (ᵞóa-dee-ᵞerm) *nt* iodine

Joegoslaaf (ᵞóō-góa-*slaaf*) *c* (pl -slaven) Jugoslav, Yugoslav

Joegoslavië (ᵞóō-góa-*slaa*-vee-er) Jugoslavia, Yugoslavia

Joegoslavisch (ᵞóō-góa-*slaa*-veess) *adj* Jugoslav

jong (ᵞong) *adj* young; **jonger** junior

jongen (ᵞo-ngern) *c* (pl ~s) boy; lad

jood (ᵞóat) *c* (pl joden) Jew

joods (ᵞóats) *adj* Jewish

Jordaans (ᵞor-*daans*) *adj* Jordanian

Jordanië (ᵞor-*daa*-nee-ᵞer) Jordan

Jordaniër (ᵞor-*daa*-nee-ᵞerr) *c* (pl ~s) Jordanian

jou (ᵞou) *pron* you

journaal (zhóor-*naal*) *nt* news

journalist (zhóor-naa-*lɪst*) *c* (pl ~en) journalist

journalistiek (zhŏŏr-naa-liss-*teek*) *c* journalism

jouw (You) *pron* your

jubileum (Yēw-bee-*lāy*-Yerm) *nt* (pl ~s, -lea) jubilee

juffrouw (Yer-frou) *c* (pl ~en) miss

juichen (Yur^{ew}-khern) *v* cheer

juist (Yur^{ew}st) *adj* right, correct, just; proper, appropriate

juistheid (Yur^{ew}st-hayt) *c* correctness

juk (Yerk) *nt* (pl ~ken) yoke

jukbeen (Yerk-bāyn) *nt* (pl ~deren, -benen) cheek-bone

juli (Yēw-lee) July

jullie (Yer-lee) *pron* you; your

juni (Yēw-nee) June

juridisch (Yēw-ree-deess) *adj* legal

jurist (Yēw-rıst) *c* (pl ~en) lawyer

jurk (Yerrk) *c* (pl ~en) frock, robe, dress

jury (zhēw-ree) *c* (pl ~'s) jury

jus (zhēw) *c* gravy

juweel (Yēw-vāyl) *nt* (pl -welen) jewel; gem; **juwelen** jewellery

juwelier (Yēw-ver-*leer*) *c* (pl ~s) jeweller

K

kaak (kaak) *c* (pl kaken) jaw

kaal (kaal) *adj* bald; naked, bare

kaap (kaap) *c* (pl kapen) cape

kaars (kaars) *c* (pl ~en) candle

kaart (kaart) *c* (pl ~en) map; card; **groene** ~ green card

kaartenautomaat (*kaar*-tern-ōa-tōa-maat) *c* (pl -maten) ticket machine

kaartje (*kaar*-t^yer) *nt* (pl ~s) ticket

kaas (kaass) *c* (pl kazen) cheese

kabaal (kaa-*baal*) *nt* racket

kabel (*kaa*-berl) *c* (pl ~s) cable

kabeljauw (kah-berl-You) *c* (pl ~en) cod

kabinet (kaa-bee-*neht*) *nt* (pl ~ten) cabinet

kachel (*kah*-kherl) *c* (pl ~s) heater; stove

kade (*kaa*-der) *c* (pl ~n) quay; embankment; dock, wharf

kader (*kaa*-derr) *nt* (pl ~s) cadre

kajuit (kaa-Yur^{ew}t) *c* (pl ~en) cabin

kaki (*kaa*-kee) *nt* khaki

kalender (kaa-*lehn*-derr) *c* (pl ~s) calendar

kalf (kahlf) *nt* (pl kalveren) calf

kalfsleer (*kahlfs*-lāyr) *nt* calf skin

kalfsvlees (*kahlfs*-flāyss) *nt* veal

kalk (kahlk) *c* lime

kalkoen (kahl-*kōōn*) *c* (pl ~en) turkey

kalm (kahlm) *adj* calm; sedate, quiet, serene

kalmeren (kahl-*māy*-rern) *v* calm down

kam (kahm) *c* (pl ~men) comb

kameel (kaa-*māyl*) *c* (pl kamelen) camel

kamer (*kaa*-merr) *c* (pl ~s) room; chamber

kameraad (kah-mer-*raat*) *c* (pl -raden) comrade

kamerbewoner (*kaa*-merr-ber-vōa-nerr) *c* (pl ~s) lodger

kamerjas (*kaa*-merr-Yahss) *c* (pl ~sen) dressing-gown

kamerlid (*kaa*-merr-lıt) *nt* (pl -leden) Member of Parliament

kamermeisje (*kaa*-merr-may-sher) *nt* (pl ~s) chambermaid

kamertemperatuur (*kaa*-merr-tehm-per-raa-tēwr) *c* room temperature

kamgaren (*kahm*-gaa-rern) *nt* worsted

kammen (*kah*-mern) *v* comb

kamp (kahmp) *nt* (pl ~en) camp

kampeerder (kahm-*pāyr*-derr) *c* (pl ~s) camper

kampeerterrein (kahm-*pāyr*-teh-rayn)

nt (pl ~en) camping site
kampeerwagen (kahm-*pāyr*-vaa-gern)
c (pl ~s) trailer *nAm*
kamperen (kahm-*pāy*-rern) *v* camp
kampioen (kahm-pee-*Yōōn*) *c* (pl ~en)
champion
kan (kahn) *c* (pl ~nen) jug
kanaal (kaa-*naal*) *nt* (pl kanalen) canal; channel; **het Kanaal** English
Channel
kanarie (kaa-*naa*-ree) *c* (pl ~s) canary
kandelaber (kahn-der-*laa*-berr) *c* (pl
~s) candelabrum
kandidaat (kahn-dee-*daat*) *c* (pl -da-
ten) candidate
kaneel (kaa-*nāyl*) *c* cinnamon
kangoeroe (*kahng*-ger-rōō) *c* (pl ~s)
kangaroo
kanker (*kahng*-kerr) *c* cancer
kano (*kaa*-nōā) *c* (pl ~'s) canoe
kanon (kaa-*non*) *nt* (pl ~nen) gun
kans (kahns) *c* (pl ~en) chance; opportunity
kansel (*kahn*-serl) *c* (pl ~s) pulpit
kant[1] (kahnt) *c* (pl ~en) side; way;
edge; **aan de andere ~ van** across
kant[2] (kahnt) *nt* lace
kantine (kahn-*tee*-ner) *c* (pl ~s) canteen
kantlijn (*kahnt*-layn) *c* (pl ~en) margin
kantoor (kahn-*tōār*) *nt* (pl -toren) office
kantoorbediende (kahn-*tōār*-ber-deen-
der) *c* (pl ~n, ~s) clerk
kantoorboekhandel (kahn-*tōār*-bōōk-
hahn-derl) *c* (pl ~s) stationer's
kantooruren (kahn-*tōār*-ēw-rern) *pl*
business hours, office hours
kap (kahp) *c* (pl ~pen) hood
kapel (kaa-*pehl*) *c* (pl ~len) chapel
kapelaan (kah-per-*laan*) *c* (pl ~s)
chaplain
kapen (*kaa*-pern) *v* hijack

kaper (*kaa*-perr) *c* (pl ~s) hijacker
kapitaal (kah-pee-*taal*) *nt* capital
kapitalisme (kah-pee-taa-*liss*-mer) *nt*
capitalism
kapitein (kah-pee-*tayn*) *c* (pl ~s) captain
kapot (kaa-*pot*) *adj* broken
kapper (*kah*-perr) *c* (pl ~s) barber;
hairdresser
kapsel (*kahp*-serl) *nt* (pl ~s) hair-do
kapstok (*kahp*-stok) *c* (pl ~ken) hat
rack
kar (kahr) *c* (pl ~ren) cart
karaat (kaa-*raat*) *nt* carat
karaf (kaa-*rahf*) *c* (pl ~fen) carafe
karakter (kaa-*rahk*-terr) *nt* (pl ~s)
character
karakteristiek (kaa-rahk-ter-*riss*-*teek*)
adj characteristic
karaktertrek (kaa-*rahk*-terr-trehk) *c* (pl
~ken) characteristic
karamel (kaa-raa-*mehl*) *c* (pl ~s, ~len)
caramel
karbonade (kahr-bōā-*naa*-der) *c* (pl
~s) cutlet, chop
kardinaal[1] (kahr-dee-*naal*) *c* (pl -na-
len) cardinal
kardinaal[2] (kahr-dee-*naal*) *adj* cardinal
karper (*kahr*-perr) *c* (pl ~s) carp
karton (kahr-*ton*) *nt* cardboard
kartonnen (kahr-*to*-nern) *adj* cardboard; ~ **doos** carton
karwei (kahr-*vay*) *nt* (pl ~en) job
kas (kahss) *c* (pl ~sen) greenhouse
kasjmier (*kahsh*-meer) *nt* cashmere
kassa (*kah*-saa) *c* (pl ~'s) pay-desk;
box-office
kassier (kah-*seer*) *c* (pl ~s) cashier
kast (kahst) *c* (pl ~en) cupboard,
closet
kastanje (kahss-*tah*-ñer) *c* (pl ~s)
chestnut
kastanjebruin (kahss-*tah*-ñer-brur[ewn])
adj auburn

kasteel (kahss-*tāyl*) *nt* (pl -telen) castle

kat (kaht) *c* (pl ~ten) cat

kathedraal (kaa-tāy-*draal*) *c* (pl -dralen) cathedral

katholiek (kaa-tōa-*leek*) *adj* catholic

katoen (kaa-*tōōn*) *nt/c* cotton

katoenen (kaa-*tōō*-nern) *adj* cotton

katoenfluweel (kaa-*tōōn*-flew-vāyl) *nt* velveteen

katrol (kaa-*trol*) *c* (pl ~len) pulley

kattekwaad (*kah*-ter-kvaat) *nt* mischief

kauwen (*kou*-ern) *v* chew

kauwgom (*kou*-gom) *c/nt* chewing-gum

kaviaar (*kaa*-vee-ᵛaar) *c* caviar

kazerne (kaa-*zehr*-ner) *c* (pl ~s, ~n) barracks *pl*

keel (kāyl) *c* (pl kelen) throat

keelontsteking (*kāyl*-ont-stāy-kıng) *c* (pl ~en) laryngitis

keelpijn (*kāyl*-payn) *c* sore throat

keer (kāyr) *c* (pl keren) time

keerpunt (*kāyr*-pernt) *nt* (pl ~en) turning-point

keerzijde (*kāyr*-zay-der) *c* (pl ~n) reverse

kegelbaan (*kāy*-gerl-baan) *c* (pl -banen) bowling alley

kegelspel (*kāy*-gerl-spehl) *nt* bowling

keizer (*kay*-zerr) *c* (pl ~s) emperor

keizerin (kay-zer-*rın*) *c* (pl ~nen) empress

keizerlijk (*kay*-zer-lerk) *adj* imperial

keizerrijk (*kay*-zer-rayk) *nt* (pl ~en) empire

kelder (*kehl*-derr) *c* (pl ~s) cellar

kelner (*kehl*-nerr) *c* (pl ~s) waiter

kenmerk (*kehn*-mehrk) *nt* (pl ~en) characteristic, feature

kenmerken (*kehn*-mehr-kern) *v* characterize, mark; **kenmerkend** characteristic, typical

kennel (*keh*-nerl) *c* (pl ~s) kennel

kennen (*keh*-nern) *v* *know

kenner (*keh*-nerr) *c* (pl ~s) connoisseur

kennis[1] (*keh*-nerss) *c* knowledge

kennis[2] (*keh*-nerss) *c* (pl ~sen) acquaintance

kenteken (*kehn*-tāy-kern) *nt* (pl ~s) registration number; licence number *Am*

Kenya (*kāy*-nee-ᵛaa) Kenya

kerel (*kāy*-rerl) *c* (pl ~s) fellow

keren (*kāy*-rern) *v* turn

kerk (kehrk) *c* (pl ~en) church; chapel

kerkhof (*kehrk*-hof) *nt* (pl -hoven) cemetery, graveyard, churchyard

kerktoren (*kehrk*-tōa-rern) *c* (pl ~s) steeple

kermis (*kehr*-merss) *c* (pl ~sen) fair

kern (kehrn) *c* (pl ~en) nucleus; heart, core; essence; **kern-** nuclear

kernenergie (*kehrn*-āy-nehr-zhee) *c* nuclear energy

kerrie (*keh*-ree) *c* curry

kers (kehrs) *c* (pl ~en) cherry

Kerstmis (*kehrs*-merss) Xmas, Christmas

kerven (*kehr*-vern) *v* carve

ketel (*kāy*-terl) *c* (pl ~s) kettle

keten (*kāy*-tern) *c* (pl ~s, ~en) chain

ketting (*keh*-tıng) *c* (pl ~en) chain

keuken (*kūr*-kern) *c* (pl ~s) kitchen

keurig (*kūr*-rerkh) *adj* neat

keus (kūrss) *c* (keuzen) pick, choice

keuze (*kūr*-zer) *c* (pl ~n) selection, choice

kever (*kāy*-verr) *c* (pl ~s) beetle; bug

kiekje (*keek*-ᵛer) *nt* (pl ~s) snapshot

kiel (keel) *c* (pl ~en) keel

kiem (keem) *c* (pl ~en) germ

kier (keer) *c* (pl ~en) chink

kies (keess) *c* (pl kiezen) molar

kiesdistrict (*keess*-dıss-trıkt) *nt* (pl

~en) constituency

kieskeurig (keess-*kūr*-rerkh) *adj* particular

kiesrecht (*keess*-rehkht) *nt* franchise, suffrage

kietelen (*kee*-ter-lern) *v* tickle

kieuw (kee°°) *c* (pl ~en) gill

kievit (*kee*-veet) *c* (pl ~en) pewit

kiezel (*kee*-zerl) *c* (pl ~s) pebble; gravel

***kiezen** (*kee*-zern) *v* *choose; pick; elect

***kijken** (*kay*-kern) *v* look; ~ **naar** look at; watch

kijker (*kay*-kerr) *c* (pl ~s) spectator

kijkje (*kayk*-Yer) *nt* (pl ~s) look

kikker (*kı*-kerr) *c* (pl ~s) frog

kil (kıl) *adj* chilly

kilo (*kee*-lōa) *nt* (pl ~'s) kilogram

kilometer (*kee*-lōa-māy-terr) *c* (pl ~s) kilometre

kilometertal (*kee*-lōa-māy-terr-tahl) *nt* distance in kilometres

kim (kım) *c* horizon

kin (kın) *c* (pl ~nen) chin

kind (kınt) *nt* (pl ~eren) child; kid

kinderjuffrouw (*kın*-derr-Yer-frou) *c* (pl ~en) nurse

kinderkamer (*kın*-derr-kaa-merr) *c* (pl ~s) nursery

kinderverlamming (*kın*-derr-verr-lahming) *c* polio

kinderwagen (*kın*-derr-vaa-gern) *c* (pl ~s) pram; baby carriage *Am*

kinine (kee-*nee*-ner) *c* quinine

kiosk (kee-*Yosk*) *c* (pl ~en) kiosk

kip (kıp) *c* (pl ~pen) hen; chicken

kippevel (*kı*-per-vehl) *nt* goose-flesh

kist (kıst) *c* (pl ~en) chest

klaar (klaar) *adj* ready

klaarblijkelijk (klaar-*blay*-ker-lerk) *adv* apparently

klaarmaken (*klaar*-maa-kern) *v* prepare; cook

klacht (klahkht) *c* (pl ~en) complaint

klachtenboek (*klahkh*-tern-bōok) *nt* (pl ~en) complaints book

klagen (*klaa*-gern) *v* complain

klank (klahngk) *c* (pl ~en) sound; tone

klant (klahnt) *c* (pl ~en) customer; client

klap (klahp) *c* (pl ~pen) blow; smack, slap

klappen (*klah*-pern) *v* clap

klaproos (*klahp*-rōass) *c* (pl -rozen) poppy

klas (klahss) *c* (pl ~sen) class; form

klasgenoot (*klahss*-kher-nōat) *c* (pl -noten) class-mate

klasse (*klah*-ser) *c* (pl ~n) class

klassiek (klah-*seek*) *adj* classical

klauw (klou) *c* (pl ~en) claw

klaver (*klaa*-verr) *c* (pl ~s) clover; shamrock

zich kleden (*klāy*-dern) dress

kleding (*klāy*-dıng) *c* clothes *pl*

kleedhokje (*klāyt*-hok-Yer) *nt* (pl ~s) cabin

kleedje (*klāy*-tYer) *nt* (pl ~s) rug

kleedkamer (*klāyt*-kaa-merr) *c* (pl ~s) dressing-room

kleerborstel (*klāyr*-bor-sterl) *c* (pl ~s) clothes-brush

kleerhanger (*klāyr*-hah-ngerr) *c* (pl ~s) hanger, coat-hanger

kleerkast (*klāyr*-kahst) *c* (pl ~en) closet *nAm*

kleermaker (*klāyr*-maa-kerr) *c* (pl ~s) tailor

klei (klay) *c* clay

klein (klayn) *adj* little, small; minor, petty, short; **kleiner** minor; **kleinst** least

kleindochter (*klayn*-dokh-terr) *c* (pl ~s) granddaughter

kleingeld (*klayn*-gehlt) *nt* change, petty cash

kleinhandel (*klayn*-hahn-derl) *c* retail trade

kleinhandelaar (*klayn*-hahn-der-laar) *c* (pl -laren, ~s) retailer

kleinood (*klay*-nōat) *nt* (pl -noden) gem

kleinzoon (*klayn*-zōan) *c* (pl -zonen) grandson

klem (klehm) *c* (pl ~men) clamp

klemschroef (*klehm*-skhrōōf) *c* (pl -schroeven) clamp

kleren (*klāy*-rern) *pl* clothes *pl*

klerenhaak (*klāy*-rern-haak) *c* (pl -haken) peg

klerenkast (*klāy*-rer-kahst) *c* (pl ~en) wardrobe

klerk (klehrk) *c* (pl ~en) clerk

kletsen (*kleht*-sern) *v* chat; talk rubbish

kleur (klürr) *c* (pl ~en) colour

kleurecht (*klūr*-ehkht) *adj* fast-dyed

kleurenblind (*klūr*-rerm-blint) *adj* colour-blind

kleurenfilm (*klūr*-rer-film) *c* (pl ~s) colour film

kleurrijk (*klūr*-rayk) *adj* colourful

kleurstof (*klūrr*-stof) *c* (pl ~fen) colourant

kleuter (*klūr*-terr) *c* (pl ~s) tot

kleuterschool (*klūr*-terr-skhōal) *c* (pl -scholen) kindergarten

kleven (*klāy*-vern) *v* *stick

kleverig (*klāy*-ver-rerkh) *adj* sticky

klier (kleer) *c* (pl ~en) gland

klimaat (klee-*maat*) *nt* (pl -maten) climate

***klimmen** (*klɪ*-mern) *v* climb

klimop (klɪ-*mop*) *c* ivy

kliniek (klee-*neek*) *c* (pl ~en) clinic

***klinken** (*klɪng*-kern) *v* sound

klinker (*klɪng*-kerr) *c* (pl ~s) vowel

klip (klɪp) *c* (pl ~pen) cliff

klok (klok) *c* (pl ~ken) clock; bell

klokhuis (*klok*-hurᵉʷss) *nt* (pl -huizen) core

klomp (klomp) *c* (pl ~en) wooden shoe

klont (klont) *c* (pl ~en) lump

klonterig (*klon*-ter-rerkh) *adj* lumpy

kloof (klōaf) *c* (pl kloven) cleft; chasm

klooster (*klōa*-sterr) *nt* (pl ~s) monastery; convent, cloister

klop (klop) *c* (pl ~pen) knock, tap

kloppen (*klo*-pern) *v* knock, tap; whip

klucht (klerkht) *c* (pl ~en) farce

kluis (klurᵉʷss) *c* (pl kluizen) safe, vault

knaap (knaap) *c* (pl knapen) boy

knalpot (*knahl*-pot) *c* (pl ~ten) silencer; muffler *nAm*

knap (knahp) *adj* smart, clever; pretty, handsome, good-looking

knappend (*knah*-pernt) *adj* crisp

knapzak (*knahp*-sahk) *c* (pl ~ken) knapsack

kneuzen (*knūr*-zern) *v* bruise

kneuzing (*knūr*-zɪng) *c* (pl ~en) bruise

knie (knee) *c* (pl ~ën) knee

knielen (*knee*-lern) *v* *kneel

knieschijf (*knee*-skhayf) *c* (pl -schijven) kneecap

***knijpen** (*knay*-pern) *v* pinch

knik (knɪk) *c* nod

knikken (*knɪ*-kern) *v* nod

knikker (*knɪ*-kerr) *c* (pl ~s) marble

knippen (*knɪ*-pern) *v* *cut

knoflook (*knof*-lōak) *nt/c* garlic

knokkel (*kno*-kerl) *c* (pl ~s) knuckle

knoop (knōap) *c* (pl knopen) button; knot

knooppunt (*knōa*-pernt) *nt* (pl ~en) junction

knoopsgat (*knōaps*-khaht) *nt* (pl ~en) buttonhole

knop (knop) *c* (pl ~pen) bud; knob

knopen (*knōa*-pern) *v* button; tie, knot

knots (knots) *c* (pl ~en) club
knuffelen (*kner*-fer-lern) *v* cuddle
knuppel (*kner*-perl) *c* (pl ~s) club; cudgel
knus (knerss) *adj* cosy
koe (kōō) *c* (pl koeien) cow
koeiehuid (*kōō*ee-er-hurewt) *c* (pl ~en) cow-hide
koek (kōōk) *c* (pl ~en) cake
koekepan (*kōō*-ker-pahn) *c* (pl ~nen) frying-pan
koekje (kōōk-Yer) *nt* (pl ~s) biscuit; cracker *nAm*
koekoek (*kōō*-kōō-kōōk) *c* (pl ~en) cuckoo
koel (kōōl) *adj* cool
koelkast (*kōōl*-kahst) *c* (pl ~en) fridge, refrigerator
koelsysteem (*kōōl*-see-stāym) *nt* (pl -temen) cooling system
koeltas (*kōōl*-tahss) *c* (pl ~sen) ice-bag
koepel (*kōō*-perl) *c* (pl ~s) dome
koers (kōōrs) *c* (pl ~en) exchange rate ; course
koets (kōōts) *c* (pl ~en) carriage, coach
koffer (*ko*-ferr) *c* (pl ~s) case, suit-case, bag ; trunk
kofferruimte (*ko*-fer-rurewm-ter) *c* trunk *nAm*
koffie (*ko*-fee) *c* coffee
kogel (*kōa*-gerl) *c* (pl ~s) bullet
kok (kok) *c* (pl ~s) cook
koken (*kōa*-kern) *v* cook ; boil
kokosnoot (*kōa*-koss-nōat) *c* (pl -noten) coconut
kolen (*kōa*-lern) *pl* coal
kolom (kōa-*lom*) *c* (pl ~men) column
kolonel (kōa-lōa-*nehl*) *c* (pl ~s) colonel
kolonie (kōa-*lōa*-nee) *c* (pl ~s, -niën) colony
kolonne (kōa-*lo*-ner) *c* (pl ~s) column
kom (kom) *c* (pl ~men) basin

komedie (kōa-*māy*-dee) *c* (pl ~s) comedy
* **komen** (*kōa*-mern) *v* *come
komfort (koam-*fōar*) *nt* comfort
komiek (kōa-*meek*) *c* (pl ~en) comedian
komisch (*kōa*-meess) *adj* comic
komkommer (kom-*ko*-merr) *c* (pl ~s) cucumber
komma (*ko*-maa) *c* (pl ~'s) comma
kompas (kom-*pahss*) *nt* (pl ~sen) compass
komplot (kom-*plot*) *nt* (pl ~ten) plot, intrigue
komst (komst) *c* coming ; arrival
konijn (kōa-*nayn*) *nt* (pl ~en) rabbit
koning (*kōa*-nɪng) *c* (pl ~en) king
koningin (kōa-nɪ-*ngɪn*) *c* (pl ~nen) queen
koninklijk (*kōa*-nɪng-klerk) *adj* royal
koninkrijk (*kōa*-nɪng-krayk) *nt* (pl ~en) kingdom
kooi (kōaee) *c* (pl ~en) cage ; bunk, berth
kookboek (*kōak*-bōōk) *nt* (pl ~en) cookery-book ; cookbook *nAm*
kool (kōal) *c* (pl kolen) cabbage
koop (kōap) *c* purchase; **te** ~ for sale
koophandel (*kōap*-hahn-derl) *c* trade
koopje (*kōap*-Yer) *nt* (pl ~s) bargain
koopman (*kōap*-mahn) *c* (pl kooplieden) dealer, merchant
koopprijs (*kōa*-prayss) *c* (pl -prijzen) purchase price
koopwaar (*kōap*-vaar) *c* merchandise
koor (kōar) *nt* (pl koren) choir
koord (kōart) *nt* (pl ~en) cord
koorts (kōarts) *c* fever
koortsig (*kōart*-serkh) *adj* feverish
kop (kop) *c* (pl ~pen) head ; headline
* **kopen** (*kōa*-pern) *v* *buy; purchase
koper[1] (*kōa*-perr) *nt* brass; copper
koper[2] (*kōa*-perr) *c* (pl ~s) buyer, purchaser

koperwerk (kōā-perr-vehrk) *nt* brass-ware

kopie (kōā-*pee*) *c* (pl ~ën) copy

kopiëren (kōā-pee-*Yāy*-rern) *v* copy

kopje (*kop*-Yer) *nt* (pl ~s) cup

koplamp (*kop*-lahmp) *c* (pl ~en) head-light, headlamp

koppeling (ko-per-lɪng) *c* clutch

koppelteken (ko-perl-tāy-kern) *nt* (pl ~s) hyphen

koppig (ko-perkh) *adj* obstinate, head-strong

koraal (kōā-*raal*) *c* (pl -ralen) coral

koren (kōā-rern) *nt* corn, grain

korenveld (kōā-rer-vehlt) *nt* (pl ~en) cornfield

korhoen (kor-hōōn) *nt* (pl ~ders) grouse

korrel (ko-rerl) *c* (pl ~s) corn, grain

korset (kor-*seht*) *nt* (pl ~ten) corset

korst (korst) *c* (pl ~en) crust

kort (kort) *adj* brief, short

korting (*kor*-tɪng) *c* (pl ~en) discount, reduction, rebate

kortsluiting (*kort*-slur^ew-tɪng) *c* short circuit

kortstondig (kort-*ston*-derkh) *adj* momentary

kosmetica (koss-*māy*-tee-kaa) *pl* cosmetics *pl*

kost (kost) *c* food, fare; livelihood; ~ **en inwoning** room and board, board and lodging, bed and board

kostbaar (*kost*-baar) *adj* precious, valuable, expensive

kostbaarheden (*kost*-baar-hāy-dern) *pl* valuables *pl*

kosteloos (*koss*-ter-lōāss) *adj* free of charge

kosten (*koss*-tern) *v* *cost; *pl* cost, expenditure

koster (*koss*-terr) *c* (pl ~s) sexton

kostganger (*kost*-khah-ngerr) *c* (pl ~s) boarder

kostuum (koss-tewm) *nt* (pl ~s) suit

kotelet (kōā-ter-*leht*) *c* (pl ~ten) chop

kou (kou) *c* cold; ~ **vatten** catch a cold

koud (kout) *adj* cold

kous (kouss) *c* (pl ~en) stocking

kraag (kraakh) *c* (pl kragen) collar

kraai (kraa^ee) *c* (pl ~en) crow

kraakbeen (*kraak*-bāyn) *nt* cartilage

kraal (kraal) *c* (pl kralen) bead

kraam (kraam) *c* (pl kramen) stand, stall; booth

kraan (kraan) *c* (pl kranen) tap; faucet *nAm*

krab (krahp) *c* (pl ~ben) crab

krabben (*krah*-bern) *v* scratch

kracht (krahkht) *c* (pl ~en) force, strength; energy, power

krachtig (*krahkh*-terkh) *adj* strong

kraken (*kraa*-kern) *v* creak, crack

kralensnoer (*kraa*-ler-snōōr) *nt* (pl ~en) beads *pl*

kramp (krahmp) *c* (pl ~en) cramp; convulsion

krankzinnig (krahngk-*sɪ*-nerkh) *adj* insane; lunatic, crazy, mad

krankzinnige (krahngk-*sɪ*-ner-ger) *c* (pl ~n) lunatic

krankzinnigheid (krahngk-*sɪ*-nerkh-hayt) *c* lunacy

krant (krahnt) *c* (pl ~en) newspaper, paper

krantenkiosk (*krahn*-ter-kee-Yosk) *c* (pl ~en) newsstand

krantenverkoper (*krahn*-ter-verr-kōā-perr) *c* (pl ~s) newsagent

krap (krahp) *adj* tight

kras (krahss) *c* (pl ~sen) scratch

krassen (*krah*-sern) *v* scratch

krat (kraht) *nt* (pl ~ten) crate

krater (*kraa*-terr) *c* (pl ~s) crater

krediet (krer-*deet*) *nt* (pl ~en) credit

kredietbrief (krer-*deet*-breef) *c* (pl -brieven) letter of credit

kreeft (krāÿft) *c* (pl ~en) lobster

kreek (krāÿk) *c* (pl kreken) creek

kreet (krāÿt) *c* (pl kreten) cry

krekel (*krāÿ*-kerl) *c* (pl ~s) cricket

krenken (*krehng*-kern) *v* offend, injure

krent (krehnt) *c* (pl ~en) currant

kreuken (*krŪr*-kern) *v* crease

kreunen (*krŪr*-nern) *v* moan, groan

kreupel (*krŪr*-perl) *adj* lame, crippled

kribbe (krı-ber) *c* (pl ~n) manger

kriebel (*kree*-berl) *c* (pl ~s) itch

***krijgen** (*kray*-gern) *v* *get; receive

krijgsgevangene (*kraykhs*-kher-vah-nger-ner) *c* (pl ~n) prisoner of war

krijgsmacht (*kraykhs*-mahkht) *c* (pl ~en) military force

krijt (krayt) *nt* chalk

krik (krık) *c* (pl ~ken) jack

***krimpen** (*krım*-pern) *v* *shrink

krimpvrij (*krımp*-vray) *adj* shrinkproof

kring (krıng) *c* (pl ~en) ring, circle

kringloop (*krıng*-lōap) *c* (pl -lopen) cycle

kristal (krıss-*tahl*) *nt* (pl ~len) crystal

kristallen (krıss-*tah*-lern) *adj* crystal

kritiek (kree-*teek*) *adj* critical; *c* criticism

kritisch (*kree*-teess) *adj* critical

kroeg (krōōkh) *c* (pl ~en) public house; pub

kroes (krōōss) *c* (pl kroezen) mug

krokodil (krōā-kōā-*dıl*) *c* (pl ~len) crocodile

krom (krom) *adj* crooked; curved, bent

kromming (*kro*-mıng) *c* (pl ~en) curve, bend

kronen (*krōā*-nern) *v* crown

kronkelen (*krong*-ker-lern) *v* *wind

kronkelig (*krong*-ker-lerkh) *adj* winding

kroon (krōān) *c* (pl kronen) crown

kruid (krŪrᵉʷt) *nt* (pl ~en) herb; **kruiden** spices; *v* flavour

kruidenier (krŪrᵉʷ-der-*neer*) *c* (pl ~s) grocer

kruidenierswaren (krŪrᵉʷ-der-*neers*-vaa-rern) *pl* groceries *pl*

kruidenierswinkel (krŪrᵉʷ-der-*neers*-vıng-kerl) *c* (pl ~s) grocer's

kruier (*krŪr*-err) *c* (pl ~s) porter

kruik (krŪrᵉʷk) *c* (pl ~en) pitcher

kruimel (*krŪrᵉʷ*-merl) *c* (pl ~s) crumb

***kruipen** (*krŪrᵉʷ*-pern) *v* *creep, crawl

kruis (krŪrᵉʷss) *nt* (pl ~en) cross

kruisbeeld (*krŪrᵉʷss*-bāÿlt) *nt* (pl ~en) crucifix

kruisbes (*krŪrᵉʷss*-behss) *c* (pl ~sen) gooseberry

kruisigen (*krŪrᵉʷ*-ser-gern) *v* crucify

kruisiging (*krŪrᵉʷ*-ser-gıng) *c* (pl ~en) crucifixion

kruising (*krŪrᵉʷ*-sıng) *c* (pl ~en) crossing, junction

kruispunt (*krŪrᵉʷss*-pernt) *nt* (pl ~en) crossroads, intersection

kruissnelheid (*krŪrᵉʷ*-snehl-hayt) *c* cruising speed

kruistocht (*krŪrᵉʷss*-tokht) *c* (pl ~en) crusade

kruit (krŪrᵉʷt) *nt* gunpowder

kruiwagen (*krŪrᵉʷ*-vaa-gern) *c* (pl ~s) wheelbarrow

kruk (krerk) *c* (pl ~ken) crutch

krukas (*krerk*-ahss) *c* crankshaft

krul (krerl) *c* (pl ~len) curl

krullen (*krer*-lern) *v* curl; **krullend** curly

krulspeld (*krerl*-spehlt) *c* (pl ~en) curler

krultang (*krerl*-tahng) *c* (pl ~en) curling-tongs *pl*

kubus (*ke‑*berss) *c* (pl ~sen) cube

kudde (*ker*-der) *c* (pl ~n, ~s) herd, flock

kuiken (*kurᵉʷ*-kern) *nt* (pl ~s) chicken

kuil (kurᵉʷl) *c* (pl ~en) hole; pit

kuis (kurᵉʷss) *adj* chaste

kuit¹ (kur^{ew}t) *c* roe

kuit² (kur^{ew}t) *c* (pl ~en) calf

kundig (kern-derkh) *adj* capable

*kunnen (ker-nern) *v* *can, *be able to; *might, *may

kunst (kernst) *c* (pl ~en) art; **schone kunsten** fine arts

kunstacademie (kernst-ah-kaa-dáy-mee) *c* (pl ~s) art school

kunstenaar (kern-ster-naar) *c* (pl ~s) artist

kunstenares (kern-ster-naa-*rehss*) *c* (pl ~sen) artist

kunstgalerij (kernst-khah-ler-ray) *c* (pl ~en) art gallery

kunstgebit (kernst-kher-bɪt) *nt* (pl ~ten) denture, false teeth

kunstgeschiedenis (kernst-kher-skhee-der-nɪss) *c* art history

kunstijsbaan (kernst-ayss-baan) *c* (pl -banen) skating-rink

kunstje (kern-sher) *nt* (pl ~s) trick

kunstmatig (kernst-*maa*-terkh) *adj* artificial

kunstnijverheid (kernst-*nay*-verr-hayt) *c* arts and crafts

kunsttentoonstelling (kerns-tern-tōan-steh-lɪng) *c* (pl ~en) art exhibition

kunstverzameling (kernst-ferr-zaa-mer-lɪng) *c* (pl ~en) art collection

kunstwerk (kernst-vehrk) *nt* (pl ~en) work of art

kunstzijde (kernst-say-der) *c* rayon

kunstzinnig (kernst-sɪ-nerkh) *adj* artistic

kurk (kerrk) *c* (pl ~en) cork

kurketrekker (kerr-ker-treh-kerr) *c* (pl ~s) corkscrew

kus (kerss) *c* (pl ~sen) kiss

kussen¹ (ker-sern) *v* kiss

kussen² (ker-sern) *nt* (pl ~s) cushion; pillow; **kussentje** *nt* pad

kussensloop (ker-ser-slōap) *c/nt* (pl -slopen) pillow-case

kust (kerst) *c* (pl ~en) coast, shore; seaside, seashore

kuur (ke̅wr) *c* (pl kuren) cure

kwaad¹ (kvaat) *adj* angry, cross; mad; ill

kwaad² (kvaat) *nt* (pl kwaden) evil; mischief, harm

kwaadaardig (kvaa-*daar*-derkh) *adj* malignant

kwaal (kvaal) *c* (pl kwalen) ailment

kwadraat (kvaa-*draat*) *nt* (pl -draten) square

kwakzalver (kvahk-sahl-verr) *c* (pl ~s) quack

kwal (kvahl) *c* (pl ~len) jelly-fish

kwalijk *nemen (kvaa-lerk *nay*-mern) resent; **neem me niet kwalijk!** sorry!

kwaliteit (kvaa-lee-*tayt*) *c* (pl ~en) quality

kwart (kvahrt) *nt* (pl ~en) quarter

kwartaal (kvahr-*taal*) *nt* (pl -talen) quarter

kwartel (kvahr-terl) *c* (pl ~s) quail

kwartier (kvahr-*teer*) *nt* quarter of an hour

kwast (kvahst) *c* (pl ~en) brush

kweken (kvā̅y-kern) *v* cultivate, *grow

kwellen (kveh-lern) *v* torment

kwelling (kveh-lɪng) *c* (pl ~en) torment

kwestie (kvehss-tee) *c* (pl ~s) matter, question, issue

kwetsbaar (kvehts-baar) *adj* vulnerable

kwetsen (kveht-sern) *v* injure; *hurt, wound

kwijtraken (kvayt-raa-kern) *v* *lose; *mislay

kwik (kvɪk) *nt* mercury

kwistig (kvɪss-terkh) *adj* lavish

kwitantie (kvee-*tahn*-see) *c* (pl ~s) receipt

L

la (laa) *c* (pl ~den) drawer
laag¹ (laakh) *adj* low; **lager** *adj* inferior
laag² (laakh) *c* (pl lagen) layer
laagland (*laakh*-lahnt) *nt* lowlands *pl*
laan (laan) *c* (pl lanen) avenue
laars (laars) *c* (pl laarzen) boot
laat (laat) *adj* late; **laatst** *adj* last; ultimate, final; *adv* lately; **later** *adv* afterwards; **te** ~ late; overdue
labiel (laa-*beel*) *adj* unstable
laboratorium (laa-boa-raa-*toa*-ree-ᵉrm) *nt* (pl -ria) laboratory
lach (lahkh) *c* laugh
***lachen** (*lah*-khern) *v* laugh
ladder (*lah*-derr) *c* (pl ~s) ladder
lade (*laa*-der) *c* (pl ~n) drawer
***laden** (*laa*-dern) *v* load; charge
ladenkast (*laa*-der-kahst) *c* (pl ~en) chest of drawers
lading (*laa*-dɪng) *c* (pl ~en) charge, load; freight, cargo
laf (lahf) *adj* cowardly
lafaard (*lah*-faart) *c* (pl ~s) coward
lagune (laa-*geᵘ*-ner) *c* (pl ~s) lagoon
lak (lahk) *c* (pl ~ken) lacquer, varnish
laken (*laa*-kern) *nt* (pl ~s) sheet
lakken (*lah*-kern) *v* varnish
lam¹ (lahm) *adj* lame
lam² (lahm) *nt* (pl ~meren) lamb
lambrizering (lahm-bree-*zay*-rɪng) *c* panelling
lamp (lahmp) *c* (pl ~en) lamp
lampekap (*lahm*-per-kahp) *c* (pl ~pen) lampshade
lamsvlees (*lahms*-flayss) *nt* lamb
lanceren (lahn-*say*-rern) *v* launch
land (lahnt) *nt* (pl ~en) country, land; **aan** ~ ashore; **aan** ~ ***gaan** land

landbouw (*lahnt*-bou) *c* agriculture; **landbouw-** agrarian
landen (*lahn*-dern) *v* land
landengte (*lahnt*-ehng-ter) *c* (pl ~n, ~s) isthmus
landgenoot (*lahnt*-kher-noat) *c* (pl -noten) countryman
landgoed (*lahnt*-khoot) *nt* (pl ~eren) estate
landhuis (*lahnt*-hurᵉʷss) *nt* (pl -huizen) country house
landkaart (*lahnt*-kaart) *c* (pl ~en) map
landloper (*lahnt*-loa-perr) *c* (pl ~s) tramp
landloperij (lahnt-loa-per-*ray*) *c* vagrancy
landschap (*lahnt*-skhahp) *nt* (pl ~pen) scenery, landscape
landsgrens (*lahnts*-khrehns) *c* (pl -grenzen) boundary
landtong (*lahn*-tong) *c* (pl ~en) headland
lang (lahng) *adj* long; tall
langdurig (lahng-*deᵘ*-rerkh) *adj* long
langs (lahngs) *prep* along; past
langspeelplaat (*lahng*-spayl-plaat) *c* (pl -platen) long-playing record
langwerpig (lahng-*vehr*-perkh) *adj* oblong
langzaam (*lahng*-zaam) *adj* slow
langzamerhand (lahng-zaa-merr-*hahnt*) *adv* gradually
lantaarn (lahn-*taa*-rern) *c* (pl ~s) lantern
lantaarnpaal (lahn-*taa*-rern-paal) *c* (pl -palen) lamp-post
las (lahss) *c* (pl ~sen) joint
lassen (*lah*-sern) *v* weld
last (lahst) *c* (pl ~en) charge; load, burden; trouble, nuisance, bother
laster (*lahss*-terr) *c* slander
lastig (*lahss*-terkh) *adj* troublesome, inconvenient; difficult
***laten** (*laa*-tern) *v* *let; allow to;

*leave; *have

Latijns-Amerika (lah-tayn-zaa-*māy*-ree-kaa) Latin America

Latijns-Amerikaans (lah-tayn-zaa-māy-ree-*kaans*) adj Latin-American

lauw (lou) adj lukewarm, tepid

lawaai (laa-*vaa*ᵉᵉ) nt noise

lawaaierig (laa-*vaa*ᵉᵉ-er-rerkh) adj noisy

lawine (laa-*vee*-ner) c (pl ~s, ~n) avalanche

laxeermiddel (lahk-*sāyr*-mɪ-derl) nt (pl ~en) laxative

ledemaat (*lāy*-der-maat) c (pl maten) limb

lederen (*lāy*-der-rern) adj leather

ledigen (*lāy*-der-gern) v empty

leed (lāyt) nt affliction, sorrow

leeftijd (*lāy*f-tayt) c (pl ~en) age

leeg (lāykh) adj empty

leek (lāyk) c (pl leken) layman

leer¹ (lāyr) c teachings pl

leer² (lāyr) nt leather

leerboek (*lāyr*-bōōk) nt (pl ~en) textbook

leerling (*lāyr*-lɪng) c (pl ~en) pupil; scholar

leerzaam (*lāyr*-zaam) adj instructive

leesbaar (*lāyss*-baar) adj legible

leeslamp (*lāyss*-lahmp) c (pl ~en) reading-lamp

leeszaal (*lāy*-saal) c (pl -zalen) reading-room

leeuw (lāyᵒᵒ) c (pl ~en) lion

leeuwerik (*lāy*ᵒᵒ-er-rɪk) c (pl ~en) lark

lef (lehf) nt guts

legalisatie (lāy-gaa-lee-*zaa*-tsee) c legalization

legatie (ler-*gaa*-tsee) c (pl ~s) legation

leger (*lāy*-gerr) nt (pl ~s) army

leggen (*leh*-gern) v *lay, *put

legpuzzel (*lehkh*-per-zerl) c (pl ~s) jigsaw puzzle

lei (lay) nt slate

leiden (*lay*-dern) v head, direct; guide, *lead, conduct

leider (*lay*-derr) c (pl ~s) leader

leiderschap (*lay*-derr-skhahp) nt leadership

leiding¹ (*lay*-dɪng) c lead

leiding² (*lay*-dɪng) c (pl ~en) pipe

lek¹ (lehk) adj leaky; punctured

lek² (lehk) nt (pl ~ken) leak

lekken (*leh*-kern) v leak

lekker (*leh*-kerr) adj good; nice, enjoyable, delicious, tasty

lekkernij (leh-kerr-*nay*) c (pl ~en) delicacy

lelie (*lāy*-lee) c (pl ~s) lily

lelijk (*lāy*-lerk) adj ugly

lemmet (*leh*-mert) nt (pl ~en) blade

lenen (*lāy*-nern) v *lend; borrow

lengte (*lehng*-ter) c (pl ~n, ~s) length; **in de ~** lengthways

lengtegraad (*lehng*-ter-graat) c (pl -graden) longitude

lenig (*lāy*-nerkh) adj supple

lening (*lāy*-nɪng) c (pl ~en) loan

lens (lehns) c (pl lenzen) lens

lente (*lehn*-ter) c (pl ~s) spring

lepel (*lāy*-perl) c (pl ~s) spoon; spoonful

lepra (*lāy*-praa) c leprosy

leraar (*lāy*-raar) c (pl leraren, ~s) master, teacher; instructor

lerares (lāy-raa-*rehss*) c (pl ~sen) teacher

leren¹ (*lāy*-rern) v *teach; *learn

leren² (*lāy*-rern) adj leather

les (lehss) c (pl ~sen) lesson

leslokaal (lehss-lōā-kaal) nt (pl -kalen) classroom

lessenaar (*leh*-ser-naar) c (pl ~s) desk

letsel (*leht*-serl) nt (pl ~s) injury

letten op (*leh*-tern) attend to, *pay attention to; watch, mind

letter (*leh*-terr) c (pl ~s) letter

lettergreep (*leh*-terr-gráyp) c (pl -grepen) syllable

letterkundig (leh-terr-*kern*-derkh) adj literary

leugen (*lūr*-gern) c (pl ~s) lie

leuk (lūrk) adj enjoyable; funny, jolly

leunen (*lūr*-nern) v *lean

leuning (*lūr*-nıng) c (pl ~en) arm; rail

leunstoel (*lūrn*-stool) c (pl ~en) easy chair, armchair

leus (lūrss) c (pl leuzen) slogan

leven[1] (*lāy*-vern) v live; **levend** alive; live

leven[2] (*lāy*-vern) nt (pl ~s) life; lifetime; **in ~** alive

levendig (*lāy*-vern-derkh) adj lively; brisk, vivid

levensmiddelen (*lāy*-verns-mı-der-lern) pl foodstuffs pl

levensstandaard (*lāy*-vern-stahn-daart) c standard of living

levensverzekering (*lāy*-verns-ferr-zāy-ker-rıng) c (pl ~en) life insurance

lever (*lāy*-verr) c (pl ~s) liver

leveren (*lāy*-ver-rern) v furnish, provide, supply

levering (*lāy*-ver-rıng) c (pl ~en) delivery, supply

***lezen** (*lāy*-zern) v *read

lezing (*lāy*-zıng) c (pl ~en) lecture

Libanees[1] (lee-baa-*nāyss*) adj Lebanese

Libanees[2] (lee-bah-*nāyss*) c (pl -nezen) Lebanese

Libanon (*lee*-baa-non) Lebanon

liberaal (lee-ber-*raal*) adj liberal

Liberia (lee-*bāy*-ree-Yaa) Liberia

Liberiaan (lee-*bāy*-ree-Yaan) c (pl -rianen) Liberian

Liberiaans (lee-*bāy*-ree-Yaans) adj Liberian

licentie (lee-*sehn*-see) c (pl ~s) licence

lichaam (*lı*-khaam) nt (pl lichamen) body

licht[1] (lıkht) adj light; pale; gentle, slight

licht[2] (lıkht) nt (pl ~en) light

lichtbruin (*lıkht*-brun^(ew)n) adj fawn

lichtgevend (*lıkht*-kher-vernt) adj luminous

lichting (*lıkh*-tıng) c (pl ~en) collection

lichtpaars (*lıkht*-paars) adj mauve

lid (lıt) nt (pl leden) member; associate

lidmaatschap (*lıt*-maat-skhahp) nt membership

lidwoord (*lıt*-vōart) nt (pl ~en) article

lied (leet) nt (pl ~eren) song

lief (leef) adj dear; sweet; affectionate, adorable

liefdadigheid (leef-*daa*-derkh-hayt) c charity

liefde (*leef*-der) c (pl ~s) love

liefdesgeschiedenis (*leef*-derss-kher-skhee-der-nıss) c (pl ~sen) love-story

***liefhebben** (*leef*-heh-bern) v love

liefhebberij (leef-heh-ber-*ray*) c (pl ~en) hobby

liefje (*leef*-Yer) nt (pl ~s) sweetheart

***liegen** (*lee*-gern) v lie

lies (leess) c (pl liezen) groin

lieveling (*lee*-ver-lıng) c (pl ~en) darling, sweetheart; favourite, pet; **lievelings-** favourite, pet

liever (*lee*-verr) adv sooner, rather; **~ *hebben** prefer

lift (lıft) c (pl ~en) lift; elevator nAm

liften (*lıf*-tern) v hitchhike

lifter (*lıf*-terr) c (pl ~s) hitchhiker

***liggen** (*lı*-gern) v *lie; ***gaan ~** *lie down

ligging (*lı*-gıng) c location; situation, site

ligstoel (*lıkh*-stool) c (pl ~en) deck chair

lijden (*lay*-dern) nt suffering

*lijden (*lay*-dern) *v* suffer
lijf (layf) *nt* (pl lijven) body
lijfwacht (*layf*-vahkht) *c* (pl ~en)
  bodyguard
lijk (layk) *nt* (pl ~en) corpse
*lijken (lay-kern) *v* seem, appear;
  look ; ~ **op** resemble
lijm (laym) *c* glue, gum
lijn (layn) *c* (pl ~en) line ; leash
lijnboot (*layn*-bōat) *c* (pl -boten) liner
lijst (layst) *c* (pl ~en) list ; frame
lijster (*lay*-sterr) *c* (pl ~s) thrush
lijvig (*lay*-verkh) *adj* bulky
likdoorn (*lik*-dōa-rern) *c* (pl ~s) corn
likeur (lee-*kurr*) *c* (pl ~en) liqueur
likken (*li*-kern) *v* lick
limiet (lee-*meet*) *c* (pl ~en) limit
limoen (lee-*mōon*) *c* (pl ~en) lime
limonade (lee-mōa-*naa*-der) *c* (pl ~s)
  lemonade
linde (*lin*-der) *c* (pl ~n) limetree, lime
lingerie (lang-zher-*ree*) *c* lingerie
liniaal (lee-nee-*Yaal*) *c* (pl -alen) ruler
links (lingks) *adj* left ; left-hand
linkshandig (lingks-*hahn*-derkh) *adj*
  left-handed
linnen (*li*-nern) *nt* linen
linnengoed (*li*-ner-gōot) *nt* linen
lint (lint) *nt* (pl ~en) ribbon ; tape
lip (lip) *c* (pl ~pen) lip
lippenboter (*li*-per-bōa-terr) *c* lipsalve
lippenstift (*li*-per-stift) *c* lipstick
list (list) *c* (pl ~en) ruse, artifice
listig (*liss*-terkh) *adj* sly
liter (*lee*-terr) *c* (pl ~s) litre
literair (lee-ter-*rair*) *adj* literary
literatuur (lee-ter-raa-*tēwr*) *c* literature
lits-jumeaux (lee-zhēw-*mōa*) *nt* twin
  beds
litteken (*li*-tāy-kern) *nt* (pl ~s) scar
locomotief (lōa-kōa-mōa-*teef*) *c* (pl
  -tieven) engine, locomotive
loeien (*lōoee*-ern) *v* roar
lof (lof) *c* glory, praise

logé (lōa-*zhāy*) *c* (pl ~'s) guest
logeerkamer (lōa-*zhāyr*-kaa-merr) *c* (pl
  ~s) spare room, guest-room
logeren (lōa-*zhāy*-rern) *v* stay
logica (*lōa*-gee-kaa) *c* logic
logies (lōa-*zheess*) *nt* lodgings *pl*, accommodation; ~ **en ontbijt** bed
  and breakfast
logisch (*lōa*-geess) *adj* logical
lokaal (lōa-*kaal*) *adj* local
lol (lol) *c* fun
lonen (*lōa*-nern) *v* *pay
long (long) *c* (pl ~en) lung
longontsteking (*long*-ont-stāy-king) *c*
  (pl ~en) pneumonia
lont (lont) *c* (pl ~en) fuse
lood (lōat) *nt* lead
loodgieter (*lōat*-khee-terr) *c* (pl ~s)
  plumber
loodrecht (*lōat*-rehkht) *adj* perpendicular
loods (lōats) *c* (pl ~en) pilot
loon (lōan) *nt* (pl lonen) wages *pl* ;
  salary, pay
loonsverhoging (*lōans*-ferr-hōa-ging) *c*
  (pl ~en) raise *nAm*
loop (lōap) *c* course ; gait, walk
loopbaan (*lōa*-baan) *c* (pl -banen) career
loopplank (*lōa*-plahngk) *c* (pl ~en)
  gangway
*lopen (*lōa*-pern) *v* walk ; *go
los (loss) *adj* loose
losgeld (*loass*-khehlt) *nt* (pl ~en) ransom
losknopen (*loss*-knōa-pern) *v* unbutton ; untie
losmaken (*loss*-maa-kern) *v* unfasten,
  *undo, detach ; loosen
losschroeven (*lo*-skhrōo-vern) *v* unscrew
lossen (*lo*-sern) *v* unload, discharge
lot[1] (lot) *nt* lot, fortune, destiny, fate
lot[2] (lot) *nt* (pl ~en) lot

loterij (lōa-ter-*ray*) *c* (pl ~en) lottery
lotion (lōa-*shon*) *c* (pl ~s) lotion
loyaal (lōa-*Yaal*) *adj* loyal
lucht (lerkht) *c* air; breath; sky
luchtdicht (*lerkh*-dıkht) *adj* airtight
luchtdruk (*lerkh*-drerk) *c* atmospheric pressure
luchten (*lerkh*-tern) *v* air, ventilate
luchtfilter (*lerkht*-fıl-terr) *nt* (pl ~s) air-filter
luchthaven (*lerkht*-haa-vern) *c* (pl ~s) airport
luchtig (*lerkh*-terkh) *adj* airy
luchtpost (*lerkht*-post) *c* airmail
luchtvaartmaatschappij (*lerkht*-faart-maat-skhah-pay) *c* (pl ~en) airline
luchtversing (*lerkht*-ferr-vehr-sıng) *c* air-conditioning, ventilation
luchtziekte (*lerkht*-seek-ter) *c* air-sickness
lucifer (*lēw*-see-fehr) *c* (pl ~s) match
lucifersdoosje (*lēw*-see-fehrs-dōa-sher) *nt* (pl ~s) match-box
lui (lur*ew*) *adj* lazy; idle
luid (lur*ew*t) *adj* loud
luidspreker (*lur*ew*t*-sprāy-kerr) *c* (pl ~s) loud-speaker
luier (*lur*ew*-err) *c* (pl ~s) nappy; diaper *nAm*
luik (lur*ew*k) *nt* (pl ~en) hatch; shutter
luis (lur*ew*ss) *c* (pl luizen) louse
luisteraar (*lur*ew*ss-ter-raar) *c* (pl ~s) listener
luisteren (*lur*ew*ss-ter-rern) *v* listen
luisterrijk (*lur*ew*ss-ter-rayk) *adj* magnificent
lukken (*ler*-kern) *v* succeed
lunch (lernsh) *c* (pl ~es) lunch
lus (lerss) *c* (pl ~sen) loop
lusten (*lerss*-tern) *v* like; fancy
luxe (*lēw*k-ser) *c* luxury
luxueus (lēwk-sēw-*ūrss*) *adj* luxurious

M

maag (maakh) *c* (pl magen) stomach; **maag-** gastric
maagd (maakht) *c* (pl ~en) virgin
maagpijn (*maakh*-payn) *c* stomach-ache
maagzuur (*maakh*-sēwr) *nt* heartburn
maagzweer (*maakh*-svāyr) *c* (pl -zweren) gastric ulcer
maal[1] (maal) *nt* (pl malen) meal
maal[2] (maal) *c* (pl malen) time
maal[3] (maal) *prep* times
maaltijd (*maal*-tayt) *c* (pl ~en) meal; **warme** ~ dinner
maan (maan) *c* (pl manen) moon
maand (maant) *c* (pl ~en) month
maandag (*maan*-dahkh) *c* Monday
maandblad (*maant*-blaht) *nt* (pl ~en) monthly magazine
maandelijks (*maan*-der-lerks) *adj* monthly
maandverband (*maant*-ferr-bahnt) *nt* sanitary towel
maanlicht (*maan*-lıkht) *nt* moonlight
maar (maar) *conj* but; yet; *adv* only
maart (maart) March
maas (maass) *c* (pl mazen) mesh
maat (maat) *c* (pl maten) size, measure; **extra grote** ~ outsize; **op** ~ **gemaakt** tailor-made; made to order
maatregel (*maat*-rāy-gerl) *c* (pl ~en, ~s) measure
maatschappelijk (maat-*skhah*-per-lerk) *adj* social
maatschappij (maat-skhah-*pay*) *c* (pl ~en) company; society
maatstaf (*maat*-stahf) *c* (pl -staven) standard
machine (mah-*shee*-ner) *c* (pl ~s) engine, machine

machinerie (mah-shee-ner-*ree*) *c* machinery

macht (mahkht) *c* (pl ~en) power; force, might; authority

machteloos (*mahkh*-ter-lōass) *adj* powerless

machtig (*mahkh*-terkh) *adj* powerful, mighty

machtiging (*mahkh*-ter-gɪng) *c* (pl ~en) authorization

magazijn (maa-gaa-*zayn*) *nt* (pl ~en) store-house, warehouse

mager (*maa*-gerr) *adj* lean, thin

magie (maa-*gee*) *c* magic

magistraat (maa-gɪss-*traat*) *c* (pl -straten) magistrate

magneet (mahkh-*nayt*) *c* (pl -neten) magneto

magnetisch (mahkh-*nay*-teess) *adj* magnetic

maillot (maa-ʸōā) *c* (pl ~s) tights *pl*

maïs (mighss) *c* maize

maïskolf (*mighss*-kolf) *c* (pl -kolven) corn on the cob

maître d'hôtel (mai-trer-dōa-*tehl*) head-waiter

maîtresse (meh-*tray*-ser) *c* (pl ~s, ~n) mistress

majoor (maa-ʸōar) *c* (pl ~s) major

mak (mahk) *adj* tame

makelaar (*maa*-ker-laar) *c* (pl ~s) broker, house agent

maken (*maa*-kern) *v* *make; **te ~ *hebben met** *deal with

makreel (maa-*krayl*) *c* (pl -relen) mackerel

mal (mahl) *adj* foolish, silly

malaria (maa-*laa*-ree-ʸaa) *c* malaria

Maleis (maa-*layss*) *nt* Malay

Maleisië (maa-*lay*-zee-ʸer) Malaysia

Maleisisch (maa-*lay*-zeess) *adj* Malaysian

*malen (*maa*-lern) *v* *grind

mals (mahls) *adj* tender

mammoet (*mah*-mōōt) *c* (pl ~en, ~s) mammoth

man (mahn) *c* (pl ~nen) man; husband

manchet (mahn-*sheht*) *c* (pl ~ten) cuff

manchetknopen (mahn-*sheht*-knōa-pern) *pl* cuff-links *pl*

mand (mahnt) *c* (pl ~en) hamper, basket

mandaat (mahn-*daat*) *nt* (pl -daten) mandate

mandarijn (mahn-daa-*rayn*) *c* (pl ~en) mandarin, tangerine

manege (maa-*nay*-zher) *c* (pl ~s) riding-school

manicure (maa-nee-*kew*-rer) *c* (pl ~s) manicure

manicuren (maa-nee-*kew*-rern) *v* manicure

manier (maa-*neer*) *c* (pl ~en) manner; way, fashion

mank (mahngk) *adj* lame

mannelijk (*mah*-ner-lerk) *adj* male; masculine

mannequin (mah-ner-*kang*) *c* (pl ~s) model, mannequin

mantel (*mahn*-terl) *c* (pl ~s) coat, cloak

manufacturier (mah-new-fahk-tew-*reer*) *c* (pl ~s) draper

manuscript (maa-nerss-*krɪpt*) *nt* (pl ~en) manuscript

marcheren (mahr-*shay*-rern) *v* march

margarine (mahr-gaa-*ree*-ner) *c* margarine

marge (*mahr*-zher) *c* (pl ~s) margin

marine (maa-*ree*-ner) *c* navy; **marine-** naval

maritiem (mah-ree-*teem*) *adj* maritime

markt (mahrkt) *c* (pl ~en) market; **zwarte ~** black market

marktplein (*mahrkt*-playn) *nt* (pl ~en) market-place

marmelade (mahr-mer-*laa*-der) *c* (pl ~s, ~n) marmalade

marmer (*mahr*-merr) *nt* marble

Marokkaan (mah-ro-*kaan*) *c* (pl -kanen) Moroccan

Marokkaans (mah-ro-*kaans*) *adj* Moroccan

Marokko (maa-*ro*-kōa) Morocco

mars (mahrs) *c* (pl ~en) march

martelaar (*mahr*-ter-laar) *c* (pl ~s, -laren) martyr

martelen (*mahr*-ter-lern) *v* torture

marteling (*mahr*-ter-lıng) *c* (pl ~en) torture

mascara (mahss-*kaa*-raa) *c* mascara

masker (*mahss*-kerr) *nt* (pl ~s) mask

massa (*mah*-saa) *c* (pl ~'s) bulk, mass; crowd

massage (mah-*saa*-zher) *c* (pl ~s) massage

massaproduktie (*mah*-saa-prōa-derk-see) *c* mass production

masseren (mah-*sāy*-rern) *v* massage

masseur (mah-*sūrr*) *c* (pl ~s) masseur

massief (mah-*seef*) *adj* solid, massive

mast (mahst) *c* (pl ~en) mast

mat[1] (maht) *adj* dull, mat, dim

mat[2] (maht) *c* (pl ~ten) mat

materiaal (maa-tree-*Yaal*) *nt* (pl -rialen) material

materie (mah-*tāy*-ree) *c* (pl -riën, ~s) matter

materieel (maa-tree-*Yāyl*) *adj* material

matig (*maa*-terkh) *adj* moderate

matras (maa-*trahss*) *c* (pl ~sen) mattress

matroos (maa-*trōass*) *c* (pl matrozen) sailor

mausoleum (mou-sōa-*lāy*-Yerm) *nt* (pl ~s, -lea) mausoleum

mazelen (*maa*-zer-lern) *pl* measles

me (mer) *pron* me; myself

mechanisch (māy-*khaa*-neess) *adj* mechanical

mechanisme (māy-khaa-*nıss*-mer) *nt* (pl ~n) mechanism; machinery

medaille (māy-*dah*-Yer) *c* (pl ~s) medal

mededelen (*māy*-der-dāy-lern) *v* notify, communicate, inform

mededeling (*māy*-der-dāy-lıng) *c* (pl ~en) communication, information

medegevoel (*māy*-der-ger-vōol) *nt* sympathy

medelijden (*māy*-der-lay-dern) *nt* pity; ~ *hebben met pity

medeplichtige (*māy*-der-*plıkh*-ter-ger) *c* (pl ~n) accessary

medewerking (*māy*-der-vehr-kıng) *c* co-operation

medisch (*māy*-deess) *adj* medical

mediteren (māy-dee-*tāy*-rern) *v* meditate

***meebrengen** (*māy*-breh-ngern) *v* *bring

meedelen (*māy*-dāy-lern) *v* communicate

meel (māyl) *nt* flour

meemaken (*māy*-maa-kern) *v* *go through

***meenemen** (*māy*-nāy-mern) *v* *take away

meer[1] (māyr) *adj* more; ~ **dan** over; **niet** ~ no longer

meer[2] (māyr) *nt* (pl meren) lake

meerderheid (*māyr*-derr-hayt) *c* majority; bulk

meerderjarig (māyr-derr-*Yaa*-rerkh) *adj* of age

meervoud (*māyr*-vout) *nt* (pl ~en) plural

meest (māyst) *adj* most

meestal (māy-*stahl*) *adv* mostly

meester (*māy*-sterr) *c* (pl ~s) master; schoolmaster, teacher

meesteres (māy-ster-*rehss*) *c* (pl ~sen) mistress

meesterwerk (*māy*-sterr-vehrk) *nt* (pl

~en) masterpiece

meetellen (*māy*-teh-lern) *v* count

meetkunde (*māyt*-kern-der) *c* ge-ometry

meeuw (māy°°) *c* (pl ~en) gull; sea-gull

mei (may) May

meid (mayt) *c* (pl ~en) housemaid, maid

meineed (*may*-nāyt) *c* (pl -eden) per-jury

meisje (*may*-sher) *nt* (pl ~s) girl

meisjesnaam (*may*-sherss-naam) *c* (pl -namen) maiden name

mejuffrouw (mer-*Yer*-frou) miss

melden (*mehl*-dern) *v* report

melding (*mehl*-dıng) *c* (pl ~en) men-tion

melk (mehlk) *c* milk

melkboer (*mehlk*-bōōr) *c* (pl ~en) milkman

melodie (māy-lōā-*dee*) *c* (pl ~ĕn) mel-ody; tune

melodieus (māy-lōā-dee-*Yūrss*) *adj* tuneful

melodrama (māy-lōā-*draa*-maa) *nt* (pl ~'s) melodrama

meloen (mer-*lōōn*) *c* (pl ~en) melon

memorandum (māy-mōā-*rahn*-derm) *nt* (pl -randa) memo

men (mehn) *pron* one

meneer (mer-*nāyr*) mister; sir

menen (*māy*-nern) *v* consider; *mean

mengen (*meh*-ngern) *v* mix

mengsel (*mehng*-serl) *nt* (pl ~s) mix-ture

menigte (*māy*-nerkh-ter) *c* (pl ~n, ~s) crowd

mening (*māy*-nıng) *c* (pl ~en) opin-ion; view; **van ~ verschillen** dis-agree

mens (mehns) *c* (pl ~en) man; **men-sen** people *pl*

menselijk (*mehn*-ser-lerk) *adj* human;

~ wezen human being

mensheid (*mehns*-hayt) *c* humanity, mankind

menstruatie (mehn-strēw-*vaa*-tsee) *c* menstruation

menukaart (mer-*nēw*-kaart) *c* (pl ~en) menu

merel (*māy*-rerl) *c* (pl ~s) blackbird

merg (mehrkh) *nt* marrow

merk (mehrk) *nt* (pl ~en) brand

merkbaar (*mehrk*-baar) *adj* noticeable, perceptible

merken (*mehr*-kern) *v* notice; mark

merkteken (*mehrk*-tāy-kern) *nt* (pl ~s) mark

merrie (*meh*-ree) *c* (pl ~s) mare

mes (mehss) *nt* (pl ~sen) knife

messing (*meh*-sıng) *nt* brass

mest (mehst) *c* dung, manure

mesthoop (*mehst*-hōāp) *c* (pl -hopen) dunghill

met (meht) *prep* with; by

metaal (māy-*taal*) *nt* (pl metalen) met-al

metalen (māy-*taa*-lern) *adj* metal

meteen (mer-*tāyn*) *adv* at once, straight away, immediately, instant-ly; presently

*meten** (*māy*-tern) *v* measure

meter (*māy*-terr) *c* (pl ~s) metre; me-ter; gauge

metgezel (*meht*-kher-zehl) *c* (pl ~len) companion

methode (māy-*tōā*-der) *c* (pl ~n, ~s) method

methodisch (māy-*tōā*-deess) *adj* meth-odical

metrisch (*māy*-treess) *adj* metric

metro (*māy*-trōā) *c* (pl ~'s) under-ground

metselaar (*meht*-ser-laar) *c* (pl ~s) bricklayer

metselen (*meht*-ser-lern) *v* *lay bricks

meubilair (mūr-bee-*lair*) *nt* furniture

meubileren (mūr-bee-*lay*-rern) *v* furnish

mevrouw (mer-*vrou*) madam

Mexicaan (mehk-see-*kaan*) *c* (pl -canen) Mexican

Mexicaans (mehk-see-*kaans*) *adj* Mexican

Mexico (*mehk*-see-kōa) Mexico

microfoon (mee-krōa-*fōan*) *c* (pl ~s) microphone

middag (*mɪ*-dahkh) *c* (pl ~en) afternoon ; midday ; noon

middageten (*mɪ*-dahkh-āy-tern) *nt* luncheon, lunch ; dinner

middel[1] (*mɪ*-derl) *nt* (pl ~en) means ; remedy ; **antiseptisch** ~ antiseptic ; **insektenwerend** ~ insect repellent ; **kalmerend** ~ tranquillizer, sedative ; **pijnstillend** ~ anaesthetic ; **stimulerend** ~ stimulant ; **verdovend** ~ drug

middel[2] (*mɪ*-derl) *nt* (pl ~s) waist

middeleeuwen (*mɪ*-derl-āy^{oo}-ern) *pl* Middle Ages

middeleeuws (*mɪ*-derl-āy^{oo}ss) *adj* mediaeval

Middellandse Zee (*mɪ*-der-lahnt-ser-zāy) Mediterranean

middelmatig (mɪ-derl-*maa*-terkh) *adj* moderate ; medium

middelpunt (*mɪ*-derl-pernt) *nt* (pl ~en) centre

middelst (*mɪ*-derlst) *adj* middle

midden (*mɪ*-dern) *nt* midst, middle ; **midden-** medium ; ~ **in** amid ; **te** ~ **van** amid ; among

middernacht (mɪ-derr-*nahkht*) *c* midnight

midzomer (mɪt-*sōa*-merr) *c* midsummer

mier (meer) *c* (pl ~en) ant

mieriks wortel (*mee*-rɪks-vor-terl) *c* (pl ~s) horseradish

migraine (mee-*grai*-ner) *c* migraine

mijl (mayl) *c* (pl ~en) mile

mijlpaal (*mayl*-paal) *c* (pl -palen) milestone ; landmark

mijn[1] (mayn) *pron* my

mijn[2] (mayn) *c* (pl ~en) mine

mijnbouw (*mayn*-bou) *c* mining

mijnheer (mer-*nāyr*) mister

mijnwerker (*mayn*-vehr-kerr) *c* (pl ~s) miner

mikken op (*mɪ*-kern) aim at

mikpunt (*mɪk*-pernt) *nt* (pl ~en) target

mild (mɪlt) *adj* liberal

milieu (meel-^y*ūr*) *nt* (pl ~s) milieu ; environment

militair[1] (mee-lee-*tair*) *adj* military

militair[2] (mee-lee-*tair*) *c* (pl ~en) soldier

miljoen (mɪl-^y*ōōn*) *nt* million

miljonair (mɪl-^yōa-*nair*) *c* (pl ~s) millionaire

min (mɪn) *prep* minus

minachting (*mɪn*-ahkh-tɪng) *c* contempt

minder (*mɪn*-derr) *adv* less

minderheid (*mɪn*-derr-hayt) *c* (pl -heden) minority

minderjarig (mɪn-derr-^y*aa*-rerkh) *adj* under age

minderjarige (mɪn-derr-^y*aa*-rer-ger) *c* (pl ~n) minor

minderwaardig (mɪn-derr-*vaar*-derkh) *adj* inferior

mineraal (mee-ner-*raal*) *nt* (pl -ralen) mineral

mineraalwater (mee-ner-*raal*-vaa-terr) *nt* mineral water

miniatuur (mee-nee-^y*aa*-tēw̄r) *c* (pl -turen) miniature

minimum (*mee*-nee-merm) *nt* (pl -ma) minimum

minister (mee-*nɪss*-terr) *c* (pl ~s) minister

ministerie (mee-nɪss-*tāy*-ree) *nt* (pl

~s) ministry

minnaar (*mi*-naar) *c* (pl ~s) lover

minst (mınst) *adj* least

minstens (*mın*-sterns) *adv* at least

minuscuul (mee-nerss-*kewl*) *adj* tiny, minute

minuut (mee-*newt*) *c* (pl minuten) minute

mis (mıss) *c* (pl ~sen) Mass

misbruik (*miss*-brur^{ew}k) *nt* misuse, abuse

misdaad (*miss*-daat) *c* (pl -daden) crime

misdadig (miss-*daa*-derkh) *adj* criminal

misdadiger (*miss*-daa-der-gerr) *c* (pl ~s) criminal

zich ***misdragen** (miss-*draa*-gern) misbehave

misgunnen (miss-*kher*-nern) *v* grudge

mishagen (miss-*haa*-gern) *v* displease

miskraam (*miss*-kraam) *c* (pl -kramen) miscarriage

mislukking (miss-*ler*-kıng) *c* (pl ~en) failure

mislukt (miss-*lerkt*) *adj* unsuccessful

mismaakt (miss-*maakt*) *adj* deformed

misplaatst (miss-*plaatst*) *adj* misplaced

misschien (mı-*skheen*) *adv* perhaps; maybe

misselijk (*mi*-ser-lerk) *adj* sick; disgusting

misselijkheid (*mi*-ser-lerk-hayt) *c* nausea, sickness

missen (*mi*-sern) *v* lack; miss; spare

misstap (*mi*-stahp) *c* (pl ~pen) slip

mist (mıst) *c* fog, mist

mistig (*miss*-terkh) *adj* foggy, misty

mistlamp (*mist*-lahmp) *c* (pl ~en) foglamp

*misverstaan (*miss*-ferr-staan) *v* *misunderstand

misverstand (*miss*-ferr-stahnt) *nt* (pl

~en) misunderstanding

misvormd (miss-*formt*) *adj* deformed

mits (mıts) *conj* provided that

mobiel (mōā-*beel*) *adj* mobile

modder (*mo*-derr) *c* mud

modderig (*mo*-der-rerkh) *adj* muddy

mode (*mōā*-der) *c* (pl ~s) fashion

model (mōā-*dehl*) *nt* (pl ~len) model

modelleren (mōā-deh-*lāy*-rern) *v* model

modern (mōā-*dehrn*) *adj* modern

modieus (mōā-dee-^y*ürss*) *adj* fashionable

modiste (mōā-*diss*-ter) *c* (pl ~s) milliner

moe (mōō) *adj* tired; weary

moed (mōōt) *c* courage

moeder (*mōō*-derr) *c* (pl ~s) mother

moedertaal (*mōō*-derr-taal) *c* native language, mother tongue

moedig (*mōō*-derkh) *adj* brave, courageous

moeilijk (*mōō*^{ee}-lerk) *adj* difficult; hard

moeilijkheid (*mōō*^{ee}-lerk-hayt) *c* (pl -heden) difficulty

moeite (*mōō*^{ee}-ter) *c* (pl ~n) trouble; pains, difficulty; **de ~ waard *zijn** *be worth-while; **~ *doen** bother

moer (mōōr) *c* (pl ~en) nut ·

moeras (mōō-*rahss*) *nt* (pl ~sen) swamp; bog, marsh

moerassig (mōō-*rah*-serkh) *adj* marshy

moerbei (*mōōr*-bay) *c* (pl ~en) mulberry

moestuin (*mōōss*-tur^{ew}n) *c* (pl ~en) kitchen garden

*moeten (*mōō*-tern) *v* *must; *have to; need to, *ought to, *be obliged to, *should

mogelijk (*mōā*-ger-lerk) *adj* possible

mogelijkheid (*mōā*-ger-lerk-hayt) *c* (pl -heden) possibility

*mogen (*mōā*-gern) *v* *be allowed;

*may; like

mogendheid (*mōa*-gernt-hayt) *c* (pl -heden) power

mohair (*mōa*-hair) *nt* mohair

molen (*mōa*-lern) *c* (pl ~s) mill; windmill

molenaar (*mōa*-ler-naar) *c* (pl ~s) miller

mollig (*mo*-lerkh) *adj* plump

moment (mōa-*mehnt*) *nt* (pl ~en) moment

momentopname (mōa-*mehnt*-op-naamer) *c* (pl ~n) snapshot

monarchie (mōa-nahr-*khee*) *c* (pl ~ën) monarchy

mond (mont) *c* (pl ~en) mouth

mondeling (*mon*-der-lıng) *adj* oral, verbal

monding (*mon*-dıng) *c* (pl ~en) mouth

mondspoeling (*mont*-spōō-lıng) *c* mouthwash

monetair (mōa-*nāy*-tair) *adj* monetary

monnik (*mo*-nerk) *c* (pl ~en) monk

monoloog (mōa-nōa-*lōākh*) *c* (pl -logen) monologue

monopolie (mōa-nōa-*pōā*-lee) *nt* (pl ~s) monopoly

monster (*mon*-sterr) *nt* (pl ~s) sample

monteren (mon-*tāy*-rern) *v* assemble

monteur (mon-*tūrr*) *c* (pl ~s) mechanic

montuur (mon-*tēwr*) *nt* (pl -turen) frame

monument (mōa-*nēw*-*mehnt*) *nt* (pl ~en) monument

mooi (mōa^ee) *adj* beautiful; pretty, fine; nice, lovely, fair

moord (mōart) *c* (pl ~en) assassination, murder

moordenaar (*mōar*-der-naar) *c* (pl ~s) murderer

mop (mop) *c* (pl ~pen) joke

mopperen (*mo*-per-rern) *v* grumble

moraal (mōa-*raal*) *c* moral

moraliteit (mōa-raa-lee-*tayt*) *c* morality

moreel (mōa-*rāyl*) *adj* moral

morfine (mor-*fee*-ner) *c* morphine, morphia

morgen[1] (*mor*-gern) *adv* tomorrow

morgen[2] (*mor*-gern) *c* (pl ~s) morning

morsen (*mor*-sern) *v* *spill

mos (moss) *nt* (pl ~sen) moss

moskee (moss-*kāy*) *c* (pl ~ën) mosque

mossel (*mo*-serl) *c* (pl ~s, ~en) mussel

mosterd (*moss*-terrt) *c* mustard

mot (mot) *c* (pl ~ten) moth

motel (mōa-*tehl*) *nt* (pl ~s) motel

motie (*mōa*-tsee) *c* (pl ~s) motion

motief (mōa-*teef*) *nt* (pl motieven) motive; pattern

motor (*mōa*-terr) *c* (pl ~en, ~s) engine, motor

motorboot (*mōa*-terr-bōat) *c* (pl -boten) motor-boat

motorfiets (*mōa*-terr-feets) *c* (pl ~en) motor-cycle

motorkap (*mōa*-terr-kahp) *c* (pl ~pen) bonnet; hood *nAm*

motorpech (*mōa*-terr-pehkh) *c* breakdown

motorschip (*mōa*-terr-skhıp) *nt* (pl -schepen) launch

motregen (*mot*-rāy-gern) *c* drizzle

mousseline (mōō-ser-*lee*-ner) *c* muslin

mousserend (mōō-*sāy*-rernt) *adj* sparkling

mouw (mou) *c* (pl ~en) sleeve

mozaïek (mōa-zaa-*eek*) *nt* (pl ~en) mosaic

mug (merkh) *c* (pl ~gen) mosquito

muil (mur^ewl) *c* (pl ~en) mouth

muildier (*mur^ewl*-deer) *nt* (pl ~en) mule

muilezel (*mur^ewl*-āy-zerl) *c* (pl ~s)
mule

muis (*mur^ewss*) *c* (pl muizen) mouse

muiterij (*mur^ew*-ter-*ray*) *c* (pl ~en)
mutiny

mul (merl) *c* mullet

munt (mernt) *c* (pl ~en) coin; token;
mint

munteenheid (mernt-āyn-hayt) *c* (pl
-heden) monetary unit

muntstuk (mernt-sterk) *nt* (pl ~ken)
coin

mus (merss) *c* (pl ~sen) sparrow

museum (mēw-*zāy*-ᵞerm) *nt* (pl ~s,
-sea) museum

musical (*m^ᵞōō*-zı-kerl) *c* (pl ~s) musical comedy, musical

musicus (mēw-zee-kerss) *c* (pl -ci)
musician

muskiet (merss-*keet*) *c* (pl ~en) mosquito

muskietennet (merss-*kee*-ter-neht) *nt*
(pl ~ten) mosquito-net

muts (merts) *c* (pl ~en) cap

muur (mēwr) *c* (pl muren) wall

muziek (mēw-*zeek*) *c* music

muziekinstrument (mēw-*zeek*-ın-
strēw-mehnt) *nt* (pl ~en) musical instrument

muzikaal (mēw-zee-*kaal*) *adj* musical

mysterie (mee-*stāy*-ree) *nt* (pl ~s)
mystery

mysterieus (mee-stāy-ree-ᵞūrss) *adj*
mysterious

mythe (*mee*-ter) *c* (pl ~n) myth

N

na (naa) *prep* after

naad (naat) *c* (pl naden) seam

naadloos (*naat*-lōass) *adj* seamless

naaien (*naa^ee*-ern) *v* sew

naaimachine (*naa^ee*-mah-shee-ner) *c*
(pl ~s) sewing-machine

naaister (*naa^ee*-sterr) *c* (pl ~s) dressmaker

naakt (naakt) *adj* nude, naked, bare

naaktstrand (*naakt*-strahnt) *nt* (pl
~en) nudist beach

naald (naalt) *c* (pl ~en) needle

naam (naam) *c* (pl namen) name;
reputation; denomination; **in ~
van** on behalf of

naar[1] (naar) *prep* to, towards; at, for

naar[2] (naar) *adj* nasty, unpleasant

naast (naast) *prep* next to, beside

nabij (naa-*bay*) *adj* near, close

nabijheid (naa-*bay*-hayt) *c* vicinity

nabijzijnd (naa-*bay*-zaynt) *adj* nearby

nabootsen (naa-*bōat*-sern) *v* imitate

naburig (naa-*bōō*-rerkh) *adj* neighbouring

nacht (nahkht) *c* (pl ~en) night; **'s
nachts** by night; overnight

nachtclub (*nahkht*-klerp) *c* (pl ~s)
nightclub, cabaret

nachtcrème (*nahkht*-kraim) *c* (pl ~s)
night-cream

nachtegaal (*nahkh*-ter-gaal) *c* (pl -ga-
len) nightingale

nachtelijk (*nahkh*-ter-lerk) *adj* nightly

nachtjapon (*nahkh*-ᵞaa-pon) *c* (pl
~nen) nightdress

nachttarief (*nahkh*-taa-reef) *nt* (pl -rie-
ven) night rate

nachttrein (*nahkh*-trayn) *c* (pl ~en)
night train

nachtvlucht (*nahkht*-flerkht) *c* (pl
~en) night flight

nadat (naa-*daht*) *conj* after

nadeel (naa-dāyl) *nt* (pl -delen) disadvantage

nadelig (naa-*dāy*-lerkh) *adj* harmful

***nadenken** (*naa*-dehng-kern) *v*
*think; **nadenkend** thoughtful

nader (*naa*-derr) *adj* further

naderen (*naa*-der-rern) *v* approach;
naderend oncoming

naderhand (naa-derr-*hahnt*) *adv* afterwards

nadien (naa-*deen*) *adv* afterwards

nadruk (*naa*-drerk) *c* stress; accent

nagedachtenis (*naa*-ger-dahkh-ter-niss) *c* memory

nagel (*naa*-gerl) *c* (pl ~s) nail

nagelborstel (*naa*-gerl-bors-terl) *c* (pl ~s) nailbrush

nagellak (*naa*-ger-lahk) *c* nail-polish

nagelschaar (*naa*-gerl-skhaar) *c* (pl -scharen) nail-scissors *pl*

nagelvijl (*naa*-gerl-vayl) *c* (pl ~en) nail-file

naïef (naa-*eef*) *adj* naïve

najaar (*naa*-Yaar) *nt* autumn

*****najagen** (*naa*-Yaa-gern) *v* chase

*****nakijken** (*naa*-kay-kern) *v* check

*****nalaten** (*naa*-laa-tern) *v* fail

nalatig (naa-*laa*-terkh) *adj* neglectful

namaak (*naa*-maak) *c* imitation

namaken (*naa*-maa-kern) *v* copy

namelijk (*naa*-mer-lerk) *adv* namely

namens (*naa*-merns) *adv* on behalf of, in the name of

namiddag (*naa*-mı-dahkh) *c* (pl ~en) afternoon

narcis (nahr-*siss*) *c* (pl ~sen) daffodil

narcose (nahr-*kōa*-zer) *c* narcosis

narcoticum (nahr-*kōa*-tee-kerm) *nt* (pl -ca) narcotic

narigheid (*naa*-rerkh-hayt) *c* (pl -heden) misery

naseizoen (*naa*-say-zōōn) *nt* low season

nastreven (*naa*-strāy-vern) *v* aim at, pursue

nat (naht) *adj* wet; damp, moist

natie (*naa*-tsee) *c* (pl ~s) nation

nationaal (naa-tshōa-*naal*) *adj* national; **nationale klederdracht** national dress

nationaliseren (naa-tshōa-naa-lee-*zāy*-rern) *v* nationalize

nationaliteit (naa-tshōa-naa-lee-*tayt*) *c* (pl ~en) nationality

natuur (naa-*tēwr*) *c* nature

natuurkunde (naa-*tēwr*-kern-der) *c* physics

natuurkundige (naa-*tēwr*-*kern*-der-ger) *c* (pl ~n) physicist

natuurlijk (naa-*tēwr*-lerk) *adj* natural; *adv* of course, naturally

natuurreservaat (naa-*tēw*-rāy-zerr-vaat) *nt* (pl -vaten) national park

nauw (nou) *adj* narrow; tight

nauwelijks (*nou*-er-lerks) *adv* hardly; scarcely, barely

nauwkeurig (nou-*kūr*-rerkh) *adj* accurate; precise, careful, exact

navel (*naa*-verl) *c* (pl ~s) navel

navigatie (naa-vee-*gaa*-tsee) *c* navigation

navraag (*naa*-vraakh) *c* inquiry; demand

*****navragen** (*naa*-vraa-gern) *v* query, inquire

*****nazenden** (*naa*-zehn-dern) *v* forward

nederig (*nāy*-der-rerkh) *adj* humble

nederlaag (*nāy*-derr-laakh) *c* (pl -lagen) defeat

Nederland (*nāy*-derr-lahnt) the Netherlands

Nederlander (*nāy*-derr-lahn-derr) *c* (pl ~s) Dutchman

Nederlands (*nāy*-derr-lahnts) *adj* Dutch

nee (nāy) no

neef (nāyf) *c* (pl neven) cousin; nephew

neen (nāyn) no

neer (nāyr) *adv* down; downwards

*****neerlaten** (*nāy*r-laa-tern) *v* lower

*****neerslaan** (*nāy*r-slaan) *v* knock down

neerslachtig (nāyr-*slahkh*-terkh) *adj*

down, low, blue, depressed

neerslachtigheid (na̅yr-*slahkh*-terkh-hayt) *c* depression

neerslag (na̅yr-slahkh) *c* precipitation

neerstorten (na̅yr-stor-tern) *v* crash

negatief (na̅y-gaa-*teef*) *adj* negative

negen (na̅y-gern) *num* nine

negende (na̅y-gern-der) *num* ninth

negentien (na̅y-gern-teen) *num* nineteen

negentiende (na̅y-gern-teen-der) *num* nineteenth

negentig (na̅y-gern-terkh) *num* ninety

neger (na̅y-gerr) *c* (pl ~s) Negro

negeren (ner-ga̅y-rern) *v* ignore

negligé (na̅y-glee-*zha̅y*) *nt* (pl ~s) negligee

neigen (nay-gern) *v* *be inclined to; ~ **tot** *v* tend to

neiging (nay-gɪng) *c* (pl ~en) inclination, tendency; **de** ~ *hebben tend

nek (nehk) *c* (pl ~ken) nape of the neck

***nemen** (na̅y-mern) *v* *take; **op zich** ~ *take charge of

neon (na̅y-Yon) *nt* neon

nergens (nehr-gerns) *adv* nowhere

nerts (nehrts) *nt* (pl ~en) mink

nerveus (nehr-*vu̅rss*) *adj* nervous

nest (nehst) *nt* (pl ~en) nest; litter

net[1] (neht) *adj* tidy, neat

net[2] (neht) *nt* (pl ~ten) net

netnummer (neht-ner-merr) *nt* (pl ~s) area code

netto (neh-to̅a) *adj* net

netvlies (neht-fleess) *nt* (pl -vliezen) retina

netwerk (neht-vehrk) *nt* (pl ~en) network

neuriën (nu̅r-ree-Yern) *v* hum

neurose (nu̅r-ro̅a-zer) *c* (pl ~n, ~s) neurosis

neus (nu̅rss) *c* (pl neuzen) nose

neusbloeding (nu̅rss-blo̅o-dɪng) *c* (pl

~en) nosebleed

neusgat (nu̅rss-khaht) *nt* (pl ~en) nostril

neushoorn (nu̅rss-ho̅arn) *c* (pl ~s) rhinoceros

neutraal (nu̅-*traal*) *adj* neutral

nevel (na̅y-verl) *c* (pl ~s, ~en) haze, mist

nicht (nɪkht) *c* (pl ~en) cousin; niece

nicotine (nee-ko̅a-*tee*-ner) *c* nicotine

niemand (*nee*-mahnt) *pron* nobody, no one

nier (neer) *c* (pl ~en) kidney

niet (neet) *adv* not

nietig (*nee*-terkh) *adj* petty, insignificant; void

nietje (*nee*-tYer) *nt* (pl ~s) staple

niets (neets) *pron* nothing; nil

nietsbetekenend (neets-ber-*ta̅y*-kernernt) *adj* insignificant

nietszeggend (neet-*seh*-gernt) *adj* meaningless

niettemin (nee-ter-*mɪn*) *adv* nevertheless

nieuw (nee⁰⁰) *adj* new

nieuwjaar (nee⁰⁰-*Yaar*) New Year

nieuws (nee⁰⁰ss) *nt* news; tidings *pl*

nieuwsberichten (*nee⁰⁰*ss-ber-rɪkhtern) *pl* news

nieuwsgierig (nee⁰⁰-*skhee*-rerkh) *adj* curious, inquisitive

nieuwsgierigheid (nee⁰⁰-*skhee*-rerkh-hayt) *c* curiosity

Nieuw-Zeeland (nee⁰⁰-*za̅y*-lahnt) New Zealand

niezen (*nee*-zern) *v* sneeze

Nigeria (nee-*ga̅y*-ree-Yaa) Nigeria

Nigeriaan (nee-ga̅y-ree-Yaan) *c* (pl -rianen) Nigerian

Nigeriaans (nee-ga̅y-ree-Yaans) *adj* Nigerian

nijptang (nayp-tahng) *c* (pl ~en) pincers *pl*

nikkel (nɪ-kerl) *nt* nickel

niks (nɪks) *pron* nothing
nimmer (*ni*-merr) *adv* never
niveau (nee-*vōā*) *nt* (pl ~s) level
nivelleren (nee-ver-*lāy*-rern) *v* level
noch ... noch (nokh) neither ... nor
nodig (*nōā*-derkh) *adj* necessary; ~
  *hebben need
noemen (*nōō*-mern) *v* call; name,
  mention
nog (nokh) *adv* still, yet; ~ **een** another; ~ **eens** once more; ~ **wat**
  some more
noga (*nōā*-gaa) *c* nougat
nogal (*no*-gahl) *adv* pretty, fairly,
  rather, quite
nogmaals (*nokh*-maals) *adv* once
  more
nokkenas (*no*-ker-nahss) *c* (pl ~sen)
  camshaft
nominaal (*nōā*-mee-*naal*) *adj* nominal
nominatie (*nōā*-mee-*naa*-tsee) *c* (pl
  ~s) nomination
non (non) *c* (pl ~nen) nun
nonnenklooster (*no*-ner-klōāss-terr) *nt*
  (pl ~s) nunnery
nood (nōāt) *c* (pl noden) distress;
  misery; need
noodgedwongen (*nōāt*-kher-*dvo*-
  ngern) *adv* by force
noodgeval (*nōāt*-kher-vahl) *nt* (pl
  ~len) emergency
noodlot (*nōāt*-lot) *nt* destiny, fate
noodlottig (*nōāt*-*lo*-terkh) *adj* fatal
noodsein (*nōāt*-sayn) *nt* (pl ~en) distress signal
noodtoestand (*nōā*-tōō-stahnt) *c*
  emergency
nooduitgang (*nōāt*-ur^(ew)t-khahng) *c* (pl
  ~en) emergency exit
noodzaak (*nōāt*-saak) *c* need, necessity
noodzakelijk (*nōāt*-*saa*-ker-lerk) *adj*
  necessary
noodzaken (*nōāt*-saa-kern) *v* force

nooit (nōā^(ee)t) *adv* never
Noor (nōār) *c* (pl Noren) Norwegian
noord (nōārt) *c* north
noordelijk (*nōār*-der-lerk) *adj* northern, northerly, north
noorden (*nōār*-dern) *nt* north
noordoosten (nōārt-*ōāss*-tern) *nt*
  north-east
noordpool (*nōārt*-pōāl) *c* North Pole
noordwesten (nōārt-*vehss*-tern) *nt*
  north-west
Noors (nōārs) *adj* Norwegian
Noorwegen (*nōār*-vāy-gern) Norway
noot (nōāt) *c* (pl noten) nut; note
nootmuskaat (nōāt-merss-*kaat*) *c* nutmeg
norm (norm) *c* (pl ~en) standard
normaal (nor-*maal*) *adj* normal, regular
nota (*nōā*-taa) *c* (pl ~'s) bill
notaris (nōā-*taa*-rerss) *c* (pl ~sen) notary
notedop (*nōā*-ter-dop) *c* (pl ~pen)
  nutshell
notekraker (*nōā*-ter-kraa-kerr) *c* (pl
  ~s) nutcrackers *pl*
noteren (nōā-*tāy*-rern) *v* note; list
notie (*nōā*-tsee) *c* notion
notitie (nōā-*tee*-tsee) *c* (pl ~s) note
notitieboek (nōā-*tee*-tsee-bōōk) *nt* (pl
  ~en) notebook
notulen (nōā-*tēw*-lern) *pl* minutes
nou (nou) *adv* now
november (nōā-*vehm*-berr) November
nu (nēw) *adv* now; ~ **en dan** now
  and then; **tot** ~ **toe** so far
nuance (nēw-*ahng*-ser) *c* (pl ~s, ~n)
  nuance
nuchter (*nerkh*-terr) *adj* sober; down-
  to-earth, matter-of-fact
nucleair (nēw-klāy-*Yair*) *adj* nuclear
nul (nerl) *c* (pl ~len) nought, zero
nummer (*ner*-merr) *nt* (pl ~s) number; act

nummerbord (*ner*-merr-bort) *nt* (pl ~en) registration plate; licence plate *Am*

nut (nert) *nt* utility, use

nutteloos (*ner*-ter-lōass) *adj* useless

nuttig (*ner*-terkh) *adj* useful

nylon (*nay*-lon) *nt* nylon

O

oase (ōā-*vaa*-zer) *c* (pl ~n, ~s) oasis

ober (*ōā*-berr) *c* (pl ~s) waiter

object (op-ᵞehkt) *nt* (pl ~en) object

objectief (op-ᵞehk-*teef*) *adj* objective

obligatie (ōā-blee-*gaa*-tsee) *c* (pl ~s) bond

obsceen (op-*sāyn*) *adj* obscene

obscuur (op-*skēwr*) *adj* obscure

observatie (op-sehr-*vaa*-tsee) *c* (pl ~s) observation

observatorium (op-sehr-vaa-*tōā*-ree-ᵞerm) *nt* (pl -ria) observatory

observeren (op-sehr-*vāy*-rern) *v* observe

obsessie (op-*seh*-see) *c* (pl ~s) obsession

obstipatie (op-stee-*paa*-tsee) *c* constipation

oceaan (ōā-*sāy*-ᵞaan) *c* (pl oceanen) ocean

ochtend (*okh*-ternt) *c* (pl ~en) morning

ochtendblad (*okh*-ternt-blaht) *nt* (pl ~en) morning paper

ochtendeditie (*okh*-ternt-āy-dee-tsee) *c* (pl ~s) morning edition

ochtendschemering (*okh*-ternt-skhāy-mer-ring) *c* dawn

octopus (*ok*-tōā-perss) *c* (pl ~sen) octopus

octrooi (ok-*trōāee*) *nt* (pl ~en) patent

oefenen (*ōō*-fer-nern) *v* practise, exercise

oefening (*ōō*-fer-nïng) *c* (pl ~en) exercise

oeroud (*ōōr*-out) *adj* ancient

oerwoud (*ōōr*-vout) *nt* (pl ~en) jungle

oester (*ōōss*-terr) *c* (pl ~s) oyster

oever (*ōō*-verr) *c* (pl ~s) river bank; bank, shore

of (of) *conj* or; whether; ~ ... **of** either ... or; whether ... or

offensief[1] (o-fehn-*seef*) *adj* offensive

offensief[2] (o-fehn-*seef*) *nt* (pl -sieven) offensive

offer (*o*-ferr) *nt* (pl ~s) sacrifice

officieel (o-fee-*shāyl*) *adj* official

officier (o-fee-*seer*) *c* (pl ~en, ~s) officer

officieus (o-fee-*shūrss*) *adj* unofficial

ofschoon (of-*skhōān*) *conj* although, though

ogenblik (*ōā*-germ-blïk) *nt* (pl ~ken) moment, instant

ogenblikkelijk (ōā-germ-*blï*-ker-lerk) *adv* instantly

ogenschaduw (*ōā*-ger-skhaa-dēwᵒᵒ) *c* eye-shadow

oktober (ok-*tōā*-berr) October

olie (*ōā*-lee) *c* oil

olieachtig (*ōā*-lee-ahkh-terkh) *adj* oily

oliebron (*ōā*-lee-bron) *c* (pl ~nen) oil-well

oliedruk (*ōā*-lee-drerk) *c* oil pressure

oliefilter (*ōā*-lee-fïl-terr) *nt* (pl ~s) oil filter

oliën (*ōā*-lee-ᵞern) *v* lubricate

olieraffinaderij (*ōā*-lee-rah-fee-naa-der-ray) *c* (pl ~en) oil-refinery

olieverfschilderij (*ōā*-lee-vehrf-skhïl-der-ray) *nt* (pl ~en) oil-painting

olifant (*ōā*-lee-fahnt) *c* (pl ~en) elephant

olijf (ōā-*layf*) *c* (pl olijven) olive

olijfolie (ōā-*layf*-ōā-lee) *c* olive oil

om (om) *prep* round, about, around;

~ te to, in order to

oma (*ōā*-maa) *c* (pl ~'s) grandmother

***ombrengen** (*om*-breh-ngern) *v* kill

omcirkelen (om-*sir*-ker-lern) *v* encircle

omdat (om-*daht*) *conj* because; as

omdraaien (*om*-draa\ee-ern) *v* turn; invert; **zich ~** turn round

omelet (ōā-mer-*leht*) *nt* (pl ~ten) omelette

***omgaan met** (*om*-gaan) associate with, mix with

omgang (*om*-gahng) *c* intercourse

omgekeerd (*om*-ger-kā̄yrt) *adj* reverse

***omgeven** (om-gā̄y-vern) *v* surround, circle

omgeving (om-*gā̄y*-ving) *c* environment, surroundings *pl*; setting

omheen (om-*hā̄yn*) *adv* about

omheining (om-*hay*-ning) *c* (pl ~en) fence

omhelzen (om-*hehl*-zern) *v* hug, embrace

omhelzing (om-*hehl*-zing) *c* (pl ~en) hug, embrace

omhoog (om-*hōākh*) *adv* up; ~ ***gaan** ascend

omkeer (*om*-kā̄yr) *c* reverse

omkeren (*om*-kā̄y-rern) *v* turn over, turn, turn round

***omkomen** (*om*-kōā-mern) *v* perish

***omkopen** (*om*-kōā-pern) *v* bribe, corrupt

omkoping (*om*-kōā-ping) *c* (pl ~en) bribery, corruption

omlaag (om-*laakh*) *adv* down

omleiding (om-*lay*-ding) *c* (pl ~en) detour

omliggend (*om*-li-gernt) *adj* surrounding

omloop (*om*-lōāp) *c* circulation

omrekenen (*om*-rā̄y-ker-nern) *v* convert

omrekentabel (om-rā̄y-ker-taa-behl) *c* (pl ~len) conversion chart

omringen (om-*ring*-ern) *v* encircle, surround, circle

***omschrijven** (oam-*skhray*-vern) *v* define

omslag (*om*-slahkh) *c/nt* (pl ~en) cover, jacket

omslagdoek (*om*-slahkh-dōōk) *c* (pl ~en) shawl

omstandigheid (om-*stahn*-derkh-hayt) *c* (pl -heden) circumstance; condition

omstreden (om-*strā̄y*-dern) *adj* controversial

omstreeks (om-*strā̄yks*) *adv* about

omtrek (*om*-trehk) *c* (pl ~ken) contour, outline

omtrent (om-*trehnt*) *prep* about, concerning

omvang (*om*-vahng) *c* bulk, size; extent

omvangrijk (om-*vahng*-rayk) *adj* bulky, big; extensive

omvatten (om-*vah*-tern) *v* comprise

omver (om-*vehr*) *adv* down, over

omweg (*om*-vehkh) *c* (pl ~en) detour

omwenteling (*om*-vehn-ter-ling) *c* (pl ~en) revolution

omwisselen (*om*-vi-ser-lern) *v* switch

omzet (*om*-zeht) *c* (pl ~ten) turnover

omzetbelasting (*om*-zeht-ber-lahss-ting) *c* turnover tax; sales tax

onaangenaam (on-*aan*-ger-naam) *adj* unpleasant, disagreeable

onaanvaardbaar (on-aan-*vaart*-baar) *adj* unacceptable

onaardig (on-*aar*-derkh) *adj* unkind

onafgebroken (on-*ahf*-kher-brōā-kern) *adj* continuous

onafhankelijk (on-ahf-*hahng*-ker-lerk) *adj* independent

onafhankelijkheid (on-ahf-*hahng*-ker-lerk-hayt) *c* independence

onbeantwoord (om-ber-*ahnt*-vōärt) *adj* unanswered

onbebouwd (om-ber-*bout*) *adj* uncultivated

onbeduidend (om-ber-*dur^ew*-dernt) *adj* petty, insignificant

onbegaanbaar (om-ber-*gaam*-baar) *adj* impassable

onbegrijpelijk (om-ber-*gray*-per-lerk) *adj* puzzling

onbehaaglijk (om-ber-*haakh*-lerk) *adj* uneasy

onbekend (om-ber-*kehnt*) *adj* unfamiliar, unknown

onbekwaam (om-ber-*kvaam*) *adj* unable, incompetent, incapable

onbelangrijk (om-ber-*lahng*-rayk) *adj* unimportant; insignificant

onbeleefd (om-ber-*lāy̆ft*) *adj* impolite

onbemind (om-ber-*mint*) *adj* unpopular

onbepaald (om-ber-*paalt*) *adj* indefinite; **onbepaalde wijs** infinitive

onbeperkt (om-ber-*pehrkt*) *adj* unlimited

onbeschaamd (om-ber-*skhaamt*) *adj* impudent, impertinent, insolent

onbeschaamdheid (om-ber-*skhaamt*-hayt) *c* impertinence, insolence

onbescheiden (om-ber-*skhay*-dern) *adj* immodest

onbeschermd (om-ber-*skhehrmt*) *adj* unprotected

onbeschoft (oam-ber-*skhoft*) *adj* impertinent

onbetrouwbaar (om-ber-*trou*-baar) *adj* untrustworthy, unreliable

onbevoegd (om-ber-*vōōkht*) *adj* unqualified; unauthorized

onbevredigend (om-ber-*vrāy*-der-gernt) *adj* unsatisfactory

onbewoonbaar (om-ber-*vōam*-baar) *adj* uninhabitable

onbewoond (om-ber-*vōant*) *adj* uninhabited

onbewust (om-ber-*verst*) *adj* unaware

onbezet (om-ber-*zeht*) *adj* unoccupied

onbezonnen (om-ber-*zo*-nern) *adj* rash

onbezorgd (om-ber-*zorkht*) *adj* carefree

onbillijk (om-bi-lerk) *adj* unfair

onbreekbaar (om-*brāyk*-baar) *adj* unbreakable

ondankbaar (on-*dahngk*-baar) *adj* ungrateful

ondanks (*on*-dahngks) *prep* despite, in spite of

ondenkbaar (on-*dehngk*-baar) *adj* inconceivable

onder (*on*-derr) *prep* under; beneath, below; among, amid

onderaan (on-der-*raan*) *adv* below

__onderbreken__ (on-derr-*brāy*-kern) *v* interrupt

onderbreking (on-derr-*brāy̆*-king) *c* (pl ~en) interruption

__onderbrengen__ (*on*-derr-breh-ngern) *v* accommodate

onderbroek (*on*-derr-brōōk) *c* (pl ~en) briefs *pl*, pants *pl*, panties *pl*; shorts *plAm*; underpants *plAm*

onderdaan (*on*-derr-daan) *c* (pl -danen) subject

onderdak (*on*-derr-dahk) *nt* accommodation

onderdeel (*on*-derr-dāȳl) *nt* (pl -delen) spare part

onderdrukken (on-derr-*drer*-kern) *v* suppress

__ondergaan__ (on-derr-*gaan*) *v* suffer

ondergang (*on*-derr-gahng) *c* destruction; ruination, ruin

ondergeschikt (on-derr-ger-*skhikt*) *adj* subordinate; secondary, minor

ondergetekende (on-derr-ger-*tāy*-kern-der) *c* (pl ~n) undersigned

ondergoed (*on*-derr-gōōt) *nt* underwear

ondergronds (on-derr-*gronts*) *adj* underground

ondergrondse (on-derr-*gron*-tser) *c*
subway *nAm*

onderhandelen (on-derr-*hahn*-der-lern)
v negotiate

onderhandeling (on-derr-*hahn*-der-
ling) *c* (pl ~en) negotiation

onderhevig aan (on-derr-*hay*-verkh
aan) subject to; liable to; **aan bederf onderhevig** perishable

onderhoud (*on*-derr-hout) *nt* upkeep;
maintenance

* **onderhouden** (*on*-derr-*hou*-dern) *v*
entertain

onderling (*on*-derr-ling) *adj* mutual

* **ondernemen** (on-derr-*nay*-mern) *v*
*undertake

onderneming (on-derr-*nay*-ming) *c* (pl
~en) enterprise, undertaking; concern, company

onderrichten (on-der-*rikh*-tern) *v* instruct

onderrok (*on*-derr-rok) *c* (pl ~ken)
slip

onderschatten (on-derr-*skhah*-tern) *v*
underestimate

onderscheid (*on*-derr-skhayt) *nt* distinction; difference; ~ **maken** distinguish

* **onderscheiden** (on-derr-*skhay*-dern)
v distinguish

onderst (*on*-derrst) *adj* bottom

ondersteboven (on-derr-ster-*boa*-vern)
adv upside-down

ondersteunen (on-derr-*stur*-nern) *v*
*hold up, support

onderstrepen (on-derr-*stray*-pern) *v*
underline

onderstroom (*on*-derr-stroam) *c* (pl
-stromen) undercurrent

ondertekenen (on-derr-*tay*-ker-nern) *v*
sign

ondertitel (*on*-derr-tee-terl) *c* (pl ~s)
subtitle

ondertussen (on-derr-*ter*-sern) *adv* in

the meantime, meanwhile

* **ondervinden** (on-derr-*vin*-dern) *v* experience

ondervoeding (on-derr-*voo*-ding) *c*
malnutrition

* **ondervragen** (on-derr-*vraa*-gern) *v*
interrogate

onderwerp (*on*-derr-vehrp) *nt* (pl ~en)
subject; topic, theme

* **onderwerpen** (on-derr-*vehr*-pern) *v*
subject; **zich ~** submit

onderwijs (*on*-derr-vayss) *nt* tuition;
education, instruction

* **onderwijzen** (on-derr-*vay*-zern) *v*
*teach

onderwijzer (on-derr-*vay*-zerr) *c* (pl
~s) schoolteacher, schoolmaster,
master, teacher

onderzoek (*on*-derr-zook) *nt* (pl ~en)
enquiry, investigation, inquiry;
check-up, examination; research

* **onderzoeken** (on-derr-*zoo*-kern) *v* enquire, investigate, examine; explore

ondeugend (on-*dur*-gernt) *adj* naughty, mischievous

ondiep (on-*deep*) *adj* shallow

ondoeltreffend (on-dool-*treh*-fehnt)
adj inefficient

ondraaglijk (on-*draakh*-lerk) *adj* unbearable

onduidelijk (on-*dur*ᵉʷ-der-lerk) *adj*
ambiguous

onecht (on-*ehkht*) *adj* false

het oneens *zijn (ert on-*ayns* zayn)
disagree

oneerlijk (on-*ayr*-lerk) *adj* crooked,
dishonest; unfair

oneetbaar (on-*ayt*-baar) *adj* inedible

oneffen (on-*eh*-fern) *adj* uneven

oneindig (on-*ayn*-derkh) *adj* infinite,
endless; immense

onenigheid (on-*ay*-nerkh-hayt) *c* (pl
-heden) dispute

onervaren (on-ehr-*vaa*-rern) *adj* inexperienced

oneven (on-*ay*-vern) *adj* odd

onevenwichtig (on-*ay*-ver-*vikh*-terkh) *adj* unsteady

onfatsoenlijk (om-faht-*soon*-lerk) *adj* indecent

ongeacht (ong-*ger*-ahkht) *prep* in spite of

ongebruikelijk (ong-ger-*brur^ew*-ker-lerk) *adj* unusual

ongeduldig (ong-ger-*derl*-derkh) *adj* impatient; eager

ongedurig (ong-ger-*dew*-rerkh) *adj* restless

ongedwongen (ong-ger-*dvo*-ngern) *adj* casual

ongedwongenheid (ong-ger-*dvo*-nger-hayt) *c* ease

ongeldig (ong-*gehl*-derkh) *adj* invalid

ongelegen (ong-ger-*lay*-gern) *adj* inconvenient

ongelijk (ong-ger-*layk*) *adj* unequal; uneven; ~ *hebben* *be wrong

ongelofelijk (ong-ger-*loa*-fer-lerk) *adj* incredible

ongeluk (*ong*-ger-lerk) *nt* (pl ~ken) accident; misfortune

ongelukkig (ong-ger-*ler*-kerkh) *adj* unhappy; unlucky, unfortunate

ongelukkigerwijs (ong-ger-ler-ker-gerr-*vayss*) *adv* unfortunately

ongemak (*ong*-ger-mahk) *nt* (pl ~ken) inconvenience

ongemakkelijk (ong-ger-*mah*-ker-lerk) *adj* uncomfortable

ongemeubileerd (ong-ger-*mur*-bee-*layrt*) *adj* unfurnished

ongeneeslijk (ong-ger-*nayss*-lerk) *adj* incurable

ongepast (ong-ger-*pahst*) *adj* unsuitable; improper

ongerief (*ong*-ger-reef) *nt* inconvenience

ongerijmd (ong-ger-*raymt*) *adj* absurd

ongerust (ong-ger-*rerst*) *adj* worried; *zich* ~ *maken* worry

ongeschikt (ong-ger-*skhikt*) *adj* unfit

ongeschoold (ong-ger-*skhoalt*) *adj* uneducated; unskilled

ongetrouwd (ong-ger-*trout*) *adj* single

ongetwijfeld (ong-ger-*tvay*-ferlt) *adv* undoubtedly

ongeval (*ong*-ger-vahl) *nt* (pl ~len) accident

ongeveer (ong-ger-*vayr*) *adv* about, approximately

ongevoelig (ong-ger-*voo*-lerkh) *adj* insensitive

ongewenst (ong-ger-*vehnst*) *adj* undesirable

ongewoon (ong-ger-*voan*) *adj* uncommon, unusual

ongezond (ong-ger-*zont*) *adj* unhealthy, unsound

ongunstig (ong-*gerns*-terkh) *adj* unfavourable

onhandig (on-*hahn*-derkh) *adj* clumsy, awkward

onheil (*on*-hayl) *nt* calamity, disaster; mischief

onheilspellend (on-hayl-*speh*-lernt) *adj* sinister; ominous

onherroepelijk (on-heh-*roo*-per-lerk) *adj* irrevocable

onherstelbaar (on-hehr-*stehl*-baar) *adj* irreparable

onjuist (oñ-*ur^ew*st) *adj* incorrect

onkosten (*ong*-koss-tern) *pl* expenses *pl*

onkruid (*ong*-krur^ewt) *nt* weed

onlangs (*on*-lahngs) *adv* recently; lately

onleesbaar (on-*layss*-baar) *adj* illegible

onmetelijk (o-*may*-ter-lerk) *adj* vast, immense

onmiddellijk (o-*mi*-der-lerk) *adj* immediate, prompt; *adv* immediately, instantly

onmogelijk (o-*mōa*-ger-lerk) *adj* impossible

onnauwkeurig (o-nou-*kūr*-rerkh) *adj* inaccurate; incorrect

onnodig (o-*nōa*-derkh) *adj* unnecessary

onontbeerlijk (on-ont-*bāyr*-lerk) *adj* essential

onopvallend (on-op-*fah*-lernt) *adj* inconspicuous

onopzettelijk (on-op-*seh*-ter-lerk) *adj* unintentional

onoverkomelijk (on-ōa-verr-*kōa*-mer-lerk) *adj* prohibitive

onovertroffen (on-ōa-verr-*tro*-fern) *adj* unsurpassed

onpartijdig (om-pahr-*tay*-derkh) *adj* impartial

onpersoonlijk (om-pehr-*sōan*-lerk) *adj* impersonal

onplezierig (om-pler-*zee*-rerkh) *adj* unpleasant

onrecht (*on*-rehkht) *nt* injustice; wrong; ~ ***aandoen** wrong

onrechtvaardig (on-rehkht-*faar*-derkh) *adj* unjust

onredelijk (on-*rāy*-der-lerk) *adj* unreasonable

onregelmatig (on-rāy-gerl-*maa*-terkh) *adj* irregular

onrein (on-*rayn*) *adj* unclean

onrust (*on*-rerst) *c* unrest

onrustig (on-*rerss*-terkh) *adj* restless

ons (ons) *pron* our; us; ourselves

onschadelijk (on-*skhaa*-der-lerk) *adj* harmless

onschatbaar (on-*skhaht*-baar) *adj* priceless

onschuld (*on*-skherlt) *c* innocence

onschuldig (on-*skherl*-derkh) *adj* innocent

ontbijt (ont-*bayt*) *nt* breakfast

***ontbinden** (ont-*bın*-dern) *v* dissolve

***ontbreken** (ont-*brāy*-kern) *v* fail; **ontbrekend** missing

ontdekken (on-*deh*-kern) *v* detect, discover

ontdekking (on-*deh*-kıng) *c* (pl ~en) discovery

ontdooien (on-*dōa*ᵉᵉ-ern) *v* thaw

ontevreden (on-ter-*vrāy*-dern) *adj* dissatisfied; discontented

***ontgaan** (ont-*khaan*) *v* escape

ontglippen (ont-*khlı*-pern) *v* slip

onthaal (ont-*haal*) *nt* reception

***ontheffen** (ont-*heh*-fern) *v* exempt; ~ **van** discharge of

***onthouden** (ont-*hou*-dern) *v* remember; deny; **zich** ~ **van** abstain from

onthullen (ont-*her*-lern) *v* reveal

onthulling (ont-*her*-lıng) *c* (pl ~en) revelation

onthutsen (ont-*hert*-sern) *v* overwhelm

ontkennen (ont-*keh*-nern) *v* deny; **ontkennend** negative

ontkoppelen (ont-*ko*-per-lern) *v* disconnect

ontkurken (ont-*kerr*-kern) *v* uncork

ontleden (ont-*lāy*-dern) *v* analyse; ***break down**

ontlenen (ont-*lāy*-nern) *v* borrow

ontmoeten (ont-*mōō*-tern) *v* encounter; ***meet**

ontmoeting (ont-*mōō*-tıng) *c* (pl ~en) encounter, meeting

***ontnemen** (ont-*nāy*-mern) *v* deprive of

ontoegankelijk (on-tōō-*gahng*-ker-lerk) *adj* inaccessible

ontploffen (ont-*plo*-fern) *v* explode

ontplooien (ont-*plōā*ᵉᵉ-ern) *v* expand

ontroeren (oant-*rōō*-rern) *v* move

ontroering (oant-*rōō*-rıng) *c* emotion

ontrouw (*on*-trou) *adj* unfaithful

ontruimen (ont-*rur*ᵉʷ-mern) *v* vacate

ontschepen (ont-*skhāy*-pern) *v* disembark

* **ontslaan** (ont-*slaan*) *v* dismiss, fire

ontslag * **nemen** (ont-*slahkh* nāy-mern) resign

ontslagneming (ont-*slahkh*-nāy-ming) *c* resignation

ontsmetten (ont-*smeh*-tern) *v* disinfect

ontsmettingsmiddel (ont-*smeh*-tings-mi-derl) *nt* (pl ~en) disinfectant

ontsnappen (ont-*snah*-pern) *v* escape

ontsnapping (ont-*snah*-ping) *c* (pl ~en) escape

ontspannen (ont-*spah*-nern) *adj* easy-going

zich ontspannen (ont-*spah*-nern) relax

ontspanning (ont-*spah*-ning) *c* relaxation; recreation

* **ontstaan** (ont-*staan*) *v* *arise

* **ontsteken** (ont-*stāy*-kern) *v* *become septic

ontsteking (ont-*stāy*-king) *c* (pl ~en) ignition; ignition coil; inflammation

ontstemmen (ont-*steh*-mern) *v* displease

* **ontvangen** (ont-*fah*-ngern) *v* receive; entertain

ontvangst (ont-*fahngst*) *c* (pl ~en) receipt; reception

ontvlambaar (ont-*flahm*-baar) *adj* inflammable

ontvluchten (ont-*flerkh*-tern) *v* escape

ontvouwen (ont-*fou*-ern) *v* unfold

ontwaken (ont-*vaa*-kern) *v* wake up

ontwerp (ont-*vehrp*) *nt* (pl ~en) design

* **ontwerpen** (ont-*vehr*-pern) *v* design

* **ontwijken** (ont-*vay*-kern) *v* avoid

ontwikkelen (ont-*vi*-ker-lern) *v* develop

ontwikkeling (ont-*vi*-ker-ling) *c* (pl ~en) development

ontwricht (ont-*frikht*) *adj* dislocated

ontzag (ont-*sahkh*) *nt* respect

* **ontzeggen** (ont-*seh*-gern) *v* deny

ontzettend (ont-*seh*-ternt) *adj* dreadful, terrible

onuitstaanbaar (on-ur^{ew}t-*staam*-baar) *adj* intolerable

onvast (*on*-vahst) *adj* unsteady

onveilig (on-*vay*-lerkh) *adj* unsafe

onverdiend (*on*-verr-deent) *adj* unearned

onverklaarbaar (on-verr-*klaar*-baar) *adj* unaccountable

onvermijdelijk (on-verr-*may*-der-lerk) *adj* unavoidable, inevitable

onverschillig (on-verr-*skhi*-lerkh) *adj* indifferent

onverstandig (on-verr-*stahn*-derkh) *adj* unwise

onverwacht (*on*-verr-vahkht) *adj* unexpected

onvoldoende (on-vol-*dōōn*-der) *adj* insufficient; inadequate

onvolledig (on-vo-*lāy*-derkh) *adj* incomplete

onvolmaakt (on-vol-*maakt*) *adj* imperfect

onvoorwaardelijk (on-vōar-*vaar*-der-lerk) *adj* unconditional

onvoorzien (on-vōar-*zeen*) *adj* unexpected

onvriendelijk (on-*vreen*-der-lerk) *adj* unkind, unfriendly

onwaar (*on*-vaar) *adj* untrue, false

onwaarschijnlijk (on-vaar-*skhayn*-lerk) *adj* unlikely, improbable

onweer (*on*-vāyr) *nt* thunderstorm

onweerachtig (*on*-vāyr-ahkh-terkh) *adj* thundery

onwel (on-*vehl*) *adj* unwell

onwerkelijk (on-*vehr*-ker-lerk) *adj* unreal

onwetend (on-*vāy*-ternt) *adj* ignorant

onwettig (on-*veh*-terkh) *adj* unlawful, illegal

onwillig (on-*vi*-lerkh) *adj* unwilling

onyx (*ōā*-niks) *nt* onyx

onzeker (on-*zāy*-kerr) *adj* doubtful, uncertain

onzelfzuchtig (on-zehlf-*serkh*-terkh) *adj* unselfish

onzichtbaar (on-*zikht*-baar) *adj* invisible

onzijdig (on-*zay*-derkh) *adj* neuter

onzin (*on*-zin) *c* nonsense, rubbish

oog (ōākh) *nt* (pl ogen) eye

oogarts (*ōākh*-ahrts) *c* (pl ~en) oculist

ooggetuige (*ōā*-kher-tur^ew-ger) *c* (pl ~n) eye-witness

ooglid (*ōākh*-lit) *nt* (pl -leden) eyelid

oogst (ōākhst) *c* (pl ~en) harvest; crop

ooievaar (*ōā*^ee-er-vaar) *c* (pl ~s) stork

ooit (ōā^eet) *adv* ever

ook (ōāk) *adv* also, too; as well

oom (ōām) *c* (pl ~s) uncle

oor (ōār) *nt* (pl oren) ear

oorbel (*ōār*-behl) *c* (pl ~len) earring

oordeel (*ōār*-dāyl) *nt* (pl -delen) judgment

oordelen (*ōār*-dāy-lern) *v* judge

oorlog (*ōār*-lokh) *c* (pl ~en) war

oorlogsschip (*ōār*-lokh-skhip) *nt* (pl -schepen) man-of-war

oorpijn (*ōār*-payn) *c* earache

oorsprong (*ōār*-sprong) *c* (pl ~en) origin

oorspronkelijk (ōār-*sprong*-ker-lerk) *adj* original

oorzaak (*ōār*-zaak) *c* (pl -zaken) cause; reason

oost (ōāst) *c* east; **oost-** eastern

oostelijk (o-ster-lerk) *adj* eastern, easterly

oosten (*ōā*-stern) *nt* east

Oostenrijk (*ōā*-stern-rayk) Austria

Oostenrijker (*ōā*-stern-ray-kerr) *c* (pl ~s) Austrian

Oostenrijks (*ōā*-stern-rayks) *adj* Aus-

trian

oosters (*ōā*-sterrs) *adj* oriental

op (op) *prep* on, upon; at, in; *adv* up; finished

opa (*ōā*-paa) *c* (pl ~'s) grandfather, granddad

opaal (ōā-*paal*) *c* (pl opalen) opal

opbellen (o-beh-lern) *v* call, ring up, phone; call up *Am*

*****opbergen** (o-behr-gern) *v* *put away

opblaasbaar (o-*blaass*-baar) *adj* inflatable

*****opblazen** (o-blaa-zern) *v* inflate

opbouw (o-bou) *c* construction

opbouwen (o-bou-ern) *v* erect; construct

opbrengst (o-brehngst) *c* (pl ~en) produce

opdat (ob-*daht*) *conj* so that

opdracht (*op*-drahkht) *c* (pl ~en) order; assignment

*****opdragen aan** (*oap*-draa-gern) assign to

opeens (op-*āyns*) *adv* suddenly

opeisen (*op*-ay-sern) *v* claim

open (*ōā*-pern) *adj* open

openbaar (*ōā*-pern-baar) *adj* public

openbaren (ōā-perm-*baa*-rern) *v* reveal

opendraaien (*ōā*-per-draa^ee-ern) *v* turn on

openen (*ōā*-per-nern) *v* unlock; open

openhartig (ōā-per-*hahr*-terkh) *adj* open

opening (*ōā*-per-ning) *c* (pl ~en) opening

openingstijden (*ōā*-per-nings-tay-dern) *pl* business hours

opera (*ōā*-per-raa) *c* (pl ~'s) opera; opera house

operatie (ōā-per-*raa*-tsee) *c* (pl ~s) operation, surgery

opereren (ōā-per-*rāy*-rern) *v* operate

operette (ōā-per-*reh*-ter) *c* (pl ~s) operetta

*opgaan (*op*-khaan) v *rise

opgeruimd (*op*-kher-rur^ew mt) adj good-humoured

opgetogen (*oap*-kher-tōa-gern) adj delighted

*opgeven (*oap*-khāy-vern) v declare; *give up

opgewekt (*op*-kher-vehkt) adj cheerful

opgraving (*op*-khraa-vɪng) c (pl ~en) excavation

ophaalbrug (*op*-haal-brerkh) c (pl ~gen) drawbridge

ophalen (*op*-haa-lern) v collect, pick up

*ophangen (*op*-hah-ngern) v *hang

ophanging (*op*-hah-ngɪng) c suspension

ophef (*op*-hehf) c fuss

*opheffen (*op*-heh-fern) v discontinue

ophelderen (*op*-hehl-der-rern) v clarify

*ophouden (*op*-hou-dern) v cease; ~ met stop; quit

opinie (ōā-*pee*-nee) c (pl ~s) opinion

opkomst (*op*-komst) c rise; attendance

oplage (*op*-laa-ger) c (pl ~n) issue

opleiden (*op*-lay-dern) v educate

opletten (*op*-leh-tern) v *pay attention; oplettend attentive

oplichten (*op*-lɪkh-tern) v cheat, swindle

oplichter (*op*-lɪkh-terr) c (pl ~s) swindler

*oplopen (*op*-lōā-pern) v increase; contract

oplosbaar (op-*loss*-baar) adj soluble

oplossen (*op*-lo-sern) v dissolve; solve

oplossing (*op*-lo-sɪng) c (pl ~en) solution

opmerkelijk (op-*mehr*-ker-lerk) adj remarkable; noticeable, striking

opmerken (*op*-mehr-kern) v notice, note; remark

opmerking (*op*-mehr-kɪng) c (pl ~en) remark

opname (*op*-naa-mer) c (pl ~n) recording; shot

*opnemen (*op*-nāy-mern) v *draw

opnieuw (op-*nee^oo*) adv again

opofferen (*op*-o-fer-rern) v sacrifice

oponthoud (*op*-ont-hout) nt delay

oppassen (*o*-pah-sern) v look out, beware

oppasser (*o*-pah-serr) c (pl ~s) attendant

opperhoofd (*o*-perr-hōāft) nt (pl ~en) chieftain

oppervlakkig (o-perr-*vlah*-kerkh) adj superficial

oppervlakte (*o*-perr-vlahk-ter) c (pl ~n, ~s) surface; area

oppositie (o-pōā-*see*-tsee) c (pl ~s) opposition

oprapen (*op*-raa-pern) v pick up

oprecht (op-*rehkht*) adj honest, sincere

oprichten (*op*-rɪkh-tern) v found; erect

*oprijzen (*op*-ray-zern) v *arise

oproer (*op*-rōōr) nt revolt, rebellion

opruimen (*op*-rur^ew-mern) v tidy up

opruiming (*op*-rur^ew-mɪng) c clearance sale

opscheppen (*op*-skheh-pern) v boast

*opschieten (*op*-skhee-tern) v hurry

opschorten (*op*-skhor-tern) v *put off

*opschrijven (*op*-skhray-vern) v *write down

*opslaan (*op*-slaan) v store

opslag^1 (*op*-slahkh) c storage

opslag^2 (*op*-slahkh) c rise; raise nAm

opslagplaats (*op*-slahkh-plaats) c (pl ~en) depot

*opsluiten (*op*-slur^ew-tern) v lock up

opsporen (*op*-spōā-rern) v trace

*opstaan (*op*-staan) v *get up, *rise

opstand (*op*-stahnt) c (pl ~en) rising, revolt, rebellion; in ~ *komen revolt

opstapelen (*op*-staa-per-lern) *v* pile

opstel (*op*-stehl) *nt* (pl ~len) essay

opstellen (*op*-steh-lern) *v* *draw up, *make up

***opstijgen** (*op*-stay-gern) *v* ascend

optellen (*op*-teh-lern) *v* add ; count

optelling (*op*-teh-lıng) *c* (pl ~en) addition

opticien (op-tee-*shang*) *c* (pl ~s) optician

optillen (*op*-tı-lern) *v* lift ; raise

optimisme (op-tee-*mıss*-mer) *nt* optimism

optimist (op-tee-*mıst*) *c* (pl ~en) optimist

optimistisch (op-tee-*mıss*-teess) *adj* optimistic

optocht (*op*-tokht) *c* (pl ~en) parade

optreden (*op*-trāy-dern) *nt* (pl ~s) appearance

***optreden** (*op*-trāy-dern) *v* act ; appear

***opvallen** (*op*-fah-lern) *v* attract attention ; **opvallend** striking

opvatten (*op*-fah-tern) *v* conceive

opvatting (*op*-fah-tıng) *c* (pl ~en) view

opvoeden (*op*-fōō-dern) *v* *bring up, educate

opvoeding (*op*-fōō-dıng) *c* education

opvolgen (*op*-fol-gern) *v* succeed

***opvouwen** (*op*-fou-ern) *v* fold

opvrolijken (*op*-frōa-ler-kern) *v* cheer up

opvullen (*op*-fer-lern) *v* fill up

***opwinden** (*op*-vın-dern) *v* *wind ; excite

opwinding (*op*-vın-dıng) *c* excitement

opzettelijk (op-*seh*-ter-lerk) *adj* deliberate, intentional ; on purpose

opzicht (*op*-sıkht) *nt* (pl ~en) respect

opzichter (*op*-sıkh-terr) *c* (pl ~s) supervisor ; warden

opzienbarend (op-seen-*baa*-rernt) *adj* sensational

opzij (op-*say*) *adv* aside ; sideways

***opzoeken** (*op*-sōō-kern) *v* look up

oranje (ōa-*rah*-ñer) *adj* orange

orde[1] (*or*-der) *c* order ; method ; **in** ~ in order ; **in orde!** okay!, all right!

orde[2] (*or*-der) *c* (pl ~n, ~s) congregation

ordenen (*or*-der-nern) *v* arrange

ordinair (or-dee-*nair*) *adj* common, vulgar

orgaan (or-*gaan*) *nt* (pl organen) organ

organisatie (or-gaa-nee-*zaa*-tsee) *c* (pl ~s) organization

organisch (or-*gaa*-neess) *adj* organic

organiseren (or-gaa-nee-*zāy*-rern) *v* organize

orgel (*or*-gerl) *nt* (pl ~s) organ

zich oriënteren (ōa-ree-Yehn-*tāy*-rern) orientate

origine (ōa-ree-*zhee*-ner) *c* origin

origineel (ōa-ree-zhee-*nāyl*) *adj* original

orkaan (or-*kaan*) *c* (pl orkanen) hurricane

orkest (or-*kehst*) *nt* (pl ~en) orchestra ; band

orlon (*or*-lon) *nt* orlon

ornamenteel (or-naa-mehn-*tāyl*) *adj* ornamental

orthodox (or-tōā-*doks*) *adj* orthodox

os (oss) *c* (pl ~sen) ox

oud (out) *adj* old ; ancient ; aged ; **ouder** elder ; **oudst** eldest, elder

oudbakken (out-*bah*-kern) *adj* stale

ouderdom (*ou*-derr-dom) *c* age ; old age

ouders (*ou*-derrs) *pl* parents *pl*

ouderwets (ou-derr-*vehts*) *adj* old-fashioned, ancient ; out of date ; quaint

oudheden (*out*-hāy-dern) *pl* antiquities *pl*

Oudheid (_out_-hayt) c antiquity

oudheidkunde (_out_-hayt-kern-der) c archaeology

ouverture (oō-verr-_teŵ_-rer) c (pl ~s, ~n) overture

ouvreuse (oō-_vrūr_-zer) c (pl ~s) usherette

ovaal (ōā-_vaal_) adj oval

oven (ōā-vern) c (pl ~s) oven ; furnace

over (ōā-verr) prep about ; over ; across ; in ; adv over

overal (ōā-verr-ahl) adv everywhere ; anywhere, throughout

overall (ōā-ver-_rahl_) c (pl ~s) overalls pl

overblijfsel (ōā-verr-blayf-serl) nt (pl ~s, ~en) remnant

*__overblijven__ (ōā-verr-blay-vern) v remain

overbodig (ōā-verr-_bōā_-derkh) adj superfluous ; redundant

*__overbrengen__ (ōā-verr-breh-ngern) v transfer

overdag (ōā-verr-_dahkh_) adv by day

*__overdenken__ (ōā-verr-_dehng_-kern) v *think over

*__overdrijven__ (ōā-verr-_dray_-vern) v exaggerate ; **overdreven** extravagant

*__overeenkomen__ (ōā-ver-_rāyng_-kōā-mern) v agree ; correspond

overeenkomst (ōā-ver-_rāyng_-komst) c (pl ~en) agreement, settlement

overeenkomstig (ōā-ver-_rāyng_-_kom_-sterkh) adj similar ; prep according to

overeenstemming (ōā-ver-_rāyn_-steh-mıng) c agreement

overeind (ōā-ver-_raynt_) adv upright ; erect

overgang (ōā-verr-_gahng_) c (pl ~en) transition

overgave (ōā-verr-gaa-ver) c surrender

*__overgeven__ (ōā-verr-_gāy_-vern) v vom-

it ; **zich** *__overgeven__ surrender

overhaast (ōā-verr-_haast_) adj rash

overhalen (ōā-verr-haa-lern) v persuade

overheersing (ōā-verr-_hāyr_-sıng) c domination

overheid (ōā-verr-hayt) c (pl -heden) authorities pl

overhemd (ōā-verr-hehmt) nt (pl ~en) shirt

overig (ōā-ver-rerkh) adj remaining

overigens (ōā-ver-rer-gerns) adv though

overjas (ōā-verr-Yahss) c (pl ~sen) topcoat, overcoat

aan de overkant (aan der ōā-verr-kahnt) across

overleg (ōā-verr-_lehkh_) nt deliberation

overleggen (ōā-verr-_leh_-gern) v deliberate

overleven (ōā-verr-_lāy_-vern) v survive

overleving (ōā-verr-_lāy_vıng) c survival

*__overlijden__ (ōā-verr-_lay_-dern) v depart, die

overmaken (ōā-verr-maa-kern) v remit

overmoedig (ōā-verr-_mōō_-derkh) adj presumptuous

*__overnemen__ (ōā-verr-_nāy_-mern) v *take over

overreden (ōā-verr-_rāy_-dern) v persuade

overschot (ōā-verr-skhot) nt (pl ~ten) surplus

*__overschrijden__ (ōā-verr-_skhray_-dern) v exceed

overschrijving (ōā-verr-skhray-vıng) c (pl ~en) money order

*__overslaan__ (ōā-verr-slaan) v skip

overspannen (ōā-verr-_spah_-nern) adj overstrung

overstappen (ōā-verr-stah-pern) v change

oversteekplaats (ōā-verr-stāyk-plaats) c (pl ~en) crossing

* **oversteken** (ōā-verr-stāy-kern) v
cross

overstroming (ōā-verr-strōā-mıng) c
(pl ~en) flood

overstuur (ōā-verr-stewr) adj upset

overtocht (ōā-verr-tokht) c (pl ~en)
crossing, passage

* **overtreden** (ōā-verr-trāy-dern) v offend

overtreding (ōā-verr-trāy-dıng) c (pl
~en) offence

* **overtreffen** (ōā-verr-treh-fern) v
*outdo, exceed

overtuigen (ōā-verr-tur^ew-gern) v convince; persuade

overtuiging (ōā-verr-tur^ew-gıng) c (pl
~en) conviction; persuasion

overval (ōā-verr-vahl) c (pl ~len)
hold-up

oververmoeid (ōā-verr-verr-mōō^eet)
adj over-tired

overvloed (ōā-verr-vlōōt) c abundance; plenty

overvloedig (ōā-verr-vlōō-derkh) adj
abundant, plentiful

overvol (ōā-verr-vol) adj crowded

overweg (ōā-verr-vehkh) c (pl ~en)
level crossing, crossing

* **overwegen** (ōā-verr-vāy-gern) v consider

overweging (ōā-verr-vāy-gıng) c (pl
~en) consideration

overweldigen (ōā-verr-vehl-der-gern) v
overwhelm

zich overwerken (ōā-verr-vehr-kern)
overwork

* **overwinnen** (ōā-verr-vı-nern) v conquer; *overcome

overwinning (ōā-verr-vı-nıng) c (pl
~en) victory

overzees (ōā-verr-zāyss) adj overseas

overzicht (ōā-verr-zıkht) nt (pl ~en)
survey

P

paal (paal) c (pl palen) post, pole

paar (paar) nt (pl paren) pair; couple

paard (paart) nt (pl ~en) horse

paardebloem (paar-der-blōōm) c (pl
~en) dandelion

paardekracht (paar-der-krahkht) c
horsepower

paardesport (paar-der-sport) c riding

* **paardrijden** (paart-ray-dern) v *ride

paarlemoer (paar-ler-mōōr) nt mother-
of-pearl

paars (paars) adj purple

pacht (pahkht) c (pl ~en) lease

pacifisme (pah-see-fiss-mer) nt pacifism

pacifist (pah-see-fist) c (pl ~en) pacifist

pacifistisch (pah-see-fiss-teess) adj
pacifist

pad[1] (paht) nt (pl ~en) path; lane,
trail

pad[2] (paht) c (pl ~den) toad

paddestoel (pah-der-stōōl) c (pl ~en)
toadstool; mushroom

padvinder (paht-fın-derr) c (pl ~s)
scout, boy scout

padvindster (paht-fınt-sterr) c (pl ~s)
girl guide

pagina (paa-gee-naa) c (pl ~'s) page

pak (pahk) nt (pl ~ken) package

pakhuis (pahk-hur^ewss) nt (pl -huizen)
warehouse

Pakistaan (paa-kee-staan) c (pl -sta-
nen) Pakistani

Pakistaans (paa-kee-staans) adj Pakistani

Pakistan (paa-kıss-tahn) Pakistan

pakje (pahk-Yer) nt (pl ~s) parcel,
packet

pakken (pah-kern) v *take

pakket (pah-*keht*) *nt* (pl ~ten) parcel

pakpapier (*pahk*-paa-peer) *nt* wrapping paper

paleis (paa-*layss*) *nt* (pl paleizen) palace

paling (*paa*-ling) *c* (pl ~en) eel

palm (pahlm) *c* (pl ~en) palm

pan (pahn) *c* (pl ~nen) pan

pand (pahnt) *nt* (pl ~en) security; house, premises *pl*

pandjesbaas (*pahn*-t^yerss-baass) *c* (pl -bazen) pawnbroker

paneel (paa-*nāyl*) *nt* (pl panelen) panel

paniek (paa-*neek*) *c* panic

panne (*pah*-ner) *c* breakdown

pantoffel (pahn-*to*-ferl) *c* (pl ~s) slipper

panty (*pehn*-tee) *c* (pl panties) pantyhose

papa (*pah*-paa) *c* (pl ~'s) daddy

papaver (paa-*paa*-verr) *c* (pl ~s) poppy

papegaai (pah-per-*gaa*ᵉᵉ) *c* (pl ~en) parrot

papier (paa-*peer*) *nt* (pl ~en) paper

papieren (paa-*pee*-rern) *adj* paper; ~ **servet** paper napkin; ~ **zak** paper bag; ~ **zakdoek** kleenex

parade (paa-*raa*-der) *c* (pl ~s) parade

paraferen (paa-raa-*fāy*-rern) *v* initial

paragraaf (paa-raa-*graaf*) *c* (pl -grafen) paragraph

parallel (paa-raa-*lehl*) *adj* parallel

paraplu (paa-raa-*plēw*) *c* (pl ~'s) umbrella

parasol (paa-raa-*sol*) *c* (pl ~s) sunshade

pardon! (pahr-*don*) sorry!

parel (*paa*-rerl) *c* (pl ~s, ~en) pearl

parfum (pahr-*ferm*) *nt* (pl ~s) perfume

park (pahrk) *nt* (pl ~en) park

parkeermeter (pahr-*kāyr*-māy-terr) *c* (pl ~s) parking meter

parkeerplaats (pahr-*kāyr*-plaats) *c* (pl ~en) car park; parking lot *Am*

parkeertarief (pahr-*kāyr*-taa-reef) *nt* (pl -tarieven) parking fee

parkeerzone (pahr-*kāyr*-zaw-ner) *c* (pl ~s) parking zone

parkeren (pahr-*kāy*-rern) *v* park

parkiet (pahr-*keet*) *c* (pl ~en) parakeet

parlement (pahr-ler-*mehnt*) *nt* (pl ~en) parliament

parlementair (pahr-ler-mehn-*tair*) *adj* parliamentary

parochie (pah-*ro*-khee) *c* (pl ~s) parish

particulier (pahr-tee-kēw-*leer*) *adj* private

partij (pahr-*tay*) *c* (pl ~en) party; side; batch

partijdig (pahr-*tay*-derkh) *adj* partial

partner (*pahrt*-nerr) *c* (pl ~s) partner; associate

pas¹ (pahss) *c* (pl ~sen) step

pas² (pahss) *adv* just

Pasen (*paa*-sern) Easter

pasfoto (*pahss*-fōa-tōa) *c* (pl ~'s) passport photograph

paskamer (*pahss*-kaa-merr) *c* (pl ~s) fitting room

paspoort (*pahss*-pōart) *nt* (pl ~en) passport

paspoortcontrole (*pahss*-pōart-kon-traw-ler) *c* passport control

passage (pah-*saa*-zher) *c* (pl ~s) excerpt; passage

passagier (pah-saa-*zheer*) *c* (pl ~s) passenger

passen (*pah*-sern) *v* try on; fit; ~ **bij** match; **passend** appropriate; convenient, adequate, proper; ~ **op** look after; attend to

passeren (pah-*sāy*-rern) *v* pass; bypass, pass by

passie (*pah*-see) *c* passion

passief (pah-*seef*) *adj* passive

pasta (*pahss*-taa) *c* (pl ~'s) paste

pastorie (pahss-tōa-*ree*) *c* (pl ~ën) parsonage, vicarage, rectory

patent (paa-*tehnt*) *nt* (pl ~en) patent

pater (*paa*-terr) *c* (pl ~s) father

patient (paa-*shehnt*) *c* (pl ~en) patient

patrijs (paa-*trayss*) *c* (pl patrijzen) partridge

patrijspoort (paa-*trayss*-pōart) *c* (pl ~en) porthole

patriot (paa-tree-*Y*ot) *c* (pl ~ten) patriot

patroon (paa-*trōan*) *nt* (pl patronen) pattern; *c* cartridge

patrouille (paa-*trōō*-Yer) *c* (pl ~s) patrol

patrouilleren (paa-trōō-*Yay*-rern) *v* patrol

paus (pouss) *c* (pl ~en) pope

pauw (pou) *c* (pl ~en) peacock

pauze (*pou*-zer) *c* (pl ~s) pause; break; interval, intermission

pauzeren (pou-*zay*-rern) *v* pause

paviljoen (paa-vil-*Yōon*) *nt* (pl ~en, ~s) pavilion

pech (pehkh) *c* bad luck

pedaal (per-*daal*) *nt/c* (pl pedalen) pedal

peddel (*peh*-derl) *c* (pl ~s) paddle

pedicure (pāy-dee-*kew*-rer) *c* (pl ~s) pedicure, chiropodist

peen (pāyn) *c* (pl penen) carrot

peer (pāyr) *c* (pl peren) pear; light bulb

pees (pāyss) *c* (pl pezen) sinew, tendon

peetvader (*pāyt*-faa-derr) *c* (pl ~s) godfather

peil (payl) *nt* (pl ~en) level

pelgrim (*pehl*-grɪm) *c* (pl ~s) pilgrim

pelikaan (pāy-lee-*kaan*) *c* (pl -kanen) pelican

pels (pehls) *c* (pl pelzen) fur

pen (pehn) *c* (pl ~nen) pen

penicilline (pāy-nee-see-*lee*-ner) *c* penicillin

penningmeester (*peh*-nɪng-māyss-terr) *c* (pl ~s) treasurer

penseel (pehn-*sāyl*) *nt* (pl -selen) paint-brush

pensioen (pehn-*shōon*) *nt* (pl ~en) pension

pension (pehn-*shon*) *nt* (pl ~s) board; boarding-house, guesthouse, pension; **vol ~** full board, board and lodging, bed and board

peper (*pāy*-perr) *c* pepper

pepermunt (pāy-perr-*mernt*) *c* peppermint

per (pehr) *prep* by

perceel (pehr-*sāyl*) *nt* (pl -celen) plot

percentage (pehr-sehn-*taa*-zher) *nt* (pl ~s) percentage

percolator (pehr-kōa-*laa*-tor) *c* (pl ~s) percolator

perfectie (pehr-*fehk*-see) *c* perfection

periode (pāy-ree-*Y*ōa-der) *c* (pl ~s, ~n) period; term

periodiek (pāy-ree-*Y*ōa-*deek*) *adj* periodical

permanent (pehr-maa-*nehnt*) *adj* permanent; *c* permanent wave

permissie (pehr-*mɪ*-see) *c* permission

perron (peh-*ron*) *nt* (pl ~s) platform

perronkaartje (peh-*ron*-kaar-tYer) *nt* (pl ~s) platform ticket

Pers (pehrs) *c* (pl Perzen) Persian

pers (pehrs) *c* press

persconferentie (pehrs-kon-fer-rehn-tsee) *c* (pl ~s) press conference

persen (*pehr*-sern) *v* press

personeel (pehr-sōa-*nāyl*) *nt* personnel

personentrein (pehr-*sōa*-ner-trayn) *c* (pl ~en) passenger train

persoon (pehr-*sōan*) *c* (pl -sonen) person; **per** ~ per person

persoonlijk (pehr-*sōan*-lerk) *adj* personal; private

persoonlijkheid (pehr-*sōan*-lerk-hayt) *c* (pl -heden) personality

perspectief (pehr-spehk-*teef*) *nt* (pl -tieven) perspective

Perzië (*pehr*-zee-Yer) Persia

perzik (*pehr*-zik) *c* (pl ~en) peach

Perzisch (*pehr*-zeess) *adj* Persian

pessimisme (peh-see-*miss*-mer) *nt* pessimism

pessimist (peh-see-*mist*) *c* (pl ~en) pessimist

pessimistisch (peh-see-*miss*-teess) *adj* pessimistic

pet (peht) *c* (pl ~ten) cap

peterselie (pāy-terr-*sāy*-lee) *c* parsley

petitie (per-*tee*-tsee) *c* (pl ~s) petition

petroleum (pāy-*trōa*-lāy-Yerm) *c* petroleum; kerosene, paraffin

peuter (*pūr*-terr) *c* (pl ~s) toddler

pianist (pee-Yaa-*nist*) *c* (pl ~en) pianist

piano (pee-Yaa-*nōa*) *c* (pl ~'s) piano

piccolo (pee-kōa-lōa) *c* (pl ~'s) pageboy, bellboy

picknick (*pik*-nik) *c* (pl ~s) picnic

picknicken (*pik*-ni-kern) *v* picnic

pick-up (pik-*erp*) *c* (pl ~s) record-player

pienter (*peen*-terr) *adj* bright, smart, clever

pier (peer) *c* (pl ~en) pier, jetty

pijl (payl) *c* (pl ~en) arrow

pijn (payn) *c* (pl ~en) ache, pain; ~ *doen **hurt; ache

pijnlijk (*payn*-lerk) *adj* sore, painful; embarrassing, awkward

pijnloos (*payn*-lōass) *adj* painless

pijp (payp) *c* (pl ~en) pipe; tube

pijpestoker (*pay*-per-stōa-kerr) *c* (pl ~s) pipe cleaner

pijptabak (*payp*-taa-bahk) *c* pipe to-

bacco

pikant (pee-*kahnt*) *adj* spicy; savoury

pil (pil) *c* (pl ~len) pill

pilaar (pee-*laar*) *c* (pl pilaren) column, pillar

piloot (pee-*lōat*) *c* (pl piloten) pilot

pils (pils) *nt* beer

pincet (pin-*seht*) *c* (pl ~ten) tweezers *pl*

pinda (*pin*-daa) *c* (pl ~'s) peanut

pinguin (*pin*-gvin) *c* (pl ~s) penguin

pink (pingk) *c* (pl ~en) little finger

Pinksteren (*pingk*-ster-rern) Whitsun

pion (pee-Yon) *c* (pl ~nen) pawn

pionier (pee-Yōa-*neer*) *c* (pl ~s) pioneer

piraat (pee-*raat*) *c* (pl piraten) pirate

piste (*peess*-ter) *c* (pl ~s) ring

pistool (peess-*tōal*) *nt* (pl pistolen) pistol

pit (pit) *c* (pl ~ten) stone, pip

pittoresk (pee-tōa-*rehsk*) *adj* picturesque

plaag (plaakh) *c* (pl plagen) plague

plaat (plaat) *c* (pl platen) plate, sheet; picture

plaats (plaats) *c* (pl ~en) place; spot, locality, site; seat; room; **in** ~ **van** instead of

plaatselijk (*plaat*-ser-lerk) *adj* local; regional

plaatsen (*plaat*-sern) *v* *lay, *put, place; locate

***plaatshebben** (*plaats*-heh-bern) *v* *take place

plaatskaartenbureau (*plaats*-kaar-ter-bew-rōa) *nt* (pl ~s) box-office

plaatsvervanger (*plaats*-ferr-vah-ngerr) *c* (pl ~s) deputy, substitute

plafond (plaa-*font*) *nt* (pl ~s) ceiling

plagen (*plaa*-gern) *v* tease

plakband (*plahk*-bahnt) *nt* scotch tape, adhesive tape

plakboek (*plahk*-bōok) *nt* (pl ~en)

scrap-book

plakken (*plah*-kern) *v* *stick; paste

plan (plahn) *nt* (pl ~nen) plan; project, scheme; **van ~ *zijn** intend

planeet (plaa-*nāyt*) *c* (pl -neten) planet

planetarium (plaa-ner-*taa*-ree-ᵞerm) *nt* (pl ~s, -ria) planetarium

plank (plahngk) *c* (pl ~en) board, plank; shelf

plannen (*pleh*-nern) *v* plan

plant (plahnt) *c* (pl ~en) plant

plantage (plahn-*taa*-zher) *c* (pl ~s) plantation

planten (*plahn*-tern) *v* plant

plantengroei (*plahn*-ter-grōoᵉᵉ) *c* vegetation

plantkunde (*plahnt*-kern-der) *c* botany

plantsoen (plahnt-*sōon*) *nt* (pl ~en) public garden

plas (plahss) *c* (pl ~sen) puddle

plastic (*pleh*-stɪk) *adj* plastic

plat (plaht) *adj* flat; even, level

platenspeler (*plaa*-ter-spāy-lerr) *c* (pl ~s) record-player

platina (*plaa*-tee-naa) *nt* platinum

plattegrond (plah-ter-*gront*) *c* (pl ~en) map, plan

platteland (plah-ter-*lahnt*) *nt* countryside, country; **plattelands-** rural

platzak (*plaht*-sahk) broke

plaveien (plaa-*vay*-ern) *v* pave

plaveisel (plaa-*vay*-serl) *nt* pavement

plechtig (*plehkh*-terkh) *adj* solemn

pleegouders (*plāykh*-ou-derrs) *pl* foster-parents *pl*

plegen (*plāy*-gern) *v* commit

pleidooi (play-*dōaᵉᵉ*) *nt* (pl ~en) plea

plein (playn) *nt* (pl ~en) square

pleister[1] (*play*-sterr) *c* (pl ~s) plaster

pleister[2] (*play*-sterr) *nt* plaster

pleiten (*play*-tern) *v* plead

plek (plehk) *c* (pl ~ken) spot; **blauwe ~ bruise**; **zere ~ sore**

plezier (pler-*zeer*) *nt* pleasure; fun

plicht (plɪkht) *c* (pl ~en) duty

ploeg[1] (plōokh) *c* (pl ~en) plough

ploeg[2] (plōokh) *c* (pl ~en) team; shift; gang

ploegen (*plōo*-gern) *v* plough

plooi (plōaᵉᵉ) *c* (pl ~en) crease

plooihoudend (plōaᵉᵉ-*hou*-dernt) *adj* permanent press

plotseling (*plot*-ser-lɪng) *adj* sudden

plukken (*pler*-kern) *v* pick

plus (plerss) *prep* plus

pneumatisch (pnūr-*maa*-teess) *adj* pneumatic

pocketboek (*po*-kert-bōok) *nt* (pl ~en) paperback

poeder (*pōo*-derr) *nt/c* (pl ~s) powder

poederdons (*pōo*-derr-dons) *c* (pl -donzen) powder-puff

poederdoos (*pōo*-derr-dōass) *c* (pl -dozen) powder compact

poelier (pōo-*leer*) *c* (pl ~s) poulterer

poes (pōoss) *c* (pl poezen) pussy-cat

poetsen (*pōo*-tsern) *v* brush; polish

pogen (*pōa*-gern) *v* try

poging (*pōa*-ging) *c* (pl ~en) try, attempt; effort

pokken (*po*-kern) *pl* smallpox

Polen (*pōa*-lern) Poland

polio (*pōa*-lee-ᵞōa) *c* polio

polis (*pōa*-lerss) *c* (pl ~sen) policy

politicus (pōa-*lee*-tee-kerss) *c* (pl -ci) politician

politie (pōa-*lee*-tsee) *c* police *pl*

politieagent (pōa-*lee*-tsi-aa-gehnt) *c* (pl ~en) policeman

politiebureau (pōa-*lee*-tsee-bēw-rōa) *nt* (pl ~s) police-station

politiek (pōa-lee-*teek*) *adj* political; *c* policy; politics

pols (pols) *c* (pl ~en) wrist; pulse

polshorloge (*pols*-hor-lōa-zher) *nt* (pl ~s) wrist-watch

polsslag (*pol*-slahkh) *c* pulse

pomp (pomp) *c* (pl ~en) pump
pompelmoes (*pom*-perl-mōōss) *c* (pl -moezen) grapefruit
pompen (*pom*-pern) *v* pump
pond (pont) *nt* pound
Pool (pōal) *c* (pl Polen) Pole
Pools (pōals) *adj* Polish
poort (pōart) *c* (pl ~en) gate
poosje (*pōa*-sher) *nt* while
poot (pōat) *c* (pl poten) leg; paw
pop (pop) *c* (pl ~pen) doll
popeline (pōa-per-*lee*-ner) *nt/c* poplin
popmuziek (*pop*-mew-zeek) *c* pop music
poppenkast (*po*-per-kahst) *c* puppet-show
populair (pōa-pew-*lair*) *adj* popular
porselein (por-seh-*layn*) *nt* porcelain, china
portefeuille (por-ter-*fur*ew-Yer) *c* (pl ~s) pocket-book, wallet
portemonnee (por-ter-mo-*nāy*) *c* (pl ~s) purse
portie (*por*-see) *c* (pl ~s) portion; helping
portier (por-*teer*) *c* (pl ~s) doorman, door-keeper, porter
portret (por-*treht*) *nt* (pl ~ten) portrait
Portugal (*por*-tew-gahl) Portugal
Portugees (por-tew-*gāyss*) *adj* Portuguese
positie (pōa-*zee*-tsee) *c* (pl ~s) position
positief (pōa-zee-*teef*) *adj* positive
post[1] (post) *c* mail, post
post[2] (post) *c* (pl ~en) entry
postbode (*post*-bōa-der) *c* (pl ~s, ~n) postman
postcode (*post*-kōa-der) *c* (pl ~s) zip code *Am*
posten (*poss*-tern) *v* mail, post
poste restante (post-rehss-*tahnt*) poste restante

posterijen (poss-ter-*ray*-ern) *pl* postal service
postkantoor (*post*-kahn-tōar) *nt* (pl -toren) post-office
postwissel (*post*-vi-serl) *c* (pl ~s) postal order; mail order *Am*
postzegel (*post*-sāy-gerl) *c* (pl ~s) postage stamp, stamp
postzegelautomaat (*post*-sāy-gerl-ōa-tōa-maat) *c* (pl -maten) stamp machine
pot (pot) *c* (pl ~ten) pot; jar
potlood (*pot*-lōat) *nt* (pl -loden) pencil
praatje (*praa*-t Yer) *nt* (pl ~s) chat
pracht (prahkht) *c* splendour
prachtig (*prahkh*-terkh) *adj* lovely, wonderful, marvellous; splendid, gorgeous, fine
praktijk (prahk-*tayk*) *c* (pl ~en) practice
praktisch (*prahk*-teess) *adj* practical
praten (*praa*-tern) *v* talk
precies (prer-*seess*) *adj* precise, very, exact; *adv* exactly; just
predikant (prāy-dee-*kahnt*) *c* (pl ~en) clergyman, minister, vicar, rector
preek (prāyk) *c* (pl preken) sermon
preekstoel (*prāyk*-stōol) *c* (pl ~en) pulpit
preken (*prāy*-kern) *v* preach
premie (*prāy*-mee) *c* (pl ~s) premium
premier (prer-m Y*āy*) *c* (pl ~s) premier, Prime Minister
prent (prehnt) *c* (pl ~en) picture; print, engraving
prentbriefkaart (*prehnt*-breef-kaart) *c* (pl ~en) picture postcard
president (prāy-zee-*dehnt*) *c* (pl ~en) president
prestatie (prehss-*taa*-tsee) *c* (pl ~s) achievement; feat
presteren (prehss-*tāy*-rern) *v* achieve
prestige (prehss-*tee*-zher) *nt* prestige
pret (preht) *c* fun; gaiety, pleasure

prettig (*preh*-terkh) *adj* enjoyable, pleasant; nice

preventief (*pray*-vehn-*teef*) *adj* preventive

priester (*pree*-sterr) *c* (pl ~s) priest

prijs (prayss) *c* (pl prijzen) price-list; charge, cost, rate; prize, award; **op ~ stellen** appreciate

prijsdaling (*prayss*-daa-lıng) *c* (pl ~en) slump

prijslijst (*prayss*-layst) *c* (pl ~en) price list

prijzen (*pray*-zern) *v* price

*****prijzen** (*pray*-zern) *v* praise

prijzig (*pray*-zerkh) *adj* expensive

prik[1] (prık) *c* (pl ~ken) sting

prik[2] (prık) *c* fizz

prikkel (*prı*-kerl) *c* (pl ~s) impulse

prikkelbaar (*prı*-kerl-baar) *adj* irritable

prikkelen (*prı*-ker-lern) *v* irritate

prikken (*prı*-kern) *v* prick

prima (*pree*-maa) *adj* first-rate

primair (*pree*-mair) *adj* primary

principe (prın-*see*-per) *nt* (pl ~s) principle

prins (prıns) *c* (pl ~en) prince

prinses (prın-sehss) *c* (pl ~sen) princess

prioriteit (pree-Yōa-ree-*tayt*) *c* (pl ~en) priority

privé (pree-*vāy*) *adj* private

privéleven (pree-*vāy*-lāy-vern) *nt* privacy

proberen (prōa-*bāy*-rern) *v* try; attempt; test

probleem (prōa-*blāym*) *nt* (pl -blemen) problem

procédé (prōa-ser-*dāy*) *nt* (pl ~s) process

procedure (prōa-ser-*dēw*-rer) *c* (pl ~s) procedure

procent (prōa-*sehnt*) *nt* (pl ~en) percent

proces (prōa-*sehss*) *nt* (pl ~sen) process; lawsuit

processie (prōa-*seh*-see) *c* (pl ~s) procession

producent (prōa-dēw-*sehnt*) *c* (pl ~en) producer

produceren (prōa-dēw-*sāy*-rern) *v* produce

produkt (prōa-*derkt*) *nt* (pl ~en) product; produce

produktie (prōa-*derk*-see) *c* (pl ~s) production; output

proef (prōof) *c* (pl proeven) experiment; trial, test

proeven (*prōō*-vern) *v* taste

profeet (prōa-*fāyt*) *c* (pl -feten) prophet

professor (prōa-*feh*-sor) *c* (pl ~en, ~s) professor

profiteren (prōa-fee-*tāy*-rern) *v* profit, benefit

programma (prōa-*grah*-maa) *nt* (pl ~'s) programme

progressief (prōa-greh-*seef*) *adj* progressive

project (prōa-Yehkt) *nt* (pl ~en) project

promenade (pro-mer-*naa*-der) *c* (pl ~s) esplanade, promenade

promotie (prōa-*mōa*-tsee) *c* (pl ~s) promotion

prompt (prompt) *adj* prompt

propaganda (prōa-paa-*gahn*-daa) *c* propaganda

propeller (prōa-*peh*-lerr) *c* (pl ~s) propeller

proportie (prōa-*por*-see) *c* (pl ~s) proportion

prospectus (pro-*spehk*-terss) *c* (pl ~sen) prospectus

prostituée (pro-stee-tēw-*vāy*) *c* (pl ~s) prostitute

protest (prōa-*tehst*) *nt* (pl ~en) protest; test

protestants (prōa-terss-*tahnts*) *adj*

Protestant

protesteren (prōa-tehss-*tay*-rern) *v* protest

provinciaal (prōa-vın-*shaal*) *adj* provincial

provincie (prōa-*vın*-see) *c* (pl ~s) province

provisiekast (prōa-*vee*-zee-kahst) *c* (pl ~en) larder

pruik (prur^{ew}k) *c* (pl ~en) wig

pruim (prur^{ew}m) *c* (pl ~en) plum; prune

prullenmand (*prer*-ler-mahnt) *c* (pl ~en) wastepaper-basket

psychiater (psee-khee-*Yaa*-terr) *c* (pl ~s) psychiatrist

psychisch (*psee*-kheess) *adj* psychic

psychologie (psee-khōa-lōa-*gee*) *c* psychology

psychologisch (psee-khōa-*lōa*-geess) *adj* psychological

psycholoog (psee-khōa-*lōa*kh) *c* (pl -logen) psychologist

publiceren (pēw-blee-*say*-rern) *v* publish

publiek (pēw-*bleek*) *adj* public; *nt* audience, public

publikatie (pēw-blee-*kaa*-tsee) *c* (pl ~s) publication

puimsteen (pur^{ew}m-stāyn) *nt* pumice stone

puistje (pur^{ew}-sher) *nt* (pl ~s) pimple

punaise (pēw-*nai*-zer) *c* (pl ~s) drawing-pin; thumbtack *nAm*

punctueel (perngk-tēw-*vāyl*) *adj* punctual

punt (pernt) *nt* (pl ~en) point; item, issue; *c* full stop, period; tip

punteslijper (*pern*-ter-slay-perr) *c* (pl ~s) pencil-sharpener

puntkomma (pernt-*ko*-maa) *c* semicolon

put (pert) *c* (pl ~ten) well

puur (pēwr) *adj* neat; sheer

puzzel (*per*-zerl) *c* (pl ~s) puzzle

pyjama (pee-*Yaa*-maa) *c* (pl ~'s) pyjamas *pl*

Q

quarantaine (kaa-rahn-*tai*-ner) *c* quarantine

quota (*kvōa*-taa) *c* (pl ~'s) quota

R

raad[1] (raat) *c* advice, counsel

raad[2] (raat) *c* (pl raden) council

raadplegen (*raat*-plāy-gern) *v* consult

raadpleging (*raat*-plāy-gıng) *c* (pl ~en) consultation

raadsel (*raat*-serl) *nt* (pl ~s, ~en) riddle, puzzle; mystery, enigma

raadslid (*raats*-lıt) *nt* (pl -leden) councillor

raadsman (*raats*-mahn) *c* (pl -lieden) counsellor; solicitor

raaf (raaf) *c* (pl raven) raven

raam (raam) *nt* (pl ramen) window

raar (raar) *adj* curious, odd, strange, queer, quaint

rabarber (raa-*bahr*-berr) *c* rhubarb

racket (*reh*-kert) *nt* (pl ~s) racquet

*****raden** (*raa*-dern) *v* guess

radiator (raa-dee-*Yaa*-tor) *c* (pl ~s, ~en) radiator

radicaal (raa-dee-*kaal*) *adj* radical

radijs (raa-*dayss*) *c* (pl radijzen) radish

radio (*raa*-dee-Yōa) *c* (pl ~'s) wireless, radio

rafelen (*raa*-fer-lern) *v* fray

raffinaderij (rah-fee-naa-der-*ray*) *c* (pl ~en) refinery

rage (*raa*-zher) *c* (pl ~s) craze

raken (*raa*-kern) *v* *hit
raket (raa-*keht*) *c* (pl ~ten) rocket
ramp (rahmp) *c* (pl ~en) calamity, disaster
rampzalig (rahm-*psaa*-lerkh) *adj* disastrous
rand (rahnt) *c* (pl ~en) edge, border; brim, rim, verge
rang (rahng) *c* (pl ~en) rank; class
rangschikken (*rahng*-skhı-kern) *v* arrange; sort, grade
rantsoen (rahnt-*soon*) *nt* (pl ~en) ration
ranzig (*rahn*-zerkh) *adj* rancid
rapport (rah-*port*) *nt* (pl ~en) report
rapporteren (rah-por-*tāy*-rern) *v* report
rariteit (raa-ree-*tayt*) *c* (pl ~en) curio
ras (rahss) *nt* (pl ~sen) race; breed; **rassen-** racial
rasp (rahsp) *c* (pl ~en) grater
raspen (*rahss*-pern) *v* grate
rat (raht) *c* (pl ~ten) rat
rauw (rou) *adj* raw
ravijn (raa-*vayn*) *nt* (pl ~en) gorge
razen (*raa*-zern) *v* rage
razend (raa-zernt) *adj* furious
razernij (raa-zerr-*nay*) *c* rage
reactie (rāy-*ᵛahk*-see) *c* (pl ~s) reaction
reageren (rāy-*ᵛah-gāy*-rern) *v* react
recent (rer-*sehnt*) *adj* recent
recept (rer-*sehpt*) *nt* (pl ~en) recipe; prescription
receptie (rer-*sehp*-see) *c* (pl ~s) reception office
receptioniste (rer-sehp-shōa-*nıss*-ter) *c* (pl ~s) receptionist
recht[1] (rehkht) *nt* (pl ~en) right; law, justice
recht[2] (rehkht) *adj* straight
rechtbank (*rehkht*-bahngk) *c* (pl ~en) court
rechtdoor (rehkh-*dōar*) *adv* straight on, straight ahead

rechter[1] (*rehkh*-terr) *adj* right-hand
rechter[2] (*rehkh*-terr) *c* (pl ~s) judge
rechthoek (*rehkht*-hōōk) *c* (pl ~en) oblong, rectangle
rechthoekig (rehkht-*hōō*-kerkh) *adj* rectangular
rechtopstaand (rehkh-*top*-staant) *adj* erect, upright
rechts (rehkhts) *adj* right-hand, right
rechtschapen (rehkht-*skhaa*-pern) *adj* honourable
rechtstreeks (*rehkht*-strāyks) *adj* direct
rechtszaak (*rehkht*-saak) *c* (pl -zaken) trial
rechtuit (rehkh-*turᵉʷt*) *adv* straight ahead
rechtvaardig (raykht-*faar*-derkh) *adj* just, righteous, right
rechtvaardigheid (rehkht-*faar*-derkh-hayt) *c* justice
reclame (rer-*klaa*-mer) *c* advertising, publicity
reclamespot (rer-*klaa*-mer-spot) *c* (pl ~s) commercial
record (rer-*kawr*) *nt* (pl ~s) record
recreatie (rāy-krāy-ᵛ*aa*-tsee) *c* recreation
recreatiecentrum (rāy-krāy-ᵛ*aa*-tsee-sehn-trerm) *nt* (pl -tra) recreation centre
rector (*rehk*-tor) *c* (pl ~en, ~s) headmaster, principal
reçu (rer-*sew*) *nt* (pl ~'s) receipt
redakteur (rāy-dahk-*tūrr*) *c* (pl ~en, ~s) editor
redden (*reh*-dern) *v* save, rescue
redder (*reh*-derr) *c* (pl ~s) saviour
redding (*reh*-dıng) *c* (pl ~en) rescue
reddingsgordel (*reh*-dıngs-khor-derl) *c* (pl ~s) lifebelt
rede[1] (*rāy*-der) *c* sense; reason
rede[2] (*rāy*-der) *c* (pl ~s) speech
redelijk (*rāy*-der-lerk) *adj* reasonable
reden (*rāy*-dern) *c* (pl ~en) reason

redeneren (rāy-der-*nāy*-rern) v reason
reder (*rāy*-derr) c (pl ~s) shipowner
redetwisten (*rāy*-der-tvɪss-tern) v argue
reduceren (rāy-dew-*sāy*-rern) v reduce
reductie (rer-*derk*-see) c (pl ~s) discount, reduction, rebate
reeds (rāyts) adv already
reekalf (*rāy*-kahlf) nt (pl -kalveren) fawn
reeks (rāyks) c (pl ~en) series; sequence
referentie (rer-fer-*rehn*-tsee) c (pl ~s) reference
reflector (rer-*flehk*-tor) c (pl ~s, ~en) reflector
reformatie (rāy-for-*maa*-tsee) c reformation
regel (*rāy*-gerl) c (pl ~s) line; rule; **in de ~** as a rule
regelen (*rāy*-ger-lern) v arrange; settle; regulate
regeling (*rāy*-ger-lɪng) c (pl ~en) arrangement; settlement; regulation
regelmatig (rāy-gerl-*maa*-terkh) adj regular
regen (*rāy*-gern) c rain
regenachtig (*rāy*-gern-ahkh-terkh) adj rainy
regenboog (*rāy*-ger-bōakh) c (pl -bogen) rainbow
regenbui (*rāy*-ger-bur^ew) c (pl ~en) shower
regenen (*rāy*-ger-nern) v rain
regenjas (*rāy*-ger-Yahss) c (pl ~sen) mackintosh, raincoat
regeren (rer-*gāy*-rern) v rule, govern, reign
regering (rer-*gāy*-rɪng) c (pl ~en) government; reign
regie (rer-*gee*) c (pl ~s) direction
regime (rer-*zheem*) nt (pl ~s) régime
regisseren (rāy-gee-*sāy*-rern) v direct
regisseur (rāy-gee-*sūrr*) c (pl ~s) director

register (rer-*gɪss*-terr) nt (pl ~s) record; index
registratie (rāy-gɪss-*traa*-tsee) c registration
reglement (rāy-gler-*mehnt*) nt (pl ~en) regulation
reiger (ray-gerr) c (pl ~s) heron
rein (rayn) adj pure
reinigen (ray-ner-gern) v clean; **chemisch ~** dry-clean
reiniging (ray-ner-gɪng) c cleaning
reinigingsmiddel (ray-ner-gɪngs-mɪderl) nt (pl ~en) cleaning fluid
reis (rayss) c (pl reizen) journey; trip, voyage
reisagent (rayss-aa-gehnt) c (pl ~en) travel agent
reisbureau (rayss-bēw-rōā) nt (pl ~s) travel agency
reischeque (ray-shehk) c (pl ~s) traveller's cheque
reiskosten (rayss-koss-tern) pl fare; travelling expenses
reisplan (rayss-plahn) nt (pl ~nen) itinerary
reisroute (rayss-rōō-ter) c (pl ~s, ~n) itinerary
reisverzekering (rayss-ferr-zāy-ker-rɪng) c travel insurance
reiswieg (rayss-veekh) c (pl ~en) carry-cot
reizen (ray-zern) v travel
reiziger (ray-zer-gerr) c (pl ~s) traveller
rek (rehk) c elasticity
rekbaar (rehk-baar) adj elastic
rekenen (rāy-ker-nern) v reckon
rekening (rāy-ker-nɪng) c (pl ~en) account; bill; check nAm
rekenkunde (rāy-kerng-kern-der) c arithmetic
rekken (reh-kern) v stretch
rekruut (rer-*krewt*) c (pl rekruten) re-

cruit

rel (rehl) *c* (pl ~len) riot

relatie (rer-*laa*-tsee) *c* (pl ~s) relation; connection

relatief (rer-laa-*teef*) *adj* relative; comparative

reliëf (rerl-*Yehf*) *nt* (pl ~s) relief

relikwie (rer-ler-*kvee*) *c* (pl ~ën) relic

reling (*rāy*-ling) *c* (pl ~en) rail

rem (rehm) *c* (pl ~men) brake

remlichten (*rehm*-likh-tern) *pl* brake lights

remtrommel (*rehm*-tro-mehl) *c* (pl ~s) brake drum

renbaan (*rehn*-baan) *c* (pl -banen) race-course; track; race-track

rendabel (rehn-*daa*-berl) *adj* paying

rendier (*rehn*-deer) *nt* (pl ~en) reindeer

rennen (*reh*-nern) *v* *run

renpaard (*rehn*-paart) *nt* (pl ~en) race-horse

rente (*rehn*-ter) *c* (pl ~n, ~s) interest

reparatie (rāy-paa-*raa*-tsee) *c* (pl ~s) reparation

repareren (rāy-paa-*rāy*-rern) *v* repair, fix ; mend

repertoire (rer-pehr-*tvaar*) *nt* (pl ~s) repertory

repeteren (rer-per-*tāy*-rern) *v* rehearse

repetitie (rer-per-*tee*-tsee) *c* (pl ~s) rehearsal

representatief (rer-prāy-zehn-taa-*teef*) *adj* representative

reproduceren (rāy-prōa-dew-*sāy*-rern) *v* reproduce

reproduktie (rāy-prōa-*derk*-see) *c* (pl ~s) reproduction

reptiel (rehp-*teel*) *nt* (pl ~en) reptile

republiek (rāy-pew-*bleek*) *c* (pl ~en) republic

republikeins (rāy-pew-blee-*kayns*) *adj* republican

reputatie (rāy-pew-*taa*-tsee) *c* reputa-

tion ; fame

reserve (rer-*zehr*-ver) *c* (pl ~s) reserve; **reserve-** spare

reserveband (rer-*zehr*-ver-bahnt) *c* (pl ~en) spare tyre

reserveren (rer-zehr-*vāy*-rern) *v* reserve; book

reservering (rer-zehr-*vāy*-ring) *c* (pl ~en) reservation ; booking

reservewiel (rer-*zehr*-ver-veel) *nt* (pl ~en) spare wheel

reservoir (rer-zerr-*vvaar*) *nt* (pl ~s) reservoir; container

resoluut (rāy-zōa-*lōōt*) *adj* resolute

respect (reh-*spehkt*) *nt* respect; esteem, regard

respectabel (reh-spehk-*taa*-berl) *adj* respectable

respecteren (reh-spehk-*tāy*-rern) *v* respect

respectievelijk (reh-spehk-*tee*-ver-lerk) *adj* respective

rest (rehst) *c* (pl ~en) rest; remainder; remnant

restant (rehss-*tahnt*) *nt* (pl ~en) remainder; remnant

restaurant (reh-stōa-*rahnt*) *nt* (pl ~s) restaurant

restauratiewagen (rehss-tōa-*raa*-tsee-vaa-gern) *c* (pl ~s) dining-car

restriktie (rer-*strik*-see) *c* (pl ~s) qualification

resultaat (rāy-zerl-*taat*) *nt* (pl -taten) result; outcome, issue

resulteren (rāy-zerl-*tāy*-rern) *v* result

resumé (rāy-zew-*māy*) *nt* (pl ~s) summary

retour (rer-*tōōr*) round trip *Am*

retourvlucht (rer-*tōōr*-vlerkht) *c* (pl ~en) return flight

reumatiek (rūr-maa-*teek*) *c* rheumatism

reus (rūrss) *c* (pl reuzen) giant

reusachtig (rūr-*zahkh*-terkh) *adj* huge;

gigantic, enormous, immense

revalidatie (rāy-vaa-lee-*daa*-tsee) c rehabilitation

revers (rer-*vair*) c (pl ~) lapel

reviseren (rāy-vee-*zāy*-rern) v overhaul

revolutie (rāy-vōa-*lēw*-tsee) c (pl ~s) revolution

revolutionair (rāy-vōa-lēw-tshōa-*nair*) adj revolutionary

revolver (rer-*vol*-verr) c (pl ~s) gun, revolver

revue (rer-*vēw*) c (pl ~s) revue

rib (rɪp) c (pl ~ben) rib

ribfluweel (*rɪp*-flew-vāyl) nt corduroy

richten (*rɪkh*-tern) v direct; ~ **op** aim at

richting (*rɪkh*-tɪng) c (pl ~en) direction; way

richtingaanwijzer (*rɪkh*-tɪng-aan-vay-zerr) c (pl ~s) trafficator, indicator; directional signal Am

richtlijn (*rɪkht*-layn) c (pl ~en) directive

ridder (*rɪ*-derr) c (pl ~s) knight

riem (reem) c (pl ~en) belt; strap; lead

riet (reet) nt reed; cane

rif (rɪf) nt (pl ~fen) reef

rij (ray) c (pl ~en) row, rank; line; file, queue; **in de ~ *staan** queue; stand in line Am

rijbaan (*ray*-baan) c (pl -banen) carriageway; roadway nAm

rijbewijs (*ray*-ber-vayss) nt driving licence

*rijden (*ray*-dern) v *drive; *ride

*rijgen (*ray*-gern) v thread

rijk¹ (rayk) adj rich; wealthy

rijk² (rayk) nt (pl ~en) kingdom, empire; **rijks-** imperial

rijkdom (*rayk*-dom) c (pl ~men) wealth, riches pl

rijm (raym) nt (pl ~en) rhyme

rijp (rayp) adj ripe, mature

rijpheid (*rayp*-hayt) c maturity

rijst (rayst) c rice

rijstrook (*ray*-strōak) c (pl -stroken) lane

rijtuig (*ray*-tur^{ew}g) nt (pl ~en) carriage; coach

rijweg (*ray*-vehkh) c drive

rijwiel (*ray*-veel) nt (pl ~en) cycle; bicycle

rillen (*rɪ*-lern) v shiver; tremble

rillerig (*rɪ*-ler-rerkh) adj shivery

rilling (*rɪ*-lɪng) c (pl ~en) chill; shiver, shudder

rimpel (*rɪm*-perl) c (pl ~s) wrinkle

ring (rɪng) c (pl ~en) ring

ringweg (*rɪng*-vehkh) c (pl ~en) bypass

riool (ree-^yōal) nt (pl riolen) sewer

risico (*ree*-zee-kōa) nt (pl ~'s) risk; chance, hazard

riskant (rɪss-*kahnt*) adj risky

rit (rɪt) c (pl ~ten) ride

ritme (*rɪt*-mer) nt (pl ~n) rhythm

ritssluiting (*rɪt*-slur^{ew}-tɪng) c (pl ~en) zipper, zip

rivaal (ree-*vaal*) c (pl rivalen) rival

rivaliseren (ree-vaa-lee-*zāy*-rern) v rival

rivaliteit (ree-vaa-lee-*tayt*) c rivalry

rivier (ree-*veer*) c (pl ~en) river

riviermonding (ree-*veer*-mon-dɪng) c (pl ~en) estuary

rivieroever (ree-*veer*-ōō-verr) c (pl ~s) riverside

rob (rop) c (pl ~ben) seal

robijn (rōa-*bayn*) c (pl ~en) ruby

roddelen (*ro*-der-lern) v gossip

roede (*rōō*-der) c (pl ~n) rod

roeiboot (*rōō*^{ee}-bōat) c (pl -boten) rowing-boat

roeien (*rōō*^{ee}-ern) v row

roeiriem (*rōō*^{ee}-reem) c (pl ~en) oar

roem (rōōm) c glory; celebrity, fame

Roemeen (rōō-*māyn*) c (pl -menen)

Rumanian

Roemeens (rōō-*mayns*) *adj* Rumanian

Roemenië (rōō-*may*-nee-ᵞer) Rumania

roep (rōōp) *c* call, cry

*****roepen** (*rōō*-pern) *v* call; cry, shout

roer (rōōr) *nt* rudder, helm

roeren (*rōō*-rern) *v* stir

roerend (*rōō*-rernt) *adj* movable

roest (rōōst) *nt* rust

roestig (*rōōss*-terkh) *adj* rusty

rok (rok) *c* (pl ~ken) skirt

roken (*rōa*-kern) *v* smoke

roker (*rōa*-kerr) *c* (pl ~s) smoker

rol (rol) *c* (pl ~len) roll

rolgordijn (*rol*-gor-dayn) *nt* (pl ~en) blind

rollen (*ro*-lern) *v* roll

rolstoel (*rol*-stōōl) *c* (pl ~en) wheel-chair

roltrap (*rol*-trahp) *c* (pl ~pen) escalator

roman (rōa-*mahn*) *c* (pl ~s) novel

romance (rōa-*mahng*-ser) *c* (pl ~s, ~n) romance

romanschrijver (rōa-*mahn*-skhray-verr) *c* (pl ~s) novelist

romantisch (rōa-*mahn*-teess) *adj* romantic

romig (*rōa*-merkh) *adj* creamy

rommel (*ro*-merl) *c* mess; litter; trash, junk

rond (ront) *adj* round; *prep* around

ronde (*ron*-der) *c* (pl ~n, ~s) round

rondom (ront-*om*) *adv* around; *prep* round

rondreis (*ront*-rayss) *c* (pl -reizen) tour

rondreizend (*ront*-ray-zernt) *adj* itinerant

*****rondtrekken** (*ron*-treh-kern) *v* tramp

*****rondzwerven** (*ront*-svehr-vern) *v* wander

röntgenfoto (*rernt*-gern-fōa-tōa) *c* (pl ~'s) X-ray

rood (rōat) *adj* red

roodborstje (*rōat*-bor-sher) *nt* (pl ~s) robin

roodkoper (*rōat*-kōa-perr) *nt* copper

roof (rōaf) *c* robbery

roofdier (*rōaf*-deer) *nt* (pl ~en) beast of prey

rook (rōak) *c* smoke

rookcoupé (*rōa*-kōo-pay) *c* (pl ~s) smoker

rookkamer (*rōa*-kaa-merr) *c* smoking-room

room (rōam) *c* cream

roomkleurig (rōam-*klur*-rerkh) *adj* cream

rooms-katholiek (rōams-kah-tōa-*leek*) *adj* Roman Catholic

roos[1] (rōass) *c* (pl rozen) rose

roos[2] (rōass) *c* dandruff

rooster (*rōa*-sterr) *nt* (pl ~s) grate; schedule

roosteren (*rōa*-ster-rern) *v* grill, roast

rot (rot) *adj* rotten

rotan (*rōa*-tahn) *nt* rattan

rotonde (rōa-*ton*-der) *c* (pl ~s) round-about

rots (rots) *c* (pl ~en) rock; cliff

rotsachtig (*rot*-sahkh-terkh) *adj* rocky

rotsblok (*rots*-blok) *nt* (pl ~ken) boulder

rouge (rōō-zher) *c/nt* rouge

roulette (rōō-*leh*-ter) *c* roulette

route (*rōō*-ter) *c* (pl ~s) route

routine (rōō-*tee*-ner) *c* routine

rouw (rou) *c* mourning

royaal (rōa-ᵞaal) *adj* generous; liberal

roze (raw-zer) *adj* rose, pink

rozenkrans (*rōa*-zer-krahns) *c* (pl ~en) rosary, beads *pl*

rozijn (rōa-*zayn*) *c* (pl ~en) raisin

rubber (*rer*-berr) *nt* rubber

rubriek (rēw-*breek*) *c* (pl ~en) column

rug (rerkh) *c* (pl ~gen) back

ruggegraat (*rer*-ger-graat) *c* spine, backbone

rugpijn (*rerkh*-payn) *c* backache

rugzak (*rerkh*-sahk) *c* (pl ~ken) rucksack

***ruiken** (*rur^ew*-kern) *v* *smell

ruil (rur^ewl) *c* exchange

ruilen (*rur^ew*-lern) *v* exchange; swap

ruim[1] (rur^ewm) *adj* broad, large; roomy, spacious

ruim[2] (rur^ewm) *nt* (pl ~en) hold

ruimte (*rur^ew*m-ter) *c* room, space

ruïne (rew-*vee*-ner) *c* (pl ~s) ruins

ruïneren (rew-vee-*nay*-rern) *v* ruin

ruit (rur^ewt) *c* (pl ~en) check; pane

ruitenwisser (*rur^ew*-ter-vɪ-serr) *c* (pl ~s) windscreen wiper; windshield wiper *Am*

ruiter (*rur^ew*-terr) *c* (pl ~s) horseman; rider

ruk (rerk) *c* (pl ~ken) tug, wrench

rumoer (rew-*moor*) *nt* noise

rundvlees (*rernt*-flayss) *nt* beef

Rus (rerss) *c* (pl ~sen) Russian

Rusland (*rerss*-lahnt) Russia

Russisch (*rer*-seess) *adj* Russian

rust (rerst) *c* rest; quiet; half-time

rusteloosheid (rerss-ter-*lōass*-hayt) *c* unrest

rusten (*rerss*-tern) *v* rest

rusthuis (*rerst*-hur^ewss) *nt* (pl -huizen) rest-home

rustiek (rerss-*teek*) *adj* rustic

rustig (*rerss*-terkh) *adj* calm, quiet; restful, tranquil

ruw (rew^oo) *adj* rough, harsh

ruzie (*rew*-zee) *c* (pl ~s) row, quarrel, dispute; ~ **maken** quarrel

S

saai (saa^ee) *adj* dull, boring

sacharine (sah-khaa-*ree*-ner) *c* saccharin

saffier (sah-*feer*) *nt* sapphire

salaris (saa-*laa*-rɪss) *nt* (pl ~sen) salary; pay

saldo (*sahl*-dōa) *nt* (pl ~'s, saldi) balance

salon (saa-*lon*) *c* (pl ~s) drawing-room, lounge; salon

samen (*saa*-mern) *adv* together

***samenbinden** (*saa*-mer-bɪn-dern) *v* bundle

***samenbrengen** (*saa*-mer-breh-ngern) *v* combine

samenhang (*saa*-mer-hahng) *c* coherence

samenleving (*saa*-mer-*lay*-vɪng) *c* (pl ~en) community

samenloop (*saa*-mer-lōap) *c* concurrence

samenstellen (*saa*-mer-steh-lern) *v* compose, compile

samenstelling (*saa*-mer-steh-lɪng) *c* (pl ~en) composition

***samenvallen** (*saa*-mer-vah-lern) *v* coincide

samenvatting (*saa*-mer-vah-tɪng) *c* (pl ~en) résumé, summary

samenvoegen (*saa*-mer-vōo-gern) *v* join

samenwerking (*saa*-mer-vehr-kɪng) *c* co-operation

***samenzweren** (*saa*-mer-zvay-rern) *v* conspire

samenzwering (*saa*-mer-zvay-rɪng) *c* (pl ~en) plot

sanatorium (saa-naa-*tōa*-ree-^yerm) *nt* (pl ~s, -ria) sanatorium

sandaal (sahn-*daal*) *c* (pl -dalen) sandal

sanitair (saa-nee-*tair*) *adj* sanitary

Saoedi-Arabië (saa-ōō-dee-aa-*raa*-bee-^yer) Saudi Arabia

Saoedi-Arabisch (saa-ōō-dee-aa-*raa*-beess) *adj* Saudi Arabian

sap (sahp) *nt* (pl ~pen) juice

sappig (*sah*-perkh) *adj* juicy

sardine (sahr-*dee*-ner) *c* (pl ~s) sardine

satelliet (saa-ter-*leet*) *c* (pl ~en) satellite

satijn (saa-*tayn*) *nt* satin

sauna (*sou*-naa) *c* (pl ~'s) sauna

saus (souss) *c* (pl sauzen) sauce

Scandinavië (skahn-dee-*naa*-vee- Yer) Scandinavia

Scandinaviër (skahn-dee-*naa*-vee-Yerr) *c* (pl ~s) Scandinavian

Scandinavisch (skahn-dee-*naa*-veess) *adj* Scandinavian

scène (*sai*-ner) *c* (pl ~s) scene

schaafwond (*skhaaf*-vont) *c* (pl ~en) graze

schaak! (skhaak) check!

schaakbord (*skhaak*-bort) *nt* (pl ~en) checkerboard *nAm*

schaakspel (*skhaak*-spehl) *nt* chess

schaal (skhaal) *c* (pl schalen) dish; bowl; scale

schaaldier (*skhaal*-deer) *nt* (pl ~en) shellfish

schaamte (*skhaam*-ter) *c* shame

schaap (skhaap) *nt* (pl schapen) sheep

schaar (skhaar) *c* (pl scharen) scissors *pl*

schaars (skhaars) *adj* scarce

schaarste (*skhaar*-ster) *c* scarcity

schaats (skhaats) *c* (pl ~en) skate

schaatsen (*skhaat*-sern) *v* skate

schade (*skhaa*-der) *c* damage; harm, mischief

schadelijk (*skhaa*-der-lerk) *adj* harmful; hurtful

schadeloosstelling (*skhaa*-der-lōa-steh-lıng) *c* (pl ~en) indemnity

schaden (*skhaa*-dern) *v* harm

schadevergoeding (*skhaa*-der-verr-gōō-dıng) *c* (pl ~en) compensation, indemnity

schaduw (*skhaa*-dew ᵒᵒ) *c* (pl ~en) shade; shadow

schaduwrijk (*skhaa*-dew ᵒᵒ-rayk) *adj* shady

schakel (*skhaa*-kerl) *c* (pl ~s) link

schakelaar (*skhaa*-ker-laar) *c* (pl ~s) switch

schakelbord (*skhaa*-kerl-bort) *nt* switchboard

schakelen (*skhaa*-ker-lern) *v* change gear

zich schamen (*skhaa*-mern) *be ashamed

schandaal (skhahn-*daal*) *nt* (pl -dalen) scandal

schande (*skhahn*-deh) *c* disgrace, shame

schapevlees (*skhaa*-per-vlāyss) *nt* mutton

scharnier (skhahr-*neer*) *nt* (pl ~en) hinge

schat (skhaht) *c* (pl ~ten) treasure; darling

schatkist (*skhaht*-kıst) *c* treasury

schatten (*skhah*-tern) *v* evaluate, estimate, value; appreciate

schatting (*skhah*-tıng) *c* (pl ~en) estimate; appreciation

schedel (*skhāy*-derl) *c* (pl ~s) skull

scheef (skhāyf) *adj* slanting

scheel (skhāyl) *adj* cross-eyed

scheepswerf (*skhāyps*-vehrf) *c* (pl -werven) shipyard

scheepvaart (*skhāyp*-faart) *c* navigation

scheepvaartlijn (*skhāyp*-faart-layn) *c* (pl ~en) shipping line

scheerapparaat (*skhāyr*-ah-paa-raat) *nt* (pl -raten) safety-razor, electric razor, shaver

scheercrème (*skhāyr*-kraim) *c* (pl ~s) shaving-cream

scheerkwast (*skhāyr*-kvahst) *c* (pl ~en) shaving-brush

scheermesje (*skhāyr*-meh-sher) *nt* (pl

~s) razor-blade

scheerzeep (*skhāyr*-zāyp) *c* shaving-soap

***scheiden** (*skhay*-dern) *v* separate; divide, part; divorce

scheiding (*skhay*-dıng) *c* (pl ~en) division; parting

scheidsrechter (*skhayts*-rehkh-terr) *c* (pl ~s) umpire

scheikunde (*skhay*-kern-der) *c* chemistry

scheikundig (skhay-*kern*-derkh) *adj* chemical

***schelden** (*skhehl*-dern) *v* scold

schelm (skhehlm) *c* (pl ~en) rascal

schelp (skhehlp) *c* (pl ~en) shell

schelvis (*skhehl*-vıss) *c* haddock

schema (*skhāy*-maa) *nt* (pl ~'s, ~ta) diagram; scheme

schemering (*skhāy*-mer-rıng) *c* twilight

schending (*skhehn*-dıng) *c* (pl ~en) violation

***schenken** (*skhehng*-kern) *v* pour; donate

schenking (*skhehng*-kıng) *c* (pl ~en) donation

***scheppen** (*skheh*-pern) *v* create

schepsel (*skhehp*-serl) *nt* (pl ~s) creature

zich *scheren (*skhāy*-rern) shave

scherm (skhehrm) *nt* (pl ~en) screen

schermen (*skhehr*-mern) *v* fence

scherp (skhehrp) *adj* sharp; keen

schets (skhehts) *c* (pl ~en) sketch

schetsboek (*skhehts*-bōōk) *nt* (pl ~en) sketch-book

schetsen (*skheht*-sern) *v* sketch

scheur (skhūrr) *c* (pl ~en) tear

***scheuren** (*skhūr*-rern) *v* rip, *tear

schiereiland (*skheer*-ay-lahnt) *nt* peninsula

***schieten** (*skhee*-tern) *v* *shoot, fire

schietschijf (*skheet*-skhayf) *c* (pl

-schijven) mark

schijf (skhayf) *c* (pl schijven) disc

schijn (skhayn) *c* semblance

schijnbaar (*skhaym*-baar) *adj* apparent

***schijnen** (*skhay*-nern) *v* appear, seem; *shine

schijnheilig (skhayn-*hay*-lerkh) *adj* hypocritical

schijnwerper (*skhayn*-vehr-perr) *c* (pl ~s) spotlight, searchlight

schikken (*skhı*-kern) *v* suit

schikking (*skhı*-kıng) *c* (pl ~en) settlement

schil (skhıl) *c* (pl ~len) skin; peel

schilder (*skhıl*-derr) *c* (pl ~s) painter

schilderachtig (*skhıl*-derr-ahkh-terkh) *adj* scenic, picturesque

schilderen (*skhıl*-der-rern) *v* paint

schilderij (skhıl-der-*ray*) *nt* (pl ~en) painting, picture

schildpad (*skhıl*-paht) *c* (pl ~den) turtle

schilfer (*skhıl*-ferr) *c* (pl ~s) chip

schillen (*skhı*-lern) *c* peel

schimmel (*skhı*-merl) *c* (pl ~s) mildew

schip (skhıp) *nt* (pl schepen) ship; boat, vessel

schitterend (*skhı*-ter-rernt) *adj* brilliant, splendid

schittering (*skhı*-ter-rıng) *c* (pl ~en) glare

schoeisel (*skhōō*ᵉᵉ-serl) *nt* footwear

schoen (skhōōn) *c* (pl ~en) shoe

schoenmaker (*skhōōn*-maa-kerr) *c* (pl ~s) shoemaker

schoensmeer (*skhōōn*-smāyr) *c* shoe polish

schoenveter (*skhōōn*-fāy-terr) *c* (pl ~s) shoe-lace

schoenwinkel (*skhōōn*-vıng-kerl) *c* (pl ~s) shoe-shop

schoft (skhoft) *c* (pl ~en) bastard

schok (skhok) *c* (pl ~ken) shock

schokbreker (*skhok*-brāy-kerr) *c* (pl ~s) shock absorber

schokken (*skho*-kern) *v* shock

schol (skhol) *c* (pl ~len) plaice

schommel (*skho*-merl) *c* (pl ~s) swing

schommelen (*skho*-mer-lern) *v* rock, *swing

school (skhōal) *c* (pl scholen) school; college; **middelbare ~** secondary school

schoolbank (*skhōal*-bahngk) *c* (pl ~en) desk

schoolbord (*skhōal*-bort) *nt* (pl ~en) blackboard

schoolhoofd (*skhōal*-hōaft) *nt* (pl ~en) headmaster, head teacher

schooljongen (*skhōal*-Yo-ngern) *c* (pl ~s) schoolboy

schoolmeester (*skhōal*-māyss-terr) *c* (pl ~s) teacher

schoolmeisje (*skhōal*-may-sher) *nt* (pl ~s) schoolgirl

schoolslag (*skhōal*-slahkh) *c* breast-stroke

schooltas (*skhōal*-tahss) *c* (pl ~sen) satchel

schoon (skhōan) *adj* clean

schoonheid (*skhōan*-hayt) *c* (pl -heden) beauty

schoonheidsbehandeling (*skhōan*-hayts-ber-hahn-der-lıng) *c* (pl ~en) beauty treatment

schoonheidsmasker (*skhōan*-hayts-mahss-kerr) *nt* (pl ~s) face-pack

schoonheidsmiddelen (*skhōan*-hayts-mı-der-lern) *pl* cosmetics *pl*

schoonheidssalon (*skhōan*-hayts-saa-lon) *c* (pl ~s) beauty salon, beauty parlour

schoonmaak (*skhōa*-maak) *c* cleaning

schoonmaken (*skhōa*-maa-kern) *v* clean

schoonmoeder (*skhōa*-mōō-derr) *c* (pl ~s) mother-in-law

schoonouders (*skhōan*-ou-derrs) *pl* parents-in-law *pl*

schoonvader (*skhōan*-vaa-derr) *c* (pl ~s) father-in-law

schoonzoon (*skhōan*-zōan) *c* (pl -zonen) son-in-law

schoonzuster (*skhōan*-zerss-terr) *c* (pl ~s) sister-in-law

schoorsteen (*skhōar*-stāyn) *c* (pl -stenen) chimney

schop (skhop) *c* (pl ~pen) kick; spade, shovel

schoppen (*skho*-pern) *v* kick

schor (skhor) *adj* hoarse

schorsen (*skhor*-sern) *v* suspend

schort (skhort) *c* (pl ~en) apron

Schot (skhot) *c* (pl ~ten) Scot

schot (skhot) *nt* (pl ~en) shot

schotel (*skhōa*-terl) *c* (pl ~s) dish; **schoteltje** *nt* saucer

Schotland (*skhot*-lahnt) Scotland

Schots (skhots) *adj* Scottish, Scotch

schouder (*skhou*-derr) *c* (pl ~s) shoulder

schouwburg (*skhou*-berrkh) *c* (pl ~en) theatre

schouwspel (*skhou*-spehl) *nt* (pl ~en) spectacle

schram (skhrahm) *c* (pl ~men) scratch

schrappen (*skhrah*-pern) *v* scrape

schrede (*skhrāy*-der) *c* (pl ~n) pace

schreeuw (skhrāy⁰⁰) *c* (pl ~en) scream, cry, shout

schreeuwen (*skhrāy⁰⁰*-ern) *v* scream, cry, shout

schriftelijk (*skhrıf*-ter-lerk) *adj* written; *adv* in writing

schrijfbehoeften (*skhrayf*-ber-hōōf-tern) *pl* stationery

schrijfblok (*skhrayf*-blok) *nt* (pl ~ken) writing-pad

schrijfmachine (*skhrayf*-mah-shee-ner) *c* (pl ~s) typewriter

schrijfmachinepapier (*skhrayf*-mah-shee-ner-paa-peer) *nt* typing paper

schrijfpapier (*skhrayf*-paa-peer) *nt* notepaper; writing-paper

schrijftafel (*skhrayf*-taa-ferl) *c* (pl ~s) bureau

schrijn (skhrayn) *c* (pl ~en) shrine

*schrijven (*skhray*-vern) *v* *write

schrijver (*skhray*-vehr) *c* (pl ~s) author, writer

schrik (skhrɪk) *c* fright, scare; ~ ***aanjagen** terrify

schrikkeljaar (*skhrɪ*-kerl-Yaar) *nt* leap-year

*schrikken (*skhrɪ*-kern) *v* *be frightened; ***doen** ~ frighten, scare

schrobben (*skhro*-bern) *v* scrub

schroef (skhrōōf) *c* (pl schroeven) screw; propeller

schroefsleutel (*skhrōōf*-slūr-terl) *c* (pl ~s) spanner

schroevedraaier (*skhrōō*-ver-draa-Yerr) *c* (pl ~s) screw-driver

schroeven (*skhrōō*-vern) *v* screw

schroot (skhrōāt) *nt* scrap-iron

schub (skherp) *c* (pl ~ben) scale

schudden (*skher*-dern) *v* *shake; shuffle

schuifdeur (*skhur*ewf-dūrr) *c* (pl ~en) sliding door

schuilplaats (*skhur*ewl-plaats) *c* (pl ~en) cover; shelter

schuim (skhur*ew*m) *nt* froth, lather, foam

schuimen (*skhur*ew-mern) *v* foam

schuimrubber (*skhur*ewm-rer-berr) *nt* foam-rubber

schuin (skhur*ew*n) *adj* slanting

*schuiven (*skhur*ew-vern) *v* push

schuld¹ (skherlt) *c* guilt; fault, blame; **de** ~ ***geven aan** blame

schuld² (skherlt) *c* (pl ~en) debt

schuldeiser (*skherlt*-ay-serr) *c* (pl ~s) creditor

schuldig (*skherl*-derkh) *adj* guilty; ~ ***bevinden** convict; ~ ***zijn** owe

schuur (skhewr) *c* (pl schuren) barn; shed

schuurpapier (*skhewr*-paa-peer) *nt* sandpaper

schuw (skhewºº) *adj* shy

scoren (*skōā*-rern) *v* score

seconde (ser-*kon*-der) *c* (pl ~n) second

secretaresse (sɪ-krer-taa-*reh*-ser) *c* (pl ~n) secretary

secretaris (sɪ-krer-*taa*-rerss) *c* (pl ~sen) secretary; clerk

sectie (*sehk*-see) *c* (pl ~s) section

secundair (sāy-kern-*dair*) *adj* secondary

secuur (ser-*kēwr*) *adj* precise

sedert (*sāy*-derrt) *prep* since

sein (sayn) *nt* (pl ~en) signal

seinen (*say*-nern) *v* signal

seizoen (say-*zōōn*) *nt* (pl ~en) season; **buiten het** ~ off season

seksualiteit (sehk-sēw-vaa-lee-*tayt*) *c* sexuality

seksueel (sehk-sēw-*vāyl*) *adj* sexual

selderij (*sehl*-der-ray) *c* celery

select (ser-*lehkt*) *adj* select

selecteren (sāy-lehk-*tāy*-rern) *v* select

selectie (sāy-*lehk*-see) *c* selection

senaat (ser-*naat*) *c* senate

senator (ser-*naa*-tor) *c* (pl ~en) senator

seniel (ser-*neel*) *adj* senile

sensatie (sehn-*zaa*-tsee) *c* (pl ~s) sensation

sensationeel (sehn-zaa-tshōā-*nāyl*) *adj* sensational

sentimenteel (sehn-tee-mehn-*tāyl*) *adj* sentimental

september (sehp-*tehm*-berr) September

septisch (*sehp*-teess) *adj* septic

serie (*sāy*-ree) *c* (pl ~s) series

serieus (sāy-ree-*Y*ūrss) *adj* serious

serum (sāy-rerm) *nt* (pl ~s, sera) serum

serveerster (sehr-vāyr-sterr) *c* (pl ~s) waitress

servet (sehr-veht) *nt* (pl ~ten) napkin, serviette

sfeer (sfāyr) *c* atmosphere; sphere

shag (shehk) *c* cigarette tobacco

shampoo (shahm-pōa) *c* shampoo

Siam (see-*Y*ahm) Siam

Siamees (see-*Y*aa-*mā*yss) *adj* Siamese

sifon (see-fon) *c* (pl ~s) syphon, siphon

sigaar (see-gaar) *c* (pl sigaren) cigar

sigarenwinkel (see-gaa-rer-vɪng-kerl) *c* (pl ~s) cigar shop

sigarenwinkelier (see-gaa-rer-vɪng-ker-leer) *c* (pl ~s) tobacconist

sigaret (see-gaa-reht) *c* (pl ~ten) cigarette

sigarettenkoker (see-gaa-reh-ter-kōa-kehr) *c* (pl ~s) cigarette-case

sigarettepijpje (see-gaa-reh-ter-payp-*Y*er) *nt* (pl ~s) cigarette-holder

signaal (see-ñaal) *nt* (pl -nalen) signal

signalement (see-ñaa-ler-mehnt) *nt* (pl ~en) description

simpel (sɪm-perl) *adj* simple

sinaasappel (see-naa-sah-perl) *c* (pl ~en, ~s) orange

sinds (sɪns) *conj* since

sindsdien (sɪns-deen) *adv* since

singel (sɪ-ngerl) *c* (pl ~s) canal

sirene (see-*rā*y-ner) *c* (pl ~s) siren

siroop (see-rōap) *c* syrup

situatie (see-tēw-vaa-tsee) *c* (pl ~s) situation

sjaal (shaal) *c* (pl ~s) shawl; scarf

skelet (sker-leht) *nt* (pl ~ten) skeleton

ski (skee) *c* (pl ~'s) ski

skibroek (skee-brōōk) *c* (pl ~en) ski pants

skiën (skee-*Y*ern) *v* ski

skiër (skee-*Y*err) *c* (pl ~s) skier

skilift (skee-lɪft) *c* (pl ~en) ski-lift

skischoenen (skee-skhōō-nern) *pl* ski boots

skistokken (skee-sto-kern) *pl* ski sticks; ski poles *Am*

sla (slaa) *c* lettuce; salad

slaaf (slaaf) *c* (pl slaven) slave

***slaan** (slaan) *v* *beat; *hit, *strike; smack, slap

slaap[1] (slaap) *c* sleep; **in ~** asleep

slaap[2] (slaap) *c* (pl slapen) temple

slaapkamer (slaap-kaa-merr) *c* (pl ~s) bedroom

slaappil (slaa-pɪl) *c* (pl ~len) sleeping-pill

slaapwagen (slaap-vaa-gern) *c* (pl ~s) sleeping-car

slaapzaal (slaap-saal) *c* (pl -zalen) dormitory

slaapzak (slaap-sahk) *c* (pl ~ken) sleeping-bag

slachtoffer (slahkht-o-ferr) *nt* (pl ~s) victim; casualty

slag[1] (slahkh) *c* (pl ~en) blow; battle

slag[2] (slahkh) *nt* sort

slagader (slahkh-aa-derr) *c* (pl ~s) artery

slagboom (slahkh-bōam) *c* (pl -bomen) barrier

slagen (slaa-gern) *v* manage, succeed; pass

slager (slaa-gerr) *c* (pl ~s) butcher

slagzin (slahkh-sɪn) *c* (pl ~nen) slogan

slak (slahk) *c* (pl ~ken) snail

slang (slahng) *c* (pl ~en) snake

slank (slahngk) *adj* slim, slender

slaolie (slaa-ōa-lee) *c* salad-oil

slap (slahp) *adj* limp; weak

slapeloos (slaa-per-lōass) *adj* sleepless

slapeloosheid (slaa-per-lōass-hayt) *c* insomnia

***slapen** (slaa-pern) *v* *sleep

slaperig (slaa-per-rerkh) *adj* sleepy

slecht (slehkht) *adj* bad; poor; ill; wicked, evil; **slechter** worse; **slechtst** worst

slechts (slehkhts) *adv* only, merely

slede (*slāy*-der) *c* (pl ~n) sledge

slee (slāy) *c* (pl ~ën) sleigh, sledge

sleepboot (*slāy*-bōat) *c* (pl -boten) tug

slepen (*slāy*-pern) *v* drag, haul; tug, tow

sleutel (*slūr*-terl) *c* (pl ~s) key; wrench

sleutelbeen (*slūr*-terl-bāyn) *nt* (pl -beenderen, -benen) collarbone

sleutelgat (*slūr*-terl-gaht) *nt* (pl ~en) keyhole

***slijpen** (*slay*-pern) *v* sharpen

slijterij (slay-ter-*ray*) *c* (pl ~en) off-licence

slikken (*sli*-kern) *v* swallow

slim (slim) *adj* clever

slip (slip) *c* (pl ~s) briefs *pl*; panties *pl*

slippen (*sli*-pern) *v* slip; skid

slof (slof) *c* (pl ~fen) slipper; carton

slokje (*slok*-Yer) *nt* (pl ~s) sip

sloot (slōat) *c* (pl sloten) ditch

slopen (*slōa*-pern) *v* demolish

slordig (*slor*-derkh) *adj* untidy; slovenly, sloppy, careless

slot[1] (slot) *nt* (pl ~en) lock; castle; **op ~** ***doen** lock

slot[2] (slot) *nt* end, issue

sluier (*slur*ew-err) *c* (pl ~s) veil

sluipschutter (*slur*ewp-skher-terr) *c* (pl ~s) sniper

sluis (slur ew ss) *c* (pl sluizen) lock, sluice

***sluiten** (*slur*ew-tern) *v* close, ***shut**; fasten

sluiting (*slur*ew-ting) *c* (pl ~en) fastener

sluw (slew oo) *adj* cunning

smaak (smaak) *c* (pl smaken) taste; flavour

smakelijk (*smaa*-ker-lerk) *adj* savoury, tasty; appetizing

smakeloos (*smaa*-ker-lōass) *adj* tasteless

smaken (*smaa*-kern) *v* taste

smal (smahl) *adj* narrow

smaragd (smaa-*rahkht*) *nt* emerald

smart (smahrt) *c* (pl ~en) grief

smartlap (*smahrt*-lahp) *c* (pl ~pen) tear-jerker

smeerolie (*smāyr*-ōa-lee) *c* lubrication oil

smeersysteem (*smāyr*-see-stāym) *nt* lubrication system

smeken (*smāy*-kern) *v* beg

***smelten** (*smehl*-tern) *v* melt

smeren (*smāy*-rern) *v* lubricate, grease

smerig (*smāy*-rerkh) *adj* dirty; foul, filthy

smering (*smāy*-ring) *c* lubrication

smet (smeht) *c* (pl ~ten) blot

smid (smit) *c* (pl smeden) smith, blacksmith

smoking (*smōa*-king) *c* (pl ~s) dinner-jacket; tuxedo *nAm*

smokkelen (*smo*-ker-lern) *v* smuggle

snaar (snaar) *c* (pl snaren) string

snavel (*snaa*-verl) *c* (pl ~s) beak

snee (snāy) *c* (pl ~ën) cut; slice

sneeuw (snāy oo) *c* snow

sneeuwen (*snāy*oo-ern) *v* snow

sneeuwslik (*snāy*oo-slik) *nt* slush

sneeuwstorm (*snāy*oo-storm) *c* (pl ~en) snowstorm, blizzard

snel (snehl) *adj* fast, swift, rapid

snelheid (*snehl*-hayt) *c* (pl -heden) speed; **maximum ~** speed limit

snelheidsbeperking (*snehl*-hayts-ber-pehr-king) *c* speed limit

snelheidsmeter (*snehl*-hayts-māy-terr) *c* speedometer

snelheidsovertreding (*snehl*-hayts-ōa-verr-trāy-ding) *c* speeding

snelkookpan (*snehl*-kōak-pahn) *c* (pl

~nen) pressure-cooker

snellen (*sneh*-lern) *v* dash

sneltrein (*snehl*-trayn) *c* (pl ~en) express train

snelweg (*snehl*-vehkh) *c* (pl ~en) motorway

****snijden** (*snay*-dern) *v* *cut; carve

snijwond (*snay*-vont) *c* (pl ~en) cut

snipper (*sni*-perr) *c* (pl ~s) scrap

snoek (snōōk) *c* (pl ~en) pike

snoep (snōōp) *nt* sweets; candy *nAm*

snoepgoed (*snōōp*-khōōt) *nt* sweets; candy *nAm*

snoepje (*snōōp*-Yer) *nt* (pl ~s) sweet; candy *nAm*

snoepwinkel (*snōōp*-ving-kerl) *c* (pl ~s) sweetshop; candy store *Am*

snoer (snōōr) *nt* (pl ~en) line, cord; flex; electric cord

snor (snor) *c* (pl ~ren) moustache

snorkel (*snor*-kerl) *c* (pl ~s) snorkel

snugger (*sner*-gerr) *adj* bright

snuit (snur^ewt) *c* (pl ~en) snout

snurken (*snerr*-kern) *v* snore

sociaal (sōa-*shaal*) *adj* social

socialisme (sōa-shaa-*liss*-mer) *nt* socialism

socialist (sōa-shaa-*list*) *c* (pl ~en) socialist

socialistisch (sōa-shaa-*liss*-teess) *adj* socialist

sociëteit (sōa-see-Yer-*tayt*) *c* (pl ~en) club

sodawater (*sōa*-daa-vaa-terr) *nt* sodawater

soep (sōōp) *c* (pl ~en) soup

soepbord (*sōō*-bort) *nt* (pl ~en) soupplate

soepel (*sōō*-perl) *adj* supple, flexible

soeplepel (*sōōp*-lāy-perl) *c* (pl ~s) soup-spoon

sofa (*sōa*-faa) *c* (pl ~'s) sofa

sok (sok) *c* (pl ~ken) sock

soldaat (sol-*daat*) *c* (pl -daten) soldier

soldeerbout (sol-*dāyr*-bout) *c* (pl ~en) soldering-iron

solderen (sol-*dāy*-rern) *v* solder

solide (sōa-*lee*-der) *adj* (pl ~en) solid

sollicitatie (so-lee-see-*taa*-tsee) *c* (pl ~s) application

solliciteren (so-lee-see-*tāy*-rern) *v* apply

som (som) *c* (pl ~men) sum; amount; ronde ~ lump sum

somber (*som*-berr) *adj* gloomy, sombre

sommige (*so*-mer-ger) *pron* some

soms (soms) *adv* sometimes

soort (sōart) *c/nt* (pl ~en) sort, kind; breed, species

sorteren (sor-*tāy*-rern) *v* assort, sort

sortering (sor-*tāy*-ring) *c* (pl ~en) assortment

souterrain (sōō-ter-rang) *nt* (pl ~s) basement

souvenir (sōō-ver-*neer*) *nt* (pl ~s) souvenir

Sovjet-Unie (sof-Yeht-ēw-nee) Soviet Union

spaak (spaak) *c* (pl spaken) spoke

Spaans (spaans) *adj* Spanish

spaarbank (*spaar*-bahngk) *c* (pl ~en) savings bank

spaargeld (*spaar*-gehlt) *nt* savings *pl*

spaarzaam (*spaar*-zaam) *adj* economical

spade (*spaa*-der) *c* (pl ~n) spade

spalk (spahlk) *c* (pl ~en) splint

Spanjaard (*spah*-ñaart) *c* (pl ~en) Spaniard

Spanje (*spah*-ñer) Spain

spannend (*spah*-nernt) *adj* exciting

spanning (*spah*-ning) *c* (pl ~en) tension; pressure, strain, stress

sparen (*spaa*-rern) *v* save; economize

spat (spaht) *c* (pl ~ten) stain, spot, speck

spatader (*spaht*-aa-derr) *c* (pl ~s,

~en) varicose vein

spatbord (spaht-bort) nt (pl ~en)
mud-guard

spatiëren (spaa-tshāy-rern) v space

spatten (spah-tern) v splash

specerij (spāy-ser-ray) c (pl ~en) spice

speciaal (spāy-shaal) adj special; particular, peculiar

zich specialiseren (spāy-shaa-lee-zāy-
rern) specialize

specialist (spāy-shaa-list) c (pl ~en)
specialist

specialiteit (spāy-shaa-lee-tayt) c (pl
~en) speciality

specifiek (spāy-see-feek) adj specific

specimen (spāy-see-mehn) nt (pl ~s)
specimen

speculeren (spāy-kēw-lāy-rern) v
speculate

speeksel (spāyk-serl) nt spit

speelgoed (spāyl-gōōt) nt toy

speelgoedwinkel (spāyl-gōōt-ving-kerl)
c (pl ~s) toyshop

speelkaart (spāyl-kaart) c (pl ~en)
playing-card

speelplaats (spāyl-plaats) c (pl ~en)
playground

speelterrein (spāyl-teh-rayn) nt (pl
~en) recreation ground

speer (spāyr) c (pl speren) spear

spek (spehk) nt bacon

spel¹ (spehl) nt (pl ~en) game

spel² (spehl) nt (pl ~len) play

speld (spehlt) c (pl ~en) pin

spelen (spāy-lern) v play

speler (spāy-lerr) c (pl ~s) player

spellen (speh-lern) v *spell

spelling (speh-ling) c spelling

spelonk (spāy-longk) c (pl ~en) cave

spiegel (spee-gerl) c (pl ~s) looking-
glass, mirror

spiegelbeeld (spee-gerl-bāylt) nt (pl
~en) reflection

spier (speer) c (pl ~en) muscle

spijbelen (spay-ber-lern) v play truant

spijker (spay-kerr) c (pl ~s) nail

spijkerbroek (spay-kerr-brōōk) c (pl
~en) jeans pl

spijskaart (spayss-kaart) c (pl ~en)
menu

spijsvertering (spayss-ferr-tāy-ring) c
digestion

spijt (spayt) c regret

spin (spin) c (pl ~nen) spider

spinazie (spee-naa-zee) c spinach

*****spinnen** (spi-nern) v *spin

spinneweb (spi-ner-vehp) nt (pl
~ben) spider's web, cobweb

spion (spee-Yon) c (pl ~nen) spy

spiritusbrander (spee-ree-terss-brahn-
derr) c (pl ~s) spirit stove

spit¹ (spit) nt (pl ~ten) spit

spit² (spit) nt lumbago

spits¹ (spits) adj pointed

spits² (spits) c (pl ~en) peak; spire

spitsuur (spits-ēwr) nt (pl -uren) rush-
hour, peak hour

*****splijten** (splay-tern) v *split

splinter (splin-terr) c (pl ~s) splinter

splinternieuw (splin-terr-nee⁰⁰) adj
brand-new

zich splitsen (split-sern) fork

spoed (spōōt) c haste, speed

spoedcursus (spōōt-kerr-zerss) c (pl
~sen) intensive course

spoedgeval (spōōt-kher-vahl) nt (pl
~len) emergency

spoedig (spōō-derkh) adv soon, shortly

spoel (spōōl) c (pl ~en) spool

spoelen (spōō-lern) v rinse

spoeling (spōō-ling) c (pl ~en) rinse

spons (spons) c (pl sponzen) sponge

spook (spōāk) nt (pl spoken) ghost,
phantom; spook

spoor (spōār) nt (pl sporen) trace;
trail, track

spoorbaan (spōār-baan) c (pl -banen)

railway; railroad *nAm*

spoorweg (*spōar*-vehkh) *c* (pl ~en) railway; railroad *nAm*

sport (sport) *c* sport

sportjasje (*sport*-Yah-sher) *nt* (pl ~s) sports-jacket, blazer

sportkleding (*sport*-klāy-dɪng) *c* sportswear

sportman (*sport*-mahn) *c* (pl ~en) sportsman

sportwagen (*sport*-vaa-gern) *c* (pl ~s) sports-car

spot (spot) *c* mockery

spraak (spraak) *c* speech; **ter sprake *brengen** *bring up

spraakzaam (*spraak*-saam) *adj* talkative

sprakeloos (*spraa*-ker-lōass) *adj* speechless

spreekkamer (*sprāy*-kaa-merr) *c* (pl ~s) surgery

spreekuur (*sprāy*-ēwr) *nt* (pl -uren) consultation hours

spreekwoord (*sprāyk*-vōart) *nt* (pl ~en) proverb

spreeuw (sprāy⁰⁰) *c* (pl ~en) starling

sprei (spray) *c* (pl ~en) counterpane, quilt

spreiden (*spray*-dern) *v* *spread

***spreken** (*sprāy*-kern) *v* *speak, talk

***springen** (*sprɪ*-ngern) *v* jump; *leap

springstof (*sprɪng*-stof) *c* (pl ~fen) explosive

sprinkhaan (*sprɪngk*-haan) *c* (pl -hanen) grasshopper

sproeier (*sprōō*ᵉᵉ-err) *c* (pl ~s) atomizer

sprong (sprong) *c* (pl ~en) jump; hop, leap

sprookje (*sprōak*-Yer) *nt* (pl ~s) fairytale

spruitjes (*sprur*ᵉʷ-tYerss) *pl* sprouts *pl*

spuit (spur ᵉʷt) *c* (pl ~en) syringe

spuitbus (*spur*ᵉʷt-berss) *c* (pl ~sen)

atomizer

spuitwater (*spur*ᵉʷt-vaa-terr) *nt* soda-water

spuug (spewkh) *nt* spit

spuwen (*spew*⁰⁰-ern) *v* *spit

staal (staal) *nt* steel; **roestvrij ~** stainless steel

***staan** (staan) *v* *stand; **goed ~** *become; suit

staart (staart) *c* (pl ~en) tail

staat (staat) *c* (pl staten) state; **in ~ stellen** enable; **in ~ *zijn om** *be able to; **staats-** national

staatsburgerschap (*staats*-berr-gerr-skhahp) *nt* citizenship

staatshoofd (*staats*-hōaft) *nt* (pl ~en) head of state

staatsman (*staats*-mahn) *c* (pl -lieden) statesman

stabiel (staa-*beel*) *adj* stable

stad (staht) *c* (pl steden) town; city

stadhuis (staht-*hur*ᵉʷss) *nt* (pl -huizen) town hall

stadion (*staa*-dee-Yon) *nt* (pl ~s) stadium

stadium (*staa*-dee-Yerm) *nt* (pl stadia) stage

stadscentrum (*staht*-sehn-trerm) *nt* (pl -tra) town centre

stadslicht (*stahts*-lɪkht) *nt* (pl ~en) parking light

stadsmensen (*stahts*-mehn-sern) *pl* townspeople *pl*

staf (stahf) *c* staff

staken (*staa*-kern) *v* *strike; stop, discontinue

staking (*staa*-kɪng) *c* (pl ~en) strike

stal (stahl) *c* (pl ~len) stable

stallen (*stah*-lern) *v* garage

stalles (*stah*-lerss) *pl* stall; orchestra seat *Am*

stam (stahm) *c* (pl ~men) trunk; tribe

stamelen (*staa*-mer-lern) *v* falter

stampen (*stahm*-pern) *v* stamp, thump

stampvol (*stahmp*-fol) *adj* chock-full

stand (stahnt) *c* score; **tot ~ *brengen** realize

standbeeld (*stahnt*-baylt) *nt* (pl ~en) statue

standpunt (*stahnt*-pernt) *nt* (pl ~en) point of view

standvastig (stahnt-*fahss*-terkh) *adj* steadfast

stang (stahng) *c* (pl ~en) rod, bar

stap (stahp) *c* (pl ~pen) step; pace; move

stapel (*staa*-perl) *c* (pl ~s) stack, heap, pile

stappen (*stah*-pern) *v* step

staren (*staa*-rern) *v* gaze, stare

start (stahrt) *c* take-off

startbaan (*stahrt*-baan) *c* runway

starten (*stahr*-tern) *v* *take off

startmotor (*stahrt*-mōa-terr) *c* starter motor

statiegeld (*staa*-tsee-gehlt) *nt* deposit

station (staa-*shon*) *nt* (pl ~s) station; depot *nAm*

stationschef (staa-*shon*-shehf) *c* (pl ~s) station-master

statistiek (staa-tiss-*teek*) *c* (pl ~en) statistics *pl*

stedelijk (*stay*-der-lerk) *adj* urban

steeds (stayts) *adv* continually

steeg (staykh) *c* (pl stegen) alley, lane

steek (stayk) *c* (pl steken) stitch; sting, bite

steel (stayl) *c* (pl stelen) stem; handle

steelpan (*stayl*-pahn) *c* (pl ~nen) saucepan

steen (stayn) *c* (pl stenen) stone; brick

steengroeve (*stayn*-grōō-ver) *c* (pl ~n) quarry

steenpuist (*stayn*-pur^{ew}st) *c* (pl ~en) boil

steigers (*stay*-gerrs) *pl* scaffolding

steil (stayl) *adj* steep

stekelvarken (*stay*-kerl-vahr-kern) *nt* (pl ~s) porcupine

*steken (*stay*-kern) *v* *sting

stekker (*steh*-kerr) *c* (pl ~s) plug

stel (stehl) *nt* (pl ~len) set

*stelen (*stay*-lern) *v* *steal

stellen (*steh*-lern) *v* *put

stelling (*steh*-ling) *c* (pl ~en) thesis

stelsel (*stehl*-serl) *nt* (pl ~s) system; **tientallig ~** decimal system

stem (stehm) *c* (pl ~men) voice; vote

stemmen (*steh*-mern) *v* vote

stemming[1] (*steh*-ming) *c* mood; atmosphere; spirits

stemming[2] (*steh*-ming) *c* (pl ~en) vote

stempel (*stehm*-perl) *c* (pl ~s) stamp

stemrecht (*stehm*-rehkht) *nt* suffrage

stenen (*stay*-nern) *adj* stone

stenograaf (*stay*-nōa-graaf) *c* (pl -grafen) stenographer

stenografie (*stay*-nōa-graa-*fee*) *c* shorthand

step-in (stehp-*in*) *c* (pl ~s) girdle

ster (stehr) *c* (pl ~ren) star

sterfelijk (*stehr*-fer-lerk) *adj* mortal

steriel (ster-*reel*) *adj* sterile

steriliseren (*stay*-ree-li-*zay*-rern) *v* sterilize

sterk (stehrk) *adj* powerful, strong; **sterke drank** spirits

sterkte (*stehrk*-ter) *c* strength

sterrenkunde (*steh*-rer-kern-der) *c* astronomy

*sterven (*stehr*-vern) *v* die

steun (stūrn) *c* assistance, support; relief

steunen (*stū̄*-nern) *v* support

steunkousen (*stū̄rn*-kou-sern) *pl* support hose

steurgarnaal (*stū̄rr*-gahr-naal) *c* (pl -nalen) prawn

stevig (*stay*-verkh) *adj* solid, firm

stichten (*stikh*-tern) v found

stichting (*stikh*-ting) c (pl ~en) foundation

stiefkind (*steef*-kint) nt (pl ~eren) stepchild

stiefmoeder (*steef*-mōō-derr) c (pl ~s) stepmother

stiefvader (*stee*-faa-derr) c (pl ~s) stepfather

stier (steer) c (pl ~en) bull

stierengevecht (*stee*-rer-ger-vehkht) nt (pl ~en) bullfight

stijf (stayf) adj stiff

stijfsel (*stayf*-serl) nt starch

stijgbeugel (*staykh*-bur̄-gerl) c (pl ~s) stirrup

*****stijgen** (*stay*-gern) v *rise; climb

stijging (*stay*-ging) c rise; climb, ascent

stijl (stayl) c (pl ~en) style

*****stijven** (*stay*-vern) v starch

stikken (*sti*-kern) v choke

stikstof (*stik*-stof) c nitrogen

stil (stil) adj silent; quiet; still

Stille Oceaan (*sti*-ler ōā-sāȳ-aan) Pacific Ocean

stilstaand (*stil*-staant) adj stationary

stilte (*stil*-ter) c (pl ~s) silence; stillness, quiet

stimuleren (stee-mēw-lāȳ-rern) v stimulate

*****stinken** (*sting*-kern) v *smell; *stink; **stinkend** smelly

stipt (stipt) adj punctual

stoel (stōōl) c (pl ~en) chair; seat

stoep (stōōp) c (pl ~en) sidewalk *nAm*

stoet (stōōt) c (pl ~en) procession

stof¹ (stof) nt dust

stof² (stof) c (pl ~fen) fabric, cloth, material; matter; **stoffen** drapery; **vaste** ~ solid

stoffelijk (*sto*-fer-lerk) adj substantial, material

stoffig (*sto*-ferkh) adj dusty

stofzuigen (*stof*-sur̄ᵂ-gern) v hoover; vacuum *vAm*

stofzuiger (*stof*-sur̄ᵂ-gerr) c (pl ~s) vacuum cleaner

stok (stok) c (pl ~ken) stick; cane

stokpaardje (*stok*-paar-tʸer) nt (pl ~s) hobby-horse

stola (*stōā*-laa) c (pl ~'s) stole

stollen (*sto*-lern) v coagulate

stom (stom) adj mute, dumb

stomerij (stōā-mer-*ray*) c (pl ~en) drycleaner's

stomp (stomp) adj blunt

stompen (*stom*-pern) v punch

stookolie (*stōāk*-ōā-lee) c fuel oil

stoom (stōām) c steam

stoomboot (*stōām*-bōāt) c (pl boten) steamer

stoot (stōāt) c (pl stoten) bump

stop (stop) c (pl ~pen) stopper, cork

stopgaren (*stop*-khaa-rern) nt darning wool

stoplicht (*stop*-likht) nt (pl ~en) traffic light

stoppen (*sto*-pern) v stop, halt; *put; darn

stoptrein (*stop*-trayn) c (pl ~en) stopping train, local train

storen (*stōā*-rern) v disturb; trouble

storing (*stōā*-ring) c (pl ~en) disturbance

storm (storm) c (pl ~en) storm; gale, tempest

stormachtig (*storm*-ahkh-terkh) adj stormy

stormlamp (*storm*-lahmp) c (pl ~en) hurricane lamp

stortbui (*stort*-bur̄ᵂ) c (pl ~en) downpour

storten (*stor*-tern) v *shed; deposit

storting (*stor*-ting) c (pl ~en) remittance, deposit

*****stoten** (*stōā*-tern) v bump

stout (stout) *adj* naughty, bad

stoutmoedig (stout-*mōō*-derkh) *adj* bold

straal (straal) *c* (pl stralen) squirt, spout, jet; ray, beam; radius

straalvliegtuig (*straal*-vleekh-tur^{ew}kh) *nt* (pl ~en) turbojet, jet

straat (straat) *c* (pl straten) street; road

straatweg (*straat*-vehkh) *c* (pl ~en) causeway

straf (strahf) *c* (pl ~fen) punishment; penalty

straffen (*strah*-fern) *v* punish

strafrecht (*strahf*-rehkht) *nt* criminal law

strafschop (*strahf*-skhop) *c* (pl ~pen) penalty kick

strak (strahk) *adj* tight; **strakker maken** tighten

straks (strahks) *adv* in a moment

strand (strahnt) *nt* (pl ~en) beach

streek (strāyk) *c* (pl streken) region; district, country, area; trick

streep (strāyp) *c* (pl strepen) line; stripe

streng (strehng) *adj* strict, harsh; severe

stretcher (*streht*-sherr) *c* (pl ~s) camp-bed; cot *nAm*

streven (*strāy*-vern) *v* aspire

strijd (strayt) *c* fight, combat, battle; struggle, strife, contest

***strijden** (*stray*-dern) *v* *fight; struggle

strijdkrachten (*strayt*-krahkh-tern) *pl* armed forces

***strijken** (*stray*-kern) *v* iron; *strike, lower

strijkijzer (*strayk*-ay-zerr) *nt* (pl ~s) iron

strikje (*strik*-Yer) *nt* (pl ~s) bow tie

strikt (strikt) *adj* strict

stripverhaal (*strip*-ferr-haal) *nt* (pl -ha-

len) comics *pl*

stro (strōa) *nt* straw

strodak (*strōa*-dahk) *nt* (pl ~en) thatched roof

stromen (*strōa*-mern) *v* stream, flow

stroming (*strōa*-ming) *c* (pl ~en) current

strook (strōak) *c* (pl stroken) strip

stroom (strōam) *c* (pl stromen) stream; current

stroomafwaarts (strōam-*ahf*-vaarts) *adv* downstream

stroomopwaarts (strōam-*op*-vaarts) *adv* upstream

stroomverdeler (*strōam*-verr-dāy-lerr) *c* distributor

stroomversnelling (*strōam*-verr-sneh-ling) *c* (pl ~en) rapids *pl*

stroop (strōap) *c* syrup

stropen (*strōa*-pern) *v* poach

structuur (strerk-*tēwr*) *c* (pl -turen) structure; fabric, texture

struik (strur^{ew}k) *c* (pl ~en) scrub, bush, shrub

struikelen (*strur^{ew}*-ker-lern) *v* stumble

struisvogel (*strurss*-fōa-gerl) *c* (pl ~s) ostrich

studeerkamer (stēw-*dāy*r-kaa-merr) *c* study

student (stēw-*dehnt*) *c* (pl ~en) student

studente (stēw-*dehn*-ter) *c* (pl ~s) student

studeren (stēw-*dāy*-rern) *v* study

studie (*stēw*-dee) *c* (pl ~s) study

studiebeurs (*stēw*-dee-būrrs) *c* (pl -beurzen) scholarship

stuitend (*stur^{ew}*-ternt) *adj* revolting

stuk¹ (sterk) *adj* broken; ~ ***gaan** *break down

stuk² (sterk) *nt* (pl ~ken) part, piece; lump, chunk; fragment; stretch

sturen (*stēw*-rern) *v* *send; navigate

stuurboord (*stēwr*-bōart) *nt* starboard

stuurkolom (*steūr*-kōā-lom) *c*
steering-column

stuurman (*steūr*-mahn) *c* (pl -lieden,
-lui) steersman, helmsman

stuurwiel (*steūr*-veel) *nt* steering-
wheel

subsidie (serp-*see*-dee) *c* (pl ~s) subsidy

substantie (serp-*stahn*-see) *c* (pl ~s)
substance

subtiel (serp-*teel*) *adj* subtle

succes (serk-*sehss*) *nt* (pl ~sen) success

succesvol (serk-*sehss*-fol) *adj* successful

suède (sēw-*vai*-der) *nt/c* suede

suf (serf) *adj* dumb

suiker (*sur*ᵉʷ-kerr) *c* sugar

suikerklontje (*sur*ᵉʷ-kerr-klon-tʸer) *nt*
(pl ~s) lump of sugar

suikerzieke (*sur*ᵉʷ-kerr-zee-ker) *c* (pl
~n) diabetic

suikerziekte (*sur*ᵉʷ-kerr-zēek-ter) *c*
diabetes

suite (*svee*-ter) *c* (pl ~s) suite

summier (ser-*meer*) *adj* concise

superieur (sēw-per-ree-ᵛ*urr*) *adj* superior

superlatief (sēw-perr-laa-*teef*) *c* (pl
-tieven) superlative

supermarkt (*sēw*-perr-mahrkt) *c* (pl
~en) supermarket

supplement (ser-pler-*mehnt*) *nt* (pl
~en) supplement

suppoost (ser-*pōast*) *c* (pl ~en) custodian, usher

surfplank (*serrf*-plahngk) *c* (pl ~en)
surf-board

surveilleren (serr-vay-ᵛ*ai*-rern) *v* patrol

Swahili (svaa-*hee*-lee) *nt* Swahili

symbool (sim-*bōal*) *nt* (pl -bolen)
symbol

symfonie (sim-fōā-*nee*) *c* (pl ~ën)
symphony

sympathie (sim-paa-*tee*) *c* (pl ~ën)
sympathy

sympathiek (sim-paa-*teek*) *adj* nice

symptoom (sim-*tōām*) *nt* (pl -tomen)
symptom

synagoge (see-naa-*gōā*-ger) *c* (pl ~ṅ)
synagogue

synoniem (see-nōā-*neem*) *nt* (pl ~en)
synonym

synthetisch (sin-*tāy*-teess) *adj* synthetic

Syrië (*see*-ree-ᵛer) Syria

Syriër (*see*-ree-ᵛerr) *c* (pl ~s) Syrian

Syrisch (*see*-reess) *adj* Syrian

systeem (seess-*tāym*) *nt* (pl -temen)
system

systematisch (seess-tāy-*maa*-teess) *adj*
systematic

T

taai (taaᵉᵉ) *adj* tough

taak (taak) *c* (pl taken) task; duty

taal (taal) *c* (pl talen) language;
speech

taalgids (*taal*-gits) *c* (pl ~en) phrase-
book

taart (taart) *c* (pl ~en) cake

tabak (taa-*bahk*) *c* tobacco

tabakswinkel (taa-*bahks*-ving-kerl) *c*
(pl ~s) tobacconist's

tabakszak (taa-*bahk*-sahk) *c* (pl ~ken)
tobacco pouch

tabel (taa-*behl*) *c* (pl ~len) chart,
table

tablet (taa-*bleht*) *nt* (pl ~ten) tablet

taboe (taa-*bōō*) *nt* (pl ~s) taboo

tachtig (*tahkh*-terkh) *num* eighty

tactiek (tahk-*teek*) *c* (pl ~en) tactics
pl

tafel (*taa*-ferl) *c* (pl ~s) table

tafellaken (*taa*-fer-laa-kern) *nt* (pl ~s) table-cloth

tafeltennis (*taa*-ferl-teh-nerss) *nt* table tennis, ping-pong

taille (*tah*-Yer) *c* (pl ~s) waist

tak (tahk) *c* (pl ~ken) branch, bough

talenpracticum (*taa*-ler-prahk-tee-kerm) *nt* (pl -tica) language laboratory

talent (taa-*lehnt*) *nt* (pl ~en) faculty, talent

talkpoeder (*tahlk*-pōō-derr) *nt/c* talc powder

talrijk (*tahl*-rayk) *adj* numerous

tam (tahm) *adj* tame

tamelijk (*taa*-mer-lerk) *adv* pretty, fairly, quite, rather

tampon (tahm-*pon*) *c* (pl ~s) tampon

tand (tahnt) *c* (pl ~en) tooth

tandarts (*tahn*-dahrts) *c* (pl ~en) dentist

tandenborstel (*tahn*-der-bors-terl) *c* (pl ~s) toothbrush

tandestoker (*tahn*-der-stōa-kerr) *c* (pl ~s) toothpick

tandpasta (*tahnt*-pahss-taa) *c/nt* (pl ~'s) toothpaste

tandpijn (*tahnt*-payn) *c* toothache

tandpoeder (*tahnt*-pōō-derr) *nt/c* toothpowder

tandvlees (*tahnt*-flāyss) *nt* gum

tang (tahng) *c* (pl ~en) tongs *pl*, pliers *pl*

tank (tehngk) *c* (pl ~s) tank

tankschip (*tehnk*-skhıp) *nt* (pl -schepen) tanker

tante (*tahn*-ter) *c* (pl ~s) aunt

tapijt (taa-*payt*) *nt* (pl ~en) carpet

tarief (taa-*reef*) *nt* (pl tarieven) rate, tariff ; fare

tarwe (*tahr*-ver) *c* wheat

tas (tahss) *c* (pl ~sen) bag

tastbaar (*tahst*-baar) *adj* palpable ; tangible

tastzin (*tahst*-sın) *c* touch

taxeren (tahk-*sāy*-rern) *v* estimate

taxi (*tahk*-see) *c* (pl ~'s) cab, taxi

taxichauffeur (*tahk*-see-shōa-fūrr) *c* (pl ~s) cab-driver, taxi-driver

taximeter (*tahk*-see-māy-terr) *c* taximeter

taxistandplaats (*tahk*-see-stahnt-plaats) *c* (pl ~en) taxi rank ; taxi stand *Am*

te (ter) *adv* too

technicus (*tehkh*-nee-kerss) *c* (pl -ci) technician

techniek (tehkh-*neek*) *c* (pl ~en) technique

technisch (*tehkh*-neess) *adj* technical

technologie (tehkh-nōā-lōā-*gee*) *c* technology

teder (*tāy*-derr) *adj* delicate, tender

teef (*tāy*f) *c* (pl teven) bitch

teen (*tāy*n) *c* (pl tenen) toe

teer (*tāy*r) *adj* gentle, tender ; *c/nt* tar

tegel (*tāy*-gerl) *c* (pl ~s) tile

tegelijk (ter-ger-*layk*) *adv* at the same time ; at once

tegelijkertijd (ter-ger-lay-kerr-*tayt*) *adv* simultaneously

tegemoetkomend (ter-ger-*mōōt*-kōā-mernt) *adj* oncoming

tegemoetkoming (ter-ger-*mōōt*-kōā-mıng) *c* (pl ~en) concession

tegen (*tāy*-gern) *prep* against

tegendeel (*tāy*-ger-dāyl) *nt* contrary, reverse

tegengesteld (*tāy*-ger-ger-stehlt) *adj* contrary, opposite

*tegenkomen (*tāy*-ger-kōā-mern) *v* *come across, *meet ; run into

tegenover (*tāy*-ger-nōā-verr) *prep* opposite, facing

tegenslag (*tāy*-ger-slahkh) *c* (pl ~en) misfortune ; reverse

*tegenspreken (*tāy*-ger-sprāy-kern) *v* contradict

tegenstander (tāy̆-ger-stahn-derr) c (pl ~s) opponent

tegenstelling (tāy̆-ger-steh-lĭng) c (pl ~en) contrast

tegenstrijdig (tāy̆-ger-stray-derkh) adj contradictory

*__tegenvallen__ (tāy̆-ger-vah-lern) v *be disappointing

*__tegenwerpen__ (tāy̆-ger-vehr-pern) v object

tegenwerping (tāy̆-ger-vehr-pĭng) c (pl ~en) objection

tegenwoordig (tāy̆-ger-vōar-derkh) adj present; adv nowadays

tegenwoordigheid (tāy̆-ger-vōar-derkh-hayt) c presence

tegenzin (tāy̆-ger-zĭn) c aversion

tehuis (ter-hurᵉʷss) nt (pl tehuizen) home; asylum

teint (taint) c complexion

teken (tāy̆-kern) nt (pl ~s, ~en) sign; indication, signal; token

tekenen (tāy̆-ker-nern) v *draw, sketch; sign

tekenfilm (tāy̆-ker-fĭlm) c (pl ~s) cartoon

tekening (tāy̆-ker-nĭng) c (pl ~en) drawing, sketch

tekort (ter-kort) nt (pl ~en) shortage; deficit; ~ *__schieten__ fail

tekortkoming (ter-kort-kōa-mĭng) c (pl ~en) shortcoming

tekst (tehkst) c (pl ~en) text

tel (tehl) c (pl ~len) second

telefoneren (tāy̆-ler-fōa-nāy̆-rern) v phone

telefoniste (tāy̆-ler-fōa-nĭss-ter) c (pl ~n, ~s) operator, telephonist

telefoon (tāy̆-ler-fōan) c (pl ~s) phone, telephone

telefoonboek (tāy̆-ler-fōan-bōōk) nt (pl ~en) telephone directory; telephone book Am

telefooncel (tāy̆-ler-fōan-sehl) c (pl ~len) telephone booth

telefooncentrale (tāy̆-ler-fōan-sehn-traa-ler) c (pl ~s) telephone exchange

telefoongesprek (tāy̆-ler-fōan-ger-sprehk) nt (pl ~ken) telephone call

telefoongids (tāy̆-ler-fōan-gĭts) c (pl ~en) telephone directory; telephone book Am

telefoonhoorn (tāy̆-ler-fōan-hōa-rern) c (pl ~s) receiver

telefoontje (tāy̆-ler-fōan-tᵞer) nt (pl ~s) call

telegraferen (tāy̆-ler-graa-fāy̆-rern) v cable, telegraph

telegram (tāy̆-ler-grahm) nt (pl ~men) cable, telegram

telelens (tāy̆-ler-lehns) c (pl -lenzen) telephoto lens

telepathie (tāy̆-lāy̆-paa-tee) c telepathy

teleurstellen (ter-lūrr-steh-lern) v disappoint; *let down

teleurstelling (ter-lūrr-steh-lĭng) c (pl ~en) disappointment

televisie (tāy̆-ler-vee-zee) c television

televisietoestel (tāy̆-ler-vee-zee-tōō-stehl) nt (pl ~len) television set

telex (tāy̆-lehks) c telex

telkens (tehl-kerns) adv again and again

tellen (teh-lern) v count

telmachine (tehl-mah-shee-ner) c (pl ~s) adding-machine

telwoord (tehl-vōart) nt (pl ~en) numeral

temmen (teh-mern) v tame

tempel (tehm-perl) c (pl ~s) temple

temperatuur (tehm-per-raa-tewr) c (pl -turen) temperature

tempo (tehm-pōa) nt pace

tendens (tehn-dehns) c (pl -denzen) tendency

tenminste (ter-mĭn-ster) adv at least

tennis (*teh*-nerss) *nt* tennis

tennisbaan (*teh*-nerss-baan) *c* (pl -banen) tennis-court

tennisschoenen (*teh*-ner-skhoō-nern) *pl* tennis shoes

tenslotte (tehn-*slo*-ter) *adv* at last

tent (tehnt) *c* (pl ~en) tent

tentdoek (*tehn*-dook) *nt* canvas

tentoonstellen (tehn-*toān*-steh-lern) *v* exhibit; *show

tentoonstelling (tehn-*toān*-steh-ling) *c* (pl ~en) exposition, exhibition; display, show

tenzij (tehn-*zay*) *conj* unless

teraardebestelling (tehr-*aar*-der-bersteh-ling) *c* (pl ~en) burial

terecht (ter-*rehkht*) *adj* just; *adv* rightly

terechtstelling (ter-*rehkht*-steh-ling) *c* (pl ~en) execution

terloops (tehr-*loāps*) *adj* casual

term (tehrm) *c* (pl ~en) term

termijn (tehr-*mayn*) *c* (pl ~en) term

terpentijn (tehr-pern-*tayn*) *c* turpentine

terras (teh-*rahss*) *nt* (pl ~sen) terrace

terrein (teh-*rayn*) *nt* (pl ~en) terrain; grounds

terreur (teh-*rūrr*) *c* terrorism

terrorisme (teh-ro-*riss*-mer) *nt* terrorism

terrorist (teh-*roā*-*rist*) *c* (pl ~en) terrorist

terug (ter-*rerkh*) *adv* back

terugbetalen (ter-*rerkh*-ber-taa-lern) *v* *repay; reimburse, refund

terugbetaling (terrerkh-ber-taa-ling) *c* (pl ~en) repayment, refund

*terugbrengen (ter-*rerkh*-brehng-ern) *v* *bring back

*teruggaan (ter-*rer*-khaan) *v* *go back, *get back

teruggang (ter-*rer*-khahng) *c* depression, recession

terugkeer (ter-*rerkh*-kāȳr) *c* return

terugkeren (ter-*rerkh*-kāȳ-rern) *v* return; turn back

*terugkomen (ter-*rerkh*-koā-mern) *v* return

terugreis (ter-*rerkh*-rayss) *c* return journey

*terugroepen (ter-*rerkh*-roō-pern) *v* recall

terugsturen (ter-*rerkh*-stew-rern) *v* *send back

*terugtrekken (ter-*rerkh*-treh-kern) *v* *withdraw

*terugvinden (ter-*rerkh*-fin-dern) *v* recover

terugweg (ter-*rerkh*-vehkh) *c* way back

*terugzenden (ter-*rerkh*-sehn-dern) *v* *send back

terwijl (terr-*vayl*) *conj* whilst, while

terylene (*teh*-ree-*lāȳn*) *nt* terylene

terzijde (tehr-*zay*-der) *adv* aside

test (tehst) *c* (pl ~s) test

testament (tehss-taa-*mehnt*) *nt* (pl ~en) will

testen (*tehss*-tern) *v* test

tevens (*tāȳ*-verns) *adv* also

tevergeefs (ter-verr-*gāȳfs*) *adv* in vain

tevoren (ter-*voā*-rern) *adv* before; van ~ in advance

tevreden (ter-*vrāȳ*-dern) *adj* satisfied, content

tewaterlating (ter-*vaa*-terr-laa-ting) *c* launching

*teweegbrengen (ter-*vāȳkh*-brehngern) *v* effect

tewerkstellen (ter-*vehrk*-steh-lern) *v* employ

tewerkstelling (ter-*vehrk*-steh-ling) *c* (pl ~en) employment

textiel (tehks-*teel*) *c/nt* textile

Thailand (*tigh*-lahnt) Thailand

Thailander (*tigh*-lahn-derr) *c* (pl ~s) Thai

Thailands (*tigh*-lahnts) *adj* Thai

thans (tahns) *adv* now

theater (tāy-*Yaa*-terr) *nt* (pl ~s) theatre

thee (tāy) *c* tea

theedoek (*tāy*-dōōk) *c* (pl ~en) tea-cloth

theekopje (*tāy*-kop-*Yay*) *nt* (pl ~s) teacup

theelepel (*tāy*-lāy-perl) *c* (pl ~s) tea-spoon

theepot (*tāy*-pot) *c* (pl ~ten) teapot

theeservies (*tāy*-sehr-veess) *nt* (pl -viezen) tea-set

thema (*tāy*-maa) *nt* (pl ~'s) theme; exercise

theologie (tāy-*Yōa*-lōa-*gee*) *c* theology

theoretisch (tāy-*Yōa*-*rāy*-teess) *adj* theoretical

theorie (tāy-*Yōa*-*ree*) *c* (pl ~ën) theory

therapie (tāy-raa-*pee*) *c* (pl ~ën) therapy

thermometer (tehr-mōa-māy-terr) *c* (pl ~s) thermometer

thermosfles (tehr-moss-flehss) *c* (pl ~sen) vacuum flask, thermos flask

thermostaat (tehr-moss-*taat*) *c* (pl -staten) thermostat

thuis (tur^ewss) *adv* home, at home

tien (teen) *num* ten

tiende (*teen*-der) *num* tenth

tiener (*tee*-nerr) *c* (pl ~s) teenager

tijd (tayt) *c* (pl ~en) time; **de laatste ~** lately; **op ~** in time; **vrije ~** spare time, leisure

tijdbesparend (tayt-ber-*spaa*-rernt) *adj* time-saving

tijdelijk (*tay*-der-lerk) *adj* temporary

tijdens (*tay*-derns) *prep* during

tijdgenoot (*tayt*-kher-nōat) *c* (pl -noten) contemporary

tijdperk (*tayt*-pehrk) *nt* (pl ~en) period

tijdschrift (*tayt*-skhrift) *nt* (pl ~en) review, periodical, journal

tijger (*tay*-gerr) *c* (pl ~s) tiger

tijm (taym) *c* thyme

tikken (*tɪ*-kern) *v* type

timmerhout (*tɪ*-merr-hout) *nt* timber

timmerman (*tɪ*-merr-mahn) *c* (pl -lieden, -lui) carpenter

tin (tɪn) *nt* tin, pewter

tiran (tee-*rahn*) *c* (pl ~nen) tyrant

titel (*tee*-terl) *c* (pl ~s) title; heading; degree

toch (tokh) *adv* still; *conj* yet

tocht (tokht) *c* draught

toe (tōō) *adj* closed

toebehoren (tōō-ber-hōa-rern) *v* belong; *pl* accessories *pl*

toedienen (*tōō*-dee-nern) *v* administer

toegang (*tōō*-gahng) *c* admittance, admission, access; entry, entrance; approach

toegankelijk (tōō-*gahng*-ker-lerk) *adj* accessible

*** toegeven** (*tōō*-gāy-vern) *v* admit, acknowledge; *give in, indulge

toehoorder (*tōō*-hōar-derr) *c* (pl ~s) auditor

toekennen (*tōō*-keh-nern) *v* award

toekomst (*tōō*-komst) *c* future

toekomstig (tōō-*kom*-sterkh) *adj* future

toelage (*tōō*-laa-ger) *c* (pl ~n) allowance, grant

*** toelaten** (*tōō*-laa-tern) *v* admit

toelating (tōō-laa-tɪng) *c* (pl ~en) admission

toelichten (*tōō*-lɪkh-tern) *v* elucidate

toelichting (*tōō*-lɪkh-tɪng) *c* (pl ~en) explanation

toen (tōōn) *conj* when; *adv* then

toename (*tōō*-naa-mer) *c* increase

*** toenemen** (*tōō*-nāy-mern) *v* increase; **toenemend** progressive

toenmalig (*tōōn*-maa-lerkh) *adj* contemporary

toepassen (*tōō*-pah-sern) *v* apply

toepassing (*tōō*-pah-sıng) *c* (pl ~en) application

toereikend (*tōō*-ray-kernt) *adj* adequate

toerisme (*tōō*-*riss*-mer) *nt* tourism

toerist (*tōō*-*rist*) *c* (pl ~en) tourist

toeristenklasse (*tōō*-*riss*-ter-klah-ser) *c* tourist class

toernooi (*tōōr*-*nōā*ᵉᵉ) *nt* (pl ~en) tournament

toeschouwer (*tōō*-skhou-err) *c* (pl ~s) spectator

*toeschrijven aan (*tōō*-skhray-vern) assign to

*toeslaan (*tōō*-slaan) *v* *strike

toeslag (*tōō*-slahkh) *c* (pl ~en) surcharge

toespraak (*tōō*-spraak) *c* (pl -spraken) speech

*toestaan (*tōō*-staan) *v* allow, permit

toestand (*tōō*-stahnt) *c* (pl ~en) state; condition

toestel (*tōō*-stehl) *nt* (pl ~len) apparatus, appliance; aircraft; extension

toestemmen (*tōō*-steh-mern) *v* agree, consent

toestemming (*tōō*-steh-mıng) *c* authorization, permission; consent

toetje (*tōō*-tᵛer) *nt* (pl ~s) sweet

toeval (*tōō*-vahl) *nt* chance; luck

toevallig (*tōō*-*vah*-lerkh) *adj* accidental, casual, incidental; *adv* by chance

toevertrouwen (*tōō*-verr-trou-ern) *v* commit

toevoegen (*tōō*-vōō-gern) *v* add

toevoeging (*tōō*-vōō-gıng) *c* (pl ~en) addition

toewijden (*tōō*-vay-dern) *v* dedicate

*toewijzen (*tōō*-vay-zern) *v* allot

toezicht (*tōō*-zıkht) *nt* supervision; ~ ***houden op** supervise

toffee (to-*fāy*) *c* (pl ~s) toffee

toilet (tvah-*leht*) *nt* (pl ~ten) toilet,

lavatory, bathroom; washroom *nAm*

toiletbenodigdheden (tvah-*leht*-ber-nōā-derkht-hāy-dern) *pl* toiletry

toiletpapier (tvah-*leht*-paa-peer) *nt* toilet-paper

toilettafel (tvah-*leh*-taa-ferl) *c* (pl ~s) dressing-table

toilettas (tvah-*leh*-tahss) *c* (pl ~sen) toilet case

tol (tol) *c* toll

tolk (tolk) *c* (pl ~en) interpreter

tolken (*tol*-kern) *v* interpret

tolweg (*tol*-verkh) *c* (pl ~en) turnpike *nAm*

tomaat (tōā-*maat*) *c* (pl tomaten) tomato

ton (ton) *c* (pl ~nen) cask, barrel; ton

toneel (tōā-*nāyl*) *nt* drama; stage

toneelkijker (tōā-*nāyl*-kay-kerr) *c* (pl ~s) binoculars *pl*

toneelschrijver (tōā-*nāyl*-skhray-verr) *c* (pl ~s) dramatist, playwright

toneelspeelster (tōā-*nāyl*-spāyl-sterr) *c* (pl ~s) actress

toneelspelen (tōā-*nāyl*-spāy-lern) *v* act

toneelspeler (tōā-*nāyl*-spāy-lerr) *c* (pl ~s) actor; comedian

toneelstuk (tōā-*nāyl*-sterk) *nt* (pl ~ken) play

tonen (tōā-nern) *v* *show; display

tong (tong) *c* (pl ~en) tongue; sole

tonicum (tōā-nee-kerm) *nt* (pl -ca, ~s) tonic

tonijn (tōā-*nayn*) *c* (pl ~en) tuna

toon (tōan) *c* (pl tonen) tone; note

toonbank (tōām-bahngk) *c* (pl ~en) counter

toonladder (tōān-lah-derr) *c* (pl ~s) scale

toonzaal (tōān-zaal) *c* (pl -zalen) showroom

toorn (tōā-rern) *c* anger

top (top) *c* (pl ~pen) peak; top, summit

toppunt (*to*-pernt) *nt* (pl ~en) height; zenith

toren (*tōā*-rern) *c* (pl ~s) tower

tot (tot) *prep* until, to, till; *conj* till; ~ **aan** till; ~ **zover** so far

totaal[1] (*tōā*-*taal*) *adj* total, overall; utter

totaal[2] (*tōā*-*taal*) *nt* (pl totalen) total; **in** ~ altogether

totalisator (*tōā*-taa-lee-*zaa*-tor) *c* (pl ~s) totalizator

totalitair (*tōā*-taa-lee-*tair*) *adj* totalitarian

totdat (*to*-*daht*) *conj* till

touw (tou) *nt* (pl ~en) twine, rope, string

toverkunst (*tōā*-verr-kernst) *c* magic

traag (traakh) *adj* slow; slack

traan (traan) *c* (pl tranen) tear

trachten (*trahkh*-tern) *v* try, attempt

tractor (*trahk*-tor) *c* (pl ~en, ~s) tractor

traditie (traa-*dee*-tsee) *c* (pl ~s) tradition

traditioneel (traa-dee-shōa-*nāy*l) *adj* traditional

tragedie (traa-*gāy*-dee) *c* (pl ~s) tragedy

tragisch (*traa*-geess) *adj* tragic

trainen (*trāy*-nern) *v* drill, train

tralie (*traa*-lee) *c* (pl ~s) bar

tram (trehm) *c* (pl ~s) tram; streetcar *nAm*

transactie (trahn-*zahk*-see) *c* (pl ~s) deal, transaction

transatlantisch (trahn-zaht-*lahn*-teess) *adj* transatlantic

transformator (trahns-for-*maa*-tor) *c* (pl ~en, ~s) transformer

transpiratie (trahn-spee-*raa*-tsee) *c* perspiration

transpireren (trahn-spee-*rāy*-rern) *v* perspire

transport (trahn-*sport*) *nt* (pl ~en) transportation

transporteren (trahn-spor-*tāy*-rern) *v* transport

trap (trahp) *c* (pl ~pen) stairs *pl*, staircase; kick

trapleuning (*trahp*-lūr-nıng) *c* (pl ~en) banisters *pl*

trappen (*trah*-pern) *v* kick

trechter (*trehkh*-terr) *c* (pl ~s) funnel

trede (*trāy*-der) *c* (pl ~n) step

*****treffen** (*treh*-fern) *v* *hit; *strike

trefpunt (*trehf*-pernt) *nt* (pl ~en) meeting-place

trein (trayn) *c* (pl ~en) train; **doorgaande** ~ through train

trek[1] (trehk) *c* (pl ~ken) trait

trek[2] (trehk) *c* appetite

*****trekken** (*treh*-kern) *v* pull; *draw; extract; hike

trekker (*treh*-kerr) *c* (pl ~s) trigger

trekking (*treh*-kıng) *c* (pl ~en) draw

treuren (*trūr*-rern) *v* grieve

treurig (*trūr*-rerkh) *adj* sad

treurspel (*trūrr*-spehl) *nt* (pl ~en) drama

tribune (tree-*bēw*-ner) *c* (pl ~s) stand

tricotgoederen (tree-*kōā*-*gōō*-der-rern) *pl* hosiery

triest (treest) *adj* depressing

trillen (*trı*-lern) *v* tremble; vibrate

triomf (tree-ˇ*omf*) *c* (pl ~en) triumph

triomfantelijk (tree-ˇom-*fahn*-ter-lerk) *adj* triumphant

troepen (*trōō*-pern) *pl* troops *pl*

trommel (*tro*-merl) *c* (pl ~s) canister; drum

trommelvlies (*tro*-merl-vleess) *nt* (pl -vliezen) ear-drum

trompet (trom-*peht*) *c* (pl ~ten) trumpet

troon (trōān) *c* (pl tronen) throne

troost (trōāst) *c* comfort

troosten (*trōāss*-tern) *v* comfort

troostprijs (*trōast*-prayss) *c* (pl -prij-zen) consolation prize

tropen (*trōa*-pern) *pl* tropics *pl*

tropisch (*trōa*-peess) *adj* tropical

trots (trots) *adj* proud ; *c* pride

trottoir (tro-*tvaar*) *nt* (pl ~s) pavement ; sidewalk *nAm*

trottoirband (tro-*tvaar*-bahnt) *c* (pl ~en) curb

trouw (trou) *adj* true, faithful

trouwen (*trou*-ern) *v* marry

trouwens (*trou*-erns) *adv* besides

trouwring (*trou*-rıng) *c* (pl ~en) wedding-ring

trui (trur^{ew}) *c* (pl ~en) jersey

Tsjech (ts^{y}ehkh) *c* (pl ~en) Czech

Tsjechisch (ts^{y}eh-kheess) *adj* Czech

Tsjechoslowakije (ts^{y}eh-khōa-slōa-vaa-*kay*-er) Czechoslovakia

tube (*tēw*-ber) *c* (pl ~s) tube

tuberculose (tēw-behr-kēw-*lōa*-zer) *c* tuberculosis

tuin (tur^{ew}n) *c* (pl ~en) garden

tuinbouw (tur^{ew}m-bou) *c* horticulture

tuinman (tur^{ew}n-mahn) *c* (pl -lieden, -lui) gardener

tuit (tur^{ew}t) *c* (pl ~en) nozzle

tulp (terlp) *c* (pl ~en) tulip

tumor (*tēw*-mor) *c* (pl ~s) tumour

Tunesië (tēw-*nāy*-zee-^{y}er) Tunisia

Tunesiër (tēw-*nāy*-zee-^{y}err) *c* (pl ~s) Tunisian

Tunesisch (tēw-*nāy*-zeess) *adj* Tunisian

tuniek (tēw-*neek*) *c* (pl ~en) tunic

tunnel (*ter*-nerl) *c* (pl ~s) tunnel

turbine (terr-*bee*-ner) *c* (pl ~s) turbine

Turk (terrk) *c* (pl ~en) Turk

Turkije (terr-*kay*-er) Turkey

Turks (terrks) *adj* Turkish ; ~ **bad** Turkish bath

tussen (*ter*-sern) *prep* between ; among, amid

tussenbeide *komen (ter-serm-*bay*-der *kōa*-mern) interfere

tussenpersoon (*ter*-ser-pehr-sōan) *c* (pl -sonen) intermediary

tussenpoos (*ter*-ser-pōass) *c* (pl -pozen) interval

tussenruimte (*ter*-ser-rur^{ew}m-ter) *c* (pl ~n, ~s) space

tussenschot (*ter*-ser-skhot) *nt* (pl ~ten) partition ; diaphragm

tussentijd (*ter*-ser-tayt) *c* interim

twaalf (tvaalf) *num* twelve

twaalfde (tvaalf-der) *num* twelfth

twee (tvāy) *num* two

tweede (*tvāy*-der) *num* second

tweedehands (tvāy-der-*hahnts*) *adj* second-hand

tweedelig (tvāy-*dāy*-lerkh) *adj* two-piece

tweeling (*tvāy*-lıng) *c* (pl ~en) twins *pl*

tweemaal (*tvāy*-maal) *adv* twice

tweesprong (*tvāy*-sprong) *c* (pl ~en) fork, road fork

tweetalig (tvāy-*taa*-lerkh) *adj* bilingual

twijfel (*tvay*-ferl) *c* (pl ~s) doubt

twijfelachtig (*tvay*-ferl-ahkh-terkh) *adj* doubtful

twijfelen (*tvay*-fer-lern) *v* doubt

twijg (tvaykh) *c* (pl ~en) twig

twintig (*tvın*-terkh) *num* twenty

twintigste (*tvın*-terkh-ster) *num* twentieth

twist (tvıst) *c* (pl ~en) quarrel

twisten (*tvıss*-tern) *v* quarrel, dispute

tyfus (*tee*-ferss) *c* typhoid

type (*tee*-per) *nt* (pl ~n, ~s) type

typen (*tee*-pern) *v* type

typisch (*tee*-peess) *adj* typical

typiste (tee-*pı*-ster) *c* (pl ~s, ~n) typist

U

u (ēw) *pron* you

ui (ur^ew) *c* (pl ~en) onion

uil (ur^ew l) *c* (pl ~en) owl

uit (ur^ew t) *prep* from, out of; for; *adv* out

uitademen (ur^ew t-aa-der-mern) *v* expire, exhale

uitbarsting (ur^ew t-bahr-stern) *c* (pl ~en) outbreak

uitbenen (ur^ew t-bay-nern) *v* bone

***uitblinken** (ur^ew t-blıng-kern) *v* excel

uitbreiden (ur^ew t-bray-dern) *v* extend, enlarge, expand

uitbreiding (ur^ew t-bray-dıng) *c* (pl ~en) extension

uitbuiten (ur^ew t-bur^ew-tern) *v* exploit

uitbundig (ur^ew t-*bern*-derkh) *adj* exuberant

uitdagen (ur^ew-daa-gern) *v* dare, challenge

uitdaging (ur^ew-daa-gıng) *c* (pl ~en) challenge

uitdelen (ur^ew-day-lern) *v* distribute; *deal

***uitdoen** (ur^ew-dōōn) *v* *put out

uitdrukkelijk (ur^ew-drer-ker-lerk) *adj* express, explicit

uitdrukken (-ur^ew-drer-kern) *v* express

uitdrukking (ur^ew-drer-kıng) *c* (pl ~en) expression; phrase

uiteindelijk (ur^ew t-ayn-der-lerk) *adj* eventual; *adv* at last

uiten (ur^ew-tern) *v* express; utter

uiteraard (ur^ew-ter-*raart*) *adv* of course, naturally

uiterlijk (ur^ew-terr-lerk) *adj* outward, external, exterior; *nt* outside; look

uiterst (ur^ew-terrst) *adj* extreme; utmost, very

uiterste (ur^ew-terr-ster) *nt* (pl ~n) extreme

***uitgaan** (ur^ew t-khaan) *v* *go out

uitgang (ur^ew t-khahng) *c* (pl ~en) way out, exit; issue

uitgangspunt (ur^ew t-khahngs-pernt) *nt* (pl ~en) starting-point

uitgave (ur^ew t-khaa-ver) *c* (pl ~n) expense, expenditure; edition, issue

uitgebreid (ur^ew t-kher-brayt) *adj* comprehensive, extensive

uitgelezen (ur^ew t-kher-lay-zern) *adj* select

uitgestrekt (ur^ew t-kher-strehkt) *adj* vast

***uitgeven** (ur^ew t-khay-vern) *v* *spend; publish, issue

uitgever (ur^ew t-khay-verr) *c* (pl ~s) publisher

uitgezonderd (ur^ew t-kher-zon-derrt) *prep* except

uitgifte (ur^ew t-khif-ter) *c* (pl ~n) issue

***uitglijden** (ur^ew t-khlay-dern) *v* slip

uithoudingsvermogen (ur^ew t-hou-dıngs-ferr-mōā-gern) *nt* stamina

uiting (ur^ew-tıng) *c* (pl ~en) expression

uitkiezen (ur^ew t-kee-zern) *v* select

***uitkijken** (ur^ew t-kay-kern) *v* watch out, look out; ~ **naar** watch for

zich uitkleden (ur^ew t-klay-dern) undress

***uitkomen** (ur^ew t-kōā-mern) *v* *come out; *come true; *be convenient; ~ **op** open on

uitkomst (ur^ew t-komst) *c* (pl ~en) issue

uitlaat (ur^ew t-laat) *c* (pl -laten) exhaust

uitlaatgassen (ur^ew t-laat-khah-sern) *pl* exhaust gases

uitlaatpijp (ur^ew t-laat-payp) *c* (pl ~en) exhaust

***uitladen** (ur^ew t-laa-dern) *v* unload, discharge

uitleg (*ur^ewt*-lehkh) *c* explanation

uitleggen (*ur^ewt*-leh-gern) *v* explain

uitlenen (*ur^ewt*-lāy-nern) *v* *lend

uitleveren (*ur^ewt*-lāy-ver-rern) *v* extradite

uitmaken (*ur^ewt*-maa-kern) *v* matter; determine; *put out

uitnodigen (*ur^ewt*-nōa-der-gern) *v* invite; ask

uitnodiging (*ur^ewt*-nōo-der-ging) *c* (pl ~en) invitation

uitoefenen (*ur^ewt*-ōō-fer-nern) *v* exercise

uitpakken (*ur^ewt*-pah-kern) *v* unpack; unwrap

uitputten (*ur^ewt*-per-tern) *v* exhaust

uitrekenen (*ur^ewt*-rāy-ker-nern) *v* calculate

uitrit (*ur^ewt*-rit) *c* (pl ~ten) exit

uitroep (*ur^ewt*-rōōp) *c* (pl ~en) exclamation

* **uitroepen** (*ur^ewt*-rōō-pern) *v* exclaim

uitrusten (*ur^ewt*-rerss-tern) *v* rest; equip

uitrusting (*ur^ewt*-rerss-ting) *c* (pl ~en) equipment; gear, kit, outfit

uitschakelen (*ur^ewt*-skhaa-ker-lern) *v* switch off; disconnect

* **uitscheiden** (*ur^ewt*-skhay-dern) *v* quit

* **uitschelden** (*ur^ewt*-skhehl-dern) *v* call names

uitslag (*ur^ewt*-slahkh) *c* (pl ~en) result; rash

* **uitsluiten** (*ur^ewt*-slur^ew-tern) *v* exclude

uitsluitend (ur^ewt-*slur^ew*-ternt) *adv* solely, exclusively

uitspraak (*ur^ewt*-spraak) *c* (pl -spraken) pronunciation; verdict

uitspreiden (*ur^ewt*-spray-dern) *v* expand

* **uitspreken** (*ur^ewt*-sprāy-kern) *v* pronounce

uitstapje (*ur^ewt*-stahp-^yer) *nt* (pl ~s) trip, excursion

uitstappen (*ur^ewt*-stah-pern) *v* *get off

uitstekend (ur^ewt-*stāy*-kernt) *adj* fine, excellent

uitstel (*ur^ewt*-stehl) *nt* delay; respite

uitstellen (*ur^ewt*-steh-lern) *v* delay, postpone; adjourn

* **uittrekken** (*ur^ew*-treh-kern) *v* extract

uitverkocht (*ur^ewt*-ferr-kokht) *adj* sold out

uitverkoop (*ur^ewt*-ferr-kōap) *c* sales

* **uitvinden** (*ur^ewt*-fin-dern) *v* invent

uitvinder (*ur^ewt*-fin-derr) *c* (pl ~s) inventor

uitvinding (*ur^ewt*-fin-ding) *c* (pl ~en) invention

uitvoer (*ur^ewt*-fōōr) *c* exportation

uitvoerbaar (ur^ewt-*fōōr*-baar) *adj* feasible

uitvoeren (*ur^ewt*-fōō-rern) *v* carry out; implement, perform, execute; export

uitvoerend (*ur^ewt*-fōō-rernt) *adj* executive; **uitvoerende macht** executive

uitvoerig (ur^ewt-*fōō*-rerkh) *adj* detailed

uitwerken (*ur^ewt*-vehr-kern) *v* elaborate

* **uitwijzen** (*ur^ewt*-vay-zern) *v* expel

uitwisselen (*ur^ewt*-vi-ser-lern) *v* exchange

* **uitzenden** (*ur^ewt*-sehn-dern) *v* *broadcast, transmit

uitzending (*ur^ewt*-sehn-ding) *c* (pl ~en) broadcast, transmission

uitzicht (*ur^ewt*-sikht) *nt* (pl ~en) view

uitzondering (*ur^ewt*-son-der-ring) *c* (pl ~en) exception

uitzonderlijk (ur^ewt-*son*-derr-lerk) *adj* exceptional

* **uitzuigen** (*ur^ewt*-sur^ew-gern) *v* *bleed

ultraviolet (erl-traa-vee-^yōa-*leht*) *adj* ultraviolet

unaniem (ēw-naa-*neem*) *adj* unanimous

unie (ēw̄-nee) c (pl ~s) union
uniek (ēw̄-*neek*) adj unique
uniform[1] (ēw̄-nee-*form*) adj uniform
uniform[2] (ēw̄-nee-*form*) nt/c (pl ~en) uniform
universeel (ēw̄-nee-vehr-*zāȳl*) adj universal
universiteit (ēw̄-nee-vehr-zee-*tayt*) c (pl ~en) university
urgent (err-*gehnt*) adj pressing
urgentie (err-*gehn*-see) c urgency
urine (ēw̄-*ree*-ner) c urine
Uruguay (ōō-rōō-gvigh) Uruguay
Uruguayaan (ōō-rōō-gvah-ᵞaan) c (pl -yanen) Uruguayan
Uruguayaans (ōō-rōō-gvah-ᵞaans) adj Uruguayan
uur (ēw̄r) nt (pl uren) hour; **om** ... ~ at ... o'clock; **uur-** hourly
uw (ēw̄ºº) pron your

V

vaag (vaakh) adj vague; faint; dim
vaak (vaak) adv often
vaandel (*vaan*-derl) nt (pl ~s) banner
vaardig (*vaar*-derkh) adj skilled, skilful
vaardigheid (*vaar*-derkh-hayt) c (pl -heden) skill; art
vaart (vaart) c speed
vaartuig (*vaar*-tur-ᵉʷkh) nt (pl ~en) vessel
vaarwater (*vaar*-vaa-terr) nt waterway
vaas (vaass) c (pl vazen) vase
vaatje (*vaa*-tᵞer) nt (pl ~s) keg
vaatwerk (*vaat*-vehrk) nt crockery
vacant (vaa-*kahnt*) adj vacant
vacature (vah-kah-*tēw̄*-rer) c (pl ~s) vacancy
vacuüm (*vaa*-kēw̄-erm) nt vacuum
vader (*vaa*-derr) c (pl ~s) father; dad
vaderland (*vaa*-derr-lahnt) nt native country, fatherland

vagebond (*vaa*-ger-bont) c (pl ~en) tramp
vak (vahk) nt (pl ~ken) profession, trade; section
vakantie (vaa-*kahn*-see) c (pl ~s) holiday, vacation; **met** ~ on holiday
vakantiekamp (vaa-*kahn*-see-kahmp) nt (pl ~en) holiday camp
vakantieoord (vaa-*kahn*-see-ōart) nt (pl ~en) holiday resort
vakbond (*vahk*-bont) c (pl ~en) trade-union
vakkundig (vah-*kern*-derkh) adj skilled
vakman (*vahk*-mahn) c (pl -lieden) expert
val[1] (vahl) c fall
val[2] (vahl) c (pl ~len) trap
valk (vahlk) c (pl ~en) hawk
vallei (vah-*lay*) c (pl ~en) valley
***vallen** (*vah*-lern) v *fall; ***laten** ~ drop
vals (vahls) adj false
valuta (vaa-*lēw̄*-taa) c (pl ~'s) currency
van (vahn) prep of; from; off; with
vanaf (vah-*nahf*) prep from, as from
vanavond (vah-*naa*-vernt) adv tonight
vandaag (vahn-*daakh*) adv today
***vangen** (*vah*-ngern) v *catch; capture
vangrail (*vahng*-rāȳl) c (pl ~s) crash barrier
vangst (vahngst) c (pl ~en) capture
vanille (vaa-*nee*-ᵞer) c vanilla
vanmiddag (vah-*mı*-dahkh) adv this afternoon
vanmorgen (vah-*mor*-gern) adv this morning
vannacht (vah-*nahkht*) adv tonight
vanwege (vahn-*vāȳ*-ger) prep on account of, for, owing to, because of
vanzelfsprekend (vahn-zehlf-*sprāȳ*-kernt) adj self-evident

*varen (*vaa*-rern) *v* sail, navigate

variëren (vaa-ree-ᵞaȳ-rern) *v* vary

variététheater (vaa-ree-ᵞaȳ-tay-taȳ-ᵞaa-terr) *nt* (pl ~s) variety theatre; music-hall

variétévoorstelling (vaa-ree-ᵞaȳ-tay-voar-steh-ling) *c* (pl ~en) variety show

varken (*vahr*-kern) *nt* (pl ~s) pig

varkensleer (*vahr*-kerss-laȳr) *nt* pigskin

varkensvlees (*vahr*-kerss-flayss) *nt* pork

vaseline (vaa-zer-*lee*-ner) *c* vaseline

vast (vahst) *adj* fixed, firm; steady, permanent; *adv* tight; ~ menu set menu

vastberaden (vahss-ber-*raa*-dern) *adj* resolute

vastbesloten (vahss-ber-sloa-tern) *adj* determined

vasteland (vahss-ter-*lahnt*) *nt* mainland; continent

*vasthouden (*vahst*-hou-dehn) *v* *hold; zich ~ *hold on

vastmaken (*vahst*-maa-kern) *v* fasten; attach

vastomlijnd (vahss-tom-laynt) *adj* definite

vastspelden (*vahst*-spehl-dern) *v* pin

vaststellen (*vahst*-steh-lern) *v* establish, determine

vat (vaht) *nt* (pl ~en) cask, barrel; vessel

*vechten (*vehkh*-tern) *v* *fight; combat, battle

vee (vaȳ) *nt* cattle *pl*

veearts (*vaȳ*-ahrts) *c* (pl ~en) veterinary surgeon

veel (vaȳl) *adj* much, many; *adv* much, far

veelbetekenend (vaȳl-ber-taȳ-ker-nernt) *adj* significant

veelomvattend (vaȳl-om-*vah*-ternt) *adj* extensive

veelvuldig (vaȳl-*verl*-derkh) *adj* frequent

veelzijdig (vaȳl-*zay*-derkh) *adj* all-round

veen (vaȳn) *nt* moor

veer (vaȳr) *c* (pl veren) feather; spring

veerboot (*vaȳr*-boat) *c* (pl -boten) ferry-boat

veertien (*vaȳr*-teen) *num* fourteen; ~ dagen fortnight

veertiende (*vaȳr*-teen-der) *num* fourteenth

veertig (*vaȳr*-terkh) *num* forty

vegen (*vaȳ*-gern) *v* *sweep; wipe

vegetariër (vaȳ-ger-*taa*-ree-ᵞerr) *c* (pl ~s) vegetarian

veilig (*vay*-lerkh) *adj* safe; secure

veiligheid (*vay*-lerkh-hayt) *c* safety; security

veiligheidsgordel (*vay*-lerkh-hayts-khor-derl) *c* (pl ~s) safety-belt; seat-belt

veiligheidsspeld (*vay*-lerkh-hayt-spehlt) *c* (pl ~en) safety-pin

veiling (*vay*-ling) *c* (pl ~en) auction

vel (vehl) *nt* (pl ~len) skin

veld (vehlt) *nt* (pl ~en) field

veldbed (*vehlt*-beht) *nt* (pl ~den) camp-bed

veldkijker (*vehlt*-kay-kerr) *c* (pl ~s) field glasses

velg (vehlkh) *c* (pl ~en) rim

Venezolaan (vaȳ-naȳ-zoa-*laan*) *c* (pl -lanen) Venezuelan

Venezolaans (vaȳ-naȳ-zoa-*laans*) *adj* Venezuelan

Venezuela (vaȳ-naȳ-zew-*vaȳ*-laa) Venezuela

vennoot (ver-*noat*) *c* (pl -noten) associate

vensterbank (*vehn*-sterr-bahngk) *c* (pl ~en) window-sill

vent (vehnt) *c* chap, guy

ventiel (vehn-*teel*) *nt* (pl ~en) valve

ventilatie (vehn-tee-*laa*-tsee) *c* (pl ~s) ventilation

ventilator (vehn-ti-*laa*-tor) *c* (pl ~s, ~en) ventilator, fan

ventilatorriem (vehn-tee-*laa*-to-reem) *c* (pl ~en) fan belt

ventileren (vehn-tee-*lāy*-rern) *v* ventilate

ver (vehr) *adj* far; remote, far-away, distant

verachten (verr-*ahkh*-tern) *v* scorn, despise

verachting (verr-*ahkh*-tıng) *c* scorn, contempt

verademing (verr-*aa*-der-mıng) *c* relief

veranda (ver-*rahn*-daa) *c* (pl ~'s) veranda

veranderen (verr-*ahn*-der-rern) *v* change; alter, transform; vary; ~ in turn into

verandering (verr-*ahn*-der-rıng) *c* (pl ~en) change; alteration; variation

veranderlijk (verr-*ahn*-derr-lerk) *adj* variable

verantwoordelijk (verr-ahnt-*vōar*-der-lerk) *adj* responsible

verantwoordelijkheid (verr-ahnt-*vōar*-der-lerk-hayt) *c* (pl -heden) responsibility

verantwoorden (verr-*ahnt*-vōar-dern) *v* account for

verband (verr-*bahnt*) *nt* (pl ~en) connection, relation; bandage

verbandkist (verr-*bahnt*-kıst) *c* (pl ~en) first-aid kit

verbazen (verr-*baa*-zern) *v* astonish, amaze, surprise; **zich** ~ marvel

verbazing (verr-*baa*-zıng) *c* astonishment, amazement, surprise

zich verbeelden (verr-*bāyl*-dern) fancy, imagine

verbeelding (verr-*bāyl*-dıng) *c* imagination

*****verbergen** (verr-*behr*-gern) *v* *hide; conceal

verbeteren (verr-*bāy*-ter-rern) *v* improve; correct

verbetering (verr-*bāy*-ter-rıng) *c* (pl ~en) improvement; correction

*****verbieden** (verr-*bee*-dern) *v* prohibit, *forbid

*****verbinden** (verr-*bın*-dern) *v* link, connect, join; dress; **zich** ~ engage

verbinding (verr-*bın*-dıng) *c* (pl ~en) link; connection; **zich in** ~ **stellen met** contact

verblijf (verr-*blayf*) *nt* (pl -blijven) stay

verblijfsvergunning (verr-*blayfs*-ferr-ger-nıng) *c* (pl ~en) residence permit

*****verblijven** (verr-*blay*-vern) *v* stay

verblinden (verr-*blın*-dern) *v* blind; **verblindend** glaring

verbod (verr-*bot*) *nt* (pl ~en) prohibition

verboden (verr-*bōa*-dern) *adj* prohibited; ~ **te parkeren** no parking; ~ **te roken** no smoking; ~ **toegang** no entry, no admittance; ~ **voor voetgangers** no pedestrians

verbond (verr-*bont*) *nt* (pl ~en) union

verbouwen (verr-*bou*-ern) *v* cultivate, raise

verbranden (verr-*brahn*-dern) *v* *burn

verbruiken (verr-*brur^ew*-kern) *v* use up

verbruiker (verr-*brur^ew*-kerr) *c* (pl ~s) consumer

verdacht (verr-*dahkht*) *adj* suspicious

verdachte (verr-*dahkh*-teh) *c* (pl ~n) suspect; accused

verdampen (verr-*dahm*-pern) *v* evaporate

verdedigen (verr-*dāy*-der-gern) *v* defend

verdediging (verr-*dāy*-der-gıng) *c* defence

verdelen (verr-*dāy*-lern) *v* divide

*****verdenken** (verr-*dehng*-kern) *v* suspect

verdenking (verr-*dehng*-king) *c* (pl ~en) suspicion

verder (*vehr*-derr) *adj* further; *adv* beyond; ~ **dan** beyond

verdienen (verr-*dee*-nern) *v* earn; *make; deserve, merit

verdienste (verr-*deens*-ter) *c* (pl ~n) merit; **verdiensten** *pl* earnings *pl*

verdieping (verr-*dee*-ping) *c* (pl ~en) storey, floor

verdikken (verr-*di*-kern) *v* thicken

verdoving (verr-*dōā*-ving) *c* (pl ~en) anaesthesia

verdraaien (verr-*draa*ee-ern) *v* wrench

verdrag (verr-*drahkh*) *nt* (pl ~en) treaty

*****verdragen** (verr-*draa*-gern) *v* endure, *bear; sustain

verdriet (verr-*dreet*) *nt* grief, sorrow

verdrietig (verr-*dree*-terkh) *adj* sad

*****verdrijven** (verr-*dray*-vern) *v* chase

*****verdrinken** (verr-*dring*-kern) *v* drown; *be drowned

verdrukken (verr-*drer*-kern) *v* oppress

verduidelijken (verr-*dur*ew-der-ler-kern) *v* clarify

verduistering (verr-*dur*ewss-ter-rehn) *c* (pl ~en) eclipse

verdunnen (verr-*der*-nern) *v* dilute

verdwaald (verr-*dvaalt*) *adj* lost

*****verdwijnen** (verr-*dvay*-nern) *v* vanish, disappear

vereisen (verr-*ay*-sern) *v* demand, require; **vereist** requisite

vereiste (verr-*ayss*-ter) *c* (pl ~n) requirement

Verenigde Staten (verr-*āy*-nerkh-der-*staa*-tern) United States, the States

verenigen (verr-*āy*-ner-gern) *v* join; unite; **verenigd** joint

vereniging (verr-*āy*-ner-ging) *c* (pl

~en) association; union, society, club

verf (vehrf) *c* (pl verven) paint; dye

verfdoos (*vehrf*-dōāss) *c* (pl -dozen) paint-box

verfrissen (verr-*fri*-sern) *v* refresh

verfrissing (verr-*fri*-sing) *c* (pl ~en) refreshment

vergadering (verr-*gaa*-der-ring) *c* (pl ~en) meeting; assembly

vergeefs (verr-*gāyfs*) *adj* vain; *adv* in vain

vergeetachtig (verr-*gāyt*-ahkh-terkh) *adj* forgetful

*****vergelijken** (vehr-ger-*lay*-kern) *v* compare

vergelijking (vehr-ger-*lay*-king) *c* (pl ~en) comparison

*****vergeten** (verr-*gāy*-tern) *v* *forget

*****vergeven** (verr-*gāy*-vern) *v* *forgive

zich vergewissen van (verr-ger-*vi*-sern) ascertain

vergezellen (verr-ger-*zeh*-lern) *v* accompany

vergiet (verr-*geet*) *nt* (pl ~en) strainer

vergif (verr-*gif*) *nt* poison

vergiffenis (verr-*gi*-fer-niss) *c* pardon

vergiftig (verr-*gif*-terkh) *adj* toxic

vergiftigen (verr-*gif*-teh-gern) *v* poison

zich vergissen (verr-*gi*-sern) *be mistaken; err

vergissing (verr-*gi*-sing) *c* (pl ~en) oversight; error, mistake

vergoeden (verr-*gōō*-dern) *v* *make good, reimburse; remunerate

vergoeding (verr-*gōō*-ding) *c* (pl ~en) remuneration

vergrootglas (verr-*grōāt*-khlahss) *nt* (pl -glazen) magnifying glass

vergroten (verr-*grōā*-tern) *v* enlarge

vergroting (verr-*grōā*-ting) *c* (pl ~en) enlargement

verguld (verr-*gerlt*) *adj* gilt

vergunning (verr-*ger*-ning) *c* (pl ~en)

licence, permit, permission; **een ~ verlenen** license

verhaal (verr-*haal*) *nt* (pl -halen) story; tale

verhandeling (verr-*hahn*-der-lıng) *c* (pl ~en) essay

verheugd (verr-*hūrkht*) *adj* glad

verhinderen (verr-*hın*-der-rern) *v* prevent

verhogen (verr-*hōā*-gern) *v* raise

verhoging (verr-*hōā*-gıng) *c* (pl ~en) rise, increase

verhoor (verr-*hōār*) *nt* (pl -horen) examination, interrogation

verhouding (verr-*hou*-dıng) *c* (pl ~en) affair

verhuizen (verr-*hur*ᵉʷ-zern) *v* move

verhuizing (verr-*hur*ᵉʷ-zıng) *c* (pl ~en) move

verhuren (verr-*hēw̄*-rern) *v* *let; lease

verifiëren (vāy-ree-fee-ᵞāy-rern) *v* verify

vering (*vāy*-rıng) *c* suspension

verjaardag (verr-ᵞaar-dahkh) *c* (pl ~en) birthday; anniversary

* **verjagen** (verr-ᵞaa-gern) *v* chase

verkeer (verr-*kāyr*) *nt* traffic

verkeerd (verr-*kāyrt*) *adj* false, wrong

verkeersbureau (verr-*kāyrs*-bēw̄-rōā) *nt* (pl ~s) tourist office

verkeersopstopping (verr-*kāyrz*-op-sto-pıng) *c* (pl ~en) traffic jam

verkennen (verr-*keh*-nern) *v* explore

* **verkiezen** (verr-*kee*-zern) *v* elect

verkiezing (verr-*kee*-zıng) *c* (pl ~en) election

verklaarbaar (verr-*klaar*-baar) *adj* accountable

verklaren (verr-*klaa*-rern) *v* state, declare; explain

verklaring (verr-*klaa*-rıng) *c* (pl ~en) statement, declaration; explanation

zich verkleden (verr-*klāy*-dern) change

verkleuren (verr-*klūr*-rern) *v* fade; dis-

colour

verknoeien (verr-*knōō*ᵉᵉ-ern) *v* muddle

verkoop (*vehr*-kōāp) *c* sale

verkoopbaar (verr-*kōā*-baar) *adj* saleable

verkoopster (verr-*kōāp*-sterr) *c* (pl ~s) salesgirl

* **verkopen** (verr-*kōā*-pern) *v* *sell; **in het klein ~** retail

verkoper (verr-*kōā*-perr) *c* (pl ~s) salesman; shop assistant

verkorten (verr-*kor*-tern) *v* shorten

verkoudheid (verr-*kout*-hayt) *c* cold

verkrachten (verr-*krahkh*-tern) *v* rape

verkrijgbaar (verr-*kraykh*-baar) *adj* obtainable, available

* **verkrijgen** (verr-*kray*-gern) *v* obtain

verlagen (verr-*laa*-gern) *v* lower, reduce; *cut

verlammen (verr-*lah*-mern) *v* paralise

verlangen¹ (verr-*lah*-ngern) *v* wish, desire; **~ naar** long for

verlangen² (verr-*lah*-ngern) *nt* (pl ~s) wish; longing

verlaten (verr-*laa*-tern) *adj* desert

* **verlaten** (verr-*laa*-tern) *v* *leave; desert

verleden (verr-*lāy*-dern) *adj* previous; *nt* past

verlegen (verr-*lāy*-gern) *adj* shy; embarrassed

verlegenheid (verr-*lāy*-gern-hayt) *c* shyness, timidity; **in ~ *brengen** embarrass

verleiden (verr-*lay*-dern) *v* seduce

verleiding (verr-*lay*-dıng) *c* (pl ~en) temptation

verlenen (verr-*lāy*-nern) *v* grant; extend

verlengen (verr-*leh*-ngern) *v* lengthen; extend; renew

verlenging (verr-*leh*-ngıng) *c* (pl ~en) extension

verlengsnoer (verr-*lehng*-snoor) *nt* (pl ~en) extension cord

verlichten (verr-*likh*-tern) *v* illuminate; relieve

verlichting (verr-*likh*-ting) *c* lighting, illumination; relief

verliefd (verr-*leeft*) *adj* in love

verlies (verr-*leess*) *nt* (pl -liezen) loss

***verliezen** (verr-*lee*-zern) *v* *lose

verlof (verr-*lof*) *nt* (pl -loven) leave; permission

verloofd (verr-*loaft*) *adj* engaged

verloofde (verr-*loaf*-der) *c* (pl ~n) fiancé; fiancée

verlossen (verr-*lo*-sern) *v* deliver; redeem

verlossing (verr-*lo*-sing) *c* (pl ~en) delivery

verloving (verr-*loā*-ving) *c* (pl ~en) engagement

verlovingsring (verr-*loā*-vings-ring) *c* (pl ~en) engagement ring

vermaak (verr-*maak*) *nt* entertainment, amusement

vermageren (verr-*maa*-ger-rern) *v* slim

vermakelijk (verr-*maa*-ker-lerk) *adj* entertaining

vermaken (verr-*maa*-kern) *v* entertain, amuse

vermeerderen (verr-*māyr*-der-rern) *v* increase

vermelden (verr-*mehl*-dern) *v* mention

vermelding (verr-*mehl*-ding) *c* (pl ~en) mention

vermenigvuldigen (verr-*māy*-nerkh-ferl-der-gern) *v* multiply

vermenigvuldiging (verr-*māy*-nerkh-ferl-der-ging) *c* (pl ~en) multiplication

***vermijden** (verr-*may*-dern) *v* avoid

verminderen (verr-*min*-der-rern) *v* decrease, lessen, reduce

vermindering (verr-*min*-der-ring) *c* (pl ~en) decrease

vermiste (verr-*miss*-ter) *c* (pl ~n) missing person

vermoedelijk (verr-*moo*-der-lerk) *adj* presumable, probable

vermoeden (verr-*moo*-dern) *v* suspect

vermoeien (verr-*moo*ee-ern) *v* tire; **vermoeid** weary, tired

vermogen (verr-*moā*-gern) *nt* (pl ~s) ability, faculty; capacity

zich vermommen (verr-*mo*-mern) disguise

vermomming (verr-*mo*-ming) *c* (pl ~en) disguise

vermoorden (verr-*moār*-dern) *v* murder

vernielen (verr-*nee*-lern) *v* wreck, destroy

vernietigen (verr-*nee*-ter-gern) *v* destroy

vernietiging (verr-*nee*-ter-ging) *c* destruction

vernieuwen (verr-*nee*oo-ern) *v* renew

vernis (verr-*niss*) *nt/c* varnish

veronderstellen (verr-on-derr-*steh*-lern) *v* assume, suppose

verontreiniging (verr-ont-*ray*-ner-ging) *c* (pl ~en) pollution

verontschuldigen (verr-ont-*skherl*-der-gern) *v* excuse; **zich ~** apologize

verontschuldiging (verr-ont-*skherl*-der-ging) *c* (pl ~en) apology

verontwaardiging (verr-ont-*vaar*-der-ging) *c* indignation

veroordeelde (verr-*ōār*-dāyl-der) *c* (pl ~n) convict

veroordelen (verr-*ōār*-dāy-lern) *v* sentence

veroordeling (verr-*ōār*-dāy-ling) *c* (pl ~en) conviction

veroorloven (verr-*ōār*-loā-vern) *v* allow, permit; **zich ~** afford

veroorzaken (verr-*ōār*-zaa-kern) *v* cause

veroveraar (verr-*ōā*-ver-raar) *c* (pl ~s)

conqueror

veroveren (verr-ōā-ver-rern) v conquer

verovering (verr-ōā-ver-rıng) c (pl ~en) conquest

verpachten (verr-pahkh-tern) v lease

verpakking (verr-pah-kıng) c (pl ~en) packing

verpanden (verr-pahn-dern) v pawn

verplaatsen (verr-plaat-sern) v move

verpleegster (verr-plāȳkh-sterr) c (pl ~s) nurse

verplegen (verr-plāȳ-gern) v nurse

verplicht (verr-plıkht) adj obligatory, compulsory; ~ *zijn om *be obliged to

verplichten (verr-plıkh-tern) v oblige

verplichting (verr-plıkh-tıng) c (pl ~en) engagement

verraad (ver-raat) nt treason

*verraden** (ver-raa-dern) v betray

verrader (ver-raa-derr) c (pl ~s) traitor

verrassen (ver-rah-sern) v surprise

verrassing (ver-rah-sıng) c (pl ~en) surprise

verrekijker (veh-rer-kay-kerr) c (pl ~s) binoculars pl

verreweg (veh-rer-vehkh) adv by far

verrichten (ver-rıkh-tern) v perform

verrukkelijk (ver-rer-ker-lerk) adj delightful, wonderful

verrukking (ver-rer-kıng) c (pl ~en) delight; in ~ *brengen delight

vers[1] (vehrs) adj fresh

vers[2] (vehrs) nt (pl verzen) verse

verschaffen (verr-skhah-fern) v furnish, provide

verscheidene (verr-skhay-der-ner) num various; several

verscheidenheid (verr-skhay-dern-hayt) c (pl -heden) variety

verschepen (verr-skhāȳ-pern) v ship

*verschieten** (verr-skhee-tern) v fade

*verschijnen** (verr-skhay-nern) v appear

verschijning (verr-skhay-nıng) c (pl ~en) apparition

verschijnsel (verr-skhayn-serl) nt (pl ~en, ~s) phenomenon

verschil (verr-skhıl) nt (pl ~len) difference; distinction, contrast

verschillen (verr-skhı-lern) v differ; vary

verschillend (verr-skhı-lernt) adj unlike, different; distinct

verschrikkelijk (verr-skhrı-ker-lerk) adj terrible; horrible, frightful, awful

verschuldigd (verr-skherl-derkht) adj due; ~ *zijn owe

versie (vehr-zee) c (pl ~s) version

versiering (verr-see-rıng) c (pl ~en) decoration

versiersel (verr-seer-serl) nt (pl ~s, ~en) ornament

*verslaan** (verr-slaan) v defeat, *beat

verslag (verr-slahkh) nt (pl ~en) report, account

verslaggever (verr-slah-khāȳ-verr) c (pl ~s) reporter

zich *verslapen (verr-slaa-pern) *oversleep

versleten (verr-slāȳ-tern) adj wornout, worn, threadbare

*verslijten** (verr-slay-tern) v wear out

versnellen (verr-sneh-lern) v accelerate

versnelling (verr-sneh-lıng) c (pl ~en) gear

versnellingsbak (verr-sneh-lıngs-bahk) c (pl ~ken) gear-box

versnellingspook (verr-sneh-lıngs-pōā) c gear lever

versperren (verr-speh-rern) v block

verspillen (verr-spı-lern) v waste

verspilling (verr-spı-lıng) c waste

verspreiden (verr-spray-dern) v scatter, *shed

*verstaan** (verr-staan) v *understand

verstand (verr-stahnt) nt brain; wits

pl, reason; **gezond** ~ sense

verstandig (verr-*stahn*-derkh) *adj* sensible

verstellen (verr-*steh*-lern) *v* patch

verstijfd (verr-*stayft*) *adj* numb

verstoppen (verr-*sto*-pern) *v* *hide

verstoren (verr-*stoa*-rern) *v* disturb; upset

***verstrijken** (verr-*stray*-kern) *v* expire

verstuiken (verr-*stur*ᵉʷ-kern) *v* sprain

verstuiking (verr-*stur*ᵉʷ-kɪng) *c* (pl ~en) sprain

verstuiver (verr-*stur*ᵉʷ-verr) *c* (pl ~s) atomizer

versturen (verr-*stew*-rern) *v* *send off, dispatch

vertalen (verr-*taa*-lern) *v* translate

vertaler (verr-*taa*-lerr) *c* (pl ~s) translator

vertaling (verr-*taa*-lɪng) *c* (pl ~en) translation; version

verteerbaar (verr-*tāȳr*-baar) *adj* digestible

vertegenwoordigen (verr-*tāȳ*-ger-*vōar*-der-gern) *v* represent

vertegenwoordiger (verr-*tāȳ*-ger-*vōar*-der-gerr) *c* (pl ~s) agent

vertegenwoordiging (verr-*tāȳ*-ger-*vōar*-der-gɪng) *c* (pl ~en) representation; agency

vertellen (verr-*ter*-lern) *v* *tell; relate

vertelling (verr-*teh*-lɪng) *c* (pl ~en) tale

verteren (verr-*tāȳ*-rern) *v* digest

verticaal (vehr-tee-*kaal*) *adj* vertical

vertolken (verr-*tol*-kern) *v* interpret

vertonen (verr-*tōa*-nern) *v* exhibit; display

vertragen (verr-*traa*-gern) *v* delay, slow down

vertraging (verr-*traa*-gɪng) *c* (pl ~en) delay

vertrek¹ (verr-*trehk*) *nt* departure

vertrek² (verr-*trehk*) *nt* (pl ~ken)

room

***vertrekken** (verr-*treh*-kern) *v* *leave; depart, *set out, pull out

vertrektijd (verr-*trehk*-tayt) *c* (pl ~en) time of departure

vertrouwd (verr-*trout*) *adj* familiar

vertrouwelijk (verr-*trou*-er-lerk) *adj* confidential

vertrouwen (verr-*trou*-ern) *nt* confidence, trust, faith; *v* trust; ~ **op** rely on

vervaardigen (verr-*vaar*-der-gern) *v* manufacture

vervaldag (verr-*vahl*-dahkh) *c* expiry

vervallen (verr-*vah*-lern) *adj* expired; due

***vervallen** (verr-*vah*-lern) *v* expire

vervalsen (verr-*vahl*-sern) *v* forge, counterfeit

vervalsing (verr-*vahl*-sɪng) *c* (pl ~en) fake

***vervangen** (verr-*vah*-ngern) *v* replace, substitute

vervanging (verr-*vah*-ngɪng) *c* substitute

vervelen (verr-*vāȳ*-lern) *v* bore; bother

vervelend (verr-*vāȳ*-lernt) *adj* dull, boring, annoying; unpleasant

verven (*vehr*-vern) *v* paint; dye

vervloeken (verr-*vlōo*-kern) *v* curse

vervoer (verr-*vōor*) *nt* transport

vervolg (verr-*volkh*) *nt* (pl ~en) sequel

vervolgen (verr-*vol*-gern) *v* continue; pursue

vervolgens (verr-*vol*-gerss) *adv* then

vervuiling (verr-*vur*ᵉʷ-lɪng) *c* pollution

verwaand (verr-*vaant*) *adj* conceited, snooty

verwaarlozen (verr-*vaar*-lōa-zern) *v* neglect

verwaarlozing (verr-*vaar*-lōa-zɪng) *c* neglect

verwachten (verr-*vahkh*-tern) *v* expect; anticipate

verwachting (verr-*vahkh*-tıng) *c* (pl ~en) expectation; outlook; **in ~ pregnant**

verwant (verr-*vahnt*) *adj* related

verwante (verr-*vahn*-ter) *c* (pl ~n) relation

verward (verr-*vahrt*) *adj* confused

verwarmen (verr-*vahr*-mern) *v* heat, warm

verwarming (verr-*vahr*-mıng) *c* heating

verwarren (verr-*vah*-rern) *v* confuse; *mistake

verwarring (verr-*vah*-rıng) *c* confusion; disturbance; **in ~ brengen** embarrass

verwekken (verr-*veh*-kern) *v* generate

verwelkomen (verr-*vehl*-kōa-mern) *v* welcome

verwennen (verr-*veh*-nern) *v* *spoil

*verwerpen (verr-*vehr*-pern) *v* turn down, reject

*verwerven (verr-*vehr*-vern) *v* acquire

verwezenlijken (verr-*vāy*-zer-ler-kern) *v* realize

verwijden (verr-*vay*-dern) *v* widen

verwijderen (verr-*vay*-der-rern) *v* remove

verwijdering (verr-*vay*-der-rıng) *c* removal

verwijt (verr-*vayt*) *nt* (pl ~en) reproach; blame

*verwijten (verr-*vay*-tern) *v* reproach

*verwijzen naar (verr-*vay*-zern) refer to

verwijzing (verr-*vay*-zıng) *c* (pl ~en) reference

verwonden (verr-*von*-dern) *v* wound, injure

verwonderen (verr-*von*-der-rern) *v* amaze

verwondering (verr-*von*-der-rıng) *c* wonder

verwonding (verr-*von*-dıng) *c* (pl ~en) injury

verzachten (verr-*zahkh*-tern) *v* soften

verzamelaar (verr-*zaa*-mer-laar) *c* (pl ~s) collector

verzamelen (verr-*zaa*-mer-lern) *v* gather; collect

verzameling (verr-*zaa*-mer-lıng) *c* (pl ~en) collection

verzekeren (verr-*zāy*-ker-rern) *v* assure; insure

verzekering (verr-*zāy*-ker-rıng) *c* (pl ~en) insurance

verzekeringspolis (verr-*zāy*-ker-rıngs-pōa-lerss) *c* (pl ~sen) insurance policy

*verzenden (verr-*zehn*-dern) *v* despatch, dispatch

verzending (verr-*zehn*-dıng) *c* expedition

verzet (verr-*zeht*) *nt* resistance

zich verzetten (verr-*zeh*-tern) oppose

verzilveren (verr-*zıl*-ver-rern) *v* cash

*verzinnen (verr-*zı*-nern) *v* invent

verzinsel (verr-*zın*-serl) *nt* (pl ~s) fiction

verzoek (verr-*zōōk*) *nt* (pl ~en) request

*verzoeken (verr-*zōō*-kern) *v* request, ask

verzoening (verr-*zōō*-nıng) *c* (pl ~en) reconciliation

verzorgen (verr-*zor*-gern) *v* look after, *take care of; tend

verzorging (verr-*zor*-gıng) *c* care

verzwikken (verr-*zvı*-kern) *v* sprain

vest (vehst) *nt* (pl ~en) cardigan; waistcoat, jacket; vest *nAm*

vestigen (*vehss*-ter-gern) *v* establish; **zich ~ settle down**

vesting (*vehss*-tıng) *c* (pl ~en) fortress

vet¹ (veht) *adj* fat; greasy

vet² (veht) *nt* (pl ~ten) fat; grease

veter (*vāy*-terr) *c* (pl ~s) lace

vettig (*veh*-terkh) *adj* greasy, fatty

vezel (*vāy*-zerl) *c* (pl ~s) fibre

via (*vee*-Yaa) *prep* via

viaduct (vee-Yaa-*derkt*) *c/nt* (pl ~en) viaduct

vibratie (vee-*braa*-tsee) *c* (pl ~s) vibration

vice-president (*vee*-ser-prāy-zee-dehnt) *c* (pl ~en) vice-president

vier (veer) *num* four

vierde (*veer*-der) *num* fourth

vieren (*vee*-rern) *v* celebrate

viering (*vee*-ring) *c* (pl ~en) celebration

vierkant (*veer*-kahnt) *adj* square; *nt* square

vies (veess) *adj* dirty

vijand (*vay*-ahnt) *c* (pl ~en) enemy

vijandig (vay-*ahn*-derkh) *adj* hostile

vijf (vayf) *num* five

vijfde (*vayf*-der) *num* fifth

vijftien (*vayf*-teen) *num* fifteen

vijftiende (*vayf*-teen-der) *num* fifteenth

vijftig (*vayf*-terkh) *num* fifty

vijg (vaykh) *c* (pl ~en) fig

vijl (vayl) *c* (pl ~en) file

vijver (*vay*-verr) *c* (pl ~s) pond

villa (*vee*-laa) *c* (pl ~'s) villa

vilt (vilt) *nt* felt

***vinden** (*vin*-dern) *v* *find; *come across; consider

vindingrijk (*vin*-ding-rayk) *adj* inventive

vinger (*vi*-ngerr) *c* (pl ~s) finger

vingerafdruk (*vi*-ngerr-ahf-drerk) *c* (pl ~ken) fingerprint

vingerhoed (*vi*-ngerr-hōōt) *c* (pl ~en) thimble

vink (vingk) *c* (pl ~en) finch

violet (vee-Yōa-*leht*) *adj* violet

viool (vee-Yōāl) *c* (pl violen) violin

viooltje (vee-Yōāl-tYer) *nt* (pl ~s) violet

vis (viss) *c* (pl ~sen) fish

visakte (*viss*-ahk-ter) *c* (pl ~n, ~s) fishing licence

visgraat (*viss*-khraat) *c* (pl -graten) fishbone

vishaak (*viss*-haak) *c* (pl -haken) fishing hook

visie (*vee*-zee) *c* vision

visite (vee-*zee*-ter) *c* (pl ~s) visit; call

visitekaartje (vi-*zee*-ter-kaar-tYer) *nt* (pl ~s) visiting-card

viskuit (*viss*-kur^{ew}t) *c* roe

vislijn (*viss*-layn) *c* (pl ~en) fishing line

visnet (*viss*-neht) *nt* (pl ~ten) fishing net

vissen (*vi*-sern) *v* fish

visser (*vi*-serr) *c* (pl ~s) fisherman

visserij (*vi*-ser-*ray*) *c* fishing industry

vistuig (*viss*-tur^{ew}kh) *nt* fishing tackle, fishing gear

visum (*vee*-zerm) *nt* (pl visa) visa

viswinkel (*viss*-ving-kerl) *c* (pl ~s) fish shop

vitamine (vee-taa-*mee*-ner) *c* (pl ~n, ~s) vitamin

vitrine (vee-*tree*-ner) *c* (pl ~s) showcase

vlag (vlahkh) *c* (pl ~gen) flag

vlak (vlahk) *adj* flat; smooth; level, plane

vlakgom (*vlahk*-khom) *c/nt* (pl ~men) rubber

vlakte (*vlahk*-ter) *c* (pl ~n, ~s) plain

vlam (vlahm) *c* (pl ~men) flame

vlees (vlāyss) *nt* meat; flesh

vlek (vlehk) *c* (pl ~ken) stain, spot, blot

vlekkeloos (*vleh*-ker-lōass) *adj* stainless, spotless

vlekken (*vleh*-kern) *v* stain

vlekkenwater (*vleh*-ker-vaa-terr) *nt* stain remover

vleugel (*vlūr*-gerl) *c* (pl ~s) wing;

grand piano

vlieg (vleekh) c (pl ~en) fly

*vliegen (vlee-gern) v *fly

vliegramp (vleekh-rahmp) c (pl ~en) plane crash

vliegtuig (vleekh-tur^{ew}kh) nt (pl ~en) aircraft, aeroplane, plane; airplane nAm

vliegveld (vleekh-fehlt) nt (pl ~en) airfield

vlijt (vlayt) c diligence

vlijtig (vlay-terkh) adj industrious; diligent

vlinder (vlin-derr) c (pl ~s) butterfly

vlinderdasje (vlin-derr-dah-sher) nt (pl ~s) bow tie

vlinderslag (vlin-derr-slahkh) c butter-fly stroke

vloed (vloot) c flood

vloeibaar (vloo^{ee}-baar) adj liquid, fluid

vloeien (vloo^{ee}-ern) v flow; **vloeiend** fluent

vloeipapier (vloo^{ee}-paa-peer) nt blot-ting paper

vloeistof (vloo^{ee}-stof) c (pl ~fen) fluid

vloek (vlook) c (pl ~en) curse

vloeken (vloo-kern) v curse, *swear

vloer (vloor) c (pl ~en) floor

vloerkleed (vloor-klayt) nt (pl -kleden) carpet

vloot (vloat) c (pl vloten) fleet

vlot (vlot) nt (pl ~ten) raft

vlotter (vlo-terr) c (pl ~s) float

vlucht (vlerkht) c (pl ~en) flight

vluchten (vlerkh-tern) v escape

vlug (vlerkh) adj fast, quick, rapid; adv soon

vocaal (voa-kaal) adj vocal

vocabulaire (voa-kaa-bew-lair) nt vo-cabulary

vocht (vokht) nt damp

vochtig (vokh-terkh) adj humid, moist; damp, wet

vochtigheid (vokh-terkh-hayt) c hu-midity, moisture

vod (vot) nt (pl ~den) rag

voeden (voo-dern) v *feed

voedsel (voot-serl) nt food; fare

voedselvergiftiging (voot-serl-verr-gif-ter-ging) c food poisoning

voedzaam (voot-saam) adj nutritious, nourishing

zich voegen bij (voo-gern) join

voelen (voo-lern) v *feel; sense

voeren (voo-rern) v carry

voering (voo-ring) c (pl ~en) lining

voertuig (voor-tur^{ew}kh) nt (pl ~en) ve-hicle

voet (voot) c (pl ~en) foot; **te** ~ on foot, walking

voetbal (voot-bahl) nt soccer

voetbalwedstrijd (voot-bahl-veht-strayt) c (pl ~en) football match

voetganger (voot-khah-ngerr) c (pl ~s) pedestrian

voetpad (voot-paht) nt (pl ~en) foot-path

voetpoeder (voot-poo-derr) nt/c foot powder

voetrem (voot-rehm) c foot-brake

vogel (voa-gerl) c (pl ~s) bird

vol (vol) adj full; full up

volbloed (vol-bloot) adj thoroughbred

*volbrengen (vol-breh-ngern) v ac-complish

voldaan (vol-daan) adj satisfied

voldoende (vol-doon-der) adj suffi-cient, enough; ~ *zijn *do, suffice

voldoening (vol-doo-ning) c satisfac-tion

volgen (vol-gern) v follow; **volgend** subsequent, next, following

volgens (vol-gerns) prep according to

volgorde (vol-gor-der) c order, se-quence

*volhouden (vol-hou-dern) v *keep up; insist

vettig (veh-terkh) adj greasy, fatty

vezel (váy-zerl) c (pl ~s) fibre

via (vee-Yaa) prep via

viaduct (vee-Yaa-derkt) c/nt (pl ~en) viaduct

vibratie (vee-braa-tsee) c (pl ~s) vibration

vice-president (vee-ser-práy-zee-dehnt) c (pl ~en) vice-president

vier (veer) num four

vierde (veer-der) num fourth

vieren (vee-rern) v celebrate

viering (vee-ring) c (pl ~en) celebration

vierkant (veer-kahnt) adj square; nt square

vies (veess) adj dirty

vijand (vay-ahnt) c (pl ~en) enemy

vijandig (vay-ahn-derkh) adj hostile

vijf (vayf) num five

vijfde (vayf-der) num fifth

vijftien (vayf-teen) num fifteen

vijftiende (vayf-teen-der) num fifteenth

vijftig (vayf-terkh) num fifty

vijg (vaykh) c (pl ~en) fig

vijl (vayl) c (pl ~en) file

vijver (vay-verr) c (pl ~s) pond

villa (vee-laa) c (pl ~'s) villa

vilt (vilt) nt felt

***vinden** (vin-dern) v *find; *come across; consider

vindingrijk (vin-ding-rayk) adj inventive

vinger (vi-ngerr) c (pl ~s) finger

vingerafdruk (vi-ngerr-ahf-drerk) c (pl ~ken) fingerprint

vingerhoed (vi-ngerr-hoot) c (pl ~en) thimble

vink (vingk) c (pl ~en) finch

violet (vee-Yōā-leht) adj violet

viool (vee-Yōāl) c (pl violen) violin

viooltje (vee-Yōāl-tYer) nt (pl ~s) violet

vis (viss) c (pl ~sen) fish

visakte (viss-ahk-ter) c (pl ~n, ~s) fishing licence

visgraat (viss-khraat) c (pl -graten) fishbone

vishaak (viss-haak) c (pl -haken) fishing hook

visie (vee-zee) c vision

visite (vee-zee-ter) c (pl ~s) visit; call

visitekaartje (vi-zee-ter-kaar-tYer) nt (pl ~s) visiting-card

viskuit (viss-kurewt) c roe

vislijn (viss-layn) c (pl ~en) fishing line

visnet (viss-neht) nt (pl ~ten) fishing net

vissen (vi-sern) v fish

visser (vi-serr) c (pl ~s) fisherman

visserij (vi-ser-ray) c fishing industry

vistuig (viss-turewkh) nt fishing tackle, fishing gear

visum (vee-zerm) nt (pl visa) visa

viswinkel (viss-ving-kerl) c (pl ~s) fish shop

vitamine (vee-taa-mee-ner) c (pl ~n, ~s) vitamin

vitrine (vee-tree-ner) c (pl ~s) showcase

vlag (vlahkh) c (pl ~gen) flag

vlak (vlahk) adj flat; smooth; level, plane

vlakgom (vlahk-khom) c/nt (pl ~men) rubber

vlakte (vlahk-ter) c (pl ~n, ~s) plain

vlam (vlahm) c (pl ~men) flame

vlees (vlāyss) nt meat; flesh

vlek (vlehk) c (pl ~ken) stain, spot, blot

vlekkeloos (vleh-ker-lōass) adj stainless, spotless

vlekken (vleh-kern) v stain

vlekkenwater (vleh-ker-vaa-terr) nt stain remover

vleugel (vlūr-gerl) c (pl ~s) wing;

grand piano
vlieg (vleekh) c (pl ~en) fly
*vliegen (vlee-gern) v *fly
vliegramp (vleekh-rahmp) c (pl ~en)
plane crash
vliegtuig (vleekh-tur^ewkh) nt (pl ~en)
aircraft, aeroplane, plane; airplane
nAm
vliegveld (vleekh-fehlt) nt (pl ~en)
airfield
vlijt (vlayt) c diligence
vlijtig (vlay-terkh) adj industrious;
diligent
vlinder (vlɪn-derr) c (pl ~s) butterfly
vlinderdasje (vlɪn-derr-dah-sher) nt (pl
~s) bow tie
vlinderslag (vlɪn-derr-slahkh) c butterfly stroke
vloed (vlŌot) c flood
vloeibaar (vlŌō^ee-baar) adj liquid,
fluid
vloeien (vlŌō^ee-ern) v flow; **vloeiend**
fluent
vloeipapier (vlŌō^ee-paa-peer) nt blot-
ting paper
vloeistof (vlŌō^ee-stof) c (pl ~fen) fluid
vloek (vlŌōk) c (pl ~en) curse
vloeken (vlŌō-kern) v curse, *swear
vloer (vlŌōr) c (pl ~en) floor
vloerkleed (vlŌōr-klāyt) nt (pl -kleden)
carpet
vloot (vlŌat) c (pl vloten) fleet
vlot (vlot) nt (pl ~ten) raft
vlotter (vlo-terr) c (pl ~s) float
vlucht (vlerkht) c (pl ~en) flight
vluchten (vlerkh-tern) v escape
vlug (vlerkh) adj fast, quick, rapid;
adv soon
vocaal (vōa-kaal) adj vocal
vocabulaire (vōa-kaa-bew-lair) nt vocabulary
vocht (vokht) nt damp
vochtig (vokh-terkh) adj humid,
moist; damp, wet

vochtigheid (vokh-terkh-hayt) c hu-
midity, moisture
vod (vot) nt (pl ~den) rag
voeden (vōō-dern) v *feed
voedsel (vŌōt-serl) nt food; fare
voedselvergiftiging (vŌōt-serl-verr-gɪf-
ter-gɪng) c food poisoning
voedzaam (vŌōt-saam) adj nutritious,
nourishing
zich voegen bij (vōō-gern) join
voelen (vōō-lern) v *feel; sense
voeren (vōō-rern) v carry
voering (vōō-rɪng) c (pl ~en) lining
voertuig (vŌōr-tur^ewkh) nt (pl ~en) ve-
hicle
voet (vŌōt) c (pl ~en) foot; **te** ~ on
foot, walking
voetbal (vŌōt-bahl) nt soccer
voetbalwedstrijd (vŌōt-bahl-veht-
strayt) c (pl ~en) football match
voetganger (vŌōt-khah-ngerr) c (pl ~s)
pedestrian
voetpad (vŌōt-paht) nt (pl ~en) foot-
path
voetpoeder (vŌōt-pōō-derr) nt/c foot
powder
voetrem (vŌōt-rehm) c foot-brake
vogel (vōa-gerl) c (pl ~s) bird
vol (vol) adj full; full up
volbloed (vol-blŌōt) adj thoroughbred
*volbrengen (vol-breh-ngern) v ac-
complish
voldaan (vol-daan) adj satisfied
voldoende (vol-dŌōn-der) adj suffi-
cient, enough; ~ *zijn *do, suffice
voldoening (vol-dŌō-nɪng) c satisfac-
tion
volgen (vol-gern) v follow; **volgend**
subsequent, next, following
volgens (vol-gerns) prep according to
volgorde (vol-gor-der) c order, se-
quence
*volhouden (vol-hou-dern) v *keep
up; insist

volk (volk) *nt* (pl ~en, ~eren) people; nation; folk; **volks-** national; popular; vulgar

volkomen (voal-kóā-mern) *adj* perfect; *adv* completely

volkorenbrood (vol-kóā-rerm-bróāt) *nt* wholemeal bread

volksdans (*volks*-dahns) *c* (pl ~en) folk-dance

volkslied (*volks*-leet) *nt* (pl ~eren) folk song; national anthem

volledig (vo-*láY*-derkh) *adj* complete

volmaakt (vol-*maakt*) *adj* perfect

volmaaktheid (vol-*maakt*-hayt) *c* perfection

volslagen (vol-*slaa*-gern) *adj* total, utter

volt (volt) *c* volt

voltage (vol-*taa*-zher) *c/nt* (pl ~s) voltage

voltooien (vol-*tóā*ᵉᵉ-ern) *v* complete

volume (vóā-*léW̄*-mer) *nt* (pl ~n, ~s) volume

volwassen (vol-*vah*-sern) *adj* adult; grown-up

volwassene (vol-*vah*-ser-ner) *c* (pl ~n) adult; grown-up

vonk (vongk) *c* (pl ~en) spark

vonnis (*vo*-nerss) *nt* (pl ~sen) verdict, sentence

voogd (vóākht) *c* (pl ~en) tutor, guardian

voogdij (vóākh-*day*) *c* custody

voor (vóār) *prep* before; ahead of, in front of; for; to

vooraanstaand (vóār-*aan*-staant) *adj* leading, outstanding

*voorafgaan (vóār-*ahf*-khaan) *v* precede

vooral (vóā-*rahl*) *adv* essentially, especially, most of all

voorbarig (vóār-*baa*-rerkh) *adj* premature

voorbeeld (vóār-*báYlt*) *nt* (pl ~en) example, instance

voorbehoedmiddel (vóār-ber-hóōt-mɪ-derl) *nt* (pl ~en) contraceptive

voorbehoud (vóār-ber-hout) *nt* qualification

voorbereiden (vóār-ber-ray-dern) *v* prepare

voorbereiding (vóār-ber-ray-dɪng) *c* (pl ~en) preparation

voorbij (vóār-*bay*) *adj* past, over; *prep* past, beyond

*voorbijgaan (vóār-*bay*-gaan) *v* pass

voorbijganger (vóār-*bay*-gah-ngerr) *c* (pl ~s) passer-by

voordat (vóār-daht) *conj* before

voordeel (vóār-*dáYl*) *nt* (pl -delen) advantage; profit, benefit

voordelig (vóār-*dáY*-lerkh) *adj* advantageous; cheap

zich *voordoen (vóār-dóōn) occur

voorgaand (vóār-khaant) *adj* previous, preceding

voorganger (vóār-gah-ngerr) *c* (pl ~s) predecessor

voorgerecht (vóār-ger-rehkht) *nt* (pl ~en) hors-d'œuvre

voorgrond (vóār-gront) *c* foreground

voorhanden (vóār-*hahn*-dern) *adj* available

voorheen (vóār-*háYn*) *adv* formerly

voorhoofd (vóār-hóāft) *nt* (pl ~en) forehead

voorjaar (vóār-ʸaar) *nt* springtime, spring

voorkant (vóār-kahnt) *c* front

voorkeur (vóār-kúrr) *c* preference; **de ~ *geven aan** prefer

voorkomen¹ (vóār-kóā-mern) *nt* look, appearance

*voorkomen² (vóār-kóā-mern) *v* occur, happen

*voorkomen³ (vóār-*kóā*-mern) *v* prevent; anticipate

voorkomend (vóār-*kóā*-mernt) *adj* obliging

voorletter (*vōar*-leh-terr) *c* (pl ~s) in-itial

voorlopig (vōar-*lōa*-perkh) *adj* provisional, temporary; preliminary

voormalig (vōar-*maa*-lerkh) *adj* former

voorman (*vōar*-mahn) *c* (pl ~nen) foreman

voornaam[1] (vōar-*naam*) *adj* distinguished; **voornaamst** *adj* principal, main, leading, chief

voornaam[2] (*vōar*-naam) *c* (pl -namen) first name, Christian name

voornaamwoord (*vōar*-naam-vōart) *nt* (pl ~en) pronoun

voornamelijk (vōar-*naa*-mer-lerk) *adv* especially

vooroordeel (*vōar*-ōar-dāyl) *nt* (pl -delen) prejudice

vooroorlogs (vōar-*ōar*-lokhs) *adj* pre-war

voorraad (*vōa*-raat) *c* (pl -raden) stock, store, supply; provisions *pl*; **in ~ *hebben** stock

voorrang (*vōa*-rahng) *c* priority; right of way

voorrecht (*vōa*-rehkht) *nt* (pl ~en) privilege

voorruit (*vōa*-rur^{ew}t) *c* (pl ~en) windscreen; windshield *nAm*

*voorschieten (*vōar*-skhee-tern) *v* advance

voorschot (*vōar*-skhot) *nt* (pl ~ten) advance

voorschrift (*vōar*-skhrıft) *nt* (pl ~en) regulation

*voorschrijven (*vōar*-skhray-vern) *v* prescribe

voorspellen (vōar-*speh*-lern) *v* predict, forecast

voorspelling (vōar-*speh*-lıng) *c* (pl ~en) forecast

voorspoed (*vōar*-spōot) *c* prosperity

voorsprong (*vōar*-sprong) *c* lead

voorstad (*vōar*-staht) *c* (pl -steden) suburb

voorstander (*vōar*-stahn-derr) *c* (pl ~s) advocate

voorstel (*vōar*-stehl) *nt* (pl ~len) proposition, proposal; suggestion

voorstellen (*vōar*-steh-lern) *v* propose, suggest; present, introduce; represent; **zich ~** conceive, fancy, imagine

voorstelling (*vōar*-steh-lıng) *c* (pl ~en) show, performance

voortaan (vōar-*taan*) *adv* henceforth

voortduren (*vōar*-dew-rern) *v* continue; **voortdurend** continuous, continual

*voortgaan (*vōart*-khaan) *v* continue; proceed

voortreffelijk (vōar-*treh*-fer-lerk) *adj* excellent; exquisite

voorts (vōarts) *adv* moreover

voortzetten (*vōart*-seh-tern) *v* carry on, continue

vooruit (vōa-*rur^{ew}*t) *adv* ahead, forward; in advance

vooruitbetaald (vōa-*rur^{ew}*t-ber-taalt) *adj* prepaid

*vooruitgaan (vōa-*rur^{ew}*t-khaan) *v* advance

vooruitgang (vōa-*rur^{ew}*t-khahng) *c* progress, advance

vooruitstrevend (vōa-rur^{ew}t-*strāy*-vernt) *adj* progressive

vooruitzicht (vōa-*rur^{ew}*t-sıkht) *nt* (pl ~en) prospect

voorvader (*vōar*-vaa-derr) *c* (pl ~s, ~en) ancestor

voorvechter (*vōar*-vehkh-terr) *c* (pl ~s) champion

voorvoegsel (*vōar*-vōokh-serl) *nt* (pl ~s) prefix

voorwaarde (*vōar*-vaar-der) *c* (pl ~n) condition; term

voorwaardelijk (vōar-*vaar*-der-lerk) *adj*

conditional

voorwaarts (*vóar*-vaarts) *adv* onwards, forward

voorwenden (*vóar*-vehn-dern) *v* pretend

voorwendsel (*vóar*-vehnt-serl) *nt* (pl ~s, ~en) pretext, pretence

voorwerp (*vóar*-vehrp) *nt* (pl ~en) object; **gevonden voorwerpen** lost and found

voorzetsel (*vóar*-zeht-serl) *nt* (pl ~s) preposition

voorzichtig (vóar-*zikh*-terkh) *adj* careful; gentle

voorzichtigheid (vóar-*zikh*-terkh-hayt) *c* caution

****voorzien** (vóar-*zeen*) *v* anticipate; ~ **van** furnish with

voorzitter (*vóar*-zi-terr) *c* (pl ~s) chairman, president

voorzorg (*vóar*-zorkh) *c* (pl ~en) precaution

voorzorgsmaatregel (*vóar*-zorkhs-maat-ráy-gerl) *c* (pl ~en) precaution

vorderen (*vor*-der-rern) *v* ***get on**; confiscate, claim

vorig (*vóa*-rerkh) *adj* last; past

vork (vork) *c* (pl ~en) fork

vorm (vorm) *c* (pl ~en) shape; form

vormen (*vor*-mern) *v* shape; form

vorming (*vor*-ming) *c* background

vorst[1] (vorst) *c* (pl ~en) ruler, monarch, sovereign

vorst[2] (vorst) *c* frost

vos (voss) *c* (pl ~sen) fox

vouw (vou) *c* (pl ~en) fold; crease

****vouwen** (*vou*-ern) *v* fold

vraag (vraakh) *c* (pl vragen) question; inquiry, query

vraaggesprek (*vraa*-kher-sprehk) *nt* (pl ~ken) interview

vraagstuk (*vraakh*-sterk) *nt* (pl ~ken) problem, question

vraagteken (*vraakh*-táy-kern) *nt* (pl

~s) question mark

vracht (vrahkht) *c* (pl ~en) freight, cargo

vrachtwagen (*vrahkht*-vaa-gern) *c* (pl ~s) lorry; truck *nAm*

****vragen** (*vraa*-gern) *v* ask; beg; **vragend** interrogative

vrede (*vráy*-der) *c* peace

vreedzaam (*vráyt*-saam) *adj* peaceful

vreemd (vráymt) *adj* strange; odd, queer; foreign

vreemde (*vráym*-der) *c* (pl ~n) stranger

vreemdeling (*vráym*-der-ling) *c* (pl ~en) foreigner; stranger, alien

vrees (vráyss) *c* dread, fear

vreselijk (*vráy*-ser-lerk) *adj* terrible; horrible, dreadful, frightful

vreugde (*vrúrkh*-der) *c* (pl ~n) gladness, joy

vrezen (*vráy*-zern) *v* dread, fear

vriend (vreent) *c* (pl ~en) friend

vriendelijk (*vreen*-der-lerk) *adj* friendly; kind

vriendschap (*vreent*-skhahp) *c* (pl ~pen) friendship

vriendschappelijk (vreent-*skhah*-per-lerk) *adj* friendly

vriespunt (*vreess*-pernt) *nt* freezing-point

****vriezen** (*vree*-zern) *v* ***freeze**

vrij (vray) *adj* free; *adv* pretty, fairly, quite, rather

vrijdag (*vray*-dahkh) *c* Friday

vrijgevig (vray-*gáy*-verkh) *adj* liberal

vrijgezel (vray-ger-*zehl*) *c* (pl ~len) bachelor

vrijheid (*vray*-hayt) *c* (pl -heden) freedom, liberty

vrijkaart (*vray*-kaart) *c* (pl ~en) free ticket

vrijpostig (vray-*poss*-terkh) *adj* bold

vrijspraak (*vray*-spraak) *c* acquittal

vrijstellen (*vray*-steh-lern) *v* exempt;

vrijgesteld exempt
vrijstelling (*vray*-steh-lıng) *c* (pl ~en) exemption
vrijwel (*vray*-vehl) *adv* practically
vrijwillig (vray-*vı*-lerkh) *adj* voluntary
vrijwilliger (vray-*vı*-ler-gerr) *c* (pl ~s) volunteer
vroedvrouw (*vrōōt*-frou) *c* (pl ~en) midwife
vroeg (vrōōkh) *adj* early
vroeger (*vrōō*-gerr) *adj* prior, previous, former; *adv* formerly
vrolijk (*vrōā*-lerk) *adj* gay, cheerful, merry, joyful
vrolijkheid (*vrōā*-lerk-hayt) *c* gaiety
vroom (vrōām) *adj* pious
vrouw (vrou) *c* (pl ~en) woman; wife
vrouwelijk (*vrou*-er-lerk) *adj* female; feminine
vrouwenarts (*vrou*-ern-ahrts) *c* (pl ~en) gynaecologist
vrucht (vrerkht) *c* (pl ~en) fruit
vruchtbaar (*vrerkht*-baar) *adj* fertile
vruchtensap (*vrerkh*-ter-sahp) *nt* (pl ~pen) squash
vuil (vur^{ew}l) *adj* filthy, dirty; *nt* dirt
vuilnis (*vur^{ew}l*-nıss) *nt* garbage
vuilnisbak (*vur^{ew}l*-nıss-bahk) *c* (pl ~ken) rubbish-bin, dustbin; trash can *Am*
vuist (vur^{ew}st) *c* (pl ~en) fist
vuistslag (*vur^{ew}st*-slahkh) *c* (pl ~en) punch
vulgair (verl-*gair*) *adj* vulgar
vulkaan (verl-*kaan*) *c* (pl -kanen) volcano
vullen (*ver*-lern) *v* fill
vulling (*ver*-lıng) *c* (pl ~en) stuffing, filling; refill
vulpen (*verl*-pehn) *c* (pl ~nen) fountain-pen
vuur (vewr) *nt* (pl vuren) fire
vuurrood (*vew*-rōāt) *adj* scarlet, crimson

vuursteen (*vewr*-stāyn) *c* (pl -stenen) flint
vuurtoren (*vewr*-tōā-rern) *c* (pl ~s) lighthouse
vuurvast (*vewr*-vahst) *adj* fireproof

W

*****waaien** (*vaa^{ee}*-ern) *v* *blow
waaier (*vaa^{ee}*-err) *c* (pl ~s) fan
waakzaam (*vaak*-saam) *adj* vigilant
waanzin (*vaan*-zın) *c* madness
waanzinnig (vaan-*zı*-nerkh) *adj* mad
waar[1] (vaar) *adj* true; very
waar[2] (vaar) *adv* where; *conj* where; ~ **dan ook** anywhere; ~ **ook** wherever
waarborg (*vaar*-borkh) *c* (pl ~en) guarantee
waard (vaart) *adj* worthy of; ~ *****zijn** *be worth
waarde (*vaar*-der) *c* (pl ~n) worth, value
waardeloos (vaar-der-lōāss) *adj* worthless
waarderen (vaar-*dāy*-rern) *v* appreciate
waardering (vaar-*dāy*-rıng) *c* appreciation
waardevol (*vaar*-der-vol) *adj* valuable
waardig (*vaar*-derkh) *adj* dignified
waarheid (*vaar*-hayt) *c* (pl -heden) truth
waarheidsgetrouw (*vaar*-hayts-khertrou) *adj* truthful
*****waarnemen** (*vaar*-nāy-mern) *v* observe
waarneming (*vaar*-nāy-mıng) *c* (pl ~en) observation
waarom (vaa-*rom*) *adv* why; what for
waarschijnlijk (vaar-*skhayn*-lerk) *adj* probable, likely; *adv* probably

waarschuwen (*vaar*-skhew⁰⁰-ern) *v*
warn ; caution ; notify

waarschuwing (*vaar*-skhew⁰⁰-ɪng) *c*
(pl ~en) warning

waas (vaass) *nt* haze

wachten (*vahkh*-tern) *v* wait ; ~ **op**
await

wachtkamer (*vahkht*-kaa-merr) *c* (pl
~s) waiting-room

wachtlijst (*vahkht*-layst) *c* (pl ~en)
waiting-list

wachtwoord (*vahkht*-vōart) *nt* (pl
~en) password

waden (*vaa*-dern) *v* wade

wafel (*vaa*-ferl) *c* (pl ~s) waffle, wafer

wagen¹ (*vaa*-gern) *c* (pl ~s) cart

wagen² (*vaa*-gern) *v* dare, venture,
risk

wagon (*vaa-gon*) *c* (pl ~s) carriage,
waggon ; passenger car *Am*

wakker (*vah*-kerr) *adj* awake ; ~
*worden wake up

walgelijk (*vahl*-ger-lerk) *adj* revolting,
disgusting

walnoot (*vahl*-nōat) *c* (pl -noten) walnut

wals (vahls) *c* (pl ~en) waltz

walvis (*vahl*-vɪss) *c* (pl ~sen) whale

wand (vahnt) *c* (pl ~en) wall

wandelaar (*vahn*-der-laar) *c* (pl ~s)
walker

wandelen (*vahn*-der-lern) *v* stroll,
walk

wandeling (*vahn*-der-lɪng) *c* (pl ~en)
stroll, walk

wandelstok (*vahn*-derl-stok) *c* (pl
~ken) walking-stick

wandkleed (*vahnt*-klāyt) *nt* (pl -kle-
den) tapestry

wandluis (*vahnt*-lur ew ss) *c* (pl -luizen)
bug

wang (vahng) *c* (pl ~en) cheek

wanhoop (*vahn*-hōap) *c* despair

wanhopen (*vahn*-hōa-pern) *v* despair

wanhopig (vahn-*hōa*-perkh) *adj* desperate

wankel (*vahn*-kerl) *adj* unsteady

wankelen (*vahn*-ker-lern) *v* falter

wanneer (vah-*nāyr*) *adv* when ; *conj*
when ; ~ **ook** whenever

wanorde (*vahn*-or-der) *c* disorder

want (vahnt) *conj* for

wanten (*vahn*-tern) *pl* mittens *pl*

wantrouwen (*vahn*-trou-ern) *nt* suspicion ; *v* mistrust

wapen (*vaa*-pern) *nt* (pl ~s, ~en)
weapon, arm

warboel (*vahr*-bōol) *c* muddle, mess

waren (*vaa*-rern) *pl* goods *pl*, wares *pl*

warenhuis (*vaa*-rer-hur ew ss) *nt* (pl -
huizen) department store

warm (vahrm) *adj* warm ; hot ; ~
*eten dine

warmte (*vahrm*-ter) *c* warmth ; heat

warmwaterkruik (vahrm-*vaa*-terr-
krur ew k) *c* (pl ~en) hot-water bottle

was¹ (vahss) *c* laundry, washing

was² (vahss) *c* wax

wasbaar (*vahss*-baar) *adj* washable

wasbekken (*vahss*-beh-kern) *nt* (pl
~s) wash-basin

wasecht (vahss-*ehkht*) *adj* fast-dyed

wasgoed (*vahss*-khōot) *nt* washing

wasmachine (*vahss*-mah-shee-ner) *c*
(pl ~s) washing-machine

wasmiddel (*vahss*-mɪ-derl) *nt* (pl ~en)
detergent

waspoeder (*vahss*-pōō-derr) *nt* (pl ~s)
washing-powder

*wassen** (*vah*-sern) *v* wash

wassenbeeldenmuseum (vah-ser-
bāyl-der-mew-zāy-Yerm) *nt* (pl ~s,
-musea) waxworks *pl*

wasserette (vah-ser-*reh*-ter) *c* (pl ~s)
launderette

wasserij (vah-ser-*ray*) *c* (pl ~en) laundry

wastafel (*vahss*-taa-ferl) *c* (pl ~s)

wash-stand

wasverzachter (*vahss*-ferr-zahkh-terr) *c* (pl ~s) water-softener

wat (vaht) *pron* what; *adv* how; ~ **dan ook** whatever; anything

water (*vaa*-terr) *nt* water; **hoog ~** high tide; **laag ~** low tide; **stromend ~** running water; **zoet ~** fresh water

waterdicht (*vaa*-terr-dikht) *adj* rainproof, waterproof

waterkers (*vaa*-terr-kehrs) *c* watercress

watermeloen (*vaa*-terr-mer-lōōn) *c* (pl ~en) watermelon

waterpas (*vaa*-terr-pahss) *c* (pl ~sen) level

waterpokken (*vaa*-terr-po-kern) *pl* chickenpox

waterpomp (*vaa*-terr-pomp) *c* (pl ~en) water pump

waterski (*vaa*-terr-skee) *c* (pl ~'s) water ski

waterstof (*vaa*-terr-stof) *c* hydrogen

waterstofperoxyde (*vaa*-terr-stof-pehr-ok-see-der) *nt* peroxide

waterval (*vaa*-terr-vahl) *c* (pl ~len) waterfall

waterverf (*vaa*-terr-vehrf) *c* water-colour

watten (*vah*-tern) *pl* cotton-wool

wazig (*vaa*-zerkh) *adj* hazy

we (ver) *pron* we

wedden (*veh*-dern) *v* *bet

weddenschap (*veh*-der-skhahp) *c* (pl ~pen) bet

wederverkoper (*vāy*-derr-verr-kōa-perr) *c* (pl ~s) retailer

wederzijds (*vāy*-derr-*zayts*) *adj* mutual

wedijveren (*veht*-ay-ver-rern) *v* compete

wedloop (*veht*-lōap) *c* (pl -lopen) race

wedstrijd (*veht*-strayt) *c* (pl ~en) competition, contest; match

weduwe (*vāy*-dew°°-er) *c* (pl ~n) widow

weduwnaar (*vāy*-dew°°-naar) *c* (pl ~s) widower

weeën (*vāy*-ern) *pl* labour

weefsel (*vāyf*-serl) *nt* (pl ~s) tissue

weegschaal (*vāykh*-skhaal) *c* (pl -schalen) weighing-machine, scales *pl*

week (vāyk) *c* (pl weken) week

weekdag (*vāyk*-dahkh) *c* (pl ~en) weekday

weekend (*vee*-kehnt) *nt* (pl ~s) weekend

weemoed (*vāy*-mōōt) *c* melancholy

weer[1] (*vāyr*) *nt* weather

weer[2] (*vāyr*) *adv* again

weerbericht (*vāyr*-ber-rikht) *nt* (pl ~en) weather forecast

*weerhouden (*vāyr*-*hou*-dern) *v* restrain

weerkaatsen (*vāyr*-*kaat*-sern) *v* reflect

weerkaatsing (*vāyr*-*kaat*-sing) *c* reflection

weerklank (*vāyr*-klahngk) *c* echo

weerzinwekkend (*vāyr*-zin-*veh*-kernt) *adj* repulsive, repellent, revolting

wees (vāyss) *c* (pl wezen) orphan

weg[1] (vehkh) *adv* gone, away; lost; off

weg[2] (vehkh) *c* (pl ~en) way; road; **doodlopende ~** cul-de-sac; **op ~ naar** bound for

*wegen (*vāy*-gern) *v* weigh

wegenkaart (*vāy*-ger-kaart) *c* (pl ~en) road map

wegennet (*vāy*-ger-neht) *nt* (pl ~ten) road system

wegens (*vāy*-gerns) *prep* because of, for

*weggaan (*veh*-khaan) *v* *go away

wegkant (*vehkh*-kahnt) *c* (pl ~en) roadside, wayside

*weglaten (*vehkh*-laa-tern) *v* omit, *leave out

*wegnemen (*vehkh*-nāy-mern) v *take out, *take away

wegomlegging (*vaykh*-om-leh-ging) c (pl ~en) diversion

wegrestaurant (*vehkh*-rehss-tōā-rahnt) nt (pl ~s) roadhouse; roadside restaurant

wegwerp- (*vehkh*-vehrp) disposable

wegwijzer (*vehkh*-vay-zerr) c (pl ~s) milepost, signpost

*wegzenden (*vehkh*-sehn-dern) v dismiss

wei (vay) c (pl ~den) meadow

weigeren (*vay*-ger-rern) v refuse; deny

weigering (*vay*-ger-ring) c (pl ~en) refusal

weiland (*vay*-lahnt) nt (pl ~en) pasture

weinig (*vay*-nerkh) adj little; few

wekelijks (*vāy*-ker-lerks) adj weekly

weken (*vāy*-kern) v soak

wekken (*veh*-kern) v *awake, *wake

wekker (*veh*-kerr) c (pl ~s) alarmclock

weldra (*vehl*-draa) adv soon, shortly

welk (vehlk) pron which; ~ ook whichever

welkom (*vehl*-kom) adj welcome; nt welcome

wellicht (veh-*likht*) adv perhaps

wellust (*veh*-lerst) c (pl ~en) lust

welnu! (vehl-*new̄*) well!

welvaart (*vehl*-vaart) c prosperity

welvarend (vehl-*vaa*-rernt) adj prosperous

welwillendheid (vehl-*vi*-lernt-hayt) c goodwill

welzijn (*vehl*-zayn) nt welfare

wending (*vehn*-ding) c (pl ~en) turn

wenk (vehngk) c (pl ~en) sign

wenkbrauw (*vehngk*-brou) c (pl ~en) eyebrow

wenkbrauwstift (*vehngk*-brou-stift) c (pl ~en) eye-pencil

wennen (*veh*-nern) v accustom

wens (vehns) c (pl ~en) wish, desire

wenselijk (*vehn*-ser-lerk) adj desirable

wensen (*vehn*-sern) v wish, desire; want

wereld (*vāy*-rerlt) c (pl ~en) world

wereldberoemd (*vāy*-rerlt-ber-rōōmt) adj world-famous

wereldbol (*vāy*-rerlt-bol) c globe

werelddeel (*vāy*-rerl-dāyl) nt (pl -delen) continent

wereldomvattend (*vāy*-rerlt-om-vah-ternt) adj global, world-wide

wereldoorlog (*vāy*-rerlt-ōar-lokh) c (pl ~en) world war

werk (vehrk) nt work; labour; occupation, employment; business; te ~ *gaan proceed; ~ in uitvoering road up

werkdag (*vehrk*-dahkh) c (pl ~en) working day

werkelijk (*vehr*-ker-lerk) adj actual, true; substantial, very; adv really

werkelijkheid (*vehr*-ker-lerk-hayt) c reality

werkeloos (*vehr*-ker-lōāss) adj unemployed; idle

werkeloosheid (vehr-ker-*lōāss*-hayt) c unemployment

werken (*vehr*-kern) v work; operate

werkgever (*vehrk*-khāy-verr) c (pl ~s) employer

werking (*vehr*-king) c operation, working; buiten ~ out of order

werknemer (*vehrk*-nāy-merr) c (pl ~s) employee

werkplaats (*vehrk*-plaats) c (pl ~en) workshop

werktuig (*vehrk*-tur^{ew}kh) nt (pl ~en) tool; utensil, implement

werkvergunning (*vehrk*-ferr-ger-ning) c (pl ~en) work permit; labor permit Am

werkwoord (*vehrk*-vòart) *nt* (pl ~en)
verb

*****werpen** (*vehr*-pern) *v* *cast, *throw

wesp (vehsp) *c* (pl ~en) wasp

west (vehst) *c* west

westelijk (*vehss*-ter-lerk) *adj* westerly

westen (*vehss*-tern) *nt* west

westers (*vehss*-terrs) *adj* western

wet (veht) *c* (pl ~ten) law

*****weten** (*vày*-tern) *v* *know

wetenschap (*vày*-ter-skhahp) *c* (pl
~pen) science

wetenschappelijk (vày-ter-*skhah*-per-
lerk) *adj* scientific

wettelijk (*veh*-ter-lerk) *adj* legal

wettig (*veh*-terkh) *adj* legal, lawful;
legitimate

*****weven** (*vày*-vern) *v* *weave

wever (*vày*-verr) *c* (pl ~s) weaver

wezen[1] (*vày*-zern) *nt* (pl ~s) creature,
being

wezen[2] (*vày*-zern) *nt* essence

wezenlijk (*vày*-zer-lerk) *adj* essential

wie (vee) *pron* who; whom; ~ **dan
ook** anybody; ~ **ook** whoever

wieg (veekh) *c* (pl ~en) cradle

wiel (veel) *nt* (pl ~en) wheel

wielrijder (*veel*-ray-derr) *c* (pl ~s) cyclist

wierook (*vee*-ròak) *c* incense

wig (vikh) *c* (pl ~gen) wedge

wijd (vayt) *adj* broad, wide

wijden (*vay*-dern) *v* devote

wijk (vayk) *c* (pl ~en) quarter, district

wijn (vayn) *c* (pl ~en) wine

wijngaard (*vayn*-gaart) *c* (pl ~en)
vineyard

wijnkaart (*vayng*-kaart) *c* (pl ~en)
wine-list

wijnkelder (*vayng*-kehl-derr) *c* (pl ~s)
wine-cellar

wijnkelner (*vayng*-kehl-nerr) *c* (pl ~s)
wine-waiter

wijnkoper (*vayng*-kòa-perr) *c* (pl ~s)
wine-merchant

wijnoogst (*vayn*-òakhst) *c* (pl ~en)
vintage

wijnstok (*vayn*-stok) *c* (pl ~ken) vine

wijs[1] (vayss) *adj* wise

wijs[2] (vayss) *c* (pl wijzen) tune

wijsbegeerte (*vayss*-ber-gàyr-ter) *c*
philosophy

wijsgeer (*vayss*-khàyr) *c* (pl -geren)
philosopher

wijsheid (*vayss*-hayt) *c* (pl -heden)
wisdom

wijsvinger (*vayss*-fi-ngerr) *c* (pl ~s)
index finger

wijting (*vay*-ting) *c* (pl ~en) whiting

wijze (*vay*-zer) *c* (pl ~n) manner, way

*****wijzen** (*vay*-zern) *v* point; direct

wijzigen (*vay*-zer-gern) *v* change, alter,
modify

wijziging (*vay*-zer-ging) *c* (pl ~en)
change, alteration

wil (vil) *c* will

wild (vilt) *adj* wild; savage, fierce; *nt*
game

wildpark (*vilt*-pahrk) *nt* (pl ~en) game
reserve

willekeurig (vi-ler-*kùr*-rerkh) *adj* arbitrary

*****willen** (*vi*-lern) *v* want; *will

wilskracht (*vils*-krahkht) *c* will-power

wimper (*vim*-perr) *c* (pl ~s) eyelash

wind (vint) *c* (pl ~en) wind

*****winden** (*vin*-dern) *v* *wind; twist

winderig (*vin*-der-rerkh) *adj* windy,
gusty

windmolen (*vint*-mòa-lern) *c* (pl ~s)
windmill

windstoot (*vint*-stòat) *c* (pl -stoten)
gust

windvlaag (*vint*-flaakh) *c* (pl -vlagen)
blow

winkel (*ving*-kerl) *c* (pl ~s) store, shop

winkelcentrum (*ving*-kerl-sehn-trerm)
nt (pl -tra) shopping centre

winkelen (*ving*-ker-lern) *v* shop

winkelier (*ving*-ker-*leer*) *c* (pl ~s) shopkeeper

winnaar (*vi*-naar) *c* (pl ~s) winner

***winnen** (*vi*-nern) *v* *win; gain

winst (vinst) *c* (pl ~en) profit; gain, winnings *pl*, benefit

winstgevend (vinst-*khay*-vernt) *adj* profitable

winter (*vin*-terr) *c* (pl ~s) winter

wintersport (*vin*-terr-sport) *c* winter sports

wip (vip) *c* (pl ~pen) seesaw

wirwar (*vir*-vahr) *c* muddle

wiskunde (*viss*-kern-der) *c* mathematics

wiskundig (viss-*kern*-derkh) *adj* mathematical

wissel (*vi*-serl) *c* (pl ~s) draft

wisselen (*vi*-ser-lern) *v* change; exchange

wisselgeld (*vi*-serl-gehlt) *nt* change

wisselkantoor (*vi*-serl-kahn-*toar*) *nt* (pl -toren) money exchange, exchange office

wisselkoers (*vi*-serl-*koors*) *c* (pl ~en) exchange rate

wisselstroom (*vi*-serl-*stroam*) *c* alternating current

wit (vit) *adj* white

wittebroodsweken (*vi*-ter-*broats*-vay-kern) *pl* honeymoon

witvis (*vit*-fiss) *c* (pl ~sen) whitebait

woede (*voo*-der) *c* anger, rage

woeden (*voo*-dern) *v* rage

woedend (*voo*-dernt) *adj* furious

woensdag (*voons*-dahkh) *c* Wednesday

woest (voost) *adj* wild, fierce; desert

woestijn (vooss-*tayn*) *c* (pl ~en) desert

wol (vol) *c* wool

wolf (volf) *c* (pl wolven) wolf

wolk (volk) *c* (pl ~en) cloud

wolkbreuk (*volk*-brurk) *c* (pl ~en) cloud-burst

wolkenkrabber (*vol*-ker-krah-berr) *c* (pl ~s) skyscraper

wollen (*vo*-lern) *adj* woollen

wond (vont) *c* (pl ~en) wound

wonder (*von*-derr) *nt* (pl ~en) wonder, miracle; marvel

wonderbaarlijk (von-derr-*baar*-lerk) *adj* miraculous

wonen (*voa*-nern) *v* live; reside

woning (*voa*-ning) *c* (pl ~en) house

woonachtig (*voan*-ahkh-terkh) *adj* resident

woonboot (*voan*-boat) *c* (pl -boten) houseboat

woonkamer (*voang*-kaa-merr) *c* (pl ~s) living-room

woonplaats (*voam*-plaats) *c* (pl ~en) domicile, residence

woonwagen (*voan*-vaa-gern) *c* (pl ~s) caravan

woord (voart) *nt* (pl ~en) word

woordenboek (*voar*-der-book) *nt* (pl ~en) dictionary

woordenlijst (*voar*-der-layst) *c* (pl ~en) vocabulary

woordenschat (*voar*-der-skhaht) *c* vocabulary

woordenwisseling (*voar*-der-vi-ser-ling) *c* (pl ~en) argument

***worden** (vor-dern) *v* *become; *go, *get, *grow

worm (vorm) *c* (pl ~en) worm

worp (vorp) *c* (pl ~en) cast

worst (vorst) *c* (pl ~en) sausage

worstelen (*vor*-ster-lern) *v* struggle

worsteling (*voar*-ster-ling) *c* (pl ~en) struggle

wortel (*vor*-terl) *c* (pl ~s, ~en) root; carrot

woud (vout) *nt* (pl ~en) forest

wraak (vraak) *c* revenge

wrak (vrahk) *nt* (pl ~ken) wreck

wreed (vrāyt) *adj* harsh, cruel

*****wrijven** (*vray*-vern) *v* rub

wrijving (*vray*-vɪng) *c* (pl ~en) friction

wurgen (*verr*-gern) *v* strangle, choke

Z

zaad (żaat) *nt* (pl zaden) seed

zaag (zaakh) *c* (pl zagen) saw

zaagsel (*zaakh*-serl) *nt* sawdust

zaaien (*zaa*^{ee}-ern) *v* *sow

zaak (zaak) *c* (pl zaken) cause; case, matter; business

zaal (zaal) *c* (pl zalen) hall

zacht (zahkht) *adj* soft; gentle, smooth, mild, mellow

zadel (*zaa*-derl) *nt* (pl ~s) saddle

zak (zahk) *c* (pl ~ken) pocket; sack, bag

zakdoek (*zahk*-dōōk) *c* (pl ~en) handkerchief; papieren ~ tissue

zakelijk (*zaa*-ker-lerk) *adj* business-like

zaken (*zaa*-kern) *pl* business; **voor** ~ on business; ~ *doen met* *deal with

zakenman (*zaa*-ker-mahn) *c* (pl -lieden, -lui) businessman

zakenreis (*zaa*-ker-rayss) *c* (pl -reizen) business trip

zakhorloge (*zahk*-hor-lōā-zher) *nt* (pl ~s) pocket-watch

zakkam (*zah*-kahm) *c* (pl ~men) pocket-comb

zakken (*zah*-kern) *v* fail

zaklantaarn (*zahk*-lahn-taa-rern) *c* (pl ~s) torch, flash-light

zakmes (*zahk*-mehss) *nt* (pl ~sen) pocket-knife, penknife

zalf (zahlf) *c* (pl zalven) ointment, salve

zalm (zahlm) *c* (pl ~en) salmon

zand (zahnt) *nt* sand

zanderig (*zahn*-der-rerkh) *adj* sandy

zanger (*zah*-ngerr) *c* (pl ~s) vocalist, singer

zangeres (zah-nger-*rehss*) *c* (pl ~sen) singer

zaterdag (*zaa*-terr-dahkh) *c* Saturday

ze (zer) *pron* she; they

zebra (*zāy*-braa) *c* (pl ~'s) zebra

zebrapad (*zāy*-braa-paht) *nt* (pl ~en) pedestrian crossing; crosswalk *nAm*

zedelijk (*zāy*-der-lerk) *adj* moral

zeden (*zāy*-dern) *pl* morals

zee (zāy) *c* (pl ~ĕn) sea

zeeëgel (*zāy*-āy-gerl) *c* (pl ~s) sea-urchin

zeef (zāyf) *c* (pl zeven) sieve

zeegezicht (*zāy*-ger-zɪkht) *nt* (pl ~en) seascape

zeehaven (*zāy*-haa-vern) *c* (pl ~s) sea-port

zeehond (*zāy*-hont) *c* (pl ~en) seal

zeekaart (*zāy*-kaart) *c* (pl ~en) chart

zeekust (*zāy*-kerst) *c* (pl ~en) sea-coast

zeeman (*zāy*-mahn) *c* (pl -lieden, -lui) seaman

zeemeermin (*zāy*-māyr-mɪn) *c* (pl ~nen) mermaid

zeemeeuw (*zāy*-māy^{oo}) *c* (pl ~en) seagull

zeep (zāyp) *c* soap

zeeppoeder (*zāy*-pōō-derr) *nt* soap powder

zeer (zāyr) *adj* sore; *adv* very, quite

zeeschelp (*zāy*-skhehlp) *c* (pl ~en) sea-shell

zeevogel (*zāy*-vōā-gerl) *c* (pl ~s) sea-bird

zeewater (*zāy*-vaa-terr) *nt* sea-water

zeeziek (*zāy*-zeek) *adj* seasick

zeeziekte (*zāy*-zeek-ter) *c* seasickness

zegel (*zāy*-gerl) *nt* (pl ~s) seal

zegen (*zāy*-gern) *c* blessing

zegenen (*zāy*-ger-nern) *v* bless

zegevieren (zāy-ger-vee-rern) v triumph

*****zeggen** (zeh-gern) v *say; *tell

zeil (zayl) nt (pl ~en) sail

zeilboot (zayl-bōat) c (pl -boten) sailing-boat

zeilclub (zayl-klerp) c (pl ~s) yachtclub

zeilsport (zayl-sport) c yachting

zeker (zāy-kerr) adv surely; adj certain, sure; ~ **niet** by no means

zekering (zāy-ker-ring) c (pl ~en) fuse

zelden (zehl-dern) adv seldom, rarely

zeldzaam (zehlt-saam) adj rare; uncommon, infrequent

zelf (zehlf) pron myself; yourself; himself; herself; oneself; ourselves; yourselves; themselves

zelfbediening (zehlf-ber-dee-ning) c self-service

zelfbedieningsrestaurant (zehlf-ber-dee-nings-rehss-tōa-rahnt) nt (pl ~s) self-service restaurant

zelfbestuur (zehlf-ber-stēwr) nt self-government

zelfde (zehlf-der) adj same

zelfmoord (zehlf-mōart) c (pl ~en) suicide

zelfs (zehlfs) adv even

zelfstandig (zehlf-stahn-derkh) adj independent; self-employed; ~ **naamwoord** noun

zelfstrijkend (zehlf-stray-kernt) adj drip-dry, wash and wear

zelfzuchtig (zehlf-serkh-terkh) adj egoistic

*****zenden** (zehn-dern) v *send

zender (zehn-derr) c (pl ~s) transmitter

zending (zehn-ding) c (pl ~en) consignment

zenit (zāy-nit) nt zenith

zenuw (zay-nēw⁰⁰) c (pl ~en) nerve

zenuwachtig (zāy-nēw⁰⁰-ahkh-terkh)

adj nervous

zenuwpijn (zāy-nēw⁰⁰-payn) c (pl ~en) neuralgia

zes (zehss) num six

zesde (zehss-der) num sixth

zestien (zehss-teen) num sixteen

zestiende (zehss-teen-der) num sixteenth

zestig (zehss-terkh) num sixty

zet (zeht) c (pl ~ten) move; push

zetel (zāy-terl) c (pl ~s) chair; seat

zetpil (zeht-pil) c (pl ~len) suppository

zetten (zeh-tern) v place; *lay, *set, *put; **in elkaar** ~ assemble

zeurpiet (zūrr-peet) c (pl ~en) bore

zeven¹ (zāy-vern) num seven

zeven² (zāy-vern) v strain, sift, sieve

zevende (zāy-vern-der) num seventh

zeventien (zāy-vern-teen) num seventeen

zeventiende (zāy-vern-teen-der) num seventeenth

zeventig (zāy-vern-terkh) num seventy

zich (zikh) pron himself; herself; themselves

zicht (zikht) nt sight; visibility; **op** ~ on approval

zichtbaar (zikht-baar) adj visible

ziek (zeek) adj ill, sick

ziekenauto (zee-kern-ōa-tōa) c (pl ~'s) ambulance

ziekenhuis (zee-ker-hur⁰ʷss) nt (pl -huizen) hospital

ziekenzaal (zee-ker-zaal) c (pl -zalen) infirmary

ziekte (zeek-ter) c (pl ~n, ~s) disease; ailment, illness, sickness

ziel (zeel) c (pl ~en) soul

*****zien** (zeen) v *see; notice; **er uit** ~ look; *****laten** ~ *show

zienswijze (zeens-vay-zer) c (pl ~n) outlook

zigeuner (zee-gūr-nerr) c (pl ~s) gipsy

zijbeuk (*zay*-būrk) *c* (pl ~en) aisle

zijde¹ (*zay*-der) *c* silk

zijde² (*zay*-der) *c* (pl ~n) side

zijden (*zay*-dern) *adj* silken

zijlicht (*zay*-likht) *nt* sidelight

zijn (zayn) *pron* his

***zijn** (zayn) *v* *be

zijrivier (*zay*-ree-veer) *c* (pl ~en) tributary

zijstraat (*zay*-straat) *c* (pl -straten) side-street

zilver (*zil*-verr) *nt* silver

zilveren (*zil*-ver-rern) *adj* silver

zilverpapier (*zil*-verr-paa-peer) *nt* tinfoil

zilversmid (*zil*-verr-smit) *c* (pl -smeden) silversmith

zilverwerk (*zil*-verr-vehrk) *nt* silverware

zin¹ (zin) *c* sense; desire; ~ *hebben in *feel like, fancy

zin² (zin) *c* (pl ~nen) sentence

***zingen** (*zi*-ngern) *v* *sing

zink (zingk) *nt* zinc

***zinken** (*zing*-kern) *v* *sink

zinloos (*zin*-lōass) *adj* senseless

zintuig (*zin*-tur^ewkh) *nt* (pl ~en) sense

zitkamer (*zit*-kaa-merr) *c* (pl ~s) sitting-room

zitplaats (*zit*-plaats) *c* (pl ~en) seat

***zitten** (*zi*-tern) *v* *sit; *gaan ~ *sit down

zitting (*zi*-ting) *c* (pl ~en) session

zitvlak (*zit*-flahk) *nt* bottom

zo (zōa) *adv* so, thus; such; **zo'n** such a

zoals (zōa-*ahls*) *conj* like, as; such as

zodat (zōa-*daht*) *conj* so that

zodra (zōa-*draa*) *conj* as soon as

***zoeken** (*zōō*-kern) *v* look for; *seek, search; hunt for

zoeker (*zōō*-kerr) *c* (pl ~s) view-finder

zoen (zōon) *c* (pl ~en) kiss

zoet (zōot) *adj* sweet; good; ~ **ma-**

ken sweeten

zoetzuur (*zōot*-sewr) *nt* pickles *pl*

zogen (*zōa*-gern) *v* nurse

zogenaamd (zōa-ger-*naamt*) *adj* so-called

zolder (*zol*-derr) *c* (pl ~s) attic

zomer (*zōa*-merr) *c* (pl ~s) summer

zomertijd (*zōa*-merr-tayt) *c* summer time

zon (zon) *c* (pl ~nen) sun

zondag (*zon*-dahkh) *c* Sunday

zonde (*zon*-der) *c* (pl ~n) sin

zondebok (*zon*-der-bok) *c* (pl ~ken) scapegoat

zonder (*zon*-derr) *prep* without

zonderling (*zon*-derr-ling) *adj* funny, queer

zone (*zaw*-ner) *c* (pl ~s) zone

zonlicht (*zon*-likht) *nt* sunlight

zonnebaden (*zo*-ner-baa-dern) *v* sunbathe

zonnebrand (*zo*-ner-brahnt) *c* sunburn

zonnebrandolie (*zo*-ner-brahnt-ōa-lee) *c* suntan oil

zonnebril (*zo*-ner-bril) *c* (pl ~len) sunglasses *pl*

zonnescherm (*zo*-ner-skhehrm) *nt* (pl ~en) awning

zonneschijn (*zo*-ner-skhayn) *c* sunshine

zonnesteek (*zo*-ner-stāyk) *c* sunstroke

zonnig (*zo*-nerkh) *adj* sunny

zonsondergang (zons-*on*-derr-gahng) *c* (pl ~en) sunset

zonsopgang (zons-*op*-khahng) *c* (pl ~en) sunrise

zoogdier (*zōa*kh-deer) *nt* (pl ~en) mammal

zool (zōal) *c* (pl zolen) sole

zoölogie (zōa-ōa-lōa-*gee*) *c* zoology

zoom (zōam) *c* (pl zomen) hem

zoon (zōan) *c* (pl ~en) son

zorg (zorkh) *c* (pl ~en) concern, worry, care; trouble

zorgen voor (*zor*-gern) look after, *take care of; see to

zorgvuldig (zorkh-*ferl*-derkh) *adj* careful

zorgwekkend (zorkh-*veh*-kernt) *adj* critical

zorgzaam (*zorkh*-saam) *adj* thoughtful

zout (zout) *nt* salt; *adj* salty

zoutvaatje (*zout*-faa-t^yer) *nt* (pl ~s) salt-cellar

zoveel (zōā-vāyl) *adv* so much

zowel ... als (zōā-*veh*...ahls) both ... and

zuid (zur^{ew}t) *c* south

Zuid-Afrika (zur^{ew}t-*aa*-free-kaa) South Africa

zuidelijk (*zur^{ew}*-der-lerk) *adj* southern, southerly

zuiden (*zur^{ew}*-dern) *nt* south

zuidoosten (zur^{ew}t-*ōāss*-tern) *nt* south-east

zuidpool (*zur^{ew}t*-pōāl) *c* South Pole

zuidwesten (zur^{ew}t-*vehss*-tern) *nt* south-west

zuigeling (*zur^{ew}*-ger-lıng) *c* (pl ~en) infant

*zuigen** (*zur^{ew}*-gern) *v* suck

zuiger (*zur^{ew}*-gerr) *c* (pl ~s) piston

zuigerring (*zur^{ew}*-ger-rıng) *c* (pl ~en) piston ring

zuigerstang (*zur^{ew}*-gerr-stahng) *c* (pl ~en) piston-rod

zuil (zur^{ew}l) *c* (pl ~en) column, pillar

zuilengang (*zur^{ew}*-ler-gahng) *c* (pl ~en) arcade

zuinig (*zur^{ew}*-nerkh) *adj* economical, thrifty

zuivelwinkel (*zur^{ew}*-verl-vıng-kerl) *c* (pl ~s) dairy

zuiver (*zur^{ew}*-verr) *adj* pure, clean

zulk (zerlk) *adj* such

*zullen** (*zer*-lern) *v* *will, *shall

zus (zerss) *c* (pl ~sen) sister

zuster (*zerss*-terr) *c* (pl ~s) sister; nurse

zuur¹ (zewr) *adj* sour

zuur² (zewr) *nt* (pl zuren) acid

zuurstof (*zewr*-stof) *c* oxygen

zwaaien (zvaa^{ee}-ern) *v* *swing; wave

zwaan (zvaan) *c* (pl zwanen) swan

zwaar (zvaar) *adj* heavy

zwaard (zvaart) *nt* (pl ~en) sword

zwaartekracht (*zvaar*-ter-krahkht) *c* gravity

zwager (*zvaa*-gerr) *c* (pl ~s) brother-in-law

zwak (zvahk) *adj* feeble, weak; faint; dim

zwakheid (*zvahk*-hayt) *c* (pl -heden) weakness

zwaluw (*zvaa*-lew^{oo}) *c* (pl ~en) swallow

zwanger (*zvah*-ngerr) *adj* pregnant

zwart (zvahrt) *adj* black

Zweden (*zvāy*-dern) Sweden

Zweed (zvāyt) *c* (pl Zweden) Swede

Zweeds (zvāyts) *adj* Swedish

zweefvliegtuig (*zvāy*-fleekh-tur^{ew}kh) *nt* (pl ~en) glider

zweep (zvāyp) *c* (pl zwepen) whip

zweer (zvāyr) *c* (pl zweren) ulcer, sore

zweet (zvāyt) *nt* sweat, perspiration

*zwellen** (*zveh*-lern) *v* *swell

zwelling (*zveh*-lıng) *c* (pl ~en) swelling

zwembad (*zvehm*-baht) *nt* (pl ~en) swimming pool

zwembroek (*zvehm*-brōōk) *c* (pl ~en) swimming-trunks, bathing-trunks, bathing-suit

*zwemmen** (*zveh*-mern) *v* *swim

zwemmer (*zveh*-merr) *c* (pl ~s) swimmer

zwempak (*zvehm*-pahk) *nt* (pl ~ken) swim-suit

zwemsport (*zvehm*-sport) *c* swimming

zwendelarij (zvehn-der-laa-*ray*) *c* (pl ~en) swindle

*zweren (*zvāy*-rern) *v* *swear, vow
*zwerven (*zvehr*-vern) *v* roam, wander
zweten (*zvāy*-tern) *v* sweat, perspire
*zwijgen (*zvay*-gern) *v* *be silent, *keep quiet; tot ~ *brengen silence; zwijgend silent

zwijn (zvayn) *nt* (pl ~en) pig
Zwitser (*zvit*-serr) *c* (pl ~s) Swiss
Zwitserland (*zvit*-serr-lahnt) Switzerland
Zwitsers (*zvit*-serrs) *adj* Swiss
zwoegen (*zvōō*-gern) *v* labour

bloemkool cauliflower
boerenkool met worst kale mixed with mashed potatoes and served with smoked sausage
boerenomelet omelet with diced vegetables and bacon
bokking bloater
boon bean
borrelhapje appetizer
borststuk breast, brisket
bosbes bilberry (US blueberry)
bot 1) flounder 2) bone
boter butter
boterham slice of buttered bread
bouillon broth
braadhaantje spring chicken
braadworst frying sausage
braam blackberry
brasem bream
brood bread
~**maaltijd** bread served with cold meat, eggs, cheese, jam or other garnishes
~**pudding** kind of bread pudding with eggs, cinnamon and rum flavouring
broodje roll
~**halfom** buttered roll with liver and salted beef
~**kaas** buttered roll with cheese
bruine bonen met spek red kidney beans served with bacon
Brussels lof chicory (US endive)
caramelpudding caramel mould
caramelvla caramel custard
champignon mushroom
chocola(de) chocolate
citroen lemon
cordon bleu veal scallop stuffed with ham and cheese
dadel date
dagschotel day's special
dame blanche vanilla ice-cream

with hot chocolate sauce
dille dill
doperwt green pea
dragon tarragon
drie-in-de-pan small, fluffy pancake filled with currants
druif grape
duif pigeon
Duitse biefstuk hamburger steak
Edam, Edammer kaas firm, mild-flavoured yellow cheese, coated with red wax
eend duck
ei egg
eierpannekoek egg pancake
erwt pea
erwtensoep met kluif pea soup with diced, smoked sausages, pork fat, pig's trotter (US feet), parsley, leeks and celery
exclusief not included
fazant pheasant
filet fillet
~**américain** steak tartare
flensje small, thin pancake
foe yong hai omelet with leeks, onions, and shrimps served in a sweet-and-sour sauce
forel trout
framboos raspberry
Friese nagelkaas cheese made from skimmed milk, flavoured with cloves
frikadel meatball
frites, frieten chips (US french fries)
gaar well-done
gans goose
garnaal shrimp, prawn
gebak pastry, cake
gebakken fried
gebonden soep cream soup
gebraden roasted
gedroogde pruim prune

Food

aalbes redcurrant
aardappel potato
~ **puree** mashed potatoes
aardbei strawberry
abrikoos apricot
amandel almond
~ **broodje** a sweet roll with al-
mond-paste filling
ananas pineapple
andijvie endive (US chicory)
~ **stamppot** mashed potato and
endive casserole
anijs aniseed
ansjovis anchovy
appel apple
~ **beignet** fritter
~ **bol** dumpling
~ **flap** puff-pastry containing
an apple slice
~ **gebak** cake
~ **moes** sauce
Ardense pastei rich pork mixture
cooked in a pastry crust, served
cold in slices
artisjok artichoke
asperge asparagus
~ **punt** tip
aubergine aubergine (US eggplant)
augurk gherkin (US pickle)

avondeten dinner, supper
azijn vinegar
baars perch
babi pangang slices of roast suck-
(l)ing pig, served with a sweet-
and-sour sauce
bami goreng a casserole of
noodles, vegetables, diced pork
and shrimps
banaan banana
banketletter pastry with an al-
mond-paste filling
basilicum basil
bediening service
belegd broodje roll with a variety
of garnishes
belegen kaas pungent-flavoured
cheese
biefstuk fillet of beef
~ **van de haas** small round fille
of beef
bieslook chive
bitterbal small, round bread
meatball served as an appeti
blinde vink veal bird; thin slic
veal rolled around stuffing
bloedworst black pudding
blood sausage
~ **met appelen** with cook/
ples

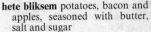

gehakt 1) minced 2) minced meat
~**bal** meatball
gekookt boiled
gekruid seasoned
gemarineerd marinated
gember ginger
~**koek** gingerbread
gemengd assorted, mixed
gepaneerd breaded
gepocheerd ei poached egg
geraspt grated
gerecht course, dish
gerookt smoked
geroosterd brood toast
gerst barley
gestoofd braised
gevogelte fowl
gevuld stuffed
gezouten salted
Goudakaas, Goudse kaas a re-
nowned Dutch cheese, similar
to *Edam*, large, flat and round;
it gains in flavour with maturity
griesmeel semolina
~**pudding** semolina pudding
griet brill
groente vegetable
Haagse bluf dessert of whipped
egg-whites, served with redcurrant sauce
haantje cockerel
haas hare
hachee hash of minced meat,
onions and spices
half, halve half
hardgekookt ei hard-boiled egg
haring herring
hart heart
havermoutpap (oatmeal) porridge
hazelnoot hazelnut
heilbot halibut
heldere soep consommé, clear
soup
hersenen brains

hete bliksem potatoes, bacon and
apples, seasoned with butter,
salt and sugar
Hollandse biefstuk loin section of
a porterhouse or T-bone steak
Hollandse nieuwe freshly caught,
filleted herring
honing honey
houtsnip 1) woodcock 2) cheese
sandwich on rye bread
hutspot met klapstuk hotch-potch
of mashed potatoes, carrots and
onions served with boiled beef
huzarensla salad of potatoes,
hard-boiled eggs, cold meat,
gherkins, beetroot and mayonnaise
ijs ice, ice-cream
inclusief included
Italiaanse salade mixed salad with
tomatoes, olives and tunny fish
jachtschotel a casserole of meat,
onions and potatoes, often
served with apple sauce
jonge kaas fresh cheese
jus gravy
kaas cheese
~**balletje** baked cheese ball
kabeljauw cod
kalfslapje, kalfsoester veal cutlet
kalfsrollade roast veal
kalfsvlees veal
kalkoen turkey
kapucijners met spek peas served
with fried bacon, boiled potatoes, onions and green salad
karbonade chop, cutlet
karper carp
kastanje chestnut
kaviaar caviar
kerrie curry
kers cherry
kievitsei plover's egg
kip chicken

kippeborst breast of chicken
kippebout leg of chicken
knakworst small frankfurter sausage
knoflook garlic
koek 1) cake 2) gingerbread
koekje biscuit (US cookie)
koffietafel light lunch consisting of bread and butter with a variety of garnishes, served with coffee
kokosnoot coconut
komijnekaas cheese flavoured with cumin seeds
komkommer cucumber
konijn rabbit
koninginnesoep cream of chicken
kool cabbage
  ~**schotel met gehakt** casserole of meatballs and cabbage
kotelet chop, cutlet
koud cold
  ~ **vlees** cold meat (US cold cuts)
krab crab
krabbetje spare rib
krent currant
kroepoek large, deep-fried shrimp wafer
kroket croquette
kruiderij herb, seasoning
kruidnagel clove
kruisbes gooseberry
kwark fresh white cheese
kwartel quail
kweepeer quince
lamsbout leg of lamb
lamsvlees lamb
langoest spiny lobster
Leidse kaas cheese flavoured with cumin seeds
lekkerbekje fried, filleted haddock or plaice
lendestuk sirloin
lever liver

linze lentil
loempia spring roll (US egg roll)
maïskolf corn on the cob
makreel mackerel
mandarijntje tangerine
marsepein marzipan
meikaas a creamy cheese with high fat content
meloen melon
menu van de dag set menu
mossel mussel
mosterd mustard
nagerecht dessert
nasi goreng a casserole of rice, fried onions, meat, chicken, shrimps, vegetables and seasoning, usually topped with a fried egg
nier kidney
  ~**broodje** roll filled with kidneys and chopped onions
noot nut
oester oyster
olie oil
  ~**bol** fritter with raisins
olijf olive
omelet fines herbes herb omelet
omelet met kippelevertjes chicken liver omelet
omelet nature plain omelet
ongaar underdone (US rare)
ontbijt breakfast
  ~ **koek** honey cake
  ~ **spek** bacon, rasher
ossehaas fillet of beef
ossestaart oxtail
oude kaas any mature and strong cheese
paddestoel mushroom
paling eel
  ~ **in 't groen** braised in white sauce garnished with chopped parsley and other greens
pannekoek pancake

~ **met stroop** pancake served with treacle (US syrup)

pap porridge

paprika green or red (sweet) pepper

patates frites chips (US french fries)

pastei pie, pasty

patrijs partridge

peer pear

pekeltong salt(ed) tongue

pekelvlees slices of salted meat

peper pepper
   ~ **koek** gingerbread

perzik peach

peterselie parsley

piccalilly pickle

pinda peanut
   ~ **kaas** peanut butter

pisang goreng fried banana

poffertje fritter served with sugar and butter

pompelmoes grapefruit

portie portion

postelein purslane (edible plant)

prei leek

prinsessenboon French bean (US green bean)

pruim plum

rabarber rhubarb

radijs radish

rauw raw

reebout, reerug venison

reine-claude greengage

rekening bill

ribstuk rib of beef

rijst rice
   ~ **tafel** an Indonesian preparation composed of some 30 dishes including stewed vegetables, spit-roasted meat and fowl, served with rice, various sauces, fruit, nuts and spices

rivierkreeft crayfish

rode biet beetroot

rode kool red cabbage

roerei scrambled egg

roggebrood rye bread

rolmops Bismarck herring

rolpens fried slices of spiced and pickled minced beef and tripe, topped with an apple slice

rookspek smoked bacon

rookworst smoked sausage

roomboter butter

roomijs ice-cream

rosbief roast beef

rozemarijn rosemary

runderlap beefsteak

rundvlees beef

Russische eieren Russian eggs; hard-boiled egg-halves garnished with mayonnaise, herring, shrimps, capers, anchovies and sometimes caviar; served on lettuce

salade salad

sambal kind of spicy paste consisting mainly of ground pimentos, usually served with *rijsttafel*, *bami* or *nasi goreng*

sardien sardine

saté, sateh skewered pieces of meat covered with a spicy peanut sauce

saucijzebroodje sausage roll

saus sauce, gravy

schaaldier shellfish

schapevlees mutton

scharretong lemon sole

schelvis haddock

schildpadsoep turtle soup

schnitzel cutlet

schol plaice

schuimomelet fluffy dessert omelet

selderij celery

sinaasappel orange

sjaslik skewered chunks of meat, grilled, then braised in a spicy sauce of tomatoes, onions and bacon

sla salad, lettuce

slaboon French bean (US green bean)

slagroom whipped cream

slak snail

sneeuwbal kind of cream puff, sometimes filled with currants and raisins

snijboon sliced French bean

soep soup

~ **van de dag** soup of the day

sorbet water ice (US sherbet)

speculaas spiced almond biscuit

spek bacon

sperzieboon French bean (US green bean)

spiegelei fried egg

spijskaart menu, bill of fare

spinazie spinach

sprits a kind of shortbread

spruitje brussels sprout

stamppot a stew of vegetables and mashed potatoes

steur sturgeon

stokvis stockfish (dried cod)

stroop treacle (US syrup)

suiker sugar

taart cake

tarbot turbot

tartaar steak tartare

~ **speciaal** extra-large portion, of prime quality

tijm thyme

tjap tjoy chop suey; a dish of fried meat and vegetables served with rice

toeristenmenu tourist menu

tomaat tomato

tong 1) tongue 2) sole

tonijn tunny (US tuna)

toost toast

tosti grilled cheese-and-ham sandwich

tournedos thick round fillet cut of prime beef (US rib or rib-eye steak)

truffel truffle

tuinboon broad bean

ui onion

uitsmijter two slices of bread garnished with ham or roast beef and topped with two fried eggs

vanille vanilla

varkenshaas pork tenderloin

varkenslapje pork fillet

varkensvlees pork

venkel fennel

vermicellisoep consommé with thin noodles

vers fresh

vijg fig

vis fish

vla custard

vlaai fruit tart

Vlaamse karbonade small slices of beef and onions braised in broth, with beer sometimes added

vlees meat

voorgerecht starter or first course

vrucht fruit

vruchtensalade fruit salad

wafel wafer

walnoot walnut

warm hot

waterkers watercress

waterzooi chicken poached in white wine and shredded vegetables, cream and egg-yolk

wentelteefje French toast; slice of white bread dipped in egg batter and fried, then sprinkled with cinnamon and sugar

wijnkaart wine list

wijting whiting
wild game
   ~ **zwijn** wild boar
wilde eend wild duck
witlof chicory (US endive)
   ~ **op zijn Brussels** chicory rolled in a slice of ham and oven-browned with cheese sauce

worst sausage
wortel carrot
zachtgekookt ei soft-boiled egg
zalm salmon
zeekreeft lobster
zeevis saltwater fish
zout salt
zuurkool sauerkraut
zwezerik sweetbread

Drinks

advocaat egg liqueur
ananassap pineapple juice
aperitief aperitif
bessenjenever blackcurrant gin
bier beer
bisschopswijn mulled wine
bittertje bitter-tasting aperitif
boerenjongens Dutch brandy with raisins
boerenmeisjes Dutch brandy with apricots
borrel shot
brandewijn brandy
cassis blackcurrant liqueur
chocolademelk, chocomel(k) chocolate drink
citroenbrandewijn lemon brandy
citroenjenever lemon-flavoured gin
citroentje met suiker brandy flavoured with lemon peel, with sugar added
cognac brandy, cognac
donker bier porter; dark sweet-tasting beer
druivesap grape juice

frisdrank soft drink
gekoeld iced
genever see *jenever*
Geuzelambiek a strong Flemish bitter beer brewed from wheat and barley
jenever Dutch gin
jonge jenever/klare young Dutch gin
karnemelk buttermilk
kersenbrandewijn kirsch; spirit distilled from cherries
koffie coffee
   ~ **met melk** with milk
   ~ **met room** with cream
   ~ **met slagroom** with whipped cream
   ~ **verkeerd** white coffee; equal quantity of coffee and hot milk
   zwarte ~ black
Kriekenlambiek a strong Brussels bitter beer flavoured with morello cherries
kwast hot or cold lemon squash
licht bier lager; light beer
likeur liqueur

limonade lemonade
melk milk
mineraalwater mineral water
oude jenever/klare Dutch gin aged in wood casks, yellowish in colour and more mature than *jonge jenever*
oranjebitter orange-flavoured bitter
pils general name for beer
sap juice
sinas orangeade
spuitwater soda water
sterkedrank liquor, spirit
tafelwater mineral water

thee tea
  ~ **met citroen** with lemon
  ~ **met suiker en melk** with sugar and milk
trappistenbier malt beer brewed (originally) by Trappist monks
vieux brandy bottled in Holland
vruchtesap fruit juice
warme chocola hot chocolate
wijn wine
  droge ~ dry
  rode ~ red
  witte ~ white
  zoete ~ sweet
wodka vodka

Dutch Irregular Verbs

The following list contains the most common strong and irregular verbs. If a compound verb or a verb with a prefix (*be-*, *con-*, *dis-*, *im-*, *in-*, *mis-*, *om-*, *on-*, *ont-*, *ver-*, etc.) is not listed, its forms may be found by looking up the basic verb, e.g. *verbinden* is conjugated as *binden*.

Infinitive	*Past*	*Past participle*	
bakken	bakte	gebakken	*bake*
barsten	barstte	gebarsten	*burst, crack*
bederven	bedierf	bedorven	*spoil*
bedriegen	bedroog	bedrogen	*deceive*
beginnen	begon	begonnen	*begin*
bergen	borg	geborgen	*put*
bevelen	beval	bevolen	*order*
bewegen	bewoog	bewogen	*move*
bezwijken	bezweek	bezweken	*succumb*
bidden	bad	gebeden	*pray*
bieden	bood	geboden	*offer*
bijten	beet	gebeten	*bite*
binden	bond	gebonden	*tie*
blazen	blies	geblazen	*blow*
blijken	bleek	gebleken	*prove to be*
blijven	bleef	gebleven	*remain*
blinken	blonk	geblonken	*shine*
braden	braadde	gebraden	*fry*
breken	brak	gebroken	*break*
brengen	bracht	gebracht	*bring*
buigen	boog	gebogen	*bow*
delven	delfde/dolf	gedolven	*dig up*
denken	dacht	gedacht	*think*
dingen	dong	gedongen	*compete (for)*
doen	deed	gedaan	*do*
dragen	droeg	gedragen	*wear*
drijven	dreef	gedreven	*float*
dringen	drong	gedrongen	*push*
drinken	dronk	gedronken	*drink*
druipen	droop	gedropen	*drip*
duiken	dook	gedoken	*dive*
dwingen	dwong	gedwongen	*force*
eten	at	gegeten	*eat*
fluiten	floot	gefloten	*whistle*
gaan	ging	gegaan	*go*
gelden	gold	gegolden	*be valid*
genezen	genas	genezen	*heal*
genieten	genoot	genoten	*enjoy*
geven	gaf	gegeven	*give*
gieten	goot	gegoten	*pour*
glijden	gleed	gegleden	*slide*
glimmen	glom	geglommen	*shine*
graven	groef	gegraven	*dig*

grijpen	greep	gegrepen	*catch*
hangen	hing	gehangen	*hang*
hebben	had	gehad	*have*
heffen	hief	geheven	*raise*
helpen	hielp	geholpen	*help*
heten	heette	geheten	*be called*
hijsen	hees	gehesen	*hoist*
houden	hield	gehouden	*keep*
jagen	jaagde/joeg	gejaagd	*chase*
kiezen	koos	gekozen	*choose*
kijken	keek	gekeken	*look*
klimmen	klom	geklommen	*climb*
klinken	klonk	geklonken	*sound*
knijpen	kneep	geknepen	*pinch*
komen	kwam	gekomen	*come*
kopen	kocht	gekocht	*buy*
krijgen	kreeg	gekregen	*get*
krimpen	kromp	gekrompen	*shrink*
kruipen	kroop	gekropen	*creep*
kunnen	kon	gekund	*can*
lachen	lachte	gelachen	*laugh*
laden	laadde	geladen	*load*
laten	liet	gelaten	*let*
lezen	las	gelezen	*read*
liegen	loog	gelogen	*tell lies*
liggen	lag	gelegen	*lie*
lijden	leed	geleden	*suffer*
lijken	leek	geleken	*seem*
lopen	liep	gelopen	*walk*
malen	maalde	gemalen	*grind*
meten	mat	gemeten	*measure*
moeten	moest	gemoeten	*must*
mogen	mocht	gemogen/gemoogd	*may*
nemen	nam	genomen	*take*
prijzen	prees	geprezen	*praise*
raden	raadde/ried	geraden	*guess*
rijden	reed	gereden	*ride*
rijgen	reeg	geregen	*thread*
rijzen	rees	gerezen	*rise*
roepen	riep	geroepen	*call*
ruiken	rook	geroken	*smell*
scheiden	scheidde	gescheiden	*separate*
schelden	schold	gescholden	*call names*
schenken	schonk	geschonken	*pour*
scheppen	schiep	geschapen	*create*
scheren	schoor	geschoren	*shave*
schieten	schoot	geschoten	*shoot*
schijnen	scheen	geschenen	*shine, seem to be*
schrijden	schreed	geschreden	*stride*
schrijven	schreef	geschreven	*write*
schrikken	schrok	geschrokken	*be frightened*

schuiven	schoof	geschoven	*shove*
slaan	sloeg	geslagen	*hit*
slapen	sliep	geslapen	*sleep*
slijpen	sleep	geslepen	*sharpen*
slijten	sleet	gesleten	*wear down*
sluipen	sloop	geslopen	*sneak*
sluiten	sloot	gesloten	*close*
smelten	smolt	gesmolten	*melt*
snijden	sneed	gesneden	*cut*
spinnen	spon	gesponnen	*spin*
splijten	spleet	gespleten	*split*
spreken	sprak	gesproken	*speak*
springen	sprong	gesprongen	*jump*
spuiten	spoot	gespoten	*squirt*
staan	stond	gestaan	*stand*
steken	stak	gestoken	*sting*
stelen	stal	gestolen	*steal*
sterven	stierf	gestorven	*die*
stijgen	steeg	gestegen	*rise*
stijven	steef	gesteven	*starch*
stinken	stonk	gestonken	*stink*
stoten	stootte/stiet	gestoten	*push*
strijden	streed	gestreden	*fight*
strijken	streek	gestreken	*iron*
treden	trad	getreden	*tread*
treffen	trof	getroffen	*hit*
trekken	trok	getrokken	*pull*
vallen	viel	gevallen	*fall*
vangen	ving	gevangen	*catch*
varen	voer	gevaren	*sail*
vechten	vocht	gevochten	*fight*
verbergen	verborg	verborgen	*hide*
verdwijnen	verdween	verdwenen	*disappear*
vergeten	vergat	vergeten	*forget*
verliezen	verloor	verloren	*lose*
vermijden	vermeed	vermeden	*avoid*
verslinden	verslond	verslonden	*devour*
vinden	vond	gevonden	*find*
vliegen	vloog	gevlogen	*fly*
voortspruiten	sproot voort	voortgesproten	*result*
vouwen	vouwde	gevouwen	*fold*
vragen	vroeg	gevraagd	*ask*
vriezen	vroor	gevroren	*freeze*
waaien	waaide/woei	gewaaid	*blow*
wassen	waste	gewassen	*wash*
wegen	woog	gewogen	*weigh*
werpen	wierp	geworpen	*throw*
werven	wierf	geworven	*recruit*
weten	wist	geweten	*know*
weven	weefde	geweven	*weave*
wijken	week	geweken	*yield*

wijten	weet	geweten	*impute*
wijzen	wees	gewezen	*show*
willen	wilde/wou	gewild	*want*
winden	wond	gewonden	*wind*
winnen	won	gewonnen	*win*
worden	werd	geworden	*become*
wreken	wreekte	gewroken	*revenge*
wrijven	wreef	gewreven	*rub*
zeggen	zei	gezegd	*say*
zenden	zond	gezonden	*send*
zien	zag	gezien	*see*
zijn	was	geweest	*be*
zingen	zong	gezongen	*sing*
zinken	zonk	gezonken	*sink*
zinnen	zon	gezonnen	*brood*
zitten	zat	gezeten	*sit*
zoeken	zocht	gezocht	*seek*
zuigen	zoog	gezogen	*suck*
zullen	zou	—	*shall, will*
zwellen	zwol	gezwollen	*swell*
zwemmen	zwom	gezwommen	*swim*
1) zweren	zwoer	gezworen	*swear*
2) zweren	zweerde/zwoor	gezworen	*ulcerate*
zwerven	zwierf	gezworven	*wander*
zwijgen	zweeg	gezwegen	*be silent*

Dutch Abbreviations

A°	*anno*	(built) in the year
afd.	*afdeling*	department
alg.	*algemeen*	general
A.N.W.B.	*Algemene Nederlandse Wielrijdersbond*	Dutch Touring Association
a.s.	*aanstaande*	next
a.u.b.	*alstublieft*	please
Bfr.	*Belgische frank*	Belgian franc
b.g.	*begane grond*	ground floor
b.g.g.	*bij geen gehoor*	if no answer
blz.	*bladzijde*	page
B.R.T.	*Belgische Radio en Televisie*	Belgian Broadcasting Company
B.T.W.	*Belasting Toegevoegde Waarde*	VAT, value added tax
b.v.	*bijvoorbeeld*	e.g.
B.V.	*besloten vennootschap*	limited liability company
C.S.	*Centraal Station*	main railway station
ct.	*cent*	1/100 of the guilder
dhr.	*de heer*	Mr.
drs.	*doctorandus*	Master of Arts
d.w.z.	*dat wil zeggen*	i.e.
EEG	*Europese Economische Gemeenschap*	EEC, European Economic Community (Common Market)
E.H.B.O.	*Eerste Hulp bij Ongelukken*	first aid
enz.	*enzovoort*	etc.
excl.	*exclusief*	exclusive, not included
fl/f	*gulden*	guilder
geb.	*geboren*	born
H.K.H.	*Hare Koninklijke Hoogheid*	Her Royal Highness
H.M.	*Hare Majesteit*	His/Her Majesty
hs	*huis*	ground floor
incl.	*inclusief*	inclusive, included
i.p(l).v.	*in plaats van*	in the place of
ir.	*ingenieur*	engineer
jl.	*jongstleden*	last
K.A.C.B.	*Koninklijke Automobiel-club van België*	Royal Automobile Association of Belgium
km/u	*kilometer per uur*	kilometres per hour
K.N.A.C.	*Koninklijke Nederlandse Automobielclub*	Royal Dutch Automobile Association

K.N.M.I.	*Koninklijk Nederlands Meteorologisch Instituut*	Royal Dutch Meteorological Institute
m.a.w.	*met andere woorden*	in other words
Mej.	*mejuffrouw*	Miss
Mevr.	*mevrouw*	Mrs.
Mij.	*maatschappij*	company
Mr.	*meester in de rechten; mijnheer*	barrister, lawyer; Mr.
N.A.V.O.	*Noordatlantische Verdragsorganisatie*	NATO
N.B.T.	*Nederlands Bureau voor Toerisme*	Dutch National Tourist Office
n.Chr.	*na Christus*	A.D.
nl.	*namelijk*	namely
n.m.	*namiddag*	afternoon
N.M.B.S.	*Nationale Maatschappij der Belgische Spoorwegen*	Belgian National Railways
N.P.	*niet parkeren*	no parking
N.S.	*Nederlandse Spoorwegen*	Dutch National Railways
N.V.	*naamloze vennootschap*	Ltd. or Inc.
p.a.	*per adres*	in care of
pk	*paardekracht*	horsepower
r.-k./R.-K.	*rooms-katholiek*	Roman Catholic
t.e.m.	*tot en met*	up to and including
t.o.v.	*ten opzichte van*	with regard to
v.a.	*volgens anderen, vanaf*	from
V.A.B.	*Vlaamse Automobilisten- bond*	Flemish Automobile Association
v.Chr.	*voor Christus*	B.C.
v.m.	*voormiddag*	morning
V.N.	*Verenigde Naties*	UN
V.S.	*Verenigde Staten*	USA
V.T.B.	*Vlaamse Toeristenbond*	Flemish Tourist Association
V.V.V.	*Vereniging voor Vreemdelingenverkeer*	tourist-information office
zgn.	*zogenaamd*	so-called
Z.K.H.	*Zijne Koninklijke Hoogheid*	His Royal Highness
z.o.z.	*zie ommezijde*	pto, please turn over

Numerals

Cardinal numbers		Ordinal numbers	
0	nul	1e	eerste
1	een	2e	tweede
2	twee	3e	derde
3	drie	4e	vierde
4	vier	5e	vijfde
5	vijf	6e	zesde
6	zes	7e	zevende
7	zeven	8e	achtste
8	acht	9e	negende
9	negen	10e	tiende
10	tien	11e	elfde
11	elf	12e	twaalfde
12	twaalf	13e	dertiende
13	dertien	14e	veertiende
14	veertien	15e	vijftiende
15	vijftien	16e	zestiende
16	zestien	17e	zeventiende
17	zeventien	18e	achttiende
18	achttien	19e	negentiende
19	negentien	20e	twintigste
20	twintig	21e	eenentwintigste
21	eenentwintig	22e	tweeëntwintigste
22	tweeëntwintig	23e	drieëntwintigste
23	drieëntwintig	24e	vierentwintigste
24	vierentwintig	25e	vijfentwintigste
30	dertig	26e	zesentwintigste
40	veertig	30e	dertigste
50	vijftig	40e	veertigste
60	zestig	50e	vijftigste
70	zeventig	60e	zestigste
80	tachtig	70e	zeventigste
90	negentig	80e	tachtigste
100	honderd	90e	negentigste
101	honderdeen	100e	honderdste
230	tweehonderddertig	101e	honderdeerste
1000	duizend	230e	tweehonderddertigste
1001	duizendeen	1000e	duizendste
1100	elfhonderd	1001e	duizendeerste
2000	tweeduizend	1100e	elfhonderdste
1 000 000	een miljoen	2000e	tweeduizendste

Time

Although official time in Holland and Belgium is based on the 24-hour clock, the 12-hour system is used in conversation.

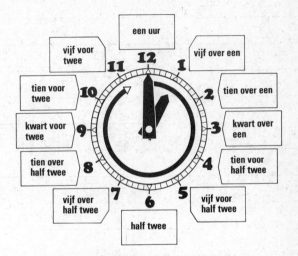

To avoid confusion, you can make use of the terms *'s morgens* (morning), and *'s middags* (afternoon) or *'s avonds* (evening).

Ik kom om vier uur 's morgens.	I'll come at 4 a.m.
Ik kom om vier uur 's middags.	I'll come at 4 p.m.
Ik kom om acht uur 's avonds.	I'll come at 8 p.m.

Days of the Week

zondag	Sunday	*donderdag*	Thursday
maandag	Monday	*vrijdag*	Friday
dinsdag	Tuesday	*zaterdag*	Saturday
woensdag	Wednesday		

Aantekeningen

Aantekeningen

Aantekeningen

Notes _____
_____
_____
_____
_____
_____
_____
_____
_____
_____
_____
_____
_____
_____
_____
_____
_____
_____
_____

Notes

Notes

BERLITZ PHRASE BOOKS

World's bestselling phrase books feature not only
expressions and vocabulary you'll need, but also travel
tips, useful facts and pronunciation throughout. The
handiest and most readable conversation aid available.

Arabic	French	Portuguese
Chinese	German	Russian
Danish	Greek	Serbo-Croatian
Dutch	Hebrew	Spanish
European	Hungarian	Latin-American
(14 languages)	Italian	Spanish
European	Japanese	Swahili
Menu Reader	Norwegian	Swedish
Finnish	Polish	Turkish

BERLITZ CASSETTEPAKS

Most of the above-mentioned titles are
also available combined with a cassette to
help you improve your accent. A helpful
32-page script is included containing the
complete text of the dual language hi-fi
recording.